HUMAN RESOURCE
MANAGEMENT

KENT SERIES IN MANAGEMENT

Barnett/Wilsted, Strategic Management: Concepts and Cases
Barnett/Wilsted, Strategic Management: Text and Concepts
Barnett/Wilsted, Cases for Strategic Management
Berkman/Neider, The Human Relations of Organizations
Crane, Personnel: The Management of Human Resources, Fourth Edition
Davis/Cosenza, Business Research for Decision Making, Second Edition
Kirkpatrick, Supervision: A Situational Approach
Klein/Ritti, Understanding Organizational Behavior, Second Edition
Kolde, Environment of International Business, Second Edition
Nkomo/Fottler/McAfee, Applications in Personnel/Human Resource
    Management: Cases, Exercises, and Skill Builders
Plunkett/Attner, Introduction to Management, Third Edition
Punnett, Experiencing International Management
Scarpello/Ledvinka, Personnel/Human Resource Management: Environments
    and Functions
Starling, The Changing Environment of Business, Third Edition
Steers/Ungson/Mowday, Managing Effective Organizations: An Introduction

KENT HUMAN RESOURCE MANAGEMENT SERIES

Bernadin/Beatty, Performance Appraisal: Assessing Human Behavior at Work
Cascio, Costing Human Resources: The Financial Impact of Behavior in
    Organizations, Second Edition
Ledvinka, Federal Regulation of Personnel and Human Resource Management,
    Second Edition
McCaffery, Employee Benefit Programs: A Total Compensation Perspective
Wallace/Fay, Compensation Theory and Practice, Second Edition

HUMAN RESOURCE MANAGEMENT
AN ECONOMIC APPROACH

Daniel J.B. Mitchell

University of California—Los Angeles

PWS-KENT Publishing Company

Boston

PWS–KENT
Publishing Company

20 Park Plaza
Boston, Massachusetts 02116

PWS-KENT Publishing Company is a division of Wadsworth, Inc.

Library of Congress Cataloging-in-Publication Data
Mitchell, Daniel J.B.
  Human resource management : an economic approach / Daniel J.B. Mitchell
    p. cm.
  Bibliography: p.
  Includes index.
  ISBN 0-534-91870-0
  1. Personnel management—United States. 2. Labor economics––United States. 3. Personnel management. 4. Labor economics.
  I. Title.
  HF5549.2.U5M56   1989   89-2983
  658.3--dc19   CIP

Editor: Rolf A. Janke
Production Coordinator: Robine Andrau
Manufacturing Coordinator: Margaret Sullivan Higgins
Interior and Cover Designer: Julia Gecha
Interior Illustration: Deborah Schneck
Typesetting: Graphic Typesetting Service
Cover Printing: Henry N. Sawyer Co., Inc.
Printing and Binding: R.R. Donnelley & Sons Company

Printed in the United States of America

89 90 91 92 93 — 10 9 8 7 6 5 4 3 2 1

To Alice, Nina, and Joshua

PREFACE

Most students in contemporary business or management programs are not planning careers in human resource management (HRM). Yet it is important that every such student—whether he or she is pursuing an undergraduate degree, an MBA, or some other degree—be exposed to the HRM field. The question for an HRM instructor is how to present the subject matter so that it grabs the attention of all students—even ones who may be taking the course as a requirement and who may not profess a special interest in it. At the same time the presentation must be thorough enough to serve as a grounding for students who do plan careers in HRM.

Unlike most other textbooks now available, *Human Resource Management: An Economic Approach* takes (as its subtitle indicates) an economic approach to HRM. Why an economic approach? Because economics, both empirical and analytical, is the language spoken by today's business or management student. Not only do most programs include a basic economics requirement—especially microeconomics—but economics is the basis of the modern study of finance. Most business or management students feel the need for a significant finance background; many consider it their major field.

In the 1940s, 1950s, and 1960s, it was not unusual to find HRM textbooks with the term "labor economics" in their titles. Those books covered some of the same ground as does this text. Not as yet appearing in the economics literature of that period, however, were the more recently developed insights encapsulated in such terms as "implicit contracts" or "efficiency wages." In the early texts the economics component often wound up in a separate section—divorced from the descriptive material that was really the heart of the book—and tended to take a macro rather than a micro perspective. With the new insights now available, however, it is possible to produce an integrated text in which economics is interwoven in every chapter and issue.

Although this textbook uses modern economics to illuminate critical issues in HRM, it is not a technical volume. It can readily be used by instructors of varied academic backgrounds in introductory HRM courses. The important institutional features of the labor market are presented and the key public policies that condition the employment relationship are discussed and analyzed. Yet by focusing on the economic approach to the various topics covered, the text avoids the common pitfalls of introductory courses.

Students who use *Human Resource Management: An Economic Approach* will not be left with the impression that HRM is a collection of traditions, folk wisdom, and rules of thumb—a view that sometimes arises when "nuts and bolts" personnel texts are used. Students will not leave the course thinking HRM is mainly a field for lawyers, as can happen if the details of public policy are overly stressed. Finally, students will not come away with the view that HRM is basically the study of the (relatively small) collective-bargaining sector, as can happen if industrial relations or labor relations texts are assigned in a survey course.

Exercises containing problems, questions for thought or discussion, and a list of key terms follow the text of the chapters. Also provided are sources for data, enabling both students and instructors to update the information as newer figures become available. Endnotes contain references to source articles and books throughout the text.

Care was taken to provide detailed references for three reasons: (1) to give credit where credit is due, (2) to enable students and instructors to follow up on important ideas and provide students with sources for the writing of term papers and similar assignments, and (3) to reinforce the point that a substantial analytical and empirical literature exists in the HRM field.

Because this book represents a new approach to an old topic, comments are welcomed by the author. Users of this text are invited to write to the author with suggestions or criticisms. The address is Daniel J.B. Mitchell, Anderson Graduate School of Management, UCLA, Los Angeles, California 90024.

Acknowledgments

Many individuals assisted in the preparation of this text. Frederick S. Hills, Virginia Polytechnic Institute and State University; Sanford M. Jacoby, University of California—Los Angeles; Bruno Stein, New York University; and George Strauss, University of California—Berkeley, were especially helpful in reviewing early versions of the manuscript. Maury Pearl, Douglas Rebne, and Ramanand Sood ably provided research assistance. Jeannine Schummer provided needed clerical skills and support. Alice Mitchell assisted with the indexing. Finally, at PWS-KENT Publishing Company, Rolf A. Janke, Laura E. Mosberg, and Robine Andrau kept the wheels turning from manuscript to completed books.

Daniel J.B. Mitchell
Santa Monica, California

CONTENTS

Chapter One

AN ECONOMIC APPROACH TO HUMAN RESOURCE MANAGEMENT

Detailed reports on financial and commodity markets are carried on a regular basis in the newspapers. The prices of particular stocks, bonds, currencies, or metals can be easily located. Traders, who cannot afford to wait for newspaper accounts, can receive almost instantaneous reports of current market transactions by electronic means. Those who are concerned about the course of these prices in the future, either to reduce risk or to speculate, have access to forward and futures markets. Other traders stand by, awaiting minor discrepancies in prices between markets, to profit through arbitrage.

1–1 How the Labor Market Differs

For many years, microeconomic models of the labor market viewed that market as basically similar to financial and commodity markets. Supply and demand were said to determine the wage in the labor market, as they did in financial and commodity markets. Yet even the most casual observation suggests that there are fundamental differences between the institutions of these types of markets. The differences do not imply that participants in the labor market are somehow "irrational," whereas those in financial and commodity markets are not. Rather, they reflect the different circumstances of the markets involved.[1]

Linking Buyers and Sellers

The labor market is reflected in the help-wanted section of daily newspapers. Yet prices (wages) are often not quoted in such ads and, where such quotes are offered, they commonly vary from firm to firm for apparently similar jobs. Indeed, the ads may specify a salary range rather than a single figure, suggesting that the firm may offer some candidates more than others for the same position. The fact that

1

candidates for employment are not homogeneous (unlike shares of a company's stock) helps explain this labor market characteristic.

Even the practice of placing help-wanted ads suggests that the labor market differs from financial and commodity markets. A person wishing to buy shares of General Motors does not place "stock-wanted" advertisements; instead, there is a well-established marketplace ready to fill the need quickly. In contrast, buyers (employers) in the labor market apparently have difficulty locating sellers (employees) and thus are forced to advertise.[2]

Lack of Market Clearing

An even more striking difference between the labor and financial/commodity markets is the chronic existence of excess supply. In the stock market anyone who wishes to sell shares of General Motors at the going price can do so. Sellers may be disappointed at the level of the going price, but not in their ability to sell at it.

The labor market situation is different. Workers often experience difficulty in finding a job, even if they are willing and able to accept a wage at or below the level that employers are paying their current employees. In an important sense the labor market does not seem to *clear* (bring demand and supply into harmony) the way financial and commodity markets routinely do.

Of course, there are examples of nonclearing behavior in other markets, too. It might be said, for example, that advertising of consumer products and similar forms of nonprice competition are symptomatic of a shortage of customers in oligopsonistic markets.[3] Even in such cases, however, there is a difference in institutional arrangements relative to the labor market. An automobile manufacturer, for example, may well sell at a price above the marginal cost of product and thus be anxious to find additional buyers.[4] But the manufacturer has the option, if it wants, to compete via price reduction and thereby increase sales volume. Generally, this option is not available to an unemployed person. He or she cannot expect to obtain work by going to employers and offering to work for less pay than current employees receive. If all jobs are filled at the wages the firm has established, unemployed persons are simply told there are no vacancies or that no help is wanted.[5]

Frequency of Price Change

Transactors in financial and commodity markets are often not content to await word of closing prices as reported in the daily newspapers. Market prices may change often in the course of a day, and opportunities could be lost unless knowledge of such changes is quickly acquired. In contrast, the prices of labor are changed very infrequently—often no more than annually. Although wages in some union contracts are changed as frequently as quarterly, prices of labor almost never change on a day-to-day or hour-to-hour basis.

There is apparently no need in the labor market for the kinds of instantaneous information services that characterize financial and product markets. Even if data on wage levels within firms were readily available (which is not typically the case in nonunion enterprises), there would be little action to report. Private labor-market information services that do exist generally ask cooperating firms about what wage-change decisions they made last *year* and about what plans they have for next year. Such information is then transmitted to subscribers infrequently, perhaps in an annual report.

Length of the Relationship

Buyers and sellers in financial and commodity markets often have no direct relationship with one another at all; they are temporarily joined by an intermediary (a broker), but otherwise have no ongoing contact. The markets are impersonal and transitory. Sellers of Treasury bills, for example, have no reason to consider the duration of their future relations with buyers; once the transaction is completed, they may never do business again.

The labor market is different. It is true that a few very brief employment relationships can be cited. For instance, in urban areas informal markets exist for day laborers, and migrant farm workers move from harvest site to harvest site. Most employees, however, expect to remain with their employers for considerable time periods, often stretching into years.

When employment histories of older workers are examined, spells of employment (job tenures) with a single employer often turn out to last twenty or more years. Moreover, most workers are concerned with (or even fearful of) the possibility of losing their jobs through layoff or discharge.[6] Such a job loss could lead to a period of unemployment with no guarantee that an eventual future employer would pay a wage as high as was received from the former employer.

Fair Treatment

Buyers in financial and commodity markets expect little more from sellers than delivery of the asset they are purchasing at the time specified. Sellers expect to be paid the agreed-upon price. Brokers generally see to it that fraud and nonperformance are rarely problems. Once again, the labor market is very different.

For example, some employers make a special point of enhancing and publicizing their reputation as good places to work. They may install practices designed to avoid or reduce layoffs, mechanisms to deal with employee concerns and grievances, and arrangements ensuring that fair standards for promotions and transfers will be applied. Management may create communications channels with employees; these may range from company newspapers to suggestion boxes and employee surveys. Such practices vary from company to company. Even unsophisticated employers with less elaborate human resource management (HRM) programs may from time to time offer a company picnic or a Christmas bonus.[7]

Employer practices are partially conditioned by social norms of fairness that have developed concerning treatment of employees. Employees are often seen as developing quasi-equity rights in their jobs that good employers should recognize. Senior workers (those who have been with the employer for many years) are commonly presumed to deserve special consideration. Indeed, in the increasing number of cases in which fired employees sue their former employers for "wrongful termination," seniority can be a factor in establishing a legal obligation of the employer to the employee.[8]

Newspaper accounts of plant closings poignantly record the complaints of long-service employees who have been laid off after giving "the best years of their lives" to the enterprise. Their employers are depicted as heartless and cruel by both the displaced workers and the reporters covering the story. In contrast, firms that protect their senior workers—say, by retraining them for other jobs within the firm or helping them move to a new location—are pictured as enlightened. These firms are seen as honoring a debt to their loyal workers, even if the debt is not strictly a legal one.

In fact, the idea that employers should be fair to their employees sometimes finds its way into law or at least sparks demands that laws be embodied to enforce the concept. Thus publicized plant closings in the 1980s sparked demands for legislation to restrict employer ability to lay off workers or shut down operations. One result was enactment of a federal law in 1988 requiring employers to give 60 days' advance notice to employees of impending plant closings or mass layoffs. Even where laws do not exist, courts have increasingly found that employers have implicit obligations to their workers.

In the absence of external law, notions of fairness may be codified in the workplace. In cases of collective bargaining with unions, labor–management contracts often express social norms in the form of formal rules regarding layoffs, discipline, promotions, and other workplace phenomena. Progressive nonunion employers may specify norms of their own behavior in documents such as employee handbooks and personnel manuals.

1–2   Concept of Organization

It would be easy to go on citing contrasts between the labor market and financial and commodity markets. Because economic analysis in the past often used financial and commodity markets as the basic model for the labor market, traditional textbooks dealing with human resource management frequently discarded the economic approach entirely (or relegated it to a few isolated chapters). Textbook writers commonly approached the subject from a legal, historical, behavioral, or simply a descriptive viewpoint.

These alternative approaches all have validity. The labor market *is* highly regulated, and labor law *does* condition market outcomes. Certainly, the legal aspect is important. Similarly, historical events such as wars, depressions, and social and political movements *have* helped create modern practices of human resource management. History should not be overlooked in the HRM context. Firms *are* complex organizations. Within an organizational context, behavioral science can provide insights into good practice. Finally, simply describing current practices and policies *is* essential to moving human resource management from the abstract to the concrete. A management subject cannot be discussed intelligently unless its key attributes are known.

Neglect of economics in human resource management, however, carries the unfortunate implicit assumption that the labor market is ultimately irrational, that good practice simply results from learning the folk wisdom of the trade, and that quantification is unlikely to improve on existing folkways of management. If such a view is accepted, HRM takes on the aura of a traditional craft, such as blacksmithing, that can only be learned on the job and that is passed on with little innovation from generation to generation. That is not the view embodied within this text. In the chapters to come, HRM is presented as consistent with rationality and efficiency and subject to quantitative analysis. In this regard, it is no different from other functional fields of management.

Beginning at the Beginning

The simple economic model of the firm found in microeconomic textbooks is misnamed. It really is a theory of a plant that has a capital stock fixed in the short run. Given the fixed capital stock, average and marginal cost curves can be drawn and profit-maximizing behavior can be predicted. Students will recognize such conclusions as "marginal revenue equals marginal cost" from the plant model.

A firm, however, can be more than a single plant. Multiplant firms, for example, are not at all uncommon. More important, the word *firm* implies an organization, not just a production decision. In the simple theory of the firm (plant), however, there is no explicit organization, just a mixing of factors of production. In the simple model it is impossible to say whether capital hires labor or labor hires capital. All that is known is that labor and capital somehow join together. Yet examples of groups of workers combining to hire factories are rare. The norm is for the owners of capital (or their management agents) to hire workers.

Moreover, the workers involved do not turn over on a daily basis. Definite authority patterns exist—employees take orders from supervisors—and the same employees, supervisors, and authority structures tend to remain in place at the firm for long periods of time. During these periods, a quality of relationship (good or bad) develops between employees and supervisors and influences the effectiveness and profitability of the firm.

The study of such human relationships has traditionally been the province of specialists in organizational design and development. If the analysis is really to begin from the beginning, fundamental questions must be asked. Why do organizations form in the first place? Why don't the owners of capital and the owners of labor (workers) meet on a daily basis in some flexible marketplace and decide—given that day's product prices—on mutually agreeable terms specifying what to produce, what should be the rental price of capital, and what should be the day's wage for labor?

Were such a flexible market actually to exist, there would be no organizations called firms. Indeed, it is unlikely that there would be any supervisors, since mutually agreeable tasks would have been determined in the market at the beginning of the day. Questions of motivation would not exist. No one would worry about promotion ladders, since every day a new deal would be cut in the marketplace. And unemployment would not be a concern, since anyone willing to supply labor at the going market wage would be hired.

Of course, such a flexible marketplace does not exist. Yet some limited labor markets approximate certain of its features. Consider, for example, the construction industry. Workers in construction often move from site to site as jobs are completed. Employees and the contractors or subcontractors who hire them do not have long-term relationships and do not form organizations in the usual sense of that word. In fact the line between employer and employee is sometimes blurred; skilled workers may sometimes act as contractors and may at other times work for someone else. Also, workers often own their own tools (capital).

Similarly, in some cities, taxi drivers may rent the cabs they drive. Independent truck drivers may also have such arrangements. In those situations labor is hiring capital rather than the other way around. Readers can certainly find other such examples of labor combining with capital without the formation of formal organizations. The key point is that these types of arrangements are the *exceptions* in the labor market, not the usual practice. It is primarily with those standard practices, rather than the occasional exceptions, that this text deals.

Why Capital Usually Hires Labor

Economics often explains phenomena and choices in terms of relative costs. If it is rare for labor to hire capital, but common for capital to hire labor, the economic explanation requires examination of the comparative costs of the two systems. Comparative costs, in turn, depend partly on consumer demand and partly on the technical characteristics of production.

Up to this point, the word *capital* has been used loosely. If capital is taken to mean plant and equipment, then it has only limited uses in production. For example, automobile factories are designed to produce automobiles, not other products. At some expense—as happened during World War II—these factories can be converted to produce aircraft or military vehicles. Converting them to produce shoes or soap, however, would entail scrapping most of the existing equipment and installing completely different machinery at heavy cost.

Thus the notion of capital meeting labor in some phantom marketplace and deciding what to produce is unrealistic. Capital in the sense of financial capital is fungible between uses. But once formed into plant and equipment, physical capital often has quite specific uses. It has what economists call putty-clay characteristics, that is, capital formation decisions are usually not reversible. Often the decisions involve not only what to produce but also the scale of production. The underlying production functions may well contain economies of scale so that, within a range, larger producers experience lower costs and have competitive advantages over smaller producers.

Such considerations mean that plants, often of considerable size, will be found in the marketplace at fixed locations producing similar or identical output from day to day. In principle, even with large, fixed plants, workers could hire capital. Yet if there are any costs at all in dealmaking, it will be much cheaper for the operator of a plant to hire 50, 100, or 1,000 workers rather than for groups of workers to coalesce and agree among themselves to hire a plant. Indeed, the notion of workers hiring capital facilities is generally not economically feasible.

Why Organizations Form

Although the nature of capital equipment explains why capital hires labor, it does not explain why organizations form. The term *organization* implies continuity. Why are the same workers employed day after day? In theory, hiring could be done on a daily basis. Workers would then be employed by firms two days in a row only by sheer coincidence.

The unusual nature of such a daily selection suggests that there are costs to rapid workforce turnover. Firms find it advantageous (cheaper) to retain workers over long periods than constantly to find new ones. Workers find it to their advantage to remain with a firm rather than to seek new employment on a daily basis.

From the viewpoint of the firm, various costs of turnover can be suggested. All workers, even in a particular occupation, are not identical. Some workers are more capable than others. Some can work cooperatively in teams; others have trouble getting along with fellow workers. Some can work without policing by (costly) supervisors; others need constant monitoring and direction. Some are trustworthy; others may be prone to steal company property. Screening workers to determine their talents and propensities can be a costly activity, involving interviewing, testing, and so on.

Even before screening can occur, a pool of potential workers must be found. In the absence of perfect knowledge and zero costs of mobility in the labor market, firms may have trouble obtaining a pool of workers to be screened in the first place. Advertising may be needed to attract such a pool. Recruiting offices may need to be established or recruitment officers sent to distant locations. Employment agencies or "headhunters" may have to be hired.

Sometimes the market may not supply workers who have the special skills needed by a firm. In such cases, expenditures on training will be required. Training may be needed over an extended period, and experienced workers may have to be diverted from regular production to provide the training to novices. When added together, recruitment, screening, and training costs can be expensive propositions for the firm and thus provide an incentive to hold down employee turnover.

There may also be turnover costs from the workers' perspective. Workplaces differ in conditions offered. Some employers offer pleasant surroundings and amiable fellow employees; others do not. Some provide training that might be useful in future employment at other workplaces; others simply use workers' existing skills. Some employers offer steady employment; others may be subject to seasonal or cyclical swings in demand. Finding a suitable job may involve the worker in a prolonged search that can be costly, particularly if the search involves a spell of unemployment during which no wage income is received.[9]

The incentives for firms and workers to stick together and avoid turnover give rise to the formation of organizations. Firm investment in workers in the sense of recruiting, screening, and training costs means that the firm will have a value beyond the price its capital equipment could fetch in the marketplace. The firm has a pool of human capital on which it may draw. If the firm is to be viable, the flow of value from this human form of capital must reflect the firm's investment in its workforce.

On the other hand, lacking perfect information, the firm may from time to time hire poor quality workers who can only be sorted out through monitoring by supervisors. In addition, the mere hiring of someone—even if he or she is highly skilled and potentially productive—does not guarantee actual performance of job duties. Supervisors will be needed to ensure that the firm receives an appropriate return from its pool of human capital. Authority relationships, combined with rewards and penalties, must be created. These relationships, rewards, and penalties are important aspects of the culture of most organizations.

Workers will typically feel they have an investment or stake in their jobs. Taking a new position is an either/or decision; a worker accepts a job offer or rejects it. A decision to accept may involve sacrificing other employment opportunities. Once hired, workers will have expectations concerning the treatment they will receive from their employer. These expectations may or may not be met. When they are not met, employee relations problems are likely to occur, perhaps adversely affecting productivity.

Since expectations may be disappointed, workers may want agents to represent them. They may seek unionization or be receptive to appeals from union organizers. In such cases, the internal union political process establishes union demands that in turn influence the firm's HRM policies. Workers may find other ways to pressure the firm to provide what is perceived to be fair treatment—that is, rather than exit (quit) their jobs, employees may find ways (possibly costly to the firm) to voice their discontent.

The kinds of firm and worker considerations outlined here give rise both to the existence of organizations and to the inherent organizational problems that ensue. The study of HRM is thus the study of organizational problems in the context of the employer-employee relationship. Since such problems have economic roots, studying HRM without reference to its economic underpinnings at best produces an incomplete picture. At worst it leads to an ad hoc approach that is ill equipped to cope with a changing environment.

One way in which firms sought to reduce commitment to employees and obtain more managerial flexibility in the 1980s was the increased use of contingent workers (part-timers, temporaries, and so on). In such cases employers, whether consciously or not, made a trade-off. Because of such workers' temporary nature and limited attachment to the firm, it did not pay for employers to make substantial investments in those workers. Also, there can be a loss of skills and loyalty available to the firm if contingent workers are used. The point is not that it is wrong for firms to rely on contingent employees; indeed, for some firms that may be the optimal approach. Rather, the key issue is to recognize and weigh the costs and benefits before embarking on such an HRM strategy.

Stockholders and Stakeholders

In the simple economic model, employees are paid the going wage for their work-time. The transaction is viewed as taking place at arms' length, that is, giving the worker no particular claim on the employer other than the agreed-upon wage for each hour worked. Indeed, the only persons with any equity in the firm are the official owners. For most firms of significant size, these owners are likely to be shareholders.

It is the shareholders (or more likely their designated agents) who are viewed as the appropriate parties to decide on the product mix, the technology of production to be employed, marketing strategy (including pricing), and plant location. Yet business critics often put forward claims that there are other stakeholders in the firm, who should have rights akin to those of shareholders. Such claims are made on behalf of communities in which production facilities are located, on behalf of consumers of the firm's output, on behalf of other businesses that may be affected by the firm's purchasing or supply decisions, and on behalf of the firm's workforce.

Economists have traditionally recognized certain grounds for government intervention on behalf of parties who are affected by firm decisions but who are not themselves stockholders in the firm. The most obvious examples are instances of air or water pollution, that is, situations in which the firm inflicts costs on area residents by treating the local atmosphere or river as if it were a free good. Certain kinds of zoning rules might also fall under the justification supplied by the theory of property rights and externalities.

In general, however, economists have not been receptive to wider notions of the social responsibility of business. They have tended to remain loyal to Adam Smith's dictum that the "invisible hand" of the marketplace would be sufficient to guide businesses devoted to maximizing the wealth of their shareholders.[10] Such wealth maximization, in the standard economic model, is seen as ultimately benefiting society at large. Given this approach, employees—like other suppliers and consumers—have no particular claim on the firm; they are free to take their business elsewhere (quit) if they become disenchanted with the pay or working conditions offered.

Despite these traditional economic views, the labor market is heavily regulated. Certain kinds of transactions are prohibited, for example, slavery, employment of prostitutes, paying less than the minimum wage, or hiring young workers below specified ages in many occupations. Elaborate legal frameworks regulate the relations among unions, employers, and workers. Special rules apply to the operation of certain fringe benefits such as pension plans and health insurance. In some cases, employers are required to provide certain benefits such as workers' compensation for employees who are injured on the job or suffer job-related illnesses.

A virtual grab bag of justifications is offered for such regulations. Some, like the bans on prostitution or slavery, are ultimately grounded in morality. Often, however, economic arguments (although not necessarily valid ones) are made in support of particular labor market regulations.

There is a common theme that runs through many of the arguments. Lawmakers and their political constituencies believe that employers have some obligation to their workers apart from paying the agreed-upon wage. They also believe that employers will tend to chisel on this obligation if not regulated. Put another way, there is a general social view that employees *are* stakeholders in their firms but that firms are reluctant to acknowledge their stakeholder rights. This view is not unique to the American labor market; most industrialized countries devote considerable regulatory effort to defining employer obligations in the employer-employee relationship.

Subsequent chapters will explore more fully the notion of the employee as a stakeholder. It is evident, however, that most employees have some stake in their jobs, a stake that typically increases with their length of service. The nature of that stake is most often not spelled out in contractual form, and indeed it might be difficult to write such a contract. To do so would require specifying how the employer and employee would behave towards each other in any foreseeable circumstance (and even in unforeseeable situations). Instead of an explicit agreement, there is thus an implicit contract—sometimes ill defined—surrounding the employment relationship.

The fact that employees are stakeholders does not mean that every legislative proposal that is made to protect an alleged stakeholder interest is optimal and appropriate. But the stakeholder relationship does explain why such proposals are so often made. From the viewpoint of HRM, acknowledging the stakeholder concept helps explain the complexity of the employer-employee attachment. It is key to understanding why there is such an attachment in the first place.

Motivation

The fact that employees are stakeholders in the firm means that the economic fortunes (or misfortunes) of the firm will have an important influence on the economic condition of its employees. In the worst case if the firm fails and ceases operation, whatever stake the employees had is wiped out. The fact that there is a connection between the economic condition of the firm and its employees does not necessarily mean that the employees will thereby automatically be motivated to act in the firm's interest, that is, to act so as to maximize profits.

Employees (and managers) are the firm's agents, hired to achieve its objectives. It costs something, however, to monitor their performance, and monitoring is imperfect. Given the limits of monitoring, employees may undertake actions that are not in the best interests of the firm. Such actions may range from inconsequential occasional goofing off to theft and embezzlement.

A long-standing goal of HRM policy has been to design systems that motivate employees, that is, systems that induce them to identify the firm's interest with their own and to work accordingly. If such motivation can be achieved, the firm can cut back on costly detailed monitoring, confident that appropriate employee performance will be forthcoming.

One possibility is to create automatic or discretionary compensation systems that provide tangible rewards for improved performance. Designing such systems without inadvertently creating perverse incentives (as will be seen in a subsequent chapter) is more difficult than may at first appear. Also, motivation can sometimes be achieved through such devices as supervisory training or developing appropriate group norms through quality circles and similar techniques. The objective is always the same, whatever tool is employed: making the goals of the agent (employee) coincident with those of the principal (firm or shareholders).[11]

1–3 Complexity of the Employment Contract

As already noted, one of the difficulties in defining the employer-employee relationship is the lack of employee homogeneity. Unlike bushels of wheat or tons of steel, workers are not easily standardized. Their productivities, skills, and attitudes vary. Some employees may be self-motivated problem solvers; others may shirk responsibility if not carefully monitored. The employee evaluation problem produces costs of turnover, since every employee who must be replaced "inflicts" on the firm the need to evaluate his or her successor. Even on the job, the question of employee output measurement is complicated. Firms may have difficulty sorting out good and bad performers.

In professional and managerial occupations, for example, employees do not turn out a simple standardized output that can be readily totaled. Is a scientist or engineer who is unable to solve an assigned problem necessarily a poor performer? Before such a question can be assessed, it is necessary to know something of the complexity of the problem and the facilities made available to seek its solution. Is a manager of a money-losing facility necessarily at fault? Surely, general economic conditions must be considered, or else one would erroneously penalize managers during general business recessions for circumstances beyond their control.

Even production workers who turn out standardized (countable) products pose evaluation problems. Workers often are employed in teams. One employee's output is dependent on that of the others. A poor worker within a team can thus reduce the output of his or her teammates. Other problems may stem from equipment unreliability, incompetent supervision, or perverse incentive systems. Again, interpreting worker output turns out to be a complex matter, even when that output can be easily measured.

The measurement and interpretation problem is a reflection of the absence of perfect information in real world firms. The problem requires the firm to devote resources to its solution. Someone has to undertake the design and operation of systems to screen and evaluate employees. Often the measurement and interpretation problem leads to a preference for filling vacancies and promotion opportunities from within the firm (a career ladder). It may be easier to evaluate employee potential among existing firm employees than among outsiders, since the firm has already had experience with the former group.

Once firms adopt the policy of internal advancement and long-term relationships with their employees, the stakeholder attribute of employees is established. At the time of hiring employees are accepting more than just a current job and wage; they are also tying their futures to the firm. They assume that satisfactory performance will be defined and recognized, and that superior performance will be appropriately rewarded. They assume that minor and isolated mistakes will not result in disproportionate penalties. But since employee evaluation is complex, uncertain, and subjective, employees will not always agree with the opinions of their evaluators. They may believe that their employer has unfairly abused the implicit understanding established at the time of hiring.

Apart from the question of individual evaluation, a complex exchange of future, as well as current, value is involved. The difficulty with a future exchange of value is that no one can foresee the future with certainty. External circumstances may result in internal changes within the firm that frustrate even recognized superior performers.

It is likely, for example, that if the firm in the future finds itself in a precarious financial situation—because of a general economic downturn, a shift in consumer tastes, a modification in government regulation, a more efficient competitor, a change in exchange rates, or a rise in material costs—worker expectations will be disappointed. Promotional opportunities may dry up, and layoffs may be threatened.

Exactly what is the employer's obligation in these circumstances? It is just not possible to specify all such contingencies and build them into the usually implicit employer-employee understanding. The future is uncertain, and risk can be shared between employer and employee. Exactly how that risk ends up being distributed—a decision which, as a formal matter, is typically in the hands of the employer—can affect the general quality of the employer–employee relationship. Even in the case of firms with written union contracts, there are often disputes about contractual interpretations and obligations.

The complexity of the employer-employee relationship is inevitable given the complexity and unpredictability of the economic environment of the real world. Within the firm, someone must undertake to deal with the inherent problems of the HRM function: recruitment, screening, training, evaluation, discipline, compensation, and rewards, as well as routine record keeping. Someone must pass judgment on the claims of the employee/stakeholders.

Of course, the "someone" does not necessarily have to be an elaborate HRM bureaucracy. According to one survey, expenditures on the HRM department run about 1% of total operating costs in a typical firm.[12] In very small firms, there may not be enough employees to justify creation of a separate HRM department. There will still be a human resource management *function* to be performed, however, whether or not there is an HRM department. The existence of the function is independent of its place on the organization chart. What the place on the organization chart influences is the effectiveness of the function's performance.

Larger firms typically find that there are sufficient economies of scale in specialization to justify a separate HRM department. The creation of a separate department, however, poses its own problems. A tension necessarily arises between line managers, who actually use most of the firm's human resources, and HRM managers, who may control and design the systems through which those human resources are obtained, evaluated, compensated, rewarded, and sometimes removed.[13] HRM managers are more prone to emphasize the claims of employees/ stakeholders than are line managers facing immediate production deadlines. A critical decision for top management, therefore, is the relative authority to be exercised by the two groups.

1–4   External Constraints

In considering the appropriate balance between the HRM manager and the line manager, top management is likely to be influenced by factors external to the firm. If the human resource area is perceived to be a potential problem, top management is more likely to place the function in the hands of professionals than if the area is quiescent. Historically, an important factor in persuading top management that the human resource area was a source of potential trouble was the perceived threat of unionization. During periods such as the 1930s and 1940s, when unions were growing rapidly, HRM professionals tended to gain authority relative to line managers.

A second source of potential difficulty in the human resource area has been government regulation. Such regulation has come in two main spurts. During the Great Depression of the 1930s, part of President Roosevelt's New Deal legislative program involved the expansion of social insurance programs such as unemployment compensation. Laws dealing with union rights were enacted, and various forms of protective regulation, such as a federal minimum wage, were adopted. Federal action, in turn, was imitated at the state level. This expansion of government regulation required expertise at the firm level to interpret the new rules and evaluate their implications for the firm's HRM policies.

Another spurt of regulatory expansion began in the mid-1960s and extended until the late 1970s. The nation's racial problems triggered the enactment of a number of civil rights statutes, including laws and regulations covering equal employment opportunity (EEO) at the workplace. At the same time, rising female participation in the workforce drew EEO regulation into sex-related issues. New regulations during this period also covered such areas as occupational safety and health standards and the provision by employers of fringe benefits such as pensions and health insurance for employees. Finally, concern about inflation in the 1970s led to episodes of wage controls and guidelines.

HRM Manager as Police Officer

While external challenges to the firm such as unionization or expanding government regulation historically created a demand for the services of HRM professionals, they also made the job of the HRM manager more difficult. When internal human resource challenges lead top management to strengthen its HRM function,

HRM managers will be viewed as integral parts of the firm's overall strategy. When the threat is external, however, HRM managers may be perceived as police officers, enforcing rules with which the firm must comply, but which cause deviations from the normal way of doing business.

There is no simple solution to this dilemma. It is often the case, however, that internal HRM policies designed to recognize the employee as a stakeholder will also help cope with the regulatory environment. For example, an employee discharged for improper conduct will frequently be disqualified from receiving unemployment compensation. The employer, which funds the unemployment compensation account from which such benefits are claimed, may wish to challenge any claims the discharged employee might make for unemployment insurance in order to hold down firm labor costs. An employer that has a system of due process, that is, a system that carefully reviews the evidence and metes out appropriate penalties, is more likely to prevail in blocking payments than one that fires employees at a whim.

In any case, it is a mistake for HRM managers to see their main roles as police officers. The external forces—union growth and regulatory expansion—that have in the past led to an upgrading of the HRM function have experienced periods of ebb and flow. During the 1980s, for example, both forces definitely ebbed. Recession and increased competition in the early to middle years of the decade put pressure on firms to concern themselves with cost controls and efficiency. Unions lost members and often made concessions to employers regarding pay and workrules. At the same time labor market regulations became less stringent, with the assent of the conservative Reagan administration.

The kind of HRM department that did well in the changed environment was one that had become part of its firm's strategic planning mechanism. HRM departments that had integrated HRM policy into the firm's overall objectives retained their status and authority. They could adapt to the new pressures. But HRM departments had primarily functioned as police lost ground.

Stakeholders and the Political Process

Even in periods such as the 1980s, when regulation ebbs, the labor market is still left with a heavy overlay of government intervention. Of course, other markets are also subject to regulation. Even the highly flexible financial and commodity markets are constrained by complex rules and procedures involving disclosure requirements, insider trading, and the like. Nevertheless, it is legitimate to ask why there is so much focus on the labor market.

The stakeholder approach has already been mentioned as a key element in fostering regulation. Employees do have a stake in their jobs, but the mutual obligations of employers and employees are not clearly specified and inevitably give rise to frictions. Since there are more employees than employers, politicians in democratic countries will devote more effort to specifying employee rights than employer rights.

Macro Social and Economic Considerations

There are other factors besides the stakeholder approach that explain the political concern with HRM issues. National welfare suffers when social harmony breaks down. Social conflict inevitably is focused on the workplace; it is the labor market, after all, from which most people derive the bulk of their incomes. Thus for most people the labor market is the most crucial market in which they participate.

Employer actions in the labor market will tend to spark debate, controversy, and demand for remedial regulation. Individual employers who pursue their own firm-level objectives may produce the kind of negative externalities toward social harmony that air pollution produces in the atmosphere. Labor laws of the 1930s and EEO laws of the 1960s were designed to calm social tensions that were produced, in part, by the then-existing employer policies and practices.

Just as macrosocial considerations have played a part in the regulatory scheme, so too have macroeconomic considerations. In general, macroeconomic policy since the end of World War II has been aimed at reducing the twin evils of inflation and unemployment. Inevitably, the actions of individual firms can have negative externalities on the objectives of low inflation and low unemployment. Wage increases at the firm level may add to inflation, but no automatic mechanism internalizes this cost to society into the firm's calculations of profit and loss. Similarly, the multiplier effects of firm hiring and layoff policies on the overall unemployment rate are not normally considered by the firm in its decision making.

Although these issues of macroeconomic policy are outside the scope of this text—since they deal with questions beyond the control or concern of firm-level managers—it is important for managers to understand that such issues exist. As long as HRM decisions have an impact on the general health of the economy, regulatory policies will be proposed and aimed at such decisions. Examples include the wage controls and guidelines of the 1970s (aimed at inflation) and the proposals for plant closing restrictions in the 1980s (aimed at unemployment). Some of these policies may be effective; others may be ineffective or perverse. But they will continue to exist or be debated.

Regulatory Constituencies

Regulatory programs create constituencies that seek to protect existing government rules and to foster new ones. Provisions in the tax code, for example, that favor employer-provided fringe benefits are supported by consultants and insurance companies that design and provide such benefits and by employers who have already incorporated such benefits into their compensation practices.

The growth of unions in the 1930s and 1940s was certainly fostered by the government regulation and policy of that period. Although the rules have not been so favorable to unions since, the establishment of a large labor movement naturally focuses public policy on issues of the labor market. Since the 1940s, unions have not been especially successful—at least with regard to the private sector—in obtaining new rules and policies that would foster their own growth. They were, however, the major political impetus behind some of the key regulatory expansions in the 1970s, notably in the field of occupational safety and health and in the regulation of pension plans.

Regulation Fosters Regulation

Finally, regulation has a tendency to create problems that call for regulatory solutions. For example, employer-provided health insurance is heavily subsidized through the tax code, since employer payments for such coverage are not subject to individual income tax. Many employees have employer coverage and, therefore, pay only a fraction of the cost of medical procedures (or nothing at all in some cases). The low marginal cost to the patient, combined with other aspects of the health care industry, has led to a substantial increase in the quantity and price of medical services. As costs of health care have risen, new regulations have expanded to encourage health care cost containment.

It is important for HRM managers to develop an appreciation of the political economy of regulation. Larger employers and employer associations have an interest in the course of regulation in the labor market. An understanding of the costs and benefits of regulation is essential to the development of an employer position with regard to proposed regulatory changes.

The external effects on the social and political atmosphere of HRM decisions taken at the firm level pose a problem for the employer's community. Actions that particular firms take in their own best interest, for example, a mass layoff at an unprofitable facility, may run contrary to social norms and create political reactions in the form of regulatory constraints. Individual firms do not internalize these downstream costs to other employers of their HRM policies. A firm may support an organization such as the Chamber of Commerce or a trade association to look after its wider interests. These organizations, however, primarily deal with proposed regulations in the legislative arena; they cannot control the actions of individual firms that may spark the proposals in the first place.

HRM Professionals and the Law

Because of the regulatory framework surrounding the labor market, many human resource professionals have legal backgrounds. Excessive concentration on the legal aspects of HRM, however, leads to overemphasis on the policing function. Simply staying out of legal trouble is not, by itself, a human resource strategy.

In terms of training, students with MBA backgrounds or other business degrees in HRM have a decided edge over individuals with exclusively legal backgrounds. The law does not provide a firm with an HRM plan. Such a plan must be a reflection of the firm's general objectives. An overall firm plan involves the various functional areas—such as marketing, production, and finance—within the firm. Students from educational programs that provide an overview of the various functional areas have an edge in making the human resource function a key element in the firm's strategic plan. Readers of this text who are considering or planning HRM careers are well advised to obtain broad training in the various management functions, regardless of the particular degree program they are following.

As an illustration of the HRM need for a broad background, consider the following circumstances and questions:

- A firm is planning to enter a product market known for its uncertainties and rapid changes. What form of compensation system for employees would be best suited to this new venture?

- A firm finds it has a shortage of labor in a given occupation. Should it intensify its recruiting efforts, raise pay levels, or train and promote existing employees into the occupation?

- A firm faces a bargaining demand from a union for an enhancement of its pension plan. Management has determined that the cost of the enhancement, along with the other demands being made, does not exceed the firm's planned labor cost increase. Apart from meeting overall cost targets, does the firm have an interest in the composition of the compensation offered to employees?

Although legal aspects may be involved in these circumstances and questions, the answers cannot be found in law books. In this regard HRM is no different from other functional areas within the firm that are subject to regulation. Marketing, for example, is constrained by regulations regarding truth in advertising. Yet a marketing strategy for the firm cannot be obtained by studying the regulations of the Federal Trade Commission. Nor can a financial plan be based exclusively on the rules of the Securities and Exchange Commission. The law is more likely to provide the don'ts than the dos.

1–5 Efficiency of HRM Policies

HRM offers guidance to a firm concerning the appropriate use of its human resources. Apart from the regulatory restrictions just discussed, the word *guidance* sometimes implies constraint. Practices that line managers might follow with regard to their employees may not be considered good policy by HRM managers.

In the simple economic view, constraints are often associated with inefficiency. Individuals and firms are assumed to be rational maximizers; if they are hindered from following their inclinations, suboptimal results are predicted to follow. For example, international trade theorists condemn quotas on imports as inefficient because quotas prevent profit maximizing importers from purchasing as much from abroad as their self-interest would otherwise dictate.

Applied within the firm, however, the view that constraints are always inefficient is misleading. Indeed, taken to an extreme, such a belief is contradicted by the existence of firms as productive organizations. Management decision making of any sort is, after all, the imposition of constraints. Someone must establish company policies, goals, and plans, and such policies, goals, and plans are themselves constraints. Firms are systems of authority, control, and decisions. Thus to say that constraints are inherently inefficient is to say that firms are inherently inefficient.

Various reasons can be cited to support the proposition that good human resource policies raise efficiency. Perhaps the most significant evidence is empirical. During the 1970s and 1980s various case studies documented that many of the most successful enterprises devoted substantial attention and resources to their HRM policies.[14] Indeed, Americans became fascinated with such HRM policies as lifetime employment and consensus decision making, which had originated with large Japanese firms that had so successfully invaded the product markets of the United States and other countries.

Theoretical reasons also support HRM policy as an efficiency booster. The real world is not characterized by perfect, costless information. Line managers are not normally HRM experts, nor is it necessarily appropriate that line managers spend their scarce time to become experts. The economies normally associated with a division of labor suggest that HRM professionals are needed as consultants to line managers.

Moreover, in a world of imperfect information and imperfect monitoring, the incentives of line managers may not always be coincident with the best interests of the enterprise. For example, a line manager might feel his or her best interest lies in showing a quick profit, even if this showing requires burning out key employees in whom the firm had previously made a significant investment. Higher management may not be able to detect the costs of the burnouts as clearly as the boost in short-term profits.

In addition, a line manager who creates human resource problems within his or her immediate area of authority may indirectly create problems for other line managers and for the firm as a whole. There are negative externalities involved and, as in other aspects of economic life, such externalities may require constraints. For example, word of a line manager who mistreats employees may spread, creating mistrust and suspicion throughout the enterprise. Or one line manager's burnouts may prove troublesome to his or her successor.

Historically, dealing with the labor problem—as it was originally called—led to the development of professional management education and to schools of business. Creation of the scientific management approach in the early part of this century was in large part focused on human resource problems. Organizations such as the American Management Association had their roots in the search for remedies to the labor problem. Underlying management education, therefore, is the belief that better ways of managing through appropriate policies and constraints can be uncovered or invented, particularly in the human resource area.

Summary

The themes set forth in this introductory chapter will reappear throughout the subsequent chapters. The following seven points, which summarize this introductory look at human resource management, are important to stress from the outset.

1. An economic approach to human resource management can provide insight into, and understanding of, the HRM field that is often lacking in traditional historical, legal, and descriptive HRM textbooks. Nevertheless, it is important to recognize that the labor market differs dramatically from the abstract perfect markets of elementary economics courses and even from the flexible financial and commodity markets of the real world. Wages are set infrequently, employees are not homogeneous commodities, measurement and information are imperfect, and the costs of employee turnover can be high.

2. Deviations of the real world labor market from the abstract perfect market explain the formation of organizations (including firms) and give rise to the organizational problems so often studied in business and management schools.

3. Employee turnover costs contribute to indefinite and often long-term employer-employee relationships. The employment contract is not simply an exchange of today's labor for today's wage. Rather, it is a complex, and often imprecise, implicit agreement whose terms can easily be misinterpreted by either side. In some cases employees may seek unions to act as their agents in defending perceived rights under these agreements.

4. Employees are stakeholders in their firms. This concept has crucial implications for human resource policy formulation. The fact that employees are stakeholders does not mean, however, that employees will see their interests as identical to those of the firm. Thus supervision, compensation systems, or other devices regulating or motivating behavior are often necessary to bring the interests of the firm and the employee closer together.

5. The view that employees are stakeholders and the importance of that stake to the income security of much of the population have given rise to substantial government regulation of the labor market. Also important in explaining the growth of labor market regulation throughout the industrialized world is the potential that individual employers can inflict negative externalities on social harmony. Once in place, labor market regulation tends to foster further regulation as regulatory problems require regulatory solutions.

6. Historically, HRM has been elevated in importance within firms by external threats, such as the growth of unions in the 1930s and 1940s or the expansion of government regulation of the labor market in the 1960s and 1970s. It is unwise, however, for HRM managers to view their roles primarily as police agents, enforcing rules that keep the firm out of trouble. HRM should be an integral part of firm policy and planning.

7. There is an inevitable tension between HRM professionals and line managers. Although line managers are agents of the firm's shareholders, their self-interests and the interests of the shareholders do not always coincide. HRM policies and constraints can be viewed as devices to prevent this discrepancy of interests from reducing firm efficiency.

EXERCISES

Problem

Following are descriptions of actions taken by two companies affecting their employees as might appear in a newspaper account. Evaluate the decisions reported to have been taken by the two companies. Were their responses appropriate, given the economic problems they faced? What impact might the actions have on employee productivity, retention, or future recruitment? Were the decisions made by company management fair?

Pay, Job Cuts at Motorparts

Motorparts, Inc., a major manufacturer of automobile parts and components, announced today that its nonunion employees would be taking a pay cut averaging 10% for at least one year. Various executive "perks," such as company-paid club memberships, are being discontinued. The company said that there would be a reduction in the number of middle management positions, which would be achieved mainly through attrition and an early retirement incentive program. But some involuntary layoffs might also be needed. Company officials met today to work out details of the early retirement incentive plan.

Queried about possible layoffs of nonunion white-collar office workers, a Motorparts representative stated that no layoffs were planned in the immediate future since the pay cut would provide sufficient savings. Should layoffs be necessary, the company would "consider" extending the early retirement program to nonsupervisory workers. However, the representative noted that many white-collar office workers have been with the company for a relatively short period of time because of turnover and, hence, would not be eligible for a pension.

The announcement of pay and job cuts followed the conclusion of negotiations between Motorparts and its unionized production workers last week. In the face of substantial operating losses over the past three years, attributed by company spokespersons largely to foreign competition, the unionized workers agreed to a 5% pay reduction, reduced holidays and other benefits, and the discontinuation of a cost-of-living pay escalator clause.

In exchange for the reduction in labor costs, union workers received a new profit-sharing plan whose details have not yet been announced. Reportedly, it will pay bonuses to workers when and if Motorparts returns to profitability in its core manufacturing operations, but will exclude sharing profits based on sales of real estate or company subsidiaries. Such sales may be needed to meet Motorparts' substantial debt service obligations.

Union workers also received "assurances" that two of Motorparts' older plants would not be closed within the next 18 months, according to union officials. Rumors of plant closures had created a political backlash within the union against the incumbent leadership. A company spokesperson verified that assurances had been given and attributed them to a need to prevent "hotheads" within the union from taking control and complicating labor relations.

Fantail Airline Employees Grumble About Long Hours

Airline traffic normally picks up substantially during the holiday season. While flight personnel have limits on the hours they may work, imposed by federal regulation, and nonsupervisory workers must be paid overtime after 40 hours, professional and middle management employees have no such restrictions. This year, Fantail Airlines announced that it would expect such employees to work a 60-hour/6-day week for the remainder of the Christmas season, with no extra pay.

Fantail has been a major force in the airline industry during the past two years, aggressively pursuing new markets with fare reductions and new routes. The new approach to the deregulated air traffic market began when a new management team was installed after an unfriendly takeover of the firm. Because of the new approach, passenger traffic this year greatly exceeded the level achieved a year ago at this time. The result, according to a company spokesperson, has been a shortage of employees "at all levels."

Although Fantail has achieved record profits during the past year, company policy is not to add new employees just because business is improving. "We are successful precisely because we hold down our labor costs," the spokesperson said. "When the new management team took over two years ago and turned this company around, it was evident that there was a history of inefficient use of our personnel. Our policy is to use our employees effectively and that means more work from the current labor force."

No affected employees wanted to comment publicly on the increased hours. A number, however, were willing to talk anonymously. One middle manager referred to the new directive as evidence that "Scrooge is now running this company." Before the new management team came in, he reported, company policies, especially at holiday time, were to allow employees time off to be with their families. Employees remember those days as a "Golden Age," he said, even if Fantail was not as big then as it is now.

A computer programmer reported that she was anxious to find work elsewhere, but that the Christmas season was not the ideal time to look around. In the meantime, she said, she would not complain about the new policy, since people who have complained about working conditions in the recent past have been fired. She noted that some people who wanted to leave were hanging on nevertheless until they reached the early retirement age under Fantail's pension program.

While acknowledging that there has been "some grumbling," a Fantail personnel executive suggested that the grumblers were from the "old regime" and hadn't adapted themselves to deregulation in the airline industry.

ENDNOTES

1. Ross notes, "if labor markets behaved like financial markets, the theories of finance would be used to study them" (Stephen A. Ross, "The Interrelations of Finance and Economics: Theoretical Perspectives," *American Economic Review*, vol. 77 [May 1987], p. 29). The fact that different approaches are taken in the modern study of these markets represents recognition of the differences in institutional structure between them.

2. Sellers of certain consumer-oriented financial assets, for example, mutual funds and insurance policies, do advertise. In the case of such assets, there may well be considerable information costs that give an incentive to advertise. Economies of scale help determine which side—buyer or seller—pays for the advertisement. An insurance company hopes to reach many potential clients just as an employer with a vacancy hopes to reach many potential applicants. The cost per client (applicant) is low. Someone in the market to buy an insurance policy is not looking for a large number of offers, thus cost considerations explain why such buyers do not place "insurance-wanted" ads. In the labor market, job seekers occasionally do place "situations-wanted" ads. Typically, however, it is cheaper for job seekers to scan the ads of employers with vacancies, determine which might suit their needs, and then make themselves known to the prospective employers.

3. An oligopsonistic market is one in which relatively few sellers compete.

4. Evidence that price generally exceeds marginal cost can be found in Robert E. Hall, "Market Structure and Macroeconomic Fluctuations," *Brookings Papers on Economic Activity* (2:1986), pp. 285–338.

5. The phenomenon of "no-help wanted" is analyzed in Arthur M. Okun, *Prices & Quantities: A Macroeconomic Analysis* (Washington; Brookings Institution, 1981), pp. 59–61.

6. The term *layoff* is generally applied to a circumstance in which a worker or workers are terminated for "economic reasons," such as a decline in demand for the firm's products. An employee is laid off not because of incompetence, poor performance, or misconduct, but because his or her services are not needed. Layoffs may be temporary, that is, the worker may expect to be recalled to the firm when demand picks up. In contrast, a *discharge* (or *firing*) usually refers to a termination based on individual incompetence, poor performance, or misconduct.

7. The phrase *human resource management* and the acronym *HRM* are sometimes used as substitutes for *personnel policy,* an older phrase. However, use of HRM is meant to express a view that the employer-employee relationship is an aspect of the firm that can be analyzed and managed, just as other aspects (such as marketing and finance) are. The label is less important than the idea, and human resource management or HRM are generally used throughout this text with that idea in mind. Students may also come across the phrase *industrial relations* in this field. Today that phrase is often used to mean union-management relations in contrast to nonunion employer-employee situations.

8. Donald W. Brodie, "Individual Contracts of Employment (Part I)," *Labor Law Journal,* vol. 39 (September 1988), pp. 585–604, especially pp. 598–599.

9. Unemployed workers may be eligible for unemployment insurance benefits (discussed in later chapters), depending on their prior work history. Benefits received by those who are eligible are generally substantially below their foregone earnings.

10. Adam Smith, *An Inquiry into the Nature and Causes of the Wealth of Nations* (New York: Modern Library, 1937 {1776}), p. 423.

11. John W. Pratt and Richard J. Zeckhauser, eds., *Principals and Agents: The Structure of Business* (Boston: Harvard Business School Press, 1985).

12. "Personnel Expenditures Are Increasing, but Staff Sizes Are Stable, BNA Survey Finds," *Daily Labor Report,* September 2, 1988, pp. A4–A5.

13. Such conflict is itself a reflection of the deviation of the firm as an organization from the simple economic model of the firm. In theory all agents of the firm, whether line managers or not, ought to be engaged in the mutual pursuit of the firm's profit-maximizing objective. The difficulty of creating incentives so that all managers work toward this end without conflict is at the root of staff–line manager tensions.

14. William G. Ouchi, *Theory Z: How American Business Can Meet the Japanese Challenge* (Reading, Mass.: Addison-Wesley, 1981); Thomas J. Peters and Robert H. Waterman, Jr., *In Search of Excellence: Lessons from America's Best-Run Companies* (New York: Harper & Row, 1982); Fred K. Foulkes, *Personnel Policies in Large Nonunion Companies* (Englewood Cliffs, N.J.: Prentice-Hall, 1980).

Chapter Two

THE U.S. WORKFORCE

For most of this century, the federal government has provided data on the makeup of the U.S. labor force. Today it is possible to obtain detailed information on the occupational, demographic, and industrial composition of employment. Such information is compiled on an aggregate basis and gives a picture of the employment environment in which each firm must make its human resource management decisions.

Each employer, of course, will have its own, unique workforce characteristics; there is no "average" firm that looks exactly like the aggregate in miniature. Starting with averages and aggregates, however, will help pinpoint major HRM issues. Depending on their workforce composition, individual firms may be more concerned about some issues than others.

Although information about the American workforce is widely available, many managers, whether in the HRM field or not, do not take advantage of this important source of data. This chapter therefore has two goals. The first is to familiarize readers with the composition and characteristics of the workforce and to draw out their implications for HRM. The second goal is to acquaint the reader with available information sources.

2–1 Management Personnel

Often, the field of human resource management is thought to focus on nonsupervisory employees—people who take orders from others. The historical focus on the "labor problem," discussed in Chapter 1, fostered this view. When the field of industrial relations (also known as labor relations, or employee relations) was originally created, most of the analytical attention was centered on blue-collar, factory workers who were regarded as prone to form unions, engage in strikes,

23

and adopt other behaviors top management saw as threatening. As will be seen, however, factory workers now constitute a distinct minority of the workforce.

As a result of the original focus, viewing management itself as a human resource is a fairly recent phenomenon. It is not uncommon for that component of the HRM function dealing with executives to be separated administratively from other elements of the HRM apparatus. Executive development is often seen as a distinct field from the rest of HRM.

Size of the Managerial Workforce

Since management is at the top of the authority pyramid in virtually all firms, starting an examination of the U.S. workforce with managerial occupations is quite appropriate. But providing a precise definition of *management* is difficult. In general terms, managerial employees are thought to be those involved in the development and execution of firm policy. For statistical purposes, the government defines a variety of occupations as falling into the classification "executive, administrative, and managerial." Such occupations include the following:

- Accountants and Auditors
- Personnel Specialists
- Purchasing Agents
- Underwriters
- Top Executives (such as CEOs)
- Public Administrators

Table 2–1, based on U.S. Bureau of Labor Statistics data and projections, shows that the managerial group accounts for about a tenth of total employment, a relatively small proportion. Moreover, even though it will be growing somewhat more rapidly than other groups, the executive, administrative, and managerial classification will still be at roughly that percentage of the workforce in the year 2000.[1]

It is well to emphasize the relative smallness of the managerial group of occupations as compared with the rest of the workforce. Often schools of management put great emphasis in courses on organizational behavior and development, which are basically managerial relations classes. The intent is to train future managers in how to lead, motivate, and coordinate other managers. Yet, important as these skills are, Table 2–1 makes it clear that they fail to involve the bulk of a firm's human resources. The managerial interaction is certainly crucial; however, even in firms in which that interaction is in some sense optimal, most HRM problems will not be solved unless other occupational groups are included in the solution.

Nevertheless, management must not be neglected as a key factor in HRM planning. Chapter 1 noted the discrepancy between financial and commodity markets and the labor market. In the latter there is substantial concern about issues such as fairness, turnover costs, and the like. How these concerns are met is typically the responsibility of management employees (who, of course, also have

TABLE 2-1 Trends in Occupational Employment

Occupational Group	Percent of Workforce		Percent Change in Employment	
	1986	*Projected 2000*	*1972–1986*	*1986–2000*
White Collar				
Executive, administrative, managerial	9.5%	10.2%	73.7%	23.7%
Professionals	12.1	12.9	57.5	27.0
Technicians, salesworkers, administrative support	32.4	32.8	45.5	20.5
Blue Collar				
Precision production, craft, repair workers	12.5	11.7	29.6	12.0
Operators, fabricators, laborers	14.6	12.6	− 1.3	2.6
Service Workers (except private household)	14.8	16.5	45.9	32.7
Other Groups				
Private household workers	.9	.7	− 31.9	− 2.6
Farming, forestry, and fishing workers	3.2	2.6	− 10.4	− 4.6
Total Employment	100.0	100.0	33.4	19.2

Source: George T. Silvestri and John M. Lukasiewicz, "A Look at Occupational Employment Trends to the Year 2000," *Monthly Labor Review*, vol. 110 (September 1987), p. 47; data for 1972–1986 growth rates from *Employment and Earnings*, vol. 31 (January 1984), p. 14, and vol. 34 (January 1987), p. 177. (*Note:* Data for 1972–1986 are not entirely consistent with those for 1986–2000.)

many other responsibilities concerning the firm's performance). But the relative smallness of the managerial group and the historic separation of management development from the rest of HRM raise important questions about the unilateral ability of management to carry out the HRM function.

Compensation

Members of the executive, administrative, and managerial grouping earn about 40% more than other full-time workers, as can be seen from Table 2–2. Even this figure is misleading, since pay increases with authority; top managerial offi-

TABLE 2—2   Median Weekly Earnings of Full-Time Wage and Salary Workers by Occupation, 1987

Occupational Group	Median Weekly Earnings
Executive, administrative, managerial	$530
Professional	518
Technical, sales, administrative support	332
Service workers	234
Precision production, craft, repair	419
Operators, fabricators, laborers	308
All Employees*	373

*Includes occupations not shown.

Source: Data from *Employment and Earnings,* vol. 34 (January 1988), pp. 224–225.

cials account for only a small portion of the grouping. At the very top echelons of management, compensation levels are likely to dwarf those of nonmanagerial employees. Thus management perceptions about the importance of pay, pay changes, fringe benefits, and the continuity of such payments through job security may be very different from those of the average employee. A potential communications and understanding gap exists.

Several areas of difference can be highlighted. Executive pay commonly consists of two elements: a salary and a bonus, which often is determined in relation to the economic performance of the firm. Table 2—3 shows the importance of top executive bonus plans by various industrial sectors. Bonuses as a proportion of salaries range from about one-third in banking to over one-half in manufacturing. Although there is much to be said for extending the concept of variable bonuses to broader groups of employees (a topic discussed in subsequent chapters), in current practice such bonuses are substantially less common for the average worker than for top executives.

The use of bonuses related to firm performance means that executive pay may be more variable from year to year than the pay of ordinary employees. Two factors can be cited as explanations for this difference. First, the overall economic performance of the firm is more closely related to the performance of top executives than it is to the efforts of individual, nonsupervisory employees. Econometric evidence indicates that the quality of the managerial input contributes importantly to productivity.[2] However, recent economic theory emphasizes the potential tension between *principals* and *agents*.[3] In this case the principals are the firm's stockholders and the agents are management officials. By linking executive pay to firm performance, shareholders hope to provide incentive for better managerial decision making. This desire of the principals (stockholders) is usually

TABLE 2–3   Importance of Executive Bonus Plans, May 1986

Sector	Percent of Surveyed Companies with Bonus Plans
Manufacturing	91%
Construction	84
Retail trade	86
Commercial banks	82
Insurance	68
Gas and electric utilities	48

Source: Charles A. Peck, *Top Executive Compensation, 1987 Edition*, Report No. 889 (New York: The Conference Board, 1987), p. 2.

put forth as the demand side of the executive pay story.

Second, on the supply side, the higher pay levels of executives make them less risk averse than other employees. Executives can afford more income fluctuation without severe consequences to their accustomed living standards.[4] Generally, even during periods of low bonus payments, higher income executives will have greater personal assets on which to draw and easier access to loan markets than do other employees.

Indeed, the risk preferences of executives may account for the process of advancement and the escalating compensation rates, as well as the widespread use of bonus pay, as position in the hierarchy increases. Some economists have modeled the way executives rise in the firm's authority hierarchy as a "tournament," a contest in which large financial "prizes" reward players who advance to the next level of the career ladder. The reward for good performance at any one level is both the pay at that level and the opportunity to compete for the next level. Since there are fewer positions for which to compete as the position in the hierarchy rises, the reward by level must escalate disproportionately.[5]

Because of their higher income levels, managerial employees tend to be in higher income tax brackets. They will place greater value on forms of compensation that avoid or defer tax liabilities. For example, when capital gains were taxed at lower rates than ordinary income, that is, until 1987, use of stock option arrangements (which provided income in the form of capital gains if the firm's stock rose in value) were particularly popular.

To some extent, stock option plans also meet the problem of principals and agents, since stock price appreciation partly reflects managerial quality and serves the interests of stockholders. Yet the volatility in overall stock market performance suggests that better compensation systems would rely on relative, not absolute, stock prices.[6] Empirical studies of executive compensation and its linkage to firm performance and stock price performance have produced mixed results, however.[7] It may be that tax considerations are sufficiently important so as to obscure other objectives in setting top executive pay.

Various "perks" (perquisites) provided to executives—such as company cars, legal consultations, expense accounts, club memberships, and the like—also reflect tax incentives. Many of these do not fit neatly into the principals and agents rationale and exist only for tax reasons. The perks have the side effect, however, of making the form of executive pay quite different from the compensation package offered ordinary employees. Advocates of reducing the apparent gap between the treatment of executives and other workers—often on the grounds that excessive perks adversely affect nonexecutive productivity—often fail to perceive the impact of the tax code in fostering such arrangements.[8]

Are the Principals Well Served by Executives?

The compensation of top executives inevitably sparks public interest. Various surveys—such as the annual listing of top executive pay by the magazine *Business Week*—respond to this public curiosity. Questions are often raised about whether top executives are really worth the high salaries, benefits, and perks they receive.

In part, this questioning is no different from the critical approach taken to the high salaries received by superstar athletes and entertainers. Some people see it as immoral that a baseball player—however talented—should be paid more than, say, a physicist. The only answer that can be given is that the labor market places a high value on an athlete who can draw substantial public interest and enthusiasm. Team owners, in bidding for players, make such calculations.

The questioning of executive pay levels, however, often involves a deeper issue of possible market failure. In the case of professional sports, it is ultimately the team owners and managers who decide how much they are willing to pay for a given player. Players can demand what they like, but their demands are evaluated in terms of benefits and costs from a commercial viewpoint. In the case of top executives, however, the charge is that the executives themselves are setting their own pay (or controlling the process by which it is set). In other words, the agents are suspected of making decisions that run counter to the interests of the shareholders (principals).

To some extent, financial markets may mitigate this problem. If executives operate contrary to the interests of owners, they may cause the firm's stock to be undervalued and thereby invite takeovers, unfriendly mergers, and their eventual replacement by more responsive managers. Indeed, those who argue for relatively unfettered takeover activity often do so on the grounds that it is a check against abusive management actions.[9]

However, the market for corporate control is itself imperfect since takeover bids involve considerable potential transactions costs. Indeed, corporate management's attempts to discourage unfriendly takeovers through "poison pills" and other such devices have triggered the same sort of debate that previously centered on executive pay. Thus the question of appropriate executive pay will inevitably remain more controversial as compared with pay levels for other employees.

Gap Between Managers and Other Employees

Managers are likely to be separated from other employees by virtue of their pay levels, authority, and discretion. They may therefore have a hard time obtaining accurate information about the concerns and performance of those they supervise. In addition, management productivity may be much more difficult to measure than that of nonmanagers. To the extent that managers are supervising nonmanagers, how may these problems be overcome? Various HRM techniques have been developed to obtain the needed information.

For example, firms can collect various statistical indicators that point to problems in the management of nonsupervisory employees. There is a long history of HRM departments developing survey instruments to obtain direct information on employee attitudes about their jobs and work situations.[10] Employee committees may be formed for similar purposes. Careful monitoring of employee grievances can be undertaken in firms that have formal grievance mechanisms.

Finally, symptoms of employee discontent—which may point to poor management—can (and should) be routinely obtained from payroll records. These measures include quit rates and absenteeism rates. A high quit rate may mean simply that pay needs to be raised relative to competitors in the labor market. But it may also mean that employees are reacting to poor supervision by seeking work elsewhere. Absenteeism problems can have a similar interpretation.

Symptoms such as high quit rates and, to some extent, absenteeism, are what economists sometimes call *exit* solutions. Workers are unhappy about their jobs, so they leave or spend less time at work. On the other hand, high grievance rates—especially in union situations—are examples of *voice* responses. Rather than leave, employees seek to achieve amelioration of their job problems at the workplace.[11]

Managers in Unionized Firms

In some countries, unionization of the workforce may extend up through the middle management level. But such unionization is virtually nonexistent in the United States in the private sector, although there are some examples in government. Most typically, therefore, management will be nonunion—along with other white-collar employees—and the union workers (if any) will be blue collar. There is thus likely to be a considerable gap between rank-and-file union workers and managers in terms of pay, social background, education, and attitude toward the firm.

By the mid-1980s, the proportion of private sector employees represented by unions had fallen to about one out of seven workers, although in the public sector the figure was over 40%. Thus many managers are employed in firms that do not deal with unions. For those who do find themselves in unionized firms, however, unionization poses a special challenge. For this reason some of the issues unionization raises for management are listed at this point, although unions and bargaining form the subject of a later chapter.

Inevitably, unionization involves a constraint on the decision-making authority of management officials. Some managers are better equipped than others to deal with such constraints. Traditionally, collective bargaining and its related processes have involved conflict or potential conflict. Again, some managers are personally better able to handle the stresses of conflict than others. Thus when a nonunion facility becomes unionized, the new pressures sometimes cause a turnover of local management personnel.

American management has generally resisted unionization whenever possible. Some of this resistance stems from the added labor costs that unionization entails. Resistance may also stem from a desire on the part of management to avoid the stresses of conflict and shared authority. As in the compensation area, this aspect of management behavior raises an interesting principals and agents problem. Are the resources that management devotes to remaining nonunion always commensurate with shareholder costs and benefits? Or does management "overspend" in this area to maintain its own comfort level?[12]

Job Security

Although news accounts of corporate restructuring often give the impression that managerial job loss has become a major factor, that impression is misleading. In 1987, when the overall civilian unemployment rate was 6.2%, the rate for executive, administrative, and managerial personnel was only 2.6%. At the bottom of the economic slump of the early 1980s, the overall unemployment rate reached 9.7%, in 1982. The rate for the executive group was only 3.3%. The fact is, the managerial group does not seem to be at untoward risk in the labor market.

A survey of employees displaced during 1981 to 1985 by plant closings, moves, slack work, or the abolishment of positions or shifts found that executives, administrators, and managers were not disproportionately displaced during this period of well-publicized restructurings. Those who were displaced seemed to find new employment at a faster rate than other employees.[13] It is not true that executives are immune from layoff during hard times. But it is also not true that, as a group, their higher pay and benefits relative to other employees reflect greater job uncertainty, although this may be the case at the very top echelons of corporate management.

Labor market figures also suggest that hours reductions due to slack work are not typically experienced by executives. Their employment hours are not tightly tied to the ups and downs of production, compared with those of other workers. In contrast, blue-collar employees may be put on part-week schedules or be temporarily laid off during business downturns.[14]

2-2   Professional Personnel

The professional worker category, like the managerial, encompasses a broad range of skills and responsibilities. This grouping includes such diverse occupations as the following:

- Engineers
- Architects
- Biologists
- Economists
- Lawyers
- Physicians
- Writers and Editors
- Registered Nurses

As Table 2–1 shows, about one out of eight members of the workforce falls under the professional classification. The group tends to be higher paid than average and to have or require higher levels of educational attainment.

Allies of Management?

Although management may see professionals as natural allies, professional employees do not necessarily have managerial authority in the firm. They do not make company policy and are often hired simply for their expertise in a particular field. Professional employees, therefore, are *employees* in the usual sense of that word. If their needs and interests are not sufficiently attended, they may exhibit the classic symptoms of other dissatisfied workers: increased turnover, reduced productivity, and hostility toward management.

As already noted, management personnel in the United States are virtually never unionized, especially in private employment. But professionals sometimes are. Various engineering associations in the aerospace industry, for example, negotiate with the management of major firms such as Lockheed. It is true, however, that professionals often see themselves as a different class of employee from other workers. And, indeed, American labor law makes special provision for them to unionize *separately* from other employees. Thus conflict with management is possible—particularly after a period of layoffs and hard times.

Professional employees may well have special concerns about their employment situation, concerns that go beyond immediate pay and conditions of work. Some may have ambitions to move eventually into managerial roles. Opportunity for such advancement (or lack thereof) can be an issue. Other professionals may simply feel that they are entitled to a significant degree of deference and consultation. They may desire academic-style "collegiality" in the workplace, a desire to which some corporate cultures respond and others do not. Economic theory suggests that employers should consider both pay and working conditions as part of the "package" they offer employees. Responding to the collegial desires of professionals can thus be good business.

Human Capital Considerations

Since professional employees are likely to have learned their occupational skills through institutions of higher education, they may feel a need for skill updating through seminars and similar programs. Fear of becoming technically outdated fosters this demand. Employee benefits that involve educational opportunities are thus likely to be important to professionals. How great a value the employer receives from providing such opportunities is an interesting question.

Human capital theory makes a distinction between *general* training and *specific* training.[15] The former is the acquisition of a skill that is of broad use to many employers in the labor market; the latter involves acquiring a skill useful only to a single employer. In making the distinction, economists have argued that employers will provide only specific training at their own expense since the return on investment in general training is likely to be captured by the employee, not the employer. For example, if an employer were to put an employee through engineering school, the employer would have no guarantee that the employee would actually come back to work for the firm at the end of the training. Even if the employee did return, he or she would be able to demand a higher salary (comparable to what competing firms were paying). The return on the human capital investment would thus go to the employee. In contrast, if an employee were trained in techniques used only by the particular employer, there would be no opportunity to exploit the skills anywhere except within the firm. Thus the return on investment could be captured by the employer in the form of higher productivity without increased wage costs.

Although the general/specific distinction is useful, its consequence for human resource management—particularly as applied to professionals—is more complex than the simple example suggests. As stressed in Chapter 1, labor markets differ from financial and commodity markets. Employees tend to remain with their employers, and employers tend to follow practices that encourage such loyalty. Although employers are unlikely to provide initial general training, for example, putting someone through engineering school, they might well provide general training as an educational benefit to employees who have been with the firm for some time. Moreover, the employer might well capture some of the return on this benefit due to employee immobility.

Indeed, for professional workers, continued employment in their field is almost inevitably a form of on-the-job general training. Outside firms will pay more for experienced lawyers, engineers, and other professionals than for novices, on the assumption that work experience involves acquisition of valuable skills. The line between specific and general skills is often vague in any case, since most learning is at least partially transferable.

Pay and Performance

Professional employees and managerial employees share some common characteristics in the compensation field. The higher pay of both groups means that both will be especially interested in benefit plans such as pensions, health insurance, and life insurance that escape or defer taxes or that create vehicles for tax-deferred saving. Firms with substantial professional workforces need to pay special attention to their benefit programs.

Aside from simply providing an income, compensation generally functions as a reward system for employee performance. In the case of professionals, there are often difficult problems in measuring productivity, since the employee's output is typically a service (such as research, advice, or design) rather than a tangible product. Measurement of productivity and performance is thus especially subjective for professionals. Yet in a professional-intensive firm, performance appraisal is a matter of critical importance.

Job Security

Professional workers share with executives and managers the characteristic of very low unemployment rates compared with other employees. During the first half of the 1980s they were substantially less likely to be displaced than their proportion of the overall workforce would suggest.[16] Of course, some professionals have been displaced by business cycle pressures. For example, an economic downturn in the aerospace industry in the early 1970s produced well-publicized job losses among engineers. Still, to the extent that professionals embody a stock of expertise and research and development that the firm has built up, layoffs will reduce that stock (and make it available to competitors). Thus mass termination of professionals may not be good HRM policy for employers, even in the face of very adverse economic conditions.

2–3 Technical, Clerical, and Sales Personnel

Professional and managerial employees form less than half of the white-collar portion of the workforce. Almost six out of ten white-collar workers (who now, in turn, form over half of the overall workforce) fall into the technical and administrative support group and into the sales group, as shown in the following list:

- Drafters
- Computer Programmers
- Emergency Medical Technicians
- Cashiers
- Retail Salesclerks
- Real Estate Agents
- Bill Collectors
- Telephone Operators
- Hotel Desk Clerks
- Secretaries
- Messengers

Although technicians earn above-average incomes, employees in the sales and administrative support occupations do not.

Until the 1970s the application of technology to raise productivity was seen largely as factory oriented. Office productivity had not undergone a technological revolution since the invention of the typewriter. However, the introduction of word-processing and data-processing equipment substantially altered that picture. For the first time, displacement by labor-saving devices became a possibility in the office. Along with the displacement threat came the opportunity for skill enhancement, that is, training to operate the new equipment. The upshot is that human resource management problems of technical, administrative, and sales workers now more closely resemble those of blue-collar workers in the past.[17]

Women are heavily concentrated in the administrative support group. They are also somewhat more represented in the technical occupations (especially those related to health care) and in the sales occupations (especially in the lower paid areas) than elsewhere in the workforce. Part-time work is more common in these fields than in others, partly reflecting the sex composition of the workforce.

Flexibility and Temporary Work

In recent years employers have sought greater flexibility in the use of their non-professional and nonmanagerial white-collar workforces. There was an upsurge in the use of temporary employees, either hired through commercial employment services or through in-house arrangements, in the aftermath of the 1982 recession.[18] Temporaries and part-timers typically receive lower benefits than do regular workers, and they are less likely to be included in any job security arrangements the employer may offer. During a difficult economic period, then, employers were apparently looking for both labor cost savings and a reduced ongoing commitment to their workforces. So-called contingent workers met that need.[19]

The general/specific skill distinction, cited earlier, helps explain this phenomenon. To the extent that the skills possessed are reasonably standard, turnover costs will not be a major consideration to employers in establishing pay levels, benefits, or other conditions of work.[20] In addition, if skill levels can be readily measured—for example, tests of typing speed—the risk to employers of mistakes in hiring is lessened. It is not surprising that the demand for employer flexibility finds special expression among these occupational groups.

In the past, unions made relatively few inroads in the nonprofessional, nonmanagerial white-collar groups in the private sector, although there were some notable exceptions, for example, supermarket clerks. The same groups, however, have been receptive to unionization in the public sector and in quasi-public health care institutions. Thus to the extent that the push for flexible working arrangements in private employment is more a matter of employer than employee preference, employers may eventually experience a backlash.

Comparable Worth

One area in which tensions arose in the 1970s was the so-called *comparable worth* issue. Proponents of comparable worth argued that jobs with heavy concentrations of female workers were systematically underpaid relative to "male" jobs. They argued for paying jobs in accordance with their comparable worth to the employer. This issue, which will be discussed in a subsequent chapter, is most commonly applied to clerical occupations.

Most of the litigation that grew out of the comparable worth question arose from the public sector. During the 1980s, however, the major court decisions in the area did not favor the concept. Nevertheless, the 1980s also saw an upgrading of female pay levels relative to male in private employment, suggesting that employers may have altered their pay policies in response to the comparable worth issue. Even though the employer position—that comparable worth should not be imposed by law—was prevailing in court cases, employers may have found it prudent to defuse the issue internally by modifying their pay-setting practices.[21] Such behavior serves to emphasize the important institutional differences between the labor market and many other types of markets; practices in the labor market are suffused with social norms and notions of fairness.

2–4   Blue-Collar Occupations

Blue-collar workers include the following:

- Carpenters
- Electricians
- Data-Processing Equipment Repairers
- Aircraft Mechanics
- Butchers and Meatcutters
- Tool and Die Makers
- Upholsterers
- Sewing Machine Operators
- Bus Drivers
- Laborers

Blue-collar occupations are not defined in the Census or similar surveys. As a proxy, the classifications "precision production, craft, and repair workers" and "operators, fabricators, and laborers" have been used.

Blue-collar workers accounted for a little over one-fourth of the overall workforce in the mid-1980s. However, because they are more likely to be unionized than others, the concerns of blue-collar workers have often received substantial popular attention. Dramatic bargaining sessions and strikes occur only where unions are involved; although nonunion workers may also have complaints, they usually lack a formal mechanism by which to voice these complaints collectively (and publicly).

Still another reason for the focus on blue-collar employment is economic. Unemployment rates are higher for blue-collar workers than for other groups. Thus the threat of layoffs and plant closings is usually pictured in the media as a blue-collar issue, although, of course, displacement can occur throughout the workforce.

Innovations in HRM and the Blue-Collar Worker

Many of the innovations in human resource management in the past have come from the blue-collar area, mainly because of the concentration of unions in this sector (or the threat of unionization as perceived by management). The widespread use of fringe benefits, for example, spread from the union sector to other employees in the 1940s and 1950s.

Perhaps more fundamentally, the field of human resource management has its historical roots in the labor problems of the late nineteenth and early twentieth century, as factory work became more common in the United States. Since factory workers during this period were often immigrants, tensions over absorption of foreigners and of importation of foreign radical ideas mixed with ordinary industrial relations issues, sometimes in an explosive manner.

Even in recent years blue-collar problems have continued to attract attention and spawn innovations. The quality of working life movement of the 1970s—with its quality circles and related devices—largely revolved around blue-collar, manufacturing workers. A shift in public policy toward occupational safety and health in the 1970s also had its origins in blue-collar employment. What started as concern for such issues as exposure to cancer-causing asbestos in blue-collar manufacturing and construction eventually widened into issues such as possible eyestrain or other adverse effects from video display terminals in white-collar settings.

Location in Key Sectors

One factor in the seemingly disproportionate concern over the HRM problems of blue-collar employment is the importance of blue-collar intensive sectors of the economy. Although manufacturing employment as a proportion of the workforce has historically declined, manufacturing *output* relative to overall output has shown no trend. In the mid-1980s, for example, manufacturing accounted for between a fifth and a fourth of gross output, approximately the same percentage as in the early 1960s.[22] More rapid growth of productivity in manufacturing relative to other sectors permitted relative employment to shrink while relative output remained steady.

Manufacturing industries loom particularly large in the international economic relations of the United States. Manufactures account for about three-fourths of merchandise exports. Other sectors using blue-collar workers (such as construction, utilities, railroads, trucking, and mining) also are key to American economic performance. Thus, if HRM's focus on blue-collar issues has seemed disproportionate in the past, it is likely to remain so in the future—and with good reason.

Yet, between management and blue-collar workers there is an especially wide social distance. At the time of the 1980 Census, for example, close to 40%

of all persons falling into the executive, administrative, and managerial occupations had completed college. Only about 5% of the workers in the more skilled blue-collar categories had finished college, and even lower rates were reported for semi-skilled and unskilled occupations. Thus management is today, as it was in the past, the furthest removed from those occupational groups where concerns over productivity and competitiveness have been most commonly centered.

Lower educational attainment among blue-collar workers poses problems for implementation of some of the more innovative schemes in employee participation in decision making. Such participation may well require facility to assimilate and interpret quantitative information, accounting data, and the like. Sometimes it proves necessary to provide training in these areas before such innovative techniques can be applied.

2–5 Service Workers

Service workers accounted for over one out of seven jobs by the mid-1980s. However, discussions of labor force trends often confuse service workers and the service industries. Service *industries* can be very broadly defined to include all industries that do not produce goods. Under this extensive definition, the service sector covers such diverse industries as railroads, construction, banking, advertising agencies, and supermarkets. More conventionally, service industries are defined as a narrower group covering such personal services as laundries, hotels, and health care, and such business services as computer consultants and credit-rating bureaus.

Service *workers,* in contrast, are employees such as the following:

- Janitors
- Bartenders
- Short-Order Cooks
- Waiters and Waitresses
- Nursing Aides
- Ticket Takers
- Guards
- Firefighters
- Barbers
- Dental Assistants

Some of these workers are typically employed in service industries (such as nursing aides in health care). Others (such as guards) are employed in many sectors of the economy.

With the exception of protective service workers such as police officers and firefighters (often associated with public employment), service occupations tend to be heavily female. The service occupations also tend to command lower-than-average wages, and they often involve either low skill levels or general (rather than specific) skills. Thus many of the same sorts of HRM issues that revolve around administrative support occupations—comparable worth, high turnover, and use of temporaries—also arise in services.

In the private sector, service workers are rarely represented by unions. They tend to be found in industries with low unionization rates. In one case—plant guards—U.S. labor law discourages unionization by requiring such workers (who are few in number and often geographically dispersed within firms) to form their own unions not including other workers. There are exceptions, such as the heavily unionized flight attendants' occupation. In the public sector, however, service workers are about as prone to unionization as blue-collar employees.

2–6   Trends in the Occupational Composition of the Workforce

Table 2–1, presented earlier, shows both the past trend and the projected trend in the occupational mix. Past trends, of course, are easy to ascertain from the historical record. Projections are a more complicated matter and involve the uncertainty always entailed in predictions. The most prominent forecaster in the employment area is the U.S. Bureau of Labor Statistics (BLS), a division of the Department of Labor.

To make its projections, the BLS starts with a general forecast of the economy.[23] It breaks this aggregate forecast into detailed industries and then uses data on employment per unit of output by industry to project job growth. Data on the occupational composition of each industry's workforce—combined with information on such factors as technological displacement of certain kinds of jobs—can then be used to project the future occupational composition of employment.

Some observers have cited the BLS projections as reasons for concern over the future distribution of American income. A crude version of this concern notes the rapid growth of low-paying service jobs and asserts that average wages will fall as Americans increasingly end up flipping hamburgers as an occupation. During the early 1980s, there did seem to be a tendency for much job creation to occur in lower paid occupations.[24] Lower wage industries expanded relative to high wage. Part of this tendency was due to the impact of foreign competition as the dollar appreciated relative to other currencies. Part was due to an acceleration of manufacturing productivity relative to other sectors; and part was due to changing patterns of demand across industries.[25]

The BLS projections, however, do *not* necessarily support such a scenario of real wage slippage over the long run. The future trends shown in Table 2–1 include both growth at the upper end of the income scale (executives, professionals) and at the lower end (service occupations). Growth of the higher paid groups offsets the downward pull of service worker wages.

A more sophisticated version of the concern over income distribution involves income inequality rather than income trends. Analysts note that the fast-growing occupations tend to be at both the higher income levels and at the lower income levels. This pattern leaves a hole in the middle consisting of better paying blue-collar jobs, which, according to some economists, will widen income inequality and could produce social tensions. Such considerations opened up a substantial debate over the "declining middle class" in the mid 1980s.[26]

There is some truth to the hole-in-the-middle view, but the effect is quantitatively small. Moreover, some studies suggest that the hole was partly formed by increased employment at the higher end of the pay hierarchy. And the trend appears to have been underway in the 1970s; it was not just a phenomenon of the 1980s.[27]

Even with its diverse occupational trends, Table 2–1 shows that the proportions of workers in the different occupational groups in the year 2000 will look much like those of the mid-1980s. Thus any tendency toward income inequality is bound to be small. The labor force generally changes form slowly. There is always a large stock of workers in any broad occupational group compared to the relatively small incremental trends, even for periods as long as a decade.

Hidden under the aggregate data are individual workers or groups of workers whose economic situation has worsened or will worsen due to economic trends. For example, the American steel industry fell into a deep recession in the early 1980s, and even after the rest of the economy began to recover, steel's economic situation worsened. Displaced steel workers, who have—or will have—difficulty finding new jobs at wage and benefit levels comparable to their old jobs, will clearly be worse off. At the same time, workers in other industries and occupational groups are experiencing improved job opportunities.

2–7   Labor Force Demographics

Up to this point the focus has been primarily on employment by occupation. An alternative view of the job market can be obtained by analyzing the demographic elements of the labor force. For example, what proportion of the labor force is male or female, white or black, young or old? As the demographic mix in the labor force changes, HRM challenges are presented to managers who must accommodate the needs of the new employees.

The labor force consists of two components: the employed (the group discussed so far) and the unemployed. Employment is an easy concept to understand; it means having a job. A few job holders are not actually at work—some are on vacation, sick leave, or on strike; but most are actually working. In contrast the unemployed are defined as individuals who are seeking work, who are on layoff awaiting recall, or who are waiting to report to a new job within thirty days. About 65% of the population aged 16 and over was in the labor force in the mid 1980s, the vast majority being employed. Those not in the labor force (the remaining 35 percent) consisted of such groups as retirees, invalids, homemakers, and full-time students.

Women in the Labor Force

The phenomenon of women in the labor force is hardly new. In the early part of the nineteenth century, for example, women were extensively used in the textile industry, the high-tech sector of that era. What is comparatively new is the widespread participation of *married* women in the labor force. Up until World War II, working women were predominantly single. Often—as in the case of the textile workers—they were teenage girls or young women awaiting marriage.

Social norms until quite recently did not emphasize job orientation for women. Until the 1960s various protective state laws (considered as progressive reforms when they were originally passed in the early part of the century) limited hours of work or type of work for female employees. The growth in the female workforce tended to be in certain types of jobs. For women looking for careers in the professions, there were jobs emphasizing children, families, or health care. These included such occupations as elementary school teachers (85% female in 1987), social workers (66%), and registered nurses (95%). Outside the professions, jobs often involved food handling (85% of the category "waiters and waitresses" were female in 1987) or lower paid sales jobs. Finally, the invention of the typewriter in the late nineteenth century brought women into office/clerical jobs such as secretaries (99% female).[28]

Economists often use the *participation rate* (or participation ratio) to illustrate the attachment of a group to the labor market. The participation rate is simply the proportion of a particular group that is in the labor force (employed plus unemployed) in a particular time period. A projection of the participation rate, combined with a projection of the underlying population, permits a projection of the number of persons in the target group who will be members of the labor force. Thus the BLS projects that in the year 2000 the number of women in the population aged 16 or older will be 106.7 million. It further projects that the participation rate for women in that year will be 61.5%. Thus its prediction for the female labor force is that it will consist of 106.7 × .615 = 66 million women.[29]

Table 2–4 shows the participation rates for female workers as compared with males over the period 1960–2000, and the proportion of the labor force that was, or will be, female. The upward trend in the propensity of women to join the labor force is apparent. Also apparent is a reverse trend for males due to such factors as enhanced opportunities for retirement and disability income (through private pension and benefit programs and Social Security). Thus, as in the past, the proportion of women in the labor force will be growing.

TABLE 2–4 Labor Force Trends, 1960–2000

Year	All Workers	Males	Females	Married Females*	Whites	Blacks	Ages 16–24
	Participation Ratio						
1960	59.4%	83.3%	37.7%	31.9%	58.8%	‡	56.4%
1972	60.4	78.9	43.9	41.4	60.4	59.9%	61.8
1987	65.6	76.2	56.0	56.0†	65.8	63.8	68.4
Projected 2000	67.8	74.7	61.5	n.a.	68.2	66.0	71.9
	Percentage of Civilian Labor Force						
1987	100%	55.2%	44.8%	23.7%	86.2%	10.8%	19.2%
Projected 2000	100	52.7	47.3	n.a.	84.1	11.8	16.3

*With husbands present.

†Figure refers to wives not living alone or with nonrelatives or wives where the husband is in the Armed Forces.

‡Data are not available for the black category prior to 1972. Before that year, the category nonwhite was used, which includes other groups, chiefly Asians.

Note: Blacks and whites do not sum to 100% because of the presence of other omitted groups, chiefly Asians, in the aggregate data.

Source: Employment and Earnings, vol. 35 (January 1988), pp. 158–168; U.S. Bureau of Labor Statistics, *Handbooks of Labor Statistics,* bulletin 2217 (Washington: GPO, 1985), pp. 8–23; Howard N. Fullerton Jr., "Labor Force Projections: 1986 to 2000," *Monthly Labor Review,* vol. 110 (September 1987), p. 24.

This growth will focus attention on certain issues in the workplace. A later chapter will discuss these in more detail but it is well to preview them here. In the compensation area, the comparable worth question will continue to arise, especially in relation to the large bloc of clerical employees. Issues will also arise in connection with the structure of fringe benefits, which sometimes continue to reflect the stereotype of a male breadwinner supporting a nonworking wife.

Time spent at work will also receive greater attention. Because married women with children are increasingly employed, issues such as provision of child care arrangements, leaves in connection with childbearing, and flexible work hours that coordinate with school hours will be increasingly raised. Many employers already offer some kind of hours flexibility, although few directly subsidize the cost of child care.[30] Sometimes such matters are raised in legal and legislative forums, and accommodating such needs may well be advantageous to employers as a recruitment incentive.

The growth of the two-earner family has implications for male employees as well as female. There is evidence to suggest that men with working spouses may prefer to reduce hours, for example, working less overtime or otherwise reduce the intensity of their work commitment. For professional/managerial families, issues arise over who moves when one spouse is transferred or has an opportunity for advancement in another geographic area. Such issues, in turn, become the concerns of human resource managers, who may find that policies requiring geographic mobility may lead to quits of valuable employees whose family situations do not permit such moves.

Similarly, job assignments that require substantial travel can play havoc with employee family responsibilities. Restructuring of such jobs or simply more use of telephones and written communication may be required. For management personnel—who were exhorted in the 1980s to get out of their offices and engage in "walking around" at distant company sites[31]—such family/work conflicts can be especially pressing.

Minority Employees in the Labor Force

The proportion of minority employees in the labor force has been growing and will continue to grow. Table 2–4 compares black versus white participation rates and shows that although overall participation of both groups has been rising, black participation has slipped relative to white. This relative slippage seems to reflect adverse labor market conditions for blacks, especially high rates of unemployment, which discourage labor force participation.

Information on minority groups other than blacks is sparser, but underlying population trends suggest that minority representation generally will rise. Hispanics, for example, constituted about 7% of the labor force in 1988, most falling in the "white" classification of Table 2–4. Asians and Pacific Islanders constituted about 1.9% of the labor force at the time of the 1980 *Census of Population,* and American Indians and related groups about 0.7%.[32]

During the 1960s and 1970s, there was a substantial upsurge in equal employment opportunity (EEO) legislation and litigation affecting minorities in the workplace (and also revolving around sex-related issues). Questions of employment discrimination and use of affirmative action programs became the focus of social and political attention and significantly affected workplace practices. Employers who were charged with discriminatory practices regarding hiring, testing, promotions, layoffs, and other standard HRM activities typically could best defend themselves by showing they used formalized, centralized, impartial HRM decision processes. Thus EEO pressures produced an unexpected byproduct: a strengthening of the HRM function within firms.

The 1980s saw a variety of steps on the part of the Reagan administration to reduce the federal role in EEO matters. However, because the judiciary is heavily involved in EEO, these initiatives—particularly in the area of affirmative action—were blunted. With continued steady increases in the minority component of the labor force, it is likely that EEO will remain an important area for HRM managers for the balance of this century. But it seems unlikely to effectuate further dramatic change in the status of the HRM function; EEO has already left its mark.

Age Composition of the Labor Force

Although Table 2–4 shows that the labor force in the year 2000 will be similar in most respects to the labor force in the late 1980s, there is one notable exception. The proportion of young people will be significantly lower by 2000. This reduction is not due to expected changes in labor force participation propensities of the young. Rather, due to the baby bust (drop in birth rates) that followed the baby boom of the post-World War II period, there will simply be fewer young people available.

Some observers in the 1970s, foreseeing this demographic trend, predicted that there would be a labor shortage at the entry level in the 1980s. Employers would find themselves bidding up the wages of young people in a desperate effort to find new recruits. Because the first half of the 1980s were characterized by deep recession and later relative high unemployment, however, no such shortages developed. Also, the increasing participation of women and migration (legal and illegal) into the United States to some extent provided a substitute for young entrants. By 1987–1988, however, as the unemployment rate dropped, there began to be renewed talk of shortages.

During the 1970s, when baby boomers crowded the entry levels of the labor force, there was a tendency for wages of young people to decline relative to those of older workers. Such a tendency could well reverse itself as the demographic effect begins to influence labor markets. To the extent that younger worker preferences become more important to employers, the mix of compensation might also be affected. Younger workers will typically be less interested in deferred benefits such as pensions, for example. And, since they are more mobile than their elders, they are likely to resent contributing directly or indirectly into benefit plans that are targeted primarily at employees who stay with the employer for a prolonged period.

In recent years young workers have been less likely to be represented by unions than have their elders. This is because the young have a tendency to work in newer industries, ranging from fast food to high tech, which were expanding at the time they entered the labor market. Unions have been notably unsuccessful at penetrating these newer industries. However, surveys indicate that nonunion younger workers are, paradoxically, more willing to join unions than are older workers.[33] The decline in the proportion of younger workers in the labor force therefore makes new organizing more difficult for unions.

Age demographics will eventually play another role after the turn of the century. At that time the baby boomers will near or reach retirement age. Issues such as Social Security payments and taxes and the status of private retirement plans will become more important in the HRM field. As the labor force ages and average mobility declines, concerns about job security will be heightened. There are already trends in some states for courts to protect employees from "wrongful" discharges, and various proposals have been made for legislation limiting discharges, plant closings, and layoffs. Presently, the push for such legislation comes primarily from the liberal end of the political spectrum. But an aging workforce could put the issue into the center of politics, adding new pressures on the HRM function.

2–8   HRM and Internal Employment Planning

This chapter has reviewed labor force trends and characteristics at an aggregate, national level. Often, however, firms will find it useful to look at the characteristics and trends of their *own* workforces. What kinds of employees will be available for hiring in the future? What tendencies are evident within the firm, such as aging of the workforce, a greater proportion of women, and so on? Do the firm's existing benefit plans match the needs of its changing workforce?

What kinds of skills will be used by the firm in the future? Will the skills be of the general variety, easily obtained from the external labor market, or will they have to be developed by the firm? If not easily obtained, should the firm undertake the needed training in its own facilities? Or can it work with local community colleges and vocational schools to provide training? In the event that the external political climate imposes constraints on the firm's current HRM practices (say, with regard to discharges and layoffs), can these practices be readily adapted to meet those constraints?

Obviously, firm size will contribute to the firm's ability to undertake such HRM planning reviews. However, even smaller firms may find such planning can be undertaken jointly through trade associations and similar groups. In the past, firms have often neglected the wealth of data on labor force characteristics and trends, which is available at nominal cost from government agencies such as the following:

- U.S. Bureau of Labor Statistics (bulletins and journals)
  Handbook of Labor Statistics
  Occupational Outlook Handbook
  Employment Projections
  Occupational Projections and Training Data
  Occupational Employment (various sectors)
  Employment and Earnings (journal)
  Monthly Labor Review (journal)

- U.S. Bureau of the Census
  Census of Population (many volumes)
  County Business Patterns
  Census of Manufactures (and periodic censuses of other sectors)

- U.S. Bureau of Economic Analysis
  Survey of Current Business, which includes data from the national income accounts relating to employment and pay by detailed industry along with other information relating to employment

The advent of computers and the ability to acquire government data on diskettes and tapes makes analysis much easier.

Government data are most helpful in analyzing the supply side of the labor market. Given a projection from within the firm of its future occupational needs, the availability of such labor can be analyzed using official data sources. However, the internal projection with regard to employment patterns can be made only if the firm has made projections of its likely production patterns. What kinds of products or services will the firm be selling? Will it be producing these products or services directly or obtaining them from other suppliers? HRM planning cannot be isolated from general strategic planning of the enterprise.

Labor force information, combined with the firm's production intentions, is also important in questions such as site selection. The firm's occupational needs might be better met in some locations than others. Often data from the *Census of Population* can give some indication of employee availability, even for relatively small geographic areas. Other sources provide information on typical wage levels, the status of labor-management relations, and the mix of employers already in the area. To the extent that a firm locates a facility in an area where the local labor force does not match its needs (say, because access to raw materials, tax incentives, or distance to markets are dominant considerations), it may have to plan on importing labor and providing housing and other social amenities. Thus HRM planning is required even when HRM considerations are not the primary motivation behind a managerial decision.

Finally, labor force information can be useful outside the HRM area, especially in marketing. The growth in female labor force participation, for example, is directly related to demand for products such as convenience foods and services such as fast-food shops and restaurants. Participation in the labor force is a major influence on the national lifestyle.

Summary

The U.S. workforce by the end of this century will have a greater proportion of white-collar workers, service workers, and female workers than it had in the mid-1980s. It will have a smaller proportion of blue-collar workers and young workers. However, the workforce changes gradually; it evolves over long periods. Thus issues relating to the changes in its composition can already be seen—for example, increased female representation in the workforce raises concerns about child care, the design of existing fringe benefit plans, and comparable worth.

Executives and managers represent a relatively small proportion of the workforce and yet have the major responsibility for setting HRM policies. Because higher level managers are different from other employees, both in terms of status and pay, they are not always close to workplace issues as seen by nonsupervisory workers. In the past when management left workplace problems unattended, the result was often unionization. By the 1980s, however, unresolved workplace frictions found expression in other forums, such as legislative pressures and litigation. Whatever the channel, problems arising from the changing composition of the workforce will find some means of expression. From the HRM perspective, it is best for management to find ways to monitor and respond to these issues rather than simply to assume that employee concerns will be inherently sensed by higher executives.

EXERCISES

Problem

Select an industry, for example, banking, steel manufacturing, retail foodstores, or trucking. A good place to start is the monthly journal *Employment and Earnings,* published by the U.S. Bureau of Labor Statistics. The journal's tables on employment and pay will give you a listing of the many U.S. industries.

Develop a human resource profile of the industry using the data sources suggested in this chapter. Consider such factors as the demographic composition of the industry's workforce, its occupational mix, and its age and education. What challenges do these characteristics pose to HRM professionals in the industry? Examine projections about the industry's likely employment growth (or decline). What HRM issues do the projections raise?

Questions

1. What has been the significance for HRM of the baby boom and baby bust?

2. What issues are raised by the increasing proportion of women in the labor force?

3. How do the job security concerns of managerial and professional employees differ from those of other employee groups?

4. How is the principal and agent theory applicable to the design of executive compensation systems?

5. What factors underlie the growth of the contingent workforce?

Terms

absenteeism	employee attitude surveys	quality of working life
affirmative action	grievances	quit rates
comparable worth	human capital	specific versus general
declining middle class hypothesis	labor force	training
	quality circles	unemployment

ENDNOTES

1. As noted, the data in Table 2–1 come from the U.S. Bureau of Labor Statistics (BLS), the preeminent source of American labor statistics. BLS produces a vast array of monthly, quarterly, and annual data on employment, unemployment, wages, and other labor market characteristics, as well as data on prices and inflation. BLS was originally created in the nineteenth century as a social uplift organization; it was assumed that bringing forth information on labor problems would lead to their solution. The modern BLS is a professional organization whose key employees are statisticians, economists, and other technicians. It maintains offices around the country and has its headquarters in Washington. These offices can provide labor market information by telephone. Information is also produced in publications, press releases, and on computer diskettes. For further information, see Joseph P. Goldberg and William T. Moye, *The First Hundred Years of the Bureau of Labor Statistics* (Washington: GPO, 1985).

2. Robert N. Mefford, "Introducing Management into the Production Function," *Review of Economics and Statistics,* vol. 63 (February 1985), pp. 96–104.

3. John W. Pratt and Richard J. Zeckhauser, eds., *Principals and Agents: The Structure of Business* (Boston: Harvard Business School Press, 1985).

4. Income security does not logically have to be an inferior good, that is, one which (other things equal) the consumer wants less of as income rises. Common sense, however, suggests that it is likely to be so.

5. Sherwin Rosen, "Prices and Incentives in Elimination Tournaments," *American Economic Review,* vol. 76 (September 1986), pp. 701–715. At each level in the hierarchy, under these models, executives give up some pay in order to play the game, that is, be able to contest for the next promotion. It should be the case, therefore, other things held constant, that CEO compensation will be an increasing function of the number of vice presidents. One empirical study of this issue did not find support for the proposition, so the tournament model remains an intriguing, although unproved, explanation of the executive pay structure. See Charles O'Reilly, Brian G. Main, and Graef S. Crystal, "CEO Compensation as Tournaments and Social Comparisons: A Tale of Two Theories," unpublished working paper, University of California, Berkeley.

6. The stock market crash of October 1987 (in which the Dow-Jones industrial average dropped 508 points in a single day) vividly illustrated this point. There was no sudden drop in managerial competence that day that could explain the decline in stock prices. Yet executives whose pay was based on absolute stock price performance were penalized by the market.

7. Kevin J. Murphy, "Corporate Performance and Managerial Remuneration: An Empirical Analysis," *Journal of Accounting and Economics,* vol. 7 (1985), pp. 11–42; Jeffrey Kerr and Richard A. Bettis, "Board of Directors, Top Management Compensation, and Shareholder Returns," *Academy of Management Journal,* vol. 30 (1987), pp. 645–664.

8. The lowering of marginal tax brackets enacted in 1986 might conceivably have some impact on the quest for non-taxable perks. However, even with the lower brackets, there is still considerable incentive for tax avoidance, especially when state income tax rates are added to federal.

9. U.S. President, *Economic Report of the President, February 1985* (Washington: GPO, 1985), pp. 187–189.

10. Sanford M. Jacoby, "Employee Attitude Surveys in Historical Perspective," *Industrial Relations,* vol. 27 (Winter 1988), pp. 74–93.

11. Richard B. Freeman, "Job Satisfaction as an Economic Variable," *American Economic Review,* vol. 68 (May 1978), pp. 135–141.

12. Ouchi and others have noted a tendency of American management to be especially concerned and disturbed about dealing with unions. But as he points out, Japanese firms, which are often held out as models of managerial behavior for Americans, seem to deal with unions without the same level of disturbance. See William G. Ouchi, *Theory Z: How American Business Can Meet the Japanese Challenge* (New York: Avon Books, 1982), pp. 97–100.

13. Francis W. Horvath, "The Pulse of Economic Change: Displaced Workers of 1981–85," *Monthly Labor Review,* vol. 110 (June 1987), pp. 3–12, especially p. 6. The survey covered only employees with a tenure of three or more years on the job from which they were displaced. About 5.1 million employees were found to be displaced by the definitions used in the study.

14. Relatively few individuals in the executive classification report that they are working part time involuntarily, that is, less than 35 hours per week, when the Bureau of Labor Statistics and the Bureau of the Census conduct their monthly survey of the population.

15. The issue of education and training is taken up in detail in a later chapter. It is briefly discussed here because of its close link to professional occupations.

16. Horvath, "The Pulse of Economic Change," *op. cit.,* p. 6.

17. It is important to note, however, that among those who attempt to project economic change there is still substantial disagreement about the eventual impact on office productivity of such computer-based innovations as word processing. See H. Allan Hunt, "Technological Change and Employment: Fears and Reality" in Barbara D. Dennis, ed., *Proceedings of the Thirty-Ninth Annual Meeting,* Industrial Relations Research Association, December 28–30, 1986 (Madison, Wisc.: IRRA, 1987), pp. 447–454.

18. Max L. Carey and Kim L. Hazelbaker, "Employment Growth in the Temporary Help Industry," *Monthly Labor Review,* vol. 109 (April 1986), pp. 37–44.

19. Bureau of National Affairs, Inc., "Special PPF Survey Report: Part-Time and Other Alternative Staffing Patterns," *Bulletin to Management,* vol. 39 (June 23, 1988), pp. 1–12; Bureau of National Affairs, Inc., *The Changing Workplace: New Directions in Staffing and Scheduling* (Washington: BNA, 1986).

20. The relationship between turnover costs and pay and other HRM decisions is discussed in a later chapter.

21. Aaron Bernstein, "Comparable Worth: It's Already Happening," *Business Week* (April 28, 1986), pp. 52, 56.

22. U.S. President, *Economic Report of the President, January 1987* (Washington: GPO, 1987), pp. 26–27.

23. Details on the projection methods of the BLS can be found in U.S. Bureau of Labor Statistics, *BLS Handbook of Methods,* bulletin 2285 (Washington: GPO, 1988), pp. 115–123.

24. Barry Bluestone and Bennett Harrison, *The Great American Job Machine: The Proliferation of Low Wage Employment in the U.S. Economy,* a study prepared for the U.S. Joint Economic Committee of Congress, available from the Committee, December 1986.

25. Richard S. Belous and Daniel J. B. Mitchell, "International Trade and Employment: Dynamic Labor Market Implications" in Barbara D. Dennis, ed., *Proceedings of the Fortieth Annual Meeting,* Industrial Relations Research Association, December 28–30, 1987 (Madison, Wisc.: IRRA, 1988), pp. 24–34, especially p. 32.

26. Frank Levy, "The Middle Class: Is it Really Vanishing?" *The Brookings Review,* vol. 5 (Summer 1987), pp. 17–21. See also the symposium on "Increasing Economic Inequality in the U.S.? Alternative Views" in Barbara D. Dennis, ed., *Proceedings of the Thirty-Ninth Annual Meeting, op. cit.,* pp. 331–357.

27. Michael W. Horrigan and Steven E. Haugen, "The Declining Middle-Class Thesis: A Sensitivity Analysis," *Monthly Labor Review,* vol. 111 (May 1988), pp. 3–13.

28. Data on the proportion of females in various occupations are taken from *Employment and Earnings,* vol. 35 (January 1988), pp. 181–185.

29. Howard N. Fullerton, Jr., "Labor Force Projections: 1986–2000," *Monthly Labor Review,* vol. 110 (September 1987), pp. 19–29.

30. U.S. Department of Labor, *Child Care: A Workforce Issue,* Report of the Secretary's Task Force (Washington: DOL, 1988), pp. 125–142.

31. Thomas J. Peters and Robert H. Waterman, Jr., *In Search of Excellence: Lessons from America's Best-Run Companies* (New York: Warner Books, 1982), pp. 288–290.

32. U.S. Bureau of the Census, *General Social and Economic Characteristics: United States Summary,* PCBO–1–C1, 1980 Census of Population (Washington: GPO, 1983), Table 144.

33. Richard B. Freeman and James L. Medoff, *What Do Unions Do?* (New York: Basic Books, 1984), p. 29.

Chapter Three

PRODUCTIVITY

Productivity is often discussed in the national context. When the growth in productivity lags, politicians and business leaders sometimes bemoan the trend and assert that America is losing the productivity race to other countries. Competitiveness, a word with clear productivity overtones, became a buzzword in the 1980s. Frequently, it is assumed that when productivity fails to advance rapidly or is not high (the two concepts are often confused in public pronouncements), it reflects a defect in national character.

In fact, as this chapter will demonstrate, while productivity has a national dimension, its analysis must be undertaken at various levels. The individual employee can be more or less productive, depending on circumstances. Human resource policies and practices can influence individual performance. Indeed, much of the justification for having an HR function stems from the potential variability of individual productivity.

Productivity can also be analyzed at the level of the plant or enterprise. At that level, important influences will include such factors as the use of capital equipment and new technology, as well as HR approaches. To assess their relative standing, firms can compare their productivity experience with that of the industries in which they operate.

Finally, when the productivity performance of all firms is aggregated, overall national productivity can be considered. At the national level, productivity growth is important because it ultimately determines what improvement in living standards and real wages is possible. To the extent that national productivity performance seems inadequate, public policies that can affect the HR function may be undertaken.

3–1   Productivity Defined

Before productivity can be discussed intelligently, however, it must be defined. At the most general level, *productivity* is simply the ratio of output to input. Although valid, this definition is hardly operational. Before productivity can be employed as an empirical concept, outputs and inputs must be specified, and they must be capable of being measured.

Inputs

Most commonly, the input utilized for measuring productivity is labor input. Hours of work is a commonly used index of labor input for this purpose. In principle, however, one could talk about capital productivity rather than labor productivity and use some index of the value of capital services as an input measure. Other productivity measures combine indices of labor and capital inputs into a single index. (These indices, known as measures of total factor productivity or multifactor productivity, are discussed later in this chapter.)

The common use of labor as the input index, even when other factors of production are involved in the output process, is largely a matter of convenience. Measures of labor input are often easier to come by and create fewer problems of interpretation than measures of capital. However, the fact that labor is so often used as the input measure does *not* mean that labor is responsible for all output. Farmers could not produce wheat without land; to perform their jobs, carpenters need saws, hammers, and other tools. If measured productivity rises—with labor used as the input index—it does not necessarily imply that employees are working harder; instead, perhaps some new technology has been introduced, permitting more output to be produced with the same labor input. Or, in the case of the wheat farmer, perhaps the weather was more favorable.

The fact that labor is frequently used as the input measure, creating the impression that productivity derives from labor alone, is perversely helpful to HRM practitioners who focus attention on the human aspects of productivity. Since the HRM function involves human resources, those carrying out that function may well be seen as the people best able to solve perceived productivity problems. But since productivity is the result of various forces, not every productivity problem is a "people problem." HRM professionals need to acknowledge that possibility and to provide accurate analysis of the different sources of productivity difficulties in their organizations.

Outputs

Measurement of output can be simple or complex, depending on the kind of output under study. If productivity regarding a standardized product is being assessed, the unit of measurement can be relatively simple, for example, tons of steel, barrels of oil, bushels of wheat. However, measurement can be complex when product quality is variable or when the product is not easily standardized.

The question, "How many workers does it take to erect a building?" has little meaning. Is the building a single family residence? An apartment house? A high-rise office unit? A warehouse? Similarly, tons of airplanes would not be a useful output measure for a productivity index.

Measurement problems also arise regarding outputs of multiple products. At the national level, output is the sum of production in many industries. Obviously, tons of steel cannot be added directly to bushels of wheat. Typically, therefore, aggregate output must be measured in value terms, since values (dollars) can be meaningfully summed. Even within industries or firms, value may be the most viable output measure because industries and firms often produce more than one product.

But value measures also raise problems, especially if the goal is to measure the *trend* in productivity. The value of the output of a product is the price of the product times the level of output in physical units. Over time, prices may change for reasons of general inflation or market conditions. In a period of general inflation, value of output per labor unit will tend to rise even if there is no change in physical productivity over time. Thus whenever value is used to measure output, a price deflator or deflators must be found to eliminate the trend in prices.[1]

3–2 Productivity at the Employee Level

In the field of human resource management, we often speak of rewarding employee productivity. What is meant by employee productivity in this sense, and why should it be rewarded? In view of the preceding discussion, might not employee productivity reflect environment, capital, and technology rather than individual effort? If so, how can individual effort and proficiency be distinguished from the external influences on productivity?

Review of the (Very) Simple Economic Model

In elementary economics texts, productivity is mentioned in connection with wages and wage determination.[2] But the standard assumptions made are often far removed from the issues facing an HRM specialist. The simple model postulates a production function, F, which relates inputs of labor, L, and capital, K—and possibly other inputs such as materials—to output, Q. That is, $Q = F(L,K)$. Often it is assumed that production takes place under "constant returns to scale" so that if L and K are increased by the same multiple (say, doubled), output will rise accordingly. That is, $2Q = F(2L,2K)$, or—more generally—$nQ = F(nL,nK)$.

Along with the assumption of constant returns to scale comes the supposition of diminishing *marginal* productivity. It is assumed that if one factor is increased while the other is held constant, the result will be positive, but diminishing, increments to output.[3] This assumption leads to a downward sloping marginal product of labor curve. This curve relates incremental output to levels of labor input. For example, with a given capital stock, if 2,000 hours of labor were used, the curve would show the extra output that would result if labor input was incremented by one hour to a total of 2,001 hours. A typical downward sloping marginal product of labor (MP_L) is shown in Figure 3–1.

The MP_L curve can be expressed in value terms by placing a value on the incremental output it represents. For a perfectly competitive firm, the value of each unit of output is simply the market price, P. For a firm with some monopoly power, the incremental output must be valued by the extra revenue the firm will obtain by selling the unit in the product market. This value, known as marginal revenue, MR, in economics, is a declining function of output because the price of output falls as the firm tries to sell more and more in the product market. Multiplying MP_L by P (in the competitive case) or MR (in the noncompetitive case) yields the marginal revenue product of labor, MRP_L. MRP_L represents the extra revenue the firm will receive due to the hiring (and resulting production) of an additional increment of labor.

The MRP_L curve is also the short-run demand for labor of the firm. At any market wage, W, the profit-maximizing firm will hire labor until $MRP_L = W$. All firms have their own MRP_L curves that, summed together, form the overall demand curve for labor. Interaction of the overall demand and supply determines W, which each firm then takes as a given. Figure 3–2 shows a firm that hires L_A units of labor when the wage per labor unit is W_A, because its MRP_L curve is equal to W_A at labor input level L_A.

Drawbacks of the Simple Model

So far, the analysis should be familiar to most students. What is often not apparent to students in elementary economics courses is the highly abstract nature of the underlying assumptions. Most importantly, from the HRM perspective, in the model, labor is assumed to be a homogeneous commodity; one unit of labor is just like another. The only source of productivity variation in the model is the ratio of capital to labor, K/L. At high values of K/L, the marginal product of labor for a specified input of L will be higher than at low values, assuming a given level of technology. This productivity effect has nothing whatsoever to do with motivation of employees; they are all assumed to be equally motivated. It has

**FIGURE 3–1
Marginal
Productivity of
Labor Schedule**

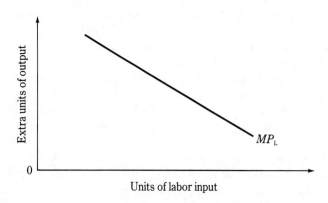

FIGURE 3–2
Marginal Revenue
Product of Labor
Schedule

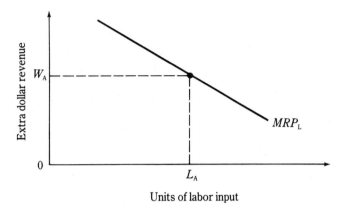

Units of labor input

nothing to do with a clever pay system that rewards individual productivity. The employees expect payment, *W,* for each unit of labor they supply. (They would like more, of course, but they know that no one will pay them more than the going market wage.)

If the real world were like the simple model, productivity would not be a matter of concern to the HRM professional. It would instead be something about which the firm's engineers alone would worry. Engineers would have to pick the *K* and *L* combination that maximizes profits. Indeed, it is not clear what role (if any) an HRM professional would have in such a world. Perhaps the professional would be needed to find out from the labor auctioneer what the going wage was each day.

The simple model has certain uses in economics. It teaches the student notions of constrained maximization, a central economic concern. But, as presented above, it is so far removed from the real world that it offers little guidance to HRM issues. We can, however, introduce more realistic assumptions into the model on a step-by-step basis that will illuminate actual HRM practices.

Complicating the Model by Recognizing Diversity

In the real world, all units of labor are *not* equivalent. Even within a narrowly defined occupational group, some workers are more effective at their jobs than others. That is, given capital and technology, certain workers in a particular occupation will add more to output than others. These differences among individuals reflect everything from inherited traits, parental upbringing, and life-style, to education, training, and work experience.

The simple model can be modified to reflect productivity differences between employees. Imagine a standard or average worker who, given capital and technology, would add ten units of output for an extra hour worked. Other workers in the labor market, under the very same conditions, might have a marginal product of only eight units. Still others might have $MP_L = 12$. How would the labor market react to such diversity in productivity? Would pay levels reflect these different productivities so that superior employees would be rewarded with superior wages and inferior employees would be penalized?

Much depends on information costs. The simple model assumes that information costs are zero. Workers and employers have no trouble finding each other and establishing wages. If that assumption is extended to the case of diverse productivity, employers will instantly and costlessly be able to differentiate between job candidates with marginal productivities of eight, ten, and twelve units. The lower productivity group will earn a wage of only 80% of the standard worker level; the higher productivity group will earn 120% of the standard wage. Effectively, with productivity diversity, the market will set a price for efficiency units of labor rather than for hours of labor.

Since workers fall into different occupational groups, yet another form of diversity can be introduced. Different occupations are not perfect substitutes for one another. When plumbing needs fixing, a plumber is called for the job, not a lawyer or a baker. Some occupations, however, may be partial substitutes (dental technicians may be used to do some of the work of dentists), while others may be complements (the more lawyers are employed, the more legal secretaries are needed).

Each occupational group will, therefore, have its own labor market within which, in turn, there may be diversity of productivity. The markets will be interconnected by means of the substitute/complement relationships. A panoply of wage differentials will emerge, reflecting alternative labor market conditions for the various occupations as well as individual productivity differences within occupations.

Still, in this modified model, there is little for the HRM professional to do other than monitor market wages. Differences in individual productivity exist, but they are apparent to employers, and the market sets differential wages accordingly. Individuals cannot be induced to change their productivity characteristics through anything the firm can control. Nor would the firm have any particular interest in changing employee productivities, since it is rendered indifferent between hiring slackers and hiring superworkers by compensating wage differentials.

Dropping the Perfect Information Assumption

Suppose firms could not tell in advance which workers had high inherent productivities and which had low. By itself, this deviation from perfect information would not at first not seem to make much difference to the eventual outcomes. However, the firm *would* now need HRM professionals to design systems that would find the lemons in the workforce it had hired. It would also need HRM specialists to create mechanisms that would verify candidates' claims that they had above-average productivity.

Low-productivity workers (the lemons) might seek employment with the firm without revealing their substandard potential. As soon as they began work, the HRM system would spot their inferior performance and offer the lemons a choice: They could leave the firm if they insisted on being paid the standard wage, or they could accept a lower wage that reflected their true productivity level. Lemons would accept the lower wage offer since they would never find a firm at which they could hold a job long enough to receive the standard wage. Their only viable option would be to accept lower wages commensurate with their lower productivity.

Workers with above-average productivity characteristics might demand a proportionately higher wage from the firm at the time of hiring. The firm could simply offer to put them on the payroll at the standard wage with a proviso that if they turned out to be above standard in productivity, their wage would be immediately increased correspondingly. HRM professionals would be available to help monitor initial performance of those who claimed to be better-than-average performers.

Adding considerations of differences in employee productivity improves the simple economic model. But even recognition of diversity of performance and imperfect information leaves the model still far removed from reality. The revised assumptions, however, do lead to wage differentials that reflect personal productivity differences and occupational differences. Yet the role of the HRM professional remains quite limited; he or she is basically an evaluation expert.

So far it has been proposed that HRM professionals could act as designers of immediate post-hiring monitoring systems to spot lemons and verify claims of superworkers. But the firm might well substitute some kind of piecework pay formula for a time-based wage system to avoid the need for (costly) HRM specialists and supervisors. If workers were paid on the basis of units of output, rather than by units of time (3¢ per widget rather than $6 per hour), lemons who produced only 80% of the standard rate would receive only 80% as much hourly pay as the standard worker. And superworkers would receive proportionately more than the standard employee. Thus a firm might decide to use an industrial engineer rather than an HRM specialist to determine the standard level of productivity and set the piece rate so that the average worker would earn the going market hourly wage for such workers.

Screening Costs

In fact the imperfect information story just described carries within it a hidden element that brings it closer to reality than first appearances suggest. Firms face the danger of hiring lemons at the standard wage. If the lemons succeed in remaining in employment at that wage, they will harm the firm. The marginal productivity of lemons will be below the wage they are paid; they will contribute less incremental value to the firm than they cost. In short, profits will be reduced if lemons sneak in and are retained undetected.

The potential presence of unidentified lemons in the labor market will induce the firm to undertake some expenditure to screen them out or appropriately reduce their pay. After all, the HRM professionals, industrial engineers, and supervisors to whom allusion has been made must also be paid. The more workers the firm hires, the more such overhead personnel it must also take on to handle the monitoring. Thus each new hire effectively imposes an implicit cost on the firm.

Workers will be hired for one of two reasons. They may be replacements for workers who have left the firm, or they may be hired to expand existing production, that is, as net new additions to the firm's workforce. Consider the first motivation: replacing departing workers.

Since each hire imposes a cost, each departure must also be costly, because in the steady state a departure requires a replacement. The firm therefore has an incentive to reduce turnover and, therefore, new hires. In other words, the presence of lemons in the labor market, that is, diversity of employee productivity, automatically gives the firm an incentive to hang on to its existing workforce, whose productivity characteristics it already knows.

The addition of the incentive to maintain a given workforce takes the story a long way (but not all of the way) towards the real world of HRM. Maintaining a given workforce means that an employer-employee relationship develops. Workers do not swirl in and out of the firm. Keeping turnover down necessarily involves catering to worker interests and concerns. If workers are unhappy, they might quit, thus imposing hiring and screening costs on the firm. It is worth expending money on HRM specialists who will cater to worker needs and tastes and reduce turnover. Employee diversity of productivity in fact extends the role of HRM beyond simple monitoring.

In addition the accidental hiring of lemons can be avoided if workers can be screened for productivity characteristics *before* they are hired. HRM professionals with expertise in interviewing (or in training other managers to interview), reviewing résumés and credentials, and administering tests can reduce the costs of post-hiring monitoring. Obviously, trade-offs are involved. Perfect pre-hiring screening would be costly and probably unattainable, and perfect post-hiring monitoring would also be very costly. The firm will therefore engage in some screening, some monitoring, and also live with the knowledge that some lemons have crept into the workforce but are hard to identify. Indeed, one of the tasks of the HRM professional in such a firm would be to identify where the trade-offs should be made through a cost/benefit analysis.

Modifying Personal Productivity

Up to this point, individual employee productivity has been assumed to be a given. Workers might change their productivity through education, or even, over time, through job experience (learning by doing).[4] But at any moment in time, workers would expend a fixed level of effort and would have fixed effectiveness characteristics.

In fact, much of the actual practice of HRM suggests that firms do *not* find the fixed productivity assumption to be valid. For example, the piece rates that were mentioned earlier are used in some modern firms, and many years ago were much more widespread than they are now. Piece rates, and related bonus systems, which gear an individual worker's pay to that worker's output, were historically designed to be more than simple measurement devices. While piece rates and bonus systems do pay low-productivity workers less than high-productivity workers, the intent in installing such systems was to *stimulate* workers to raise their own productivities, that is, to expend more effort. Piece rates and bonus systems (discussed in a later chapter) were intended to be motivational tools.

The fact that such pay systems have declined in usage does not mean that managers have abandoned the notion that employees can be motivated. To the contrary, other devices, which are believed to be more effective (but not perfect) motivators, have replaced automatic incentive systems. These motivators include merit pay systems, opportunities for promotion and advancement (career ladders), and other methods both of recognizing superior employee performance and of penalizing substandard work.

All such rewards and penalties require an evaluation system. Evaluation systems, which HRM specialists classify under the heading *performance appraisal,* will be discussed in a subsequent chapter. At this point it should be noted that performance appraisal is a measurement device designed to gauge employee productivity. It is used even when output is not easily quantified, as is often the case with professional, technical, managerial, and service employees.

Impact of Teamwork

The simple economic model has begun to look more realistic as more reasonable assumptions have been added. However, one element may have struck the reader as peculiar. Up to this point, workers identified by the employer as substandard are not fired. Rather, their wages are simply lowered to the point at which the firm is indifferent between using these workers and using higher quality workers. In the real world substandard workers are likely to be terminated, especially after they have been warned. This practice is particularly widespread with regard to workers who exhibit low productivity shortly after hiring. Indeed, firms often have formal probationary periods, during which termination is easier under company rules than it would be later, precisely to weed out poor performers.

Why do firms use termination rather than reduced pay when lemons are uncovered? One answer lies in the concept of *teamwork*.[5] Employees often must work in groups. The most obvious example is an assembly line in which work is passed from one employee to the next. A lemon anywhere in the line will reduce the productivity of all of the group. If a standard worker can process 100 widgets per hour, but another worker in the line can process only 80 widgets, the overall line speed cannot exceed the 80-widget constraint. Assume the line consists of nine standard productivity (100-widget) workers and one 80-widget lemon. The one lemon has effectively turned nine standard workers into lemons!

Lemons, in short, can have multiplier effects. They may so drastically lower overall productivity of the group that there is no positive wage at which it would pay to hire them. In such cases, the firm will elect termination rather than a pay reduction when it uncovers a lemon.

The assembly line example is an extreme one because it involves passing work in a linear fashion from one worker to the next. However, the team concept has more general applications. There are relatively few cases, in fact, where employees work in total isolation so that a lemon does not reduce the productivity of others. For example, scientists, engineers, and managers often form task forces and similar groups to accomplish goals and projects. If one member of the task force does not pull his or her weight, costs are inflicted on the entire team.

Even apart from assembly lines and task forces, employees usually work in proximity to one another. Social groups often form at the workplace. Employees who are rude, disruptive, or who have other personal problems may adversely affect the productivity of others and may induce costly turnover of fellow employees. This problem will be especially acute if the poor performer is a supervisor or manager. Thus, problem workers—once identified—may be subject to dismissal because they produce what economists call negative *externalities*. They inflict costs on others that may outweigh any contribution the problem employee may make to firm output.

The measurement of individual employee productivity therefore involves an estimate, whether quantitative or qualitative, of two factors—(1) the incremental personal contribution the employee makes to output, and (2) the positive or negative external impact the employee has on other workers. Since workplaces are organizations, the externalities may be the more important consideration for many types of jobs.

3–3   Productivity at the Plant and Firm Level

It would be unusual for a multiproduct firm to wish to compute global productivity measures covering all divisions. However, such productivity indexes can be useful on a more local basis. If there are productivity problems, managers are likely to want to know which divisions, plants, or products are involved. At these disaggregated levels, productivity calculations can be useful for certain purposes, although it is important to note certain drawbacks.

Productivity, Profitability, and Unit Labor Costs

Productivity is basically an efficiency concept in the technical sense, not in the economic or commercial sense. A plant may be highly efficient compared to others, and yet may not be economically viable. Decisions to open or close plants will hinge importantly on the costs of inputs (including labor) as well as on the technical efficiency with which inputs are combined.

Ultimately, in evaluating a plant in terms of its contribution to the firm, what matters is profitability, not productivity. Profitability, however, will reflect productivity even though the two concepts are not the same. If a plant seems to be substandard in profitability, it is important to find out whether the poor performance is due to substandard productivity or to high costs of inputs.

Ideally, in investigating productivity of a plant, it would be best to use a measure of input that includes all factors of production—labor, capital, materials—broken down in as much detail as possible. Such calculations may well be too complex for practical purposes. A handy concept, when labor is used as the input measure, is *unit labor cost* (*ULC*). Unit labor cost is defined as total labor costs per unit of output. Using the earlier notation, $ULC = WL/Q$.[6] The *ULC* formula can be rearranged as $W/(Q/L)$, that is, unit labor cost is equal to the average wage divided by the level of productivity. Thus a plant that pays relatively high wages can still be economically viable *if* it can also achieve an offsetting relatively high productivity level.

For this reason much of the world's manufacturing capacity, for example, still operates in relatively high-wage countries. Were wage levels the only consideration in determining costs, world manufacturing would long since have relocated to extremely low-wage nations. As it is, low-wage countries tend to succeed in world markets mainly with products for which technology and productivity are sufficiently comparable across countries so that the remaining element in competitiveness is the cost of labor.

Uses of Productivity Data

Multiplant firms may find it useful to compare plant productivity and unit labor costs within product lines. Wage levels can easily be obtained from payroll records, as can labor input. Assuming the plant produces output that can be reasonably quantified, productivity measures can be easily calculated. Of course, a plant that is relatively high cost, but that does not turn out to be poor in productivity performance, may not be viable economically. On the other hand, a high-cost plant with low productivity may have a problem, either technical or involving employee relations, which could (or should) be addressed.

Firms often fail to make productivity evaluations, even when data to do so are readily available. Sometimes, when such measurement is undertaken, other data are still needed to pinpoint the source of productivity problems. On the HRM side, symptoms such as high employee turnover, heavy absenteeism, and high rates of employee grievances may indicate that the solution to a productivity problem lies with improved HRM rather than with technical areas such as replacement of antiquated machinery. In a multiplant firm, the hypothesis that, say, grievance rates are negatively associated with productivity might be checked statistically.[7]

At unionized firms, productivity calculations can be useful for *workrule bargaining*. Typically, union contracts specify a variety of workrules to which the employer must adhere. For example, the number of machines to be operated by an employee may be stated in the contract. As technology changes, such workrules often become outdated and a source of added costs to management.

Some companies have estimated the productivity improvement that would accrue from a relaxation of workrules and have then used these figures to buy out the rules from the union. The unit labor cost saving that results can be used to offer higher pay, severance benefits, and early retirement options in exchange for greater management flexibility. Obviously, in such situations, measurements of productivity and estimates of potential cost savings are critical to intelligent bargaining.

Comparisons with External Data Sources: Trends

Generally, even if firms compute productivity data for internal use, they will be reluctant to share them with outsiders, especially competitors. Within a product line, however, a firm might find it useful to compare its productivity performance with those of other firms in the industry. Data on industry-level productivity trends are being made increasingly available by the U.S. Bureau of Labor Statistics (BLS). Examples of such trends, reported from selected industries by the BLS, are shown in Table 3–1.

The industries selected for Table 3–1 illustrate various influences on productivity. For example, in the bituminous coal industry, productivity moved in an erratic fashion in the 1970s and 1980s, first falling and then rising. The shift toward high-productivity western strip mining, and away from eastern underground mining tended to raise output per hour in the coal mining industry. This positive effect was offset by deteriorating union–management relations in the eastern states.

An aggravating factor was an internal political struggle for leadership of the Mine Workers union during this period. Toward the end of the 1970s, however, both labor and management made a concerted effort to ameliorate their relationship, and the productivity situation improved. The coal experience thus illustrates how the labor relations climate can influence productivity trends.[8]

A contrasting picture emerges from the telephone communications industry. Output per hour has rapidly and steadily increased in this sector. (The output index is derived from revenue for various telephone services deflated by appropriate price measures.) Here, the story is dominated by rapidly improving technology, including adoption of electronic switching systems, satellite communications, and computer applications. Technology at the leading edge has long been

TABLE 3–1   Output per Employee Hour in Selected Industries, 1959–1986

Type of Industry	*Annual Rates of Change*			
	1959–1969	*1969–1973*	*1973–1979*	*1979–1986*
Bituminous coal mining (SIC 121)	5.3%	–3.4%	–3.9%	7.7%
Telephone communications (SIC 4811)	5.7	4.9	6.8	5.3
Steel (SIC 331)	1.7	4.3	0.0	4.1
Commercial banking (SIC 602)	n.a.	3.4	.6	1.6*

*Data for 1979–1985.

Source: U.S. Bureau of Labor Statistics, *Productivity Measures for Selected Industries and Government Services, 1958–86,* bulletin 2296 (Washington: GPO, 1988), pp. 15, 86, 140, 151.

a feature of the telephone industry, going back to the development of the dial telephone in the 1920s, and the productivity numbers reflect this tradition.

Banking output is defined by the BLS in terms of demand deposit transactions, loans, and fiduciary, or trust, activity. Productivity in banking was also positively affected by computerization. However, elements of banking, which is a service industry, have proved resistant to automation. The cashless and checkless society, with transactions occurring entirely through electronic means, remains in the future. Thus banking productivity trends have been positive but not extraordinary. Banking's record illustrates some of the difficulties in raising productivity in service-oriented sectors.

Finally, the steel industry showed dramatic productivity increases after a recession-related slump in the early 1980s. The productivity improvement occurred at a time of great economic distress in the industry, due largely to import competition. As a result of the strong competitive pressures, the industry reduced its capacity by closing its least-productive facilities. The steel industry's productivity record thus illustrates the influence that product market pressures can have in forcing an efficiency improvement.

Although the story behind the productivity trends varies from industry to industry, the availability of published data about trends now allows firms to compare their productivity performance with that of the overall industry within product lines. Unfortunately, most human resource professionals have not caught up with the substantial expansion of productivity statistics from the BLS and other sources. Many have not taken advantage of the ability of computers to extract useful information from personnel and payroll records. However, the newer generation of quantitatively oriented managers now emerging from the nation's business and management schools will be in an advantageous position to make use of the new data sources. Utilization of productivity statistics within firms can thus be expected to increase.

Absolute Productivity Information

The nation's gross national product (GNP) is the total value of goods and services produced. Firms contribute to the GNP by buying materials and using capital and labor to produce a more refined product. Each advance in the stages of production from iron ore to steel to automobiles, for example, represents "value added" by the processing enterprise. That is, a firm will (it is hoped) produce output that is worth more to its consumers than are the materials put into that output.

Valued added can be viewed in two ways. It can be seen as the difference between the revenues the firm receives for its product and the costs of the materials that went into the production process. Alternatively, value added can be viewed as the sum of the rewards to the factors of production that added value to the product, with rewards in the form of wages and benefits to employees and profits, depreciation, and interest to capital owners.

Table 3–2 shows GNP per full-time equivalent (FTE) employee for various sectors. The table includes four industries (coal mining, primary metals, telephone and telegraph, and banking), which correspond to the sectors discussed in the

TABLE 3–2   GNP per Full-Time Equivalent Employee in Selected Industries, 1986

Sector	GNP/FTE (in dollars)
All private industries	$47,270
Coal mining	79,532
Primary metals	46,900
Telephone and telegraph	105,992
Banking	41,768
Apparel and other textile products	19,714
Oil and gas extraction	166,136

Source: Survey of Current Business, vol. 67 (July 1987), pp. 57, 60.

previous section. As can be seen from the table, the GNP produced per FTE in the sectors covered varies widely. These differences, however, do not necessarily reflect efficiency differentials between industries. For the most part, the differences are the result of variations in the importance of the nonlabor input across industries. Industries that are capital-intensive will have a proportionately higher payment to capital included in value added.

Two industries added to Table 3–2—apparel and oil and gas extraction — provide extreme illustrations of this principle. The apparel industry utilizes labor-intensive technology and thus produces a small share of capital in value added.[9] In addition it tends to use relatively cheap, unskilled labor so that its labor return is also low. In contrast, oil and gas extraction involves substantial investment in both equipment and land or mineral rights, and workers in the industry are comparatively well paid. Thus its contribution to GNP per FTE is at the other end of the spectrum from apparel.

While the differences *across* industries would not be especially useful managerial information, *within*-industry comparisons can be helpful. Firms have (or should have) information from their internal accounting systems to generate comparable data for their own operations. These data can be compared with the industry averages to point to superior or inferior productivity performance.

3–4   National Productivity

This chapter began by noting the tendency of politicians to bemoan lagging productivity trends. Why should there be this concern? More specifically, while productivity performance is obviously of interest to managers at the microlevel, why should anyone be concerned with aggregate productivity trends at the national level? In the following paragraphs some answers to these questions are suggested. Also presented are data on the actual course of national productivity.

Productivity as Ability to Pay

One reason for the concern about national productivity, perhaps the most crucial, is living standards. In 1986 the GNP per full-time equivalent worker in the private sector was 1.8 times higher in "real" terms (that is, adjusted for inflation) than it was in 1947. Labor compensation (wages, fringes, and payroll taxes) accounted for 52% of the GNP in 1947 and only a slightly higher fraction in 1986 (54%).

If wages in 1947 had somehow been raised to the purchasing power standards of 1986, almost all of GNP would have gone to labor, leaving nonwage income at an unsustainably low level for a capitalist economy.[10] Although data for carrying out the precise calculation are not available, it is evident that going back a few years before 1947 would have produced a situation in which more than 100% of GNP would have had to go to labor to maintain 1986 purchasing standards. Such a situation could not exist under any economic system.

Private GNP per FTE is a measure of productivity at the national level. The data just cited show that productivity is not simply an efficiency index; it also has much to do with living standards. It is the rise in productivity that has made the long-term advance of real wages possible. Thus a period of poor productivity growth, such as set in after the early 1970s, is also going to be a period in which living standards will not advance much. Clearly, that situation is something about which politicians (and all citizens) must be concerned. Management, in particular, must be concerned, since the business community is often held responsible for adverse economic developments.

Rising productivity, in short, means rising economy-wide ability to pay. A period in which productivity performance deteriorates is likely to create difficulties in the workplace. Workers will not experience the increases in real wages during such periods that they may previously have come to expect. If real wages are pushed up in some sectors in spite of the productivity trend, wage rates in those sectors will progressively become more and more out of line with others. Such a process took place in the union sector of the workforce in the 1970s, with dramatic and adverse consequences for unions in the 1980s.

Productivity and Inflation

It is often said that "wages should rise with productivity." Sometimes, this proposition is advanced as a moral prescription, since it suggests that workers ought not to expect pay increases unless they work for them. Despite the appeal of the Puritan ethic, we already know that productivity trends reflect many influences, including growth in the stock of capital, technological advances, and so on. Thus the proposition—although valid—turns out to be more empirical than moral.

Earlier it was noted that the share of labor compensation in private GNP was about the same in 1947 and 1986 (52% vs. 54%). It is from this constancy that the linkage between (real) wages and productivity develops. The value of total output (GNP) can be expressed as the multiplicative product PQ, where P is a price index for output and Q measures the volume of output. Similarly, the value of labor compensation can be expressed as WL, where W is a wage index (including all forms of labor compensation) and L is an index of the volume of labor employed. If s is the share of labor compensation in the value of output, then $s = WL/PQ$.

Given the definition of s, by simple rearrangement of the terms it is easy to see that $W/P = s(Q/L)$. The real wage is W/P and Q/L is labor productivity. If s is relatively constant—as we know it is—then real wages *will* move with productivity as an empirical fact, regardless of the morality or ethics involved. The simple equation also contains another lesson. Since W/P is fixed by productivity (as an empirical matter), then periods in which W rises faster than productivity will be periods in which P must also be rising. Put another way, periods in which wages rise faster than productivity will also be periods of inflation.

On occasion this observation has been used in government wage-control programs aimed at preventing or reducing inflation.[11] For example, during the Kennedy/Johnson administrations in the early 1960s, federal policymakers urged that businesses (and unions) not raise wages faster than productivity. It was thought that if this prescription were followed, the economy could expand without accelerating inflation.

Although this policy statement, known as the wage/price guideposts, had some transitory effect on wage setting, it was not ultimately successful in preventing rising inflation. The subsequent Nixon administration, after grappling with inflation for several years, eventually imposed mandatory wage and price controls, using the productivity rule as a guide. In an effort to reduce price inflation from about 5–6% per year to 2–3% a year, the Nixon administration proposed that wages should rise at a 5.5% annual rate. Using the simple equation described above, the reader can easily deduce that the underlying assumption of this program was that productivity growth of about 3% per annum could be expected.

The interrelationship between wage change, productivity change, and inflation is an empirical fact. However, the ability to use that fact to control inflation is another matter. Ultimately, neither the Kennedy/Johnson administrations nor the Nixon administration was able to reduce inflation permanently via productivity guidelines. Nor was a subsequent attempt in the late 1970s by the Carter administration successful. Thus, unless there is both a sharp change in political climate and a resurgence of inflation, it is unlikely that productivity guidelines will again be imposed on wage setters in the near future.

Competitiveness and Productivity

The connection between productivity, wages, and unit labor costs has already been noted at the level of the plant. The same concept can be applied at the national level. We already know that $s = WL/PQ$ and that $ULC = WL/Q$. Thus $ULC = sP$. Since s is roughly constant in the long run, unit labor costs can be expected to rise at about the same rate as the price level over extended periods.

Trends of American unit labor costs relative to other countries will be examined in a subsequent chapter. However, it should be noted that unit labor costs are particularly important as determinants of success for labor-intensive products in the international marketplace. General upward pressure on unit labor costs will make American goods less competitive relative to foreign goods, and thus tend to reduce exports and increase imports. Such changes in the international balance of trade will either cause job losses in American industries or lead to offsetting devaluations of the U.S. dollar in currency exchange markets.

More rapid productivity growth—other things being equal—tends to slow the rise of unit labor costs. Thus better productivity performance can lead to improved competitiveness of American firms in world markets. This linkage between competitiveness and productivity is still another factor behind official concern over national productivity trends.

3–5   Trends in U.S. Productivity

Reference has been made to a deterioration of American productivity performance in the 1970s. It is useful, at this point, to examine the evidence surrounding this deterioration. When did it happen? What caused it? What can be done, if anything, to improve national productivity growth?

Empirical Record

Table 3–3 shows a quarter-century review of American productivity performance. The dip in the productivity trend is clearly visible from the top row of the table. Output per labor hour rose at almost a 3% annual rate from the late 1950s until the early 1970s. But during the remainder of the 1970s, productivity growth averaged less than 1% per annum. Some pickup in productivity growth occurred in the 1980s, but the pre-1970s rate has never been restored. As has already been suggested, the growth in real wages during the period of the productivity slowdown was drastically reduced.

Various explanations have been put forward to explain the dip in productivity growth.[12] Some have argued that the problem is illusionary, and that productivity is not being properly measured in the growing service sector. There *are* difficult problems involved in measuring service productivity. Table 3–3 shows that the productivity slowdown occurred in manufacturing as well as other sectors in the 1970s, but that a pickup occurred thereafter. Even if we are having trouble getting the numbers exactly right, there is no doubt that the 1970s saw slower productivity growth than in earlier periods and that the 1980s did not bring forth a complete productivity growth recovery for the economy as a whole.

It has also been argued that the productivity slowdown was rooted in insufficient investment in the 1970s. As noted previously, the simple economic model predicts that labor productivity will be linked to the capital/labor ratio. Table 3–3 shows that there was a slowdown in the growth of this ratio in the 1970s.

TABLE 3–3   Annualized Trends in Labor Productivity, Multifactor Productivity, and the Capital/Labor Ratio, 1959–1986

	1959–1973	1973–1979	1979–1986
*Labor Productivity**			
Private sector	2.9%	.8%	1.4%
Private nonfarm	2.8	.6	1.2
Manufacturing	3.2	1.5	3.4
Multifactor Productivity†			
Private sector	1.9	.4	.5
Private nonfarm	1.7	.3	.3
Manufacturing	2.7	.7	2.6
Capital/Labor Ratio‡			
Private sector	2.6	1.2	2.5
Private nonfarm	2.2	1.1	2.6
Manufacturing	1.8	2.9	3.5

*Output per hour of all persons.

†Output divided by an index of capital and labor inputs.

‡Capital services per hour of all persons.

Source: U.S. Bureau of Labor Statistics, *Trends in Multifactor Productivity, 1948–81,* bulletin 2178 (Washington: GPO, 1983), pp. 22–24; *Monthly Labor Review,* vol. 111 (June 1988), p. 105.

But it also suggests that the trend in the capital/labor ratio cannot be the chief explanation of the slowing of productivity growth.

In the private, nonfarm sector, the capital/labor ratio rose at the same rate in the 1960s and 1980s. Yet productivity in the 1980s did not recover its pre-1970s pace of advance. Indeed, in manufacturing the growth of the capital/labor ratio progressively accelerated, but productivity growth did not.

Multifactor Productivity

The impact of capital on productivity can be further quantified. Consider a production function, $Q = F(K,L)$, where Q = real output, K = capital input, and L = labor input. Differentiated, this relationship implies that:

$$dQ = [(\partial Q/\partial K)dK] + [(\partial Q/\partial L)dL] \tag{1}$$

Let P represent the price level. Divide both sides of equation (1) by Q, multiply the first bracketed term of the right-hand side by PK/PK and the second bracketed term by $PL/PL,$ and rearrange terms. The result is:

$$dQ/Q = [(\partial Q/\partial K)PK(dK/K)]/PQ + [(\partial Q/\partial L)PL(dL/L)]/PQ \tag{2}$$

Note the following: $dQ/Q, dK/K,$ and dL/L are, respectively, the percent change in output, the percent change in capital input, and the percent change in labor input over some relevant time period. PQ is the value of output. In economic theory, $\partial Q/\partial K$ and $\partial Q/\partial L$ are the marginal products of labor and capital, which are equal, respectively, to the real price of capital (the rental rate) and the real wage. Multiplying these real quantities by P converts them into nominal terms, that is, the money price of capital, R, and the money wage, W. Thus equation (2) can be rewritten:

$$\text{percent change in output} = [(RK/PQ) \times \text{percent change in capital}] \\ + [(WL/PQ) \times \text{percent change in labor}]. \quad (3)$$

The respective shares of capital and labor in the value of output are RK/PQ and WL/PQ. Thus in the absence of any effects on output other than from capital and labor, if the change in capital and the change in labor are weighted by their respective shares in the value of output, the change in output can be predicted using equation (3). If the percent change in output is greater than can be explained by equation (3), there is a rise in *multifactor productivity* (or *total factor productivity*), which is defined simply as the left-hand side of equation (3) divided by the right-hand side.

The middle panel of Table 3–3 shows trends in multifactor productivity, which accounts for the influence on output of both capital and labor. As can be seen from the table, the same productivity slowdown that appeared when the labor productivity definition was used appears when multifactor productivity is used. Thus the slowdown cannot be fully explained by changes in the capital/labor ratio, since these changes are reflected in the multifactor measure. The productivity slowdown problem, in short, cannot be attributed simply to inadequate investment flows.

Of course, other things being equal, growth in the capital/labor ratio will raise productivity, even if other forces are retarding productivity growth. The fraction of GNP devoted to nonresidential gross investment did not decline in the 1980s, relative to other periods. But, because of substantial dissaving on the part of the federal government (a budget deficit), foreign capital inflows were required to sustain the level of investment.[13] By the mid-1980s, there was concern among economists that net foreign borrowing by the United States for domestic investment might prove unsustainable in the long run. Resulting high interest rates would then choke off business investment, ultimately harming productivity growth.

Proposed Explanations of the Slowdown

Given the importance of productivity movements, it is not surprising that considerable effort has been expended by economists to explain the productivity slowdown. Quantitative estimates have been made of such factors as the impact of government regulation (antipollution and safety requirements imposed on business, which diverted resources from production), changes in the education and experience levels of the workforce, and the reduction in research-and-development expenditures that occurred in the 1970s. None of the obvious explanations appears to go very far toward explaining the slowdown.

Perhaps this is not surprising. Much of the productivity growth rate prior to the 1970s was not explained by measurable influences in statistical studies. Economists simply attributed the large, unexplained portion of productivity growth to technological advance and improved managerial techniques. Thus, when productivity growth slowed, the reason was largely unknown.[14]

HRM Element in Productivity

There have been suggestions that the slowdown in productivity growth was linked to a deterioration in employee relations that began in the late 1960s. The evidence we have on this deterioration comes from the union sector of the economy. During the late 1960s, strike activity rose sharply. Not only did union members seem more defiant of their employers; they also became more likely to defy their union officials. Contracts that were negotiated by union leaders were more frequently voted down by union members in this period than previously.

Unfortunately we have no handy indexes to gauge the climate of HRM among nonunion employers. However, it is obvious that the late 1960s were generally years in which authority of all kinds was increasingly questioned, not only in the United States but also abroad. There were outbreaks of student demonstrations and protests on university campuses, and signs of intergenerational conflict. Juvenile delinquency rates rose. Racial tensions increased. Anecdotal evidence suggests that these social strains were eventually felt in the workplace, and complicated the HRM function.

No easy way exists for quantifying the effect of these broad social influences on productivity. Efforts to do so have foundered on a lack of hard data.[15] Inability to quantify, however, does not imply that the human element in productivity should be dismissed as irrelevant. In the absence of alternative explanations, in fact, it must be assumed that improving the HRM climate at the employer (micro) level would improve macro productivity performance. But caution is also required. As already noted, there is a tendency—simply because productivity is usually measured using only labor as the input—to attribute all productivity problems to human resource issues. Excessive claims ultimately do a disservice to the improvement that can come from improved HRM techniques.

One of the outgrowths of the 1970s was the development of the *quality of working life* (QWL) movement, an effort to address the human side of productivity.[16] Although the QWL label has been stretched to encompass many workplace innovations and experiments, its general theme has been employee involvement in traditional management decisions. QWL programs often involve cooperative employer/employee committees, such as quality circles, to address workplace problems and enhance productivity.

These efforts have most often taken place at the local workplace, but have sometimes extended into areas of upper management. In a few cases, they have included placement of employee or union representatives on corporate boards of directors. The guiding thought behind QWL programs is that workers have a stake in "their" firm and the current generation wants formal recognition of that stake through participative channels into management. Note that this stakeholder premise is in line with the position taken in Chapter 1.

Of course, had the productivity challenge simply evaporated after the 1970s, there would have been little pressure to continue or extend QWL experiments in the 1980s. But the challenge still exists, and QWL appears to have taken permanent root as a result. Even so, not all QWL experiments are destined to succeed. Econometric evidence at the plant level suggests that simply imposing QWL features on the existing climate of employee relations does not produce benefits.[17] What can be said is that QWL experimentation is warranted, provided that it is combined with changes in the organization's HR system.

3–6 Policies to Promote Productivity Growth

The productivity slowdown led to various suggestions for federal government action to reverse it. (See Figure 3–3 for various sources of productivity information.) However, the inability to point quantitatively to a specific cause of the slowdown has hindered efforts to produce convincing proposals for such action. Generally, suggestions have fallen into four categories: setting up investment incentives, promoting industrial policy, fostering a better climate of HRM at the workplace, and improving the educational system.

Investment Incentives

Although there are some programs of direct federal subsidy to certain forms of investment, much of the efforts to encourage investment have been made through the tax code. Perhaps the most prominent example has been periodic creation of accelerated depreciation allowances for capital equipment. Such incentives were increased in the early 1980s and were credited with maintaining investment in the face of high real interest rates.

Raising the rate of investment would undoubtedly improve productivity performance. Over the long run, the multifactor productivity technique tells us that the effect will be moderate, however. Increases in the capital-to-labor ratio are but one influence on productivity, and the effect of capital is filtered through its share in value added. In any case, Congress repealed much of the tax-incentive program for investment in 1986, in an effort at tax simplification and reform.

Industrial Policy

There has been a strain of support for economic planning in the United States, at least since the 1930s when—at the bottom of the Great Depression—a form of such planning was briefly tried as part of the Roosevelt administration's New Deal policies. The New Deal's planning component was terminated as unconsti-

FIGURE 3–3
Sources of
Productivity
Information

Macroeconomic Trends
1. *Economic Report of the President* (annual)
2. *Handbook of Labor Statistics* (periodic publication of the U.S. Bureau of Labor Statistics)

Industry Level Data
1. *Productivity Measures for Selected Industries* (annual publication of the U.S. Bureau of Labor Statistics)
2. *Survey of Current Business* (contains national income account data, with annual industry breakdowns usually in the July issue)

Studies
1. Edward F. Denison, *Accounting for Slower Economic Growth: The United States in the 1970s* (Washington: Brookings Institution, 1979).
2. Edward F. Denison, *Trends in American Economic Growth, 1929–1982* (Washington: Brookings Institution, 1985).
3. Sar A. Levitan and Diane Werneke, *Productivity: Problems, Prospects, and Policies* (Baltimore: Johns Hopkins University Press, 1984).
4. *Monthly Labor Review* (periodic reports and articles about productivity)
5. Marta Mooney, *Productivity Management,* number 127 (New York: The Conference Board, 1982).
6. U.S. Bureau of Labor Statistics, *A BLS Reader on Productivity,* bulletin 2171 (Washington: GPO, 1983).
7. U.S. Bureau of Labor Statistics, *Trends in Multifactor Productivity, 1948–81,* bulletin 2178 (Washington: GPO, 1983).
8. White House Conference on Productivity, *Productivity Growth: A Better Life for America* (Springfield, Va.: National Technical Information Service, 1984).

tutional by the Supreme Court in 1935. Its only remaining legacy is the current structure of American labor law with regard to unions and collective bargaining, an issue to be discussed in a later chapter.[18]

During World War II, however, a massive military buildup was accompanied by substantial government intervention in the economy. Prior to the war, productivity had been virtually stagnant for a decade. But from 1940 to 1945, real GNP per full-time equivalent employee rose at a 3% annual rate, despite the influx to the workforce of inexperienced young and female workers and the disruption of male employment by conscription. The impressive conversion to war production in the early 1940s—with the cooperation of government, business, and labor—has remained in the American political memory and contributed to the industrial policy proposals of the 1970s and 1980s.

Proponents of industrial policy generally argue that economic performance could be improved if concerted, cooperative efforts were made to develop key industries. Usually, some kind of tripartite mechanism is envisioned, involving representatives of business, government, and unions, to identify which industries are key ones. Some proposals call for creation of a special investment bank to channel funds to such industries. Often cited in support of these arrangements are examples of such cooperation in Japan.[19]

Opponents of industrial policy have countered that such a program would likely evolve as a protective device for older, declining industries that have been hurt by import competition and deregulation. These opponents have been fearful of excessive government involvement in the direction of the economy and have expressed skepticism about the importance of industrial policy in Japan. Even if the program did not become a captive of older industries, opponents argue, government would have trouble identifying winners among new industries.[20]

Apart from these economic considerations, the management community is unlikely to give enthusiastic support to creation of a mechanism that would give labor unions a new, prestigious role in economic policy. For much the same reason, unions and liberal Democrats have found the idea of industrial policy appealing. Thus political factors will play a strong role in determining whether the United States ever embarks on such a program.

Fostering an Improved HRM Climate

Various government programs in Western Europe have required medium- to large-sized firms to establish works councils through which management is supposed to consult with elected worker representatives. In some cases, government regulations also require that worker representatives sit on corporate boards. Such systems are sometimes termed *co-determination*. The effectiveness of these mandatory arrangements in either raising productivity or furthering industrial democracy has been questioned. However, these policies can be viewed as an attempt to impose a QWL-type framework on business by fiat.

From time to time, there have been proposals in the United States that the federal government should either require or foster European-style productivity consultation committees in American firms. While mandatory programs have received little serious support, there has been increased attention to creating a climate supportive of *voluntary* cooperative and participative programs. Although the Reagan administration generally eschewed government intervention in the workplace, it did encourage educational efforts aimed at fostering productivity-enhancing cooperative experiments. Agencies such as the Federal Mediation and Conciliation Service and the Bureau of Labor-Management Relations and Cooperative Programs (a division of the U.S. Department of Labor) became the main instruments of this effort.[21]

To some extent, the tax code has been used to foster forms of financial participation in the enterprise by employees. For example, various tax subsidies provide substantial incentives to establish Employee Stock Ownership Plans (ESOPs). Under ESOPs, stock in the firm is accumulated for employees, often as part of a retirement savings program. Most ESOPs own only a small share of their company's stock. But there are some examples of enterprises that became worker-owned through the ESOP mechanism. Certain types of profit-sharing plans also receive indirect subsidies through the tax code.[22]

Financial participation of employees and participation in management decision making have some obvious linkages. If employee pay is tied partly to the economic performance of the firm, employees may want some voice in how management decisions, which affect performance, are made. Put another way, the stakeholder position of the employee is enlarged by financial participation in the firm. However, the empirical fact is that most financial participation plans do not have accompanying managerial participation mechanisms.

Improving Education

The American workforce has experienced a long-term rise in educational attainment. Presumably, this increasing stock of human capital that is embedded in the typical employee contributes to higher productivity.[23] However, concern has been expressed that the U.S. educational system could do a better job of preparing students for entering the workforce. While the quantity of education has risen, there may be a lag in quality, as evidenced by such measures as declining Scholastic Aptitude Test (SAT) scores in the 1970s.

In the United States, the funding of education—especially elementary and secondary education—occurs at the state and local levels. The federal government can exercise some leverage through conditional subsidies to local educational authorities; but it cannot directly change course content or other educational policies. When concerns do arise at the national level, they thus tend to be expressed through exhortations from official study groups.[24] The notion that American productivity and competitiveness could be better served by its educational system began to be widely expressed in the 1980s. However, as in the case of investment in physical capital, the short-run effects of improvements in the stock of human capital on measured productivity are inherently very small.

Summary

It is evident from this survey that the initiative with regard to productivity improvement in the United States currently lies at the level of the firm. But as in many fields, the actual practice of HRM often lags behind the latest, most innovative practice. Even obvious first steps toward productivity improvement, such as productivity measurement and use of available data sources, are not always taken. If, as has been suggested, there is considerable scope for improving productivity through enhancement of the HRM climate at the level of the firm, younger managers now entering the workforce have a challenge before them.

A good understanding of the productivity issue is important in meeting that challenge. This chapter has demonstrated that raising productivity involves both HR approaches and approaches outside the HR field (such as investment and general education). Where the focus is on the individual, HR techniques clearly have the major role to play. Assessing and rewarding individual productivity are the subjects of the next chapter. Even at the national level, however, public policies undertaken to address shortfalls in productivity performance will affect the

HR function. It is important for managers to recognize and anticipate these external influences.

EXERCISES

Problem

Use information available from the U.S. Bureau of Labor Statistics to gather productivity trends for several industries. See what influences you think may have contributed to trend differences. If there are firms from these industries in your local area, talk with their HRM executives about their views on productivity performance in their companies.

Questions

1. Does the simple marginal productivity model provide guidance to firms about their wage policies?

2. What are the implications of teamwork for compensation systems?

3. Why might changes in national productivity trends have implications for HRM within firms?

4. What is the relationship between competitiveness and productivity?

5. How might external social forces affect productivity within firms?

6. Can information on measures such as grievance rates be of use in evaluating the productivity of different work units within an organization? Explain.

Terms

bonus systems	marginal product	unit labor costs
co-determination	marginal revenue product	value added
Employee Stock Ownership Plan (ESOP)	multifactor productivity	workrule bargaining
industrial policy	piece rates	works councils
	quality of working life	

ENDNOTES

1. Prices do not always rise, although since the end of World War II general indexes of prices have almost always risen on a year-to-year basis. Even during periods of general inflation, some prices may fall absolutely. Price deflators for value-based measures of output are needed as long as prices vary, whether the variation is up or down.

2. The analysis that follows should be familiar to students who have had an elementary course in economics. If it does not seem familiar, review any standard microeconomics textbook.

3. That is, $\partial Q/\partial L > 0$—where $\partial Q/\partial L$ is the marginal product of labor—and $\partial/\partial L^2 < 0$.

4. Productivity enhancement through education, training, and experience is discussed in a later chapter.

5. Issues of teamwork are discussed in Armen A. Alchian and Harold Demsetz, "Production, Information Costs, and Economic Organization," *American Economic Review,* vol. 62 (December 1972), pp. 777–795, especially pp. 779–781.

6. Suppose, for example, a plant uses 4,000 hours of labor per week at an hourly wage of $10. Its weekly labor costs are thus $40,000. If the plant produces 1,000 widgets, its unit labor cost per widget is $40,000/1,000 widgets = $40/widget.

7. For some research in this area, see Casey Ichniowski, "The Effects of Grievance Activity on Productivity," *Industrial and Labor Relations Review,* vol. 40 (October 1986), pp. 75–89; J. R. Norsworthy and Craig A. Zabala, "Worker Attitudes, Worker Behavior, and Productivity in the U.S. Automobile Industry, 1959–1976," *Industrial and Labor Relations Review,* vol. 38 (July 1985), pp. 544–557.

8. William H. Miernyk, "Coal" in Gerald G. Somers, ed., *Collective Bargaining: Contemporary American Experience* (Madison, Wisc.: Industrial Relations Research Association, 1980), pp. 1–48.

9. Of course, the *rate* of return to capital in labor-intensive industries need not be lower (and would not be expected to be lower) than in other industries.

10. The private GNP deflator was used to make this calculation.

11. Craufurd D. Goodwin, ed., *Exhortation & Controls: The Search for a Wage-Price Policy: 1945–71* (Washington: Brookings Institution, 1975); John Sheahan, *The Wage-Price Guideposts* (Washington: Brookings Institution, 1967); Arnold R. Weber and Daniel J. B. Mitchell, *The Pay Board's Progress: Wage Controls in Phase II* (Washington: Brookings Institution, 1978).

12. A list of readings on productivity appears at the end of this chapter.

13. U.S. President, *Economic Report of the President, January 1987* (Washington: GPO, 1987), pp. 107–113.

14. Perhaps part of the problem in economic research has been the concentration on aggregate data rather than industry studies. By the 1980s, however, some attention had been turned on industry level research, for example, Martin Neil Baily and Alok K. Chakrabarti, "Innovation and Productivity in U.S. Industry," *Brookings Papers on Economic Activity* (2:1985), pp. 609–632. Baily and Chakrabarti argue that the slowdown has been caused by a reduced pace of technological advance, based on detailed study of the chemical and textile industries.

15. An attempt to measure the effect of workplace disharmony on productivity—and an argument that increased dishar-

mony reduced productivity growth—can be found in Thomas E. Weisskopf, Samuel Bowles, and David M. Gordon, "Hearts and Minds: A Social Model of U.S. Productivity Growth," *Brookings Papers on Economic Activity* (2:1983), pp. 381–441.

16. Louis E. Davis and Albert B. Cherns, eds., *The Quality of Working Life,* two volumes (New York: The Free Press, 1975).

17. Harry C. Katz, Thomas A. Kochan, and Jeffrey H. Keefe, "Industrial Relations and Productivity in the U.S. Automobile Industry," *Brookings Papers on Economic Activity* (3:1987), pp. 685–715.

18. The initial New Deal policy was embodied in the National Industrial Recovery Act (NIRA) of 1933, which was found unconstitutional two years later. Elements of NIRA regarding unions were incorporated in the Wagner Act of 1935 which, unlike NIRA, was found to be constitutional.

19. See, for example, Lester C. Thurow, "A World-Class Economy: Getting Back into the Ring," *Technology Review,* vol. 88 (August/September 1985), pp. 27–37: Lester C. Thurow, *The Case for Industrial Policies,* occasional paper, Alternative for the 1980s (Washington: Center for National Policy, 1984); Report of a Study Group, *Restoring American Competitiveness: Proposals for an Industry Policy,* report no. 11, Alternatives for the 1980s (Washington: Center for National Policy, 1984). The study group that authored the last citation was chaired by Lane Kirkland, president of the AFL-CIO, Irving Shapiro, former chairman and CEO of Du Pont, and Felix Rohatyn of Lazard Freres & Co. A survey of the industrial policy issue can be found in Kenan Patrick Jarboe, "A Reader's Guide to the Industry Policy Debate," *California Management Review,* vol. 27 (Summer 1985), pp. 198–219.

20. Charles L. Schultze, "Industrial Policy: A Dissent," *The Brookings Review,* vol. 2 (Fall 1983), pp. 3–12; U.S. President, *Economic Report of the President, February 1984* (Washington: GPO, 1984), pp. 87–111.

21. The program took the form of sponsorship of publications and conferences on innovative HRM practices and attempts to stimulate labor-management cooperative committees.

22. ESOPs and other compensation systems are discussed in a later chapter.

23. Education and training are taken up in a subsequent chapter.

24. See, for example, National Commission on Excellence in Education, *A Nation at Risk: The Imperative for Educational Reform* (Washington: U.S. Department of Education, 1983), known as the "Gardner Report."

Chapter Four

EMPLOYEE APPRAISAL AND REWARD

In the previous chapter, it was noted that labor is not a homogeneous factor of production. Even within narrowly defined occupations, labor can differ in productivity and value to the employer for many reasons. Two are particularly important for this chapter. First, employees have different "endowments" of skills, talents, innate traits, and learned behavioral characteristics. Second, employees may *choose* to vary their behavior in response to conditions at the workplace, including incentives and disincentives that may be built into the reward system.

It is evident that the variability in employee quality—which may not be detectable or predictable at the time of hiring—will require some type of policy response from the employer. One possibility is simply to gear wages directly to productivity so that, for example, a worker who is 10% more productive than another will enjoy a 10% premium relative to his or her fellow employee. Such payment systems are possible only in the case of well-defined and measurable output.

This chapter deals with employee evaluation and reward, even when output is not easily measured, since for many types of jobs piece rates or other pay plans tied to measured production are not feasible. In fact, historically, the long-term trend has been *away* from such pay formulas and toward time-based wages such as hourly pay, or weekly, monthly, or yearly salaries. However, use of time-based pay does not preclude differential rewards.

Chapter 3 also indicated that the team element in production often rendered output-linked pay differentials impractical when there were large behavioral differences between employees. A poor worker, who spread negative externalities to his or her fellow employees, may so adversely affect productivity that no positive wage, no matter how low, could make it worthwhile for the employer to continue the employment relationship.

4–1   Performance Appraisals

Given these considerations, some mechanism in the workplace must be established to evaluate performance. When conducted on a formal basis, such systems are often described by HRM professionals as *performance appraisals*. Once performance is evaluated, various employer responses are possible. In cases of favorable reviews, rates of pay can be increased through a merit plan. In addition, highly rated employees can be promoted or rewarded with bonuses. Where negative reviews occur, employees may be denied a merit pay increase, warned to correct their deficiencies, or even be disciplined or dismissed.

Table 4–1 presents the results of a survey, taken in the early 1980s, of employer practice with regard to performance appraisal systems. Ninety-two percent of the respondents reported that their firms had at least one performance appraisal system in place.[1] As can be seen from the table, the use of formal performance appraisal is very common—indeed, close to universal—except in two cases: appraisal of top management and of unionized production workers. In the former case there is a question of who should do the appraisal; in the latter, unions may resist the subjective element in performance appraisals and may push for rewards based on nonsubjective seniority.

Since performance appraisals will have desirable or undesirable consequences for workers, the performance appraisal system must be seen as part of the incentive arrangements at the workplace. If good reviews lead to rewards, employees will strive to receive such reviews. Similarly, they will attempt to avoid unfavorable reviews, if these lead to penalties.

**TABLE 4–1   Use of Formal Performance Appraisal Systems
by Type of Employee**

Occupational Group	*Percent of Employers with Formal Plans*
Top management	67%
Middle management	87
First-level supervisors	91
Professional, technical	88
Office, clerical	88
Production workers	63
Union	42
Nonunion	84

Note: Table shows results of a survey of private and public employers based on the responses of 264 HRM executives.

Source: The Bureau of National Affairs, Inc., *Performance Appraisal Programs,* PPF Survey no. 135 (Washington: BNA, 1983), p. 4.

Ideally, the performance appraisal system will lead to higher employee productivity, since that is supposed to be the behavioral response that is rewarded. As with any rating system, however, problems of design and implementation inevitably arise. Any professor who has designed and administered an exam, or any student who has taken one, will have no difficulty in understanding these problems!

Loose Links in the Chain

In a performance appraisal system, the reward that the employee hopes to achieve is linked only indirectly to his or her productivity. In theory, high productivity leads to a superior rating that, in turn, leads to a reward. But there are two loose links in the chain between productivity performance and reward. The productivity performance must in fact be recognized, and must be reflected in the employee's official rating, before a reward is possible. Even then, someone must examine the rating and decide to link it to the reward.

If either link in the chain is broken (productivity $\longrightarrow$ rating, or rating $\longrightarrow$ reward or penalty), the performance appraisal system will not provide an economic incentive toward higher productivity.[2] Nor will it be a deterrent to improper conduct. In the real world there are reasons why the chain might be broken at one or both points. Indeed, there are incentives in the workplace that can damage or prevent the proper functioning of a performance appraisal system.

Supervisors as Performance Raters

Most employees have supervisors, and in most organizations supervisors form part of a larger, hierarchical authority structure. Supervisors have supervisors, who—in turn—have supervisors. One role of a supervisor is simply to provide instructions, that is, to tell people what tasks to perform. However, the role of a supervisor is far more complex than simply being an order giver.

Trying to define the supervisory role is difficult, since the role varies from employer to employer. However, a legal definition that illustrates the nature and scope of the role does exist. In 1947 Congress amended basic U.S. labor law by passing the Taft-Hartley Act in order to remove existing protections for supervisors who wished to engage in collective bargaining.[3] At that time the management community, afraid that unionized supervisors would not adequately represent their employers' interests, pressed for legislation. To make this legal modification, Congress had to define a supervisor. Since that time, a *supervisor* has been defined as:

> ... any individual having authority, in the interest of the employer, to hire, transfer, suspend, lay off, recall, promote, discharge, assign, reward, or discipline other employees, or responsibly to direct them, or to adjust their grievances, or effectively recommend such action ...[4]

Supervisors may perform some or all of the above-listed tasks. Regardless of the scope of their duties, however, virtually all supervisory employees are capable of taking actions that can enhance or harm the welfare of their subordinates. Determining the productivity of subordinates and playing some role in linking that determination to tangible rewards is an important element of supervision. Poor supervisory training may hinder this process. Apart from training, if there is a potentially defective link in the connection between performance and rating, its roots are likely to be found in the incentives and disincentives facing supervisors. Even the best system cannot avoid this problem entirely.

Agents, Principals, and Performance Appraisals

If information were perfect and costless, supervisors would have little role to play in the firm. But because information is not perfect and costless, the firm must delegate to an individual (the supervisor) responsibility for local operations. Decentralization of authority is to some degree unavoidable. In this regard the internal workings of the firm mirror the decentralized, external market.

Just as ordinary workers cannot be perfectly monitored, neither can supervisors. Supervisors can sometimes abuse their positions, that is, take actions that benefit themselves at the expense of their employer. Since they have authority to take actions that can benefit or harm subordinates, supervisors could demand personal favors from subordinates. Such supervisory behavior, of course, is detrimental to the employer's interest, but may not be detected by the employer in a world of imperfect information. It is a classic illustration of the difficulty principals have in controlling their agents.

Cases of overt monetary kickbacks from employees to their supervisors are not common but are certainly not unknown. More common is the vague impression around many workplaces that employees who do favors for supervisors may receive rewards. This impression about the agent (supervisor) may or may not work in the interest of the principal (employer). A rule that to get ahead, you should please your boss is fine for the employer *if* what pleases the supervisor-boss is congruent with advancing the employer's agenda. But congruence of interests between employer and supervisor is not always perfect and certainly is not guaranteed.

In the early part of this century, for example, production workers often viewed their foremen as repressive, arbitrary, and exploitative figures.[5] This resentment, in fact, contributed to the growth of HRM, when employers experienced high costs of turnover from dissatisfied workers during the tight labor markets of World War I.[6] In addition, employers feared (and sometimes still do) that such resentments would provide footholds for union organizers among their workforces. More recently, the rash of litigation involving claims of sexual harassment—often from women workers claiming that male supervisors demanded sexual favors in exchange for good ratings or career advancements—dramatically illustrates the fact that supervisors do not always act in their employer's best interests.[7]

Obviously, a performance appraisal system will be sabotaged if supervisors use their power to give good or bad ratings to extract personal rents from workers. However, such blatant supervisory misconduct need not be present for a performance appraisal system to fail in its mission of providing incentives for high productivity among employees. Other, more subtle, influences can have that effect and are far more pervasive.

Performance Appraisal and the Rating of Raters

Supervisors are judged, in part, by the quality of their subordinates. Since supervisory workers are supposed to motivate subordinates and to correct or eliminate their subordinates' mistakes and misconduct, a supervisor must be concerned about the effects of reporting an abnormally high number of problem employees. The consequences of such a report could adversely affect the supervisor's own interests.

Even if a supervisor simply drew an unlucky hand in the workforce he or she must supervise, accurately reporting that fact poses a certain risk. In a world of imperfect information, and imperfect appraisal of supervisors, rules of thumb such as "where there's smoke, there's fire" could undermine a supervisory career. A supervisor may feel it is best not to advertise workplace problems. Indeed, the worse the problems, the greater may be the incentive to hide them. Cover-ups are not unique to some high government officials!

For the same reason, a department or production unit whose employees are highly rated is a positive reflection on its supervisor. In the absence of perfect information, those higher in the management structure may believe that a department or work unit with a highly rated staff must have a superior supervisor. There are, in short, incentives for supervisors to overstate the positive qualities of subordinates and to downplay subordinate deficiencies in any formal documentation.

Supervisors may feel that they can handle difficult or incompetent workers on an informal basis, bypassing the official performance appraisal mechanism and the scrutiny of superiors. Those supervisors who elect the unofficial approach may find themselves embarked on a perilous course if the informal route fails (as will be seen in a later chapter). Nevertheless, the temptation is there.

One exception to the supervisory incentive to avoid negative ratings involves fear of up-and-coming subordinates. A supervisor may worry that he or she will be upstaged and bypassed by a subordinate and may attempt to block the subordinate by means of low ratings. Or the supervisor may appropriate the ideas of the subordinate without giving credit where credit is due. In this case, although supervisory misincentives produce low, rather than high, ratings, they still distort the performance appraisal process.

Performance appraisal systems are often linked to pay. Good ratings can lead to merit increases for the employee. Generally, in organizational hierarchies, supervisors are expected (and themselves expect) to be paid more than subordinates. In the absence of perfect information on marginal productivity, it is assumed—not unreasonably—that supervisors contribute more incremental value to the employer than those whom they direct. Thus a supervisor who succeeds in raising the average pay of subordinates may succeed in raising his or her own pay level.

Employee Influence on Ratings

The tendency of higher management to consider a problem-infected workforce to be the consequence of an ineffective supervisor creates yet another incentive to produce inaccurate ratings. Subordinates are made aware of their evaluations, usually as a formal part of the performance appraisal process.[8] Complaints stemming from the dissatisfaction of poorly rated employees can produce a climate a supervisor would prefer to avoid. Supervisors thus tend to boost ratings of subordinates' performances to misleading levels. Employees may know that worker complaints could undermine management confidence in supervisors. Even if they do not recognize this possibility, their supervisor will surely be aware of it. One way of averting such problems is not to give poor ratings, even when they are merited, except in extreme cases. In addition, to avoid inter-employee jealousies and tensions, supervisors may give relatively undifferentiated ratings.

Most medium- to large-sized firms have some kind of grievance mechanism, whereby workers can file complaints if they feel mistreated by their supervisors. In unionized firms these systems are usually highly formalized and typically provide for arbitration by a neutral, outside arbitrator if the grievance cannot be resolved internally. Larger nonunion firms, especially those that emphasize the HRM function, are likely to have formal grievance mechanisms too (although only a few nonunion firms provide for an outside arbitrator as a final step in the process).[9]

Under a grievance system the filing of a complaint by an employee inevitably will come to the attention of management. The supervisor involved will be questioned about the validity of the grievance and about his or her actions that precipitated the complaint. If many grievances arise from within a particular supervisor's jurisdiction, questions may be raised about the quality of supervision.

Higher management may begin to wonder why the supervisor does not solve problems *before* they arise. Even if the supervisor is not the cause of the initial complaints, perhaps he or she is poor at resolving conflict. Perhaps there is an adverse impact on productivity and morale caused by the workplace friction that the grievances are indicating.

Apart from monitoring formal grievances, larger firms may also conduct employee attitude studies to uncover areas of employee dissatisfaction. These studies sometimes involve periodic polling of workers to determine the nature and source of their workplace concerns. Supervisors in firms that conduct attitude surveys are aware that such reviews might reflect dissatisfaction if many unfavorable performance appraisals are given. Unfavorably rated subordinates are unlikely to have kind words to say about their supervisors. Again, an incentive exists for supervisors to give ratings that are too high and too uniform.

Finally, it is important to note that giving subordinates poor ratings may create an actual productivity problem for the supervisor, not just the appearance of one. Employees and supervisors are really engaged in team production. Disgruntled employees may withhold cooperation from the team and reduce the unit's output. Moreover, supervisors are ultimately held accountable by management for their work unit's output.

Causes of Perverse Incentives

That perverse incentives can create perverse behavior on the part of supervisors can hardly be a controversial proposition. But from the economic perspective, *why* does a profit-maximizing firm permit such misincentives to exist or even create them in the first place? Surely, by correcting the improper incentives and obtaining accurate performance appraisals, firms could enhance productivity and reduce unit labor costs. Are not top managers aware of these potential profit-enhancing cost savings?

The answer is "yes"; top managers (including HRM managers) are aware of the difficulties inherent in performance appraisals. They even have evolved some remedies for the problem (discussed in the next section). But the ultimate answer to the question of why perverse incentives are allowed to exist and persist is one of trade-offs. The difficulties associated with performance appraisal are part of a general class of problems inherent in organizations. In general these problems intensify as organizations grow larger. Because of imperfect and costly information channels, larger organizations require that more and more delegations of authority must be made.

Balanced against the costs associated with organizational size and control are the gains in coordination of operations that size brings. The firm effectively encloses a set of functions within its organizational structure and takes them out of the external marketplace. As noted in Chapter 1, in a perfect market of the type characterized in elementary economics textbooks, there would really be no firms. Rather, through a daily, costless, auctionlike process, workers and owners of capital would organize themselves into temporary production units, based on prevailing prices and costs.

In the real world, however, forming such units on a daily basis would be prohibitively expensive. Firms (organizations) have evolved instead as the most efficient units of production. Although the creation of firms entails costs associated with imperfect incentives, bureaucracy, and so on, firms that succeed show themselves to be more efficient than the outside market alternative. HRM professionals within successful firms attempt to minimize organizational costs, including misincentives, but cannot entirely eliminate them. Trade-offs between competing objectives must be made.[10]

As a simple example, top management might decide that by reducing the number of middle and first-line supervisors, replacing them with a smaller number of trusted management agents, more accurate performance appraisals would result. Perhaps such benefits would accrue, but even if they did, the firm would simultaneously lose the economies previously gained by delegation and decentralization. Management's role is to balance the two objectives: information accuracy and reduced misincentives versus decentralized efficiency.

As another example, management could decide to stop monitoring signs of employee dissatisfaction because such monitoring provides a perverse incentive to supervisors to avoid giving poor ratings to low-productivity workers. (Some firms have abandoned formal performance appraisals for just such reasons.) A decision of this type deprives the employer of a source of information that sometimes *does* indicate poor supervision. Alternatively, the employer could retain the monitoring mechanism, but expend more resources to distinguish between poor supervisors and poor employees. Unfortunately, resources are scarce and expenditures must be limited. Real world systems of performance appraisal will always be imperfect.

In any case, employers may want to retain performance appraisal systems—

even if they provide inaccurate information—because of the signaling effect they provide. To not have a system, however imperfect, might signal to employees that the employer does not place much weight on quality performance. Having an appraisal system, even if all involved understand its deficiencies, at least communicates the message that performance is important to the employer. The medium is the message.

4–2   Reducing Perverse Incentives of Performance Appraisal

Two basic types of rating error have been outlined, both related largely to incentives surrounding supervisors. First, supervisors might take advantage of their position of authority and discretion and award ratings in exchange for "favors" from employees. Second, supervisors might find it advantageous to be overgenerous and undifferentiated in giving subordinates ratings in order to further personal career objectives. Various techniques have been tried to reduce these perverse behaviors that may otherwise undermine a performance appraisal system.

Documentation

The more documentation that is required to back up ratings and the more that ratings are tied to verifiable criteria, the less leeway there is for false or inflated reports. For these reasons performance appraisal forms are often accompanied with detailed instructions to supervisors, defining the various rating scales as precisely as possible, and—in some cases—providing examples of behaviors that should receive high or low ratings. Such scales are known as behaviorally anchored rating scales. In some cases supervisors may be required to cite specific instances (or critical incidents) of either superior or inferior performance on the part of the employee being rated.

Some rating systems rely partly or completely on essay-type responses, rather than on numerical scales. Proponents argue that use of the essay format will capture components of employee behavior that simple rating scales can miss. This argument is made especially for higher managerial and professional jobs, in which check-the-box answers are not informative. In addition proponents insist that writing an essay requires more care than simply filling out a numerical form of the type shown in Figure 4–1.

The reader will immediately see that a trade-off is involved in completing performance appraisals. Elaborate instructions, detailed requirements for documentation, and lengthy essays all consume substantial time. Moreover, the time involved is typically that of the higher paid employees who perform the rating function. Of course, care and accuracy are not necessarily proportional to the time consumed; but again, signaling is involved. If the performance appraisal system requires elaborate documentation, supervisors are given a sense that accurate appraisal is considered important by their superiors.

Rankings

Since there are incentives to rate most employees as being above average, performance appraisal systems can be structured to provide constraints on such tendencies. Supervisors can be asked, for example, to *rank* employees rather than give them absolute ratings, or limits can be placed on the proportion of employees who can be top ranked. The result is similar to grading on a curve in the educational setting.

The pitfalls are the same as in systems of grading on a curve; superior (inferior) employees who are located in departments in which there happen to be high concentrations of high- (low-) productivity workers will tend to be rated lower (higher) than in the average department. Thus rankings and constraints create problems of "horizontal equity" across departments. They create incentives, moreover, for high-productivity employees to seek to transfer out of departments in which there are other good performers.

Reviewing the Review

Rather than rely on the design of the appraisal form to minimize misleading ratings, some firms prefer to subject the ratings to further review. Filled-out performance appraisals can be scrutinized by professionals employed in the HRM department. These reviewers may question results that appear out of line with past reports on the employee in question. Supervisors may also be questioned if their average ratings seem high relative to other departments. (Can everyone really be better than average?)

Such HRM reviews amount to a monitoring of the monitors by individuals who do not have an immediate, personal stake in the supervisor's relations with his or her employees. There is an obvious expenditure involved in hiring monitors to monitor other monitors, and HRM professionals themselves are subject to potential misincentives. They do not want to appear to be constantly criticizing, and interfering with, the work of line managers. The goal of the organization is production, after all, not perfect appraisal.

Another commonly used option, which does not involve hiring professional monitors, is to have the rated employee read the completed form and add any comments he or she believes relevant. Indeed, in systems such as management by objectives, the employee is asked in advance to help designate the relevant criteria to be rated. Such employee review will tend to prevent false negative information from becoming part of the record without challenge. On the other hand this approach is less likely to correct false positive information. And, since some systems require the supervisor to discuss the form personally with the employee, they may add to the incentive to inflate ratings and avoid distasteful confronta-

FIGURE 4–1   Excerpt from a Simple Performance Appraisal Form

CLERICAL EVALUATION

For each work attribute you are given five possible characterizations. Circle the characterization that best describes the employee you are rating. Indicate any additional comments you have in the spaces provided.

A. Work Quality (accuracy, neatness, thoroughness)

    a. Excellent b. Above Average c. Average d. Need for Improvement e. Unsatisfactory

    Comments: _____

    _____

B. Productivity (amount of work produced per day)

    a. Excellent b. Above Average c. Average d. Need for Improvement e. Unsatisfactory

    Comments: _____

    _____

C. Job Knowledge (degree of skill, awareness of duties)

    a. Excellent b. Above Average c. Average d. Need for Improvement e. Unsatisfactory

    Comments: _____

    _____

D. Relations with Others (ability to work effectively with fellow employees and supervisors)

    a. Excellent b. Above Average c. Average d. Need for Improvement e. Unsatisfactory

    Comments: _____

    _____

E. Dependability (quality of work, ability to carry through an assignment)

    a. Excellent b. Above Average c. Average d. Need for Improvement e. Unsatisfactory

    Comments: _____

    _____

F. Work Habits (care of office equipment, adherence to company and department policies, attendance, punctuality)

    a. Excellent b. Above Average c. Average d. Need for Improvement e. Unsatisfactory

    Comments: _____

    _____

G. Other _____
                        (specify)

    a. Excellent b. Above Average c. Average d. Need for Improvement e. Unsatisfactory

    Comments: _____

    _____

_____

Overall Rating (should be consistent with ratings on items A–G)

    a. Excellent b. Above Average c. Average d. Need for Improvement e. Unsatisfactory

    Comments: _____

    _____

    _____

_____   _____
  Supervisor's signature   Employee's signature*

Your signature means only that you have read your supervisor's ratings. It does not mean you agree with them.

tions. Even if a supervisor is skilled at giving constructive criticism, the subordinate may not be skilled at receiving it.

Alternative Raters

Although the vast majority of performance appraisal systems rely on supervisors to function as raters, other options are available for employers. A few companies ask employees to rate themselves, and provide a detailed list of questions for the employee to answer. On the surface, it might seem that employees would have strong incentives to overrate their performance. However, the incentives are more complex.

An employee who rates himself or herself uniformly high on all dimensions will immediately be suspect. To appear honest, the employee has an incentive to identify *some* fault. Having done so, he or she is then under pressure to correct the self-identified problem. The exercise bears a resemblance to confession in the religious setting or the self-criticism practiced in communist countries.

Still another alternative is to have co-workers rather than supervisors do the rating. Such systems of peer review are extremely rare, but they have traditionally been used for faculty in institutions of higher learning. Where workers are part of teams, shirkers impose costs on others in the team. Thus fellow team members may not take kindly to inferior performance. Co-workers are often less understanding of substandard behavior than are supervisors.[11] However, the incentives are again complex; cliques of workers can take advantage of their authority just as supervisors sometimes do, and fear of retaliation can undermine worker-rater systems.

4–3   Rewards and Performance Appraisal

There are obvious reasons for linking the results of performance appraisal with some tangible economic consequence, positive or negative, for employees. However, it is a common—but not a universal—practice, to separate the appraisal process from the reward system. Employers may insist that there is one process for performance appraisal and another for rewards. The reason for this (surprising) separation is linked to fear of exacerbating the misincentives discussed earlier.

As indicated, supervisors have an incentive to manage highly paid subordinates, since having highly paid subordinates may tend to boost their own pay. In addition, supervisors will prefer that their subordinates be content with their pay level. Discontented workers could make achievement of the supervisor's production targets difficult, either through turnover or through low productivity. A supervisor might thus be tempted to pay a premium (which comes out of the employer's pocket) to ensure workplace tranquility. This premium might be higher than the employer would find optimal. It is often felt, therefore, that separating the appraisal process from the reward decision will keep the latter more honest.

Still, as Table 4–2 shows, simply keeping reference to rewards off the performance appraisal form does not necessarily sever the connection between ratings and rewards. Most firms that use appraisal systems report that they do use them as a guide for individual pay adjustments and for promotions, even if the linkage is informal. Although promotion opportunities may be limited and infrequent, many companies have merit pay systems—effectively tied to performance appraisals—that provide the opportunity for regular pay advances. An interesting question is how important performance appraisals are as a source of internal pay advancement within the firm.

TABLE 4–2   Uses of Performance Appraisals

	Percent of Employers Using Performance Appraisal	
Occupational Group	*To Determine Wage/Salary Adjustments*	*To Make Promotion Decisions*
Top management	8%	8%
Middle management	87	80
First-level supervisors	87	80
Professional, technical	87	79
Office, clerical	86	79
Production workers	78	75

Note: Table shows results of a survey of private and public employers based on the responses of 264 HRM executives.

Source: The Bureau of National Affairs, Inc., *Performance Appraisal Programs*, PPF Survey no. 135 (Washington: BNA, 1983), p. 12.

Alternative Progression Systems

Various systems of "wage progression" are in use. Under such systems, a rate *range*—rather than a single wage rate—is established for an occupation. Typically, employees enter the occupation at (or towards) the bottom of the range, and then have an opportunity to work their way to the top. Although the systems vary in detail, there are two basic options for determining the rate of advancement of the individual employee: time (seniority) and/or merit.

    A mechanism of advancement by virtue of time or seniority is formula-driven. It is easy to verify whether an employee should receive a pay increase by applying the simple rules of the system; all that is needed is an accurate record of the date of entry into the job. In contrast a system of pay advances on the basis of merit requires a subjective judgment (performance appraisal) by a management representative.

    Table 4–3 shows that a merit-based approach is used by employers for most occupational groups. The plant/service category, however, is substantially less likely to be under a merit system than the other groups, and is more likely than the others to be rewarded on a seniority basis. Further, Table 4–3 shows that much of the discrepancy regarding the plant/service occupations revolves around union status. Union-represented workers are less likely than others to have a merit plan and are more likely to have seniority used as a criterion for wage progression.

    The use of seniority is stronger in the union sector than in the nonunion sector for two basic reasons. First, the internal union political mechanism tends to be dominated by more senior worker/members, who naturally prefer to tilt

TABLE 4-3   Use of Wage Increase Plans, Late 1980

Occupation Group	Percent of Respondents Reporting Use of Each Wage Increase Plan	
	Automatic, Length-of-Service Increases	Merit Pay Plan
Plant, service	29%	44%
Union	39	16
Nonunion	22	60
Office, clerical	15	81
Professional, technical	10	85
Sales	4	83
First-level supervisors	8	88
Middle managers	6	88

Source: The Bureau of National Affairs, Inc., *Wage & Salary Administration,* PPF Survey no. 131 (Washington: BNA, 1981), pp. 10, 13.

workplace rules and benefits in their own favor. Second, unions prefer to limit management discretion on matters of pay.

Numerous empirical studies suggest that unions have the effect of boosting the average pay of the workers they represent above levels employers would otherwise choose. This pay advantage for union workers could be eroded if management had the unilateral discretion to influence pay through subjective merit decisions. Average pay could be reduced by management simply through a finding that few employees were meritorious. To avert employer decisions that could lower pay back to market levels, unions will either push for an objective seniority-based system or insist that whatever merit systems the employer operates be tightly controlled to avoid back-door pay reductions. Without tight control, the employer might be tempted to give low ratings to hold down pay artificially.

Merit Versus Seniority: An Implicit Contracts Approach

Although Table 4-3 reveals a strong employer preference for using merit rather than seniority as a guide to pay advancement, there can be a discrepancy between stated preference and actual result. For example, in the public sector, civil service procedures for pay progression are often nominally based on merit. Yet it is frequently the case that so-called merit decisions are routinely made after the employee serves a designated time on the job, and almost all employees are found to be meritorious on a regular basis. Thus, in practice, a supposedly merit-based system can easily operate as a seniority system.

Private employers are more likely to insist that their merit plans do, in fact, function on the basis of merit. However, some empirical studies based on internal company data suggest that seniority is often a critical factor, even in the nonunion sector. In other words, time on the job shows up as an important variable in determining the pace of pay advancement for individual employees.

Exactly why seniority and pay are positively correlated remains a matter of some debate in economic circles. Some researchers argue that the association is a statistical illusion, caused by a process of job matching. According to this view, those employees who tend to remain with the firm have (unmeasured) characteristics that meet the firm's needs, and their own. Poor matches, in contrast, leave the firm because they are unhappy with their situations—perhaps because they have failed to advance—or in some cases they may be terminated. The good matches are rewarded with pay and promotions, creating the correlation between pay and seniority. Essentially, the sample of workers at the firm is biased towards good matches as seniority increases.[12]

Unfortunately, because this view depends on unmeasured matching characteristics, it is difficult to prove or disprove. If there is a causal relationship between seniority and pay, *implicit contracting* provides a possible explanation.[13] It could be that employers reward seniority with pay as a motivational device, paradoxical though that seems.

Under implicit contracting theory, the employee's pay profile and marginal revenue product profile are viewed as separated—that is, implicit contracting departs from the simple economic theory that wage = marginal revenue product of labor (MRP_L) at every moment of time. Instead, under implicit contracting, the employee is paid less than marginal revenue product in the initial phase of his or her career with the employer and more than marginal revenue product towards the end. Thus the equality of wage and MRP_L is maintained on average (with appropriate adjustment for discounting) over the expected career life, but not instantaneously.

Figure 4–2 provides an illustration of typical pay and MRP_L profiles over a career. At time t_M the employee enters employment and is paid less than his or her incremental value to the firm, although at a high enough level for the firm to

FIGURE 4–2
Hypothetical Profile of Pay and Marginal Revenue Productivity over Career Life

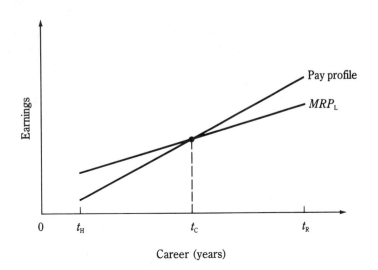

be able to recruit and retain workers. The firm effectively makes an implicit contract with the employee that if his or her performance is satisfactory, pay will gradually be raised so that eventually—by the time of retirement, t_R—pay will exceed the level justified by productivity. In short the theory of implicit contracts puts a kind face on the so-called Peter Principle, which states that "in a hierarchy every employee tends to rise to his level of incompetence."

Various explanations have been put forward for such implicit contracts. On the supply side, the pay profile (low at first, high at career's end) is said to accommodate employee needs for income; in other words, young workers have few dependents whereas older ones support families and must make provision for retirement. This argument must be accompanied by a presumed constraint on the ability of employees to save when they are young for later expenses.[14]

On the demand side employers will experience lower turnover costs since employees, once hired, must remain with the firm to gain the eventual rewards of seniority. Young employees will also have an incentive to perform at least at a satisfactory level to avoid being terminated before collecting the reward.[15] Older employees will have a strong incentive to maintain their performance level, since such workers will know that, if terminated, they would have to find work in the outside market where their productivity-based wages would be significantly lower. For this implicit contract system to work, however, there are two requirements: an honestly run wage progression (and possibly promotion) system and an employer who remains in business long enough to honor the implicit contract.

Rules and Employer Reputation

At time t_C in Figure 4–2, the employee reaches a crossover point in his or her career. After that time, the employee is overpaid; before that time, the employee is underpaid relative to productivity. Employers would therefore have the temptation to entice job seekers into underpaid, entry-level service with promises of eventual pay progression. But when the employees actually reached time t_C, they would be terminated, preventing worker recoupment of the promised return for loyal service.

Given this problem of moral hazard on the part of the employer, potential employees might be reticent to accept an implicit contract of the type represented in Figure 4–2 without some assurance that the contract would not be broken. Having formal progression plans—and establishing a reputation for not abusing their discretion—is one way that employers can provide such assurance. If an employer had a merit system in which pay advancements were commonly denied, potential employees might be reluctant to accept employment, once they learned of the firm's poor reputation as a keeper of commitments. Moreover, morale problems might develop among current employees, who might fear that the deals they thought they had made with the firm were being, or were likely to be, dishonored.

The theory of implicit contracting, therefore, suggests that seniority could play an important role in determining pay advancement, whether or not a merit system is used. It also suggests that when layoffs are made, firms may prefer to let junior workers go before seniors, since terminating seniors before retirement age would tend to violate longstanding implicit agreements. Or seniors might be offered special retirement incentives to compensate them for early separation from the firm.

Finally, implicit contracting suggests that firms—if unconstrained by legal barriers—would want to establish some kind of mandatory retirement age (say, at t_R). Such an age would avoid having employees over-recoup their initial investments made as junior workers. For most employees, however, Congress forbade mandatory retirement after 1986. Hence firms might instead have an incentive to offer financial retirement inducements.[16] Or they might have an incentive to offer less of an upward sloping pay profile initially. A later chapter will return to some of these points.

Employer Stability and Corporate Restructuring

Implicit contracting theory was partly inspired by case studies of actual HRM practices. Observations included the paternal employer policies such as "lifetime" employment at major Japanese companies, "full" employment policies at certain progressive American employers such as IBM, the general social ethos that condemns employers who fire long-service employees, and studies that suggest that older workers have a hard time starting over when they are terminated because of the career ladders at other potential employers. Regardless of initial intent, it is clear that career-oriented commitments of any character are unlikely to be met if the employer ceases to exist before an employee's working life has ended.

Employers may cease to exist because market conditions no longer can maintain them profitably in business. Even before actual shutdown occurs, such employers may effectively cease to defer to seniority, since maintaining a reputation as a good employer no longer matters. Companies may also cease to exist as independent entities if they are swallowed by, or merged with, other firms. The new owner/operators may not feel constrained by the implicit commitments of their predecessors.

During the 1980s, there was a considerable acceleration of merger activity and corporate restructuring. This instability in the business sector was partly due to changes in antitrust policy, increased international competition, deregulation in some industries, and the severity of the recession in the early years of the decade. Such volatility must inevitably have an effect on the credence employees can put in corporate HRM policies, including those related to merit systems, progression, and promotion opportunities.

Rapid change in corporate ownership may have the effect of prodding management to greater efficiency; this is often seen as the social function of the market for corporate control.[17] Usually, the issue of wealth redistribution is debated when so-called greenmail is paid to potential raiders. Presumably, takeovers, mergers, spin-offs, and the like could generate wealth for those undertaking these activities by improving corporate management and efficiency. It is also possible that such activity can benefit its undertakers by *transferring* wealth, rather than generating it.[18] Since employees are stakeholders in the firm, it is possible that a wealth transfer from employees to new owners could occur. Instances in which wages or benefits are reduced, or other conditions of work deteriorate, may fall into this category.

The critical issue is whether the enterprise was viable at the old pay rates and conditions. For example, suppose a newly deregulated business finds itself burdened with pay and benefit obligations established during the prior period of regulation and protection. If it faces new-entrant competition at lower rates of pay that would make the firm uncompetitive, new owners may enter the picture and proceed to lower labor standards. In this case, there is no transfer of wealth from employees to the new owners; *rather, deregulation has transferred wealth from employees to consumers.* Although employee anger may focus on the new owners, they were simply the instruments and reflection of a change in government policy (deregulation).

Alternatively, if new owners simply renege on past implicit commitment to employees in the absence of a tangible deterioration in the economic conditions facing the firm, higher short-run profits may be generated. In such cases there may be a wealth transfer from employees to new owners. Much depends on the specific circumstances.

Consider first a circumstance in which previous owners—through their managers—adopted HRM policies on compensation and other matters that turned out to be excessively generous from the firm's viewpoint. In other words, the extra productivity, loyalty, and so on generated by the policies did not outweigh their costs at the margin even though the firm could nevertheless operate at a reasonable profit. If a change in ownership results in a take-away of the policies, there is a simple wealth transfer from employees to the new owners.

If, however, the previous HRM policies—though seemingly generous—were optimal, a shift toward reduced pay and conditions might still generate short-run accounting profits. In the long term, it might be argued, the external valuation of the firm should be lower; even if short-run accounting profits increase, because of the departure from optimal HRM practice. The situation is analogous to a firm that generates short-term accounting profits by neglecting optimal maintenance of equipment.

Economic theory suggests that external evaluators—those buying and selling the company's shares in the case of a publicly traded firm—would see through the veil of accounting data. In the case of the maintenance deferral, they would realize that the firm was accelerating depreciation of actual physical capital in a nonoptimal fashion. In the case of the deterioration in pay and conditions for employees, the evaluators would realize that the firm was nonoptimally depreciating its stock of human capital. But given information costs—and the difficulty of determining precisely the optimal level of maintenance expenditures or HRM generosity—the external market may not always pierce the accounting veil. Still, the market does exert some discipline, and it does not appear that mergers are generally based on putting employees at a disadvantage.[19]

Where collective bargaining is involved in setting the firm's HRM policies, shifts in bargaining power can lead to transfers of wealth back and forth between employees and owners. For a variety of reasons (discussed in a later chapter), employer bargaining power increased in the 1980s. Sometimes the changes in management that accompanied restructuring were the vehicle through which the increase in employer bargaining power was expressed. New management came in, demanded, and often received wage, benefit, and workrule concessions from the union or unions involved.[20]

In any case if the volatility of corporate ownership and control that developed in the 1980s continues indefinitely, changes are likely to occur in the implicit contracts offered to or accepted by workers in the future. Lack of trust in, or ability to make, forward employment contracts would cause the pay profile of Figure 4-2 to rotate clockwise towards the MRP_L line. In effect employees would be paid what they are worth, *when* they are worth it. Performance appraisal and merit rewards would continue, but the rewards might be weighted towards current year bonuses rather than permanent upward shifts in an individual employee's pay rate.

Some symptoms of a shift in this direction developed in the 1980s as the use of temporary employees increased. Temporary employees—whether hired through a personnel supply agency or directly by the employer—typically are employed under spot contracts. They are paid for the work they do at the time they do it; there is no commitment by either party to a continuing employment relationship. Employers who wish to maintain forward implicit contracts with a core group of employees may find it desirable, in a volatile world, to rely more heavily on such spot arrangements with a second tier of temporary employees than has been the practice in the past. The temporaries can absorb the peaks and valleys of production, thereby insulating the core group.[21]

4-4 Cost of Merit and Promotion Systems

Given the importance of labor costs to most firms, it is essential that HRM professionals develop the ability to project such expenses. Unfortunately, the existence of systems of merit pay (and, to some extent, promotion) seems to be a source of endless confusion for those charged with such costing. The costs of merit are often overstated by the very professionals who should know better.

It is important to start with the observation that in a steady state, that is, a situation in which the firm maintains its employment level over a long period of time in the face of normal turnover, a merit system should not cost anything. This surprising conclusion holds despite the fact that individual employees under the system are receiving regular merit pay increases. Although the case of promotions is not explicitly elaborated below, the reader will quickly see that the issues of merit awards and promotions are closely related.

Numerical Example

Table 4-4 presents a hypothetical example of a job with a rate range spread between $10/hour and $14/hour in five equal steps. Employees enter the occupation in step 1 ($10) and progress annually to the next step. (A seniority-based

TABLE 4–4   Hypothetical Example of Gross and Net Costs of Merit Pay

	Hourly Wage	Employee Distribution Year 1	Employee Distribution Year 2	Incremental Cost of Merit Pay Adjustments, Year 1 to Year 2	
				Gross Cost Basis	Net Cost Basis
Entry Step 1	$10	A	F		− $4*
Step 2	$11	B	A	$1	$1
Step 3	$12	C	B	$1	$1
Step 4	$13	D	C	$1	$1
Top Step 5	$14	E	D	$1	$1
Total hourly payroll	$60				
Mean hourly payroll	$12				
Increment to payroll				$4	$0
Increment/payroll				6.7%	0%

*Difference between wage of newly hired employee F and departing employee E.

pay system is being assumed for pedagogical purposes, but there will be no difference between merit and time advancement if, under the former, employees progress "on average" one step per year.) In year 1, employees A, B, C, D, and E are spread over the five steps. The following year, employee E retires and a replacement, employee F, is hired. Also, employees A, B, C, and D are advanced one step.

It can be easily seen that the total hourly payroll will be the same in year 1 and in year 2 ($60 = $10 + $11 + $12 + $13 + $14), as will the average hourly wage ($12 = $60/5). Although the four employees who remain with the firm in year 2 (A, B, C, and D) each get $1 raises ($4 in total), the replacement of E at $14 by F at $10 saves the firm an equivalent amount (−$4 = $10 − $14). The *net* cost of the merit system is, therefore, zero in a steady state situation.

Of course, at any point in time, an employer will probably not be in precisely the steady state. However, the basic principle holds. What determines the net costs of merit is the change (if any) in the proportions of workers at each step. In the steady state, the proportions remain unaltered from year to year. In the real world, there could be modest shifts in the proportions depending on surges in new hiring (which increase the "weight" of the lower step), hiring freezes (which decrease the entry weight), the age distribution of employees (which will determine how long they stay in the top step before retiring), and so on. As long as there is a clear distinction made between net and gross costs, none of these departures from the steady state poses analytical problems.

Gross Versus Net Confusion

The arithmetic in Table 4–4 is so simple that the reader may have difficulty understanding why confusion should ever exist. Nevertheless, there is ample evidence that merit pay systems are a source of confusion. As an example, during the anti-inflation wage controls program of the Nixon administration, the rules proposed for costing merit plans provoked substantial controversy. Yet the various participants in the dispute, including the rule makers themselves, seemed to have great difficulty understanding the difference between gross and net costs.[22]

A second bit of evidence comes from the responses of HRM specialists to various private surveys concerning the wage increases they have awarded or are planning to award. Compared with other data on wage trends, the responses appear consistently too high. This upward bias suggests that respondents have trouble differentiating the net and gross costs of merit, and report the latter when they should use the former.[23]

In Table 4–4, the gross cost of merit is $4, the equivalent of 6.7% of payroll. Thus unless the savings of replacing expensive employee E with cheap employee F are recognized, it might appear (erroneously) that having a merit system raises average pay by 6.7%. This arbitrary gross amount, of course, simply results from the assumptions of the example. A more typical annual gross cost of merit pay in real world plans is 1–2% of payroll. Regardless of the amount, the gross cost is not appropriate for judging the impact on employer expenditures. Only the net amount—zero in the steady state example of Figure 4–2—is appropriate.

There appear to be two reasons for the common confusion between net and gross merit costs. The first has to do with the problem of supervisor misincentives, discussed earlier in this chapter. The second is related to the propensity of firms to mix merit pay with general, across-the-board pay adjustments.

Merit Budgets and Misincentives

The merit plan of Table 4–4 is tightly controlled, with "normal" annual steps carefully delineated. However, even in such a system considerable supervisory discretion might be allowed. For example, a supervisor might be allowed to decide that a particularly meritorious employee could jump a step, say, move from step 3 to step 5. Since there are pressures on supervisors (in the absence of other constraints) to give out merit increases, such discretion might cause the supervisor to raise the average pay level from step 3 in year 1 to, say, step 4 in year 2.

For example, suppose employee A were jumped to step 4 ($13) and B and C were boosted to step 5 ($14). Suppose, as in the previous example, that D advanced normally to step 5, E retired, and F entered employment at step 1 ($10). The average wage in the unit would rise from $12, the equivalent of step 3, to $13, the equivalent of step 4. Such an increase would represent a rise in *net* costs of $5 or 8.3% of payroll, as shown on Table 4–5 (including the $4 savings of replacing E with F). Gross costs would rise by $9 or 15% of payroll.

To guard against profligate awards of merit increases, firms will often ration supervisors through the imposition of merit budgets. A supervisor in the example just cited might be constrained by assignment of a merit budget of $4. Within

TABLE 4-5   Hypothetical Example of Gross and Net Costs of Merit Pay with Supervisory Discretion

	Hourly Wage	Employee Distribution Year 1	Employee Distribution Year 2	Incremental Cost of Merit Pay Adjustments, Year 1 to Year 2	
				Gross Cost Basis	Net Cost Basis
Entry Step 1	$10	A	F		− $4*
Step 2	$11	B			
Step 3	$12	C			
Step 4	$13	D	A	$3	$3
Top Step 5	$14	E	B, C, D	$3 + $2 + $1	$3 + $2 + $1
Total hourly payroll	$60				
Mean hourly payroll	$12				
Increment to payroll				$9	$5
Increment/payroll				15%	8.3%

*Difference between wage of newly hired employee F and departing employee E.

that budget the supervisor might exercise discretion by awarding more to one candidate than to another. For example, employee A might receive a $2 increase, B and C a $1 increase each, and D might be bypassed. Or the awards could be spread evenly, as in Table 4−4. Either way, the $4 merit budget constraint holds the net cost of the merit system to zero, given the $4 turnover savings.

The accounting artifact of $4, however, can easily become a source of confusion. A supervisor who spends (allocates) a $4 merit budget might believe that he or she had raised pay by 6.7%, since the merit budget is presented on a gross basis. As noted, this confusion is surprisingly common.

Mixing of Merit and Other Pay Adjustments

Compounding the confusion created by merit budgets is the temptation to mix merit pay and across-the-board pay adjustments. In the example just cited, the rate range for the job ($10 to $14) was unchanged from year 1 to year 2. However, external market wages typically rise from year to year, especially during periods of general inflation. Thus the firm might feel the need to raise the rate range by, say, 40¢, thus increasing the steps to $10.40, $11.40, and so on. Spread over the five steps, the net cost would be $2, that is, 40¢ × 5, or 3.3% of payroll.

Often, nonunion employers prefer to insist that *all* their pay increases are based on merit. Sometimes this assertion is maintained even during periods of inflation when there is clearly an across-the-board market factor included in wage decisions. In a period of generally rising wages, such an employer might raise the top and bottom step in Table 4–4 by 40¢ and give the supervisor a $6 budget to award increases. Implicitly, $2 of the $6 is for inflation and $4 is for merit. The $2, however, is part of the supervisor's discretionary adjustment fund and is not nominally being awarded to all workers.

Unfortunately, throwing both types of monies into the same pot and calling the entire sum a merit budget inevitably creates ambiguity. The average wage is raised by 3.3%; but the supervisor has a (gross) budget for increases of $6, creating the misleading appearance of a 10% average increase.

The impact of inflation and other factors on internal wage policies will be discussed more fully in a later chapter. However, the examples just reviewed indicate that periods of inflation have a cost beyond the nominal dollars expended for labor. Inflationary periods have the effect of distorting merit systems that do not clearly separate the amount being awarded for merit from that which reflects the upward trend in market wages. Of course, these costs could be minimized by a more careful (and realistic) segregation of merit pay decisions from other forms of pay adjustment.[24]

Summary

The evaluation of performance and pay turns out to be a complex matter. Although the general notion that better performers should be rewarded is not controversial, the actual workplace implementation of that principle faces many obstacles. Good performance must be evaluated by someone, typically a supervisor, who acts as an agent for the employer. Yet, it is difficult in practice for the principal (employer) to create the incentives necessary for the agent to act in the best interests of the firm.

Linking the evaluations produced by performance appraisals to merit pay and other forms of advancement is also a complicated process. Although employers (in the absence of union pressure) often eschew seniority as a criterion for wage progression and advancement, there are reasons to suspect that seniority is actually an important consideration. Implicit contract theory suggests that pay and productivity may not be tied tightly together, except over an extended horizon. However, changes in the economy in the 1980s may force a closer tie between individual performance and pay.

Finally, the use of merit pay systems seems to create confusion about the trend in labor costs. The gross costs of a merit system exceed its net costs, because the former exclude turnover savings. But control systems designed to limit supervisory discretion and external inflation can blur the important gross/net distinction.

EXERCISES

Problem

Obtain a sample of performance appraisal forms of the type shown in Figure 4–1 from employers in your area. Evaluate these forms with regard to the degree of useful information they are likely to produce.

Questions

1. Can alternative performance rater systems, such as peer reviews, provide more accurate information on performance appraisal than the more common system of rating by supervisors? Explain.

2. What should be the role of HRM departments and line managers in determining monetary rewards and promotions for employees?

3. What should be the importance of seniority in determining pay?

4. What impact may corporate restructuring have on the pay-seniority profile?

5. How can merit systems be better structured to deal with periods of inflation?

6. What is the importance of the distinction between the gross and net costs of merit programs?

Terms

behaviorally anchored rating scales	implicit contracting	sexual harassment
employee attitude surveys	mandatory retirement	supervisor
grievances	piece rates	wage progression systems
	principal and agents theory	

ENDNOTES

1. As in the case of most such surveys, respondents tend to come from larger firms. Small firms are more likely to have informal performance appraisal methods than large ones.

2. Some employees may be positively motivated by a complimentary review, even if it does not produce an automatic financial reward.

3. Collective bargaining arrangements are discussed in later chapters. Private sector supervisors after 1947 could form unions if they wish, but they had (and still have) little or no legal protection for such activity—that is, they can be fired for being union members or for attempting to form unions. However, some statutes covering public sector employees give supervisors some protected rights to unionize.

4. Taft-Hartley Act, Sec. 2(11).

5. Sanford M. Jacoby, *Employing Bureaucracy: Managers, Unions and the Transformation of Work in American Industry: 1900–1945* (New York: Columbia University Press, 1985), chapter 1.

6. A "tight" labor market is one in which unemployment is very low and vacancies are plentiful, that is, it is one that benefits the employee. The opposite situation—when

unemployment is high and jobs are scarce—is known as a "loose" labor market.

7. The topic of sexual harassment is part of the general subject of equal employment opportunity (EEO), which will be discussed in a later chapter.

8. Keeping the rating secret from the employee would subvert the notion that the evaluation will induce improvements in behavior. An employee cannot be expected to respond to an evaluation of which he or she is not aware.

9. Fred K. Foulkes, *Personnel Policies in Large Nonunion Companies* (Englewood Cliffs, N.J.: Prentice-Hall, 1980), chapter 15; Industrial Relations Department, National Association of Manufacturers, *Settling Complaints in the Union-Free Environment* (Washington: NAM, 1982); Ronald Berenbeim, *Nonunion Complaint Systems: A Corporate Appraisal* (New York: The Conference Board, 1980); Bureau of National Affairs, Inc., *Policies for Unorganized Employees,* PPF Survey No. 125 (Washington: BNA, 1979). Employee complaints and systems for handling them are discussed in a later chapter.

10. The question of the optimal size of firms—which cannot be discussed further here—is obviously linked to the trade-off between efficiencies of centralized control and diseconomies of hierarchical delegation of authority.

11. Professors often discover that student teaching assistants are harsher in grading fellow students than regular faculty would be.

12. See Katharine G. Abraham and Henry S. Farber, "Job Duration, Seniority, and Earnings," *American Economic Review,* vol. 77 (June 1987), pp. 278–297.

13. There are many facets of implicit contracting theory. A review can be found in Sherwin Rosen, "Implicit Contracts: A Survey," *Journal of Economic Literature,* vol. 23 (September 1985), pp. 1144–1175.

14. Such arguments are sometimes made in connection with public policies that provide for retirement incomes, such as Social Security, or tax-favored treatment for pension plans. It is argued that individuals are shortsighted and will not on their own provide for later income needs. Of course, if young employees are shortsighted, they might not look kindly on an employer that cuts pay now in exchange for more pay later.

15. This approach is part of the "efficiency wage" model discussed in a later chapter.

16. In principle the worker would not retire unless the firm compensated him or her for the discounted value of all potential future "overpayment." But, if that is the price for retirement, the firm would not gain any cost saving. Never-

theless, since workers cannot be sure of their health or life-expectancy and since they are likely to be risk-averse, an offer of a financial inducement of less expected value than the stream of future overpayments might still produce a retirement.

17. U.S. President, *Economic Report of the President, February 1985* (Washington: GPO, 1985), pp. 187–216, presents a standard economic appraisal of this activity.

18. Much debate over this issue arose in the 1980s. A symposium concerning economic research in the field of corporate takeovers appears in *Journal of Economic Perspectives,* vol. 2 (Winter 1988), pp. 3–82.

19. One study of mergers found mixed results on wages and employment. Research in this area is in a preliminary stage. However, it is clear that not all mergers have the same results, and in some cases it appears that wage decreases are associated with employment gains. See Charles Brown and James L. Medoff, "The Impact of Firm Acquisitions on Labor," working paper no. 2273, National Bureau of Economic Research, June 1987.

20. Critics of corporate restructuring have argued that it is a device to "discipline" labor. See, for example, Barry Bluestone, "Deindustrialization and Unemployment in America" in Paul D. Staudohar and Holly E. Brown, eds., *Deindustrialization and Plant Closure* (Lexington, Mass.: Lexington Books, 1986), pp. 3–15, especially pp. 12–14.

21. Bureau of National Affairs, Inc., *The Changing Workplace: New Directions in Staffing and Scheduling* (Washington: BNA, 1986); Max L. Carey and Kim L. Hazelbaker, "Employment Growth in the Temporary Help Industry," *Monthly Labor Review,* vol. 109 (April 1986), pp. 37–44.

22. Arnold R. Weber and Daniel J. B. Mitchell, *The Pay Board's Progress: Wage Controls in Phase II* (Washington: Brookings Institution, 1978), pp. 89–93.

23. Sanford M. Jacoby and Daniel J. B. Mitchell, "Alternative Sources of Labor Market Data" in Barbara D. Dennis, ed., *Proceedings of the Thirty-Eighth Annual Meeting,* Industrial Relations Research Association, December 28–30, 1985 (Madison, Wisc.: IRRA, 1986), pp. 42–49, especially pp. 46–48.

24. Economists often have difficulty explaining, in terms of standard theory, why inflation is a problem. In principle, if all prices rise at the same rate, and the rate of inflation is recognized, no one should be made any better or worse off. However, it is sometimes argued that inflation causes confusion among actors in the economic system. General price (and wage) increases are perceived incorrectly as relative price (wage) increases. The merit problem regarding inflation is an example of such confusion.

Chapter Five

ALTERNATIVE PAY SYSTEMS

The goal of pay for performance can be pursued through subjective appraisals and discretionary rewards. But an alternative, mentioned in Chapter 4, is to build incentives into the pay system so that employees will be rewarded automatically for desirable behavior. Much of the *scientific management* movement of the late nineteenth and early twentieth century involved the development of appropriate incentives. Frederick W. Taylor, the founder of the movement, sought to develop a pay system that would provide the proper motivation for employees.[1]

Even today, writers and consultants in the HRM field will sometimes make glowing (if uncritical) comments about what incentive pay can accomplish. Witness the following excerpt from a recent HRM text:

> There are no losers with incentive pay systems. The organization gains through cost reductions, increased productivity and improved employee attitudes. The long-run benefits are increased productivity and organizational survival. Eventually, depending upon the performance variables used in the incentive pay system, other results occur such as an increase in sales due to employees' ideas to improve the utility of a product or service.
>
> Customers also benefit from incentive pay systems through lower prices, better quality products and services, and improved product features. The lower prices result from productivity and efficiency improvements. . . .
>
> Stockholders also gain through incentive pay systems by sharing in some of the productivity and efficiency increases. Stockholders benefit through increased dividends and an appreciation in the price of their stock. . . . Citizens or taxpayers gain in public organizations through an improvement in service and lower taxes and fees.[2]

The difficulty with such views is not that they are necessarily wrong—quite the contrary. Incentive pay systems *can* be useful in some circumstances. But incentives, like performance appraisals, have their pitfalls. They often do not turn out to be cheaper and more effective than conventional systems of pay. This chapter explores the potential advantages and disadvantages of incentive pay systems and other innovative approaches to compensation.

5–1   Basic Alternative Pay Systems

When they are initially hired, employees generally do not make formal contracts with their employers. Even in companies in which employers are unionized, the written contract that is negotiated is between the union and the employer and not with the individual worker. The absence of a written contract, however, does not mean that the employee–employer relationship is a simple one. As suggested in the previous chapter, when an employee is hired a complex, implicit exchange is arranged.

Derived Demand for Labor

The employer's demand for labor is what economists call a "derived demand"— that is, with the possible exception of certain personal service occupations (some of which are better left unnamed), the employer does not directly "enjoy" the labor being hired. Rather, the labor services that are purchased are a means to an end. Labor is an input to the production process; from the resulting production the employer's profits flow. Thus what the employer wants is not merely the employee's presence at the work site but the employee's presence combined with productive activity.

It is not just worker time that is being bought but time and what can be generally described as *effort*. When the employee accepts a job offer, he or she is implicitly agreeing to both the sacrifice of "leisure" time and a willingness to take direction and meet standards. Those who argue for use of incentive pay systems are basically proposing that, since the employer is buying more than just time, the pay system should reflect more than time alone in providing rewards.

Apart from output and productivity, employers may want *loyalty* from employees. Loyalty can be interpreted in various ways, for example, not giving the company's products or services a bad name but instead boosting their reputation, not giving away trade secrets to competitors, and so on. Also included under the loyalty label is a commitment to remain with the company for some indefinite period.

Loyal employees reduce hiring and turnover costs for the firm. For this reason employers are often reluctant to hire employees whose résumés suggest they are opportunistic job hoppers. A job hopper may not remain long enough to permit the firm to recoup its investment in that employee.

Time-based, Incentive, and Share Systems

Given the employer's objectives of obtaining a productive and loyal workforce, various compensation systems suggest themselves. First is the *time-based system*. Under such a system, workers' pay is based on time spent on the job. As Chapter 4 showed, time systems are often combined with subjective performance appraisals and related merit plans. Thus employees are not literally being paid merely to make an appearance at the workplace.

A second option is an *explicit incentive system*. Under incentive plans, pay (or a portion of pay) is automatically tied to the achievement of some tangible objective, such as a level of production, by the individual employee. In cases in which the employee is part of a work team, the incentive payment may be linked to group achievement rather than individual performance.

A third category is a *share system*. Under such a plan, the employee benefits from the overall performance of the establishment or enterprise. Since the individual's contribution to the overall establishment or enterprise is likely to be small, HRM specialists often view such share arrangements as loyalty generators rather than as direct incentives to productivity.

Empirical Evidence: Time-based Versus Incentive Systems

Table 5–1 shows the incidence of time-based and incentive pay systems for various occupational groups, based on a survey of private and public employers. It is apparent from the table that incentive systems are not the norm. On the contrary, only two groups give evidence of any significant coverage by incentive plans: plant or service occupations and sales occupations. Even among these two classifications, however, only a small minority of the employers surveyed reported using either individual or group incentive systems.

TABLE 5–1   Percentage of Employers Reporting Alternative Time and Incentive Pay Systems, 1980

	Plant and Service	Office and Clerical	Professional and Technical	Sales	First-Level Supervisors	Middle Managers
Time Systems						
Hourly rate	86%	43%	16%	9%	11%	6%
Weekly rate	5	21	19	17	18	13
Monthly rate	8	30	40	43	36	40
Annual rate	5	11	28	26	34	39
Incentive Systems						
Individual	11	—	*	7	*	*
Group	5	—	*	3	*	2

*Less than 1%.

Note: Percentages may sum to more than 100% due to multiple plans used by an employer for a particular occupational group.

Source: The Bureau of National Affairs, Inc., *Wage & Salary Administration*, PPF Survey no. 131 (Washington: BNA, 1981), p. 6.

It is not surprising that plant and service and sales workers would be more likely to be covered by incentive plans than other employees. In both cases output that is subject to measurement and verification is commonly available. Plant/service workers often are employed in manufacturing establishments that produce tangible, countable outputs. (Within manufacturing, 18% of the employers responding reported that they had individual incentives covering plant and service workers; 8% reported group incentives.)

For sales workers, there is an additional reason for use of incentives. Often sales workers are employed in situations in which close supervision simply is not possible. Sales personnel who operate away from their offices are obvious examples. Sales workers who wait on customers may also fall into this category. If supervision is not a feasible option, commission sales arrangements can be used as a substitute.

Unfortunately, surveys regarding incentive and other pay systems are sporadic and often cover unrepresentative samples. A study conducted by the Conference Board at about the same time as the survey shown in Table 5–1 suggested that 36% of manufacturing firms had wage incentive and bonus plans covering "production or operations" workers.[3] This percentage suggests a more extensive use of incentives than Table 5–1. There is no way to reconcile the conflicting evidence. The neglect of employer pay systems and other HRM practices constitutes an important hole in official government surveys of the labor market. All recent surveys, however, suggest incentives are not used for determining the pay of the vast majority of employees.

Studies based on employer responses to questionnaires such as those just cited often fail to indicate the proportion of workers in the workplace who are covered by particular HRM practices. Instead, these studies report the number of employers who have examples of the HRM practices, even though relatively few employees within the reporting firm may be affected. An exception was a 1970 BLS study that found that only 14% of urban plant workers in medium to large firms were covered by incentive systems (20% in manufacturing). Virtually no office workers were found to have incentive arrangements.[4]

Perhaps most revealing about the 1970 BLS survey was its finding that use of incentives declined during the 1960s. A subsequent BLS study, relating only to manufacturing industries, indicated that use of incentives continued to decline in the 1970s.[5] This downward trend appears to be part of a long-term process. In the 1920s, use of incentives was extremely widespread, reflecting both the popularity of scientific management and employer disdain for alternative motivational devices. Thereafter, however, time-based pay systems became much more common.

A Union Influence?

One factor sometimes cited for the decline in the popularity of incentives after the 1920s is the subsequent rise of unions. In the past many unions, although not all, opposed incentive plans. Despite this history, it is not clear that contemporary unions inherently oppose incentive systems as a method of pay. In the mid-1980s, for example, one study found pay incentives included in almost a third of 400 union contracts, with the ratio rising to 47% in manufacturing.[6]

In theory, if unions are successful in capturing some of the returns that would otherwise go to profits, they could be expected to take a pragmatic view of incentives. For example, they would favor pay incentives when such incentives were more efficient than other arrangements, assuming that some of the efficiency gains could be "captured" by their members. The fact that use of incentives has varied substantially over time, however, suggests that opinions about such efficiency are often subjective and prone to fads. Given this history, union officials may sometimes be suspicious of management claims on behalf of incentives.

If workers are risk-averse, unions might oppose those incentives that appear likely to create income variability for their members. The union push in the 1940s and 1950s for a "guaranteed annual wage" may still be associated with a union distaste for incentives in some instances. The guaranteed annual wage idea was meant to address income variability caused by periodic layoffs, rather than fluctuations in the rate of pay. Unions wanted their blue-collar members to be paid annual salaries, rather than per-hour wages, thereby making income less dependent on production. A system that gears pay directly to production is the antithesis of this idea.[7]

Unions might also oppose those incentive programs that make it more difficult for them to exercise group control over the pace of work. Indeed, one of the original goals of scientific management was to wrest control over output from factory workers. The pace of work, however, is a condition of employment, and unions can normally be expected to wish to influence *all* such conditions, not just pay.

HRM Influence

Apart from actual policies regarding incentives, unions probably indirectly affected members of management who favored the time-based alternative to incentive pay. As unions grew in strength in the 1930s, management responded by strengthening the HRM function inside the firm. In their own self-interest, the new HRM specialists may have supported pay systems that required discretion rather than formulas. Formula systems leave authority in the hands of industrial engineers, who set the accompanying production norms. Discretionary systems, in contrast, strengthen the HRM function within the firm, since they require the employment of experts with knowledge of evaluation and motivation techniques. In short, there was an incentive for HRM professionals not to be keen on incentives.

By the 1980s, however, the HRM function was more firmly ensconced in the typical enterprise than it was in the 1930s. There was pressure to respond to competitive pressures through devices that enhanced productivity. Moreover, the computer revolution brought with it an improved data-handling capacity and an orientation toward quantitative studies to determine the best HRM techniques. These developments could and should lead to a revived interest in incentive arrangements. Demonstrated effectiveness of incentives relative to time-based pay systems, rather than preconceptions, should be the determining factor in the adoption, retention, or rejection of incentive systems. The use or nonuse of an incentive pay system should be a pragmatically determined, empirical matter.

5—2 Time-based Systems

Table 5—1 shows that one of the options to be selected under a time-based system is the unit of time on which pay is based. Hourly rates tend to be most commonly used in the plant or service occupational group. White-collar workers are more likely to be paid on the basis of a longer unit of time such as a week, month, or year. Generally, the higher the job hierarchy ladder is ascended, the longer is the unit of time on which pay is based.

The data in Table 5—1 were reinforced by a 1984 survey by the U.S. Bureau of Labor Statistics, which found that about one-fourth of professionals and less than one-fifth of managers were paid on an hourly basis. For workers in blue-collar occupations, however, hourly rates characterized 75% to 90% of the work-force. All told, about six out of ten wage and salary earners were found to be paid on an hourly basis.[8]

Time Units and Employment Stability

It might initially appear that the varying practices regarding time units are inconsequential. After all, hourly rates can always be expressed in weekly, monthly, or annual terms by simply multiplying by some appropriate number of normal hours. Annual, monthly, or weekly salaries can be similarly expressed in hourly equivalents. However, the time specification indicates a component of the implicit employment contract, as evidenced by the distinction HRM professionals often make between their policies for hourly workers and their policies for others. The hourly choice is not simply a matter of arbitrary arithmetic.

Typically, those whose pay is based on short time units—particularly hours—are more subject to employment instability and layoffs than those whose pay is based on longer time units. The demand for the services of the former is seen as closely linked to production levels that may vary, even within a weekly period. If production falls, whether due to recession, bad weather, or mechanical breakdown, hourly workers are the most likely to be laid off. They may be told not to report for work for the remainder of a week, or they may be told not to report at all unless and until further advised.

Such indefinite layoffs do not necessarily mean that the employer–employee relationship ends. Many firms have systems of recall from layoff so that when production picks up, laid-off workers are rehired. However, except for a relatively small number of union-represented workers who receive supplemental unemployment benefits from their employers while awaiting recall, laid-off workers cease being paid and suffer a significant drop in income.[9]

Table 5—2 provides insights into the relative employment stability of different occupational groups. The first two columns show trends in employment

TABLE 5-2   Some Measures of Employment Stability by Occupational Group

Occupational Group	Percent Change in Employment During Recession Periods		Civilian Unemployment Rates		Proportion Experiencing Some Unemployment*
	1973–75	*1979–82*	*1982*	*1987*	*1987*
Managerial and professional occupations	+6.6%	+8.8%	3.3%	2.3%	5.9%
Technical, sales, administrative support	+6.9	+4.1	6.1	4.3	10.5
Service occupations	+5.2	+4.4	10.8	7.7	15.4
Precision production, craft, and repair	−2.6	−6.5	10.6	6.1	17.4
Operators, fabricators, and laborers	−8.4	−12.1	16.7	9.4	21.4
Total†	+.9	+.7	9.7	6.2	12.9

*Individuals are assigned to occupational groups by occupation of the job they held longest in 1987.

†Includes farming, forestry, and fishery workers not shown separately.

Source: Data from *Employment and Earnings,* vol. 31 (January 1984), pp. 14, 167; *Employment and Earnings,* vol. 35 (January 1988), p. 170. Data for right-hand column supplied by U.S. Bureau of Labor Statistics from unpublished tables.

over two recession periods: 1973 to 1975 and 1979 to 1982. In both cases, employment fell only for the blue-collar and service occupational groups, the groups most likely to be paid on an hourly basis.

Unemployment rates provide still another measure of potential job instability. Most persons who are officially counted as unemployed are either actively seeking work or on layoff awaiting recall.[10] The unemployment *rate* is defined simply as the proportion of the labor force that is unemployed—that is, U/LF or, equivalently, $U/(E + U)$, where U = the number of unemployed, LF = the number of people in the labor force, and E = the number of employed workers. As Table 5-2 shows, the blue-collar and service groups consistently show above-average unemployment rates, not only in years at the bottom of a recession (such as 1982), but also in years of recovery and economic growth (such as 1987).

Ideally, the best measure of employment stability would be the probability that an employed worker in a particular occupational classification would lose his or her job in a given year. There are no published data that precisely indicate those probabilities; however, the right-hand column of Table 5-2 presents an approximation. The column shows the proportion of workers who had a job at some time in 1987, but who also experienced one or more spells of unemployment during that year. Although the average monthly civilian unemployment rate in 1987 was 6.2%, 12.9% of persons who had jobs experienced at least one unemployment spell. The proportions of managers and professionals with some unemployment fell in the 5% to 11% range, whereas for the blue-collar and service groups the range was 15% to 22%. These data suggest a positive association between hourly pay status and likelihood of job loss.

Varying Hourly Pay Rates

There is no requirement that workers who are paid on an hourly basis receive the same rate of pay for each hour worked. In fact, it is a standard practice to pay higher rates of pay for overtime hours than for regular hours. This practice is required by the federal Fair Labor Standards Act (FLSA), which requires time and a half (a 50% premium) for weekly hours exceeding forty for nonexempt workers.[11] (Nonexempt workers in HRM terminology are those subject to the FLSA; exempt employees are generally higher paid professionals and managers to whom overtime requirements do not apply.) Similar regulations are found in state labor codes.

Although the 50% overtime premium has a basis in law, it is likely that some overtime differentials would be paid even if the law were not in place, especially to workers paid hourly. The overtime features of the FLSA were originally passed in 1938 as an antidepression measure designed to encourage employers to hire more workers rather than use overtime. Early surveys reveal that in the 1920s overtime premiums were offered to employees (although typically after longer regular workweeks than the forty-hour standard found in the FLSA).

Figure 5–1 provides an economic rationale for the use of an overtime pay premium. Consider a worker who in a given period (say, a week) has H_A hours available that could be used for work or leisure. The worker must chose between leisure and work-related income. If the hourly wage (W) is constant (the same for each hour worked), the worker will face a simple linear trade-off between

FIGURE 5–1
Effects of
Overtime Pay on
Leisure–Work
Trade-Off

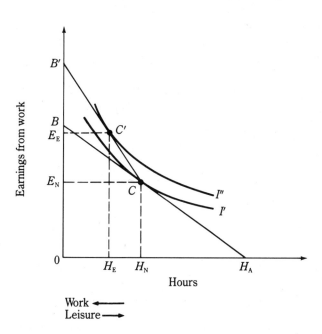

earnings and leisure. Each hour worked subtracts one hour from potential leisure time, but adds W to total earnings. Given a free choice, the worker would chose to work until the earnings–leisure trade-off line BH_A reached his or her highest possible indifference curve.[12]

Such a situation is shown at point C, where the earnings–leisure trade-off line is just tangent to indifference curve I'. Thus the worker is employed for H_A–H_N hours, has OH_N leisure, and receives total earnings of E_N. Let this configuration be regarded as reflecting a normal work time duration. If the employer wishes to purchase more hours from the worker, a pay premium could be offered for extra hours. The extra or overtime hours could be paid at a rate $W(1 + X)$, where X is the premium pay as a proportion of W, for example, .5.

With the premium the earnings–leisure trade-off line now is represented by $B'CH_A$. The worker would now maximize utility at point C', where the new earnings–leisure trade-off line is just tangent to indifference curve I''. An extra H_N–H_E would be worked, raising the worker's total earnings to E_E.[13]

Generally, workers are not free to pick and choose their normal hours for a given employer. Unexcused absence is grounds for discipline. The proportion of working time lost to absences is typically small, about 3% to 4% among full-time workers; about two-thirds of such absences are related to illness and injury.[14] Thus once hired, employees have limited hours at their discretion.

Yet workers do have some choice in seeking full-time or part-time work. Those who take positions as temporaries can vary their hours to suit personal preferences and family responsibilities.[15] For workers seeking longer hours and added income, moonlighting—holding more than one job—is an option. About 5% of all employees are moonlighters, and their median weekly hours substantially exceed those of single job holders.[16] Through choice of the kinds of jobs they accept, workers can thus influence their hours, although they are not always able to find the job of their choice.

The degree to which production is a team activity is important in explaining the limits employers place on employee choice of hours. People whose productivity depends on one another cannot come and go on the basis of personal whims.[17] However, given that working especially long hours, or weekend hours, or holiday hours is often more distasteful to employees than working regular hours, it is not surprising that pay premiums are often offered.

In some firms overtime and other "irregular" hours are assigned; in others, employment during such hours is voluntary. In effect, the employment contract states to the employee that while there may be involuntary assignments of hours, an attempt will be made to offer some compensation for the possible unpleasantness involved.

5–3 Incentive Pay Systems

Although incentive pay systems cover only a relatively small portion of the workforce, such systems seem to be paying directly for performance. Why is it that automatic pay for performance (as opposed to discretionary pay for performance under merit plans) is used infrequently? Why has the popularity of incentive pay declined?

Although difficulties in measuring the output of an increasingly white-collar workforce play an obvious role in answering these questions, they do not provide the whole explanation. Finding the right incentive plan—one that creates just the incentives the employer wants to engender—can be a complex matter. Maintaining the incentives at the correct setting once they are installed also poses problems.

Incentive Design

Suppose you wanted to have a house built. You face the problem of making a contract that will meet your objectives and those of the builder. The builder wants to make an adequate profit. You want to have the house built to your basic design at a reasonable cost. In a sense, both you and the builder have the common goal of working out a satisfactory agreement. But you are also adversaries, a situation found in any buyer-seller relationship, including the employment relationship. More for one party probably means less for the other.

One possibility would be for you to make a contract to pay the builder on the basis of time and materials. The builder would bill you for all materials used and for all work time expended. Another option would be for you to agree on a fixed price for the entire project before the job begins. Which option is better from your perspective?

The builder, of course, might prefer the option of having you pay for time and materials. This approach would mitigate the risk of having to absorb unexpected cost increases such as a sudden jump in the price of lumber or in the cost of labor. You, on the other hand, would probably choose a fixed price, fearing that simply paying for time and materials would leave you open to contractual abuse. The builder might work excessively slowly and wastefully, running up large bills. With the price fixed, you would at least know the cost of construction in advance.[18]

Yet the matter is really not so simple. If the price is fixed, there may be an incentive for the builder to hold down costs by skimping on quality. In short, with a fixed-price contract you might end up with a house at the agreed-upon price, but it might not be quite the quality of house you had in mind.

One solution would be for you to hire a monitor (an additional expense) who would watch for quality deficiencies and insist they be corrected. You could offer to accept the builder's preferred option of "pay as you go" *if* the monitor were given authority to police quality standards. Of course, supposing a satisfactory monitor could be found, some definition of quality would need to be established and agreed upon in the contract with the builder. Even with such a definition, there could still be a disagreement between the monitor and one of the parties to the transaction over whether quality standards were adequately met.

Apart from the quality issue, there are other contingency problems to be considered. For example, suppose bad weather were to delay the project, or to cause damage to the partially completed structure. Who would shoulder the resulting expense? With a time/materials contract, the customer would presumably absorb the cost. With a fixed-price contract, the builder would bear the risk. But suppose that weather damage was arguably due to negligence of the builder, who should have covered the structure with a tarpaulin in case of rain. Or what if weather damage occurred because you had insisted on the redesign of certain elements of the house, delaying its completion until after the rainy season had begun?

Designing just the right contract that will perfectly satisfy you and your builder under all contingencies is difficult, if not impossible. Of course, commercial contracts, often containing ambiguities and unresolved issues, are written in spite of these imperfections. As a result, contractual disputes are a regular feature of the marketplace. There are analogies between these disputes and the problems that arise with pay incentive systems in the workplace. Additional complications stem from the ongoing nature of the employer–employee relationship.

Quality and Contingency

In the house construction case, a contract guaranteeing a fixed price for completion of a project could create perverse incentives for the builder to skimp on quality. The same problem arises in the case of incentive pay for employees. If the incentive payment is geared to the quantity produced, there will be a built-in temptation for employees to increase quantity at the expense of quality.

Of course, it would be possible to try to include quality in the incentive formula. For example, the payment for quantity could be subject to some type of quality inspection. Only items passing a quality test would be included in the payment formula. Adding quality tests, however, requires a costly monitoring process, as in the house construction example. Such a process might have a subjective element that could lead to friction. Even when quality can be precisely measured, questions of fault for quality deficiencies arise.

Failure to meet a standard of quality does not always result from improper or inadequate workmanship. If a batch of output does not pass a quality test, the failure could be due to inferior materials (provided by the employer) or to mechanical breakdowns (on machines owned and maintained by the employer). Should employees be required to sacrifice income because of quality deficiencies in such cases? Or should the employer bear the burden? And who should determine whose fault the quality shortfall was?

As in the house example, unforeseen contingencies can upset the working of a pay formula. Suppose a power failure causes workers in a plant to be idle. Or suppose needed materials do not arrive at the plant due to bad weather, a strike at a supplier, or poor inventory control. What payments should workers receive if production stops for reasons beyond their control?

Of course, it is possible to spell out rules governing such contingencies, but it is unlikely that such rules will produce incomes exactly equal to what would have been received in the absence of a production disruption. Thus further sources of friction arise. These frictions are really disagreements over what the employer–employee contract provides. The more potential frictions there are, the more supervisors and overhead personnel will be required to deal with them. As such overhead cost accumulates, the advantages of a pay incentive system over an ordinary time-based system erode.

Incentives and the Ongoing Employment Relationship

The house construction example is essentially a one-shot transaction. Even though imperfect, a contract is eventually drawn up to cover the building of a particular structure. Once construction is completed, the buyer–seller relationship ends, amicably or not.

In a workplace incentive system, however, there is an ongoing relationship between employer and employee. The indefinite duration of the employer–employee association means that the contract will have to be periodically updated. Changes in technology, in particular, pose dynamic problems for incentive systems. These problems arise because improved technology is likely to increase worker productivity even if employee effort levels remain constant.

Generally, as technology raises productivity, the rates of incentive pay per unit of output will have to be decreased. Each arrival of new equipment and each improvement in technique will require rate changes. Otherwise, pay rates per unit of production would become excessive. If, for example, new machinery raises output by 10%, a 10% reduction in the pay rate per piece would be required to hold equivalent hourly pay constant. Thus new norms will have to be established periodically and errors in judgment regarding norm setting may lead to over- or underpayments of workers.

Since workers know that standards probably will be increased if they continually outperform the expected norms, they may restrict output to levels that will not trigger reevaluations of expected normal productivity. Incentives, in short, can easily become disincentives as employees respond to the rules of the game in rational economic fashion.

Discontinuities in the Productivity/Pay Relationship

Determining norms of production is important in the design of incentive rates because simple piece rate formulas may not provide the correct incentives for workers. As noted, a criticism of time-based systems is that the employer is really trying to buy a time–effort combination, but pays only for time. A similar problem exists with incentives: the employer is not directly paying for effort under a piece rate system, only an output *proxy* for effort.

It is commonly assumed that—ignoring the dynamic problems discussed in the previous section—installing a piece rate marries the employer's interest with the employee's. When a piece rate is in effect, according to this view, both parties want more output. However, Figure 5–2 shows that the appealing notion of creating mutual interests can be very misleading. A piece rate can *separate* the interests of employer and employee.

To understand this point, it is necessary to make some assumptions about the conditions of production. Assume that the employee can generally produce more widgets per period of time by expending more effort. However, diminishing returns to effort are likely to be present. Eventually, at exceedingly high effort levels, productivity may actually begin to decrease as exhaustion sets in.

FIGURE 5–2
Effect of Incentive System on Level of Effort

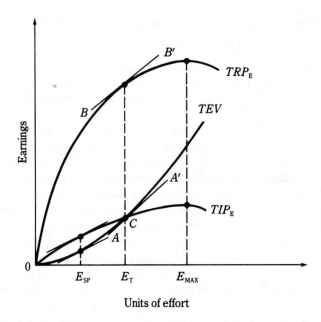

Assume further that the widgets produced can be sold in the marketplace for a fixed price, P. Then, in value terms, the relationship between individual employee effort per period can be expressed in Figure 5–2 by function TRP_E, the total revenue product of effort. This function shows the value of effort in the product market, that is, the gross revenue received by the employer resulting from widget sales. The function has the form of an inverted U with a peak at effort level E_{MAX}, the point at which exhaustion overwhelms additional output and productivity begins to fall.

Although increases in effort below the exhaustion point produce added revenue for the employer, the same increases result in disutility for the employee. Translated into value terms, this disutility is expressed by function TEV, the total effort value for the employee. TEV represents the total dollar value that must be paid to the employee to produce a willingness to work at a given effort level. The increasing marginal disutility of effort is reflected in the steepening slope of TEV as the effort level rises.

Suppose now that the employee and employer made a time-based bargain, with an effort level also explicitly specified. Suppose further that effort could be costlessly monitored so that the bargain would be honestly kept. The effort level upon which both parties would agree in this time bargain would be E_T. In a welfare economics sense E_T is optimal, since the slopes of TEV and TRP_E are identical at that level of effort. In other words, the marginal "cost" of effort to the worker is exactly equal to the marginal value of effort to the employer. Graphically expressed, tangent BB' is exactly parallel to tangent AA'.

Of course, such bargains involving effort are difficult to enforce in the real world. Indeed, the enforcement problem is the justification usually presented for incentive rates. Incentive systems are supposed to induce appropriate employee effort without monitoring. Suppose, then, that the employer instead offers a simple piece rate (either X cents per widget or Y% of sales revenue) to the worker. Assume that this rate is set at a level that at effort E_T would produce exactly the same income for the worker that he or she would receive under the optimal contract just discussed. The total incentive payment for the worker, as a function of effort level, is shown by the TIP_E curve.

TIP_E has the same general shape as TRP_E (an inverted U), but is flatter, since the piece rate gives only a portion of the value of output to the worker. Although TIP_E intersects TEV at point C (corresponding to optimum effort level E_T), neither the employer nor the employee will want effort to remain at that level. Under a simple piece rate, the employer's *net* revenue, after subtracting TIP_E from TRP_E, is maximized at E_{MAX}. Thus the employer will want the employee to expend effort right up to the exhaustion point. *Use of the simple piece rate therefore causes the employer to want a too-high level of effort.*

The opposite effect occurs for the employee. Under a simple piece rate, employee welfare will be maximized when the marginal income received by the worker is just equal to the marginal disutility cost of effort. Such maximization occurs at effort level E_{SP}. At that effort level, the slope of TIP_E is just equal to the slope of TEV. *Use of the simple piece rate causes the employee to offer a too-low level of effort.* Thus the simple piece rate system of Figure 5–2 does not marry the interests of employer and employee; rather it spreads them apart.[19]

This aberrational behavior occurs because the piece rate does not reflect the marginal value of effort to the employer. Only if the employer set the rate so that all value went to the worker, would optimum effort (E_T) be expended. But the employer cannot offer such a rate in the simple terms that have been presented up to this point. There would be nothing left for profits at a piece rate per widget of P (the market price) or a share rate of 100% of revenue.[20]

To overcome this paradox of contracting, the employer must offer a more complex piece rate, whose average value is less than its marginal value at effort level E_T. In practical terms such an offer will entail a piece rate with a step function providing higher incentive payments above E_T than below it. For example, the employer could provide a simple hourly wage, but no incentive bonus, for output below the level corresponding to E_T. A bonus could be offered for output at or exceeding that level.

Real-world incentive systems often do include such step functions, with bonuses occurring at particular output levels. Frederick W. Taylor, previously mentioned in connection with scientific management, proposed a *differential piece rate* that would assign a high rate to be paid above a specified output. Other, similar pay systems were proposed and implemented early in this century. The Bedaux Point System, the Halsey Plan, the Rowan Plan, Merrick multiple piece rate, and the Emerson Plan are among the examples.[21]

All of these systems, however, present a measurement problem. Since E_T is not readily observable, industrial engineers must try to establish the productivity levels at which the bonus should be given. In the absence of perfect information, which would obviate any need for an incentive pay system in the first place, such norm setting is likely to be accomplished through rules of thumb, past trends, or other fallible techniques.

Incentive Pay and the Firm

As already noted, it is in the interest of employees to have norms and step points set at comparatively low effort levels. The arrival of a time-and-motion analyst to establish such criteria was a common source of labor unrest when incentive pay was in vogue. The same problem exists today. Time can be measured and the quantity of output can be measured. But effort cannot be directly verified. One of the most widely cited deficiencies of piece rates is that workers have an incentive to hold back output in an attempt to fool management into accepting a lower-than-optimal work norm.[22]

The motivation for worker restrictions of output is simple enough. Workers assume that management (or its agent) estimates production norms from historical data on what worker output has been previously. Thus, working hard today will lead to an increase of the norm and pressure to work still harder tomorrow, a ratchet effect. The larger the ratchet is believed to be, the less is the value of an incentive bonus to workers.[23] Under some economic models, management can, in principle, offset the incentive to restrict output with an appropriate increase in the piece rate.[24] Such an increase involves greater cost to the firm; hence, the incentive for output restriction reduces the attraction of piece rates and similar systems relative to ordinary time rates.[25]

Any incentive payment system must therefore involve the hiring of overhead personnel—supervisors, industrial engineers, time-and-motion specialists, and so on—to (partially) overcome this measurement deficiency. The more overhead and frictions the process entails, the less likely it is that employers will prefer incentive pay over conventional time-based compensation systems. After all, the idea of an incentive system is that it economizes on the need for supervision, relative to time-based systems.

Despite the long-term trend away from incentives, and despite the drawbacks discussed above, there is one important piece of evidence suggesting that firms that use incentives receive a net payoff from them. Comparisons of piece rates and time rates within occupations consistently show that piece rates, when converted to average hourly equivalents, are higher than time rates.[26] If firms are willing to pay more to incentive workers, there must be a net benefit to them in the form of higher productivity or reduced supervisory costs, compared to what would occur with time workers.

5–4   Share Systems

Share systems are almost always used in conjunction with some other form of payment plan, whether time-based or incentive. There are three basic types of share systems: (1) productivity gain-sharing plans that divide the savings from improved productivity between the employer and the employees, (2) profit-sharing plans that give employees a portion of company profits, and (3) employee stock-ownership plans that entail giving some equity ownership rights to workers. Each type of plan is briefly discussed in the following paragraphs.

Productivity Gain-sharing Plans

Productivity gain-sharing plans are designed to stimulate worker productivity by dividing the gains from added productivity between the employees and employer according to a formula. Such plans are often installed at the plant level. There are three commonly cited forms of productivity gain sharing. In addition, firms may design their own customized gain-sharing programs.[27]

It is always difficult to determine when an HRM innovation such as productivity gain sharing was first initiated. Modern gain sharing, however, is usually credited to Joseph Scanlon, a union official who designed such a plan in the 1930s as part of a deal to save a financially distressed company.[28] The *Scanlon Plan* is based on the ratio of payroll to production value (sales plus inventory accumulation). A base level of this ratio is established from historical company or plant data. A decrease in the ratio below the base level is viewed as a labor cost saving and the total value of the saving (in the form of a bonus payment) is divided between the firm and the employees. Scanlon payouts typically occur on a monthly or quarterly basis.

Refinements are sometimes added to the Scanlon method. For example, the impact of product market prices is sometimes factored out, since a rise in product value might result simply from product price inflation. As with incentive plans, the base ratio is sometimes adjusted when significant changes in technology occur.

Generally, modern Scanlon Plans are implemented as part of a series of quality of working life (QWL) measures. Forums and mechanisms are provided for employee participation in managerial decisions and for suggestions. Because of Scanlon's union background, however, the plans are generally used in unionized settings only, and efforts are made not to disrupt existing collective-bargaining processes. Little is known about the incidence of Scanlon Plans other than that they are infrequently used and tend to be found in smaller firms. One study estimated that about 400 such plans were in place in the early 1980s.[29]

Rucker Plans were also developed in the 1930s. They are similar to Scanlon Plans, except that production value is measured by value added, that is, sales plus inventory accumulation minus the cost of materials. The proportion of savings that is shared between employees and the company is set equal to the base period ratio of labor costs to production value.

The use of value added rather than sales in Rucker Plans is closer to the way economists measure the activity of a plant, firm, or industry. For example, in the national income accounts, the proportion of GNP originating in an industry is estimated using a value-added measure. In practice, however, there will be little difference in the results of using a sales measure (as in Scanlon Plans) or a value-added measure if the ratio of materials costs to total sales is not highly variable.

No estimate is available of the number of Rucker Plans in operation. As with Scanlon Plans, only a small proportion of employers are believed to use them.

Improshare Plans are based on physical productivity rather than on value-based indexes of output. Figures showing base period output per labor hour are set on a product line basis using historical data. If productivity rises by, say, 5% relative to the base level, the saving is divided equally between the firm and the workers. Thus, the 5% saving would translate into a 2½% bonus. Improshare Plans are not designed to be part of quality of working life or worker involvement programs. Their incidence is unknown but small. Payouts under Improshare are often as frequent as weekly.[30] In effect, Improshare plans are a cross between gain sharing and some of the more elaborate piece rate systems described earlier, but are applied on a group basis.

External Market and Productivity Gain Sharing   Productivity gain-sharing plans are linked in the minds of their proponents with internal company developments—that is, it is implicitly assumed either that forces that affect productivity are the result of influences within the company, or that the formulas used will filter out external factors such as inflation. There is reason to believe, however, that productivity gain sharing is not isolated from general economic trends.

One of the stylized facts of productivity at the national level is its procyclical movement—that is, productivity tends to decrease or decelerate during recessions and to increase or accelerate during periods of economic expansion. Table 5–3 illustrates this cyclical phenomenon during the 1970s and the 1980s. During recession periods, the rate of productivity advance has tended to be lower than

TABLE 5–3   Productivity and the Business Cycle, 1969–1987
(Nonfarm, Business Sector)

	Annual Rate of Change in Output Per Hour	
Time Period	*As Recorded*	*Detrended**
Recession 1969–71	2.0%	.5%
Expansion 1971–73	2.5	1.3
Recession 1973–74	−2.1	−3.3
Expansion 1974–79	1.1	−.1
Recession 1979–82[†]	0.0	−1.1
Expansion 1982–87	1.6	.7

*Over the entire period, 1969–87, output per hour rose at about a 1.1% annual rate. Productivity figures were detrended by subtracting the 1969–87 rate from them.

[†]There were actually two back-to-back recessions during this period.

Source: Data from U.S. President, *Economic Report of the President, February 1988* (Washington: GPO, 1988), p. 300.

during subsequent expansions. The procyclical effect is particularly apparent from the right-hand column of Table 5–3, in which the 1969–1987 productivity trend has been removed from the data.

When first discovered, the fact that productivity was procyclical was viewed as a paradox. Surely, when the economy falls into recession and labor is laid off, the capital/labor ratio must rise. In microeconomic theory, increases in the capital/labor ratio are associated with increases in productivity. So why does measured productivity fall in recessionary periods?

There is a twofold answer to this riddle. First, if capital is measured as a stock, that is, the value of plant and equipment, then movements in the capital/labor ratio will be anticyclical.[31] However, the relevant measure for capital is the *flow* of services, not the stock. If a plant works fewer hours per week (for example, if overtime is eliminated), its capital will be used that much less. Thus, as a first approximation, the flow-based capital/labor ratio will be constant over the business cycle.

Second, firms will retain certain workers when orders and production levels decline. Some employees, ranging from guards to accountants, are overhead workers. The need for their services is largely a reflection of maintaining an organization, not of the amount of activity in the organization.

In addition to overhead workers, other employees, even those more closely linked to production, may be retained to avoid turnover costs.[32] If the fall-off in business is considered temporary, the firm may prefer to retain the services of those workers who would be expensive to replace during the coming upturn. Such employees might be used to carry out maintenance projects that had been deferred during the period of high production.[33] Firm inventory policies, which reflect the costs of carrying currently unsold or unused goods, will be related to layoff policies. If carry-over costs are not too high, layoffs can be reduced.

Since productivity is likely to be procyclical for these reasons, productivity gain-sharing plans will tend to pay bonuses (or to pay higher bonuses) during boom periods. They will pay no bonus (or pay a smaller bonus) during business downturns. Through these plans the firm acquires another advantage—procyclical labor costs. Traditionally, this advantage has not been stressed (or even recognized) by plan proponents. It means that the firm pays most to labor when its ability to pay is greatest and receives relief from labor costs during hard times.

Hiring Plans: Employer Versus Worker Interests   Although productivity tends to be procyclical, at any moment in time the conventional microeconomic wisdom is likely to apply—that is, the marginal productivity of labor will decline as more labor is added to the production process while other inputs are held constant. If employers are simply increasing working hours (say, by adding a second shift), the flow-based capital/labor ratio need not fall. But if more workers are added per unit of time, marginal productivity will be decreased as the flow-based capital/labor ratio is reduced.

When combined with a productivity gain-sharing plan, this phenomenon has the potential for creating a division between the interests of employees and management. Adding workers to the workforce tends to lower productivity and thus to decrease the gain-sharing bonus. The bonus-lowering effect can be expected to separate workers into what economists call insider and outsider interests.[34] Insiders (workers who already have jobs with the firm) would feel in conflict with outsiders (those who might seek jobs). Profit-sharing plans—discussed later in this chapter—raise similar problems, at least in theory.

Unfortunately, because studies of productivity gain-sharing plans are so rare—and are often produced by advocates of such plans—little evidence is available on the severity of this conflict. One study did report "active resistance (by workers) to any talk of increasing the size of the work force. . . ."[35] Anecdotal evidence thus supports the existence of an insider/outsider conflict.

As will be seen in the discussion of profit sharing, although employees may favor restrictions on new hires, employers are likely to feel quite differently. Studies of wage determination have found that wages are much less flexible, particularly in a downward direction, than simple textbook economics would suggest. In a conventional wage system that has no productivity gain sharing or profit sharing, employers will limit their hiring. The limits are based on their (inflexible) wage levels. Even if there are outside job applicants willing to work for less than the going inside wage, this outsider willingness and availability will not create additional jobs without a share system.

With a productivity gain-sharing plan, or any system with similar characteristics, however, the firm has an incentive to hire more employees, if any are available. The additional hires "dilute" the bonus pool, thus lowering labor costs per worker. This dilution effect occurs because the marginal productivity of the added workers will be less than the average productivity of the firm's workforce.

If the bonus is based on average productivity, then adding more workers will pull down the bonus. In effect, the added workers end up working for less than the previous inside pay level (counting the bonus), even though the hourly wage component of total pay is not lowered. At the same time the new hires also reduce pay for others in the employer's workforce.

Macroeconomic Benefits of Productivity Gain Sharing   Like simple incentive pay plans, productivity gain-sharing plans turn out to have more complex potential impacts on the employment relationship than might be initially supposed. These plans cannot always be assumed to create harmony of interests between employer and employee. However, some of the effects of productivity gain sharing are beneficial to society external to the firm.

Whenever an activity has external benefits that are not captured by those responsible, economic theory suggests not enough of the activity will take place. With productivity gain sharing —at least in some forms—the externally beneficial activity is more flexible pay and (potential) additional hiring. Additional hiring and more stable employment of existing workers are social benefits in a world in which chronic unemployment problems persist. In a subsequent chapter, it will be seen that the added wage flexibility that accompanies productivity gain sharing could improve macroeconomic performance. If the employer incentive for additional hiring prevails, lower unemployment could also result.[36]

Stakeholders and Productivity Gain Sharing   It has been noted that employees are stakeholders in the firm. In other words, because mobility is costly to both the firm and the worker, employees find their welfare linked to the economic viability of their employers. Productivity gain sharing partially recognizes this employee interest. Since productivity and profitability are not identical, however, the stakeholder aspect of the employer–employee relationship is only imperfectly reflected by such plans.

Despite their imperfections, it is possible that gain-sharing plans could raise productivity or lower net costs. Unfortunately, because the plans are not widely used, there has been little hard research concerning their effects. Firms that use gain sharing tend to be strong proponents of the approach. Case study evidence, which may be biased toward plans that are successes on some dimension, tends to report positive results. Workers under such plans tend to receive higher total pay, suggesting that—as in the case of incentives—firms find that economic benefits accrue from the use of gain sharing.[37]

Profit Sharing

Profit-sharing plans, as defined in this chapter, include only compensation systems that use a formula (either specified in writing or solidified by ongoing practice) to provide a share of profits to employees. It is important to stress this definition. Unfortunately, the term *profit sharing* has come to be used loosely by compensation administrators to cover a variety of tax-deferred savings/retirement plans, some of which have little to do with profits. One study of 411 firms that reported they had profit sharing found that many did not in fact use a fixed formula to determine the bonus. This practice was especially common in small and medium-sized firms, but less so for plans covering 1,000 or more employees.[38]

Loose terminology regarding profit sharing has a long history. For example, in the early part of this century, Henry Ford referred to his firm's policy of paying higher wages to employees who met company standards of moral character as "profit sharing." To be meaningful, however, the practice of paying high wages that do not vary with profits cannot be included under the profit-sharing label.

The actual bonus formulas used in profit-sharing plans vary widely. Some plans provide first dollar coverage, sharing each dollar of profits with employees according to a fixed percentage or schedule. Others have hurdle rates of return, in which only profits above a given level will be shared. In some cases certain adjustments to profits are made before the employee share is calculated. For example, profits received from foreign subsidiaries may be removed from the pot before any sharing takes place.

Unfortunately, there are no comprehensive surveys of the types of formulas in use. If the definition of profit sharing is confined to plans that use a profit-based formula to determine the bonus, one study suggests that one-fourth of such plans have a hurdle element in the formula.[39] This estimate should be taken only as a general indication.

Empirical Evidence   The BLS began collecting information on the proportion of employees covered by various fringe benefit plans in the early 1980s. Unfortunately, the survey is limited to medium and large firms, which accounted for only 29% of private, nonfarm payroll employment in 1986. Since small firms typically have less sophisticated HRM practices, it is likely that the BLS survey overstates coverage of the various benefits it reports, including profit sharing. In other words, the proportion of workers in the entire economy who are covered by profit sharing is probably smaller than it is at medium-sized and large firms.

Table 5–4 summarizes the coverage of profit-sharing plans by broad occupational groups from the BLS survey. Twenty-two percent of employees included in the report participated in profit sharing. At one time production workers were somewhat less likely than white-collar workers to be under profit sharing. The data in Table 5–4, however, suggest that by 1986 this tendency no longer applied, at least for medium-sized and large firms.

Union Wage Concessions and Profit Sharing   The blue-collar/white-collar distinction with regard to profit sharing probably eroded in the 1980s because of developments in the union sector of the economy. Until the 1980s profit sharing was extremely rare in union contracts. In the early 1980s, however, unions found themselves forced to negotiate concessions on wages and workrules. In some cases, they were able to obtain profit sharing in return. Large numbers of workers in the automobile industry, for example, were covered by profit-sharing plans negotiated as part of concession deals at General Motors and Ford in 1982. Since that time, profit sharing has spread among union members in such industries as lumber, airlines, and steel.[40]

TABLE 5–4   Profit-Sharing and Employee Stock-Ownership Plans in Medium-sized to Large Firms, 1986

	Percentage of Employees in Profit-Sharing Plans				Percentage of Employees in ESOP Plans	
Type of Employee	*All*	*Cash*	*Deferred*	*Cash and Deferred*	*Tax Credit*	*Other*
All employees	22%	1%	18%	3%	28%	2%
Professional, administrative	22	1	18	3	30	3
Technical, clerical	22	1	18	4	31	2
Production	22	1	17	4	26	2

Note: For profit-sharing plans, details may not sum to totals because some employees participate in more than one type of plan.

Source: U.S. Bureau of Labor Statistics, *Employee Benefits in Medium and Large Firms, 1986,* bulletin 2281 (Washington: GPO, 1987), p. 81.

We will have more to say about unions and profit sharing in a later chapter. However, it should be noted at this point that although unions were not receptive to profit sharing plans until the 1980s, unions actually offer *potential* advantages to their members regarding such plans.[41] (These advantages are not available to nonunion workers.) The degree to which unions actually undertake to offer these potential services remains to be seen.

First, since profit sharing involves a calculation of profits, unions can perform an auditing function to ensure that appropriate bonuses are paid. Profits are subject to alternative estimation practices. Creative accounting can raise or lower measured profitability. Without their own auditor, workers may be unable to determine whether they are receiving adequate profit-sharing payments.

Second, if profit sharing becomes a significant portion of total compensation, worker interest in the managerial decisions that affect profitability may rise. Unions could offer a mechanism for worker participation in such decisions. In the past, unions resisted the suggestion that they should take on a managerial role, preferring instead a traditional adversarial relationship with management. In the 1980s, however, there was evidence of a shift in this attitude among certain key union leaders. For those officials profit sharing has a newfound appeal, at least relative to previous attitudes.[42]

Influence of Tax Preferences   Certain types of profit sharing are eligible for preferential tax treatment. Basically, if the profit-sharing bonus is paid into a trust fund used for retirement purposes, it may be deducted as a business expense by the firm. The employee has no tax liability until the contribution is paid out—typically at the time of retirement or upon separation from the firm. Thus the employee benefits by way of a tax deferral.[43]

The influence of these tax provisions is clear from Table 5–4. Profit-sharing plans that pay out only a current cash bonus (and thereby receive no tax preferences) account for a mere 1% of total employment in the BLS survey. Most of the profit-sharing coverage involves plans that provide deferment of the bonus, such as payment into a trust fund, or that offer the employee a choice of cash or deferred features.

Although the tax code undoubtedly tilts the mix of profit-sharing plans toward the deferred variety, it probably has little effect on the basic decision of whether to have a profit-sharing plan in the first place. There are other savings plans that employers can provide to employees and that offer similar tax deferral features but do not involve a formula geared to profits. If the employer's objective is simply to provide a savings or retirement vehicle, alternatives to profit sharing are available that have equally attractive tax implications.

Conventional HRM View of Profit Sharing   Profit sharing, particularly in a large firm, may cover a broad range of corporate activities and products. This company-wide aspect of profit sharing means that the connection between individual employee effort and profit-sharing bonuses is remote. A worker in one division of a firm may receive a smaller or larger bonus based on developments in another division. Profits may fluctuate due to product market conditions, changes in interest rates, and other external factors. Or they may vary due to managerial decisions regarding marketing, investments, and other areas that do not reflect employee effort.

Because of the loose connection between effort and profits, HRM specialists have generally not viewed profit sharing as an incentive plan. Rather, its benefits—as seen by proponents—are said to be in the area of general morale boosting. In addition, profit sharing is viewed as having the potential to create a more loyal workforce. Loyal workers are more likely to remain with the firm and thus reduce the costs of turnover.

Traditional proponents of profit sharing have argued that the firm should not view the expected share bonus as a substitute for a wage. Rather, it should pay the going wage and allow the bonus to be perceived as something extra. In modern economic parlance, what is being proposed is a "gift exchange," that is, extra pay from the employer serves as a gift in exchange for extra effort and loyalty from the employees.[44]

Because profits may fluctuate for many reasons, an extensive communications program is often seen as a necessary companion to profit sharing. The causes of profit variations need to be explained to employees, particularly in years when the bonus paid out mysteriously declines or disappears entirely. In the past, therefore, profit sharing was often the province of large, nonunion firms, with progressive HRM policies encompassing elaborate communications mechanisms.

Having profit sharing was sometimes seen by employers as part of a strategy for remaining nonunion. Although there is little evidence on the effectiveness of this strategy, one study did report lesser union success in winning representation elections at companies in which profit sharing was being used.[45] This history of union avoidance accounted, in part, for the one-time tradition of union aversion to profit-sharing arrangements.

As in the case of productivity gain sharing, much of the evidence on the effectiveness of profit sharing from the HRM perspective is anecdotal and is often produced by proponents. Since profit sharing appears to be much more widespread than productivity gain sharing, it can be assumed that many employers have found it to be useful as part of an overall HRM program. But it remains limited to a minority of the workforce. Many employers apparently do not believe that it would be in their interest to install profit sharing as a motivational device.

Some economists have argued that the fact that profit sharing is not used for a large majority of the workforce proves that it is generally not an effective motivational device.[46] It is possible, however, to take a more agnostic viewpoint. For example, there is evidence that the Japanese practice of paying workers large bonuses is really a type of profit sharing.[47] If Japanese firms find such schemes in their interest, it is not clear why U.S. firms would not.

Previous references to implicit employer–employee contracting suggest that fairness is an important consideration in defining the relationship. However, fairness is a vague concept. If profit sharing were the norm, firms not offering it might appear unfair. Perhaps this is the case in Japan. And perhaps profit sharing could become the norm in the United States if it received encouragement, say, from additional tax preferences. There is a natural tendency, in the labor market and elsewhere, to feel that what exists is normal.

Macroeconomic Side of Profit Sharing   Recently, some economists have argued that profit sharing should be encouraged, not because it is particularly effective as an HRM device, but because it offers macroeconomic benefits. Since macroeconomic benefits flow to society at large and not to the individual firm, it has been proposed that the government should provide encouragement in the form of special tax incentives. In effect, profit sharing is said to have positive social externalities; thus it will be underutilized from a social welfare viewpoint unless it is subsidized.

The most prominent advocate of this position is MIT economist and professor Martin L. Weitzman.[48] (A full exploration of the Weitzman position will be deferred to a later chapter.) Weitzman argues that widespread profit sharing (and a variety of similar share plans, including some of the productivity gain-sharing plans) would create an incentive for employers to increase hiring and to stabilize employment. If many firms actually did increase their employment levels, the national unemployment rate could be reduced.

Firms would increase their hiring, according to Weitzman, because the marginal cost of adding a worker would fall under profit sharing and would be below the average cost. Each additional worker would contribute some extra output and therefore some extra profits. Only a fraction of these profits would be shared with workers, so that it would usually pay to hire more employees.[49]

According to Weitzman, the effect of a generalized demand for workers would be a permanent labor shortage. Even if aggregate demand tended to fall, firms would hang on to their workers because of the shortage. The result, he claims, would be a full-employment, recession-proof economy, without inflationary tendencies.

Weitzman's proposal for massive encouragement of profit sharing has stimulated considerable debate in economic circles. One of the criticisms is that inside workers would resist new hires (outsiders). Just as in the productivity gain-sharing case, new hires would tend to dilute the bonus payment and lower average compensation for all workers already employed. If this resistance were severe, it might lead to restrictions on hiring and thwart Weitzman's goal of lowered unemployment. This counterargument is discussed further in a later chapter.

Stakeholders and Profit Sharing   Profit sharing comes closer to recognizing employees' stakeholder interests in their enterprises than productivity gain sharing. The basis of the bonus under (true) profit sharing is profitability—the ultimate measure of the firm's economic health—and not productivity. Because profit-sharing plan formulas vary widely, however, their impacts may differ substantially from company to company. Productivity gain-sharing plans typically aim at making the bonus a significant element of total pay. Some profit-sharing plans, in contrast, may pay out relatively small bonuses.

Some studies have sought to determine if profit sharing is profitable to the firms that offer it.[50] They have uncovered some evidence of increased profitability and productivity. However, as in the cases of gain sharing and incentives, the linkage between the pay system and the firm's bottom line is an under-researched topic.

Employee Stock-Ownership Plans

Examples of firms encouraging their employees to purchase their stock have existed for many years. Such programs go back at least to the 1920s, when some firms with advanced HRM policies offered stock-ownership incentives to employees as part of what was then called welfare capitalism. Plans of that era sometimes offered stock at a discount or waived brokerage fees. Similar plans still exist today, through which employees as individuals can accumulate company stock.

Redistributing Wealth Through ESOPs   Over the years, a number of social reformers have argued that corporate stock should be more widely owned than is actually the case. The good society, according to this view, is one in which every worker is a mini-capitalist. It has also been argued, along the lines used by profit-sharing proponents, that if workers owned the stock of their own employer, they would be more loyal, more concerned about the well-being of their firm, and so on.

During the 1950s, such a position was advocated by Louis Kelso.[51] Under what became known as the Kelso Plan, federal tax incentives would be given to the establishment, by employers, of stock trusts for their workers. By the mid-1970s, this idea had captured the fancy of Senator Russell Long, chair of the Senate Finance Committee. Beginning in 1974, Long fostered changes in the tax code designed to favor establishment of Employee Stock Ownership Plans (ESOPs) and related arrangements. The result was a substantial expansion of these programs.

Tax Subsidies to ESOPs   Perhaps the high point of the tax subsidy to ESOP plans came with the formation of so-called Payroll-based Stock Ownership Plans (PAYSOPs) that provided a tax credit up to 1% of payroll if an equivalent amount of stock were given to the PAYSOP trust. Additional benefits were available to employers who matched employee contributions to PAYSOP. As the President's Office of Management and the Budget noted, the total subsidy from the taxpayer to this arrangement was in excess of 100% of the costs![52] Not surprisingly, when Congress decided to reform the tax code in 1986, the tax subsidy to PAYSOPs was eliminated.

Regular ESOPs also receive special tax considerations. There are two basic types of ESOPs. In an unleveraged ESOP, the employer simply contributes stock to a trust fund for the benefit of employees, up to limits specified in the tax code. The employer deducts the value of the stock from corporate taxes as a business expense. The employees' tax liability is deferred until they withdraw the contributions (at retirement or separation from the firm). Thus, an unleveraged ESOP is not much different in tax treatment from a conventional defined contribution pension plan.[53]

It was the leveraged ESOP that particularly excited Kelso and Long. As originally established in 1974, the leveraged ESOP was seen as a financial tool for employers as well as a share-the-wealth mechanism for workers. Employers would create trust funds for ESOPs and use them as financial intermediaries for raising capital.

Instead of the employer borrowing from a bank directly, for example, the ESOP trust borrows from the bank; the trust receives an equivalent value of stock from the employer in exchange for passing on the proceeds of the loan. The employer thereafter makes contributions to the trust to pay off the loan. Since the contributions are made to an employee benefit plan and not directly to the bank, the employer is able to deduct both principal and interest payments from corporate income taxes. In contrast, in a conventional loan transaction without an ESOP, only interest can be deducted.

Is the ESOP Game Honestly Played? Proponents of ESOPs have touted the advantage the firm receives through the tax deduction of the loan principal. But is it really an advantage? Suppose the loan from the bank is for $1 million. When all is said and done, the employer has (1) paid the bank its interest, which is a tax deduction with or without an ESOP, (2) repaid the bank its principal of $1 million, and (3) given away $1 million in stock to the employees via the ESOP.

If the stock is in fact worth $1 million, *there is no subsidy* involved in allowing a tax deduction of $1 million plus interest. The stock contribution represents a claim on the company and an asset to the employees. Just as the firm deducts the cost of the money it pays out in wages (another kind of asset given to employees), so it should be able to deduct the cost of giving away stock.

Thus, despite the hoopla, the tax provision permitting deduction of principal should not have been a strong enticement to create leveraged ESOPs. Nor should there have been a strong inducement to create unleveraged ESOPs, since the shares given to employees through the trust are costs to the firm's other shareholders. Yet as Table 5–5 shows, the net formation of ESOPs, as recorded in reports filed with the Internal Revenue Service, rose rapidly after the tax code was revised in 1974.

If the firm's stock is publicly traded so that an outside market value can be easily verified, there will be little opportunity for abuse in valuation of the stock given to the plan. But when stock is closely held—as in many smaller, family owned companies—there is a danger that the value of the stock contributed to the ESOP trust could be artificially inflated to obtain an excessive tax deduction. A 1987 report based on 210 ESOPs found that only 7% were associated with firms whose stock was publicly traded.[54] Another survey put the figure at one-fourth in 1983.[55]

Concerns that the ESOP mechanism was being abused were reflected in a 1980 government report. Excess stock valuations (and, therefore, excess tax deductions) were apparently being encouraged by the tax code. Apart from the question of valuation of stock contributed, the report noted problems related to the marketability of nontraded stock, and the limited voting rights allowed to employees for "their" shares.[56] Perhaps hoping to attract more firms into the ESOP pool—including larger, publicly traded enterprises—Congress passed a further tax incentive for ESOPs in 1984. The 1984 rules allow banks and other lenders to exclude half of the interest they receive from ESOPs from corporate income taxes. Borrowing through an ESOP is thus made cheaper than borrowing

TABLE 5–5   Cumulative Number of Stock Bonus and ESOPs, 1975–1986

Time Period	Sum of Approvals Minus Terminations of ESOP and Stock Bonus Plans
Summer 1975	275
Dec. 1976	1,033
Dec. 1977	1,874
Dec. 1978	2,682
Dec. 1979	3,225
Dec. 1980	3,670
Dec. 1981	4,175
Dec. 1982	4,516
Dec. 1983	4,957
Dec. 1984	5,467
Dec. 1985	6,017
Dec. 1986	6,698

Note: Figures are based on reports to the Internal Revenue Service.

Source: Estimates provided to the author by the Profit Sharing Research Foundation.

directly, since lenders will give reduced interest rates to ESOPs reflecting the tax subsidy.[57]

Future of ESOPs   In 1986, according to Table 5–4, 30% of employees at medium and large firms were covered by some form of ESOPs. The vast majority of these workers were under tax-credit ESOPs (the PAYSOPs previously discussed). Given the 100 + % tax subsidy then provided to PAYSOPs, it is surprising that the figure was not much higher. Regular ESOPs covered only 2% of the employees within the scope of the survey.

ESOPs have strong proponents, and much of the research done on the plans has been by proponents.[58] But there is mixed evidence on their contribution to firm productivity or profitability.[59] A study by the U.S. General Accounting Office found that ESOPs had no effect on profitability; some indication of a positive effect on productivity was found only when ESOPs were combined with worker participation in management decision making.[60]

Apart from any effect on corporate performance, there was a surge of interest during the 1980s in the use of ESOPs to transfer full or majority ownership to employees. In some cases workers (and their unions) have bought failing enterprises and attempted to put them back into viable financial condition to preserve jobs. Some of these efforts have produced well-publicized successes, such as Weirton Steel in West Virginia.[61] Less publicity has accrued to cases in which worker ownership has failed, such as Rath Packing, a meatpacking company that went bankrupt under an ESOP.[62]

As long as some provisions of the tax code continue to favor ESOPs, they will remain on the scene. But their impact on productivity or employee loyalty remains uncertain. Nor have they transferred substantial stock to employees. And while ESOP success stories will inevitably attract favorable coverage, ESOPs will also receive unfavorable publicity when, for example, they are used by management to fend off hostile takeovers. With their close cousins, the PAYSOPs (now stripped of tax incentives), ESOPs seem destined to remain an interesting but not very important form of compensation.

There is an economic justification for this limited role for ESOPs. From a microeconomic viewpoint, ESOPs reflect, although imperfectly, the stakeholder interests of employees in the firms that employ them. Once an employee's connection with the firm is severed—through retirement, quit, or permanent layoff—that stake ceases to exist. Yet with an ESOP, the employee who leaves the firm takes his or her equity as stock, cash, or as an annuity. With profit sharing or productivity gain sharing, in contrast, claims on the company exist only for current employees. Thus, profit sharing and productivity gain sharing better recognize employee stakeholder interests relative to ESOPs.

ESOPs are also defective from a macroeconomic viewpoint. The advantages that Weitzman has argued accompany profit sharing and similar arrangements do not accrue from ESOPs. ESOPs, at least as they are structured in the United States, create more stockholders, but do not make compensation more flexible or change the firm's hiring incentives.[63] Profit-sharing plans thus have a better claim than ESOPs on the tax subsidy that ESOPs currently receive.

Summary

Firms face compensation decisions that are much more complicated than simply determining the average wage. How to pay is as important as what to pay. A variety of alternative ways of structuring pay are in use, some based on time units of labor input, and others based on output, revenue, value added, or profits. The alternative systems serve complex functions of monitoring and motivating the workforce. Systems that involve the employee in economic sharing may or may not be linked to quality of working life arrangements, which also provide for a share in decision making.

All of the alternative systems have their proponents. Generally, all could do with more research on their ultimate effects on firm economic performance.[64] The case for ESOPs is probably the shakiest of all of the alternatives, since ESOPs seem to be mainly dependent on tax advantages rather than clear-cut evidence of a positive impact on profitability or productivity. Incentive workers seem usually to earn more than comparable time workers, suggesting that firms that use incentive systems receive a payoff in higher productivity or reduced costs.

EXERCISES

Problem

Imagine you are a human resource executive in a large firm with many plants and operating units. Your workforce is paid on a time-based system and you are considering the installation of an alternative system of pay. Because you have many plants in your company, you have the opportunity to experiment with alternative systems at different locations. Develop a research design so that you will be able to determine if installation of a particular plan will improve company performance. Be sure to specify what objectives you are seeking.

Questions

1. What factors have contributed to the long-term decline in the use of incentive systems relative to time-based pay?

2. What impact did the phenomenon of union concession bargaining in the 1980s have on pay plans in the union sector?

3. Do piece rates marry the interests of employer and employee? Explain.

4. What can be inferred from the average wage differential between incentive workers and time workers?

5. How has the tax code influenced the choice of pay systems?

6. How does the business cycle affect productivity?

Terms

derived demand for labor	leveraged ESOP	team production
exempt employee	moonlighting	time and motion study
Fair Labor Standards Act	Scanlon Plan	unemployment rate
insider-outsider model	scientific management	

ENDNOTES

1. Frederick W. Taylor, *The Principles of Scientific Management* (New York: Harper & Brothers Publishers, 1911). Taylor's interests went beyond pay systems into all manner of managerial innovation. In many respects, the notion that management could be systematically studied and improved developed from Taylor's work. If you are a student in a business school, much of what you are learning goes back to that notion.

2. Donald W. Myers, *Human Resources Management: Principles and Practice* (Chicago: Commerce Clearing House, 1986), p. 787.

3. Harriet Gorlin, *Personnel Practices II: Hours of Work, Pay Practices, Relocation*, no. 92 (New York: Conference Board, 1981), p. 25.

4. John Howell Cox, "Time and Incentive Pay Practices in Urban Areas," *Monthly Labor Review*, vol. 94 (December 1971), p. 54.

5. Norma W. Carlson, "Time Rates Tighten Their Grip on Manufacturing Industries," *Monthly Labor Review,* vol. 105 (May 1982), pp. 15–22.

6. The Bureau of National Affairs, Inc., *Basic Patterns in Union Contracts,* eleventh edition (Washington: BNA, 1986), p. 125.

7. Unions did not achieve the goal of a guaranteed annual wage. Their demand evolved instead into the supplemental unemployment benefit systems discussed below.

8. Earl F. Mellor and Steven E. Haugen, "Hourly Paid Workers: Who They Are and What They Earn," *Monthly Labor Review,* vol. 109 (February 1986), p. 21.

9. Supplemental Unemployment Benefit Plans (SUB Plans) are basically privately negotiated systems of unemployment insurance under which covered workers receive benefits in addition to the unemployment insurance benefits paid by state agencies. These plans began to be negotiated in significant volume in the 1950s in certain manufacturing industries in which layoffs were a widely used practice.

10. A small additional number of the unemployed are individuals who have found a job that they have not yet started and that they will start within thirty days. To be counted as employed or unemployed, an individual must be part of the noninstitutional population (not in a jail, hospital, or similar institution) and at least sixteen years of age.

11. The Fair Labor Standards Act is better known as the "minimum wage law" since it specifies the federal minimum wage. The act also contains provisions limiting the use of child (and teenage) labor.

12. The concept of a map of indifference curves is drawn from consumer theory. Each curve represents a menu of alternative combinations—in this case of leisure and earnings—that leave the worker's utility (state of welfare or well-being) unchanged. The curves are concave, representing diminishing marginal utility of the two "goods." Students who have had an elementary microeconomics course should be familiar with indifference curve analysis. If the concept is unfamiliar, consult any standard microeconomics textbook.

13. It will be seen in the next chapter that the employer benefits from paying a premium for incremental hours worked rather than simply raising the basic hourly wage.

14. Daniel E. Taylor, "Absences from Work among Full-Time Employees," *Monthly Labor Review,* vol. 104 (March 1981), pp. 68–70.

15. Martin J. Gannon, "Preferences of Temporary Workers: Time, Variety, and Flexibility," *Monthly Labor Review,* vol. 108 (August 1984), pp. 26–28.

16. Daniel E. Taylor and Edward S. Sekcenski, "Workers on Long Schedules, Single and Multiple Jobholders," *Monthly Labor Review,* vol. 105 (May 1982), pp. 47–53.

17. An alternative explanation of employer control of hours relates to the implicit contracting notion described in the previous chapter. If workers are underpaid early in their careers and overpaid later, they will tend to want to underwork and later overwork, given their hourly pay rates. Hence, employers would have to set hours as part of the implicit contract. Empirical information on desired hours, however, does not suggest that young workers want to reduce hours while senior workers want to increase them. See Edward P. Lazear, "Agency, Earnings Profiles, Productivity, and Hours Restrictions," *American Economic Review,* vol. 71 (September 1981), pp. 606–620; Susan E. Shank, "Preferred Hours of Work and Corresponding Earnings," *Monthly Labor Review,* vol. 109 (November 1986), pp. 40–44; and Kevin Lang, "Understanding Over- and Underemployment," *NBER Reporter* (Summer 1988), pp. 6–9.

18. One consideration for you would be whether or not you had good information on alternative jobs available to the builder. If other jobs were waiting, the builder would be less likely to dawdle on your job.

19. The model presented in Figure 5–2 was originally designed to analyze contingency fees charged by lawyers in personal injury cases. In such situations, the lawyer receives a percentage of the revenue obtained from the defendant (typically an insurance company) with the rest going to the plaintiff. In effect, the lawyer is on a revenue-based piece rate. See Daniel J. B. Mitchell and Murray L. Schwartz, "Theoretical Implications of Contingent Legal Fees," *Quarterly Review of Economics and Business,* vol. 12 (Spring 1972), pp. 69–76; and Murray L. Schwartz and Daniel J. B. Mitchell, "An Economic Analysis of the Contingency Fee in Personal-Injury Litigation," *Stanford Law Review,* vol. 22 (June 1970), pp. 1125–1162. An elaboration of the model appears in Kevin M. Clermont and John D. Currivan, "Improving on the Contingent Fee," *Cornell Law Review,* vol. 63 (April 1978), pp. 529–639.

20. Strictly speaking, this statement should be modified to take account of the materials input into production. The employer cannot give away 100% of value added, that is, net rather than gross revenue after deduction of materials cost. Nor can the employer set a piece rate such that it consumes the margin between output price and unit materials cost.

21. For details on these systems, see Benjamin W. Niebel, *Motion and Time Study,* fourth edition (Homewood, Ill.: Irwin, 1967), chapter 25.

22. A classic study is Stanley B. Mathewson, *Restriction of Output among Unorganized Workers* (Carbondale, Ill.: Southern Illinois University Press, 1969 [1931]). Before this study, it had often been assumed that worker restrictions of output were a phenomenon only of the union sector. Mathewson showed that nonunion workers also can implement such restrictions.

23. Martin L. Weitzman, "The 'Ratchet Principle' and Performance Incentives," *Bell Journal of Economics,* vol. 11 (Spring 1980), pp. 302–308.

24. Edward P. Lazear, "Salaries and Piece Rates," *Journal of Business,* vol. 59 (July 1986), pp. 405–431, especially pp. 422–425.

25. The fact that the cost of piece rates rises relative to time rates does not mean that using a piece rate will necessarily be uneconomical for a given firm. Each firm must weigh the costs and benefits of alternative systems.

26. Eric Seiler, "Piece Rates vs. Time Rates: The Effect of Incentives on Earnings," *Review of Economics and Statistics,* vol. 66 (August 1984), pp. 363–376. Another study finds that the differential between incentive and time workers lies across, rather than within, establishments—that is, workers at the same establishment receive similar pay, regardless of the pay system used. Some establishments specialize in incentive pay, while others use mainly time pay. See John H. Pencavel, "Work Effort, On-the-Job Screening, and Alternative Methods of Remuneration" in Ronald G. Ehrenberg, ed., *Research in Labor Economics,* vol. 1 (Greenwich, Conn.: JAI Press, 1977), pp. 225–259, especially pp. 241–248.

27. Firms that report gain-sharing programs indicated in a survey that many of the plans were not of the Scanlon, Rucker, or Improshare types described in the text. Some were described as "profit sharing," but geared to a subunit of the firm such as division. See Carla O'Dell and Jerry McAdams, *People, Performance, and Pay* (Houston: American Productivity Center, 1987), pp. 43–44.

28. Frederick G. Lesieur, ed., *The Scanlon Plan: A Frontier in Labor-Management Cooperation* (Cambridge, Mass.: MIT Press, 1958).

29. U.S. General Accounting Office, *Productivity Sharing Programs: Can They Contribute to Productivity Improvement?,* report AFMD–81–22 (Washington: GAO, 1981), p. 9.

30. O'Dell and McAdams, *People, Performance, and Pay, op. cit.,* p. 43.

31. That is, the capital-to-labor ratio (with capital measured as a stock) will fall as the economy picks up and more employees are hired to work with the given amount of capital. Similarly, the ratio will fall during economic downturns.

32. For example, a six-month lag was found even in the adjustment of the hours of production workers in manufacturing (a group that should be very sensitive to output). And since hours per worker can be adjusted to meet labor demand, the employment of production workers was always less than proportionate to output. See Christopher A. Sims, "Output and Labor Input in Manufacturing," *Brookings Papers on Economic Activity* (3:1974), pp. 695–728.

33. Jon A. Fay and James L. Medoff, "Labor and Output Over the Business Cycle: Some Direct Evidence," *American Economic Review,* vol. 75 (September 1985), pp. 638–655.

34. Assar Lindbeck and Dennis J. Snower, "Wage Setting, Unemployment, and Insider–Outsider Relations," *American Economic Review,* vol. 76 (May 1986), pp. 235–239.

35. Ellen Wojahn, " 'Gainfully' Employed," *Inc.,* vol. 5 (December 1983), p. 152.

36. One way of looking at this issue is to consider price (and, therefore, wage) rigidity as having a negative externality on other firms. If a firm's prices are rigid (unresponsive to demand) because of wage rigidity, the firm will adjust to demand fluctuations exclusively through output. But its larger output swings make demand more variable for other firms, especially suppliers. The firm does not bear the cost of this negative external effect, creating (macro)economic inefficiency. To the extent that flexibility is increased, as might occur through gain sharing, efficiency is improved. The externality approach can be found in Laurence Ball and David Romer, "Are Prices Too Sticky?," working paper no. 2171, National Bureau of Economic Research, February 1987.

37. R. J. Bullock and Edward E. Lawler, "Gainsharing: A Few Questions, and Fewer Answers," *Human Resource Management,* vol. 23 (Spring 1984), pp. 23–40.

38. Hewitt Associates, *1987 Profit Sharing Survey (1986 Experience),* joint bulletin with Profit Sharing Council of America (Lincolnshire, Ill.: Hewitt Associates, 1987), p. 13.

39. *1987 Profit Sharing Survey, op. cit.,* p. 13. The estimate is based on the percentage of plans with hurdles out of a sample of firms with bonuses based on profits with a hurdle, profits, and profits plus a discretionary element.

40. Daniel J. B. Mitchell, "Shifting Norms on Wage Determination," *Brookings Papers on Economic Activity* (2:1985), pp. 575–599.

41. Daniel J. B. Mitchell, "The Share Economy and Industrial Relations: An Overview of the Weitzman Proposal," *Industrial Relations,* vol. 26 (Winter 1987), pp. 1–17.

42. The reader should not be left with the impression that unions have completely turned around in their views on profit sharing. There is still skepticism, but it is mixed with a pragmatic attitude that in some cases profit sharing may be beneficial. See John L. Zalusky, "Labor's Collective Bargaining Experience with Gainsharing and Profit-Sharing" in Barbara D. Dennis, ed., *Proceedings of the Thirty-Ninth Annual Meeting,* Industrial Relations Research Association, December 28–30, 1986 (Madison, Wisc.: IRRA, 1987), pp. 174–182.

43. The employee may also be in a lower tax bracket upon retirement than he or she would be during working life.

44. George A. Akerlof, "Labor Contracts as Partial Gift Exchanges," *Quarterly Journal of Economics,* vol. 97 (November 1982), pp. 543–569. There is a potential conflict between the gift view of profit sharing and the Weitzman argument for macroeconomic benefits. Part of Weitzman's argument depends on the firm reducing the wage and substituting the profit-sharing bonus.

45. Edgar R. Czarnecki, "Profit Sharing and Union Organizing," *Monthly Labor Review,* vol. 92 (December 1969), pp. 61–62.

46. Armen A. Alchian and Harold Demsetz, "Production, Information Costs, and Economic Organization," *American Economic Review,* vol. 62 (December 1972), p. 786.

47. Richard B. Freeman and Martin L. Weitzman, "Bonuses and Employment in Japan," working paper no. 1878, National Bureau of Economic Research, 1986.

48. Martin L. Weitzman, *The Share Economy: Conquering Stagflation* (Cambridge, Mass.: Harvard University Press, 1984).

49. These tendencies have already been described in this chapter with regard to gain sharing.

50. Bion B. Howard and Peter O. Dietz, *A Study of the Financial Significance of Profit Sharing* (Chicago: Profit Sharing Research Foundation, 1969); Edward Morse II, *The Effects of Profit Sharing on Productivity,* doctoral dissertation, Department of Economics, Boston College, 1986.

51. Louis Kelso, *The Capitalist Manifesto* (New York: Random House, 1958). Kelso authored or coauthored a series of books thereafter. The most recent is Louis O. Kelso and Patricia Hetter Kelso, *Democracy and Economic Power: Extending the ESOP Revolution* (Cambridge, Mass.: Ballinger Publishing Co., 1986). In it the authors argue for all manner of stock ownership arrangements under such names as MUSOP, CSOP, GSOP, ICOP, COMCOP, and PUBCOP and proclaim that "it is time that we do for economic power what the founding fathers did for political power; put it on the road to democracy." (p. 9)

52. U.S. Office of Management and Budget, *Special Analyses: Budget of the United States Government, Fiscal Year 1987* (Washington: GPO, 1986), pp. G29–G30.

53. Pension programs and other forms of fringe benefits are discussed in a later chapter.

54. ESOP Association, *ESOP Survey, 1987* (Washington: ESOP Association, 1987), p. 5.

55. U.S. General Accounting Office, *Employee Stock Ownership Plans: Interim Report on a Survey and Related Economic Trends,* report no. GAO–PEMB–86–4BR (Washington: GAO, 1986), p. 19.

56. U.S. General Accounting Office, *Employee Stock Ownership Plans: Who Benefits Most in Closely Held Companies?,* report no. HRD–80–88 (Washington: GAO, 1980).

57. A review of the tax aspects of ESOPs can be found in U.S. General Accounting Office, *Employee Stock Ownership Plans: Benefits and Costs of ESOP Tax Incentives for Promoting Stock Ownership,* GAO/PEMD–87–8 (Washington: GPO, 1986).

58. See, for example, Corey Rosen, Katherine J. Klein, and Karen M. Young, *Employee Ownership in America: The Equity Solution* (Lexington, Mass.: Lexington Books, 1986).

59. Joseph R. Blasi, *Employee Ownership: Revolution or Ripoff?* (Cambridge, Mass.: Ballinger, 1988), chapter 8.

60. U.S. General Accounting Office, *Employee Stock Ownership Plans: Little Evidence of Effects on Corporate Performance,* GAO/PEMD–88–1 (Washington: GAO, 1987).

61. Steven Greenhouse, "Employees Make a Go of Weirton," *New York Times,* Section F, January 6, 1985, p. 4.

62. Tove H. Hammer and Robert N. Stern, "A Yo-Yo Model of Cooperation: Union Participation in Management at the Rath Packing Company," *Industrial and Labor Relations Review,* vol. 39 (April 1986), pp. 337–349.

63. It is possible to imagine ESOPs with different structures than those currently in use. For example, it has been proposed that ESOPs could issue shares to workers that were contingent on continued employment. See J. E. Meade, *Alternative Systems of Business Organization and of Workers' Remuneration* (Boston: Allen & Unwin, 1986), pp. 115–119.

64. For a review of the research issues, see Ronald G. Ehrenberg and George T. Milkovich, "Compensation and Firm Performance" in Morris M. Kleiner, Richard N. Block, Myron Roomkin, and Sidney W. Salsburg, eds., *Human Resources and the Performance of the Firm* (Madison, Wisc.: IRRA, 1987), pp. 87–122.

Chapter Six

ANALYSIS OF PAY SETTING

Setting pay is one of the key human resource management decisions for an organization. As has been seen, the pay *system* functions partly as a reward/incentive system. It is closely intertwined with procedures for employee evaluation. Once a pay system is established, however, the pay *level* must be determined. The pay level will be a critical determinant of the firm's success in employee recruiting and employee retention. If pay is set too low, then regardless of the system in which it is embedded, the firm will suffer from excessive vacancies and turnover. If pay is set too high, excess direct labor costs will result. Too high wages may also make it difficult to bring new blood into the organization, since voluntary quit rates of existing employees will be extremely low.

This chapter presents the classical economic supply/demand model of pay determination.[1] The model is shown to have substantial analytical problems, and its predictions do not accord with many real world phenomena. On the other hand, there are some applications for the traditional framework. Next, some recent modifications to the classical model are presented. These newer approaches help explain the actual practice of pay determination, which is discussed in the next chapter. They also suggest some HRM methodology that ought to be followed, but often is not, in the pay-setting process.

Throughout this chapter the words *wage* and *pay* are used to refer to labor compensation. These terms include fringe benefits such as pensions, health insurance, and life insurance, as well as cash wages. Chapter 7 analyzes HRM strategies regarding the mix of compensation among wages, benefits, and work conditions.

6-1 Demand in the Classical Model of Pay Determination

The classical economic model depicted the labor market as just another product market, the main difference being that what is called a *price* in the goods market

132

is relabeled a *wage* in the labor market. Chapter 2 on productivity reviewed the demand side of the classical labor market model. The model begins with the proposition that the demand for labor by employers is a derived demand; labor is not wanted for direct consumption, but only as a necessary input into the production process.

Labor Demand in the Short Run

In the labor market, despite this distinction between a direct demand and a derived demand, a normal downward sloping demand curve results. The short-run demand curve for labor at the level of the firm is the firm's marginal revenue product of labor (MRP_L) schedule. This schedule is, in turn, derived from the marginal product of labor (MP_L) function by placing a value on the marginal product.

The resulting demand curve for labor is described as short run because of the definition of marginal product. The marginal product of labor is the incremental production of an extra unit of labor, holding capital (and other factor inputs) *fixed*. It is a convention in economics to view capital as fixed in the short run, although variable in the long run. In the short run, factory or office management must work with the capital equipment already installed and must vary output mainly by varying labor input. Over a longer period the capital employed can be increased through new purchases and installation or decreased through sales, depreciation, or scrapping.

Recapitulating, the basic short-run formulas for labor demand are

$$MP_L = \partial Q/\partial L, \tag{1}$$

where Q is physical output and L is labor input,

$$MRP_L = MP_L \times P, \tag{2}$$

where P = price of the final product (or marginal revenue, in the case of an imperfectly competitive firm).

Due to diminishing marginal returns, the MRP_L schedule will have a downward sloping profile (as depicted in Figure 3–2). The firm will add units of labor to its workforce until it reaches the point at which

$$W = MRP_L, \tag{3}$$

where W is the wage per unit of labor. At the point corresponding to equality (3), profit maximization occurs.

If the firm hired fewer units of labor than correspond to equality (3), adding an additional unit would cost less than the incremental revenue that acquiring that unit would produce. A simple cost/benefit analysis indicates that the extra labor units should be added. Similarly, if the firm hired more units of labor than indicated by equality, the marginal units of labor will cost more than they are worth to the firm and should therefore be severed from the workforce.

Labor Demand in the Long Run

In the long run, both labor and capital are variable. The firm's capital/labor ratio can be changed in response to changes in the wage rate (W) relative to the rental cost of capital (R).[2] Common assumptions used to analyze this decision in microeconomics are that the firm's production function exhibits both constant returns to scale (for example, doubling all inputs will double output) and diminishing marginal productivity. Under these assumptions, a given level of output (say, level Q^*) has an associated *isoquant* curve relating all possible combinations of capital and labor inputs that could be used to produce that output.

Such an isoquant is shown in Figure 6–1 by curve I_1. The curve is downward sloping because labor and capital are assumed to be substitutes. If one factor is decreased, the other must be increased to maintain production at level Q^*. In addition, the isoquant is concave because of the diminishing returns assumption. For example, if units of capital are successively removed from the production process, progressively larger increments of labor will be required to maintain an unchanged level of output.

There is a family of isoquants representing alternative production levels. Higher isoquants represent more output, lower isoquants represent less. Due to the assumption of constant returns to scale, the isoquants have a proportional relationship to one another; that is, each isoquant is a radial projection of the others.

The slope of a ray from the origin represents a given capital/labor ratio. Isoquants intersecting such rays will all have the same slope at the intersection points because the curves are radial projections. The distance of these intersection

**FIGURE 6–1
Factor Selection in
the Long Run**

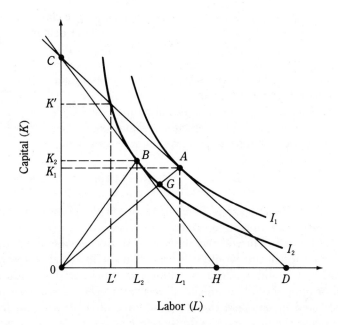

points from the origin is in direct relation to the output associated with the isoquant. For example, if isoquant I_2 represents 80% of output level Q^*, then OG in Figure 6–1 will be 80% of the length of OA.

Profit maximization implies producing the maximum output for a given expenditure on factor inputs. Total expenditure on such inputs will be $WL + RK$, where L is the level of labor input and K is the level of capital input. A given expenditure level (say, E^*), can be represented by a downward sloping straight line such as CD in Figure 6–1. Given E^*, the firm could purchase capital and labor inputs at any point along CD. For example, it would be feasible to purchase OK' of capital and OL' of labor and produce at the output level corresponding to I_2. But to do so would not be optimal, since higher isoquant curves can be reached with E^* expenditure.

The highest output will be Q^*, which is associated with isoquant I_1. Production will occur at point A, where the isoquant is just tangent to the expenditure line. Given expenditure E^*, the firm will purchase OK_1 of capital and OL_1 of labor. Its capital/labor ratio will be the slope of ray OA.

If labor became more expensive (an increase in wage W), the expenditure line would rotate clockwise around point C. The new expenditure line OH represents combinations of capital and labor that can be bought given the higher wage. Now the highest isoquant that can be reached is I_2 at point B. The new capital input will be OK_2 and the new labor input will be OL_2.

Note that usage of both capital and labor is decreased because of the wage increase but that the labor reduction is proportionately larger than the capital reduction. As a result, the capital/labor ratio (shown by the slope of ray OB) increases. When labor costs rise relative to capital costs, the firm substitutes capital for labor.

In the long run, then, a wage increase in the classical model sets in motion a complex set of forces that tend to reduce the demand for labor. First, firms substitute capital for labor. Second, since production costs have increased, prices will rise, leading to reductions in demand for output. Output will therefore be lower for the typical firm in the industry depicted and less labor will be needed as a result.[3]

Total Labor Market Demand

To determine the wage in the classical model, it is necessary to consider more than one firm, and to encompass both supply and demand in the analysis. In the labor market, many firms—often from many industries—are competing for available labor. Their individual demand curves must be summed to obtain the schedule for overall market demand for labor. Figure 6–2 illustrates how the demand curves of firm A and firm B (D_A and D_B) can be summed to produce a joint demand curve for the two firms (D_{A+B}).

At a wage of W^*, firm A would hire L_A units of labor and firm B would hire L_B units. The two firms together would hire $L_A + L_B = L_{A+B}$, a point on

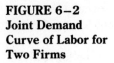

FIGURE 6–2
Joint Demand
Curve of Labor for
Two Firms

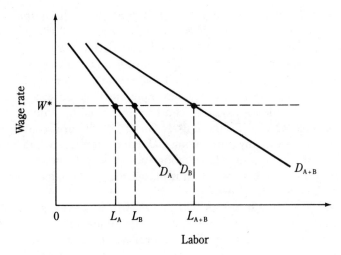

the D_{A+B} schedule. A similar calculation can be made for all possible wage levels, and the joint labor demand curve can be traced. This horizontal summation process can be repeated for all firms in the labor market to produce the total market demand curve for labor (D_T), which is shown in Figure 6–3.

Some Criticisms of Classical Demand Analysis

Over the years various criticisms have been leveled at classical labor demand analysis. A longstanding complaint about the classical model relates to its marginalist assumptions. Can firms really make the precise marginal calculations that are assumed in the short-run model? Do they really know whether the marginal revenue product of labor equals the wage? There is certainly little trace of such marginalist calculations in the ordinary day-to-day operations of real world firms or in their HRM practices. Typically, where cost estimates are made, they are likely to be total cost or average cost estimates rather than marginal.[4]

It may well be that production technology, once embodied in the capital equipment of the firm, is essentially of the fixed coefficient variety. That is, there is a basic capacity constraint imposed by the capital stock. Output below that capacity is varied on a roughly proportional basis through changes in labor and material inputs. The marginal product of labor may be a positive constant up to the capacity constraint and then fall to zero when the capacity limit is reached.[5]

Some analysts have argued that even in the long run the classical model as depicted in Figure 6–1 does not well describe the production decision process. For a given level of technological sophistication, capital and labor may be complements rather than substitutes, so that the capital/labor ratio is more or less fixed by technological imperatives. A boost in labor costs relative to capital costs may trigger innovations, so that new equipment involving a higher capital/labor ratio is ultimately developed. But the process of innovation is discontinuous, not

**FIGURE 6–3
Labor Market
Demand and
Supply Curves**

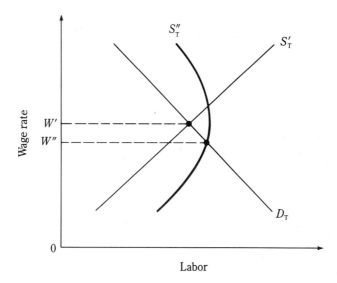

the smooth adjustment depicted in Figure 6–2. Further, many innovations may
be regarded as accidents unrelated to the relative costs of capital and labor. Once
installed, they become locked into the production process for long periods of
time.[6] (Other criticisms of the strict classical model are reviewed later in this
chapter.)

Some Uses of the Classical Labor Demand Model

In spite of these (valid) objections, classical labor demand theory still has an
important message. Generally, labor demand will be downward sloping as in
Figure 6–2, no matter what theories or models are put forward. A downward
sloping demand curve implies that less labor will be used as the wage is raised,
whether the demand curve under consideration is taken to represent a plant, a
firm, an industry, or all employers in a given area. This conclusion has important
implications for understanding labor market developments. Two examples are
discussed here: minimum-wage floors and union membership trends.

Legal Minimum-Wage Floors   Since 1938, the United States has set a federal
minimum wage forbidding covered employers from paying less than a designated
wage rate (originally 25¢ per hour). From time to time, Congress has seen fit to
raise the minimum. In the early 1980s the Fair Labor Standards Act (FLSA)
designated the minimum-wage level as $3.35 per hour. (The FLSA also requires
time and a half for hours over 40 worked per week, as discussed in the previous
chapter.)

The coverage of the FLSA was steadily widened, especially in the 1960s,
and by 1986 an estimated 87% of private sector nonsupervisory workers fell
under the FLSA's minimum-wage regulation.[7] Thanks to Congressional action in
the 1970s, and subsequent Supreme Court interpretation, nonsupervisory government workers are also covered. Many states have minimum-wage laws as well;

in fact, state minimums can exceed the federal level. When state minimums are higher than the federal, they supersede the FLSA. In addition, state laws apply to employers who are otherwise exempt from FLSA coverage.

Most covered workers in fact earn substantially more than the minimum wage. But certain industries, such as fast food restaurants, use significant numbers of minimum-wage workers, especially in periods immediately following a minimum wage increase. For industries that make heavy usage of relatively unskilled workers, the minimum wage is an effective constraint on their internal pay policies; such employers would pay a lower wage were such payments not illegal. Thus the FLSA is but one of many examples of legal restrictions on HRM practices.

Reduction of poverty is the most common argument made in favor of minimum-wage laws. Yet economists have generally been skeptical of the use of minimum-wage laws as antipoverty devices, precisely because the demand for labor is believed to be negatively sloped.[8] With a negatively sloped labor demand curve, a wage floor will result in less employment than would be offered in the absence of any constraint. Thus some potential low-wage workers may not be able to find work with covered employers because of the minimum wage.[9]

If workers are unable to find work at covered employers, they could conceivably shift their job searching to the uncovered sector. Were they to do so, however, wages would tend to be *lower* than otherwise in that sector because of the artificial increase in labor supply. Moreover, the uncovered sector is small and is further narrowed by state minimum-wage laws that reach small employers who do not meet the coverage standards of the FLSA.[10] Workers who do not find work at the minimum wage thus may simply be disemployed, that is, either unemployed and looking for work or simply out of the labor force entirely.

How large this disemployment effect may be has long been subject to empirical controversy. The size of the effect depends on the slope of the demand curve for unskilled workers. But to argue there is *no* disemployment effect whatsoever, minimum-wage proponents must come up with one of three types of arguments: They must (1) find a rationale for a vertical demand curve for labor, (2) produce a reason (or reasons) why the minimum wage would cause the labor demand curve to shift upwards sufficiently to offset disemployment, or (3) argue that the minimum wage is so low as to be ineffective.

It is difficult—if not impossible—to find a rationale for a vertical demand for labor curve. The negative slope of the classical model comes from two influences: (1) the substitution in production potential, for example, of capital for labor and (2) the negative slope of the demand for the outputs produced by labor. Even if the scope for production substitution is small, it is difficult to imagine why product market demand curves should not be negatively sloped. Hence the notion of a vertical demand curve for labor is not defensible. Of course, it might be argued—based on empirical evidence—that the elasticity of the demand for labor is low.

The second argument—that imposing a minimum wage raises the demand for labor curve—can be made in two ways. One is to argue that raising the minimum will redistribute income to low-wage workers, who will then spend more on the products they themselves produce than would otherwise be spent.

The difficulty with this approach is that the proportion of minimum-wage workers is small, so any income effects will also be small. Moreover, the argument is based on income redistribution, not creation. Any added spending of minimum-wage recipients must be netted against reduced spending by their employers.

Another possible argument revolves around what some economists have called X-efficiency. X-efficiency—or more appropriately for the purpose at hand, X-inefficiency—represents a departure from the classical economic model.[11] It refers to a margin of potential profit maximization that firms do not exploit unless "shocked" into doing so.

Actually, arguments that X-inefficiencies exist have a long history in business cycle analysis. Business cycle theories formulated in the early part of this century viewed depressions as periods in which business would be stimulated to end wasteful practices and cut costs. Booms were seen as periods when business became lazy. These ideas have lingered; reports that the economic slump of the 1980s and foreign competition made U.S. business "lean and mean" are really expressions of the X-inefficiency notion.

Some minimum-wage proponents have argued that imposing or raising a minimum wage acts as a shock, and causes employers who pay low wages to become more efficient (in other words, reduce their X-inefficiency), thus raising the demand for labor. Perhaps this was what President Lyndon Johnson had in mind when he defended a minimum-wage increase in the mid-1960s with the statement, "If a businessman can't do well with this minimum wage in our booming economy that we have today, perhaps he might not be just a good businessman."[12]

The shock approach, like the income approach, raises an analytical problem. There may well be X-inefficiency in the economy, contrary to the assumptions of the classical economic model. Assuming that there is such inefficiency, however, it is unclear why shocks to eliminate it would necessarily result in *more* employment.

Suppose an X-inefficient employer were neglecting to utilize a profitable, labor-displacing technology. If shocked into more efficient operation, the employer would *reduce* its workforce, not increase it. In other words, there is no a priori reason to believe that shock effects must create more jobs, even assuming that such shock effects occur in the first place.

A third possible argument by minimum-wage proponents is that the wage is so low that very few workers will be affected. This argument was particularly prominent in the late 1980s, because the $3.35 minimum wage had remained unchanged for a long period while the general wage level rose.[13] In the limiting case, if market wages drifted upward to the point where no one earned as low as the minimum, an incremental adjustment in that minimum would have no effect. Indeed, employers interviewed in 1988, seven years after the previous hike in the minimum wage, reported that an increase in the minimum wage was expected to have little effect on employment.[14]

There are some difficulties with the low minimum argument. Even if relatively few workers at a firm earn the minimum, raising it will lead to a compression of the wage structure at the bottom. Employees at somewhat higher wages may feel that a narrowing of their wage premium relative to the lowest paid workers creates an inequity, and employers may respond by pushing up their wages. Some evidence exists that this effect occurs.[15] Thus the minimum may affect more workers than just those legally required to receive an adjustment.

More important, if few people are covered by the minimum, then raising it will also benefit relatively few. Under such circumstances, the benefit of raising the minimum, which is usually thought of as a reduction in poverty, must also be very small. The fact that the cost is small may be outweighed by an offsetting small benefit.

There are other elements in the minimum-wage debate. For example, most workers employed at or below the minimum wage come from families with incomes above the official poverty line.[16] Teenagers from middle class families, for example, may work at the minimum. Raising the minimum may cause employers to make substitutions between different low-wage groups, thus redistributing income in complex ways.[17] Similarly, lowering the minimum wage just for teenagers—as has been proposed from time to time—may cause adult workers to lose jobs.[18]

Despite these other important considerations, the debate over the impact of the minimum wage illustrates the use of the classical economic model of demand to analyze a pay-setting issue. In spite of the model's weaknesses, it does provide a framework for the debate. Proponents of minimum-wage increases must ultimately answer the question: Why won't raising the wage reduce the demand for low-wage labor or particular kinds of low-wage labor? The answers can be judged in terms of their plausibility and supporting empirical evidence.

Union Membership Trends   A variety of issues related to unions and collective bargaining will be discussed in a subsequent chapter. By way of preview, one of the most important phenomena in the private union sector has been its shrinkage relative to nonunion employment. In the mid-1950s unions represented as many as 40% of private, nonfarm wage and salary employees.[19] By 1987 the proportion had fallen to only 15%.[20]

At the same time that the proportion of unionized workers was falling, union pay rates were generally rising compared with nonunion. Only in the 1980s did the widening of the union/nonunion pay differential notably reverse, as part of a general movement toward union pay concessions. The classical approach to labor demand illuminates the relationship between the rising wage and the decline in the unionization rate.

Classical demand theory would predict that rising union pay differentials would trigger a relative fall in the demand for services of union workers. The market would tend to substitute cheaper nonunion workers for more expensive union workers. Nonunion employers would attempt to avoid unionization; unionized employers would attempt to convert to nonunion status.[21] Eventually shrinkage of the union sector would weaken unions sufficiently so that the widening union pay differential could no longer be maintained.

Obviously it will be important to look further into the phenomenon of declining union representation in a later chapter. However, the fact that classical labor demand theory helps explain developments in the union sector is well worth noting. It illustrates that such theory, despite its many unrealistic elements, can nevertheless be useful in understanding actual labor market trends.

6–2 Supply in the Classical Model of Pay Determination

In the complete classical model, the wage is determined by the interaction of demand and supply. Whereas demand ultimately is a byproduct of the production processes used by the many firms in the labor market, labor supply is a matter of the tastes and preferences of individual workers or potential workers. The labor market offers workers a choice—a trade-off—between income and leisure. They can supply their services to the labor market and receive wage income. Or they can forgo working and have more leisure.

In textbook presentations of supply in a goods market, the supply curves are often depicted with the general upward-sloping shape of line S_T' in Figure 6–3. The notion is that the more the market pays for something, the more of that good will be produced. This proposition is intuitively appealing. In the labor case, however, there can be very different results. It is possible for labor supply to *diminish* as the wage is raised.

Consider Figure 6–4, which represents an individual's choice between leisure and labor-generated income. As noted in the previous chapter, at a constant wage per unit of time, the individual faces a linear trade-off, such as line AB, between leisure and work-related income. The individual has an endowment of

**FIGURE 6–4
Individual Labor
Supply Decisions**

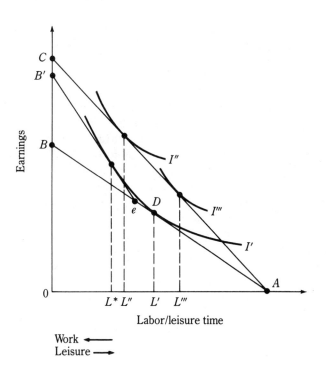

potential labor time, *OA,* which can be divided between work and leisure. Given the trade-off line *AB,* the individual will supply labor corresponding to the point where his or her highest indifference curve between income and leisure is reached. In Figure 6−4, this level of labor supply is *L'* and the highest attainable indifference curve is *I'*.

At a given level of utility, the individual would indeed provide more labor, if marginal income gains were higher than the wage rate underlying line *AB*— that is, the slope of indifference curve *I'* is steeper, going leftwards from point *D,* and flatter going rightwards. Raising (lowering) the wage, however, raises (lowers) the potential level of utility. At a high wage the individual can receive more income from a given level of labor supplied than at a lower wage. Thus two effects are operating: a substitution effect between leisure and income (reflected in the convex shape of the indifference curve) and an income effect.

If leisure is what economists call a superior good, an increase in income (other influences held constant) will produce a greater relative demand for leisure, that is, an increase in the amount of potential income spent on leisure. But if leisure is an inferior good, a boost in income will reduce the relative consumption of leisure time. Only in the inferior case will the substitution effect and the income effect work in the same direction when wages are increased or decreased. If leisure is inferior, for example, a wage increase will always lead to an increase in labor supply. But when leisure is superior, a wage increase could lead to a cutback in labor supply, if the income effect overcomes the substitution effect.

To illustrate, in Figure 6−4 the individual depicted is shown as experiencing a wage increase, thus rotating his or her leisure−income trade-off line in a clockwise direction to *AC.* If the individual's higher indifference curves are similar to *I'',* labor supply will increase from *AL'* to *AL''.* But if the higher indifference curves are similar to *I''',* then labor supply will drop from *AL'* to *AL'''* when wages are increased.

Neither result shown in Figure 6−4 should be regarded as irrational or illogical; each result is simply a question of individual preference. A person characterized by more of the Puritan work ethic will have indifference curves such as *I'',* and will increase labor supplied as wages rise. An individual who just wants to earn enough to get by or to live comfortably will cut labor supply beyond a certain wage level as pay rates continue to rise. This reduction occurs because the individual's target income can be achieved with reduced labor and more leisure when wage rates increase.[22]

Figure 6−5 shows the segments of the individual supply curve that can be derived from the indifference curve analysis of Figure 6−4. Let W_B correspond to the wage underlying line *AB* in Figure 6−4 and W_C correspond to the wage underlying *AC.* The individual with higher indifference curve *I''* will have a normal supply curve segment that looks like *ab* of Figure 6−5. The individual with indifference curve *I'''* will have segment *ac.* Because of its negative slope, economists refer to supply schedules such as *ac* as backward bending.

Just as the firms' demand curves were summed up to produce an overall market demand curve, so the individual labor supply curves of all workers or

FIGURE 6–5
Segments of
Individual Labor
Supply Curves

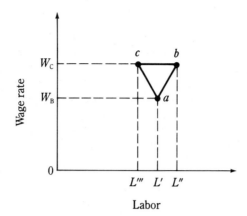

potential workers can also be summed to produce a total labor supply schedule. If many individuals have backward bending supply curves, the aggregate market labor supply schedule may look like S_T'' in Figure 6–3. But if there are more Puritan-ethic types, the labor supply will look like S_T'.

6–3 Some Uses for the Classical Labor Supply Concept

The preceding analysis of labor supply behavior is highly abstract. And, as will be noted in later chapters, the classical economic model of the labor market obscures and distorts many aspects of real world behavior. For example, the decision to supply labor is not affected by considerations of job availability or unemployment in the classical model, because the labor market is assumed always to clear. Nevertheless, the model has some interesting implications for HRM policy.

Voluntary Overtime

In the classical economic model, the individual employer has no labor market power. As a small player in a vast labor market, the employer simply accepts the going market wage and hires accordingly or refrains from hiring. But the real world employer does have power relative to employees and a certain scope for changing wages at the firm level. Consider a firm that wants to induce its current employees to work more hours per week than they have in the past. Given the indifference curve analysis just presented, what kind of a pay schedule would best induce workers to supply more labor hours to the firm on a voluntary basis?

One possibility would be for the employer simply to raise wage rates across the board and then wait to see if more labor were offered at the new, higher wage. Figure 6–4 suggests that this strategy might not be successful. If the workforce was characterized by workers with indifference curves such as I''', the income effect would more than offset the substitution effect. Thus, at a higher wage, workers might prefer to put in *fewer* hours on the job, not more.

Faced with a backward bending labor supply schedule, the employer might, of course, consider reducing wages instead of increasing them. Such a reduction, however, might raise worker turnover, reduce morale, or in other ways produce counterproductive results. Yet there is an alternative to both across-the-board wage cuts or wage increases, one that we have already discussed.

Even if the labor supply curve is not backward bending, raising the general wage rate might not be in the best interests of the employer, who is seeking extra hours of labor. If wages are raised, the employer will pay higher wages not only for the extra hours, but also for hours that are already being supplied at the current wage rate.

As a solution, the employer could pay a premium wage applicable only to the *incremental* hours that the firm needed. Paying overtime is a form of such a premium. An overtime pay premium breaks the leisure–income trade-off line into two differently sloped segments, illustrated by the broken line AeB' in Figure 6–4. The premium-related segment eB' emphasizes the substitution effect embodied in indifference curve I'. But it also avoids triggering the offsetting income effect, since the premium wage applies only to the incremental labor hours, and not to the regular hours that were previously worked. The income effect is not triggered because if the employee chooses not to supply extra labor time, he or she will not receive any income increase.

As shown in Figure 6–4, the worker will be just indifferent between working the old AL' level of labor input and the higher level AL^*. A slight increase in the overtime pay premium above that underlying line segment eB' will induce the worker to prefer the longer hours and to volunteer for overtime. Thus the classical model of labor supply provides a rationale for overtime pay premiums, which— as noted in the previous chapter —employers often paid even before they were required to do so under federal law. A premium for overtime hours, as opposed to a general wage increase, avoids much of the income effect, thus guaranteeing a willingness to supply more hours of work. This premium also targets the extra pay just to the incremental hours needed by the employer.[23]

Absenteeism

Employers in the real world do not usually permit employees to select how many hours to work per week free of any constraints. Some individual flexibility may be allowed, for example, the decision whether or not to work overtime, but typically there are normal hours per week during which the employee is expected to be on the job. Since such constraints do exist, individual workers may not be entirely free to reach their highest indifference curves, given their pay rates.

If a firm has rules about normal work hours, employees who violate those rules through unexcused absences can be disciplined or terminated. Repeated exercise of discipline and termination as HRM policies may be costly. Moreover, an employer who detects a severe absenteeism problem should view it as a symptom of inequality of marginal rewards for labor hours supplied and the value of those hours to employees. If employees are effectively reducing their labor supply via absenteeism, there may be a remedy available in the pay system.

As in the overtime case, one solution might be to raise pay across the board. But, it is not clear that higher pay would necessarily induce reduced absenteeism. It could have the reverse effect, if workers' preferences are basically to earn a target income. In some cases higher pay might lead to a greater demand for leisure and more absenteeism.

In principle the firm could try to produce an elaborate pay schedule with rising wages for each hour of work supplied. Rather than just a straight time rate and an overtime rate, there could theoretically be many progressively higher, in-between rates. Such a proliferation of wage rates, however, would be difficult for the employer to administer.

Some employers find a compromise solution by using a bonus system. Employers can offer lump-sum financial rewards to those workers who have good attendance records. Such bonuses effectively add a wage premium to those hours that might otherwise be lost to absenteeism. A bonus system is not especially difficult to administer, assuming that employee absenteeism records are kept. The analysis presented here suggests that employers *should* keep such records, since rising or too-high absenteeism indicates the presence of a pay problem that needs to be addressed.

Influence on Worker Preferences

The indifference curves shown in Figure 6–3 are reflections of individual tastes. However, such preferences can be influenced. Use by economists of the word *leisure* to represent the alternative to work is misleading. Leisure suggests that nonworking hours are spent at the beach or the golf course or just "goofing off." In fact, employees' nonworking hours are often programmed with family responsibilities, which are reflected in employee tastes.

Worker preferences with regard to work hours reflects the *scheduling* of those hours as well as the total number of hours. By adjusting the schedule of working hours to accord with external demands on worker time, the employer can effectively reduce the marginal value of leisure. Some firms, for example, have experimented with flexitime (or flextime) arrangements under which employees are permitted some freedom in scheduling the time of day they work, even though total hours are designated by the employer. Other firms have rescheduled work to permit more concentrated family time, for example, allowing for four 10-hour days rather than five 8-hour days per week. Finally, some employers provide or subsidize child care arrangements to alleviate household demands on worker hours.[24] These policies reduce the value of nonworking time relative to working time for employees, thus cutting absenteeism costs to the employer.

6–4   Interaction of Demand and Supply in the Classical Model

The simple classical model of demand and supply in the labor market produces a single, going-wage rate. An auctionlike process is assumed to operate, similar to what is observed in financial and commodity markets. Suppose the wage rate were somehow set too low, so that there is an excess demand for labor (a shortage). The wage would be quickly bid up to the market clearing level where demand equals supply. Similarly, if there were a too high wage, so that supply exceeded demand (a glut), the wage would be bid down to the market clearing level. Thus in Figure 6–3 the market clearing wage will be W', if the supply schedule is S_T'. If the supply schedule is instead represented by S_T'', the market clearing wage will be W''.

In this simple demand/supply framework, firms do not have their own wage policies. From the viewpoint of the firm, the wage is simply given by the market. The firm does not offer a wage below the going rate, since no workers will accept jobs at below-market pay levels. Workers always have the opportunity to accept jobs at the market wage from other employers; why should they work for less than that rate of pay?

Just as workers would not see any advantage in accepting below-market wages in the classical economic model, so firms would not benefit by offering above-market wages. Any firm that did pay above the market could easily hire all the workers it wanted; indeed, all workers in the market would be most anxious to work at the firm. The lucky job recipients would be enjoying what economists call rents (windfalls) for their services. If it paid above the market, the firm would simply be paying more than was necessary to obtain labor. It would be putting itself at a cost disadvantage relative to its product market competitors, and it would be cutting into its own profits.

Critical Assumptions of the Classical Model

The single wage rate conclusion from the simple classical model follows from a number of key assumptions, some of which were discussed in earlier chapters as unrealistic. The conclusion assumes there is perfect labor market information, that is, firms and workers have no trouble locating each other. Everyone knows the market wage rate immediately; there are no wage differentials resulting from ignorance because there is no ignorance.

In addition the classical model assumes that all labor in the relevant market is homogeneous; there is no variation in individual characteristics that might affect the employee's value to the firm. There is no cheating or shirking in the market. All aspects of the labor market contract are understood by employers and workers, and everyone fulfills his or her part of the bargain.

Two Key Problems with the Model

It is easy to criticize the assumptions underlying the classical economic model because they clearly depart from reality. Workers, we know, are not homogeneous. There are problems and costs involved in acquiring information in the labor market. And there may be employee cheating and shirking, which require costly incentive corrections or supervision. Similarly, employers may not always keep their side of the employment bargain, whether that bargain is implicit or explicit.

Of course, all models are oversimplified and depart from reality in some respects. A key issue is what the empirical evidence shows about the model's predictions. There are really two predictions from the classical model of pay determination. First, it is predicted that there is only one rate of pay in the marketplace (although we must worry about exactly what we mean by *market*). Second, the model predicts that the labor market always clears; there is no excess demand or supply (except in certain deviant cases involving market power, which are discussed below).

Diversified Rates of Pay

One of the most striking features of labor market data is the diversity of observed pay rates. For example, data from the decennial Censuses of Population show large variations in earnings across occupations, regions, age brackets, and educational levels. According to Table 6–1, for example, mean earnings of full-time, year-round workers varied substantially, as reported in the 1980 Census. In 1979 waitresses averaged $6,554, whereas accountants and auditors received $23,835.

Clearly, Table 6–1 does not show a single rate of pay for labor. Yet there is a quick comeback for someone defending the classical model. The response would be that the different occupations are not part of the same labor market; they involve different skills, different levels of education, and so on. Of course

TABLE 6–1   Mean Annual Earnings of Full-Time, Year-Round Workers, 1979

Category of Workers	*Males*	*Females*
Accountants and auditors	$23,835	$13,629
Receptionists	13,642	8,792
Waiters and waitresses	9,673	6,554
Aircraft engine mechanics	20,481	14,849
Upholsterers	12,452	8,082

Source: Data from U.S. Bureau of the Census, *1980 Census of Population, Earnings by Occupation and Education*, PC80–2–8B (Washington: GPO, 1984), Table 2.

there are pay differentials across such a diverse group, it can be argued, because workers across occupations are not perfect substitutes for one another.

This defense of the classical model is certainly valid, as far as it goes. The differentials shown on Table 6–1 are not necessarily inconsistent with the single-wage prediction of the classical model. Adam Smith, the father of classical economic analysis, would have been quick to point out that occupational wage differentials should be expected. Indeed, in his famous *Wealth of Nations* (originally published in 1776), Smith cited various reasons for pay differentials, even apart from occupational skills. He expected conditions of work, pleasant or unpleasant, to result in what are now called compensating wage differentials, holding other influences constant.[25] If other things were constant, more pleasant jobs would pay less than unpleasant jobs.[26]

Although there are obvious causes of wage differentials that do not violate the classical model, Table 6–1, even with its overly broad occupational selection, poses some problems for the single wage rate prediction. Why do males consistently earn more than females within occupations in the table? Are there hidden skill differences that explain the differences in pay between the sexes? Certainly, there have been attempts to reconcile such sex-linked differences with classical theory. As will be seen in a later chapter, such attempts have not answered all of the questions raised.

If a labor market is to be defined empirically, which would approximate the market of the classical model, the analysis must be confined to a single occupation. It should also remain within a relatively narrow geographical region so that employee mobility between employers could occur at low cost. As Table 6–2 illustrates, even when such narrow definitions are used, what emerges is a range of pay rates, not a single number.

Table 6–2 is derived from one of many area wage surveys regularly conducted by the U.S. Bureau of Labor Statistics in about seventy urban areas. The survey used for Table 6–2 was confined to the Los Angeles–Long Beach Metropolitan area. Occupations reported are precisely defined for survey purposes in terms of skills and responsibilities. Yet for the two occupations shown in the table—"level-1" secretaries and drivers of light trucks—the dispersion of pay rates reported is very wide.[27]

Some employers evidently pay substantially above or below the median wage for a given occupation. Although there is some clumping of observations near the median wage, the median does not correspond to the going wage in the classical sense. It is simply a measure of central tendency within a scattered distribution.

Table 6–2 also reveals that larger firms often pay more for the same kind of occupation than do smaller firms. Median truck driver wages for larger firms are 64% higher than the level for all surveyed employers. This gap may well reflect a greater tendency for larger firms to be unionized at the blue-collar level. For secretaries, who are rarely unionized even in large firms, there is a much smaller relative pay premium associated with bigger employers.

Of course, it is always possible to argue that even narrow labor market definitions, such as those underlying Table 6–2, are not narrow enough. Accord-

TABLE 6–2 Range of Earnings of Secretaries and Truckdrivers in the Los Angeles–Long Beach, California Metropolitan Area, October, 1987

Weekly Earnings	Number of Surveyed Secretaries Level-1*	Straight-Time Hourly Earnings	Number of Surveyed Truckdrivers, Light Trucks
$200–219	31	$4.50–5.99	7
220–239	31	5.00–5.49	71
240–259	—	5.50–5.99	517
260–279	29	6.00–6.49	464
280–299	185	6.50–6.99	615
300–319	158	7.00–7.49	98
320–339	215	7.50–7.99	34
340–359	312	8.00–8.49	124
360–379	291	8.50–8.99	14
380–399	294	9.00–9.49	4
400–419	151	9.50–9.99	8
420–439	151	10.50–10.99	15
440–479	74	11.00–11.99	110
480–519	16	12.00–12.99	19
520–559	8	13.00–13.99	2
		14.00–14.99	18

Type of Firm	Median Weekly Wage	Type of Firm	Median Hourly Wage
All firms in survey	$361.00	All firms in survey	$6.70
Firms with at least 500 workers	$369.00	Firms with at least 500 workers	$10.94

*Nonmanufacturing.

Source: Data from U.S. Bureau of Labor Statistics, *Area Wage Survey: Los Angeles–Long Beach, California, Metropolitan Area, October 1987*, bulletin 3040–45 (Washington: GPO, 1988), pp. 3, 11, 16, 22.

ing to such views, the observed pay differences are simply the result of unmeasured variations in worker skills or occupational titles. The problem with such defenses is that they are untestable. They can neither be affirmed nor refuted. By definition, the unmeasurable cannot be measured.

A simpler and more sensible approach is to recognize that firms in fact have differentiated pay policies. For internal reasons, some employers choose to pay more than others, even within narrowly defined occupations. Other employers are compelled to pay more than they would like because of union pressures. Before considering the concept of pay policy, which will be developed later, it would be useful to discuss the other prediction of the classical economic model—namely, market clearing. Does the pay determination mechanism within labor markets cause them to clear?

Market Clearing and Shortages

From time to time employers complain that they can't get enough good help, or they report continuing vacancies for particular occupations. Such complaints generally do not accord with the classical economic model of wage determination. If an employer needs more workers in a given occupation, why not simply raise the pay level until such workers are attracted?

Indeed, occupations affected by labor shortages normally will experience above-average pay increases. But the adjustment process may be slow, unlike the instantaneous market clearing suggested by the classical model. In the face of a shortage, employers may first try to make do with the workers they have, perhaps assigning individuals whose skill levels do not quite meet normal standards to perform the work. They may increase overtime hours for current employees despite the premium pay involved. Or they may offer training to workers to produce the skills needed, although before the shortage they relied on the market to supply the required skills.[28] "We don't go through applications to pick the most qualified any more. Now we hire anybody, and say 'Be all that you can be.' "[29]

In short, employers first look for ways to avoid wage increases when they experience labor shortages. Indeed, the historical evidence suggests that labor shortages during World War I were responsible for the first big surge in adoption of modern HRM policies. Employers looked at HRM as an alternative to wage increases in the face of excess demand for labor sparked by the war.[30]

Sometimes the reluctance to raise wages of a particular occupational group is linked to notions of inter-occupational equity that become embedded in the workforce. Employers may feel that if they raise the wage of one group, other groups (that are not in short supply) will want comparable increases. In such situations, morale and productivity might suffer, or possibly union organizers would be attracted by the employee discontent. Rather than upset workplace relations, the employer may decide to cope with the shortage through means other than overt wage increases.

Where unions are already present, the potential workplace discontent over advancing pay of one group relative to another has a channel of expression. For example, school boards complained in the early 1980s of chronic shortages of math and science teachers, who could earn superior incomes in industry. The market solution would have been to raise the salaries of just math and science teachers, but not those of others. However, teacher unions, which represent all specialties, were reluctant to see the traditional, uniform pay schedule disturbed.

If math and science teachers received pay increases, they argued, perhaps history and English teachers would become resentful, both at their employer and at their union. Cross-sectional equity was a concern. In addition, teacher unions may have hoped to use the shortages of math and science teachers as a bargaining tool to induce school boards to grant across-the-board pay increases for all teachers.

One rationale employers sometimes offer for reluctance to raise wages in the face of a shortage is that they end up bidding against one another for a limited labor supply. As one employer put it, "All that happens is that one business is 'stealing' from another business."[31] While this rationale is valid for all employers taken together, in a competitive labor market no one employer should be large enough for this rationale to matter. The fact that wage-raising can lure employees from other employers should keep the bidding going and clear the market. Only in the special case of monopsony (a market with one buyer)—discussed later in this chapter—does such an explanation fit into the classical model.

Although labor shortages may not accord with the classical economic model of pay determination, many analysts have found advantages for society in such shortages. During the two world wars, for example, anyone who wanted to work could readily find a job. Indeed, employers were literally begging for labor to meet military production goals. As noted in the previous chapter, profit-sharing plans have been advocated as devices to produce artificial labor shortages that would simulate such wartime-type conditions.

The fact that wartime periods of labor shortage are viewed as golden ages for workers is a reflection of the tendency of the labor market more often to fail to clear in the other direction. When regional labor shortages have developed in peacetime, as in the case of parts of New England during the mid-1980s, the rest of the country became envious. It is more common for the economy to face significant unemployment problems than to have generalized labor shortages. Shortages are seen as good news, except to the extent they bring about inflation.

Market Clearing and Unemployment

Shortages may be seen as good news, but unemployment never is. The degree to which the political system has regarded unemployment as a major policy issue has varied. But unemployment has traditionally been viewed as an important social problem.

A cleared labor market should not exhibit unemployment. Unemployed workers represent excess supply, a sign the labor market has failed to clear. The existence of unemployment has always been a thorn in the side of classical economic theory. Ultimately, it cannot be reconciled with a simple demand/supply framework of the type shown in Figure 6–3.

Most economists ignored the unemployment issue until the Great Depression of the 1930s. There were two basic reasons for avoiding the subject. One was that there were no good measures of unemployment available, especially in the United States. The measurement of unemployment in a rigorous fashion by government statistical agencies did not begin in the United States until the 1940s. (Reported figures on unemployment during the 1930s, which now appear in statistical handbooks, are guestimates made long after that period had passed.)

A second reason that unemployment was largely ignored was that joblessness was taken to be a temporary aberration in the labor market, a transitory maladjustment that would be resolved. Or it was assumed that unemployment could usefully be viewed as a voluntary condition. According to this latter view, if the unemployed truly wanted to work, they would bid down the prevailing wage until someone offered to hire them.

The Great Depression was so severe and so extended in duration, however, that the maladjustment or voluntary unemployment views became indefensible. A theory of macroeconomics developed, associated with the British economist John Maynard Keynes.[32] This new theory sought to remove the focus from wage setting as the solution to unemployment.

Keynes insisted that the wage mechanism could not clear the labor market. He argued that the solution to the problem of the labor market lay, paradoxically, outside that market. Details of Keynesian theory—and criticisms of it—are best left to macroeconomics courses. But Keynes's essential point was simple enough.

Classical microeconomic theory, as we already know, predicts that firms will operate where $W = MRP_L = MP_L \times P$. Thus $W/P = MP_L$. W/P is the real wage, that is, the wage expressed in terms of its purchasing power over the final product.[33] According to Keynes, if wages were cut in the face of unemployment, prices would fall proportionately, because wages are ultimately the major factor in costs. If wages and prices fell proportionately, their ratio W/P would be unchanged, and no new employment would be created. Thus, only government, according to Keynes, through monetary and fiscal policies, could cause the labor market to clear by maintaining adequate aggregate demand in the economy.[34]

Although unemployment has never returned to the very high levels of the 1930s, its continued existence after World War II remained a challenge to economic thought. By the 1970s, a substantial body of theoretical literature regarding the failure of the labor market to clear had produced insights valuable to the understanding of HRM practice. Some of this literature was meant as a criticism of Keynesian views. Other elements were intended to rationalize or supplement the Keynesian explanation of labor market failure. These new views, involving implicit contracting and efficiency wages, will be discussed in later sections.

There are few today who would argue that the simple demand/supply framework of Figure 6–3 adequately describes the overall functioning of the labor market.[35] Some would argue that the classical story is basically correct, but simply needs to be modified and extended. Others would say that the modifications needed are so extensive as to require a completely new theory. Despite its weaknesses in explaining macroeconomic phenomena, however, the older classical theory can provide insights into certain micro issues.

6–5   Supply/Demand Analysis and General Wage Trends

Although the labor market does not clear in the manner suggested by classical economic theory, supply and demand pressures do influence pay trends. At the micro level, prolonged shortages will raise wages of those groups affected relative to others, and prolonged surpluses will have the opposite effect. At the macro level, generalized labor shortages will eventually lead to wage inflation. Large-scale unemployment, in contrast, will be associated with reduced wage inflation and can even lead to wage cuts.

Demographic Influences on Wage Trends

Two illustrations will serve to demonstrate both the uses and the limitations of supply/demand analysis at the micro level. (The macro evidence is discussed in a subsequent chapter.) Table 6–3 shows the ratio of the wages of young people (16–24 years olds) to the wages of older people (25 years and above), from the late 1960s to the mid-1980s. Demographic changes in the population (the post–World War II baby boom) caused a bulge of young people to enter the labor market during the 1970s. Other things being equal, this increase in relative supply would be expected to depress wages of younger workers relative to those of older workers.[36] Indeed, that is precisely what occurred in the 1970s.

On the other hand, the bulge phenomenon reversed in the 1980s as the generation of the baby bust (low birthrates in the 1960s) came of labor market age. It might have been expected that wage trends of the 1980s would have responded to this demographic reversal. But, in fact, the relative wage of younger workers went on declining.

Some influences behind this continued trend were the freezing of the minimum wage after 1980 and the general state of the labor market during the early

TABLE 6–3   Demographic Influences on Wages, 1967–1987

Year	Median Weekly Earnings of Full-Time Workers (Ratio: Wage for Younger Workers to Wage for Older Workers*)		Young People as Percent of the Civilian Labor Force[†]
	Males	Females	
1967	74%	94%	20%
1972	66	87	23
1977	62	81	24
1982	56	75	22
1987	54	70	19

*Younger workers are those aged 16–24 years; older workers are those aged 25 years or more.

[†]Young people are those aged 16–24 years.

Source: Data from U.S. Bureau of Labor Statistics, *Labor Force Statistics Derived from the Current Population Survey: A Databook, Volume 1,* bulletin 2096 (Washington: GPO, 1982), p. 726; U.S. Bureau of Labor Statistics, *Handbook of Labor Statistics,* bulletin 2217 (Washington: GPO, 1985), p. 10; U.S. Bureau of the Census, *Statistical Abstract of the United States: 1987* (Washington: GPO, 1987), pp. 378, 402; *Employment and Earnings,* vol. 35 (January 1988), pp. 160, 216.

1980s. The 1980s initially saw very high unemployment. Thereafter, as the economy recovered from recession, unemployment did not fall to pre-recession levels until early 1987. Since young people were new entrants into the labor market, their pay was particularly sensitive to labor market slackness.[37]

Another factor that adversely affected young people's pay in the 1980s was the changing composition of the workforce. New jobs tended to open in lower paid service and retail trade industries. Foreign competition, among other factors, created stagnation in higher paying manufacturing. Thus entry into higher paying jobs was made more difficult than had been the case previously.[38]

If wage trends for young people are to be understood, a *combination* of influences must be considered. Demographic influences in the 1970s are consistent with the classical supply/demand model. On the other hand, periods of extended unemployment such as that from the early to mid-1980s—although relevant to demographic wage trends—are not consistent with the simple demand/supply economic model. Also inconsistent are hiring systems that establish entry jobs geared to young people and make hiring in those jobs especially sensitive to product market conditions. In other words, in the simple model, employers would not seek to shield incumbent senior workers (insiders) from labor market conditions at the expense of potential new hires (outsiders).

Occupational Wage Analysis

Table 6–4 illustrates an occupational wage trend, a second example of the use of demand/supply analysis. The table shows wages for elementary and secondary school teachers as a percentage of economy-wide wages from the early 1960s to the mid-1980s. Until the early 1970s baby boomers caused school enrollments to rise rapidly. Thereafter the baby bust led to declining enrollments. If other factors held constant, we would expect the period of increasing enrollments to boost the demand for teachers and to pull up their relative wages. Similarly, declining enrollments should reverse this wage trend.

According to the table, relative teacher salaries generally moved as expected until the mid-1980s. By that time two factors seemed to be boosting teacher pay. First, there was general concern, as expressed in reports of official commissions, that the quality of the American educational system was declining.[39] Such factors as falling SAT scores were often cited as evidence of this decline. It was argued that raising teacher pay would lead to an increase in teacher quality.

A second influence was what is sometimes called a "cobweb" effect.[40] The decline in teacher pay, with a lag, discouraged young people from entering the teaching profession. Eventually, shortages began to appear for certain specialties, triggering pay increases for both new hires and incumbents. Undoubtedly, as information about teacher pay opportunities spreads, more young people will decide to make careers in the field. If teacher salaries continue their relative rise, perhaps a rush to enroll in teacher training programs will produce a future labor market glut. In other words, lags in market perceptions—and those caused by the time involved to complete training programs—can produce cycles of excess demand and supply.[41]

TABLE 6-4   Trends in Pay of Teachers and in Elementary and Secondary School Enrollments, 1960-1986

Year	Annualized Percent Change in Enrollments from Prior Year Shown	Average Teacher Salary*	Teacher Salary as Percent of Wages and Salaries per Full-Time Equivalent Employee[†]
1960	+3.6%	$5,000	104%
1965	+2.8	6,200	107
1970	+1.1	8,600	111
1975	−.6	11,700	108
1980	−1.6	16,000	102
1986	−.4[‡]	25,200	115

*Refers to 12-month period ending in June in year listed.

[†]Wages and salaries per full-time equivalent employee refers to all-industry average.

[‡]Estimate.

Source: Data from U.S. Bureau of the Census, *Statistical Abstract of the United States: 1988* (Washington: GPO, 1988), pp. 122, 130; U.S. Bureau of Economic Analysis, *The National Income & Product Accounts of the United States, 1929–82, Statistical Tables* (Washington: GPO, 1986), Table 6.8B; *Survey of Current Business,* vol. 67 (July 1987), p. 61.

Using demand/supply analysis can be helpful to HRM practitioners. Employers can make projections of their future labor costs and hiring problems if they can forecast labor market trends for the kinds of occupations and groups they typically hire. Thus operators of fast-food chains could have foreseen that the labor on which they depend, based on demographic projections in the 1960s, would be widely available and relatively cheap during the following decade. School boards in the 1980s, with knowledge of recent public demands for higher quality, as well as an upcoming baby "boomlet" (as baby boomers have babies), must now plan for higher labor costs until the teacher labor market comes into a better balance.

6-6   Exercise of Labor Market Power

One exception to classical competitive assumptions that still falls within the spirit of the classical model involves labor market monopsony power on the part of employers. Another exception is union bargaining power. These special cases could result respectively, in labor shortages or surpluses that can be understood through simple supply/demand analysis.

Employer Monopsony Power and Labor Shortages

The classical labor market, with many buyers and sellers, is generally pictured as competitive. However, there can be exceptions to this structure. Given costs of mobility to workers, situations could arise in which an employer or a relatively small number of employers could influence wage rates by deliberately limiting their demands on the job market. Such HRM strategies are called *monopsonistic* by economists. The word refers to a market with one buyer, just as the more common term *monopoly* refers to a market with one seller.

Perhaps the best illustration of such a market would be a company town in which a single employer is the only demander of labor. If mobility into or out of the town is costly (perhaps the town is in a remote location), the employer will have monopsony power over the workforce. Figure 6–6 depicts the result.

Line D_L on Figure 6–6 is the demand for labor in the town. The assumed supply curve is S_L.[42] The competitive wage for this case would be W_1, where demand meets supply. Similarly, the competitive employment level would be L_1. However, the situation is not competitive. For the employer each unit of labor hired is more costly than the wage at which hiring occurs. This extra cost is incurred because the employer must raise the wages of previously hired workers in order to attract the incremental labor unit. Thus the marginal cost of labor schedule (M_L) lies above S_L at every point to the right of the vertical axis.

A profit-maximizing employer will hire labor until the marginal revenue resulting from the hire just equals its marginal cost (m). For the employer of Figure 6–6, this equality occurs at employment level L_2, which is less than the competitive level L_1. The employer pays a wage of W_2 ($W_2 < W_1$) to hire L_2 units

FIGURE 6–6
Employer
Monopsony Power

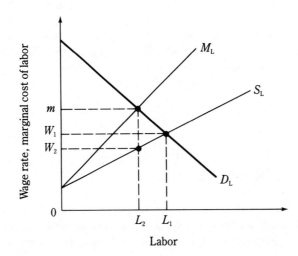

of labor. By repressing its own demand for labor, the employer raises the level of profits.

True company towns are comparatively rare today, although they form part of the historical folklore of industrial unrest, particularly in natural resource-oriented industries such as coal mining. However, there may be circumstances in which, even in comparatively large metropolitan areas, there are few enough employers of a particular occupational group to depress wages through cartel-type actions.

For example, over the years it has been alleged that hospital associations have been able to depress nurses' wages in some cities by agreeing on wage levels below what the competitive market would produce.[43] Where more than one employer is involved, such collusive arrangements produce a labor shortage. Each employer would like to hire more workers than can be found at the agreed-upon wage. But each refrains from raising wages to hire more workers, knowing that the collusive arrangement would be undermined by competitive bidding for labor. Informal no raid agreements may help maintain the arrangement.

Assuming all employers stick to the arrangement (despite the temptation to cheat present in any cartel), a chronic labor shortage would develop. Indeed, for many years the "nursing shortage" has been discussed by hospital administrators. This type of labor shortage is in keeping with the classical model, modified to reflect monopsony.

Employers may find it possible to exert monopsony power in situations in which a relatively small number of individuals with a unique skill are being hired. The most visible example is in the professional sports field. Top professional athletes have great value to their team owners, because they win games and attract fans. Yet the athletes' alternative earnings outside their sport are often low, leaving a potentially large margin for bargaining over wages.

Team owners have typically tried to enforce collusive arrangements aimed at holding down pay and preventing bidding wars. Historically, team owners have enjoyed various legal arrangements, such as antitrust law exemptions, that have facilitated collusion, although their monopsony power tended to erode in the 1970s.[44] The result of this erosion has been the phenomenon of spectacular salaries for certain superstars.

In contrast to the nurses' case, references are not made to shortages of athletes because the market is very thin. Professional teams incur considerable expenditure, however, in locating and enticing potential players. In that respect they behave in the same way as do other employers in shortage situations.

Union Bargaining Power and Labor Surpluses

In a similar way unions might influence wages. If unions can inflict costs on employers (through strikes or other job actions), they may be able to induce employers to agree to higher than market wages. Figure 6–7 illustrates such a case. A particular employer's demand for labor is depicted as D_L. The going market wage, in the classical sense, is assumed to be W^*. At that wage, any other pressures being absent, the employer would hire L_1 units of labor.

FIGURE 6–7
Impact of an
Above-Market
Union Wage in
Classical Economic
Analysis

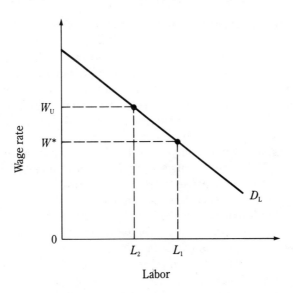

Suppose a union is able to induce the employer to agree to a higher wage, W_U. The employer will hire L_2 units of labor: $L_2 < L_1$. Those lucky workers supplying the L_1 units will enjoy a union wage premium, a "rent", of $W_U - W^*$ for each unit supplied. Since the employer's wage is now above the market, other workers will be attracted by the premium.

However, employment will not be available for these outside job seekers. Instead, there will be a chronic labor surplus, a queue of people waiting for vacancies to open at the premium wage.[45] This type of labor surplus is reconcilable with classical labor market theory, modified to include union bargaining power. It could also result from minimum-wage laws and certain other government policies that constrain employers to pay higher wages than they otherwise would.[46]

Finally, it should be noted that in the case of wage setting by a monopsonistic employer, a union could raise wages above what would otherwise be paid without creating a labor surplus. Consider a union that raised the wage in Figure 6–6 from W_2 (the monopsony level) to W_1. No surplus would result because supply = demand at the higher wage. If the union raised wages still higher, however, a surplus would result. At any wage the union negotiated above W_1 and below m, however, there would actually be more employment for union members than at the L_2 level. Perhaps it is not surprising that unions have made significant inroads among nurses and athletes, unlike the experience for most other professionals. Employees in these specialized fields may perceive that employer monopsony power can be offset by union bargaining power.

6–7   Alternative Models of Pay Determination

Recent economic models of pay determination have included costs and benefits that are neglected in the simple, classical approach. As stressed in earlier chapters, merely hiring labor does not guarantee optimum production. Once the labor is on the payroll, the employer needs to take steps to motivate workers. Use of incentive systems and of supervisor/auditors has been discussed as mechanisms used to ensure "a fair day's work for a fair day's pay." However, some economists have argued that the absolute level of pay itself is an important mechanism designed to avoid excessive employee shirking. Such models are generally put under the heading of efficiency wage theories.

Still another approach emphasizes the cost of employee turnover. An employee who quits imposes costs on the firm, especially if a replacement must be hired. The replacement must be recruited, screened, and trained, all costly activities. These costs can be viewed as employer investments in the workforce, which depreciate as employees depart. Since wage policy can affect the rate of employee turnover, the setting of a wage is more complicated than simply determining the going market rate.

Efficiency Wages

Imagine that the labor market initially did function in accordance with the classical economic model. Employees and employers would not be attached; rather they would negotiate daily agreements through a market process that ultimately produced a uniform wage for all employees of a given classification.

The employer in such a marketplace would face the standard principal–agent problem: How should the employer (as principal) make sure that the employee (as agent) performs as the employer desires? One possibility, as noted in a previous chapter, would be to offer an incentive compensation system. This route entails many complications and has generally declined empirically as the option chosen by employers. Another possible approach to resolving the principal/agent problem is to offer merit rewards, with meritorious behavior determined by supervisors through performance appraisals. This method *is* widely used, but it, too, poses significant problems of effective implementation.

A major difficulty, starting from a classical labor market, is that an employee whose performance is substandard really suffers no penalty. Such an employee can be dismissed if unsatisfactory conduct is uncovered; but the dismissal itself simply rids the firm of the employee. It imposes no penalty on the worker, since the auction process provides easy access to another job with some other firm at the going market wage.

Bonding   In such a market an employer might want to create a penalty system to provide an incentive for employees to avoid improper behavior. Theoretically the employer could request that employees post a bond of some type against poor performance. Such a system poses a difficult contracting problem. If the employer were the sole judge of whether performance was satisfactory, there would be an incentive for the employer to impose artificially high standards in order to disqualify workers and appropriate their bonds. On the other hand if the employee were made the sole judge, bonds would never be forfeited, regardless of how poor actual performance turned out to be.

Of course, the judge could be some neutral, outside person on whom the employer and employee would agree, prior to implementing the employment contract. Under union contracts there are systems of arbitration that handle employee grievances relating to discipline and dismissal. Even if such a system could be made applicable to all employees, including the large, nonunion majority, there would still be two barriers to a bonding system. First, the value of the bond would need to be mutually negotiated by the employer and employee. Second, the employee would have to raise the funds needed to post the bond in financial markets, if he or she did not have the money handy.

Obviously, a very small bond would not provide much incentive for shirking avoidance, and a large bond might be difficult for workers to finance. Many employees have little collateral for potential lenders. Moreover, lenders would have to make judgments, in setting interest rates or determining loan eligibility, on the likely future performance of the potential employee. Considerable risks might be entailed that would be difficult for lenders to reduce in the face of imperfect and costly information.

The bonding system is thus a theoretical nicety but not a practical solution to the principal–agent problem in the labor market. The absence of such systems in most employer–employee relationships is adequate testimony to the difficulty they would pose. While certain employees—for example, armored truck drivers— are bonded, the bonding is provided to the employer by an outside insurance carrier in order to insure against employee theft. The employer, not the employee, pays for the bonding service, so that no employee incentive effects are involved.

Single-Employer Wage Premium   An alternative approach to bonding—again, starting from a classical economic labor market—would be for some imaginative employer to offer a wage premium to employees who performed satisfactorily. An employer might announce that it would offer a wage of, say, 20% above the going market wage, to satisfactory employees. It would guarantee workers that the premium pay policy would be continued indefinitely and that the firm would not dismiss employees except for "just cause," that is, clearly unsatisfactory conduct.[47]

Under such a policy, the employer could not gain by appropriating something from employees after subjecting them to artificially high standards. While a bonding system would provide a temptation for employers to cheat, the wage premium system has no such perverse incentives. If an employer fired a worker without just cause, a replacement employee would have to be hired at the premium wage. Improper termination would gain nothing for the employer.

However, the wage premium system *would* provide an incentive to perform satisfactorily on the part of the employee. If the employee were fired, he or she would not have another opportunity to earn the premium working for this employer again. (Remember, as the story has been told so far, this employer is the only one offering the premium.) The fired employee would immediately find another job through the auction labor market, but not at the premium wage. Lifetime income for the employee would thus be reduced as the penalty for inadequate performance or misconduct.

Spread of the Wage Premium   Of course, if one employer successfully solved the principal/agent problem through a wage premium, other employers would imitate the solution. Once the innovation became general, however, the entire functioning of the labor market would be transformed. If every employer attempts to pay more than the going wage, the going wage would itself begin to escalate. It would rise above the level that would clear the labor market, producing a labor surplus (unemployment).

With unemployment now in the picture, the nature of the firing penalty is automatically changed. The penalty for employee misconduct becomes joblessness for some period, rather than a mere loss of a wage premium. A fired worker experiences a drop of wage income to zero during the job search period, which may have an extended duration.[48] Since this penalty is potentially heavy, the new going wage would not have to be much above the market clearing rate to enforce employee discipline. The wage would have to be just high enough to create a sufficient margin of unemployment to make the threat of firing for misconduct significant.

There is ample, anecdotal evidence that the level of unemployment does influence employee discipline. During wartime periods, when unemployment was very low, employers complained about inability to maintain standards. ("You just can't get good help nowadays.") During recessions, when the level of joblessness is high, security-conscious employees are less likely to take actions that might threaten their positions. In the union sector, for example, periods of elevated unemployment seem to be associated with reduced strike activity.[49]

Differentiated Pay Policies   The model is now beginning to look more like the real world. Employees do not wish to be fired. Unemployment exists. But the story continues to lack an important element of realism, namely, a dispersion of wages— that is, the modified model still has a uniform wage rate, although this wage is above the market-clearing level for efficiency wage reasons. Yet we know that actual labor markets exhibit a range of wages for a given occupation.

Efficiency wage theory offers some insight into the variegated pattern of firm wage policies. Different employers will have different inherent discipline problems. In some cases, employee misconduct will be more costly to the firm than in others. Where team production is involved, for example, poor performance of a single employee might upset the performance of many other workers. For some employers, it may be especially difficult to detect misconduct, particularly in large, bureaucratic firms.

Thus some firms will end up paying higher wages than others. Those with the highest wages—abstracting from any union pressures—will be employers that find employee misconduct especially costly and hard to detect. Larger firms, that rely on hierarchies of supervisors to maintain discipline, might well fall into this category; such firms therefore would be expected to pay particularly high wages. Small firms, in which the boss is near the shop floor and only relatively small teams can exist, would be likely to follow lower wage policies.

Discipline or Incentive?   Employee discipline has been emphasized in the efficiency wage story. The theory seems to present a negative aspect. Workers are pictured as lazy shirkers who must be deterred from their potential cheating by crafty employers. However, it is easy to place the story in a more positive perspective.

After all, the high-wage employer is really indicating to workers that the firm is an especially good place to work because of the premium compensation it offers. The employer is saying "You do right by me, and I'll do right by you." Efficiency wage theory, in other words, can be presented as the golden rule, applied to the labor market.

The golden rule need not be exclusively expressed as a pay premium. The employer might chose to offer career opportunities to satisfactory workers, that is, opportunities for promotions and advancements. An employee might expect that satisfactory performance would yield an upward sloping wage profile. At the entry level, wages would be comparatively low. As the employee proved himself or herself, pay would increase by means of advances up a defined job ladder or through merit adjustments.

The reader might stop at this point and consider what he or she regards as a "good" job. It probably has many of the aspects just discussed. A good job is generally viewed as one with good pay and benefits, opportunities to progress, and fair treatment and evaluation by the employer. Such attitudes are entirely in accord with the efficiency wage approach.

Turnover Costs

The costs of employee turnover provide another rationale for wage premiums.[50] If the firm has an investment in its incumbent employees (the total of their recruitment, screening, and training costs), each voluntary quit imposes a loss on the employer. The investment in the departing employee is lost and new investment must be made in the replacement. In a classical economic labor market, however, employees are leaving all the time; there is no formal employer/employee linkage.

An innovative employer in such a market might decide to pay a wage premium to employees in order to hold on to them and avoid human resource investment losses. The premium would be a windfall to workers, who would otherwise earn the lower, going wage in the market. Thus paying a premium would dramatically cut quits.

To protect their human resource investments, all employers would then begin to pay premiums. As in the efficiency wage case, the going market wage would begin to escalate, until the labor market no longer cleared. A labor surplus would develop and would, in turn, influence the amount of premium an employer had to pay. An employee who resigned might face a spell of costly joblessness, thus deterring such quits in the first place.

Since different employers have different levels of investments in their employees, there would be differences in firm wage policies. Firms with heavy investments would pay more than those with low investments in employees. Generally, it would be expected that relatively low wage policies (and high employee turnover) would characterize occupations in which investments were low. Workers whose productivity could be easily judged (keeping screening costs low) or who had skills provided in the external labor market (such as typing and shorthand) would have higher turnover rates than others.

The turnover cost approach, like the efficiency wage model, is consistent with employer policies other than simple wage premiums. Career ladders and opportunities for advancement can be part of employer strategies to retain employees and reduce turnover. Once employees are retained by such policies, they develop an ongoing relation with their employers. The arm's length impersonal transaction disappears.

In a world with ongoing relationships, career ladders make great sense. Career ladders foster ongoing relationships, and ongoing relationships foster career ladders. Since employees are likely to remain with the firm for an extended duration, firm investments in the workforce have a better chance of being recouped by the employer. The employer might thus provide training for workers to enable them to advance.

Formal Solution

In the classical economic model, the employer does not have a wage policy. Wages are set by the market, not the firm. The only choice for the employer is to determine the level of employment (in the short run) and the level of both labor and capital (in the long run). Labor will be hired such that wage = marginal revenue product of labor.

It is easy to modify the classical model to incorporate both efficiency wage considerations and turnover costs. Consider an employer using labor and capital in the short run to produce some output. Let P = the product price, Q = the level of output, W = the wage, L = the labor input, π = profits, and t = the rate of turnover costs per employee. Then firm profits can be expressed as follows:

$$\pi = PQ - WL - tL - \text{fixed capital costs} \qquad (4)$$

The employer must maximize π, using W and L as instruments.[51]

In order to solve for the optimum solution, it is necessary to specify the production process as it relates to labor input and efficiency (employee effort). It is important to consider how the wage level chosen affects efficiency and turnover. As long as the employer pays a wage within reasonable range of the market average, L can be maintained at a target level. Low wages, however, will mean that heavy turnover must be sustained to maintain L, whereas high wages will permit maintaining L with low turnover.

Thus t is a function of W such that $\partial t/\partial W < O$ and $\partial^2 t/\partial W^2 > O$ in the relevant range surrounding W^*, the average rate of wages for the class of worker under consideration. The relationship between t and W is represented by the downward sloping curve shown in the upper panel of Figure 6–8. At a wage such as W_1, which is less than the average wage, turnover would be high and the marginal effects of reducing the turnover rate by increasing wages would be considerable. But at high wages (relative to the market average) such as W_2, turnover would be low and the gains from further wage increases in reducing turnover would be low.

Finally, turnover rates might reach an irreducible minimum at some high wage, such as W_3. Due to deaths and family pressures, some departures from the

FIGURE 6–8
Turnover Costs
and Wage Rates

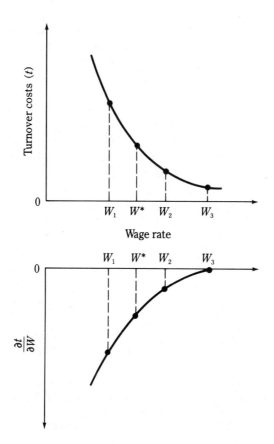

firm's workforce are inevitable, regardless of the wage level. Thus the marginal effect of wages on turnover, $\partial t/\partial W$, becomes zero at some very high wage.

A similar analysis can be made of the efficiency effect of wage levels. In the short run, output's relation to labor input can be written $Q = eF(L)$, where e is an efficiency factor that is, in turn, a function of W. $F(L)$ is the short-run production function, that is, the total product of labor with capital held fixed. Within the relevant range, we assume that $\partial e/\partial W > 0$ and $\partial^2 e/\partial W^2 < 0$. The efficiency factor's relation to the wage is represented by the curve on the upper panel of Figure 6–9. The lower panel of the figure represents $\partial e/\partial W$.

It is assumed that efficiency will be very low at wages such as W_1, which are well below the market average wage W^*. High incremental efficiency gains can be achieved by raising the wage from those very low levels. At above-average wage levels, such as W_2, marginal efficiency gains are positive, but much reduced. Finally, at some very high wage (such as W_3), it is assumed that no further efficiency gains can be achieved by wage raising. At that wage $\partial e/\partial W = 0$.

To determine the optimum, profit-maximizing decisions regarding L and W, the usual differentiation of equation (4) can be performed. The result is

$$\partial\pi/\partial L = P[e(\partial Q/\partial L)] - W - t = 0, \tag{5}$$

FIGURE 6–9
Efficiency and
Wage Rates

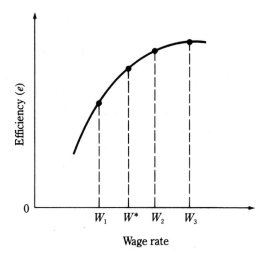

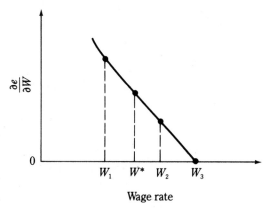

and

$$\partial\pi/\partial W = PF(L)(\partial e/\partial W) - L - (\partial t/\partial W)L = 0 \qquad (6)$$

The term in brackets [] in equation (5) is the marginal product of labor. When multiplied by P, it becomes the marginal revenue product of labor (MRP_L). Hence, equation (5) specifies that the firm should set its employment level so that $MRP_L = W + t$. This condition is eminently sensible. Each labor unit added to production involves a cost to the firm of the direct wage payment to the worker *plus* an expected turnover cost. In making a marginal cost/benefit analysis, the firm is simply equating the marginal benefit of added labor with the incremental cost of labor acquisition. The reasoning is precisely the same as that underlying the classical economic model, except that the classical model omitted consideration of turnover costs.

Equation (6) can be rewritten as follows:

$$[PF(L)(\partial e/\partial W)/L] - \partial t/\partial W = 1 \qquad (7)$$

The bracketed [] term on the left-hand side of equation (7) is the marginal increase in revenue per labor unit from efficiency gains associated with wages, while the next expression, $-\partial t/\partial W$, is the marginal saving in turnover costs per labor unit. Thus equation (7) says that the firm should raise wages by \$1 (or 1 dime or 1 cent) increments until the marginal revenue per labor unit from the wage increase, plus the marginal turnover saving per labor unit, just equals the \$1 (or 1 dime or 1 cent) cost per labor unit of the incremental wage increases. This equation, although sensible, has no counterpart in the classical model, since the firm in that model is not assumed to have its own wage policy.

Employee as Stakeholder

The model presented above provides for an extended employer–employee relationship. Employees remain with the firm for indefinite periods, possibly for entire careers. They are aware of the firm's policy of promised fair treatment and potential advances in pay and status for employees who meet specified work standards. Such employees are likely to be willing to make their own personal investments in meeting the firm's required standards. For example, they may undertake training in pursuit of the rewards promised in the firm's HRM policy.[52]

In addition, in a labor market characterized by unemployment, accepting a job offer carries with it a certain risk to the employee. If the job does not turn out as expected, or if the employer breaches its own HRM policies, the worker may have to quit or may be terminated. Either outcome could result in a spell of costly unemployment. Thus the employee has a stake in the successful outcome of his or her job decision and a stake in the overall economic condition of the enterprise.

This stake is accentuated in a labor market with entry-level job openings and internal career ladders. If a worker loses his or her job in mid-career, it may be necessary—even if another job is quickly located—to start at the bottom. It may not be possible to carry over the status and pay from the old job into the new one. Studies of job losses due to mass layoffs in the 1980s demonstrate that displaced career workers often experienced significant spells of unemployment or nonemployment or, if they found jobs, often had to accept lower pay compared with their previous employment.[53] Incumbent workers with considerable seniority on their jobs thus have a special stake in retaining those positions.

Summary

This chapter has explored both the uses of the classical model of pay determination and the important limitations of that model. Simple supply/demand analysis, with its implicit assumptions of one wage rate in the labor market and complete clearing of the market, can be useful for certain purposes. But it is necessary also to include the impact of wages on worker efficiency and turnover before the model produces a generally realistic picture of the labor market.

The fact that the labor market is different from financial and commodity markets, however, does not mean that participants in the labor market are somehow irrational. It has been assumed throughout this chapter that there are rational actors (employers and employees) in our modified model of labor market behavior. It is simply that the principal/agent problem and the difficulty in obtaining information are sufficiently powerful in the labor market to create different institutional arrangements than are found in other types of markets. Rational people will operate differently when faced with different circumstances.

Although this chapter formally presents a model of a firm that recognizes efficiency and turnover, it does not consider whether that model can be applied to improve HRM policy. For example, can some of the concepts that have been introduced be quantified for use by employers? The next chapter will explore the issue of implementation. It will also consider the mix of alternative kinds of pay, for example, wages versus fringe benefits and other conditions of work, as a matter of HRM policy.

EXERCISES

Problem

Consider the advertisement shown in Figure 6–10. What incentive is this firm offering to prospective employees? What relation does this firm's hiring strategy have to turnover costs? Examine help wanted ads in your local newspaper and see if you can determine the employment strategy of the firms placing them.

Questions

1. What insights are available from the classical demand-and-supply model of the labor market?

2. What are the deficiencies in the simple classical model?

3. What types of strategies do employers follow when they experience labor shortages?

4. What role does unemployment play as a disciplinary device?

5. What factors might influence an employer to pay wages above or below the market average?

6. What influence might changing demographic characteristics have on the national wage structure?

7. Under what circumstance might a union push up wages without fear of adverse employment effects?

FIGURE 6–10
Advertisement
for Labor

We're Looking for Top Performers

We're Public Department Stores and we're looking for career-minded staff who will help us continue our reputation for the best customer service in the industry.

We want people who will grow with us in our new location in sales, alterations, stock handling, and building maintenance. We want people with ideas, people oriented toward customer assistance.

We want people who enjoy working with others, and with our clients.

And the rewards? We have an open-ended commission earnings system that lets our employees determine their own incomes. And we offer a company-paid profit-sharing plan. Benefits include health and life insurance and more.

But most of all, we offer opportunity to work with top performers. Opportunity to advance through our promote-from-within policy.

If what we offer appeals to you, and you think you meet our standards, call us at 555-1000 for an appointment.

PUBLIC DEPARTMENT STORES
an equal opportunity employer

Terms

backward bending labor supply

clearing of the labor market

cobweb model

compensating wage differentials

derived demand for labor

Fair Labor Standards Act

flextime

income versus substitution effects

indifference curve

isoquant

shirking

shock effects

stakeholder

turnover costs

X-efficiency

ENDNOTES

1. Some economists might prefer to term the analysis of this chapter "neoclassical."

2. The rental cost of capital is the sum of foregone interest and net depreciation (subtracting any price increase in the value of the equipment) in a given time period. Thus, suppose the purchase of a $100 machine that depreciates (net) by $10 per year. Suppose further than the relevant annual interest rate is 5%. The cost of owning the machine is $5 (.05 × $100) plus $10. So R = $15. A capital renting company under competitive conditions would charge this annual price to a firm that rented its equipment. A firm that owned and operated the machine would still need to view the opportunity cost of the machine as the implicit rental rate of $15.

3. The text is following the convention of referring to the theory embodied in Figure 6–1 as the theory of the firm. In fact, it is really a theory of the plant. With constant returns to scale, firm size is really indeterminate—and irrelevant—in the model. (A firm might own more than one plant.) For that matter, with constant returns to scale, even plant size is indeterminate.

    In theory, it is possible to create models in which the preferences of workers are biased towards labor-intensive products. Then, pushing up wages might create more demand for such products and more demand for labor. Such a model would be unstable, since wage increases would generate pressure for further wage increases.

4. Richard A. Lester, "Shortcomings of Marginal Analysis for Wage-Employment Problems," *American Economic Review,* vol. 36 (March 1946), pp. 63–82; Gerald R. Faulhaber and William J. Baumol, "Economists as Innovators: Practical Products of Theoretical Research," *Journal of Economic Literature,* vol. 26 (June 1988), pp. 577–600, especially pp. 592–594.

5. Strictly speaking, if labor and materials must be fed into the production process in a fixed ratio, neither one has a marginal product (or, put another way, the marginal product of each separately is zero). There would be a positive, constant marginal product of a combined unit of labor and materials. Readers who are familiar with input-output analysis will recognize such production assumptions.

6. The development of the modern typewriter/computer keyboard is an example. Current key arrangements were determined in the nineteenth century in response to key jamming problems of early typewriter models and a desire of a manufacturer to have salespeople be able to type the brand name "Type Writer" on the top line of letter keys. Touch typing subsequently locked in the arrangement of the keys, since typists needed to be able to use any typewriter model that an office might use. With modern computers, the keyboard could easily be rearranged to facilitate faster typing. But until mechanical typewriters have totally disappeared, and until all computers have the ability to allow simple user key rearrangements, the standard QWERTY arrangement will prevail. For a history, see Paul A. David, "Clio and the Economics of QWERTY," *American Economic Review,* vol. 75 (May 1985), pp. 332–337. One study, based on cases, investigated the impact of relative labor costs (between different kinds of labor) on the techniques employed in manufacturing production. Changes in relative wages were not found to play a role in such choices, since estimates of cost savings were not precise enough to warrant the use of such information. See Michael J. Piore, "The Impact of the Labor Market Upon the Design and Selection of Productive Techniques Within the Manufacturing Plant," *Quarterly Journal of Economics,* vol. 82 (November 1968), pp. 602–620. Piore did find, however, that average wages (for all grades of labor) were used in estimating cost savings, thus leaving open the possibility that general increases in labor costs relative to capital costs could influence capital/labor substitutions.

7. U.S. Bureau of the Census, *Statistical Abstract of the United States: 1988* (Washington: GPO, 1988), p. 395.

8. The standard analysis can be found in George J. Stigler, "The Economics of Minimum Wage Legislation," *American Economic Review,* vol. 36 (June 1946), pp. 358–367. More recent references are Finis Welch, *Minimum Wages: Issues and Evidence* (Washington: American Enterprise Institute, 1978); Donald O. Parsons, *Poverty and the Minimum Wage* (Washington: American Enterprise Institute, 1980); Masanori Hashimoto, *Minimum Wages and On-the-Job Training* (Washington: American Enterprise Institute, 1981); Belton M. Fleisher, *Minimum Wage Regulation in Retail Trade* (Washington: American Enterprise Institute, 1981); Belton M. Fleisher, *Minimum Wage Regulation in the United States* (Washington: National Chamber Federation, 1983); U.S. General Accounting Office, *Minimum Wage Policy Questions Persist,* GAO/PAD–83–7 (Washington: GAO, 1983); Charles Brown, Curtis Gilroy, and Andrew Kohen, "The Effect of the Minimum Wage on Employment and Unemployment," *Journal of Economic Literature,* vol. 20 (June 1982), pp. 487–528.

9. Employers might also reduce nonwage benefits, such as provision of training for those low-wage workers who do find employment, relative to what they would have received at a lower wage.

10. Under the U.S. Constitution, Congress has regulatory power only over interstate or foreign commerce. In practice, since the 1930s, very broad definitions of interstate commerce have been applied by the Supreme Court. Coverage under the FLSA is determined partly by the nature of the activities performed by the employer or employee and by the dollar level of the employer's business.

11. Harvey Leibenstein, *General X-Efficiency Theory and Economic Development* (New York: Oxford University Press, 1978).

12. "President Signs FLSA Amendments," *Daily Labor Report* (September 23, 1966), p. 2.

13. Sar A. Levitan and Isaac Shapiro, "The Working Poor: A Missing Element in Welfare Reform," working paper 1987–5, Graduate School of Arts and Sciences, George Washington University, 1987, pp. 16–19.

14. "Minimum Wage Hike Won't Cause Layoffs, Many Employers Say," *Daily Labor Report* (July 11, 1988), pp. A1–A4.

15. Jean Baldwin Grossman, "The Impact of the Minimum Wage on Other Wages," *Journal of Human Resources,* vol. 18 (Summer 1983), pp. 359–378.

16. About a fifth of such workers were below the poverty line as of March 1985. Ralph E. Smith and Bruce Vavrichek, "The Minimum Wage: Its Relation to Incomes and Poverty," *Monthly Labor Review,* vol. 110 (June 1987), pp. 24–30, especially p. 28.

17. Edward M. Gramlich, "Impact of Minimum Wages on Other Wages, Employment, and Family Incomes," *Brookings Papers on Economic Activity* (2:1976), pp. 409–451.

18. Albert Rees, "An Essay on Youth Joblessness," *Journal of Economic Literature,* vol. 24 (June 1986), pp. 613–628, especially pp. 624–625.

19. Estimates for unionization of the overall workforce, including government employees, in this period peak at about 35%. See U.S. Bureau of Labor Statistics, *Handbook of Labor Statistics,* bulletin 2070 (Washington: GPO, 1980), p. 412. The text figure is an approximation that excludes government workers.

20. *Employment and Earnings,* vol. 35 (January 1988), p. 223.

21. Richard B. Freeman and James L. Medoff, *What Do Unions Do?* (New York: Basic Books, 1984), p. 239. A qualification is that when unions first organize an employer, they may not be able to obtain the same wage premium found at firms that had been unionized for many years. See Richard B. Freeman and Morris M. Kleiner, "The Impact of New Unionization on Wages and Working Conditions: A Longitudinal Study of Establishments under NLRB Elections," working paper no. 2563, National Bureau of Economic Research, 1988.

22. Employers in less developed countries sometimes complain about labor force commitment. Workers recruited from rural areas are said to quit and return home after earning a target income, thus causing substantial labor turnover.

23. An important qualification is that many workers do not work the hours they want, or are assigned hours by their employer. The issue of work hours will be discussed in a later chapter.

24. U.S. Department of Labor, *Child Care: A Workforce Issue,* Report of the Secretary's Task Force (Washington: DOL, 1988), pp. 125–136.

25. Adam Smith, *An Inquiry into the Nature and Causes of the Wealth of Nations* (New York: Modern Library, 1937), pp. 100–110.

26. Of course, the gross correlation between pay and pleasantness runs in the opposite direction. The least pleasant jobs tend to be low paying. However, such correlations do not hold other influences constant.

27. Detailed definitions of these jobs are provided by the U.S. Bureau of Labor Statistics. A level-1 secretary carries out recurring office procedures independently and selects the guidelines or references that fit the specific case. The secretary's supervisor provides specific instructions on new assignments and checks completed work for accuracy. A variety of specified duties are mentioned such as responding to routine telephone requests and maintaining supervisor's calendar. A light truck driver drives a truck weighing less than 1½ tons within a city or industrial area. The precise details appear in the source to Table 2.

28. The benefits to employees in a labor-shortage economy are discussed in Arthur M. Okun, "Upward Mobility in a High-Pressure Economy," *Brookings Papers on Economic Activity* (1:1973), pp. 207–252.

29. Human resource executive quoted in Paul Richter, "Northeast U.S. Frustrated by Acute Labor Shortage," *Los Angeles Times,* December 23, 1986, Part 4, pp. 1, 20.

30. Sanford M. Jacoby, *Employing Bureaucracy: Managers, Unions, and the Transformation of Work in American Industry, 1900–1945* (New York: Columbia University Press, 1985), chapter 5.

31. "Employers Resort to Variety of Measures to Cope with Shrinking Pool of Workers," *Daily Labor Report* (July 26, 1988), p. A9.

32. John Maynard Keynes, *The General Theory of Employment, Interest, and Money* (New York: Harcourt, Brace & World, 1936).

33. Dividing the wage by a price gives the consumption power of the wage in terms of the product being priced. Thus, if the hourly wage is $10 and apples cost 50¢, then the hourly wage expressed in terms of apples is $10/50¢ = 20 apples.

More commonly, we divide wages by a price *index* and express the result as a real wage index. (The relations of wages and prices are discussed more fully in a later chapter.)

34. Daniel J.B. Mitchell, "Wages and Keynes: Lessons from the Past," *Eastern Economic Journal,* vol. 12 (July–September 1986), pp. 199–208.

35. For a survey of views, see Thomas J. Kniesner and Arthur H. Goldsmith, "A Survey of Alternative Models of the Aggregate U.S. Labor Market," *Journal of Economic Literature,* vol. 25 (September 1987), pp. 1241–1280.

36. Finis Welch, "Effects of Cohort Size on Earnings: The Baby Boom Babies' Financial Bust," *Journal of Political Economy,* vol. 87 (October 1979), Part 2, pp. S65–97; Richard B. Freeman, "The Effect of Demographic Factors on Age-Earnings Profiles," *Journal of Human Resources,* vol. 14 (Summer 1979), pp. 289–318. There have also been attempts to forecast the impact of the baby boom on the demographic structure of wage. as it ages into the next century. See Phillip B. Levine and Olivia S. Mitchell, "The Baby Boom's Legacy: Relative Wages in the 21st Century," working paper no. 2501, National Bureau of Economic Research, 1988.

37. An anticyclical movement of the wage differential between experienced workers and new entrants has long been noted. See Melvin W. Reder, "The Theory of Occupational Wage Differentials," *American Economic Review,* vol. 45 (December 1955), pp. 833–852. There may be a differential sectoral impact with some high-wage, job rationing industries able to recruit even as the labor market tightens while low-wage, more market sensitive industries are forced to raise wages to compete for new labor. See also Michael L. Wachter, "Cyclical Variations in the Interindustry Wage Structure," *American Economic Review,* vol. 60 (March 1970), pp. 75–84; Sanford M. Jacoby and Maury Y. Pearl, "Labor Market Contracting and Wage Dispersion," *Journal of Labor Research,* vol. 9 (Winter 1988), pp. 65–77.

38. The issue of changing workforce composition was discussed in Chapter 2.

39. National Commission on Excellence in Education, *A Nation at Risk: The Imperative for Educational Reform* (Washington: U.S. Department of Education, 1983). Known as the "Gardner Report."

40. The cobweb effect will be discussed in a later chapter.

41. Richard B. Freeman, "A Cobweb Model of the Supply and Starting Salary of New Engineers," *Industrial and Labor Relations Review,* vol. 29 (January 1976), pp. 236–246.

42. In principle, the supply curve could be backward bending. However, it can be shown that a monopsonistic employer will only operate on the upward sloping portion of a labor supply curve.

43. See Charles R. Link and John H. Landon, "Monopsony and Union Power in the Market for Nurses," *Southern Economic Journal,* vol. 41 (April 1975), pp. 649–659; and Richard W. Hurd, "Equilibrium Vacancies in a Labor Market Dominated by Non-Profit Firms: The 'Shortage' of Nurses," *Review of Economics and Statistics,* vol. 55 (May 1973), pp. 234–240. It has also been argued that hospitals collude in a manner that lowers nurses' return to additional education, thus intensifying the shortage of nurses with 4-year degrees relative to those with 2- or 3-year degrees. See Lavonne A. Booton and Julia I. Lane, "Hospital Market Structure and the Return to Nursing Education," *Journal of Human Resources,* vol. 20 (Spring 1985), pp. 184–195.

44. For a review of the economic and legal environment surrounding professional sports, see Roger G. Noll, ed., *Government and the Sports Business* (Washington: Brookings Institution, 1974).

45. Among longshoremen on the West Coast, for example, union members have first crack at available work at the union hiring hall, which dispatches workers to the various stevedoring companies as ships require loading and unloading. When sufficient union labor is not available, other workers can be dispatched. There are inevitably queues for such peak vacancies because of the high union wage paid.

46. The federal government requires contractors on government-financed construction projects to pay prevailing wages as determined by the U.S. Department of Labor, pursuant to the Davis-Bacon Act. Such wages may be above levels nonunion employers would otherwise pay.

47. Models of the type discussed in this section can be found in George A. Akerlof and Janet L. Yellen, eds. *Efficiency Wage Models of the Labor Market* (New York: Cambridge University Press, 1986); and Joseph E. Stiglitz, "The Causes and Consequences of the Dependence of Quality on Price," *Journal of Economic Literature,* vol. 25 (March 1987), pp. 1–48. Analysis has also turned to the historical evidence, notably Henry Ford's decision to pay a wage of $5/day— a princely sum at the time—in 1914. Ford argued that raising wages was actually a cost-saving device, a position in line with the efficiency wage approach (within limits). See Daniel M.G. Raff and Lawrence H. Summers, "Did Henry Ford Pay Efficiency Wages?," working paper no. 2101, National Bureau of Economic Research, December 1986.

48. The existence of unemployment insurance in the real world may partially mitigate the penalty for dismissal. However, employers may challenge unemployment insurance benefit claims for workers who are fired for cause. In any case, the benefits are likely to be substantially less than the wage the worker previously received. (Unemployment insurance is discussed in a later chapter.)

49. David Card, "Strikes and Wages: A Test of a Signaling Model," working paper no. 2550, National Bureau of Economic Research, April 1988.

50. A model of the type developed in this section can be found in Arthur M. Okun, *Prices & Quantities: A Macroeconomic Analysis* (Washington: Brookings Institution, 1981), pp. 26–133.

51. A competitive firm with price fixed by the market at P is assumed. Modification of the model to include imperfect competitors is not difficult.

52. Employee training is discussed in a later chapter.

53. U.S. Bureau of Labor Statistics, *Displaced Workers, 1979–83,* bulletin 2240 (Washington: GPO, 1985); Richard M. Devens, Jr., "Displaced Workers: One Year Later," *Monthly Labor Review,* vol. 109 (July 1986), pp. 40–43, and "errata" for this article in the September 1986 issue, p. 41. A later study can be found in U.S. Bureau of Labor Statistics, *Displaced Workers, 1981–85,* bulletin 2289 (Washington: GPO, 1987).

Chapter Seven

THE COMPENSATION DECISION

The previous chapter analyzed various analytical approaches to pay setting and labor market adjustment. This chapter, in contrast, explores three key issues faced by employers in making pay decisions. In order to establish a pay policy, firms must establish the general level of pay at other employers. Thus the first issue is where to find information about the external labor market. Since some jobs within the firm do not have counterparts in the outside market, the second issue is the setting of pay for workers in such jobs within the firm's internal labor market. The third issue is determining the appropriate mix of wages versus fringe benefits for all jobs within the firm.

7–1 Using External Information for Setting Pay

Most employers will find that many jobs in the firm can be compared to jobs in the external market. Job titles such as lawyer, chemist, tool and die maker, carpenter, receptionist, secretary, and janitor are well recognized and have broadly similar duties across firms. This recognition does *not* mean that all workers in these occupations are identical. Previous chapters have stressed the variation among workers with regard to skill, attitude, and other attributes. If the employer advertises for workers in these positions, however, most of the resulting applicants will have at least the potential to do the required work. They are likely to be plausible candidates.

An important point emphasized in earlier chapters is that the market for labor is different from financial and commodity markets. In a financial or commodity market, it is obvious why a participant (either a buyer or a seller) will want to know the current market price for an asset. Although a participant will generally be unable to influence that price, the price information is important in deciding whether or not to transact. A potential buyer in the stock market, for example, might decide whether a particular stock—based on a price quotation— was a bargain or overpriced. In the labor market, which has an array of prices, is there any use in finding out the level of the average wage for an occupation?

The analysis in Chapter 6 suggests that such measures can indeed be very useful to employers. At wages below the average, employers can expect to experience relatively high turnover rates and lower worker efficiency. At higher wage levels, the reverse will be true; other things being equal, turnover will be low and worker efficiency high. The employer will need a benchmark from which wage policy can be gauged. The decision to be a high or low payer must be made relative to some measure of central tendency in the relevant labor market.

7–2   Obtaining Information

One element of pay setting common to employers is the gathering of some type of external wage data. Table 7–1 shows the results of a 1981 survey of employer practices. Virtually all employers surveyed obtained outside wage information. Over half characterized the information as "essential/absolutely necessary" to the ultimate pay decision. Moreover, many employers had multiple sources of information.

Data from BLS

Only about one-third of the employers surveyed used data available from the U.S. Bureau of Labor Statistics (BLS) as part of their wage-setting process. This failure to use BLS data is surprising, since most of its information is available for free or at very low cost. BLS information also tends to be more accurate statistically than private surveys of wages, since the bureau pays more attention to statistical sampling and data reliability.[1]

On the other hand, BLS data often are more aggregated than most employers would like. Often the aggregate data are the series that are produced most frequently. Aggregates are of special interest to economic policy makers, but detailed information is generally what HR executives need. Moreover, although detailed information is available, there are often publication lags involved. These drawbacks may cause employers to look for other data sources. Simple ignorance of what BLS offers may also be a factor.

Establishment Wage Data   One of the most commonly cited series from the BLS is the establishment survey reporting average hourly and weekly earnings. These data have a history going back to the early part of this century. Over the years, industry coverage has been broadened so that available information now covers the entire private, nonfarm sector on a monthly basis. Approximately 290,000 establishments are covered by the survey, which is conducted jointly by the BLS and state government agencies.

TABLE 7–1   Use and Evaluation of Wage Surveys by Employers

	Proportion of Employers Surveyed
Proportion Using Wage and Salary Surveys in Setting Pay	93%
*Sources of Wage and Salary Data Used**	
In-house staff	78%
Outside consultant	35%
Local employer association	50%
Industry association	48%
Other employer in area	36%
Other employer in industry	32%
U.S. Bureau of Labor Statistics	34%
State or local government agency	25%
Other	20%
*Evaluation of Wage and Salary Surveys**	
Essential/absolutely necessary	55%
Very helpful	30%
Of some use as a guideline	15%

*Percentages of those employers using wage and salary surveys.

Note: Data based on survey of 183 personnel executives whose employers are members of the Personnel Policies Forum of The Bureau of National Affairs, Inc.

Source: The Bureau of National Affairs, Inc., *Wage & Salary Administration*, PPF Survey No. 131 (Washington: BNA, 1981), p. 3.

The establishment survey produces data on employment, hours, and earnings. Earnings data apply to production and related workers in manufacturing industries, construction trade workers in the construction industries, and non-supervisory workers in other sectors. Average hourly earnings (AHE) data are obtained by dividing the weekly payroll by average weekly hours paid for (AWH). Average weekly earnings (AWE) are obtained by dividing the payroll by the number of employees. AHE $\times$ AWH = AWE.[2] Average hourly earnings data are available for manufacturing only, adjusted by BLS to produce an estimate of straight-time hourly earnings, that is, earnings excluding the effects of overtime. Sample data from the establishment series are shown in Table 7–2.

The establishment wage data provide no occupational detail. Because payrolls are used as the measure of compensation, the data exclude payments that employees do not receive directly in their paychecks. Employer contributions to pension plans, health and life insurance, and social insurance programs (Social Security, Railroad Retirement,[3] unemployment insurance, and workers' compensation) are omitted. Information is available on earnings by states and metropolitan areas, but only for manufacturing.

TABLE 7–2 Selected Data from BLS Establishment Survey, Production and Nonsupervisory Workers, 1987

Industry	Average Hourly Earnings (AHE)	Average Weekly Hours (AWH)	Average Weekly Earnings (AWE)	Straight-Time Hourly Earnings*
Coal mining	$15.75	41.9	$654.78	n.a.†
Highway and street construction contractors	11.92	41.9	499.45	n.a.
Fabricated metal products	10.03	41.5	416.25	$9.59
Metal cans	14.01	44.1	617.84	n.a.
Food and kindred products	8.92	40.2	358.58	8.49
Meat-packing plants	8.37	41.7	349.03	n.a.
Class 1 railroads	14.26	43.0	613.18	n.a.
Department stores	6.80	27.9	189.72	n.a.
Banking	7.50	36.1	270.75	n.a.
Motion picture production and services	16.28	29.3	605.62	n.a.

*Average hourly earnings excluding the effect of overtime wage premiums (at time and a half).

†n.a. = not available.

Source: Data from U.S. Bureau of Labor Statistics, *Employment and Earnings*, vol. 35 (March 1988), pp. 83–99.

Despite these limitations, earnings figures from the establishment survey can be used to compare a firm's average wages with those of other firms in its industry. Such comparisons will be especially useful if the firm seems to have an occupational pattern similar to the average for the industry and to devote a roughly similar proportion of total compensation to fringe benefits. It should be possible, based on internal firm payroll records, to produce a company estimate of average hourly and weekly earnings using methodology similar to that of the BLS. This internal estimate can be compared with BLS data on industry earnings to determine if the firm is a relatively high-, average-, or low-paying employer.

Area and Industry Wage Surveys Since pay differs by occupation, firms may want to compare specific occupational wage rates paid internally with those paid by other firms in the area or industry. The previous chapter provided examples of occupational wage data for an area (see Table 6–2). In the late 1980s area wage surveys were available for about seventy standard metropolitan statistical areas. Data in these surveys apply to selected occupations in the clerical, professional, technical, maintenance, toolroom, powerplant, material movement, and custodial occupational groups. Occupations selected are those common to many firms, such as secretarial work. Certain information is also included on pay-related practices such as the incidence of paid holidays and other fringe benefits.

Smaller firms with less than 50 to 100 workers (depending on the industry) are excluded from area wage surveys. Since smaller firms tend to pay lower than average wages, the occupational wage data from area wage surveys are somewhat upward biased. Nevertheless, area wage reports can give firms an idea of their relative wage standing compared with others in their geographical area. The main difficulty with using area wage data is the lag involved in obtaining the figures. Area wage surveys are conducted on an annual or biennial cycle, and several months may elapse between data collection and publication.

Industry wage surveys provide substantially more occupational detail than area wage surveys, since the occupations included are those of importance to the industry studied, even if they are not widely found in other sectors. Forty industries were included in the survey program in the mid-1980s. Because industries are surveyed on a three- to five-year cycle, the resulting wage data appear too infrequently for employers to use them in annual pay reviews. However, when relevant surveys do appear, HRM specialists in surveyed industries can take the opportunity to compare their company's wage rates with those of the survey. Table 7–3 presents sample data from a typical industry wage survey.

Earnings Data from the Current Population Survey   Unlike the data series discussed thus far, data from the Current Population Survey (CPS) are obtained from individuals, not employers. The CPS was originally created in the 1940s to mon-

TABLE 7–3   **Selected Data from Industry Wage Survey on Wood Household Furniture, June 1986**

Occupation and Region	Average Hourly Earnings
Rip-saw operators	
U.S.	$6.03
New England	6.96
Middle Atlantic	7.07
Southeast	5.92
Southwest	4.07
Great Lakes	7.01
Middle West	6.16
Mountain	5.09
Pacific	6.19
Inspectors, final, U.S.	6.20
Sprayers, U.S.	5.81

Note: Data refer to nonupholstered furniture.

Source: Data from U.S. Bureau of Labor Statistics, *Industry Wage Survey: Wood Household Furniture, June 1986,* bulletin 2283 (Washington: GPO, 1987), pp. 9–10.

itor monthly trends in employment and unemployment. Earnings questions were added to the survey on a regular basis beginning in the 1960s. The 1980s brought a considerable expansion in the CPS gathering and presentation of earnings information. Almost 60,000 households were involved each month in the CPS as of the late 1980s.

Respondents to the CPS are asked about the earnings of employed members of their households. For wage and salary earners—that is, those not self-employed—respondents are asked about usual earnings per week. Information is also obtained about usual hourly earnings and hours worked per week for individuals paid by the hour. *Usual* includes premiums for overtime if these are received on a regular basis. Also included are tips and commission payments.

Certain CPS occupational data for broad classifications were shown in Chapter 2 (Table 2–2). More detailed occupational data are published periodically. Examples of such data are shown in Table 7–4. As with some other series, publication lags make these data useful primarily for retroactive comparisons.

Other BLS Wage Information   Because most employees are covered by mandatory, government-provided unemployment insurance (UI), information on their wages is collected by BLS as a byproduct. (An unemployed worker's previous wage history plays an important role in determining the weekly unemployment benefit to which he or she is entitled.) Data on annual wages per worker and average weekly wages are available by industry and state. Unlike the establishment survey, information is available on wages for state and local government workers and for agricultural workers.[4] Reports on UI-based wage estimates appear in BLS press releases and are published annually in bulletins entitled *Employment and Wages*.

White-collar occupational wages are surveyed annually by BLS as an input into the process of setting pay for federal civil servants. This procedure, known as the National Survey of Professional, Administrative, Technical, and Clerical Pay (PATC) covers medium to large sized private establishments. Information is published in BLS press releases and bulletins showing wages within occupations, for example, alternative pay rates for different levels of skill and responsibility of accountants or computer programmers.

Because of periodic controversy over whether federal civil servants are overpaid, demands have been made that the survey include smaller establishments, more services, and state and local governments. Such changes could be expected to lower the average salaries reported. Some of these suggestions have been implemented. In 1987, however, establishments with as few as twenty workers were included, and coverage of the service sector was improved. Given the unresolved issues related to federal pay, users of the PATC survey need to watch for coverage changes that may occur in the future.

Other Official Wage Information

Although the BLS is the major government agency in the collection of employment and wage statistics, other agencies do have useful data. As noted, the BLS hourly earnings data omit the costs of fringe benefits. Often employers want to compare

TABLE 7–4 Median Weekly Earnings for Selected Occupations from Current Population Survey, 1986 (Full-Time Workers)

Occupations	Median Weekly Earnings
Financial managers	$584
Accountants and auditors	478
Chemical engineers	721
Registered nurses	460
Economists	704
Editors and reporters	425
Radiologic technicians	383
Cashiers	181
File clerks	239
Telephone operators	315
Bank tellers	231
Police and detectives, public service	478
Janitors and cleaners	247
Office machine repairers	376
Electricians	473
Tool and die makers	506
Bakers	292
Welders and cutters	376
Bus drivers	272
Operating engineers	410
Garbage collectors	286

Source: Earl F. Mellor, "Weekly Earnings in 1986: A Look at More Than 200 Occupations," *Monthly Labor Review,* vol. 110 (June 1987), pp. 41–46.

their wage levels with others on a total compensation basis, that is, including fringe benefits and payroll taxes for social insurance. On the other hand, they may want to compare the proportion of their total compensation bills that go to fringes and payroll taxes with those of other employers.

One source of such information is the national income (GNP) accounts published by the Bureau of Economic Analysis (BEA), a component of the U.S. Department of Commerce. The BEA annually publishes estimates of the costs of wages and salaries and total compensation on a detailed industry basis. Also provided are estimates of the number of full-time equivalent (FTE) employees by industry. (Two half-time workers count as one full-time equivalent.)

Dividing wages and salaries or total compensation by FTE yields an estimate of annual pay rates in the industry. These figures appear annually in the *Survey of Current Business* and in related supplementary publications. Table 7–5 presents an illustrative sample of such data for selected industries.

TABLE 7–5   Selected Data on Compensation and Wages and Salaries from the National Income Accounts, 1986

Industry	Total Compensation* per Full-Time Equivalent Employee	Wages and Salaries per Full-Time Equivalent Employee	Other Labor Income† as Percent of Total Compensation
Coal mining	$45,029	$35,053	22%
Construction	28,499	23,567	17
Fabricated metal products	30,481	24,672	19
Food and kindred products	27,911	22,634	19
Railroad transportation	48,379	37,463	23
Retail trade	16,183	14,042	13
Banking	27,152	21,778	20
Motion pictures	33,196	29,095	12

*Total compensation = wages and salaries plus other labor income.

†Other labor income = employer contributions to social insurance (including workers' compensation), to pension and profit-sharing plans, to group health and group life insurance, to supplemental unemployment benefit plans, and for miscellaneous purposes.

Source: Survey of Current Business, vol. 67 (July 1987), pp. 59–61.

The national income account data provide information on the pay of government workers as well as private, unlike the pay figures from the establishment series exclusively for private sector workers. Public employers seeking wage data to use for comparative purposes, however, will probably want geographical and programmatic detail that is not available from the national income accounts. The Bureau of the Census, another branch of the Commerce Department, conducts annual surveys of state and local governments; these surveys include information on the monthly pay of public workers. Geographic and programmatic breakdowns are available from various publications derived from these surveys. Every five years the bureau conducts a *Census of Governments* that provides still more detail on pay in the public sector. As with many other sources cited, the principal difficulty in using these data is the lag between collection and publication.

Employers can also find wage information in the decennial *Census of Population,* the *Census of Manufactures,* and specialized data collected by regulatory agencies and state statistical bureaus. Some of the earliest sources of information about the labor market were state agencies in the late nineteenth century. Many state statistical bureaus today, however, rely on the BLS for their labor market data. Nevertheless, state bureaus often provide convenient tabulations focused on their own jurisdiction. A few continue to collect their own information.

Also available from the BLS are index numbers that indicate the rate of wage change (but not the absolute wage) over various time periods. Other data sources apply only to the unionized sector of the economy. These specialized series will be discussed in later chapters.

Private Data Sources

Many of the employers surveyed in Table 7–1 reported using sources of information other than official government data. Private data suppliers attempt to fill gaps in wage data left by government agencies.[5] Two notable gaps are in the fields of executive compensation, particularly for higher echelon executives, and in salary intention surveys. (The latter, discussed in the next chapter, are surveys in which HRM managers are asked what wage adjustments are being planned for next year.) It is useful to discuss executive compensation at this point, however.

Executive compensation is a relatively neglected area of official data collection by agencies such as the BLS, because relatively few employees are involved. Although some information on managerial salaries can be obtained from the CPS, the occupational categories used are too broad for use by anyone interested in setting pay for top level executives. An additional problem is that executive compensation arrangements are complex and often include bonuses linked to company performance as well as various types of stock options.

This complexity of pay arrangements for executives has partially reflected tax considerations; since top executives tend to be in a higher tax bracket than the average employee, tax avoidance strategies attain special significance. Prior to the 1986 tax law modifications, there was an incentive to turn current income into capital gains where possible because capital gains were taxed at significantly lower rates than other income. Another factor in the complexity of executive pay is the adoption of executive bonus arrangements linked to profitability or other measures of company performance. The various compensation devices used for executives mean that information on straight salary is of limited utility to those responsible for determining executive compensation levels.[6]

To determine executive pay, pay setters must rely on survey information provided by management-consulting firms such as Hewitt, Hay, and Wyatt. Such private surveys may be available only from expensive publications or be made available only to clients.[7] Users must be more cautious about the interpretation of such surveys than they are about data from BLS and other government agencies, since the surveys are often vague on the methodology—the precise questions asked, the occupational definitions, and the sampling techniques used by private data sources.

Other Forms of Data Gathering

It is evident from Table 7–1 that employers commonly use informal methods of gathering wage data. Such methods may involve simply making a phone call to another firm in the area to acquire anecdotal information. Employers may also find that trade associations to which they belong conduct periodic pay surveys on behalf of their members.

In the public sector, state and local governments may have formal, reciprocal arrangements to exchange wage data with other jurisdictions. These practices become particularly important for jobs that are not found in the private sector, for example, police work. In some cases public employers may have a legal obligation to pay no less than the level indicated by such wage surveys or at least to conduct a survey before making wage decisions.

Apart from the use of surveyed data purely for information, association surveys may help employers exercise monopsonistic power in the labor market. The previous chapter pointed out that it may be to the benefit of employers to hold down wages, even if labor shortages are a result. If employers in a geographic area tacitly agree not to pay more than the survey indicates, the survey becomes a wage coordination device. This mechanism is similar to the price or cost surveys employed in the product market in order to coordinate industry pricing. Like other cartel-type arrangements, however, incentives to cheat can thwart the objectives of any wage coordination strategy, particularly since successful coordination will engender labor shortages.

7–3   Using Other Methods for Setting Pay

There are many jobs that are either unique to a firm or that do not have broad labor markets. In these cases, survey information will not produce quotes of typical market wages. How can pay be set for such jobs?

Pragmatic Comparison Approach

Faced with the need to set pay rates for jobs without obvious outside markets, employers often do the obvious. They find ways of linking pay in such jobs to wages and salaries for other jobs where clearer markets exist. Firms may have hierarchies of job classifications, for example, and may simply place jobs into families of similar positions. Thus all jobs in Grade 1 may have the same rate of pay or the same range of pay rates. Some jobs in Grade 1 may be easily subject to external survey, whereas others are not. Alternatively, jobs may be characterized by certain attributes that permit comparisons with other jobs, and pay can be set by placing a monetary value on these designated attributes.

Put another way, where no market quote is available for a particular job, employers seek indirect market information. Doing so, particularly in larger firms where many job titles are involved, requires subjective judgments about which market is relevant to which jobs. These subjective elements mean that the pay assigned to many jobs has an arbitrary facet. Pay for a given job title might be set somewhat higher or lower than its actual rate and still fall within the bounds of reasonableness.

Job Analysis   Linking nonmarket jobs to market jobs is an appealing notion in the abstract. By itself, however, the notion hardly provides guidance on precisely what to do. Over the years HRM practices have developed specific steps that can be followed, although the analytical underpinning for the various approaches is often unclear. For example, HRM departments frequently use *job analysis* as a first step in evaluating and classifying jobs. Essentially, job analysis involves the preparation of a detailed description of the position in question, typically obtained by observing what employees in that position actually do. As in the case of other HRM techniques, job analysis has an inherent pitfall. It can create misincentives and engender conduct that is not in the employer's best interest.

Employees will realize that job analysis can influence their rates of pay. If their jobs appear complex and demanding to the analyst, they are likely to be more highly compensated. The job analyst thus faces a problem of imperfect and biased information if he or she relies heavily on the employee for information. Reliance on supervisors for accurate information does not necessarily resolve this dilemma. As noted earlier, principal/agent problems often arise when supervisors are involved.

In particular, it will generally be in the interests of supervisors to demonstrate that their subordinate employees should be highly rated. A supervisor's own pay is likely to reflect the pay of subordinates. There may well be an incentive, therefore, for the supervisor to inflate subordinate job descriptions. Moreover, subordinates may be more cooperative if they are highly paid, which helps the supervisor carry out assignments successfully.

There are no ways to avoid such misincentives and misinformation completely. As a partial insulation against job description inflation, job analysts will often follow elaborate checklists and guidelines. In addition they are trained to take a skeptical approach to claims of substantial job responsibilities or claims of a substantial increase in responsibilities since a previous review.

On the other hand, there are limits to the skepticism that can be brought to bear when jobs are being analyzed. If, for example, a supervisor is insistent that the requirements of a certain job have been upgraded, the cause may be that there has been a problem in attracting candidates into that position. Inflating the job description may help inflate the job's designated salary to a competitive level. The job analyst may be reluctant to hinder a line supervisor in this subterfuge, since blocking the effort could intensify line-versus-staff tension. Organizations require a certain level of mutual cooperation, and an action that helps or hinders today may be remembered when cooperation is requested tomorrow.

Once jobs are described (accurately or not), comparisons across jobs can be made. Jobs can be put into families and then placed in pay grades, or more elaborate job evaluation plans can be undertaken.

Job Evaluation   In HRM textbooks *job evaluation* is usually described as a two-step process. First, jobs are ranked or graded by key attributes. Second, a monetary unit is designated for each point of the resulting grades. In other words, such factors as skill, responsibility, and physical strength are evaluated for each job. Then points are given according to the degree to which each attribute is required. Jobs with higher point values will receive higher pay.

Such formula-type plans can be created within the firm by its own HRM department. Sometimes, outside management-consulting firms, such as Hay Associates, can be brought in to perform the evaluation. Use of outsiders for such purposes is not unusual, although many firms do not find it necessary. One study reported, for example, that almost a third of surveyed employers used outside consultants to establish pay structures for their management personnel and almost one-fourth used them for other employees.[8]

Hedonic Pricing and Job Evaluation   Is there a theoretical justification for formal job evaluation plans? In certain respects, such evaluation can be regarded as a type of what economists call *hedonic pricing*. Hedonic pricing attempts to divide up the value of an item into subvalues that are placed on its attributes or components. The attributes of a job could thus be treated as independent factors that each carry implicit market values. The price of the overall job is determined by summing up the values of its attributes.

As an example outside the HRM field, consider a portfolio of stocks. If you were offered such a portfolio, you would probably value it as the sum of the values of the individual shares of which it was comprised. Your justification for doing so would be that markets exist for the individual shares, which readily specify their values. Once having obtained the portfolio, you would be free to buy or sell individual shares at market prices to change the portfolio mix as you saw fit. There would be no reason not to price the portfolio simply as the sum of its component worth.

Although the component approach is easily justified as a method of pricing stock portfolios, it may not be so readily applied in other areas. Consider the price of a home. Homes are more complex to price than stock portfolios because many of their attributes are dependent on the context in which they reside. It might be found—perhaps through regression analysis—that the price of a home in a particular real estate market varied with such attributes as the number of bathrooms, the number of bedrooms, the overall square footage of the structure, the size of the lot, the proximity to transportation, and so on. Suppose the transaction prices of particular houses sold in the market are regressed against measures of these attributes. The resulting regression coefficients would provide an indication of the incremental market values of the attributes. It might be learned, for example, that the market placed a value of, say, $10,000 on an extra bedroom.

However, there is no actual market for bedrooms by themselves; bedrooms only come attached to houses. A more sophisticated regression analysis might indicate that there are diminishing values placed on successive bedrooms—that is, a three-bedroom house might be valued at $10,000 more than a two-bedroom house, but a four-bedroom house might be worth only $8,000 more than an otherwise comparable three-bedroom house. There would be no more justification for saying that a bedroom is worth $10,000 in the abstract than that it is worth $8,000. The value of the bedroom variable, in fact, depends on its own magnitude.

Regression analysis might also indicate that there are interaction effects between the explanatory variables. Extra bedrooms might turn out to be worth more in larger houses than in smaller houses. Market participants might prefer that smaller houses devote proportionately more space to common areas such as living rooms than to bedrooms. Again, no unique value of a bedroom would be indicated. A bedroom could be valued only in the context of other key variables.

Finally, the results of a regression analysis for one real estate market might not be valid for some other market. An incremental bedroom added to a standardized house in Detroit might be worth more or less than the same bedroom added to the identical house in Omaha. Tastes of housing consumers and input prices facing housing construction contractors might well be different in the two cities.

It should be clear that the real estate example is more relevant to the job market than the stock portfolio example. There is no market for abstract units of skill (or responsibility or reliability or physical strength). Assuming measurement is possible, the value of skill (or other attributes) may well have diminishing returns at some point. Skills come embedded in people along with other attributes. The presence or absence of other attributes will determine the value of skills. In addition, people fall into different job markets depending on their occupations, and different markets may place different values on skill.

Unlike stock portfolios, it is often not possible to adjust "portfolios" of employees for imbalances. An investor with a portfolio weighted excessively with stocks of high-risk companies can easily acquire less-risky shares to mix with the initial endowment. These new shares would correct the imbalance. In the case of a job, however, combining, say, a stupid person with a smart one on a team may not produce the equivalent of two persons of average intelligence.

Naive application of job evaluation techniques assumes that there is an implicit market for the job attributes being measured, and that somehow it is possible to buy or sell increments of these attributes at a uniform price. Fortunately, most employers who use job evaluation do not apply it so naively. More typically, after jobs are initially priced, a subjective review process leads to adjustment of the initial results. Some pay rates designated by the formula may seem too far above (or too far below) the level needed to attract and retain labor.

Job Evaluation and Comparable Worth   There is an empirical tendency for jobs that are heavily female dominated to pay lower wages than male-dominated jobs. Yet it is not unusual to find that women in female-dominated jobs have higher educational levels than males in higher paid, male-dominated jobs. Table 7–6 provides some examples. The table shows that in 1986 median usual weekly earnings of construction laborers (male dominated) were almost 38% higher than those of hairdressers (female dominated). Yet hairdressers had higher educational attainment than the laborers. A similar comparison is made of secretaries and automobile mechanics; both earned the same wages, but secretaries had higher educational attainment.

If a job evaluation plan were applied across broad occupational groups, it is quite possible that female-dominated jobs would be designated for higher pay rates than are often observed in the marketplace. The outcome would depend on the weight the plan gave to white-collar and education-correlated characteristics. Since some plans do contain such weights, there have been demands for application of job evaluation to raise female pay relative to male.[9]

TABLE 7–6   Selected Occupational Wage Comparisons

Occupation	Median Usual Weekly Earnings in 1986*	Percent Female in 1986*	Percent with Completion of High School in 1980†
Hairdressers	$208	85%	80%
Construction laborers	287	3	54
Secretaries	288	99	95
Automobile mechanics	324	2	66

*Wage and salary workers who usually worked full time.

†Persons 18 years of age and older who worked year round, full time in 1979 in the civilian labor force.

Source: Earl F. Mellor, "Weekly Earnings in 1986: A Look at More Than 200 Occupations," *Monthly Labor Review,* vol. 110 (June 1987), pp. 41–46; U.S. Bureau of the Census, *1980 Census of Population: Earnings by Occupation and Education,* PC80–2–8B (Washington: GPO, 1984), Table 1.

The 1963 federal law known as the Equal Pay Act requires that employers provide equal pay rates to men and women in the same (or essentially the same) jobs.[10] However, the 1963 act is quite narrow; it does not apply to comparisons of dissimilar jobs (such as secretaries and automobile mechanics). Advocates of "comparable worth" as a pay-setting method usually rely on another law: Title 7 of the Civil Rights Act of 1964 (as amended in 1972). Title 7 applies to virtually all forms of job discrimination—in hiring, promotions, testing, training opportunities, layoffs, and so on. It forbids such discrimination on the basis of race, sex, religion, or national origin.

Comparable worth proponents propose that jobs of comparable worth— even if dissimilar—should be paid comparable wages. Job evaluation plans provide a way of making comparisons across diverse jobs. Hence use of job evaluation has tended to be viewed as *the* method by which comparable worth could be put into effect.

As a matter of strict litigation victories, comparable worth is at best an unapproved theory. Some out-of-court settlements have been achieved, however, particularly in the public sector, that have raised pay in "women's" jobs. The agitation surrounding comparable worth may also have had some impact on employer wage policies (public and private). Even in the absence of court approval, women's average pay tended to rise relative to men's during the period from the late 1970s to the late 1980s.[11] A later chapter will discuss this trend and other aspects of equal employment opportunity (EEO) policies. At this point it is useful to note the difficulties facing courts that might lean towards the comparable worth approach.

One problem is that there are many types of job evaluation plans in use. It has already been seen that the analytical foundation of job evaluation is weak. Choosing among plans on a scientific basis is thus not possible. It has also been noted that firms will often use job evaluation as an initial guide, and then flexibly adjust the formula's outcome to fall in greater accord with perceived labor market conditions. Such subjective adjustment would be difficult to defend were job evaluation to be made mandatory. A flexible pay-setting approach might be changed by legal constraint into a mechanical application of a questionable formula.

The fact that job evaluation is arbitrary does not mean that it would be impossible to require employers to use such systems. For example, the Canadian province of Ontario enacted such a law in 1987. Significant administrative problems are entailed in such an approach, however; undoubtedly the Canadian experience will be watched carefully in the United States.

American courts have been reluctant to enter the wage-setting business, especially in the absence of a clear-cut legislative directive to do so. This reluctance does not mean that some form of comparable worth could not be implemented through a court system. A version of comparable worth *was* applied in Australia in the early 1970s and resulted in substantial relative wage gains for female employees.[12] However, Australia has something the United States lacks: a complex system of wage courts that set minimum pay rates for the vast majority of the workforce and for most occupations. These courts were already in the wage-setting business; including comparable worth as a criterion in the wage-setting process did not require a major shift in their focus. Such activity would, however, be a major undertaking for the U.S. judiciary system.

Economic theory suggests that implementation of comparable worth might cause job displacement for women.[13] For example, raising the relative wage of female-dominated jobs compared with that of male-dominated jobs might lead employers to substitute 'male" jobs for "female" jobs in the production process. Or, were female pay to be pushed up, there might be more pressure to apply automation to replace female jobs, for example, to substitute word and data processors more extensively for clerical occupations.

Although economic theory points toward a direction of effect, it does not indicate the magnitude. In the Australian case some studies suggested that the *increase* of women in the workforce was slowed by implementation of the comparable worth approach. This impact was a relatively mild effect, compared with what many economists would have expected. Really dramatic adverse impacts on female employment were not in evidence.

Some observers argued that this lack of a large effect in Australia was due to limited substitution possibilities. Hairdressers do not make good substitutes for construction laborers, nor do secretaries make good substitutes for automobile mechanics. Concerning technology and automation, there is some evidence that relative wages do not play a major role in machine design and specification.[14] Perhaps these factors explain the Australian results.

Alternative to Comparison Approach

The previous chapter noted that the level of pay can both affect efficiency and reduce turnover. Profit maximization was associated with the rule that wages should be raised until the cost of doing so (that is, the direct addition to payroll), was just offset by savings resulting from efficiency and turnover. For employers actually to make such calculations, they would need to be able to obtain the relevant cost and savings data. Is it possible for employers to make these computations?

Quantification of Firm Data Experiments have been undertaken in some firms to quantify the concept of turnover savings. For example, Table 7–7 displays the results of a survey conducted by an employer association that requested information on turnover and replacement costs of employees in the Los Angeles area. The study suggests that average turnover costs ranged from just under $2,300 in 1979 to over $10,000 for salaried exempt workers, presumably managers and professionals. If these costs rose at the same rate as wages generally, by 1988 they would have risen by a factor of over 63%.[15] The range of turnover and replacement costs—were the study to have been undertaken in 1988—might have been $3,700 to $16,900.

Perhaps the key point is that the study was not undertaken again. It appears that most employers do not attempt to quantify their turnover costs on a regular

TABLE 7–7   Costs of Turnover from an Employer Survey, 1979

	Production and Maintenance	Office and Technical	Salaried Exempt
Separation costs			
Lost production between decision to terminate and effective date	$100.00	$25.00	$200.00
Exit interview	78.50	19.67	13.33
Paperwork processing	54.75	11.00	7.00
Severance pay	—	260.00	1,020.00
Replacement costs			
Advertising	$351.25	$288.33	$693.33
Travel of recruiters and/or applicants	27.50	—	6,000.00
Administrative (interviews, reference checks, paperwork, testing)	489.00	182.67	150.00
Medical examination	403.00	270.00	—
Induction procedures	207.75	72.33	22.50
Substandard production of new employees	1,000.00	762.50	1,550.00
Time spent by supervisors or fellow workers performing on-the-job training	900.00	400.00	700.00
Total turnover costs	$3,611.75	$2,291.50	$10,356.16

Note: Data based on responses of companies that had adequate data to answer detailed questions on turnover costs. A second sample of companies could not answer the questions in detail but provided the following estimates of total turnover costs: production & maintenance, $1,029.09; office & technical, $1,332.84; salaried exempt, $4,260.39.

Source: Merchants and Manufacturers Association, *Turnover and Absenteeeism Manual* (Los Angeles: M&M Assn.: 1980), Section III, pp. 11–12.

basis. Moreover, even the data in Table 7–7 raise substantial questions. It is not clear, for example, what is meant by the cost of "substandard production of new employees." Does this mean the market value of wasted materials that had to be discarded? Or does it indicate that because of initial low productivity, newly hired workers received more in wages than they produced in value of output? As in the case of many private surveys, precise methodological statements are not available.

The Los Angeles study does not provide any estimate of how much turnover (and therefore turnover costs) would decrease if wages were raised. This absence of information is an important gap. A complete understanding of the optimal response to turnover requires information on turnover costs and the responsiveness of these costs to wages.

Human Resource Accounting   Professor Eric G. Flamholtz of UCLA has been a pioneer in developing human resource accounting techniques with regard to turnover. His approach suggests that Table 7–7 may omit some important turnover costs, thus widening the possible range of discretion rather than narrowing it. Flamholtz notes that since firms have career ladders, some of the costs of developing an employee to a given level may arise before the employee assumed the job title being studied.[16] Moreover, since some employees leave the firm after being partially developed, but before attaining the studied rank, it may be necessary to develop more than one entering employee to obtain a single finished product.[17] Using this career concept, Flamholtz provides examples of the development costs of two senior accounting positions and finds that the costs of nurturing someone in these positions amounted to $23,000 for one job and $45,000 for another.[18]

Although it cannot be argued that these measurements are perfect (what measurements are?), they do indicate that firms *can* produce useful cost measures relating to turnover.[19] Merely the act of collecting such information on a regular basis can help make pay setters more sensitive to the turnover implications of their decisions. The substantial spread of computers and data processing capability should permit quantitative studies to be undertaken at lower cost than in the past. The spread into HRM positions of recent graduates of management school programs that stress quantitative and computer skills should further encourage such techniques.

Determining the degree to which turnover would decline if pay were raised or determining the efficiency gain from higher pay, as developed in the previous chapter, is a more complex task than measuring current turnover costs. However, the barriers to making at least ballpark estimates are not insurmountable by any means. Since firms change pay only infrequently (say, annually), there may have been periods in which company wages fell behind trends in the external labor market. Examination of such periods might give some clues to the turnover (and, possibly, the efficiency) effect of a relative wage slippage.

Even if competitors are not willing to supply information, impressionistic evidence about turnover might be obtained by observing turnover and productivity of other firms that are low or high payers in the area or industry. (HRM professionals may move from firm to firm, acting as carriers of information when they make career transitions.) Apart from such an informal information network, trade associations might survey such information on a confidential basis, providing still another data source. Finally, it is even possible to obtain experimental data within the firm, if the firm has multiple divisions or plants at which pay can be adjusted independently. In a given year, the firm might raise pay at a plant by somewhat more or less than the normal practice would suggest and then observe the results.

Quantification and Comparable Worth   As noted, advocates of the comparable worth concept have generally tied it to job evaluation, a subjective and uncertain technique. Usually, the debate over comparable worth on economic grounds is between those who argue that the market should set wages and those who argue for the questionable comparative approach. The difficulty with the market approach is that it is also subjective. While firms establish pay policies within a market context, they have discretion over whether they will be high or low payers relative to the market averages.

Direct analysis of wage effects on efficiency and turnover is a way of assessing the appropriate worth of a job. In the simple classical model, a job is always worth what it receives, since the firm simply expands hiring until wage = marginal revenue product of labor. The quantitative efficiency/turnover approach suggests that a given job might be worth more or less to a firm than the average market wage for that occupation.

Of course, there is no guarantee that if a firm studied its turnover and other costs, the ultimate result would be a raising of pay in female-dominated jobs relative to others. Indeed, the data of Table 7–7 suggested that turnover costs for office and technical positions (which have heavy concentrations of women) were lower than for other occupations. Given the uncertainty surrounding those data, however, the actual effect of applying the efficiency/turnover approach to relative female pay cannot be predicted. Results will differ in each firm.

In any case, employers who conduct job evaluations and then fail to implement the indicated pay scales risk potentially expensive lawsuits. They may be called to explain why they did not do what their own job evaluation plan suggested was appropriate. Employers may thus be more reticent about use of conventional job evaluation in the future, unless they are compelled by law to do so.

If the alternative turnover/efficiency approach came into widespread use, it would be less likely to raise this problem. Suppose the approach did indicate that pay of certain female-dominated jobs should be raised to boost company profits. Why would an employer hesitate to implement a step that would raise profitability?

7–4   Equity and Fairness as Pay Standards

None of the approaches to pay setting so far discussed involved considerations of fairness. Yet there certainly is a history of such considerations in discussions of pay. Ideas about the just wage for workers go back thousands of years. Usually of pay. Ideas about the just wage for workers go back thousands of years. Usually the concept of fairness relates to the ability of the wage earner to enjoy a decent standard of living. Until the late nineteenth century and early twentieth century, this notion could not be quantified, since information on living costs was not easily available. As the possibility of collecting the needed data became more real, advocates of its use for wage-setting purposes became more vocal.

The Australian wage courts mentioned earlier had their roots in the idea that wages could be set fairly by impartial judges who would consider what minimum income was needed for a worker with dependents. Periodic attempts were made to collect information on worker budgets to make this minimum income determination. Eventually, the budget information was collected on a regular basis. It was also seen as fair that jobs requiring more skills should be paid more than the basic minimum income. The judges considered traditional wage differentials and tended to preserve them as equitable in making their decisions on pay structure.

Australia's motivation in creating wage courts was to reduce industrial unrest and strikes in the early part of this century. Such unrest was regarded as a threat to the country's social stability. It was felt that employee discontent would be reduced if pay setting were made fair. Australians still debate whether judicial wage setting has had this intended effect in their country. In most other Western nations, even in the face of industrial unrest, such extensive official intervention in pursuit of fairness has not taken place in the labor market. More typically, some form of minimum wage was imposed at the bottom, such as the American Fair Labor Standards Act of 1938 (see Chapter 6). Wages above the minimum were (and are) left to private determination.

It should not be assumed, however, that privately set wages omit notions of fairness. The efficiency/turnover model of wage setting suggests that such notions *ought* to influence wage setting. If employees believe that wages are unfair, they are more likely to leave, and they may become less productive and cooperative. In making pay decisions it is in the interests of employers to consider employee concepts of fairness. Of course, where unions are involved, employees may have a mechanism of enforcing their views of fair pay practices on the employer.

Concepts of fairness, however, are not independent of actual practice in the workplace. Sometimes practice influences perceptions of fairness. As productivity has raised real wages and living standards, notions of what constitutes a decent minimum income have also risen. The Australian judges who accepted traditional skill differentials as fair were using existing employment standards in their decision making. Even without judges and courts, employers are well aware that changes in traditional pay structure can lead to workplace frictions.

For example, when job evaluation plans are applied, it sometimes turns out that particular jobs are pinpointed as being overpaid. In cases where the employer elects to lower pay for these jobs, it is a common practice to "red circle" the pay of incumbent workers, that is, to continue to pay existing workers the old wage, rather than cut their pay. Of course, as other wages in the organization generally rise, the incumbents will slip in their position in the wage structure. Eventually their pay will fall to the relative pay level the job evaluation plan says they should receive. The red circle method is a way of cushioning the impact because immediate and overt pay cuts would be perceived as unfair.

The previous chapter noted that rational employer practices often lead to long-term employer/employee relationships featuring pay premiums, career ladders, and reward for loyal service. Economists have sometimes referred to such arrangements as implicit contracts because they are usually not written down as formal contractual obligations.[20] Only when unions are involved—or in specialized occupations such as professional sports—are written contracts the norm in private employment.[21] Nevertheless, social standards of fairness tend to reinforce the implicit agreement.

For example, employers are usually viewed as having greater obligations to long-service employees than to recent hires. Terminating long-service workers or cutting their pay is more likely to be seen as unfair than if the same policies were applied to junior workers. In the 1980s, for example, when unions negotiated wage concessions, two-tier wage plans were developed in which incumbent workers retained their old rates of pay, but new hires entered the firm at a lower wage. Senior (long-service) workers were thus protected from market pressures.[22]

Of course, the existence of social standards of fairness does not prevent employers from taking steps that their workers (or customers) regard as unfair.[23] Wages *are* sometimes cut. Long-service workers *are* sometimes dismissed without notice. The point is that the fairness standards have an inhibiting effect on such behavior. Fairness standards are yet another reason why the labor market differs substantially from financial and commodity markets.

The common use of fairness as a decision-making criterion in the labor market suggests that there are some circumstances in which it may *not* be used. Labor markets differ from financial and commodity markets because the buyer and seller relationship in the labor market is ongoing. Less concern about fairness is likely to be evidenced in situations in which the employer knows the relationship will not be ongoing. The cost of being unfair is much lower. For example, employment conditions in a plant that management knows will be permanently closed might well deteriorate during its final days.[24]

7–5 Benefits Versus Wages

Various forms of fringe benefits are offered by employers as part of their compensation packages for employees. These include pension and retirement savings programs, health and life insurance, group legal services, and many others. Note, however, that such programs are available through sources other than the workplace. Individuals can save for retirement, purchase health and life insurance, and arrange for legal services on their own.

Apart from benefits that can be purchased externally, fringes also include various arrangements that are specifically linked to the workplace. Examples are the various forms of time off (such as vacations, holidays, bereavement leave, jury duty leave), items provided at the workplace such as parking and subsidized cafeterias, and miscellaneous benefits such as discounts on company-produced merchandise. Indeed, it is difficult to draw a precise line between benefits and general conditions of work.

Why do employers provide benefits? In the cases of benefits that employees could purchase individually, this question is particularly puzzling. Why not simply pay employees cash wages and let them determine how much, if any, life insurance or health insurance they wish to purchase, or how much they wish to save for retirement? Why should employers undertake to support the expenses and bureaucracy entailed in administering complex benefit programs?

Two answers are usually given to these questions. First, it is argued that there are economies to be obtained in benefit administration by employers. These economies occur because fixed administrative costs—at least for larger employers— can be spread over large numbers of people, thus reducing unit costs. Also, insurance programs require risk pooling. The second answer has to do with tax incentives for employer-provided benefits.

Scale Economies and Risk Pooling

If an individual applies to an insurance company for a health plan, there is always a possibility that the individual wants the coverage because he or she is already in bad health. Carriers attempt to protect themselves from such risks through various devices, such as requiring medical exams of applicants. But there is still the possibility that individual purchase of insurance will lead to an accumulation of bad risks by the carrier. For example, medical exams may not catch all high-risk applicants. In contrast, if an employer simply enrolls its *entire* workforce in a health plan, the insurance carrier is likely to obtain a cross section of risks. The costs of coverage per enrollee will thus be lower because good risks from the general employee population will offset the bad.

The risk-pooling approach helps explain why employers often constrain benefit choices offered to employees. For example, as just noted, the employer may simply enroll every employee in a particular benefit plan, regardless of individual employee preference. There are exceptions to these employer-imposed constraints, but the exceptions can prove to be expensive.

As an example of an unconstrained program, consider arrangements known as cafeteria plans, or flexible spending accounts. Under these plans, the individual employee is given substantial choices concerning what benefits he or she wishes to select. In its simplest form, the cafeteria plan allocates a pool of benefit dollars to each employee, and the employee then distributes the pool across the menu of benefits offered. Some employees might buy dental insurance with their benefit dollars, others might buy life insurance.

Cafeteria plans are very appealing, since they permit consumer choice. Their drawback is that they encourage adverse selection. Employees whose children are about to need braces will pick dental insurance. Those employees with serious illnesses in their families will opt for comprehensive health insurance. The premiums for these separate programs will be expensive compared to levels prevailing at firms where everyone must take all of the benefits offered, regardless of preference.

With constrained choices, therefore, it is likely that there are some economies associated with risk pooling. Although every employee may not be pleased with the benefit package, the average employee receives benefits at a bargain rate. To maintain a reasonable matching of employee preference and the compensation package, sophisticated employers will periodically examine their benefit offerings and the desires of their employees. If the workforce's composition shifts toward parents with young children, for example, the employer might consider offering some form of child care benefit. Monitoring and reflecting the preferences of the average employee may enable the employer to economize on labor costs.

Figure 7–1 illustrates this point. The figure shows indifference curves of an average worker who faces a trade-off between cash wages and benefits. If given only a cash wage income of *0A* with no employer-provided benefits, the individual worker would reallocate his or her dollars and purchase benefits in the external market along budget line *AB*.[25] At point *a* on Figure 7–1, the employee depicted maximizes his or her welfare.

If the firm can obtain benefit plans more cheaply than the individual employee and makes such benefits available, the resulting budget line for the worker shown in Figure 7–1 would rotate in a clockwise direction to a new line such as *AB'*. Were the employer to continue to pay out compensation dollars equal to *0A*, the worker would enjoy higher welfare on line *AB'* by purchasing benefits through

FIGURE 7–1
Employee
Preferences:
Benefits Versus
Wages

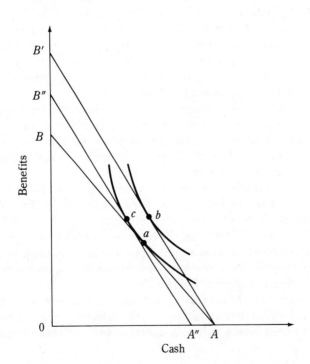

the employer at point *b*. However, there is no need for the employer to provide compensation dollars as high as *0A*, given the welfare improvement. Compensation dollars can be reduced to *0A″*, leaving the individual with a cash/benefit mix at point *c*. At point *c*, the individual has the same welfare as at *a*, but at a lower cost to the employer.

This analysis suggests that larger employers would be more likely than smaller employers to offer rich benefit packages. Larger employers would have the advantage of scale economies in benefit administration.[26] And, indeed, larger firms *do* tend to offer richer packages than do other firms.[27] However, the analysis still leaves some basic questions unanswered.

Despite the bias toward large firms, smaller firms often offer some benefits. Why is this so, if smaller firms cannot achieve administrative scale economies?[28] The analysis of Figure 7–1 does not indicate whether it is the *employer* or the *employee* who is required to pay for benefits. Determining just who pays for the benefits may not seem important in the analysis just presented, since the employee will end up at point *c* of Figure 7–1 regardless of who is the payer.[29] The fact is that employers typically are formally responsible for paying for benefits. Why should this situation be the norm?

Finally, the economies of scale and risk-pooling arguments could be applied to any large group, not just a group consisting of employees. Employees might buy benefits through professional organizations, unions, fraternal orders, religious bodies, and so on. Although some benefits are purchased through such groups, employed individuals are likely to obtain most of their benefits through their employers. It is apparent, therefore, that there is another influence that tilts preferences toward employer-provided and employer-paid benefits.

Tax Considerations

Until World War II, income taxes were not a major consideration for the average person. With the expansion of government in the 1930s and the growing use of income taxes as a financing tool for federal expenditures, income taxes became more important in affecting individual and business behavior. During World War II, the federal government grew especially rapidly. Congress began to discover that it could encourage or discourage activities by providing incentives or disincentives through manipulation of the individual and corporate income tax codes.

A benefit will be discouraged if the employer is not permitted to deduct its cost as a business expense. Making the benefit cost deductible for the employer puts the benefit on an equal footing with cash wages, if the recipient of the benefit must pay current taxes on its value. Permitting the recipient to defer taxes on the benefit beyond the current year provides a net subsidy to the benefit. The employee avoids current taxation, thus earning implicit interest on the taxes saved and possibly deferring taxation to a future period when he or she will be in a lower tax bracket. A greater net subsidy can be provided if the benefit is *never* subject to personal income taxation. It is possible to increase the subsidy even more if the cost of the benefit can be taken as a tax *credit* by the employer rather than just as a deduction.[30]

The tax treatment of benefits varies substantially. Often, Congress will specify certain attributes the benefit must have in order to be "qualified" for favorable tax treatment. A common rule is that the benefits should be offered to employees in a nondiscriminatory manner, that is, offered to most employees, not just high-paid executives. Over the years Congress has incorporated more and more complex requirements into the tax code. Indeed, Congress has tended to view employer-provided benefits partly as a national social welfare program over which it exercises certain supervisory authority. Pressure to move in this direction intensified in the 1980s, due to large federal government budget deficits. Rather than spend government funds, Congress may prefer to spend employer monies by adjusting the tax code or mandating certain benefits.

Generally, tax rules for plans such as pensions that involve saving for retirement permit employer deductions and employee tax deferral until the benefits are actually paid out. Health and life insurance plans, up to a specified limit, are deductible to the employer and not taxable to the employee. The precise rules change, however, whenever Congress modifies the tax code. It is the tax code that has provided the greatest incentive for benefit expansion in the post-World War II period.

The influence of the tax code can also be seen in Figure 7–1. Imagine that the employee starts as before with a cash-only wage of $0A$. If the employer or employee can obtain a tax break by purchasing benefits at work, the effective cost of benefits falls. This fall is reflected in a new budget line, AB', that would enable the employee to reach point b. However, the employer will be able to reduce cash outlays (to $0A''$), and the employee will maximize welfare at point c. Congress generally insists that tax breaks will be available only if the employer is the formal payer of the benefits. Hence employer-paid and -provided benefits have become the standard practice.[31]

Union Influence

Acknowledging the influence of the tax code on benefits raises still another question. What led Congress to use the tax code to stimulate certain kinds of benefits? It is sometimes said that the initial impetus came from a government desire to stimulate saving rather than consumption during World War II.[32] Benefits such as life insurance and pensions are forms of saving. A close examination of the record reveals that these benefits were not widely available during the war,[33] and really active use of the tax code by Congress was largely a postwar development.

The push for tax-favored fringe benefits seems to have mirrored developments in the union sector. In the late 1930s various forms of government-operated social insurance benefits (such as Social Security) were adopted as part of the New Deal program of the Roosevelt administration.[34] Unions, particularly those with liberal/left orientations, initially believed that this trend would continue after World War II and that programs such as national health insurance would soon be adopted. But the postwar period brought a more conservative mood in Congress, and the expected rapid expansion of social insurance did not occur. Unions began to try to obtain social benefits directly from employers—partly in what they saw as an interim step—rather than wait for the federal government to provide those benefits.

Employers initially resisted fringe benefit demands of unions. Those employers that had such benefits viewed them as symbols of employer goodwill that they wanted employees to appreciate. Employers wanted benefits to be perceived by workers as something that did not arise from unions and bargaining. A U.S. Supreme Court decision in the late 1940s, however, declared that employers had to bargain with unions over their benefit offerings.[35] As a result certain unions became leaders in the innovation of new and expanded benefits.

As unions found themselves more and more in the fringe benefit business, the question of the tax status of these benefits arose. Unions pushed to have benefits either be exempt from income taxation, or for taxation to be at least deferred until payments were actually received by workers. In the postwar period, unions were important influences in Congress, and so the preferential tax treatment of benefits became ingrained in national policy.

Fringe benefits have special features that appeal to unions. First, they are particularly visible outcomes of bargaining and can convince workers of the union's ability to improve conditions. If union bargaining strength is used to obtain, say, another 1% to 2% wage increase, workers have no way of ascertaining whether such an increase might have been forthcoming in any case. But if the union can come up with a new, highly visible benefit, worker loyalty to the union can be strengthened. The union simply is following the same strategy often used by sellers of consumer products: rather than cut the price directly, the seller relies on visible rebates, coupons, gifts, and the like so that the consumer will perceive and appreciate the bargain being offered.

Second, fringe benefits often favor senior workers over juniors. Pension plans, for example, often provide no benefit at all to short-service employees who leave the company after a few years. Typically, pension formulas require a significant period of attachment to the firm before benefit entitlement ('vesting') occurs. Actual retirement benefits, even after vesting, are frequently tilted towards long-service employees in the defined benefit plans favored by unions.[36]

As we will see in the chapter on collective bargaining, unions have built-in political incentives to favor senior workers. Fringe benefits have become a means to this end. Thus it is not surprising that the union sector provided a substantial impetus for the growth of fringe benefits and for reinforcement of such growth through the tax code.

Benefit Lobby

As benefits expanded, unions were joined by other interests in maintaining and enlarging the tax preferences for fringes. Insurance companies and management-consulting firms that sold or administered benefit plans became a component of the fringe benefit lobby. Employers, whose compensation system became more and more tilted towards benefits, also joined the effort. Finally, as the number of covered employees rose, these employees themselves became an element in the politics of fringes.

Although Congress has tinkered with the tax treatment of benefits, the basic structure that arose after World War II has remained intact. From time to time, the question of why employers should be the providers of benefits is raised by academics. But the issue has become just that—an academic question. Modern HRM administrators correctly assume that benefit management will be part of their responsibility indefinitely.

Advantages to Employers

In 1929 wages and salaries accounted for 99% of employee compensation in the private sector. Fringe benefits paid by the employer were virtually nonexistent, although some large firms did offer limited—and well-publicized—benefits.[37] The historical evidence suggests that employers did not rush into the offering of fringes until subjected to external pressures and incentives. In some cases benefit plans were seen as a way of holding off unions in the early twentieth century.[38] Generally, however, employers did not see an advantage in providing significant benefit compensation before the 1930s, 1940s, and 1950s brought strong union pressure and tax incentives.

The fact that employers probably would not have initiated the proliferation of benefits that is now common does not mean that no advantages accrued to employers from offering fringes. At the time, however, these advantages were not perceived to exist (or were not perceived as being sufficiently important) for employers to develop modern complex compensation arrangements unilaterally.

Advantages from Pension Plans   Economic analysis has been applied to the provision of benefits from the employer's perspective (apart from the tax, scale, and risk-pooling aspects already discussed). The emphasis in this analysis has been on cost savings and productivity improvements resulting from benefit-related turnover reduction and incentives. Generally, these effects have been associated with *deferred* benefits such as pensions, particularly those for which there is a significant waiting period before benefit eligibility occurs. For convenience, this section concentrates on pension plans as examples.

Pension plans come in two basic varieties: defined contribution and defined benefit. (The latter are associated with larger firms, unionization, and situations in which large employer investments have been made in employees.[39]) Under a *defined contribution plan*, the employer regularly contributes a sum on behalf of the employee to a trust fund. The contributed sum is typically fixed by formula and geared to the employee's current wage, for example, 5% of the wage. When the worker retires or leaves the firm, he or she receives the employer contributions plus whatever has been earned as a return on the investment.

At the time of separation, the funds accumulated under a defined contribution plan can be rolled over into another tax-deferred vehicle (such as an IRA account) by the departing employee or can be used to purchase an annuity at retirement age. The monthly income received from the annuity will depend on actuarial considerations—age and health of the worker—and the relevant market returns on funds then prevailing.[40] The worker has no guarantee concerning the eventual monthly payment that will be received. He or she thus assumes the risk resulting from uncertainty over future market interest rates and over his or her future health condition.

Under a *defined benefit plan*, in contrast, it is the employer (or, more accurately, the plan) that assumes the risk.[41] The employee's monthly pension is set by a formula. Such formulas typically reflect the wage, years of service to the firm, and age, each of which tends to increase the pension. Under the Employee Retirement Income Security Act of 1974 (ERISA), the employer is supposed to put aside sufficient resources today to fund tomorrow's liabilities.[42] But since the actual cost of the obligation will depend on the future course of earnings of the pension fund portfolio, the age composition of the workforce, and so on, the amount put aside can only be an estimate.

Defined contribution plans typically do not have prolonged vesting periods. Often, vesting under such plans is immediate. The employee can take whatever is in his or her account upon departure from the firm. Defined benefit plans, however, often do have long vesting periods. Until 1986 a common rule was that vesting would not occur until ten years of service. This type of vesting is known as cliff vesting because all the vesting occurs on a single date. In 1986 new legislation brought the maximum cliff vesting period down to five years in private employment.[43] Even with a 5-year rule, many workers may enter and leave the firm's employment without picking up any pension entitlement.

Even apart from vesting, the formulas of defined benefit plans tend to discriminate against short-service employees. If an employee quits soon after the vesting period, he or she will be entitled to something. But that something will probably be less than the discounted value of the future pension, had employment continued. The combination of significant vesting periods and formulas that discriminate against short-service job leavers thus creates an incentive for workers to stay with the firm. Put another way, defined benefit pension plans tend to reduce employee quits, which can be expensive to the employer, by creating what are poetically called golden handcuffs.

Defined benefit pensions increase in value to the employee as service increases. They thus create an incentive for continued productivity, in the presence of imperfect monitoring by the employer's supervisory agents. If a worker were to be terminated for inadequate performance, he or she would pay a heavy penalty in terms of partially forfeited pension entitlements. The pension right, which is in fact contingent on satisfactory job performance, functions as a quasi-performance bond.

Note also that the magnitude of the bond rises with age and service. This feature ties pensions into efficiency wage theory. Under that theory, as discussed in the previous chapter, employers adjust wages so that a penalty is suffered by a worker fired for malfeasance, shirking, or inadequate performance. As a worker approaches the end of his or her working life, the bond must become progressively higher, since lost income associated with job termination could extend for only a few remaining years.

Efficiency wage theory suggests that employers would create upward sloping seniority/wage profiles to make nonperformance at the end of working life sufficiently costly for the employee. Defined benefit pension formulas create similar incentives by establishing a large reward (penalty) for high (low) productivity. Offering a defined benefit pension is thus a partial substitute for an upward sloping wage profile.[44] It has been found, for example, that unionized employers offer flatter wage profiles than others but are more likely to have defined benefit pensions. Thus pension/wage profile substitution may be occurring.

Still another aspect of efficiency wage theory links it to employer pension policy. If the earnings profile is tilted upward for reward/penalty purposes, there comes a point late in working life in which the gap between current wage and actual value to the firm becomes excessive.[45] According to this view, older workers will earn substantially more than their current value to the firm. The employer will be increasingly tempted to replace them with younger (new entrant) workers.

Simply firing older workers capriciously (were it legal) would violate the implicit contract that underlies the profile. To avoid such violations, some advance understanding about when the contract ends could be included in the implicit arrangement. Efficiency wage and implicit contracting considerations thus suggest that, with an upward sloped earnings profile, the firm will want to specify a mandatory retirement age.[46]

What the firm wants, however, and what it may legally do can diverge. For various reasons—including fears of inadequate Social Security revenue if too many elderly workers retired and drew benefits rather than paid taxes—Congress has legislated against age-related mandatory retirement. The federal Age Discrimination in Employment Act (ADEA) of 1967 originally forbade mandatory retirement below age 65 for most employees. In the late 1970s this floor was raised to 70. And in 1986 ADEA was further amended to forbid mandatory retirement for almost all employees at *any* age.

Because of these constraints, employers may need some device to induce employees to retire without the firm's actually requiring it.[47] A retirement benefit that peaks in value to the employee at the age at which the employer would otherwise want to require retirement may be that device. In this view, then, pensions are an important part of overall HRM policy.

Despite the advantages of defined benefit pensions, nonunion employers more typically offer the defined contribution alternative. The latter is, as already noted, less risky for the employer and cheaper to administer. Moreover, Social Security—which provides defined benefits—creates retirement incentives in the age range around 65 years.[48] Given Social Security incentives, many employers may feel that added inducements from their own plans are unnecessary. They see some advantage from defined benefit plans but not enough to outweigh the disadvantages.

Although ERISA places a variety of legal restraints on underfunding of defined benefit pension plans, significant underfunding is common. By underfunding, the firm is sharing the risks of the marketplace with its employees.[49] Employees in such firms are in effect placing their trust in the ability of the firm to survive in the marketplace and cover benefit obligations.

Such a situation enhances the stake employees have in the firm and its continuation.[50] There may be an advantage to employers in unionized situations to have this group stake in the firm's economic health accentuated through a defined benefit pension. The union is less likely to take actions that might undermine the firm's economic well-being. On the other hand, since ERISA requires that defined-benefit pension plans be insured against bankruptcy by a government-sponsored agency—the Pension Benefit Guaranty Corporation (PBGC)—these incentives are somewhat weakened. Should the plan go bankrupt, workers would receive at least some of their pensions because of the presence of "termination insurance."[51]

Defined benefit pensions are not the only employee benefit plans that accord some advantages to the employer, but they are the most prominent example. Furthermore, many other benefits really do not closely match the efficiency wage/ implicit contracting model (although they can be justified by scale/risk-pooling/ tax incentive considerations). Moreover, the regulation of benefits by Congress makes their use for long-term HRM policy difficult. As the history of the ADEA indicates, Congress can easily override employer inclinations. For example, Congress is already concerned about excessive inducements to retire under pension formulas.

Advantages from Wellness and Health Benefits   The auction market model of the labor market—in which no ongoing relationship exists between employer and employee—is incompatible with the phenomenon of employer wellness efforts. In an auction world the employer would always hire those workers who were in adequate health and avoid others or pay them lower wages. Since no ongoing employer–employee relationship exists in an auction world, employers would not be concerned about the future health of workers they had on the payroll at a particular moment.

In the real world, however, employers increasingly offer programs to help employees stop smoking, end alcohol or drug dependencies, or resolve family or personal problems through counseling. Today such programs are often known as—or associated with—Employee Assistance Programs (EAPs). Some observers trace the origins of wellness programs all the way back to the welfare work that certain firms undertook early in this century.[52]

Employee health problems can affect employers adversely in several ways. They may reduce productivity, cause safety problems and accidents, lead to increased absenteeism, or run up health insurance and workers' compensation costs. None of these adverse effects could occur, of course, if the employer felt completely free to terminate any employee whose productivity fell below standard, assuming such falls could be perfectly and immediately detected. The existence of EAPs is yet another sign of the ongoing employer/employee linkage.[53]

As in many other aspects of HRM practice, the employee wellness area could benefit from a substantial dose of quantification. There are no good data on exactly how many EAPs actually exist, let alone what their effect has been. A 1984 study by the Conference Board surveyed senior human resource officers and found that about one-fifth reported significant EAP activity in their firms.[54] Another study reports that a typical EAP has saved employers far more than its operating costs and suggests that employers who do not install EAPs are at best shortsighted.[55] Yet, since few studies have been undertaken, it is difficult to accept these conclusions uncritically.

Perhaps the lack of hard data on wellness programs and EAPs should not be surprising. Firms may well be reluctant to provide information on their EAP experience. For example, even if very successful EAP experience has occurred, reports that a firm "solved its drug problem" risk public disclosure that a drug problem once existed. Concerns about drug usage on the job could make such information damaging.

Despite difficulty in obtaining survey information from other firms, employers can use their own internal data sources to monitor the before and after effects of EAPs. They can examine records on absenteeism, accidents, and health insurance, for example. Use of individual employee data, however, poses problems, since EAP experts insist that strict confidentiality is a key ingredient of success. EAP operations typically fall within the purview of the HRM department, which should be making cost/benefit analyses of all such programs.

7–6   Empirical Look at Benefits

There are two types of data available on fringe benefits. Cost data provide information on the expense of fringe benefits paid by the employer. Such data are inevitably based on actual, out-of-pocket expenses. (The incurring of unfunded liabilities will not be reflected.) In addition to cost data, information is available on the incidence of particular benefits, that is, the proportion of the workforce covered by various plans. Cost data are available from the national income accounts and a BLS survey. Incidence data also appear in reports of the Bureau of Labor Statistics.

Data on Benefit Costs

The national income (GNP) accounts provide only very aggregative information on benefits, as illustrated in Table 7–8. Table 7–8 shows that the nonwage element of compensation has historically risen. By the mid-1980s roughly half of nonwage compensation was legally required. This component includes Social Security taxes paid by the employer, unemployment insurance taxes, and premiums paid to private workers' compensation carriers or state-operated workers' compensation funds. The remainder of nonwage compensation, as defined in the national income accounts, includes such items as payments to pension plans and insurance programs.

Although national income account data are useful for pointing to general trends, their lack of detail means that they are of only limited use for benefit planning within the firm. More detailed information on benefit costs is provided in an annual survey taken by the BLS. Examples of the data obtained are shown in Table 7–9. Similar tables from BLS break down compensation expenditure by region, broad occupational group, and union status.

Table 7–8   Trends in Nonwage Compensation, 1929–1986

| Year | *Nonwage Compensation as Percent of Total Compensation* | | |
	Total	Legally Required*	All Other†
1929	1%	n.a.	n.a.
1939	5	n.a.	n.a.
1949	5	3%	2%
1959	8	4	4
1969	10	5	5
1979	16	8	8
1986	17	9	8

*Social Security, Railroad Retirement, unemployment insurance, and workers' compensation.

†Private, public, and military pensions, health insurance, life insurance, supplementary unemployment benefit plans, and other.

Source: Data from U.S. Bureau of Economic Analysis, *The National Income & Product Accounts of the United States, 1929-82: Statistical Tables* (Washington: GPO, 1986), Tables 6.4B, 6.5A, 6.12, 6.13; *Survey of Current Business,* vol. 67 (July 1987), pp. 59, 62-63.

Table 7–9   Composition of Compensation Reported by U.S. Bureau of Labor Statistics, March 1988

Type of Payment	Payment as Percent of Private Compensation	Payment as Percent of Private Benefits
Wages and salaries	72.7%	—
Legally required payments	8.8	—
Private benefits	18.5	100.0%
Pensions and savings	3.3	17.6
Insurance	5.6	30.6
Vacation pay	3.5	18.8
Holiday pay	2.4	12.9
Sick leave	.9	4.7
All other	2.8	15.3
Total Compensation	100.0	—

Note: Total private benefits = $2.55; legally required payments = $1.22; average hourly earnings = $10.02.

Source: U.S. Bureau of Labor Statistics, "Employer Costs for Employee Compensation–March 1988," press release USDL: 88-293, June 16, 1988, Table 2.

Table 7–9 indicates that over a fourth of compensation is nonwage. This figure is higher than the level indicated by the national income accounts because it includes such items as vacation, holiday, and sick-leave pay. If the table were adjusted to national income definitions by placing such items under wages and salaries, the two series would be generally comparable.

The BLS did not produce data on the compensation mix until 1987.[56] Hence, pay setters often relied on a private survey published by the U.S. Chamber of Commerce.[57] Yet users of Chamber of Commerce data need to be cautious about casually citing summary data. The Chamber generally reports benefits as a percent of *payroll*, rather than as a percent of total *compensation*. Use of the smaller denominator inflates the quoted estimates. Although the reason for the Chamber's peculiar style of presentation is not entirely clear, there may be a public relations factor behind it. Chamber data are often cited to show the great burden (or generosity) that benefits represent to business. Publicizing a large fraction may therefore appear advantageous.

Incidence Data

Because the design of employee benefits is highly complex, compensation planners will have only limited use for cost data. Such data are mainly useful as a benchmark against which a firm's own overall benefit costs can be measured. Also, cost data are only a rough guide, since—due to variations in demographic factors—the identical benefit may produce different costs at different firms.[58] Of greater interest will be the frequency with which particular plans are offered and the specific formulas embodied in particular plans.

During the 1980s the U.S. Bureau of Labor Statistics developed a benefit survey designed to capture information of this type. The survey applies only to medium- and large-sized firms, thus biasing the sample toward employers likely to have richer benefit packages.[59] It also limits its coverage to full-time workers. (Part timers are less likely to enjoy fringe benefits.) Thus only about a fourth of the private sector workforce is reflected.

A sample of the BLS data is presented in Table 7–10. As can be seen, certain types of benefits—such as retirement plans and health insurance—are nearly universal for full-time workers in firms of significant size. Disability plans are less common. An HRM compensation specialist in a firm whose benefit package looked very different from the average might well want to examine the reasons for the deviation. Is there some motive of corporate strategy that accounts for the difference?

Table 7–10 also illustrates some of the more detailed information on particular benefit plans available from the BLS survey. For example, one measure of pension adequacy is the ratio of initial pension benefit to final year's earnings. This measure, the replacement ratio, is simulated for various earnings/years of service profiles by the BLS. As the lower panel of the table shows, a worker with twenty-five years of service can expect to replace roughly half of preretirement income from a combination of Social Security and pension.

This replacement ratio represents a potentially drastic fall in income. A firm

**Table 7–10   Sample Data from BLS Survey of Employee Benefits in Medium-
and Large-Sized Firms, 1986**

Type of Benefit	Percent of Full-Time Employees Receiving Benefits
Retirement plan(s)	89%
Health insurance	95
Short-term disability	49
Long-term disability	48
Paid vacations	100
Paid holidays	99

First Annual Earnings	Earnings Replacement Ratios for Employees with 25 Years of Service	
	Pension Only	Pension Plus Social Security
$15,000	26%	69%
$30,000	23	53
$40,000	24	46

Source: Data from U.S. Bureau of Labor Statistics, *Employee benefits in Medium and Large Firms, 1986,* bulletin 2281 (Washington: GPO, 1987), p. 4 (upper panel), p. 67 (lower panel).

hoping to encourage retirements as a way of making a voluntary workforce reduction might thus meet resistance. Special severance pay arrangements or pension supplements might also be required. With the outlawing of mandatory retirement, firms might want to consider encouraging employee use of additional savings arrangements.

For example, the BLS study reports that less than a third of the employees within the scope of the survey had available 401(k) plans (tax-deferred savings arrangements). Such savings plans can supplement retirement income from pension and Social Security. Their availability may also help induce retirements of older workers who can no longer be retired mandatorily.

The complexity of the benefit field poses an empirical problem for those who would provide data and those who would use it. Even the best external surveys can provide only a general guide for internal benefit planning. Ultimately, a firm's benefit package should reflect the needs of its employees and its HRM objectives (such as turnover control or retirement encouragement). What others are doing is useful, but not decisive, information.

Summary

In this chapter, the compensation decision was examined from various perspectives. In establishing its general pay policy, a firm needs to determine if it wants to be a relatively high-, low-, or average-paying employer. It needs also to establish an internal wage structure, that is, pay differentials between jobs. Moreover, the firm needs to determine its preferred mix of wages versus benefits.

An important element in pay and benefit setting is the determination of what other employers are doing. A variety of data sources are available to pay setters, both from government agencies such as the BLS and from private sources. However, for jobs that are unique to the firm, outside market information will not be available. Firms commonly use some form of job evaluation in these cases to establish their internal pay structures. Employers would do well, however, to consider other approaches involving human resource accounting and consideration of turnover costs.

The widespread use of fringe benefits as an element of compensation has several roots, including economies of scale, risk pooling, union pressures, tax treatment, and the benefit lobby. Employers derive certain benefits from plans that reduce worker turnover. However, benefit administration has grown very complex and considerable expertise is needed to keep up with changing congressional tax regulation. A later chapter will point out that benefit administration has also been importantly affected by federal equal employment opportunity policy.

Once basic decisions are made on the level, structure, and wage-versus-benefit mix of pay, general pay adjustments must be considered. Even during periods of low inflation, nominal compensation levels creep upward. Chapter 8 addresses the issue of regular increase in the general pay level.

EXERCISES

Problem

Obtain data from the national income accounts on the proportion of nonwage pay relative to total compensation by detailed industry. (These data typically appear annually in the July issue of the *Survey of Current Business*.) The proportion will vary from industry to industry. See if you can come up with plausible explanations for the variation.

Questions

1. What kinds of information do employers usually obtain when setting wages?

2. If you wanted information about the general level of wages paid in a particular city, what might be a possible source?

3. What is the difference between job evaluation and performance appraisal?

4. Why might large firms tend to pay a higher percentage of their compensation in the form of fringe benefits?

5. What advantages might accrue to an employer from providing a pension program?

6. What has been the influence of the tax code on employee benefits? How have unions influenced benefits?

Terms

adverse selection	Equal Pay Act	job analysis
cafeteria plan	ERISA	Pension Benefit Guarantee
comparable worth	establishment survey	Corporation
defined benefit pension	401(k)	mandatory retirement
defined contribution	golden handcuffs	red circling
pension	human resource	two-tier wage plan
EAPs	accounting	vesting
efficiency wage model	implicit contracting	

ENDNOTES

1. Information on BLS wage data and methodology can be found in U.S. Bureau of Labor Statistics, *BLS Measures of Compensation,* bulletin 2239 (Washington: GPO, 1986).

2. The earnings, hours, employment, and payroll data apply to the pay period containing the 12th of the month.

3. Railroad Retirement, a government-run retirement program for railroad employees, is similar to Social Security. It was established during the Great Depression of the 1930s when private railroad pension plans failed.

4. Some state and local workers and agricultural workers are not covered by UI and thus are excluded from the data.

5. Sanford M. Jacoby and Daniel J.B. Mitchell, "Alternative Sources of Labor Market Data" in Barbara D. Dennis, ed., *Proceedings of the Thirty-Eighth Annual Meeting,* Industrial Relations Research Association, December 28–30, 1985 (Madison, Wisc.: IRRA, 1986), pp. 42–49.

6. Not all the information available on executive pay is aimed at serious pay setters, however. An annual survey by *Business Week* magazine, for example, seems largely designed to appeal to the public's appetite for information on the wealthy. In many respects curiosity about executive pay

mirrors that relating to the incomes of professional athletes, movie stars, and other celebrities.

7. An exception is the *Top Executive Compensation* series published annually by the Conference Board.

8. Bureau of National Affairs, Inc., *Wage & Salary Administration,* PPF Survey No. 131 (Washington: BNA, 1981), p. 4.

9. See Donald J. Treiman and Heidi I. Hartman, eds., *Women, Work, and Wages: Equal Pay for Jobs of Equal Value* (Washington: National Academy Press, 1981); Donald J. Treiman, *Job Evaluation: An Analytic Review,* interim report to the Equal Employment Opportunity Commission, staff paper (Washington: National Academy of Sciences, 1979); Henry J. Aaron and Cameran M. Lougy, *The Comparable Worth Controversy* (Washington: Brookings Institution, 1986); U.S. Commission on Civil Rights, *Comparable Worth: An Analysis and Recommendations* (Washington: U.S. Commission on Civil Rights, 1985); Daniel R. Fischel and Edward P. Lazear, "Comparable Worth and Discrimination in Labor Markets," *University of Chicago Law Review,* vol. 53 (Summer 1986), pp. 891–918; James D. Holzhauer, "The Economic Possibilities of Comparable Worth,"

University of Chicago Law Review, vol. 53 (Summer 1986), pp. 919–933. The views of an official of Hay Associates, which provides job evaluation services for employers, can be found in The Bureau of National Affairs, Inc., *The Comparable Worth Issue* (Washington: BNA, 1981), pp. 44–46.

10. Walter A. Fogel, *The Equal Pay Act: Implications for Comparable Worth* (New York: Praeger, 1984).

11. Aaron Bernstein, "Comparable Worth: It's Already Happening," *Business Week* (April 28, 1986), pp. 52, 56.

12. For information on the Australian case, see Daniel J.B. Mitchell, "The Australian Labor Market" in Richard E. Caves and Lawrence B. Krause, eds., *The Australian Economy: A View from the North* (Washington: Brookings Institution, 1984), 127–193; Robert G. Gregory and Ros K. Anstie, "Equal Pay in Australia: Can Women Do Better than 88 Cents in the Hourly Male Dollar?," working paper prepared for Pacific Rim Comparative Labour Policy Conference, Vancouver, B.C., Canada, June 1987.

13. Perry C. Beider, B. Douglas Bernheim, Victor R. Fuchs, John B. Shoven, "Comparable Worth in a General Equilibrium Model of the U.S. Economy," working paper no. 2090, National Bureau of Economic Research, December 1986.

14. Peter B. Doeringer and Michael J. Piore, *Internal Labor Markets and Manpower Analysis* (Lexington: Mass.: Heath, 1971).

15. The Employment Cost Index for wages and salaries in the private sector was used for this computation.

16. Eric G. Flamholtz, *Human Resource Accounting,* second edition (San Francisco: Jossey-Bass, 1985), chapter 12.

17. Some employees may not quit, but may simply not be found capable of rising to the higher position. Or it may turn out that a qualified, lower-level employee is simply not needed in the higher job.

18. Flamholtz, *Human Resource Accounting, ibid.,* pp. 347–378.

19. There is a problem in allocating development costs. For example, an entry level employee may receive some initial training that is partly useful in the initial job, but that also would be useful in the eventual job at the top of the career ladder. The firm may recapture some of the training cost in the entry position, even if the employee quits before rising through the hierarchy.

20. Employers may have personnel manuals in which some of the rules are written down. In some cases, courts have treated these manuals as contractual obligations.

21. Workers in government jobs may be covered by written civil service procedures that serve as quasi-contractual protections.

22. Richard S. Belous, "Two-Tier Wage Systems in the U.S. Economy," report no. 85–165 E, Congressional Research Service, August 12, 1985; Sanford M. Jacoby and Daniel J.B. Mitchell, "Management Attitudes Toward Two-Tier Pay Plans," *Journal of Labor Research,* vol. 7 (Summer 1986), pp. 221–237.

23. There may be conflicting notions of equity in some cases. For example, the two-tier wage systems mentioned above may create resentment among the lower-paid new hires. See James E. Martin and Melanie M. Peterson, "Two-Tier Wage Structures: An Equity Theory Approach," working paper, Department of Management, Wayne State University, undated. In some cases, however, workers in the lower tier were reported to have positive work attitudes, perhaps because they attribute their hiring to the creation of the lower tier. See Peter Cappelli and Peter D. Sherer, "Assessing Worker Attitudes Under a Two-Tier Wage Plan," working paper no. 726, Wharton School, University of Pennsylvania, November 1987.

24. There have been complaints about the absence of notice, or of very short notice, prior to plant closings. Since long advance notice might help workers obtain alternative jobs, absence of notice is viewed as unfair by employees. From the employer's perspective, if everyone began to depart— including the best (and most marketable) employees—plant operations would suffer in the pre-closing period. The employer's advantage in not disclosing the shutdown in advance is not tempered by future employee morale deterioration, since the employment relation is about to end. This may account for the finding of one study that median advance notification of plant closures and permanent layoffs was only seven days, with many firms giving no notice at all. See U.S. General Accounting Office, *Plant Closings: Limited Advance Notice and Assistance Provided Dislocated Workers,* GAO/HRD–87–105 (Washington: GAO, 1987), pp. 34–39. Some companies that do provide significant advance notice for shutdowns report doing so to maintain morale of other employees (those not affected by the layoff) or because of community relations concerns. See Ronald E. Berenbeim, *Company Programs to Ease the Impact of Shutdowns,* report no. 878 (New York: The Conference Board, 1986), p. 11. The plant closing issue will be discussed in a later chapter.

25. The slope of AB is the inverse of the price of benefits.

26. In some cases, mainly in the union sector, employers are grouped into large multiemployer pension plans. One study revealed significant scale economies in such plans. Presumably, these economies are also to be found in single-employer plans. See Olivia S. Mitchell and Emily S. Andrews, "Scale Economies in Private Multi-Employer Pension Systems,"

Industrial and Labor Relations Review, vol. 34 (July 1981), pp. 522–530.

27. Until the late 1970s, the BLS published a series providing a breakdown of compensation that included data by size of establishment. Establishment size and firm size are not the same thing, since firms may have more than one establishment. However, the two concepts are positively correlated, and the BLS series indicated an association of size with relative expenditure of nonwage compensation. See, for example, U.S. Bureau of Labor Statistics, *Employee Compensation in the Private Nonfarm Economy, 1974,* bulletin 1963 (Washington: GPO, 1977), p. 30. The evidence suggests that firms which have richer (absolute) benefit expenditures do not simply deduct the cost of these on a dollar-for-dollar basis from regular wages. It is not surprising that firms that pay more in benefits also pay more in wages. See Steven G. Allen and Robert L. Clark, "Pensions and Firm Performance" in Morris M. Kleiner, Richard N. Block, Myron Roomkin, and Sidney W. Salsburg, eds., *Human Resources and the Performance of the Firm* (Madison, Wisc.: Industrial Relations Research Association, 1987), pp. 195–242, especially pp. 198, 224–227.

28. It should be noted that small employers can still offer risk-pooling economies to insurance carriers. If employees are automatically enrolled in a benefit program, regardless of preference, adverse selection will not occur. By soliciting business from many small employers, the carrier can achieve a broad cross section of risks. Dealing with many small employers will raise administrative costs. Small employers, particularly in firms in which unions are involved, may band together into associations and provide benefits through these groups, thus reducing administrative costs.

29. Disregarding the tax considerations discussed in the next section, there is no difference in welfare between a $500 per week employee who must contribute $50 to a benefit plan and a $450 per week employeee whose employer contributes $50 toward the same benefit. As will be seen, however, under existing tax law the welfare difference could be considerable.

30. As noted in a previous chapter, in the early 1980s Congress created a benefit, known as the PAYSOP plan, under which employees were given stock in their firms. The stock was to be held by a trust for employees for retirement and similar purposes. Employer contributions to the PAYSOP trust were taken as a tax credit, that is, the employer's tax liability was reduced dollar for dollar for each dollar of stock contributed. Thus the federal government effectively bought the stock for employees. The employees paid no income tax on shares received until the stock was withdrawn. As a result, the subsidy to PAYSOPs exceeded 100% of their

cost. Not surprisingly, Congress decided to end this subsidy as part of tax modifications passed in 1986.

31. Certain qualifications need to be made to this statement. In some cases, employers want to share costs with employees (despite tax incentives) to limit excessive usage of the benefit. This issue arises particularly with regard to health care costs. Employers may feel that if employees pay a deductible or receive only partial reimbursement of medical expenses, they will economize on the use of medical services. Another point is that employers can offer plans under which salaries are reduced for tax purposes and the resulting money diverted into benefits that the employee would otherwise need to fund. The employee thus pays for benefits on a pre-tax basis, blurring the distinction between an employer-paid and an employee-paid benefit.

32. World War II involved a substantial reallocation of production away from consumption goods and toward military output. If consumers saved more, the argument went, they would spend less on scarce consumer goods, thus facilitating the reallocation. The argument, of course, neglects the possibility that if employees have savings put away from them through work-related benefit plans, they may reduce saving from their own cash incomes. The latter effect could, at the limit, offset the former.

33. John T. Dunlop, "An Appraisal of Wage Stabilization Policies" in U.S. Bureau of Labor Statistics, *Problems and Policies of Dispute Settlement and Wage Stabilization During World War II.* bulletin 1009 (Washington: GPO, 1950), pp. 155–186, especially pp. 166–167.

34. Irving Bernstein, *A Caring Society: The New Deal, the Worker, and the Great Depression* (Boston: Houghton Mifflin, 1985).

35. *Inland Steel Co. v. NLRB* (1948).

36. Richard B. Freeman and James L. Medoff, *What Do Unions Do?* (New York: Basic Books, 1984), pp. 129–132.

37. Sometimes, insurance companies saw an opportunity to sell policies to employees of larger firms and would induce the employer to cooperate.

38. Sanford M. Jacoby, *Employing Bureaucracy: Managers, Unions, and the Transformation of Work in American Industry, 1900–1945* (New York: Columbia University Press, 1985), p. 52–53. When benefits such as nonvested pensions are at stake, employees might be reluctant to take actions, such as joining a union, that might lead to their dismissal.

39. Stuart Dorsey, "The Economic Functions of Private Pensions: An Empirical Analysis," *Journal of Labor Economics,* vol. 5 (October 1987), Part 2, pp. S171–S189.

40. Under a Supreme Court decision, an annuity offered through an employer cannot be based on separate actuarial tables for males and females, although women on average live significantly longer than men. This aspect of public policy will be discussed in a later chapter.

41. By law, pension plans are established as independent entities with their own trustees. The employer, however, has liability for underfunding. In potential mergers and acquisitions, the pension liabilities of the target firms are routinely evaluated along with other assets and liabilities. Sometimes, pension liabilities are crucial elements in determining the success or failure of such deals and/or the prices involved.

42. In fact, pension plans are often underfunded. Many plans were not fully funded when ERISA went into effect and were given time to correct their underfunding. In addition, firms in shaky financial situations can sometimes win approval to delay full funding. Public policy in this area will be discussed in a later chapter.

43. ERISA privides alternatives to the five-year rule.

44. Robert M. Hutchens, "A Test of Lazear's Theory of Delayed Payment Contracts," *Journal of Economic Literature,* vol. 5 (October 1987), Part 2, pp. S153–S170.

45. Robert Hutchens, "Delayed Payment Contracts and a Firm's Propensity to Hire Older Workers," *Journal of Labor Economics*, vol. 4 (October 1987), pp. 439–457.

46. Lazear, Edward, "Why is There Mandatory Retirement?," *Journal of Political Economy,* vol. 87 (December 1979), pp. 1261–1284.

47. Studies of retirement decisions of employees suggest that pension formulas have a significant influence on these decisions. See Olivia S. Mitchell and Gary S. Fields, "The Economics of Retirement Behavior," *Journal of Labor Economics,* vol. 2 (January 1984), pp. 84–105.

48. Gary Burtless and Robert A. Moffitt, "The Joint Choice of Retirement Age and Postretirement Hours of Work," *Journal of Labor Economics,* vol. 3 (April 1985), pp. 209–236.

49. Rebecca A. Luzadis, "Defined Benefit, Defined Contribution, or No Pension?" in Barbara D. Dennis, ed., *Proceedings of the Thirty-Ninth Annual Meeting,* Industrial Relations Research Association, December 28–30, 1986 (Madison, Wisc.: IRRA, 1987), pp. 222–225.

50. One qualification is that there is some evidence that employees are often unaware of the type of pension they have: defined benefit or defined contribution. However, knowledge of pension provisions rises with seniority. See Olivia S. Mitchell, "Worker Knowledge of Pension Provisions," *Journal of Labor Economics,* vol. 6 (January 1988), pp. 21–39.

51. The presence of the PBGC raises a host of problems related to pension fund risk management which are not considered in this chapter. Employee benefits under a bankrupt pension plan are not completely insured, so there remains some risk of default. On the other hand, given the way the program is structured, there can be incentives for employers in precarious financial situations to *want* to bankrupt their underfunded pension plans and push the liability to the PBGC. The result of these misincentives has been escalating insurance premiums for other (nonbankrupt) plans. Suggestions have been made to vary the premiums charged for insurance according to the riskiness of the plan, that is, its unfunded liability. However, Congress has been fearful that raising premiums to the most underfunded plans would push them into bankruptcy.

A host of special problems are also related to multiemployer plans and pension termination insurance. Small employers who may belong to such plans may find themselves saddled with large bills for unfunded liabilities should they attempt to withdraw. In some cases this development has given unions leverage to prevent employers from attempting to withdraw from multiemployer bargaining situations.

52. Donald W. Myers, *Human Resources Management: Principles and Practice* (Chicago: Commerce Clearing House, 1986), pp. 612–619.

53. Employers may have other motivations for having EAPs as well. Federal regulations restricting discrimination against the handicapped by federal contractors can play a role, since EAPs deal partly with alcohol- and drug-dependency problems. Employers may be concerned that such problems might be considered protected handicaps, although, in fact, individuals with active dependencies (as opposed to those who had a problem in their past) can be discharged. On the other hand, testing individual workers for drugs has raised many controversial issues, and employers who conduct such tests may prefer to have an EAP option for individuals found to have used drugs.

54. Helen Axel, *Corporations and Families: Changing Practices and Perspectives,* report no. 868 (New York: Conference Board, 1985), p. 49.

55. Bureau of National Affairs, Inc., *Alcohol & Drugs in the Workplace: Costs, Controls, and Controversies* (Washington: BNA, 1986), pp. 45–49.

56. An earlier BLS series was discontinued in the 1970s. A discussion of the new series can be found in Felicia Nathan, "Analyzing Employers' Costs for Wages, Salaries, and Benefits," *Monthly Labor Review,* vol. 110 (October 1987),

pp. 3–11. The new series is part of the Employment Cost Index program.

57. The data are published annually in booklets available from the Chamber. Unfortunately, it is difficult to obtain a detailed methodological statement concerning the survey, a common problem with private sources of data.

58. Workforce demographics will play a role in determining costs. An older workforce, for example, will raise the costs of a health care plan.

59. The size cutoff varies from 50 to 250 workers, depending on industry.

Chapter Eight

MAKING GENERAL PAY ADJUSTMENTS

Over time, pay levels in the labor market change, and a firm must regularly update its wage levels to keep pace with the market. In the period after World War II, average pay levels generally rose. Aggregate pay has not declined since the Great Depression of the 1930s. Hence updating pay typically means raising pay.

What is typical across the economy does not necessarily apply to every firm, of course. In the 1980s examples of pay cuts became far more commonplace than at any time since the 1930s. These cuts were generally associated with union wages that (it will be argued in a later chapter) were affected by special circumstances. Nevertheless, even in the nonunion sector, pay setters are not bound to follow general pay trends mechanically.

Moreover, pay trends of a firm must be differentiated from pay trends experienced by any particular employee within that firm. Employees may receive merit pay adjustments based on their own performance. These adjustments are intended as individual awards. This chapter, however, will deal with across-the-board pay adjustments that affect all (or many) members of the firm's workforce.

8–1 Determining When to Make Adjustments

There are no good data on the frequency with which firms consider general pay adjustments. In the union sector labor–management contracts are usually negotiated for multiyear periods, three years being the most common duration. Under these agreements, wage adjustments are generally provided at the beginning of the contract and at each anniversary date, although many variations exist. Sometimes, wage adjustments under union contracts are more frequent than annual;

quarterly adjustments are occasionally made, especially if wages are linked to prices by an escalator clause.

In the nonunion sector there is some evidence that annual pay review cycles are the most common practice. Relatively few nonunion workers appear to be covered by multiyear pay decisions.[1] A Conference Board study found that pay increases for clerical workers, who are largely nonunion, were considered annually by proportions of employers ranging from two-thirds to three-fourths, depending on sector.[2] Furthermore, surveys taken by management-consulting firms regarding prospective pay decisions generally assume a one-year cycle.

Of course, the fact that earth has traveled once again around the sun is no reason that pay must be readjusted or even reviewed. However, little alternative practical advice can be given concerning the optimum frequency of adjustment or review. All that can be said is that reviews should be made more frequently during periods in which the relevant factors determining pay adjustments are changing rapidly. Generally, an annual review will prove adequate unless unusual conditions are occurring, either externally or internally. An annual pay review cycle will also tend to be linked to other budgetary and planning processes within the firm.

Some nonunion firms claim that they do not make general pay increases at all. It appears that this approach is more likely to be taken for white-collar than blue-collar employees, and that it is more common the higher up the pay/responsibility ladder one climbs.[3] Essentially, the argument is, "We pay only on merit." In effect, the employer is asserting that if employees are not found meritorious, they will not experience any upward nominal wage adjustment. Since consumer prices are generally rising, such employees will in fact find that their real wages have fallen.

Such a merit-only policy may, on the surface, seem appealing to the employer. It raises serious problems, however, particularly during periods when external pay is rising rapidly. A firm's pay must ultimately be kept in some relationship to the outside market, whether the firm wishes to acknowledge it or not. Thus the firm risks corrupting its merit system by repeatedly having to find that virtually all workers were especially meritorious in order to keep them apace with the external market. Such artificial merit pay raises will make employees skeptical about the degree to which their performance has anything to do with their pay. In the following discussion, therefore, it will be assumed that firms either make general pay adjustments explicitly, or that they find some covert way of doing so.

8–2 Criteria for Pay Adjustments

Although the point has frequently been made, it is nevertheless important to stress that the issue of *setting* pay arises only because the real-world labor market departs from the classical auction-style model of wage determination. In the classical model, firms do not worry about how to set pay any more than stockbrokers worry about how to set stock prices. The market makes all decisions, and the firm simply meets the market.

Once there is departure from the classical model, however, and recognition of the ongoing employer/employee attachment that characterizes the labor market, discretionary pay setting becomes important. Employees at the time of hire agree to a designated pay level. They know that, over time, this level will be altered. Workers may well expect that the criteria that will be used to adjust the level of pay will be reasonable and fair. Thus it is important to examine commonly cited criteria for pay adjustments.

Five possible criteria are usually cited for making adjustments: price trends, productivity trends, profitability, labor market conditions, and the general pace of pay adjustments being made by other employers. Each of these criteria seems to be relevant to the pay decision. Yet exactly what role each plays (or should play) is at the heart of pay policy. The following sections discuss these five criteria.

8–3   Price Trends

The notion that general price inflation should have some bearing on pay adjustments is deeply ingrained. Common parlance refers to general, across-the-board pay adjustments as cost-of-living increases, even if criteria other than changes in the cost of living were used in their determination.[4] Figure 8–1 suggests that there is good empirical reason for this perception.

Three indexes of wage change are plotted on the figure along with a broad index of price change. The solid line plots the annual percentage change in wages and salaries for all workers in the private nonfarm sector. The dotted line covers wage changes experienced by union workers, and the dashed line applies to nonunion workers. Finally, annual percent changes in the nonfarm business price deflator are marked with a dotted-and-dashed line.[5]

Figure 8–1 clearly shows that periods in which price inflation is high (such as 1979 to 1981) are also periods in which wage inflation is high. Similarly, when price inflation is low (as during 1983 to 1987), wage inflation is also low.

The correlation tells us nothing about causation. Moreover, the precise relationship between wages and prices may vary across sectors (compare the union and nonunion sectors). Still, the reason for the perception that general pay adjustments are "cost-of-living" increases is obvious from the figure. Thus pay raises are larger and more likely when the cost of living, that is, the price level, is rising.

Wage Push or Price Pull?

Labor costs are an important element of aggregate pricing. This fact is obscured at the firm level because much of the cost of production is simply the expenditure on materials and inputs purchased from other firms. In the manufacturing industries listed in Table 8–1, for example, labor costs fell into a range of roughly one-tenth to one-third of sales in 1982. At the aggregate level, however, one company's

FIGURE 8–1
Wage and Price
Trends 1976–1987

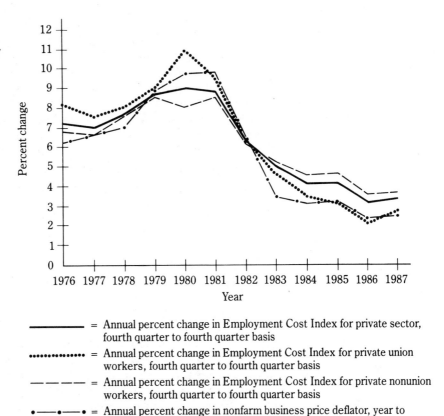

———————— = Annual percent change in Employment Cost Index for private sector,
fourth quarter to fourth quarter basis

•••••••••••••• = Annual percent change in Employment Cost Index for private union
workers, fourth quarter to fourth quarter basis

— — — — = Annual percent change in Employment Cost Index for private nonunion
workers, fourth quarter to fourth quarter basis

•——•——• = Annual percent change in nonfarm business price deflator, year to
year basis

**TABLE 8–1 Employee Compensation as a Percent of the Total Value of
Output in Selected Industries, 1982**

Industry	Employee Compensation as Percent of Value of Output
Tobacco manufactures	11%
Chemical products	21
Motor vehicles and equipment	22
Apparel	24
Furniture and fixtures	32
Leather and leather products	34

Source: Data from U.S. Bureau of Economic Analysis, *The National and Income Product Accounts of the
United States, 1929–82* (Washington: GPO, 1986), p. 264; Interindustry Economics Division, "Annual Input-
Output Accounts of the U.S. Economy, 1982," *Survey of Current Business,* vol. 68 (April 1988), Table 1.

material purchases are another company's sales, and the intermediate transactions net out. Thus labor compensation in 1987 accounted for 84% of the net domestic income in the corporate sector.[6]

Given the importance of labor costs in total costs, it is evident that periods can occur in which wages push up prices rather than prices pulling up wages. It would be a serious mistake, however, to assume that this direction of causation is the normal state of affairs, that is to say, that wage setting is the usual cause of inflation. An important element in the price inflation surge of the 1979–1981 period was the boost in world oil prices administered by the OPEC cartel, an event having little to do with American wage determination. Similarly, the drop in oil prices in the subsequent period—as OPEC lost control of the international oil market—played a very significant role in bringing down the general rate of price inflation in the United States. During that episode wages were again followers, rather than leaders.

Prices from the Employer's Perspective

The classical model of wage determination indicates that firms will hire labor until wage equals marginal revenue product of labor (MRP_L). In a competitive firm, $MRP_L = MP_L \times P$, where MP_L = the marginal product of labor and P is the price of the firm's output. For a noncompetitive firm, $MRP_L = MP_L \times MR$, where MR = marginal revenue, a value that moves in a positive relation to the price.[7] The classical model thus suggests that prices should have something to do with the level of labor demand (the MRP_L schedule).

Implicit contracting models of the employee–employer relationship also suggest a connection between labor demand and prices. The relationship is long term, so that the firm's demand for labor would depend on the MRP_L over the expected duration of the relationship rather than in the immediate period. Profits would be maximized at the point where the expected flow of wages (appropriately discounted) equals the expected incremental flow of revenue over the duration. However, the incremental revenue is still a function of the price level. Changes in the price level would thus move the curve showing the firm's demand for labor in the same direction, just as in the classical model.[8]

Based on the preceding analysis, if prices are generally increasing due to domestic demand pressures, wages can be expected to move up along with them. Another way to explain this expectation is that employer ability to pay, as indicated by the price or marginal revenue, has risen. As the oil price example illustrates, however, prices may increase for reasons other than an expansion of general demand. Thus an oil price increase due to foreign developments may actually *reduce* labor demand, as firm profits are squeezed by energy costs.[9]

Another important qualification to the linkage between prices and wages must be recognized. Price developments may have *diverse* effects on employer wage policies, even if they are domestically caused. In any period of time, certain firms are more likely to experience faster rates of price increases of their outputs than other firms are experiencing. Part of the implicit contract between employer and employee may be that some elements of this firm-specific demand fluctuation will be shared with employees. Thus wages might rise more rapidly or more slowly than the market average for firms experiencing above- or below-average price increases (or decreases) for their products.

As an example, in the wake of the first major OPEC price increases in the mid-1970s, major oil companies reopened their labor contracts voluntarily and gave extra wage increases to their employees. In contrast, in the mid-1980s when oil prices fell, pay increases in the industry were very moderate. The 1986 wage agreements in the petroleum industry called for no basic wage increase in the first year of the contract, and only a small increase in the second year.[10] Examples can also be found in mining pay systems in the United States and abroad, in which an element of pay is explicitly linked to the price of the product being mined.

Price Increases from the Employee's Perspective

The classical formula can be rewritten as $W/P = MP_L$. W/P is the real wage *in terms of the product made by the employer,* or what economists call the product wage.[11] However, since employees consume many products other than those made by their firms, the price index they will consider relevant to their welfare must cover the outputs of many industries. Various price indexes are available that include many products. The most widely used price measure that is applied to worker welfare is undoubtedly the Consumer Price Index (CPI), which is reported monthly by the U.S. Bureau of Labor Statistics (BLS).

Consumer Price Index and Worker Welfare. The history of the CPI goes back to the time of World War I, when government tribunals felt they needed data on price changes to settle wartime wage disputes.[12] The idea that wages should be set to provide decent standards of living gained currency during that era. A corollary position was that, since prices were generally rising during the war, wage decisions had to be regularly updated for price changes to account for the increased cost of a decent standard.

Although the methods of collecting price data by the BLS are far more sophisticated than those of the World War I years, certain elements remain. First, the CPI is based on a periodic budget survey in which actual consumption patterns are observed. Second, prices of items representative of the consumption pattern are tracked by BLS field agents on a regular basis.[13] The index thus reflects changes in the cost of maintaining the original reference budget.

In fact, the CPI since the late 1970s has really been two indexes. One version is the Consumer Price Index for All Urban Consumers (CPI-U); the other applies to Urban Wage Earners and Clerical Workers (CPI-W). These indexes differ in the consumption baskets they measure, that is, they have somewhat different weights. The former index is considered a good measure of general price inflation. The CPI-W is most often used for union wage escalator clauses, that is, contractual clauses that automatically link wages to prices.[14]

Because it prices a fixed basket of goods and services based on past consumption patterns, the CPI is what is called a Laspeyres price index. In that index let period 0 be the reference period during which the consumption pattern has been surveyed. Then the index's basic formula in subsequent period 1 can be expressed as

$$\frac{\sum\limits_{i}^{n} P_{i1}Q_{i0}}{\sum\limits_{i}^{n} P_{i0}Q_{i0}}$$

where the denominator of the fraction is the cost of the consumption pattern at period 0 prices of goods $i = 1, 2, 3, \ldots n$ and the numerator is the cost of the *same* pattern of consumption at period 1 prices.[15]

The CPI is expressed as a pure index number, set equal to 100 in an arbitrary base period. In 1988 that period was established as an average of 1982 to 1984.[16] The index's value in December 1986 was 110.5 and in December 1987, 115.4, using CPI-U. Thus, the CPI-measured rate of price inflation for all areas from the end of 1986 to the end of 1987 was 4.4% $= [(115.4/110.5) - 1]$. If it was desired to protect the purchasing power of someone earning $10.00 per hour in December 1986, it would have been necessary to have raised his or her wage to $10.44 a year later.

CPIs are available for many cities, giving the option of adjusting local wages on the basis of a corresponding local index.[17] For example, from December 1986 to December 1987 CPI-U rose 5.2% in the Los Angeles area and 5.9% in the New York City area. To protect the real value of a December 1986 $10.00 wage, an increase would be needed of $10.52 in Los Angeles and $10.59 in New York. A national firm with workers all around the country might use the national CPI if it had a centralized wage policy. Local firms, or national firms that make wage policy on a decentralized basis, can use local indexes.

Index Number Problem.   Economists and statisticians are fond of pointing out that the percentage wage adjustments cited above (4.4%, 5.2%, and 5.9%) may not be quite accurate if the goal is to maintain welfare standards. Specifically, the increases may be bigger adjustments than necessary to maintain worker well-being unchanged. The difficulty with the method of adjusting wages proportionately to movements in a price index is often called the index number problem. Its conceptual basis is illustrated by Figure 8–2.

Consider a consumer who chooses between two goods: "soup" and "nuts." Initially, the consumer has a budget line represented by AA' and consumes at point a on indifference curve I_1. Suppose that the price of nuts rises, so that the budget line now drops to BA'. If the consumer is to continue consuming at point a, his or her budget must be raised to CC'. This raise is analogous to giving the worker a 4.4% raise because "prices" rose by 4.4% in the previous example.

Figure 8–2 shows, however, that such a budget increase would actually *raise* welfare, not just maintain it. With budget line CC', the consumer shifts consumption to point b and reaches a higher indifference curve, I_2. The consumer does not consume at point a (even though it is possible to do so) because point b is superior. If the goal is simply to maintain the consumer's welfare, the budget

FIGURE 8–2
Consumer Welfare
and the Index
Number Problem

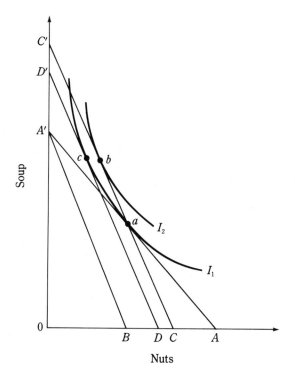

should be raised only to DD', allowing consumption at point c on the original indifference curve I_1.[18]

The reason for the discrepancy between maintaining purchasing power (going to CC') and maintaining welfare (going to DD') is that the former fails to recognize the ability of consumers to make *substitutions* away from a product whose price has increased. Thus, when gasoline prices rose very dramatically in the 1973–1974 and 1979–1980 periods, a pure purchasing power adjustment would have assumed that worker welfare could be protected only if workers were given sufficient wage increases to allow them to maintain previous driving habits *unchanged*. The welfare approach recognizes that when gasoline prices rise, it is possible to buy smaller cars, take vacations closer to home, use public transportation, and so on, thus cushioning the shock.[19]

In reality, however, the discrepancy between the purchasing power approach and the welfare approach is not likely to be large. It arises only when certain products experience dramatic price increases *relative* to other items. Empirical studies have not found the discrepancy to be of major importance.[20] During periods of inflation, however, unhappiness with the state of the economy tends to give rise to complaints about the ways in which prices are measured, and the index number problem is inevitably raised. Nevertheless, other objections to moving wages up mechanically with price inflation are of greater practical significance.

Alternative Price Indexes. Among the problems relating to gearing wages to prices is the availability of various price indexes. Table 8–2 presents some of the

TABLE 8–2 Price Trends According to Selected Indexes, 1970–1987

Price Index	Annualized Percent Change in Prices	
	1970–1980	1980–1987
Consumer Price Index (CPI)		
All urban consumers (CPI-U)	n.a.	4.7%
Urban wage earners and clerical workers (CPI-W)	7.8%	4.5
All items excluding food, energy, and shelter	7.1	5.5
GNP deflator	7.4	4.6
Nonfarm business deflator	7.3	4.3
Deflator for personal consumption expenditures	7.3	4.6
Producer Price Index (PPI) for finished goods	8.4	2.6

Source: Data from *Economic Report of the President: February 1988* (Washington: GPO, 1988), pp. 252, 300, 316–317, 319; *Monthly Labor Review,* vol. 111 (June 1988), p.98.

alternatives. Even the two CPIs—CPI-U and CPI-W—do not always coincide.[21] Nor do they agree precisely with price indexes constructed using other methodologies. Which is the best index to use, CPI-U or CPI-W? Actually, the choice between the two CPIs is not very important since they will not diverge by a large margin. Either one, however, is likely to be superior to alternative (non-CPI) price indexes as a wage indicator.

As examples of alternative indexes, the table shows three price deflators from the national income accounts: the deflator for the entire GNP,[22] for nonfarm business, and for personal consumption expenditures. Note that none of these deflators produces results drastically different from the CPIs for the periods reported.[23] Thus the availability of reasonable alternatives from the national income accounts is not a good argument for discarding the CPI as the key indicator of price trends.

Moreover, the deflators from the national income accounts all are subject to continuing revision, as the accounts themselves are revised. In contrast, the CPIs are almost never revised once issued, precisely because BLS recognizes their use in wage setting and wage escalation. This lack of revision is useful in avoiding after-the-fact arguments about how much wages should have been adjusted.

The only index shown on Table 8–2 that is in widespread use and that differs significantly from the two CPIs is the Producer Price Index (PPI) for finished goods. This index, an outgrowth of what was once termed the Wholesale Price Index, shows a higher rate of inflation for the 1970s than the other indexes and a lower rate for the 1980s. The PPI is widely used as a barometer of inflation by economists, but it has only limited value as a measure of worker purchasing power.[24]

First, the PPI measures prices charged by producers, not retailers. Second, the index omits the service sector and includes only goods and commodities. Since consumption of services is an important element of the typical worker's budget, omission of services makes the Producer Price Index unsuitable as a wage guide. Despite the attention often paid to the PPI for economic forecasting purposes, it is thus of little use for setting pay policy.

Given the methodological improvements made by BLS in the 1980s, the Consumer Price Index (either one) should be regarded as the best measure of price change to use as a guide for wage setting.[25] The index was designed specifically for that purpose and, although it is not perfect in a theoretical sense, it represents a pragmatic, reasonable attempt to provide necessary information. There is little to choose between CPI-U and CPI-W. CPI-W has weights that come closer to the budgetary patterns of the typical nonsupervisory worker than CPI-U. On the other hand, CPI-U is more widely cited in the popular press and will be the index workers will hear most about. The choice between them is largely a matter of taste.[26]

The fact that the CPIs *can* be used as guides to wage setting does not mean that their indicated price trends *should* be used for that purpose. The analysis so far has examined the price issue separately from the employer's and employee's perspectives. Perhaps the greatest problem with the use of prices as a wage guide is that these two perspectives need not coincide.

Employee Perspective Versus Employer Perspective

Any broad-based price index, including the CPIs, will contain volatile elements. In the main, these elements are commodities, typically agricultural products and energy products, sold in auction-style markets. If prices of these volatile elements rise, pressures inevitably will ensue to protect real wages from fluctuations by granting nominal wage increases. Such wage increases are in line with the employee's viewpoint. From the average employer's viewpoint, however, the fact that, say, oil prices have risen does not increase ability to pay for wage hikes (except for oil producing companies). Indeed, if oil prices rise, employer ability to pay may actually be *reduced* due to the added costs of energy.

The third row of Table 8–2 shows price movements recorded by the CPI, *excluding* its volatile elements.[27] As can be seen, the difference in the inflation rates of the 1970s and early 1980s turns out to have been concentrated in the volatile components. When these components are removed, the two periods exhibit a significantly smaller difference in rates of price increase. Yet, from the employee's perspective, wage pressures varied considerably as the volatile prices shifted.

Nonvolatile price movements of the CPI, sometimes termed the underlying rate of inflation by economists, approximate the ability-to-pay concept. Given the relative constancy of the underlying rate during the periods shown in Table 8–2, it must be concluded that attempts to adjust wages by prices in the 1970s would have produced a cost squeeze from the employer's perspective. In the 1980s, this tendency reversed; gearing wages to prices would have permitted a profit expansion.

From the HRM perspective, therefore, there can be no single, unchanging policy regarding the significance of price changes for wage setting. Because of the importance of volatile elements in the CPI, employers are unlikely to want to guarantee to maintain real wages—regardless of which prices are rising—in the face of inflation. The price trends that employers consider relevant (namely, the price trends of their outputs) are not necessarily going to accord with the price trends relevant to employee consumption patterns.

Not surprisingly, given the analysis above, explicit employer guarantees to protect the real wage are rarely found in the nonunion sector. Only the union sector, in which pressure to reflect the employee's viewpoint is greatest, commonly has automatic escalator formulas.

Escalation of Wages

As already noted, an escalator clause is a contractual device in a union–management agreement that links wage changes to recent price changes. In principle, a nonunion employer could offer such an adjustment to its workers. Yet escalators are rare in the nonunion sector. Nonunion employers are free to change wages whenever they want and for whatever reason, since they are not bound by a contract with their employees. There is little reason for a mechanical formula in such cases.[28] When nonunion escalation does exist, it is usually a reflection of a union element elsewhere in the company. Thus if a company has a union contract with escalation for blue-collar workers, it may sometimes offer the same feature to nonunion white-collar employees.[29]

Escalators exist in the union sector for two primary reasons. First, as already indicated, the notion that purchasing power should be protected is basically an employee perspective. Since unions represent that perspective, it is not surprising that they have pushed for escalation (sometimes termed indexation) in their contracts.

Second, unions typically negotiate long-term contracts with employers. In the absence of escalation, negotiators may have to guess the rate of inflation over the next two or three years. Forecasting inflation is difficult, so including an escalator clause provides a way to avoid the risks of forecast errors.

Five stylized facts can be reported about escalation in the United States:

1. *Occurs in long term contracts.* Escalators are more likely to be found in long-term union-management contracts than in short-term ones. In a short-term contract, the risks of an inflation forecast error are smaller than in a contract of longer duration. Even if an error is made, a short-term contract will soon reopen and the error can be corrected. Also, employers historically have sought long-term contracts from unions as a way of lowering the risk of strikes by reducing the frequency of negotiations. Management used escalators as a carrot to win union acceptance of long-term contracts.[30]

2. *Increases under inflation.* The use of escalation tends to increase during periods of relatively high inflation and to diminish during periods of low inflation. Escalation thus diminished during the early 1960s when inflation was very low,

but rose in the 1970s when inflation was high. Escalation again diminished in the 1980s as inflation fell.

Although economists acknowledge this empirical correlation between the frequency of escalation and the rate of inflation, they prefer to explain the relationship as one of inflation *uncertainty*.[31] They argue that what matters is the risk of forecast error, which should be a function of uncertainty about inflation's future variation rather than of its magnitude. Since periods of high inflation have also been periods in which inflation has been variable and uncertain, it is difficult empirically to disentangle the two influences.

3. *Varies across industries.* The use of escalation varies considerably across industries. Escalation has tended to be strongly resisted by unionized employers when either the prices of their own products are volatile (as in the petroleum industry) or when prices are fixed in advance in nominal terms (as in construction). Under such circumstances, an employer who undertook to gear wages to general prices would be bearing a substantial risk. Wages might rise rapidly relative to the employer's product price because inflation of other prices was pushing up the CPI. However, employers who have resisted escalation often must live with union–management contracts of relatively short duration.

4. *Involves complex formulas.* Escalator formulas are almost never simple. The obvious formula is that each 1% price index increase should translate into a 1% wage increase. *Such simple approaches are virtually never found in union–management contracts.* Escalator clauses have been qualified with limitations, especially in the 1980s. Sometimes a given amount of inflation (a corridor) must occur before the escalator comes into operation. A contract might thus indicate that no escalator payments will be made unless inflation exceeds 5%. Still another common type of limitation is a cap that limits the escalator payout to some maximum level, regardless of the inflation rate.

Basic escalator formulas often link a 1¢ wage increase to a given *index point* rise.[32] As an example, the escalator negotiated in the automobile industry in 1987 provided for quarterly 1¢ increases for each .26 point increase in CPI-W (at that time based on 1967 = 100).[33] An index point's value will change, depending on the base of the index and the period of time that has elapsed since the base. When the CPI stood at 200 on a base of 1967 = 100 (as it did around 1978), each index point rise was equivalent to a 0.5% increase in inflation (1/200 = 0.5%). When the CPI reached 340 (around the time of the 1987 auto settlement), each index point increase translated into only a 0.3% increase (1/340).[34]

Often these complex formulas serve to disguise the fact that the average worker will receive *less* than a 1% wage increase for each 1% price index increase.[35] In the 1970s the net effect of the formulas then in use was that each 1% price increase translated into roughly a 0.6% wage increase. Concession bargaining in the 1980s reduced this ratio to an average of about 0.5%. The reason for this formula obfuscation is to be found in the bargaining process itself, which is one of compromise. As the formula departs (in a downward direction) from proportionality, the employer assumes less risk. The end result is that some risk is assumed by the employer and some by the employees. In other words, the compromise over escalation is one of *de facto* risk sharing by both sides.[36]

5. *Uses CPI as indicator.* Escalator formulas almost always use the CPI as the price inflation indicator. Most use CPI-W. National contracts (involving firms with facilities in multiple areas) use the national CPI. Some purely local contracts use the local index, if one is available.

Among major union–management contracts in the private sector in late 1987 (those involving 1,000 or more workers), 38% of the workers covered had some form of escalator.[37] A smaller, but unknown, proportion under nonmajor contracts also had escalators. Escalators also exist, but cover relatively few workers, in the state and local government sector. Under major state and local contracts, only 2% of covered employees had escalation in late 1987.[38] All told, therefore, even with generous allowance for escalated agreements among nonmajor contracts, it is doubtful that more than 4% of wage and salary earners had formal escalation of their pay. A majority of union workers did not have escalator coverage in 1987, and less than a fifth of wage and salary workers were unionized.[39]

Money Illusion

Given that formal escalation is comparatively rare in the United States, an interesting question is whether workers actually think in real terms when evaluating their pay. Do they consider W/p, where p is a price index such as the CPI, or do they just worry about W?[40] Economists term the tendency to consider only W as *money illusion*, an obviously pejorative phrase suggesting unawareness of real purchasing power.

Money illusion, as a concept, has been an important element in macroeconomic theory. The originator of modern macroeconomic theory, John Maynard Keynes, postulated that workers would accept a real wage cut brought about by a price increase (with no change in the nominal wage), but that a nominal wage cut in the face of a stable price level would be less acceptable.[41] This seemingly peculiar behavior of employees was attributed to their concern about their wages *relative* to those of other workers.

Workers would be content, in the Keynesian view, as long as their wages were not decreased relative to those of other workers. A nominal wage cut at any moment of time will be a cut in wages relative to someone else's wages that were not then experiencing a cut. Nominal wage decreases would thus meet with resistance. On the other hand, a real wage cut caused by a general increase in prices is experienced by everyone simultaneously and is therefore acceptable. It causes no change in wage relativities.

Calling such behavior the product of an illusion is unnecessarily harsh terminology. When inflation is low, it is reasonable that workers, like everyone else, would tend to rely on the official yardstick of value, that is, nominal money. Moreover, there is nothing inherently irrational about judging one's position relative to that of others. Indexes such as the CPI are abstractions to most people. As a result most wage contracts are set in money units, which people have learned to accept, rather than CPI units. Only when inflation (or deflation) becomes so pronounced that it can no longer be ignored does the official system of value measurement break down.

Within a nominally based, monetary economy, an employer who cuts wages is viewed as taking an overt act against the employees involved. It is not surprising that the overt nature of the act, and the fact that it takes place *within* the firm, triggers a hostile employee reaction. In contrast, an employer who lets real wages erode by not giving wage increases—or by giving nominal wage increases below the rate of inflation—does not have to take an overt act against the employees.

Workers view price inflation as *external* to the firm. In their opinion if other firms had not raised prices, real purchasing power would not have been eroded. Thus anger over the real wage erosion is directed outside the firm, against the greedy "them" who raised prices or perhaps against the government that let the increase happen.

Although Keynes never cited empirical evidence for this nominally oriented behavior, its symptoms are apparent. During periods of high inflation, it is not unusual for significant groups of workers to find their wages falling substantially behind the inflation rate. During periods of low inflation, real wage erosion is limited since nominal wage decreases are inhibited.[42]

Survey evidence also suggests that nominal wage cuts are viewed as unfair even if they produce no more of a real wage erosion than an equivalent situation caused by price inflation. A sample of the general public was asked to respond to a hypothetical situation in which a company making a small profit in an area with high unemployment, but no inflation, cut wages by 7%. Sixty-two percent said such a pay cut would be unfair. When asked if the same firm could give only a 5% wage increase when inflation was 12%, 78% thought the policy was fair.[43] Yet, in terms of real purchasing power, a 7% wage cut with zero inflation is equivalent to a 5% wage hike with 12% inflation; both amount to a 7% real-wage reduction.

When evaluating such attitudes, it is important to designate clearly the horizon over which wage decisions are being judged. In the short run, with moderate price inflation, it is likely that real wage erosion can occur without a major employee counterreaction. Over the long run, however, or with high price inflation, workers will come to understand that they are losing purchasing power. Money illusion is thus likely to be only a temporary phenomenon.

Indeed, one of the reasons that inflation becomes a major domestic political issue is that people eventually come to understand that price increases are distorting the nominally oriented implicit contract in the workplace. Suppose the implicit contract has a rule that nominal-dollar wage cuts should be undertaken only in dire circumstances. Then workers' real wages will be protected only so long as inflation is not too high and does not continue for too long.

If price inflation is high and/or prolonged, however, the rule loses its meaning, and the labor market begins to resemble an auction market, with large swings in real wages becoming a possibility. At that point democratic societies either elect new political leaders pledged to disinflation, or adopt widespread escalation, effectively recasting the no-wage-cut rules in real, rather than nominal, terms. In other words, continued high inflation is likely to accentuate the nominal/real difference, and lead to an end of money illusion.

8−4   Productivity Trends

Productivity has been discussed in various contexts in previous chapters. This chapter is concerned not with individual productivity and its rewards but with whether productivity can be a guide for making *across-the-board* wage adjustments. Two types of productivity trends — national and firm — can be distinguished.

It had already been seen that real wages across the economy tend to rise with national productivity over long periods of time. As a rough approximation nominal wage changes equal price changes plus national productivity changes.[44] Indeed, a famous labor contract between General Motors and the United Automobile Workers union in 1948 adopted this formula as a basic pay policy. It was believed that wages would follow the price/productivity trend anyway, and that explicitly adopting the formula would help avert labor disputes and strikes.

The 1948 GM-UAW contract provided for a 3¢ nominal wage increase in each year of a two-year contract, plus an escalator clause. Three cents, converted to a percentage, was considered a rough approximation of the trend rate of increase in national productivity at the time and was dubbed the annual improvement factor.[45] The escalator clause, or cost of living adjustment (COLA), was designed to protect the annual improvement factor from being eroded by price inflation. Eventually, 3% became the accepted annual productivity growth estimate in such formulas. Up until the 1980s, union circles commonly held the notion that "3% plus COLA" was the normal rate of pay increase to be expected.

The 3% plus COLA formula illustrates the pitfalls of using national productivity as a guide to wage setting. Although it is true that, in the aggregate over long periods, productivity plus inflation equals wage increase, such need not be the case for any particular industry or group of workers or given period. In addition a formula such as 3% plus COLA, if followed universally, would produce a rigid, unchanging wage structure in which all workers received exactly the same increase, regardless of demand conditions in their firms, industries, or occupations.

Moreover, the trend of national productivity improvement need not be a constant, such as 3% per year. For example, productivity growth slowed markedly in the 1970s relative to earlier decades. Even if past productivity can be accurately observed, future productivity is difficult to forecast. The locking in of the 3% productivity assumption in the auto and other unionized industries was one of the factors causing union wages to rise faster than nonunion in the 1970s, when actual productivity growth stagnated. This relative union wage rise contributed to the dramatic wage concession movement of the 1980s and to accompanying substantial losses of union membership and unionized employment.[46]

An alternative to national productivity as a guide for pay policy is firm productivity. The use of gain-sharing plans that build firm (or plant) productivity improvements into pay formulas has been discussed. However, arguments that firm productivity should be used for wage setting have been criticized by economists. They assert that such a policy, if widely followed, would lead to excessively divergent wage trends between firms and industries.

Some firms are in industries—such as telephone communications—in which technical change happens to permit long-term, above-average productivity improvements. Others are in the position of barbershops, in which the scope for productivity improvement is extremely limited. Taking the example to its logical conclusion, wages geared exclusively to firm productivity would eventually produce both impoverished barbers (or severe shortages of barbers) and wealthy telephone operators (with large queues of anxious job seekers applying to the telephone company for work).

It is not necessary, however, to use firm productivity as a guide to pay setting all the way to its logical conclusion. Employers in firms with inherently low productivity improvement will obviously not base their wage adjustments on internal productivity trends. In firms with favorable productivity trends some employers will take the opportunity to follow a *high* wage policy (but not an indefinitely faster-than-average wage *increase* policy). In other words, a trend toward rapid productivity growth may be shared with employees *for a time*. The stakeholder relationship of employees in the firm makes this a reasonable policy, one that is reflected in the use of profit-sharing and gain-sharing plans among some employers.

Still, most employers are unlikely to commit themselves to *permanent* productivity sharing. Such policies could result in wage levels substantially out of line with those of other firms. Perhaps this consideration is part of the reason why formal productivity gain-sharing plans (such as the Scanlon plans) are so rare. Employers are unwilling to let their pay levels be dictated by internal considerations that are largely independent of the outside labor market.

8–5 Profitability

Use of profitability as a guide to adjusting wages raises some of the problems found with the productivity criterion. Wages might rise substantially above the external labor market average in firms in which profitability was high and improving. The opposite would occur in firms in which profits were low and declining. Despite this problem, there are some offsetting considerations.

A firm whose profitability is high and rising may well be in an expansion mode, and thus in need of more workers. Having a pay advantage relative to other employers could help in recruitment of high quality workers. Similarly, firms that have low and declining profits may well be reducing production. Having lower wages would tend to induce needed voluntary quits, thus reducing the necessity of employer-sponsored layoffs.

Despite these tendencies, the critical variable is expansion or contraction rather than profitability. A firm with low and declining profits may need to recruit new workers if it sees the prospects of reversing its fate by developing new markets or lines of business. It may also want to retain its best workers to help it change direction toward better future productivity.

A highly profitable firm may need to shrink its workforce if, say, the technology it is using is highly labor displacing. To the extent that pay policy is being dictated by recruitment, retention, or displacement, profitability should not be a direct consideration in making wage rate adjustments. But profit sharing can accomplish other goals, such as having flexible labor costs.

Most profit-sharing plans involve the payment of a bonus, either in cash or into a deferred savings arrangement, rather than an adjustment of the wage rate. A typical profit-sharing compensation system includes both a basic wage and a bonus. The basic wage rate can be adjusted by the same criteria used by firms without profit sharing, but the bonus is geared to internal firm profitability.

Making the profit-related element of pay into a bonus is helpful in dealing with the variability of profits. Economists usually view profits as a residual, that is, what is left over after expenses are deducted from receipts. Both receipts and expenses can vary substantially, thus making profits especially volatile. If wage rates were geared to profits, wages would rise and fall frequently, violating the implicit contract rule of avoiding nominal wage cuts.

Labeling the profit-sharing element a bonus alerts employees that the resulting payment will be variable. If the bonus is used to finance a deferred savings plan, employees will not directly and immediately feel the impact of the fluctuations. Over a period of time, the ups and downs of the bonus will tend to net out, thus providing a supplement to other retirement savings arrangements.

In theory American firms could pay bonuses to employees without directly referencing profits as their determinants, while nevertheless considering profits as a guide to bonus determination. Some researchers have argued that the Japanese compensation system, under which bonuses are a significant element of total pay, functions as a de facto profit-sharing plan, without the profit-sharing label.[47] In the United States employers who use profitability as a guide to pay setting are likely to do so through an explicit profit-sharing plan. Even when there is no such plan, firms that experience severe financial reverses may freeze (or occasionally cut) pay.

The fact that pay is sometimes affected by profit reversals, even in firms without profit-sharing plans, illustrates the stakeholder relationship workers have with their employers. Ultimately, workers' jobs depend on the economic success of the firms that employ them. Although equity owners assume much of the fluctuation in the form of changes in share prices, pay policy is unlikely to insulate the stakeholder/workforce completely from variations in profitability.

8–6   Labor Market Conditions

Suppose a firm making reasonable profits discovers that it could hire workers at lower wages than it is currently paying. Perhaps other firms in the area have had to lay off their workforces, creating a pool of desperate job seekers. Should the firm cut the wages of its incumbent or inside workers?

Insiders and Outsiders

Economists oriented toward the classical model might well argue that the employer should gear pay policy to outsiders (job seekers) rather than insiders.[48] In this view inside workers should simply accept the external market price of labor as the determinant of their pay. Survey evidence suggests, however, that public opinion would find that cutting wages of inside workers because of the presence of outsiders was unfair.[49]

In effect society—and therefore the inside workforce—expects employers to protect insiders from outsiders whose competition would pull down their wage levels. Of course, employers do not always provide such protection. But the fact that society and the inside workforce have such an expectation constrains employer wage-setting behavior.

Two-Tier Pay Plans

Perhaps the most dramatic example of an attempt to reconcile the insider/outsider conflict occurred in the union sector in the 1980s with the development of *two-tier pay plans*. Under these plans, pay levels of inside workers were retained, but new hires (outsiders) were brought in at lower wage scales as vacancies occurred. Two-tier plans became widely used in industries such as air transportation, where deregulation of the product market had undermined the earlier wage structure.

Unionized airlines faced competition from new nonunion firms that enjoyed lower wage scales. By negotiating lower pay for new hires, unionized carriers received a reduction in the *marginal* cost of hiring, while inside workers (who were the constituents of their unions at the time of negotiation) received pay protection. Two-tier plans were not confined to deregulated industries, however. They became common in other industries, such as retail foodstores, that faced lower-wage nonunion competition.[50]

The two-tier approach was found mainly in the union sector, where inside employees could pressure employers to afford them some protection from general wage cuts. A few cases of two-tier plans did occur in nonunion firms as well.[51]

The two-tier approach to compensation has also been used in other contexts. For example, when the federal government decided that the pension program for its incumbent workers was becoming too expensive in the mid-1980s, it instituted a less costly plan for new hires.[52] Because retirement planning is inherently a long-term strategy for employees, it was felt to be unfair for the federal government, as employer, to cut back on already promised pension benefits. But new employees, hired after the less costly program was initiated, had received no such promises and hence, it could be argued, could more fairly be given reduced retirement benefits.

The Phillips Curve

Labor market conditions do have some effect on wage change decisions, although the effect is attenuated by implicit contracts and insider/outsider considerations.

An abundance of econometric literature describes this effect. The relevant literature has its roots in work begun in the late 1950s.

Much of the econometric research on wage-change equations stems from the finding by A.W. Phillips that, over a period from the middle of the nineteenth century to the middle of the twentieth, British wages rose more slowly when unemployment was high than when it was low.[53] If unemployment rates were sufficiently high, nominal wages might even decline. The so-called Phillips curve, which summarizes these conclusions, is illustrated by line PP in Figure 8–3.

As originally put forward, the Phillips curve was seen as a stable relationship. At a low unemployment rate, U_1 in Figure 8–3, annual wage inflation (%W) would be quite rapid. However, an increase in the unemployment rate to U_2 could greatly moderate the rate of wage inflation. If unemployment rose to U_3, nominal wages would not change at all. Finally, at a very high unemployment rate, such as U_4, nominal wages would actually decline.

To the extent that unemployment can be viewed as a measure of excess supply of labor, the Phillips curve bears a superficial resemblance to the auction model of the labor market. The apparent resemblance is misleading. With an auction labor exchange, the market always clears. Any excess supply would immediately cause the wage to plummet; excess demand would result in extremely fast wage increases.

In contrast to the classical approach, the Phillips curve suggests that excess supply simply slows down the rate of wage increase and that only at extreme levels will it trigger general wage reductions. Put another way, the Phillips curve includes unemployment as a variable explaining the wage inflation rate. The classical model operates so that unemployment should not exist, and certainly should not persist.

FIGURE 8–3
The Phillips Curve

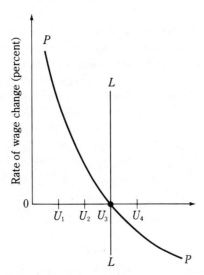

Unemployment rate

The Phillips curve is more an empirical description than a theoretical model. Much of the work that developed in its aftermath has been an ad hoc search for empirical relationships. Most researchers who applied the Phillips approach to post-World War II data found that wage change equations needed to be more complicated if they were to fit the data reasonably well. The basic Phillips curve can be expressed as follows:

$$\%W = F(u),$$

where u is the unemployment rate and $d\%W/du < 0$. Subsequent work generally expressed the equation as:

$$\%W = F(u, X_1, X_2, \ldots X_n),$$

where $X_1, X_2, \ldots X_n$ are other variables found to be statistically significant in explaining wage inflation. Virtually all studies find it necessary to include some measure of lagged price inflation in the equation. Sometimes roles are also found for variables related to profitability or productivity.

Five basic findings have emerged from the wage equation literature. They are described in the following paragraphs.

1. *Increases in unemployment reduce wage inflation.* Unemployment rate increases have a modest but significant effect on the pace of wage change. Over the course of a year an increase in the unemployment rate of one percentage point might reduce wage inflation by, say, one-half to one percentage point. This limited impact is a far cry from the classical auction model. It suggests that employers are constrained from cutting wages, or even rapidly reducing the rate of wage increase because there are more outsiders seeking work.

2. *Wage inflation shifts by less than price inflation in the short run.* In the short run, an increase of one percentage point in the rate of inflation typically triggers something less than a one percentage point increase in the rate of wage inflation. This finding supports the notion of money illusion (or nominal orientation) in wage determination. Wages are not mechanically determined in relation to the CPI or any other wage index.

3. *Wage inflation fully reflects price inflation in the long run.* Eventually, price inflation is recognized by pay setters and, in the long run, an increase in price inflation produces the same increase in wage inflation. Exactly how long the "long run" is, however, is not clear. Many economists believe that the Phillips curve, eventually evolves into a vertical line such as *LL* in Figure 8–3. At the natural rate of unemployment (U_3 in Figure 8–3), whatever rate of inflation there is will tend to maintain itself. For this reason, the natural rate is sometimes termed the Non-Accelerating Inflation Rate of Unemployment or NAIRU by macroeconomists.[54] If unemployment falls above U_3, inflation (both wage and price) will accelerate; if unemployment falls below U_3, inflation will decelerate.

4. *Other variables may affect wage inflation.* The empirical literature suggests that variables other than the unemployment rate (or some measure closely correlated with it) and lagged price inflation may affect wage change. Possibly this uncertainty is due to measurement problems. Profitability, for example, might

be measured by a profits-to-sales ratio or a return on equity or a marginal return to new investment. Adjustments of profits for inflation may be needed.

Because the theory of wage equations is vague, it is unclear which concept of a variable should be used. Perhaps profits or productivity play a stronger role in setting wages than econometric studies have so far indicated. Some studies have found limited effects.[55] There may be other relevant variables the literature has so far failed to capture.

5. *Shifts in wage norms occur.* There appear to be seemingly exogenous shifts in wage equations in certain periods. During the early 1960s, for example, there seemed to be less push behind wages than in the 1950s or 1970s. The 1980s seemed to reflect a downward shift again in wage norms.[56] These shifts in wage norms appear to be more concentrated in the union sector than elsewhere, and seem to reflect swings in relative bargaining power between management and labor.[57]

Some observers relate such swings to legal and political variables; others relate them to economic forces that are not well captured by time series wage equations. The complete explanation is not known. Both the early 1960s and the early 1980s, however, were periods when unemployment was comparatively high and persistent. Thus it may be that prolonged unemployment pressure ultimately forces a downward wage norm shift.

8–7   Wage Adjustments of Other Employers

Most employers make comparisons between their wages and the wages of other employers as part of the wage-setting process. Similarly, obtaining a sense of the going rate of wage increase is an important component of determining wage adjustments. However, examining outside wage increases does not imply a commitment to follow the external market mechanically. Finding out what others are doing is simply one more piece of information relevant to making a decision to change wages.

Market Versus Equity Considerations

The making of comparisons might be viewed as a purely market-oriented process.[58] A firm that collects information on the outside market may simply be trying to maintain its wage level at a competitive level with other employers in order to avoid recruitment/retention problems. It is important, however, not to underestimate the equity or fairness element that is also involved.

In a recession, for example, the firm might not need to match other employers' pay increases in order to attract and retain labor in the short run. Many unemployed job seekers may be willing to work, even if the firm does not keep its wages in line with the external market. Inside employees may not feel that outside opportunities exist that would warrant quitting.

A failure to grant wage increases comparable to those of other employers in such a period, however, might be viewed as unfair by employees. Employees might feel that the employer was taking advantage of a temporary situation (the recession) to hold down costs at their expense. Resentment could take the form of reduced morale and productivity in the short run, and a rise in the quit rate in the long run, as the economic situation improved. The making of outside comparisons by employers thus has a more complex motivation behind it than simply meeting the market for competitive reasons.

Internal Comparisons of Union Versus Nonunion Pay

Employers may also make internal comparisons in determining wages, especially if the firm is partially unionized. A survey in the late 1970s found that one-fifth of such firms had a policy of granting the same wage increase to nonunion employees that they had negotiated for unionized workers. Over 60% of respondents indicated that they made comparisons of the wages of their union and nonunion employees in determining wage adjustments for the latter group, even though they had no standard policy of keeping both groups in a fixed relationship.[59]

Internal comparisons between union and nonunion workers can be based on two considerations. The first is the general equity argument made above: Nonunion workers who receive smaller pay increases than their union counterparts might become resentful, creating a variety of HRM problems. A second motivation may be union avoidance. Employers may feel that their nonunion employees will be less likely to want to unionize if their pay keeps pace with union wage increases. Economists sometimes term such motivation — as it affects wage decisions — the *threat effect* of unions. Through the threat effect, nonunion workers may benefit indirectly from union pay gains.

As previously noted, union wage rates rose relative to nonunion in the 1970s. It appears that this tendency existed within partially unionized firms as well as across firms.[60] Thus, although the threat effect may have been operative for some employers, it was certainly not universally felt. Moreover, in the 1980s the union organizing threat weakened, and union membership fell sharply. The threat effect probably became less of a factor in employer wage-setting practices than it previously had been.

Pattern Bargaining in the Union Sector

From the end of World War II until the 1980s, *pattern bargaining* was a prominent feature of the union sector. Under pattern bargaining, a wage settlement between a union and an employer in one location was imitated at other firms. For example, a settlement reached by the United Automobile Workers (UAW) and one of the Big Three automobile manufacturers (General Motors, Ford, and Chrysler) would be eventually adopted by the other two. Once the pattern was established at the Big Three, it tended to spread into automobile-related firms, such as auto parts companies and farm machinery manufacturers, with whom the UAW also bargained.

Generally, pattern bargaining has involved a fair degree of flexibility; more flexibility, in any case, than the literature on the subject often recognized. As the pattern spread from the lead settlement, it became increasingly varied. For example, smaller firms might make the same wage adjustment as the lead settlement, but be less generous with fringe benefits. Or wages might be absolutely lower at such firms, even if their wage increases followed the pattern.

In the 1980s pattern bargaining broke down in many industries, or simply shrank to encompass a smaller sphere of imitative contracts.[61] A Conference Board survey, published in 1985, found that firms had generally become more inward looking in making pay adjustments than they were in the 1970s.[62] Broad, industry-wide patterns became less important than other considerations in making wage decisions.

The major factor behind this phenomenon of eroding and shrinking patterns was increased nonunion competition. As union membership declined within industries, newer lower-wage firms and plants undermined the earlier wage patterns. But even in the adverse climate of the 1980s, some patterns persisted. Ford and General Motors, for example, continued to follow one another in their negotiations. And Chrysler, which had deviated from the auto pattern beginning in 1979, was gradually brought back into line by the UAW.

As with wage imitation generally, pattern bargaining partly reflects equity considerations. Workers may simply ask, "If someone else has received an X% wage increase, why shouldn't I receive one?" Unions, as political institutions, must respond to such pressures.

Another important consideration in the union sector is taking wages out of competition. If the union succeeds in raising wages above market levels at a given firm, that employer will be placed at a competitive cost disadvantage in the product market unless other firms are forced to make the same wage adjustments. To strengthen its bargaining position with any one employer, the union must be able to make wages at other relevant employers move according to the same pattern.

Indeed, unionized employers can be expected to press the union to make sure that their competitors make wage settlements similar to their own. In a few contracts this expectation is formalized in union agreements in so-called "most-favored-nation clauses" (MFN). Under such clauses, if the union settles for a less costly package at a rival firm, it may be compelled to offer the more favorable terms to others with the MFN clauses in their contracts.[63]

In most cases, however, the pressure for common costs is not formalized into an agreement; it simply exists as a feature of the union–management relationship. This factor explains why pattern bargaining tends to be strongest *within* a given industry (such as automobile manufacturing) and less prominent *across* industries. And it will erode within industries if nonunion firms (whose wages the union cannot control) enter the product market.

Available Data on Pay Adjustments

For employers who wish to determine what kinds of pay adjustments have recently occurred in the labor market, a variety of measures are available from the U.S. Bureau of Labor Statistics. BLS wage data can be readily obtained from press releases and statistical journals published by the bureau. However, the pay adjustment data produced by BLS tend to be oriented toward national averages, not detailed local labor markets.

Table 8–3 presents examples of BLS data on pay adjustments. Average hourly earnings data (discussed in the previous chapter) are available on a monthly basis for production and nonsupervisory employees. These data are published on a detailed industry basis, as the table shows. However, they can be distorted by shifts in the mix of overtime and nonovertime hours, shifts in the proportions of high- and low-paid workers, and—at the aggregate level—shifts in employment between high- and low-paying industries. Such shifts can affect average hourly earnings, even if wage *rates* are unchanged. Yet it is wage rate decisions that are of concern to employers.[64]

Average hourly earnings do not reflect fringe benefits such as pensions and health insurance and do not include data for supervisory workers. There are no monthly sources for these missing data. On a quarterly basis, however, the BLS

TABLE 8–3 Selected Measures of Pay Change, 1987

Pay Index and Sector or Group	*Wages and Salaries*	*Total Compensation*
Average hourly earnings* (M)	3.0%	—
Meat-packing plants	1.9	—
Eating and drinking places	2.5	—
Banking	3.8	—
Compensation per hour† (Q)	—	2.8%
Employment Cost Index‡ (Q)	3.5	3.6
Private sector	3.3	3.3
White-collar	3.7	3.7
Professional and technical	4.5	4.1
Manufacturing	3.4	3.1
Union	2.6	2.8
Nonunion	3.6	3.6
West	2.6	2.6
State and local government workers	4.2	4.4
White-collar	3.3	4.6
Elementary and secondary schools	4.8	5.0

Note: Indexes denoted (M) are available monthly; percentage pay changes shown for monthly indexes are on a December-to-December basis. Indexes denoted (Q) are available quarterly; percentage pay changes shown for quarterly indexes are on a fourth quarter to fourth quarter basis.

* Production and nonsupervisory workers in the private, nonfarm sector.
† Nonfarm, business sector.
‡ Civilian workers excluding farm, household, and federal government employees.

Source: Data from *Current Wage Developments, Monthly Labor Review, Employment and Earnings,* various issues.

has for many years published the compensation per hour index. This index includes fringes and payroll taxes as well as wages and includes all occupational groups. Unfortunately, compensation per hour is distorted—as are average hourly earnings—by shifts in overtime, occupational mix, and industry composition.

The BLS began publishing the quarterly Employment Cost Index (ECI) in 1976 in an attempt to remedy the deficiencies of the other available wage measures. In the 1980s the ECI was widened to include data on fringes and payroll taxes and on state and local government workers. Although its industry detail is limited to broad sectors, unlike the other pay indexes, it does provide some occupational detail as well as a union–nonunion breakdown.

Table 8–3 shows that in 1987 private sector workers as a whole received increases in total compensation of a little over 3%. Nonunion workers received larger increases than union workers. Total compensation rose at about the same rate as wages, a pause in a longstanding trend under which benefits had tended to rise faster than wages. Finally, state and local government workers received larger pay increases than private sector workers.

Given these trends, a private nonunion employer contemplating a pay increase in early 1988 could have viewed an adjustment in pay of 3% as falling in the normal range. A public employer might have considered 4% to 5% as the going rate of pay adjustment. As stressed earlier, such norms need not have been automatically followed. But an employer who was considering an adjustment outside these limits would probably have wanted to look carefully at the reasons for the deviation and the possible consequences.

For unionized employers, the BLS publishes data on major union settlements in both the private and public sectors. For purposes of wage change statistics, *major* refers to settlements covering 1,000 or more workers. Where data are published on a total compensation basis, *major* refers to settlements covering 5,000 or more workers. Smaller bargaining units are omitted.

Table 8–4 summarizes information on union settlements in 1987. In interpreting such data, it is important to keep in mind the existence of escalator clauses in the union sector. BLS notes the presence of such clauses, but does not attempt to estimate what wage increases will occur pursuant to them. (To do so would require forecasting the rate of CPI inflation, which the bureau hesitates to attempt.) As a result the data understate the wage adjustment that will actually be experienced.

Because of the escalator problem, it is a good idea to start by looking at those settlements that do not have escalator clauses. The table shows that such agreements provided for total compensation adjustments of 2% to 3% per annum over the contract's life. These modest settlements were influenced by the wage concession movement that sometimes involved giving up, or freezing, the escalator clause.

As noted earlier, escalator clauses in the 1980s yielded roughly a 0.5% wage increase for each 1% CPI increase. Suppose that CPI inflation of about 4% per year were expected over the following two to three years. Then a very crude estimate of the adjustment to be experienced under settlements with escalator clauses would have been about two percentage points above the levels shown in

Table 8–4. The escalated contracts, which were less likely to involve concessions, thus could be projected to provide roughly 4% pay increases per annum over the contract's life.

Generally, a unionized employer entering negotiations in early 1988 would have known that pay adjustments of about 2% to 4% per annum could be considered normal. Of course, the employer might plan or expect to negotiate a settlement outside that range. Knowing the averages, however, gives guidance for bargaining strategy and cost projections.

Pay Intention Surveys

BLS data on pay changes are always retrospective. Unless economic conditions are changing drastically, such retrospective information may be a sufficient guide to the future. Pay changes made in one year generally do not differ dramatically from the previous year unless, for example, the rate of inflation is markedly accelerating or decelerating. Even so, for planning purposes pay setters may want to know what other employers are considering as likely pay adjustments in the future.

Possible sources to meet this need are the various major economic forecasting services. These services, such as Data Resources, Inc. (DRI), use econometric wage-change equations to forecast wage changes as part of their larger economic

TABLE 8–4   Selected Pay Change Measures Related to the Union Sector, 1987

	First Year		Contract Life	
	Wages Only	Compensation	Wages Only	Compensation
U.S. Bureau of Labor Statistics data for major settlements*				
All private settlements	2.2%	3.0%	2.1%	2.6%
Settlements with escalator clauses	2.3	3.2	1.5	2.3
Settlements without escalator clauses	2.1	2.7	2.5	2.9
All state and local government settlements	4.9	4.9	5.1	4.8
Bureau of National Affairs, Inc. data[†]				
All settlements	2.4%[‡]	—	—	—

* Major settlements for the wages only columns are those involving 1,000 or more workers. For the compensation columns, major settlements are those involving 5,000 or more workers.
[†] Settlements involving 50 or more workers.
[‡] With lump sums included, figure would be 3.0%.

Source: Data from *Current Wage Developments*, vol. 40 (March 1988), pp. 7, 11, 34; *Daily Labor Report*, January 15, 1988, p. B3.

models. The wage equations in these models play an important role in the forecasting of general inflation trends.

Larger firms often subscribe to economic forecasting services through their economic research departments. Pay setters within the HRM department may have access to such information, and certainly should take advantage of it. However, economic forecasters typically provide no disaggregated information about wages. Generally, they forecast only compensation per hour at the aggregate level.

To acquire more detail, employers must rely on various private surveys conducted by management and compensation consulting firms such as Hewitt Associates. These surveys usually ask subscribing employers what kinds of wage and salary increases they gave for various occupations groups during the past year and what they are contemplating as probable adjustments for the following year.

Pay intention surveys are not always readily available to firms that are not in a commercial relationship with the consultants. The surveys are sometimes summarized, however, by reporting services such as the *Daily Labor Report*. In addition, the Human Resources Outlook Panel of the Conference Board publishes its own forecast of likely pay adjustments and includes data from various pay intention surveys.

Users of pay intention surveys must be wary of interpreting the resulting data at face value. In a previous chapter it was noted that confusion often arises concerning the cost effects of merit increases. In a steady-state situation, a properly functioning merit system should not raise average pay. However, HRM managers often confuse two concepts: the average pay adjustment that will be experienced by current employees who stay with the firm and the average adjustment in pay for all workers (including those who arrive and those who depart).[65]

The former concept will include the gross cost of merit increases for those employees eligible for them as well as any general across-the-board pay increase. The latter, which includes only the across-the-board adjustment, is the most relevant concept for an employer considering budgeting for future pay increases.

In many surveys, the respondents seem to include the gross cost of merit pay systems in their answers about future pay adjustments. The result is an upward bias in the reported figures of about one to two percentage points. A user unaware of this bias could gain a misleadingly high estimate of the likely rate of wage inflation. One way to probe for possible bias is to look at the pay adjustments the respondents say they have already given and to compare them with appropriate retrospective BLS data. If the survey results seem high relative to BLS figures, merit bias is probably present.

8–8   A Single Formula?

When there are multiple guides to a decision, the question of weighting the guides inevitably arises. In the case of making pay adjustment decisions, this chapter has shown that various factors are relevant, including price inflation, labor market conditions, pay adjustments at other employers, and profitability and productivity. Is there some formula that incorporates all of the various factors and indicates percisely what decision an individual employer should make? The answer is "no." As is often the case in business decision making, quantification has both its benefits and limits. Ultimately, a subjective judgment, based on available data, is required.

Nevertheless, employers should have a general, long-term strategy concerning their pay policies. Such a strategy might simply be to pay average wages for given occupations in the local labor market over the long run. In any given year, however, there may be reason to deviate from the long-range strategy. From time to time, the strategy itself must be reexamined. Neither the annual decision, nor the periodic strategy determination, should be undertaken without reference to the indicators and considerations discussed in this chapter.

Summary

From time to time employers must make decisions that adjust the general level of pay. The frequency of such adjustments will vary with the speed at which the criteria for adjustments are changing. In normal times most firms review the issue of making general pay changes on an annual basis.

Various factors are relevant for pay-change decisions. Generally, increases in prices create pressure for wage increases. Most nonunion employers, however, do not mechanically adjust wages in accordance with consumer prices. Even in the union sector, where cost-of-living escalator clauses are not unusual, the formulas used do not provide a one-for-one linkage between wage and price increases. There is a sharing of risk between employer and employee implicit in the formulas.

Increased demand in the labor market, leading to reduced unemployment and increased unfilled job vacancies, also puts upward pressure on wages. During periods of high unemployment and few external job opportunities, however, employers do not typically slash wages of their incumbent, insider workforces. Employers sometimes share with their workers increases in the firm's ability to pay, as reflected in their profit or productivity increases. This sharing may occur through formal profit- or gain-sharing plans, or it may simply take place via more generous pay adjustments over a period of time.

In the long run the average real wage of the American worker increases with national productivity. Put another way, the nominal wage increase in the long run is approximately the sum of the trend increase in prices and the trend increase in national productivity. As their economic circumstances change, individual firms and industries may, however, exhibit rates of pay adjustment that deviate from the national average.

In making their own pay decisions, employers commonly look at pay adjustments elsewhere in the labor market. In the union sector this approach to pay setting sometimes takes the form of pattern following, a feature of collective bargaining that was weakened in the 1980s but continues to exist. Nonunion employers are less likely to follow patterns. But, for a combination of market and equity reasons, they do try to avoid excessive deviation between their pay levels and those of other employers.

EXERCISES

Problem

Use the statistical sources described in this chapter to determine the most recent 12–month increase in (1) CPI-U, (2) CPI-W, (3) average hourly earnings, and (4) the Employment Cost Index. Find out what has been the average first-year wage adjustment for major private contracts in the union sector. Analyze the relative pace of wage trends and price trends you have found.

Questions

1. Why are wage trends correlated with price trends?

2. Why are nominal wages seldom cut?

3. Why are escalator clauses rare among nonunion employers?

4. Does the CPI measure employer ability to pay? Explain.

5. What should be the role of profitability in adjusting wages?

Terms

caps and corridors in
  escalator clauses
index number problem
insider/outsider model
Laspeyres price index

merit bias in pay intention
  surveys
money illusion
most-favored-nation
  clauses

norm shifts in wage setting
pattern bargaining
Phillips curve
threat effect of unions
two-tier wage plan

ENDNOTES

1. A now-discountinued survey by the Bureau of Labor Statistics covered nonunion manufacturing and indicated that virtually all pay increases experienced by nonunion workers occurred pursuant to decisions made within the same year. See Sanford M. Jacoby and Daniel J.B. Mitchell, "Does Implicit Contracting Explain Explicit Contracting?" in Barbara D. Dennis, ed., *Proceedings of the Thirty-Fifth Annual Meeting.* Industrial Relations Research Associa- tion, December 28–30, 1982 (Madison, Wisc.: IRRA, 1983), p. 323.

2. Harriet Gorlin, *Personnel Practices II: Hours of Work, Pay Practices, Relocation,* information bulletin no. 92 (New York: Conference Board, 1981), p 24.

3. Bureau of National Affairs, Inc., *Wage & Salary Admin-*

istration, PPF Survey no. 131 (Washington: BNA, 1981), p. 10.

4. This usage should not be confused with the escalator clauses discussed later in this chapter. Employees will often refer to cost-of-living adjustments—meaning general wage increases—when no escalator is involved.

5. The ECI-based series are on a fourth quarter to fourth quarter basis; the price deflator series is on a year-to-year basis.

6. See *Survey of Current Business,* vol. 68 (June 1988), p. 5.

7. Total revenue $(TR) = PQ$, where P = price and Q = quantity. Differentiating both sides by Q yields the following equation:

$$\text{(a)} \quad MR = [Q(dP/dQ)] + P$$

The elasticity of demand (e) is $(dQ/dP)(P/Q)$. Thus it is easy to show that

$$\text{(b)} \quad MR = P[(1 + e)/e]$$

Note that e is a negative number (since a demand curve is downward sloping) and that a profit-maximizing firm will always operate where $e < -1$. For example, if $e = -2$, marginal revenue will be one-half the price.

8. Other deviations from the classical model still are consistent with a positive effect of price on demand. For example, it has been proposed that employers—for reasons of employee perceptions of equity—compress the earnings distribution between high- and low-productivity workers. Even in such cases, however, there is an average equality between price (or marginal revenue) and marginal product. For such a model, see Robert H. Frank, "Are Workers Paid Their Marginal Products?," *American Economic Review,* vol. 74 (September 1984), pp. 549–571.

9. An important consideration is whether labor is a complement to, or a substitute for, energy in production.

10. A lump-sum bonus was paid in the first year in lieu of a wage increase.

11. As noted earlier, the classical formula can be modified to deal with implicit contracting in terms of flows of wages and revenues.

12. See Sanford M. Jacoby, "Cost-of-Living Escalators: A Brief History" in Barbara D. Dennis, ed., *Proceedings of the Thirty-Seventh Annual Meeting,* Industrial Relations Research Association, December 28–30, 1984 (Madison, Wisc.: IRRA, 1985), pp. 396–403.

13. Price data were collected from 21,000 retail eatablishments and 60,000 housing units in 91 urban areas as of mid-1988. The coverage of the CPI is sometimes varied due to budgetary pressures at the BLS.

14. CPI-U is estimated to cover the consumption habits of 80% of the noninstitutional population; CPI-W represents about 32%.

15. Details concerning the actual construction of the CPI can be found in U.S. Bureau of Labor Statistics, *BLS Handbook of Methods,* bulletin 2285 (Washington: GPO, 1988), chapter 19. Actually, the BLS does not need to collect data on precise quantities of goods and services consumed in the reference period. Rather, it is sufficient to determine the proportion of expenditure devoted to different classes of goods. These proportions become the reference period weights of the index. Goods and services that are "representative" of the expenditure class are then selected, and the price changes of these representatives are collected from period to period. These price "relatives" form the heart of CPI data collection.

The rationale for this method of data collection can be seen by rearranging the formula in the text. That formula can be rewritten as:

$$\sum_{i}^{n} (P_{i1}/P_{i0}) \, [P_{i0}Q_{i0}/\sum_{i}^{n} P_{i0}Q_{i0}],$$

where the term in parentheses ( ) is the price relative of good i from period 0 to period 1 and the term in brackets [ ] is the expenditure weight for good i in period 0.

Note that it is possible to apply this formula period after period as long as the expenditure weights are continuously updated by price trends (not consumption patterns). The weights for good i will increase if the price of good i rises faster than the average of other prices. To compute the index from period 10 to period 11, it is only necessary to have the weight for period 10 and the price relatives for period 10 to 11.

16. The arbitrary base period does not necessarily have to be the same as the period in which the consumer expenditure weights were established. Beginning in 1988, the two periods coincided (1982–84). Prior to 1988, however, the periods generally were different. A user can convert the base period to any arbitrary date simply by dividing all values of the index by the value at the arbitrary date and multiplying by 100. For discussion of the changes in the CPI introduced in 1987–88, see Bureau of National Affairs, Inc., *New Consumer Price Index Provides Updated Measure of Household Spending* (Washington: BNA, 1987).

17. It is important to note, however, that city CPIs cannot be used to compare absolute living costs. Thus, in December 1987, the Los Angeles area CPI-U stood at 118.5 while the Philadelphia area CPI stood at 118.9, both based on 1982 to 1984 = 100. These index values do not indicate that it cost less to live in Los Angeles in December 1987 than Philadelphia; they meant only that prices *rose* less rapidly in Los Angeles than in Philadelphia from 1982–84 to December 1987.

18. Remaining on the same indifference curve is, by definition, equivalent to leaving consumer welfare unchanged.

19. Of course, if all prices rise by the same percentage amount, the index number problem does not arise, since substitution effects are not triggered.

20. Steven D. Braithwait, "The Substitution Bias of the Laspeyres Price Index: An Analysis Using Estimated Cost-of-Living Indexes," *American Economic Review,* vol. 70 (March 1980), pp. 64–77; Daniel J.B. Mitchell, "Should the Consumer Price Index Determine Wages?," *California Management Review,* vol. 25 (Fall 1982), pp. 5–21; Marilyn E. Manser and Richard J. McDonald, "An Analysis of Substitution Bias in Measuring Inflation, 1959–82," working paper 142, U.S. Bureau of Labor Statistics, May 1984.

21. In the late 1970s, the CPI suffered from an acute problem relating to housing costs and the treatment of mortgage interest payments. This problem was remedied in the early 1980s, but at different times for CPI-U and CPI-W. Hence, the two indices diverged for a time due to the separate treatments of housing, a problem that no longer exists. Discrepancies between CPI-U and CPI-W now are due only to the different weighting schemes of the two measures.

22. Part of the GNP consists of government services that are measured at wage costs. Thus, the GNP deflator has a wage component for the government sector; it is not a pure price index.

23. Deflators from the national income accounts are Paasche indexes rather than Laspeyres. Their quantity weights are based on the end period rather than some fixed reference period. In principle, Paasche indexes have reverse index number problems; they will underestimate the degree of budget increase needed to maintain welfare. The fact that they do not greatly diverge from the CPIs is another indication that the index number problem is not a major difficulty in practice. It might be noted that fixed-weight (Laspeyres) versions of the national income account deflators are available as are "chain-linked" versions. The latter use the previous period's consumption as the base for the current period.

24. The Producer Price Index is weighted by shipment values in a reference period. It contains components for different stages of production, of which finished goods is the highest. Thus, it can be used to trace the movement of an inflationary or deflationary shock from crude materials to intermediate goods to finished goods. About 3,100 commodities were included as of mid-1988.

25. These improvements eliminated an unrealistic measure of housing costs involving use of mortgage interest rates.

26. Because Social Security benefits are indexed to the CPI, there has been pressure on the BLS to produce a special version of the CPI for retired people. It is not evident that such an index would necessarily rise faster than the general index. One study over the period 1961 to 1981 found little difference between a retiree index and a general index. See Michael J. Boskin and Michael D. Hurd, "Are Inflation Rates Different for the Elderly?," working paper no. 943, National Bureau of Economic Research, 1982. Similar conclusions were reached in U.S. General Accounting Office,

A CPI for Retirees Is Not Needed Now But Could Be in the Future, GAO/GGD–82–41 (Washington: GAO, 1982). Lobbyists concerned with retiree welfare, however, suspected that a retiree CPI would rise faster in the 1980s, and ultimately Congress required the BLS to study the problem and produce an experimental index. As might be expected, the weights for the experimental retiree CPI were higher in the medical care area than in the general index. Since health care prices have risen relative to others, this factor tends to push up the retiree index.

Private employers rarely have formal escalator clauses in their pension plans, and, hence are not likely to be much affected, even if a retiree index is ultimately used for Social Security purposes. (Unions might cite the retiree index in making demands for improvements for pensioners.) However, some public sector pensions do have formal escalation, and government employers may come under pressure to switch to a retiree index at some point in the future.

The BLS study is reproduced in the *Daily Labor Report* (July 1, 1988), pp. D1–D14.

27. Shelter has been excluded along with food and energy because of the treatment of mortgage interest rates in the CPI through the early 1980s. The index shown combines the original CPI-W with CPI-U, once the latter became available in 1978.

28. To the extent that nonunion employers provide health benefits, they might be said to have a limited form of escalation. If the health benefits are offered in such a way that the employer bears some or all of the cost of increases in health care prices, then an element of labor compensation is being geared to an outside source of price determination.

29. It should be noted that the CPI is used to index various forms of government benefits such as Social Security payments. A 1983 study suggested that a 1% increase in the CPI triggered $2 billion in federal outlays. See U.S. General Accounting Office, *Funds Needed to Develop CPI Quality Control System,* report GGD–83–32 (Washington: GAO, 1983), p. 2. See also U.S. Congressional Budget Office, *Indexing with the Consumer Price Index: Problems and Alternatives* (Washington: GPO, 1981).

30. Although escalators were used on occasion before World War II, they became widespread after a 1948 settlement between General Motors and the Auto Workers union. This contract is discussed in the text.

31. David Card, "Microeconomic Models of Wage Indexation" in Barbara D. Dennis, ed., *Proceedings of the Thirty-Seventh Annual Meeting,* Industrial Relations Research Association, December 28–30, 1984 (Madison, Wisc.: IRRA, 1985), pp. 404–412. It has also been argued that the apparent correlation of inflation and escalation usage is illusory and that the correlation was really an artifact of the wage–price controls program of the early 1970s, which gave preference to escalated agreements. See Stephen G. Cecchetti, "Indexation and Incomes Policy: A Study of Wage Adjustment in Unionized Manufacturing," *Journal*

of Labor Economics, vol. 5 (July 1987), pp. 391–412. When price inflation fell in the 1980s, a period of no wage controls, use of escalation also fell. This fact suggests that the illusion hypothesis is overstated. Other relevant references include Wallace Hendricks and Lawrence M. Kahn, "Cost-of-Living Clauses in Union Contracts: Determinants and Effects," *Industrial and Labor Relations Review,* vol. 36 (April 1983), pp. 447–460; Stuart E. Weiner, "Union COLA's on the Decline," *Federal Reserve Bank of Kansas City Economic Review,* vol. 71 (June 1986), pp. 10–25; Jo Anna Gray, "On Indexation and Contract Length," *Journal of Political Economy,* vol. 86 (February 1978), pp. 1–18.

32. Note that giving a flat cents-per-hour increase to all workers—as most escalators do—tends to flatten the spread of wage differentials between skilled and unskilled workers. The escalator thus functions as a backdoor method of redistributing income among the workforce. However, as skill differentials become depressed, pressure arises from skilled workers (and sometimes from management) to increase the differential in the course of subsequent negotiations.

33. The automobile formula also permits wage decreases if prices fall. Some brief episodes of escalator-triggered wage decreases did occur in the 1980s.

34. When the CPI is rebased, as occurred in 1988, the BLS continues publishing the series using the old base for a considerable period. This practice enables contracts reached before the change, such as the 1987 automobile settlements, to continue with the existing formula. It also permits the parties yet another degree of freedom in designing escalator formulas, since they can link them to the CPI under the old or new base.

35. Escalators generally cover wages, not fringe benefits. Often, the escalator money is kept separate from the base wage, so that certain benefits—such as pensions—that reflect the base wage, are not adjusted by the escalator. From time to time, a negotiation may move some of the escalator money into the base wage, thus triggering a benefit increase.

36. Ronald G. Ehrenberg, Leif Danzinger, and Gee San, "Cost-of-Living Adjustment Clauses in Union Contracts: A Summary of Results," *Journal of Labor Economics,* vol. 1 (July 1983), pp. 215–245.

37. Joan Borum, James Conley, and Edward Wasilewski, "The Outlook for Collective Bargaining in 1988," *Monthly Labor Review,* vol. 111 (January 1988), p. 13.

38. Federal postal workers did have escalation, however.

39. A total of 2,473,000 workers had escalators, out of 8,697,000 union-represented workers in the major private and state-and-local sectors. There were 19,051,000 union-represented wage and salary workers in 1987. Hence, 10,354,000 workers were under nonmajor or federal contracts. If we assume that these workers had a rate of esca-

lator coverage equal to half the rate for those under major private and state-and-local agreements (14% vs. 28%) and take the resulting estimate of escalator workers as a percent of all wage and salary workers (union and nonunion), the result is about 4%. Estimates regarding workers under major contracts are from Borum, Conley, and Wasilewski, *op. cit.,* p. 13. Other estimates are from *Employment and Earnings,* vol. 35 (January 1988), p. 222.

There has been concern from time to time that wages geared to prices through escalator clauses could themselves contribute to inflation. Actually, the macroeconomic effects are complex; under some circumstances, such linkage could enhance the ability of monetary policy to bring inflation under control. The small proportion of the U.S. workforce under escalation, however, suggests that whatever the sensitivity of wages to prices, escalators can play only a small part in the inflation process. See Wayne Vroman, "Cost-of-Living Escalators and Price-Wage Linkages in the U.S. Economy, 1968–1980," *Industrial and Labor Relations Review,* vol. 38 (January 1985), pp. 225–235; Daniel J.B. Mitchell and Larry J. Kimbell, "Labor Market Contracts and Inflation" in Martin Neil Baily, ed., *Workers, Jobs, and Inflation* (Washington: Brookings Institution, 1982), pp. 199–238.

40. A lower-case p represents the price level; the upper-case P was used previously to designate the price of the particular product the worker produces.

41. This assumption is implicit in Keynes's definition of involuntary unemployment. See John Maynard Keynes, *The General Theory of Employment, Interest, and Money* (New York: Harcourt, Brace & World, 1936), p. 15. See also Daniel J.B. Mitchell, "Wages and Keynes: Lessons from the Past," *Eastern Economic Journal,* vol. 12 (July-September 1986), pp. 199–208.

42. Daniel J.B. Mitchell, "Explanations of Wage Inflexibility: Institutions and Incentives" in Wilfred Beckerman, *Wage Rigidity and Unemployment* (Baltimore: Johns Hopkins University Press, 1986), pp. 41–76, especially pp. 46–47.

43. Daniel Kahneman, Jack L. Knetsch, and Richard Thaler, "Fairness as a Constraint on Profit Seeking: Entitlements in the Market," *American Economic Review,* vol. 76 (September 1986), p. 731.

44. This formula ignores compounding. The reader is referred to the chapter on productivity for more precise analysis.

45. Robert H. Ferguson, *Cost-of-Living Adjustments in Union-Management Agreements,* ILR Bulletin no. 65 (Ithaca, N.Y.: New York State School of Industrial and Labor Relations, Cornell University, 1976), p. 5.

46. Some discussion of this point occurred in an earlier chapter. It will also be discussed in more detail in a later chapter.

47. Production workers in Japanese manufacturing received about one-fifth of their compensation in the form of bonuses in the late 1970s. The corresponding figure for American workers was less than 1%. See U.S. Bureau of Labor Sta-

tistics, *Handbook of Labor Statistics,* bulletin 2217 (Washington: GPO, 1985), p. 439. See also Richard B. Freeman and Martin L. Weitzman, "Bonuses and Employment in Japan," *Journal of the Japanese and International Economies,* vol. 1 (1987), pp. 168–194.

48. The insider/outsider terminology has become common in economic literature. See, for example, Assar Lindbeck and Dennis J. Snower, "Wage Setting, Unemployment, and Insider-Outsider Relations," *American Economic Review,* vol. 76 (May 1985), pp. 235–239.

49. Kahneman et al, "Fairness as a Constraint on Profit Seeking," *op. cit.,* p. 730.

50. Some two-tier plans were permanent so that new hires could never work their way up to the pay scales of incumbent workers. More common were temporary plans in which the pay scales eventually merged after a specified period on the job. Of course, under either plan, the outsiders become insiders once hired, creating the possibility of friction within the workforce. For more details on the two-tier phenomenon, see Sanford M. Jacoby and Daniel J.B. Mitchell, "Management Attitudes Toward Two-Tier Pay Plans," *Journal of Labor Research,* vol. 7 (Summer 1986), pp. 221–237; Richard S. Belous, "Two-Tier Wage Systems in the U.S. Economy," report no. 85–165 E, Congressional Research Service, August 12, 1985; Peter Cappelli and Peter D. Sherer, "Assessing Worker Attitudes Under a Two-Tier Wage Plan," working paper no. 726, Wharton School, University of Pennsylvania, November 1987.

51. Delta Airlines, which is largely nonunion except for its pilots, instituted a two-tier plan at the same time other, unionized airlines did so. It ended the plan in 1988.

52. "New Retirement System for Federal Employees," *Monthly Labor Review,* vol. 104 (October 1986), p. 34.

53. A.W. Phillips, "The Relation Between Unemployment and the Rate of Change of Money Wage Rates in the United Kingdom, 1861–1957," *Economica,* vol. 25 (November 1958), pp. 283–299.

54. Some economists would object to the use of the terms interchangeably. Since the issue involves a debate in macroeconomics and is not directly relevant here, it is simply acknowledged here. See Anthony Myatt, "On the Non-Existence of a Natural Rate of Unemployment and Kaleckian Micro Underpinnings to the Phillips Curve," *Journal of Post-Keynesian Economics,* vol. 8 (Spring 1986), pp. 447–462.

55. For a study finding that above-normal profits added to union wage increases, see Daniel J.B. Mitchell, *Unions, Wages, and Inflation* (Washington: Brookings Institution, 1980), pp. 151–152. Reference to other profit-related stud-

ies can be found in this source. On productivity, see E. Kuh, "A Productivity Theory of Wage Levels—An Alternative to the Phillips Curve," *Review of Economic Studies,* vol. 34 (October 1967), pp. 333–360.

56. George L. Perry of the Brookings Institution is the originator of the concept of discrete shifts in wage norms. See George L. Perry, "Inflation in Theory and Practice," *Brookings Papers on Economic Activity* (1:1980), pp. 207–241; George L. Perry, "What Have We Learned About Disinflation?," *Brookings Papers on Economic Activity* (2:1983), pp. 587–602; George L. Perry, "Shifting Wage Norms and Their Implications," *American Economic Review,* vol. 76 (May 1986), pp. 245–248.

57. Daniel J.B. Mitchell, "Shifting Norms in Wage Determination," *Brookings Papers on Economic Activity* (2:1985), pp. 575–599.

58. John T. Addison and John B. Chilton, "Wage Patterns: An Evolutionary Perspective," *Journal of Labor Research,* vol. 9 (Summer 1988), pp. 207–219.

59. Bureau of National Affairs, Inc., *Policies for Unorganized Employees,* PPF Survey no. 125 (Washington: BNA, 1979), p. 13.

60. Daniel J.B. Mitchell, *Unions, Wages, and Inflation, op. cit.,* pp. 175–177.

61. Audrey Freedman and William E. Fulmer, "Last Rites for Pattern Bargaining," *Harvard Business Review,* vol. 60 (March–April 1982), pp. 30–48.

62. Audrey Freedman, *The New Look in Wage Policy and Employee Relations,* report no. 856 (New York: Conference Board, 1985), pp. 7–10.

63. The term comes from international trade jargon. In that context it refers to an agreement between countries A and B under which they undertake to offer to each other any tariff-lowering concessions they might later give to a third country. MFN clauses in the union context can also refer to situations in which an employer agrees to give the union the advantage of a better (higher) settlement it (the employer) might make with some other union.

64. For many years the BLS offered an adjusted version of average hourly earnings that controlled shifts in employment between high- and low-paying industries. However, BLS decided to discontinue this adjusted index in favor of the Employment Cost Index discussed later.

65. The merit bias in pay intention surveys is discussed in Sanford M. Jacoby and Daniel J.B. Mitchell, "Alternative Sources of Labor Market Data" in Barbara D. Dennis, ed., *Proceedings of the Thirty-Eighth Annual Meeting,* Industrial Relations Research Association, December 28–30, 1985 (Madison, Wisc.: IRRA, 1986), pp. 42–49.

Chapter Nine

INSTITUTIONS OF COLLECTIVE BARGAINING

Although previous chapters have referred to the union sector, unions and collective bargaining have not been explicitly analyzed. Unions represented less than a fifth of American wage and salary workers as of the late 1980s. During the first half of that decade, unions lost substantial membership and strength, although the proportion of the workforce organized, that is, represented by unions, had been declining gradually since the mid-1950s. Despite this downward trend, unions retained a significant influence on the employment relationship in a number of private industries and in government, especially at the state and local levels.

Historically, the union sector has been the source of much innovation in the employment relationship. The widespread use of fringe benefits, for example, was popularized initially at unionized firms, and then spread throughout the economy.[1] Moreover, unions have often played an important role in the political process. At the federal level, for example, the passage of occupational health and safety regulation legislation (OSHA) in 1970 was largely the product of union lobbying efforts.[2] Similarly, the establishment of federal regulation of private pension plans under ERISA in 1974 stemmed essentially from union concerns about the safety of the defined benefit pension plans they were negotiating.[3]

Unions are often important political influences at the state and local level as well. State laws regulate such programs as workers' compensation and unemployment insurance, which affect virtually all employers.[4] In addition, local laws and ordinances on such topics as zoning can be important to both employers and unions, for example, in the building industry. Unions frequently play a major role in determining state and local policies, especially in states where large numbers of union workers reside. Managers thus ignore developments and trends in the union sector at their peril, even if they find themselves in totally nonunion firms.

Moreover, the figures on overall unionization of the workforce can be misleading. Large firms (that are disproportionately the employers of the graduates of MBA programs) are much more likely to deal with unions than small firms.

In a period when mergers and acquisitions are common, nonunion firms will often acquire an interest in, or control of, an enterprise that is unionized. For all of the preceding reasons, it is important to devote attention to unions and collective bargaining and their influence on management. Both this chapter and the next one focus on these topics.

9–1   Unions Defined

In simplest terms, unions are associations of employees that are formed to represent workforce concerns and interests in negotiations with management. Often American unions are associated with the AFL-CIO, a central union body that acts as a voice for organized labor and as a lobbying organization.[5] With the reaffiliation of the Teamsters union in 1987, about eight out of ten union members were in unions belonging to the AFL-CIO.[6]

Increasingly, as unions found themselves facing both loss of membership and a severe crisis in their relations with employers, the AFL-CIO began to play a coordinating role in the search for appropriate union responses.[7] As can be seen in Table 9–1, however, some unions, such as the large and influential National Education Association, are not AFL-CIO members.[8] Various small, independent unions, sometimes representing workers at a single firm or plant, are also outside the AFL-CIO framework.[9] In the past, management occasionally encouraged the formation of such independent unions, hoping to keep out national unions. This tactic is no longer common, but some older independent unions that resulted still exist.[10]

American unions most commonly come to represent a group of employees by means of an election process conducted by a government agency.[11] If a union wins the election, it becomes the exclusive bargaining representative for the workers in the "appropriate bargaining unit" (the election district). No other union may represent those workers with management. For its part, management is legally obligated to bargain in "good faith" about terms and conditions affecting the represented workers. This exclusive representation system contrasts with that found in many other countries. Abroad, it is not unusual to find systems under which multiple unions vie to represent the same group of workers.

Representation of workers by unions takes two forms. First, unions negotiate with employers for contracts that specify wages, benefits, workrules, and other workplace procedures. Second, within the contractual framework negotiated, there is typically a mechanism whereby employee and union grievances can be aired and adjudicated. (Since nonunion firms also often have some form of grievance system, discussion of this latter function is left to a later chapter.)

Unions are able to influence management decisions through the bargaining power they possess. At the core of this power is the union's ability to carry out a strike, which can impose significant costs on the enterprise. If management makes concessions under traditional collective bargaining, it does so to avoid

TABLE 9-1 Membership of Major Labor Organizations, 1987

Organization	Claimed Membership	Affiliation	Major Sectors Covered
National Education Association	1,700,000	Independent	School systems
International Brotherhood of Teamsters	1,600,000	AFL-CIO	Trucking, food stores, construction, various manufacturing
United Food and Commercial Workers	1,270,000	AFL-CIO	Food stores, meatpacking
American Federation of State, County, and Municipal Workers	1,100,000	AFL-CIO	State and local government
United Automobile Workers	1,002,675	AFL-CIO	Autos, auto parts, aerospace
Service Employees International Union	850,000	AFL-CIO	Health care, building services, local government
International Brotherhood of Electrical Workers	790,000	AFL-CIO	Construction, electrical manufacturing
International Association of Machinists	750,000	AFL-CIO	Aerospace, machinery
United Steelworkers	730,400	AFL-CIO	Metal manufacturing
Communications Workers	700,000	AFL-CIO	Telephone communication
American Federation of Teachers	660,000	AFL-CIO	School systems
Carpenters and Joiners	609,000	AFL-CIO	Construction, lumber

Source: Courtney D. Gifford, ed., *Directory of U.S. Labor Organizations,* 1988–89 edition (Washington: The Bureau of National Affairs, Inc., 1988), Part III.

these costs. That process may sound harsh. But were the ability to impose costs on the firm absent, unions would be little more than consultative bodies.

Indeed, analogies have often been made between union–management relations and relations between nations. In both cases, if diplomacy fails, one party can influence another's behavior by actual or threatened infliction of costs. The weapons in the international setting include everything from trade embargoes, to stirring up subversion, terrorism, and military action. In the union–management setting, the older weapons on the union side include work slowdowns, boycotts, and strikes. Newer weapons may include pressure on financial institutions and other companies that deal with the target employer. On the management side, there may be firings, plant shutdowns, and lockouts.

Of course, some unions are better positioned to inflict strike and other costs on the employers they deal with than are others. But even unions that are well equipped to inflict costs must be aware that the strike threat is costly to themselves and their members, just as nations should remember that war is a two-edged sword. To inflict economic pain requires the ability to endure economic pain.

The strike weapon will be examined in more detail in the next chapter. But it is extremely important to stress that traditional union–management relations in the United States have been conducted within an adversarial framework. That framework coexists with notable (and routine) examples of union–management cooperation. There is nothing remarkable about this coexistence, since it is built into the employer–employee relationship. Both parties to that relationship are adversaries, as are all buyers and sellers. Both also have an investment, a stake, in having their relations endure. When a union is present these aspects of the relationship become more overt and explicit.

9–2 Legal Framework Surrounding Unions

An elaborate legal framework, beginning with legislation enacted during the Great Depression of the 1930s, has been erected to regulate unions and collective bargaining. Three major pieces of legislation have been adopted to cover most of the private sector.[12] This regulatory mechanism has been imitated in related legislation dealing with unionization of government workers at the federal, state, and local level.

The initial piece of major federal regulatory legislation dealing with unions was the Wagner Act of 1935, also known as the National Labor Relations Act.[13] This act gave employees the right to organize into unions, provided an election mechanism for workers to choose whether or not they wanted a particular union to represent them, and forbade various employer practices considered to be anti-union ("unfair labor practices"). A federal agency, the *National Labor Relations Board* (NLRB), was created to oversee the new employee rights, to prevent unfair labor practices by employers, and to hold representation elections. The NLRB responds to petitions and complaints from unions, employers, and workers; it does not have independent inspectors who look for violations of the law on their own initiative.

Although the original Wagner Act aimed at promoting unions and collective bargaining, subsequent federal legislation pulled back from this objective. By the late 1940s the balance of political forces had shifted in a more conservative direction, and the public was aroused and angered by a series of major strikes following World War II. The outcome of these pressures was the 1947 Taft-Hartley Act (also known as the Labor–Management Relations Act).[14]

Taft-Hartley modified the Wagner Act by creating a series of prohibitions on unfair labor practices by unions. These regulations paralleled the forbidden employer practices specified in the Wagner Act. Taft-Hartley created NLRB decertification elections whereby employees could *remove* unions as their representatives, as well as install them. Responding to public concerns about major strikes, Taft-Hartley created a mechanism whereby the president could enjoin strikes for a temporary period. Finally, union–management contracts were made into legally enforceable documents; either party could sue the other for damages if it felt the contract was being breached.

In the 1950s a series of congressional investigations into complaints of undemocratic and corrupt practices in certain unions led to still more federal intervention. The Landrum-Griffin Act of 1959 (officially titled the Labor–Management Reporting and Disclosure Act) provided certain rights to union members within their organizations and regulated unions' internal financial and political affairs. In addition, Landrum-Griffin further refined the election and unfair labor practice procedures of the National Labor Relations Board.

This volume will not undertake a detailed examination of the federal regulatory system surrounding unions and bargaining beyond the above description.[15] The student should be aware, however, that union–management relations have over the years taken on an aura of legalism that extends far beyond anything the original Wagner Act framers could have imagined. Many observers have decried this tendency toward legalism.[16] Indeed, concerns have been expressed that the existing legal regulatory system may interfere with innovative experiments in worker participation and labor–management cooperation.[17] But barring a sweeping revision of the amended Wagner Act framework, the trend is irreversible.

The laws regarding unions extend to union members and organizers employed in nonunion companies and to situations in which workers engage in "concerted activity," even if they are not unionized. For example, a group of workers who form an informal group to complain to management about poor ventilation in the workplace are undertaking protected concerted activity that is protected by law. Management reprisals against them for their complaint could be an unfair labor practice. Thus *nonunion employers are affected by the amended Wagner Act in important ways even though they do not engage in collective bargaining.* For this reason academic training for specialists in the HRM field inevitably includes a careful examination of the laws surrounding unions and bargaining.

9–3 Political and Legal Influences on Unionization

How important have the periodic changes in the legal system been as determinants of union membership? What influence does the political climate have? What other factors may affect the degree to which the workforce is unionized? Out of the substantial literature devoted to these questions, several points emerge.

First, historically, wartime periods have been conducive to union growth. Union membership as a proportion of the workforce rose during World Wars I and II and during the Korean War, as can be seen in Table 9–2. Only during the Vietnam War did this pattern fail to emerge. The wartime effect appears to be due to the position taken by the federal government with regard to union–

TABLE 9-2   Labor Organization Membership Trends, 1915-1969

Period	Year	Members as Percent of Nonagricultural Employment		
		Unions Only, Wolman Series*	Unions Only, BLS Series	Unions and Associations, BLS Series
World War I and immediate aftermath	1915	11.0%	—	—
	1920	17.5	—	—
Conservative era/employer resistance to unionization				
	1929	9.7	—	—
Onset of Great Depression				
	1933	10.6	11.3%	—
Swing to left/New Deal era/Wagner Act				
	1940	—	26.9	—
World War II				
	1945	—	35.5	—
Conservative swing in Congress/Taft-Hartley Act				
	1950	—	31.5	—
Korean War				
Moderate Republican administration (Eisenhower)/ Landrum-Griffin Act	1954	—	34.7	—
	1960	—	31.5	—
Liberal era (Kennedy and Johnson)/Vietnam War				
	1969	—	27.0	29.5%

See *Sources* and *Notes* for Table 9-3.

management disputes. During major war efforts, government officials were anxious to maintain uninterrupted military and related production. Since contractors were under pressure to settle labor disputes and since they could pass the costs of the settlement on to government, union bargaining positions were enhanced during wartime. In addition the government was not sympathetic to employers who provoked strikes by resisting unionization.

A second point that emerges from Table 9-2 is that the passage of the Wagner Act was at least coincident with a substantial expansion of unionization. Taft-Hartley, on the other hand, is associated with slippage of the union penetration rate (although the Korean War temporarily pulled the ratio up again).

TABLE 9–3 Labor Organization Membership and Representation Trends, 1969–1985[†]

Period	Year	Members as Percent of Nonagricultural Employment, BLS Series	Workers Represented as Percent of Wage and Salary Employment, CPS Series		
			Total	Private	Public
Moderate Republican administration (Nixon and	1969	29.5%	—	—	—
Ford)/end of Vietnam War	1975	28.9	—	—	—
Liberal era (Carter)	1979	25.1	25.7%[‡]	21.7%[‡]	43.4%[‡]
Conservative era (Reagan)	1987	—	19.2	14.4	42.5

— = data not available.

[*]Membership series developed by economist Leo Wolman, divided by an estimate of the nonfarm employed labor force.

[†]Includes unions and associations.

[‡]Data as of May 1980.

Note: The Wolman series are based on union-reported membership and originally appeared in Leo Wolman, *Ebb and Flow in Trade Unionism* (New York: National Bureau of Economic Research, 1936), pp. 172–193. The BLS (Bureau of Labor Statistics) series are also based on membership. Figures before 1954 are based largely on union reports to the AFL and CIO. Thereafter, the series is based on a BLS-conducted membership survey. The CPS (Current Population Survey) series is based on responses by households and includes some workers who are represented by labor organizations but are not members.

Sources: Data from U.S. Bureau of the Census, *Historical Statistics of the United States: Colonial Times to 1970,* Part 1 (Washington: GPO, 1975, pp. 126, 178; U.S. Bureau of Labor Statistics, *Directory of National Unions and Employee Associations, 1979,* bulletin 2079 (Washington: GPO, 1980), p. 59; Courtney D. Gifford, ed., *Directory of U.S. Labor Organizations,* 1982–83 edition (Washington: The Bureau of National Affairs, Inc., 1982), pp. 1, 55, 63; *Employment and Earnings,* vol. 35 (January 1988), pp. 222–223.

Finally, the Landrum-Griffin Act preceded a prolonged period of gradual slippage of unionization.

It is difficult, however, to disentangle the strictly legal effects from the impacts of shifts in the political climate. Unions benefited from the sympathetic climate of political and public opinion in the 1930s. In less liberal periods they lost ground relative to the overall workforce. During the conservative era of the Reagan administration in the 1980s, union membership tumbled absolutely as well as relative to the workforce, as Table 9–3 demonstrates.

Examining data such as those contained in Tables 9–2 and 9–3, leads to a strong impression that changes in the political–legal climate matter a great deal in determining unionization. Some econometricians have sought to explain changes in union representation using regression analysis and have created variables (such as the proportion of Democrats in Congress) to capture political shifts.[18] Even in the absence of such evidence, however, few practitioners on either the union or management sides would doubt the importance of the political and legal environment to union success (or lack thereof) in organizing.

For unions, success in organizing is linked to success in bargaining. If a union represents most of the workers in an industry, its bargaining position is substantially improved. It need not fear competition from low-wage nonunion employers. If a union is unable to organize substantial portions of an industry, however, competition will inevitably weaken its bargaining position relative to that of the unionized employers with which it deals.

The interconnection between unionization and bargaining power explains much of the rash of concession bargaining in the 1980s. As unions found themselves facing more and more nonunion competition, they were forced to accept wage freezes, wage cuts, and workrule relaxations at unionized worksites. In economic terms, the linkage can be viewed as a *substitution effect*. The possibility of substituting nonunion for union workers acts as a check on union bargaining power. Whether the substitution is made by a union employer who switches to nonunion labor sources, or whether the product market makes the substitution by switching demand to employers that have the advantage of a lower labor cost, pressures will eventually arise that limit what unions can obtain for their members.

Both management and labor seek political influence. Although an individual employer cannot by itself influence the political–legal climate, management as a group finds it useful to do so. Groups such as the Chamber of Commerce and the National Association of Manufacturers articulate the management interest at the national level, and trade associations perform a similar function at the industry level. Organized labor is also active in the political arena, supporting both legislation and candidates.

The fact that such activity occurs is perhaps the best proof of the impact of the political–legal climate on the outcomes of collective bargaining. Both sides are convinced of the importance of political activity in pursuing the goals of their constituents. In view of this fact of life, managers at the firm level must analyze the general environment for labor relations in formulating their collective-bargaining agenda.

9–4   Economic Policy and Unions

Discussions about public policy toward unions and collective bargaining often revolve around such concepts as industrial democracy. However, prevailing economic theories and economic objectives have also influenced the course of public policy. Indeed, the economic motivation is stronger than many casual observers believe. Changing views on macroeconomic policy have influenced the legal climate surrounding unions, and that, in turn, has affected unionization.

The original Wagner Act was passed in 1935, when the country was still in deep depression, and when the appropriate economic policies to escape that depression seemed elusive. Macroeconomics as an idea was just being born.[19] The economic debate concerning how to raise economic activity and lower unemployment was confused. Most economists of the period did not have the tools to state their assumptions about economic relationships clearly. Moreover, the collection of economic statistics was embryonic, making empirical analysis difficult.[20] Even the most critical economic and social concern of the period—unemployment—was not measured.[21]

During the Great Depression a popular economic theory held that if wages were boosted, the economy could be lifted from its slump. It was argued that if workers were paid higher wages, they would spend more on consumption and thus stimulate economic activity. Some commentators argued that the Great Depression had actually been caused by too low wages in the 1920s. Given this theory, the Roosevelt administration followed policies aimed at pushing up wages, even before passage of the Wagner Act.[22]

Since unions could be expected to demand higher wages, the passage of the Wagner Act to promote unions was viewed in part as an economic policy.[23] Indeed, the preamble to the Wagner Act contains the wage-purchasing power theory as a justification for the new law. It argues that "the inequality of bargaining power between employees . . . and employers . . . burdens and affects the flow of commerce, and tends to aggravate recurrent business depressions, by depressing wage rates and the purchasing power of wage earners. . . ."[24]

Numerous criticisms were made of the wage-purchasing power view during the 1930s and afterwards. For example, it was pointed out that if wages were pushed up relative to prices, profit margins would be squeezed and workers might be laid off. Thus aggregate worker purchasing power might be reduced, instead of increased, by raising wages. Rather than attempt to review this issue further, let it be said that the wage-purchasing power theory was questionable, and that the debate over it was conducted, often in polemical terms, in the absence of formal models or empirical evidence.

A sharp shift in economic thinking and goals occurred after World War II. Generally, in the postwar period, there has been much more concern about limiting inflation than there was in the 1930s, when mass unemployment was the key problem. In addition the rise of macroeconomics has led to the view that it is federal government policy (monetary and fiscal) that should be used to deal with inflation and unemployment. Private parties—businesses, unions, employees, and consumers—are viewed as micro-actors who should not be expected to cure macro-problems in the economic system on their own.

In the postwar atmosphere, encouraging unions to push up wages was often seen as inflationary, that is, contrary to public policy rather than supportive of it. During the Kennedy and Johnson administrations, a "voluntary" guidepost for holding back wage increases was therefore issued. In the Nixon years formal wage controls were instituted, and during the Carter administration, wage guidelines were again announced. Although each of these programs also placed limits on price increases and each covered nonunion as well as union wages, all ended up focusing special attention on union wage settlements. Furthermore, each featured notable confrontations between the President's program and particular unions whose wage settlements exceeded the official standards.[25]

Whether fairly or not, unions tended to be seen as the villains in these confrontations. The general public, moreover, often viewed union wage settlements as contributing to inflation. Thus in the postwar period—unlike the 1930s— pro-union legislation could no longer be depicted as furthering macroeconomic objectives. It is not surprising, therefore, that organized labor opposed most of the key postwar legislation relating to unions and bargaining that was passed at the federal level. The resulting less favorable legal climate for organizing new members also meant that the unionization rate slipped.

9–5 Patterns of Unionization

Table 9–4 shows the pattern of unionization in the United States as of the late 1980s. In the private sector, only about one out of seven wage and salary earners was represented by a union. The sectors with greater than average unionization

TABLE 9–4   Union Representation Rates, 1987

Industry	Percent of Wage and Salary Workers Represented by Unions	Selected Industries with Higher-Than-Average Private Major Union Representation Rates*
Agriculture	2.5%	
Private nonagricultural	14.6	
Mining	19.5	Coal, metal mining
Construction	22.2	
Manufacturing	24.7	Tobacco products, apparel, petroleum, leather, stone-clay-glass, primary metals, electrical equipment, transportation equipment
Transportation	34.0	Railroads, trucking, air transport, water transport
Communications and utilities	39.0	Telephones, electricity, gas
Wholesale trade	9.1	
Retail trade	7.4	Food stores
Finance, insurance, real estate	3.2	
Services	7.6	
Government	42.5	
All Sectors	19.2	

*Industries listed are those in which the ratio of workers estimated to be covered by major union agreements (those covering 1,000 or more employees) to total payroll employment exceeded the average rate of 8.5% in 1987. The number of workers under major union agreements is reported as of November 1987. Total payroll employment is the average for the entire year.

Source: Representation rates from *Employment and Earnings*, vol. 35 (January 1988), pp. 222–223. Coverage by major union agreements is from Joan R. Borum, James R. Conley, and Edward J. Wasilewski, "The Outlook for Collective Bargaining in 1988," *Monthly Labor Review*, vol. 111 (January 1988), pp. 11, 13. Total payroll employment is from *Employment and Earnings*, vol. 35 (March 1988), Table B–2.

were mining, construction, manufacturing, transportation, communications, and utilities. These were the sectors in which unions primarily expanded in the 1930s and 1940s. The unionized portion of the workforce thus reflects employment patterns of an earlier era, when the economy had more of an industrial base.

Industrial Detail

Union representation rates in Table 9–4 are drawn from the Current Population Survey (CPS). Because CPS data are not published according to detailed industry classifications, another data set has been used to identify more narrowly defined industries that had above-average unionization. The right-hand column of the table lists those industries in which the ratio of workers estimated to be covered by major agreements (those involving 1,000 or more employees) to total payroll employment was above the private, nonfarm average.[26]

By providing more detail, especially in manufacturing, the table shows that unionization is not evenly spread around the various sectors. For example, unionization is low in the textile and furniture industries within manufacturing, but is high in certain heavy industries including primary metals (such as steel and aluminum production) and transportation equipment (motor vehicles, aerospace, shipbuilding, railroad rolling stock production).

The pattern of unionization that emerged in the 1930s and 1940s partly reflected firm size. If relatively few large firms dominated an industry, unions could make substantial gains with a limited number of concentrated organizing campaigns. Geographic location also had an effect. The textile industry, for example, is heavily based in the South, where resistance to unions was especially intense and limited union successes in organizing that industry.

Particularly noteworthy in Table 9–4 is the high degree of unionization in the government sector.[27] Government employment was the major sector of union membership expansion in the 1960s and 1970s. Laws were passed that facilitated this development in various states and at the federal level. Generally, union organizers found government employers less resistant to organization (although not necessarily less resistant to bargaining demands once organized). The fact that the union wage premium generally seems smaller in the public than the private sector may be a factor in this lesser resistance.[28] Also significant are the facts that strikes in the public sector are often prohibited by law, that existing HRM procedures (even for nonunion workers) tend to be formal and unionesque in government, and that it is more difficult to fire workers in the public sector.[29]

Unions in the public sector have had significant success in organizing white-collar workers, including professionals (especially teachers). Unions in the private sector, with some exceptions, have traditionally been concentrated in blue-collar occupations. The exceptions in the private sector include such groups as foodstore clerks, airline and railroad clerks, telephone operators, and some aerospace engineers and insurance company personnel.

These exceptions, plus the public sector experience, suggest that union organizing of white-collar employees is by no means impossible. Indeed, unions have tended to win a higher proportion of white-collar representation elections than others.[30] But because unions met early resistance in the white-collar field[31] and thus limited their organizing efforts there, they found themselves representing occupations that today make up a declining fraction of the workforce.[32] As the earlier chapter on the workforce indicates, such occupational trends are expected to continue in the future.

Employer and Union Detail

For larger collective-bargaining units (those involving 1,000 or more workers), information is available concerning the schedule and outcomes of negotiations and whether a strike or lockout occurred in the process of producing those outcomes. A collective-bargaining unit could be comprised of a relatively small group of employers (as will be discussed). In many sectors larger bargaining units are usually found in larger firms. It is thus usually easier to obtain information about the bargaining relationship at larger firms than at smaller ones.

Information for Potential Investors.   Apart from individuals directly involved in collective bargaining, information on firm-level industrial relations could be of use to anyone considering investing in, or conducting a business relationship with, a particular firm. For example, a firm with a history of rocky labor relations and disruptions of production might prove to be an unreliable supplier. In a contemplated merger or acquisition situation, the labor relations climate could be an important consideration in appraising the value of the firm in question. Finally, there is empirical evidence that bargaining settlements produce corresponding reductions in stock market valuations of firm worth.[33]

It may be easier to obtain information about human resource management policies in unionized firms than in nonunion firms. For example, union–management agreements can often be obtained from the U.S. Bureau of Labor Statistics (BLS). Private organizations, such as the Bureau of National Affairs, Inc. (BNA), may also be able to supply a copy of the agreement. Because union–management settlements at prominent firms are often in the public eye, information may also be available from business periodicals and daily newspapers. In contrast, nonunion firms often deliberately avoid publicity concerning the details of their human resource practices.

Sometimes, the presence of a union can be a proxy for other conditions that may affect the firm's value. For example, as will be noted, unionized firms are especially likely to have defined benefit pension plans. Such programs may entail significant unfunded liabilities, that is, there may be less in the pension trust than the actuarial value of promised future pension benefits. These liabilities are the responsibility of the employer (even if it is only one of many firms paying into a common multiemployer pension plan). In mergers and acquisitions considerable attention must be devoted to determining who will carry the burden of the unfunded liability.[34]

Unions may also have an interest in the outcomes of merger and acquisition efforts. Successor owners may not be obligated, and may sometimes decline, to honor an existing union–management contract.[35] They may redeploy corporate assets in ways that adversely affect the interests of union-represented workers and the union itself. In the 1980s, as unions became more sensitive to the effects of mergers and acquisitions, they became more likely to intervene as active players in such situations. Unions have been known to oppose takeovers through litigation and to make counteroffers to buy a target company.

Bargaining Calendars.   The U.S. Bureau of Labor Statistics maintains a file of major union agreements. Included in the file is the employer and union name, the Standard Industrial Classification (SIC) of the firm, the number of workers covered by the contract, and the contract's beginning and expiration date. Computer listings of this file are available by special order, and bargaining calendars are published by the BLS on an annual basis.

Bargaining calendars appear first as a preliminary press release in late fall, next in summary form in the *Monthly Labor Review* (usually in the December or January issue), and then as a final bulletin. Each calendar lists the contracts that will expire during the year. Since union–management agreements rarely run more than three years, a virtually complete listing of major contracts can be obtained from any three consecutive calendars. (The private BNA also prints its own calendar.) A good beginning step to determine if a larger firm is unionized is to check for its name in the calendars.

Bargaining Outcomes.   The BLS reports information on negotiated major settlements in a monthly journal, *Current Wage Developments* (CWD). Generally it can be expected that a settlement will be reached at roughly the time the contract expires. In any case CWD contains an annual index that can be used to locate particular settlements. CWD listings usually indicate the basic wage adjustment (for example, an increase of 10¢ per hour, or 3%, or no wage change), the presence of an escalator clause and its formula, and changes in other benefits. Apart from the listing at settlement time, CWD lists deferred and escalator adjustments as they occur.

The private BNA publishes a similar listing of settlements and deferred and escalator adjustments on a biweekly basis in the *Daily Labor Report*. BNA's contract file includes smaller bargaining units—those involving 50 to 999 workers—as well as the major contracts reported by BLS. However, even with the BNA file, it is likely that the smaller the bargaining unit, the greater the chance it will escape any listing.

Work Stoppages.   Strikes and lockouts are not the only measure of tensions in labor relations, but they are the most visible symptoms and the only ones systematically reported. A poor climate of labor–management relations may adversely affect a firm's productivity level. More important, it may suggest difficulties in implementing new technologies and procedures.

The BLS lists strikes involving 1,000 or more workers in *Current Wage Developments* and in press releases. Listings show the starting date of the dispute, the number of workers involved, and the number of workdays lost. Prior to the 1980s information was also available on strikes involving fewer than 1,000 workers.

If a strike occurs as the result of a bargaining impasse, it is likely to occur at roughly the contract expiration date. Hence bargaining calendars can be combined with listings of work stoppages to determine whether peaceful settlements of new contracts are the norm. Of course, labor disputes at prominent firms are often discussed in the news media.

Union Information.   Background information on particular unions is available from various sources. Specialized reference books provide descriptions of the history of unions and their leadership.[36] Most major unions publish newspapers at the national level, and local unions also publish papers. These sources provide information on current union activities and policies and often give background on union bargaining objectives. In addition, the BLS's *Monthly Labor Review* and the BNA's *Daily Labor Report* carry articles on leadership changes and policy resolutions and discussions at union conventions. Finally, data on membership and financial information of particular unions are available from specialized directories.[37]

9–6   Union Structure and Governance

Unions are membership organizations that select their leaders through an election process. On a de facto basis, some unions are more democratic than others. Whatever the internal reality of their union's governance, union leaders must take cognizance of member opinions and interests, particularly in negotiations and dealings with employers.

Members of unions, like employees generally, have a stakeholder relationship with their employer. In certain respects, however, their stake may be greater than that of similar nonunion workers. The union political process will particularly represent the preferences of senior workers. Within a voting-type process, it is the median voter—the voter who can provide the 50%-plus-1 margin—whose needs will be reflected.[38] In the union setting, such a voter will have been on the job for a significant period.

Unions are thus likely to negotiate arrangements that favor senior workers. The stake of employees in their firm becomes greater and greater the longer they remain with the employer. In periods when plant closings are occurring or seem likely to occur, as in the early to mid-1980s, emphasis in union bargaining demands reflects the senior preference. To a senior worker, a plant closing or a complete shutdown of the employer would involve a substantial capital loss, that is, a loss of the capitalized value of his or her seniority-augmented stake. In such periods the internal political process of unions will tend to shift demands towards those emphasizing job security and related issues.

The nature of the employee stake will vary with such factors as age, seniority, occupational category, family status, and location of work. What serves one group may not serve another. The fact that unions are political organizations, often comprised of diverse factions and conflicting interest groups, complicates the collective-bargaining process. Managers, especially those accustomed to top-down decision making, commonly find it hard to adjust to this complexity.

For example, it sometimes happens that management reaches a tentative settlement with union officials only to find that the union membership rejects the deal in a ratification vote. As in the wider political environment, elected leaders sometimes misjudge their constituents and find that their programs (and even they!) are repudiated at the polls. Generally, negotiating with a union on the terms of a labor–management agreement is a more difficult prospect than negotiating with a supplier about the prices of inputs or with a customer about output prices.

Within a union, the structure of authority tends to reflect the industries and employers with which it deals. National unions (often called internationals if they have members in Canada as well as the United States) are divided into regional bodies and locals. In industries such as automobile manufacturing, in which only a few national employers sell in a large domestic market, the industry–employer pattern dictates a union structure that puts substantial authority over bargaining goals in the hands of the national union leadership. However, if employers are generally local contractors operating in separate product markets, such as in the construction industry, local unions play the major role in negotiating contracts and determining policy.

Even in cases where the national union exercises strong authority, locals will still have a significant voice regarding local issues. Furthermore, the day-to-day climate of industrial relations in a particular plant of a large firm will reflect the state of relations between local plant management and the local union leadership. It is quite possible, for example, for a relatively cordial relationship to exist between top management and the national union leadership at the same time substantial frictions exist in particular plants or divisions at the local level.

Empirical studies suggest that the quality of the labor–management relationship can have an important impact on productivity. Top managers must therefore be concerned about both national and local levels of their relationship with the union.[39] Of course, local management must be especially concerned about relations with the local union. Ultimately, poor productivity performance stemming from a hostile relationship will reflect badly on local management personnel. The question will be (rightly) asked whether another management team is needed to improve the labor-relations climate.

9–7   Bargaining Structure

Various negotiating formats have developed in different industries. In some cases, negotiations are predominantly between a single union and a firm. Once a settlement is reached, its terms may be imitated at other firms with which the union deals in the industry. This is the so-called pattern bargaining discussed in the previous chapter. Sometimes, however, a large firm may deal with various unions primarily on a local basis. In instances in which multiple unions deal with a single employer, the unions may form a bargaining coalition to present proposals to management as a unified bargaining team. In other instances the individual unions may coordinate their demands but present them separately.

Employers may also form coalitions, especially in industries in which many small employers deal with a particular union. Examples of such employer associations exist in construction and longshoring. Some employer associations have been formed at the behest of the union. It simplifies the union's administrative task to negotiate a single master contract with an association rather than a host of individual agreements on a company-by-company basis. Sometimes small employers themselves will form an association, hoping that a unified front will strengthen their position in multiemployer bargaining. If firms negotiate independently, the union can strike them one at a time, diverting their sales and customers to their competitors. Faced with such union "whipsaw" tactics, each individual firm would be under great pressure to make concessions to the union.

Employer unity, however, may force the union to strike many firms at once. Even if the union tries to strike a single firm to whipsaw the others into accepting its terms, allied employers may call a *lockout,* that is, cease production and employment (or cease use of union members and hire nonunion replacements). Such a lockout effectively converts a single-firm strike into an industry-wide strike.

Individual employers—just as buyers or sellers in the product market—can enhance the profitability of their labor market strategy through coordination. Just as in the case of a product market cartel, however, there are always pressures to break away from the group and negotiate side deals that undermine group unity. For example, an employer might decide it would prefer to see its competitors do battle with the union while it sits quietly on the sidelines. The employer might negotiate an interim agreement with the union during a strike, maintain its production, and profit from sales diverted from its less fortunate rivals. It could simply agree with the union that after the strike against its competitors ends, it will sign a contract equivalent to theirs.[40]

Employer bargaining associations are not the exclusive province of small employers. In a few cases larger employers such as railroads have formed bargaining associations. More commonly, however, larger employers have agreed to cooperate loosely in their bargaining positions, rather than completely delegate their negotiations to an association. Larger firms have occasionally been known to establish "mutual assistance pacts," whereby firms that are struck receive aid from other (nonstruck) firms in the industry.[41]

One of the features of collective bargaining in the 1980s was the breakdown of longstanding negotiating structures. In many cases multiemployer bargaining associations were weakened or collapsed.[42] More generally, employers became less willing to engage in pattern-following settlements and tended to stress firm-specific goals in labor-relations strategies.[43] These changes reflected the erosion of union bargaining strength, which had been a force for uniformity in many industries. With the arrival of new, nonunion entrants and foreign competitors, unions could no longer guarantee to employers that every firm in the product market would pay the same wages and benefits.[44]

9–8   Representation Structure

There have been two traditional models of union representation. *Craft unions* represent workers on the basis of occupations. Examples are the various construction crafts (carpenters, painters, electricians, and so on), the film and TV crafts (writers, actors, and so on), and professional groups such as nurses, teachers, and airline pilots. Generally, management finds dealing with a multiplicity of craft unions to be a complicating factor in labor relations. The different unions may have rivalries that need to be considered, and jurisdictional disputes sometimes arise between the unions. For example, one craft union in construction may claim the work performed by another.

The alternative to craft unionization is representation of a group of workers regardless of their occupations. Such multi-occupational representation is called *industrial unionism*. It is found in such areas as manufacturing, mining, telephone communications, and the civil service. Much of the growth in unionization in the 1930s and 1940s came in the industrial format. Many unions that were once craft unions—even those that still have names suggesting their original crafts (Teamsters, Machinists)—are in reality industrial unions today.[45]

In the private sector managerial and supervisory workers are almost never represented by unions in the United States. Indeed, the American labor law framework excludes such employees from its protections (although it does not forbid them from unionizing).[46] In other countries, such managerial and supervisory unionization does occasionally occur. Sometimes supervisors and administrators in the public sector do have limited representation in the United States.

9–9   Compensation Provisions in Union–Management Agreements

Virtually any matter that might be the subject of a HRM policy in a nonunion firm may be covered in a collective-bargaining agreement. Often, economic models of union behavior have framed the analysis in terms of bargaining over a wage. This approach can be a useful simplification for modeling purposes. Even in the wage area, however, much more complexity is involved.

Union Wage Effects

A common question about union wages is whether they are higher than nonunion. Table 9–5 uses data from the Current Population Survey on median usual weekly earnings to answer that simple question. Union workers are typically higher paid than nonunion, although the ratio varies considerably from one group to another. Generally, the ratios of union to nonunion pay are highest for groups likely to

TABLE 9–5   Ratio of Union to Nonunion Usual Weekly Earnings of Full-Time Wage and Salary Earners, 1987

Category	Ratio
All wage and salary earners	134%
Males	121
Females	134
White	134
Black	147
Hispanic	150
Private nonfarm	133
Government	121
Managerial/professional	99
Technical and related support	117
Sales	105
Administrative support, including clerical	136
Protective service workers	159
Other service workers	152
Precision production, craft and repair workers	137
Operatives, fabricators, and laborers	155
Farming, forestry, fishing workers	176

Note: Union workers are those represented by unions and include some workers who are not union members.
Source: Data from *Employment and Earnings,* vol. 35 (January 1988), pp. 224–225.

receive lower-than-average wages, that is, women, blacks, and unskilled and semi-skilled blue-collar workers (operatives, fabricators, and laborers).

Of course, data such as those in Table 9–5 do not prove conclusively that unions *cause* wages to be higher than they otherwise would be. In theory unions might simply happen to represent workers whose personal characteristics would earn them higher pay than nonunion workers in their groupings.[47] The evidence, however, is to the contrary. There have been detailed studies of this issue in which other characteristics, both personal and industrial, are controlled. The consensus among economists as a result of such studies is that unions commonly do cause wages to be higher than employers would otherwise pay. Moreover, the effects of unions on wages seem to be greater for minority workers, blue-collar occupations, and private sector workers, than for (respectively) whites, white-collar occupations, and government employees.[48]

Even disregarding the statistical studies, two casual pieces of evidence strongly suggest that unions affect wages. First, management resistance to unions is strong. Nonunion managements do not want their workers organized and expend considerable sums and energy to prevent unionization when it is threatened. If unions had no effect on wages, it is hard to understand why such employer resistance would occur.[49]

Second, during the wage concession movement in the 1980s, there were notable cases in which unions accepted wage cuts and benefit reductions. If union wages and benefits had been no higher than what the employer would otherwise have determined, why should employers have demanded such cuts? Given the evidence, both statistical and casual, it will be assumed throughout the remainder of this chapter and the next that unions do raise wages relative to market levels. The effect may well develop over time, however, so that newly unionized firms may pay lower premiums than those with a long history of bargaining.[50]

Wages and Premiums in Union–Management Contracts

Typically, a union–management contract—especially outside the craft union arena—will cover the wage rates for a variety of occupations. There is thus not one wage but a multiplicity of wages to be negotiated. Moreover, rates of pay will vary according to the circumstances under which they are earned. A BNA survey of union contracts in the mid-1980s found that 86% included pay premiums for late shifts. Seventy-four percent of contracts provided for "reporting pay" in cases when workers arrived at work, but found none available. Eleven percent provided for extra pay in hazardous situations. Contracts often also provided for reimbursement of employee expenses for travel, work clothes, and tools.[51]

Wage Schedules and Systems

Often workers in a given occupation have a wage schedule rather than a single wage rate. Wage progression plans were discussed in detail in a previous chapter. It was noted that an occupation may have a rate range, that is, a minimum and maximum wage, under which new entrants begin at the minimum and work their way up to the maximum on the basis of merit and/or length of service.

Union contracts are more likely than nonunion pay systems to emphasize length of service, rather than merit, as the criterion for advancement. In the BNA survey previously cited, 71% of the contracts studied used length of service alone as the criterion for progression. Only 5% used merit only, with the remainder specifying a mix of service and merit.[52]

The service versus merit distinction between the union and nonunion sectors illustrates the impact of the bargaining process on negotiated outcomes. As noted above, there is substantial evidence that unions do succeed in raising wage and benefit levels of the workers they represent. In other words, unionized employers often pay more for labor than they otherwise would unilaterally determine to do. Whenever a price is raised relative to market levels, opportunities for avoiding and evading the floor may arise.

As an example, in the airline industry prior to deregulation a federal government agency kept airline fares above market levels on many routes. Airline carriers, therefore, had an incentive to find de facto ways of lowering the effective price to attract business from competitors without overtly appearing to do so. To do this, they might offer discounts on nonairline services such as hotels and rental cars, or they might look the other way (or even encourage) the arrangement of phony charter flights. Periodically, federal regulators had to crack down on such devices by defining new and more complex rules, for example, strictly defining a charter flight.[53]

The same potential for erosion of the union's bargaining advantage arises in the collective-bargaining sphere. If the union raises wages, employers might attempt to get around the higher wage indirectly. For example, if merit—an inherently subjective judgment—determines pay progression, an employer might be tempted to be especially critical in making merit judgments in the face of union-raised wages. By limiting pay advances for individual workers, the employer could hold down the average rate of pay in the firm, partly offsetting the union wage advantage.

Thus, the union must respond—as did federal regulators in the airline example—with more elaborate rules, in this case concerning pay progression. To avoid the risks of leaving subjective judgments to the employer, the union will press for an objective criterion for advancement, with length of service being the obvious index. More generally, unions will seek to limit managerial discretion over a wide range of issues to avoid employer chiseling away of negotiated gains.

Progression in pay by seniority also fits with another aspect of union motivation. As a political process, union policy on wages and other matters will be determined by coalitions that can control just over 50% of the union's electorate. Thus the views of the median voter are especially significant. Because senior voters have the greatest stake in workplace affairs (since they are least likely to depart voluntarily), the median voter will be a worker with significant seniority, rather than a new entrant. A pay progression plan that explicitly rewards seniority will have obvious appeal to the median voter. Studies have also found that promotions, as well as merit rewards, are more likely to be based on seniority in the union sector than in the nonunion sector.[54]

Two-Tier Pay Systems

As noted in an earlier chapter, the wage concession movement of the 1980s brought with it the development of two-tier pay systems. These systems arose out of the clash between demands by unionized employers for across-the-board pay cuts and union resistance to such demands. The compromise solution was the establishment of a dual wage arrangement in which current workers retained their existing wage scales (or in some cases even received an increase in pay) while new hires were paid at a new, lower scale. In the BNA survey of union contracts in the mid-1980s cited earlier, 17% contained two-tier plans.[55]

As a pay scheme the two-tier approach is perhaps the ultimate recognition of the union's political realities and the insider/outsider division of interests. New hires are outside the union's political system until they become employees. They therefore do not vote in ratification of two-tier pay plans (since they are not yet hired). So it is easy to see why—if offered a choice between cutting the pay of current voters and cutting the pay of not-yet-voters—unions would pick the latter.

Even so, union political mechanisms influenced the type of two-tier plan negotiated. Sixty-one percent of the surveyed contracts had temporary two-tier plans under which the wage schedule for new hires (the lower tier) would eventually merge with the wage schedule for current workers (the upper tier). Under such arrangements, the new hires eventually reach the higher pay scale; they do not remain second-class citizens indefinitely.

The remainder of contracts had permanent two-tier plans under which the lower tier would never catch up with the upper tier. Since the lower tier workers would eventually become a majority in the union's political process, it is easy to see why unions would opt for temporary rather than permanent plans when it was possible to affect the choice. Of course, the eventual outcome reflects a mix of both union and management preferences.[56] But instances of eliminations of two-tier plans (or of a narrowing of the wage gap between the tiers) began to be reported by the late 1980s.

Lump Sum Bonuses

Concession bargaining in the 1980s also brought with it growing use of lump sum bonuses in lieu of wage increases. For example, instead of three 3% annual wage increases in a three-year contract, an employer might negotiate three 3% bonuses. Three 3% wage increases would raise wages about 9% over the course of the agreement. Three 3% bonuses, however, do not raise wage rates at all and leave compensation paid out only 3% higher in the last year of the contract than in the year just before the contract.

Lump sum bonuses can be specified in many wages. Sometimes, a flat bonus, for example, $1,000 is paid out to all workers regardless of pay level. In other cases, the bonus may be proportionate to annual salary. Bonuses may also have quasi–two-tier elements. For example, the contract may indicate that only those who have been on the payroll a full year are eligible for the annual bonus. Thus new hires must wait at least a year before receiving a bonus payment.

Until the 1980s bonuses were rarely used in union–management agreements. By 1987, however, over half the workers under major new settlements in the private sector had lump sum bonuses as part of their pay packages.[57] The presence of bonuses on a large scale has distorted some commonly used indexes of wage levels and wage change. Bonuses are excluded, for example, from the calculation of average hourly earnings.

It may be that lump sum bonuses will evolve as a flexible element of pay in the union sector in the future. In principle, unions might negotiate a relatively inflexible base wage but add a bonus to it that reflected economic circumstances prevailing at the time the bargain was reached. This type of system would amount to de facto profit sharing. It is too early, however, to tell whether such a development will actually come about.

Benefits

The union emphasis on seniority and the median voter helps explain the richness of benefit packages of unionized workers compared with nonunion. In March 1988, for example, one-third of private-sector union pay went to benefits (private and legally required) as compared to one-fourth in the nonunion sector.[58] Some benefits, such as vacation plans, are commonly linked to seniority. Typically, workers with longer service are entitled to longer vacations. Such benefits would have an obvious appeal to unions.[59]

Other benefits are of greater utility for senior workers, even though they are not explicitly linked to seniority. For example, health care benefits will be of greater appeal to older workers (who are more likely to become ill and more likely to have dependents) than to younger workers. Age and seniority are likely to be correlated.

Finally, some plans may actually be indirect mechanisms for transfers from junior to senior workers. Union workers are much more likely than nonunion to be covered by pensions, and the plans they have are much more likely to be defined benefit (rather than defined contribution) plans.[60] As noted in a previous chapter, defined benefit plans typically have vesting rules that exclude the most junior employees if they leave the firm or are permanently laid off. Even when vested, workers who depart before retirement age generally take away a lump sum payment that is worth less than the actuarially adjusted value of their defined benefit.

Thus union pension plans favor the most senior workers. Moreover, junior workers—on whose behalf contributions to the pension fund are made—may not receive any component of those contributions unless they at least become vested. Contributions of junior workers who depart are effectively reallocated to support the pensions of seniors.

In terms of retirement benefits actually paid, the union effect seems to be a leveling influence. Half of the pension plans studied as part of the survey cited earlier paid a flat dollar benefit per year of service, regardless of the earnings level of the pensioner before retirement.[61] Notions of equity, expressed through the union bargaining mechanism, may account for this leveling effect.[62]

Summary

Unions are representation devices, developed independently by employees, whose major function is collective bargaining with employers. The modern legal machinery that surrounds union organizing and collective bargaining developed during the Great Depression of the 1930s but was subsequently modified importantly in the 1940s and 1950s. Since that time basic federal policy regarding unions and bargaining has changed little, although the interpretations of the law by the National Labor Relations Board and the courts have varied with the political tides. The law provides an election process to determine if a group of employees wants union representation. A variety of unfair labor practices of employers and unions are forbidden.

Membership in unions as a proportion of the workforce has declined since the mid-1950s. During the 1980s union membership fell significantly in absolute numbers as well. The pattern of unionization across private sector industries and occupations reflects the structure of employment that existed during the years of union expansion, that is, the 1930s, 1940s, and 1950s. Heavy manufacturing employees in blue-collar jobs are disproportionately represented, for example. During the 1960s and 1970s, however, union membership grew in the public sector, including among white-collar civil servants.

Some unions are organized on a craft basis, although most union members belong to industrial unions that cross occupational lines. The authority structure within unions varies with the structure of the industry. When bargaining is conducted with a few large firms, major union policy decisions are made at the national level. When bargaining is primarily with small local employers, the locus of authority is with the local unions that make up the national organization. Within unions the political mechanism tends to tilt bargaining goals towards items that are of special benefit to more senior workers.

The structure of bargaining also varies substantially. Sometimes unions coordinate their negotiations with other unions facing the same employers. On the management side, employers sometimes group themselves into multi-employer bargaining associations or coordinate their actions in other ways. The scope of pattern bargaining shrank in the 1980s, but pattern bargaining continues to exist in some industries. Negotiated outcomes in the 1980s became more favorable to the management side, as reflected in a rash of concession bargaining.

Many features of union–management contracts do not involve the specification of wages and benefits. Rather, they reflect the stake of the employee in maintaining the employer–employee relationship and the stake of the union in maintaining the union–management relationship. The next chapter reviews these features and explores the processes of bargaining and conflict resolution in the context of the union–management relationship.

EXERCISES

Problem

Select a prominent bargaining situation (such as the automobile industry negotiations). Using data sources described in this chapter, trace through the last few rounds of bargaining that have occurred. How many workers were involved? Did strikes occur? What settlements were reached? What can you find out about the background of the union(s) and the industry?

Questions

1. Within the private sector, what factors seem to account for the change in the level of unionization over time?

2. What factors account for the divergence in unionization between the public and private sectors?

3. Within the private sector, what influences account for the variations in unionization rates between industries?

4. What is the unionization status of white-collar workers?

5. In merger and acquisition situations, what information related to unionization is useful to obtain?

6. What influence does seniority have in the union political process?

7. Why did two-tier pay plans develop in the union sector in the 1980s?

8. What influence do unions have on the level of pay and benefits?

Terms

appropriate bargaining unit	insider-outsider model	representation election
coalition bargaining	jurisdictional dispute	Taft-Hartley Act
concerted activity	lockout	unfair labor practice
concession bargaining	median voter model	wage controls and guidelines
craft union	multiemployer bargaining	wage-purchasing power theory
industrial union	mutual assistance pacts	Wagner Act
decertification election	National Labor Relations Board	whipsaw tactics
employees as stakeholders	pattern bargaining	
Landrum-Griffin Act		

ENDNOTES

1. Although fringe benefits did not originate in the union sector, they did not become widespread until the advent of unionization in the 1930s, 1940s, and after.

2. OSHA stands for the Occupational Safety and Health Act. It will be discussed in a later chapter.

3. ERISA stands for the Employee Retirement Income Security Act. References to it have been made in a previous chapter. ERISA sets basic standards for pension funding and investment, requires that defined-benefit pension plans carry government-sponsored termination insurance, and sets standards for pension eligibility and vesting. Because of its complexity and technical nature, ERISA is not discussed in detail in this text.

4. States also enact laws dealing with minimum wages, employment of minors, safety on the job, and equal employment opportunity. Such laws may overlap (and be stricter than) federal legislation in these areas.

5. The AFL-CIO stands for American Federation of Labor–Congress of Industrial Organizations. The American Federation of Labor was originally founded in 1881. A dissident group split from the AFL and formed the CIO as a separate organization in 1935. The two groups subsequently merged in 1955.

6. Leo Troy and Neil Sheflin, *Union Sourcebook: Membership, Structure, Finance, Directory,* first edition 1985 (West Orange, N.J.: Industrial Relations Data and Information

Services, 1985), Table 3.31, modified to account for the Teamsters. In the late 1950s the Teamsters were ejected from the AFL-CIO on charges of corruption. Although there have been continued allegations of corruption, the AFL-CIO sought to form a more united labor movement in the 1980s and reaffiliation was arranged.

7. Perhaps the most visible sign of this change in the position of the AFL-CIO was the issuance of its report *The Changing Situation of Workers and Their Unions* (Washington: AFL-CIO, 1985). This report was disseminated to member unions and used as a basis for discussion of future policy and actions.

8. The National Education Association (NEA) for many years considered itself a professional association, not a union, representing teachers and other educators. It did not engage in collective bargaining, unlike its AFL-CIO rival, the smaller American Federation of Teachers (AFT). This history partly explains why the NEA has remained outside the AFL-CIO structure. NEA affiliation with the AFL-CIO would require a merger of the NEA and the AFT. Although there have been some cases in which locals of the two unions have merged, national merger would be difficult to accomplish. In this volume, no distinction is made between unions and associations that act like unions.

9. Less than 4% of total private sector union membership was estimated to belong to independent local unions in 1983. Source: Troy and Sheflin, *Union Sourcebook, op. cit.,* Tables 3.35, 3.31.

10. Sanford M. Jacoby and Anil Verma, "Company Unions in the Modern Era: A Case Study of Corporate Compensation and Industrial Relations Strategies," working paper, Anderson Graduate School of Management, UCLA (undated).

11. Employers may recognize unions without the formality of an election. For example, sometimes employers will agree that new facilities they open will become part of the union-represented bargaining unit. However, management most typically will insist on formal elections in representation disputes. Representation elections may include more than one union on the ballot if more than one is seeking representation rights. Where no choice receives a clear majority, run-off elections between the top two choices are held. The initial election always includes the choice of "no union" and "no union" will appear on the ballot in a run-off, if it is among the top two choices in the initial vote.

12. There are three major exclusions from this framework. First, the Railway Labor Act, originally passed in 1926 and significantly amended in 1934, regulates union–management relations in the railroad and airline industries. Unions and bargaining in those sectors are not covered by the laws described below in the text, although the Railway Labor Act has many similarities to those laws. Second, agriculture is excluded from federal regulation of union–management relations, but can be regulated at the state level. Some states, such as California, do have regulatory systems for agriculture, and these largely parallel the federal model for non-agricultural industries. Third, small employers are excluded from coverage by federal regulation, although they may be subject to state laws. Standard for exclusion from federal coverage vary from industry to industry, but are based on dollar volume of business.

13. An earlier piece of legislation, the Norris-LaGuardia Act of 1932, limited the authority of federal courts to issue injunctions (orders to discontinue some activity) in cases of labor disputes. At the time the law was passed, it was felt by Congress that the federal courts too often issued injunctions that supported the management side in such disputes. Passage of the Norris-LaGuardia Act signaled a change in the political climate in Congress to a more pro-union attitude than had previously existed. Part of the reason for this shift stemmed from anger at the business sector, which was blamed for the worsening Great Depression.

14. When considered by Congress, the Taft-Hartley bill was an extremely controversial piece of legislation. It was vetoed by President Truman but passed by Congress over his veto. The Taft-Hartley Act became a major political issue in the 1948 presidential election that Truman narrowly won. However, its major features have never been repealed.

15. Many sources of legal information are available. As examples, Commerce Clearing House, Inc., puts out periodic reference books entitled *Labor Law Course* and publishes the monthly *Labor Law Journal*. In addition, textbooks on labor law, aimed primarily at law and business students, are available from various publishers.

16. Douglass V. Brown, "Legalism and Industrial Relations in the United States" in Gerald G. Somers, ed., *Proceedings of the Twenty-Third Annual Winter Meeting,* Industrial Relations Research Association, December 28–29, 1970, pp. 2–10.

17. U.S. Bureau of Labor-Management Relations and Cooperative Programs of the U.S. Department of Labor, *U.S. Labor Law and the Future of Labor-Management Cooperation,* BLMR 113 (Washington: U.S. Department of Labor, 1987). The current regulatory system is based on a sharp division between supervisory employees and nonsupervisory employees, with the former assumed to be agents of management and only the latter to be protected in their union rights. Some cooperative arrangements, however, blur the supervisor-nonsupervisor distinction. In addition, because under the law unions and employers are supposed to have an arms' length relationship, devices such as quality circles might be challenged if the circle was considered to be a legal labor organization. It should be noted that these problems are hypothetical; to date they have not been a significant inhibitor of cooperation.

18. Orley Ashenfelter and John H. Pencavel, "American Trade Union Growth: 1900–1960," *Quarterly Journal of Economics,* vol. 83 (August 1969), pp. 434–448; William J. Moore and Douglas K. Pearce, "Union Growth: A Test of the Ashenfelter-Pencavel Model," *Industrial Relations,* vol. 15 (May 1976), pp. 244–247; Farouk Elsheik and George Sayers Bain, "American Trade Union Growth: An Alternative Model," *Industrial Relations,* vol. 17 (February 1978), pp. 75–79.

19. Macroeconomics as a field is usually dated from the writings of the British economist, John Maynard Keynes. Keynes chief book on macroeconomics, *The General Theory,* did not appear until 1936 although elements of his views were becoming known in the United States before then. Much of macroeconomics developed as a refinement and a debate of Keynesian economics, a process that took many years. See John Maynard Keynes, *The General Theory of Employment, Interest, and Money* (New York: Harcourt, Brace & World, 1936). The state of economic thinking in the 1930s, particularly in regard to labor market issues, is discussed in Daniel J.B. Mitchell, "Wages and Keynes: Lessons from the Past," *Eastern Economic Journal,* vol. 12 (July–September 1986), pp. 199–208.

20. Econometrics was in its infancy in the 1930s, so that even if substantial empirical information had been available, the techniques for interpreting it would have been primitive. And, of course, the computers that are so commonly used for empirical analysis today did not exist.

21. Although historical sourcebooks often present unemployment rates going back to the 1930s, these statistics were not collected at the time. The Current Population Survey—from which modern unemployment and other labor force data are collected—did not begin until 1940. Earlier figures are at best crude estimates.

22. There were, in fact, various economic theories floating around, and it is difficult to say precisely which ones were most favored by the Roosevelt administration at any one time. Some theories suggested that the goal should be raising prices rather than wages. Initial policies of the New Deal seemed aimed at raising both prices and wages. Under the National Industrial Recovery Act (NIRA) of 1933, industries were organized into cartel-like groups and the antitrust laws were suspended. Increased wages and prices were encouraged through the codes of conduct these cartels established with government blessing.

23. See Daniel J.B. Mitchell, "Inflation, Unemployment, and the Wagner Act: A Critical Reappraisal," *Stanford Law Review,* vol. 38 (April 1986), pp. 1065–1095.

24. Wagner Act, ch. 372, SEc. 1, 49 Stat. 449, 449 (1935) [current version at 29 U.S.C., Sec. 151 (1982)].

25. On these issues, see Crauford D. Goodwin, ed., *Exhortation & Controls: The Search for a Wage-Price Policy, 1945–1971* (Washington: Brookings Institution, 1975);

John Sheehan, *The Wage-Price Guideposts* (Washington: Brookings Institution, 1967); and Arnold R. Weber and Daniel J.B. Mitchell, *The Pay Board's Progress: Wage Controls in Phase II* (Washington: Brookings Institution, 1978). Comparatively little has been written about the Carter program. However, see Daniel J.B. Mitchell, "The Rise and Fall of Real Wage Insurance," *Industrial Relations,* vol. 19 (Winter 1980), pp. 64–73, for an analysis of one aspect of the Carter wage guideline and U.S. General Accounting Office, *The Voluntary Pay and Price Standards Have Had No Discernible Effect on Inflation,* PAD–81–02 (Washington: GAO, 1980), for a general review.

26. The Bureau of Labor Statistics maintains a data file of major union agreements in order to keep track of contract expirations and scheduled wage adjustments.

27. References concerning economic and other factors explaining differences in public and private sector unionization include Edward P. Lazear, "Symposium on Public and Private Unionization," *Journal of Economic Perspectives,* vol. 2 (Spring 1988), pp. 59–62; Richard B. Freeman, "Contraction and Expansion: The Divergence of Private Sector and Public Sector Unionism in the United States," *Journal of Economic Perspectives,* vol. 2 (Spring 1988), pp. 63–88; Melvin W. Reder, "The Rise and Fall of Unions: The Public Sector and the Private," *Journal of Economic Perspectives,* vol. 2 (Spring 1988), pp. 89–110; Richard B. Freeman, "Unionism Comes to the Public Sector," *Journal of Economic Literature,* vol. 24 (March 1988), pp. 41–86; Richard B. Freeman and Casey Ichniowski, eds., *When Public Sector Workers Unionise* (Chicago: University of Chicago Press, 1988).

28. On wage premiums, see Daniel J.B. Mitchell, "Collective Bargaining and Compensation in the Public Sector" in Benjamin Aaron, Joyce M. Najita, and James L. Stern, eds., *Public-Sector Bargaining,* second edition (Washington: BNA, 1988), pp. 124–159.

29. In the private sector, it is an unfair labor practice to fire union organizers and activists. The penalties, however, are low and remedies may be slow in coming. In contrast, in the public sector a host of civil service procedures makes it difficult to terminate workers.

30. Unions won about 55% of white-collar representation elections in the late 1970s and early 1980s. This figure was roughly 10 percentage points above the all-election win rate. See Bureau of National Affairs, Inc., *1983 Briefing Sessions on Collective Bargaining: Workbook* (Washington: BNA, 1983), pp. 38–39.

31. C. Wright Mills, *White Collar: The American Middle Classes* (New York: Oxford University Press, 1956 [originally 1951]), pp. 301–323.

32. It might be noted that the Taft-Hartley Act singles out professional employees with regard to union representation. Such workers may not be placed in a bargaining unit

with nonprofessionals unless the professionals agree to be so included in a special election.

33. John M. Abowd, "Collective Bargaining and the Division of the Value of the Enterprise," working paper no. 2137, National Bureau of Economic Research, January 1987.

34. Firms with pension systems sometimes provide health care benefits to retirees, but typically do not pre-fund these benefits. Changes in accounting standards will require such unfunded liabilities to be appropriately reported on company financial statements. Hence unfunded health care as well as pension liabilities must be considered in merger and acquisition situations.

35. In general, the legal rule is that if the successor continues the basic business, it must continue to recognize the union as the bargaining representative. However, a new contract may have to be negotiated unless the union's contract with the previous owner specified that it would sell the business only to a new owner who agreed to abide by the existing agreement.

36. See Gary M. Fink, ed., *Labor Unions* (Westport, Conn: Greenwood Press, 1977); Gary M. Fink, ed., *Biographical Dictionary of American Labor* (Westport, Conn.: Greenwood Press, 1984).

37. See Leo Troy and Neil Sheflin, *Union Sourcebook: Membership, Structure, Finance, Directory,* first edition, 1985 (West Orange, NJ: Industrial Relations Data and Information Services, 1985); Courtney D. Gifford, ed., *Directory of U.S. Labor Organizations,* 1986–87 edition (Washington: BNA, 1986).

38. This statement is an obvious oversimplification. Some unions are more democratically run than others. And it is often the case in unions—as in many other private associations—that many members do not vote, leaving policy in the hands of a smaller, committed group. However, the point of the text is unaffected. Some readers may prefer to substitute the words "inframarginal voter" for "median voter."

39. Casey Ichniowski, "The Effects of Grievance Activity on Productivity," *Industrial and Labor Relations Review,* vol. 40 (October 1986), pp. 75–89; J.R. Norsworthy and Craig A. Zabala, "Worker Attitudes, Worker Behavior, and Productivity in the U.S. Automobile Industry, 1959–1976," *Industrial and Labor Relations Review,* vol. 38 (July 1985), pp. 544–557; Harry C. Katz, Thomas A. Kochan, and Jeffrey H. Keefe, "Industrial Relations and Productivity in the U.S. Automobile Industry," *Brookings Papers on Economic Activity* (3:1987), pp. 685–715.

40. Each breakaway firm weakens the position of the remaining struck firms, eventually contributing to a settlement that is less favorable from the employer viewpoint. There is a close analogy between such behavior and that of members of a sellers' cartel, such as OPEC, who produce and sell more than their agreed-upon quota in the expectation

that others in the cartel will cut back production and keep prices high. Each defection makes it less likely that the remaining sellers will abide by cartel rules.

41. A mutual assistance pact (MAP) existed in the airline industry until the 1970s when it was effectively outlawed by the same legislation that deregulated air transportation. Under the airline MAP, struck firms received financial aid from others in the pact. Many problems arose, however, since the formula for determining the aid sometimes appeared to make being on strike more profitable than operating. Firms contributing the aid did not have a direct voice in determining the bargaining posture of the struck firm. A MAP also existed in the rubber industry, whereby nonstruck firms supplied tires to struck firms so that they could meet their customers' needs.

42. In the steel industry, the major producers formed a bargaining association to negotiate master contracts with the United Steelworkers union in the mid-1950s. This arrangement was abandoned in the 1980s, under the pressure of severe foreign competition. Deregulation in the telephone industry, and the breakup of the Bell System, led to decentralized (company-by-company) bargaining in the 1980s, rather than the uniform agreements that had prevailed in the 1970s. Deregulation also influenced negotiations in interstate trucking, in which many employers dropped out of the major employer association although a master agreement format was maintained. Numerous other examples of similar types can be cited.

43. Audrey Freedman, *The New Look in Wage Policy and Employee Relations,* report no. 856 (New York: The Conference Board, 1985), pp. 7–10.

44. The implications of this development will be explored in the next chapter.

45. The Taft-Hartley Act imposed certain limitations on industrial unionism. For example, professional employees cannot be forced into a bargaining unit with nonprofessionals unless the professionals vote separately for such incorporation. Plant guards cannot be part of a union of nonguard employees. In the former case, Congress sought to protect what it saw as a separate community of interests of professionals and non-professionals. In the latter case, it was felt that plant guards, who might be called upon to protect employer property during a labor dispute, should not be part of the union engaged in the dispute. Requiring a separate union for guards made them difficult to unionize, since guards represent only a small fraction of a typical employer's workforce, and may be employed at scattered locations. Generally, private sector professionals have been resistant to unionization, as have other white-collar workers.

46. The Taft-Hartley Act specifically defines supervisors in order to exclude them from its protections. Management employees (other than supervisors) have been excluded by NLRB interpretation. These exclusions are based on the assump-

tion that top management needs loyal administrative subordinates, particularly in the event of a labor dispute.

47. Some have argued that higher paid workers might simply have a taste for union services, thus causing the correlation between pay and unionization. However, it is unclear what services might be provided by a union so bereft of bargaining power that it cannot affect wages.

48. For surveys, see H. Gregg Lewis, "Union Relative Wage Effects: A Survey of Macro Estimates," *Journal of Labor Economics*, vol. 1 (January 1983), pp. 1–27; H. Gregg Lewis, *Union Relative Wage Effects: A Survey* (Chicago: University of Chicago Press, 1986); H. Gregg Lewis, *Unionism and Relative Wages in the United States* (Chicago: University of Chicago Press, 1963); and Richard B. Freeman and James L. Medoff, *What Do Unions Do?* (New York: Basic Books, 1984), pp. 43–60; Daniel J.B. Mitchell, *Unions, Wages, and Inflation* (Washington: Brookings Institution, 1980), chapter 3; Richard B. Freeman, "Longitudinal Analyses of the Effects of Trade Unions," *Journal of Labor Economics*, vol. 2 (January 1984), pp. 1–26.

49. Some observers have argued that management might resist unionization—even with no wage effect present—because unions might impose restrictive workrules and limit managerial discretion in decision making. However, while it is true that managers are concerned about such nonwage issues, it is difficult to conceive of a union that had the bargaining power to impose workrules and other limits on management, but that didn't choose to use any of that power to raise wages.

50. Richard B. Freeman and Morris M. Kleiner, "The Impact of New Unionization on Wages and Working Conditions: A Longitudinal Study of Establishments Under NLRB Elections," working paper no. 2563, National Bureau of Economic Research, April 1988.

51. Bureau of National Affairs, *Basic Patterns in Union Contracts*, eleventh edition (Washington: BNA, 1986), pp. 119–122.

52. Bureau of National Affairs, *Basic Patterns, op. cit.*, p. 118.

53. It is easy to cite similar examples from other regulated fields. For example, when federal regulations limited financial institutions by placing ceilings on interest rates that could be paid on deposits, the institutions competed by giving away gifts such as toasters and TV sets to depositors. These *de facto* interest payments had to be restricted by regulation when the gift giving became excessive. Similarly, where rent controls are imposed, landlords react by cutting back maintenance and other services. It then becomes necessary to develop regulations specifying what services will be provided, for example, how often apartments must be repainted.

54. Katherine G. Abraham and James L. Medoff, "Length of Service and the Operation of Internal Labor Markets" in Barbara D. Dennis, ed., *Proceedings of the Thirty-Fifth Annual Meeting*, Industrial Relations Research Association, December 28–30, 1982 (Madison, Wisc.: IRRA, 1983), pp. 308–318.

55. Bureau of National Affairs, *Basic Patterns, op cit.*, p. 118.

56. On management attitudes, see Sanford M. Jacoby and Daniel J.B. Mitchell, "Management Attitudes Toward Two-Tier Pay Plans," *Journal of Labor Research*, vol. 7 (Summer 1986), pp. 221–237. See also Peter Cappelli and Peter D. Sherer, "Assessing Worker Attitudes Under a Two-Tier Wage Plan," working paper no. 276, Wharton School, University of Pennsylvania, November 1987; James E. Martin and Melanie M. Peterson, "Two-Tier Wage Structure: An Equity Theory Approach," working paper, Department of Management, Wayne State University, no date.

57. "Major Collective Bargaining Settlements in Private Industry, 1987," *Current Wage Developments*, vol. 40 (March 1988), p. 7.

58. U.S. Bureau of Labor Statistics, press release USDL: 88–293, June 16, 1988, Table 3.

59. Ninety percent of the vacation plans in contracts in the BNA data base we have been citing use length of service to determine vacation periods. See Bureau of National Affairs, *Basic Patterns, op. cit.*, p. 107.

60. For discussion of union versus nonunion pension behavior, see Alan L. Gustman and Thomas L. Steinmaier, "Pension, Unions, and Implicit Contracts," working paper no. 2036, National Bureau of Economic Research, October 1986.

61. Pension plans are often included in a supplementary contract rather than in the basic union–management agreement. For this reason, the survey was confined only to those pension plans for which sufficient information was available. See Bureau of National Affairs, *Basic Patterns, op. cit.*, pp. 27–28.

62. On the influence of an equity-related leveling effect on pay, see Robert H. Frank, "Are Workers Paid Their Marginal Products," *American Economic Review*, vol. 74 (September 1984), pp. 549–571.

Chapter Ten

THE COLLECTIVE-
BARGAINING
RELATIONSHIP

The previous chapter introduced the institutions of collective bargaining, discussed the influences that determined its growth and decline, and examined the types of compensation arrangements commonly found in union–management agreements. This chapter considers other types of contractual features that are aimed at maintaining the employer–employee relationship and the union–management relationship. It also analyzes the bargaining process, labor disputes, and dispute resolution. Finally, in view of the decline in union membership and the weakened bargaining power of unions, which developed in the 1980s, the chapter poses an important long-term question for management: Will employers be better off if the erosion of union power continues indefinitely?

10–1 Employee and Union Security

Both employees and unions have a stake in maintaining their relationship with their employers. For employees, loss of the relationship, that is, job loss, can impose significant costs, particularly since the value of continuing the relationship rises with seniority.[1] For unions, loss of representation rights at an employer means a decline in membership and related dues revenue, possible loss of bargaining strength at competing employers (if the representation rights are lost at a firm that continues to produce on a nonunion basis), and eventually a threat to the survival of the union as a viable institution. Not surprisingly, union–management contracts reflect these employee and union interests.

Job and Income Security

The Bureau of National Affairs (BNA) survey of union contracts (cited in the previous chapter) reports that contractual provisions aimed at increasing job and income security for employees generally increased in frequency from the mid-

1960s to the mid-1980s. Thirteen percent of the contracts in the BNA sample provided for guaranteed minimum hours of work or guaranteed minimum levels of pay for eligible workers in 1986. Forty-one percent provided severance pay—a one-time bonus for those permanently laid off. And 16% had Supplemental Unemployment Benefit (SUB) plans that provide laid-off workers with weekly payments beyond the unemployment insurance they receive from the state.[2]

Certain workers under union contracts are more insulated from layoffs than others. Under the median voter hypothesis the union political mechanism will be especially responsive to more senior employees. Seniority therefore plays a major role in determining the order of layoff and the degree of insulation from layoff. Generally, junior workers are the first to be let go when labor demand falls. The BNA survey found that seniority was an explicit criterion for layoffs in 89% of the contracts; the proportion was 98% in the cyclically sensitive manufacturing sector.

Of those contracts making explicit reference to seniority as a layoff criterion, over half made it the *sole* factor determining the order of termination. About a third indicated that juniors would be laid off first unless a senior worker was unqualified for the available job. If particular jobs were being eliminated, senior workers were often given the right to "bump" (replace) junior workers in other jobs of comparable or lower status.

When bumping is allowed, however, there is a managerial concern to prevent wholesale disruption in the workforce. Frequently bumping rights are restricted to a subgroup of the workforce such as the plant, division, or job classification in which the senior worker is employed. In a large firm that has operations in many locations the absence of a limit on bumping rights could mean that a worker being laid off might bump some other employee in a plant thousands of miles away. Such wholesale bumping could be disruptive to operations and morale.

Half of the contracts specified that advance notice of layoffs should be given by management, either to employees or to the union. However, often the advance notice specified was a matter of only a few days.[3] These short notice periods reflect a management interest. Congressional action taken in 1988—two years after the BNA survey was conducted—now generally requires sixty days' notice for plant closings and mass layoffs.

The management community generally opposed mandatory long advance notice periods, arguing that firms might not be able to lay off workers quickly in the event of an unanticipated drop in labor demand. In such a case the firm might find itself having to pay for unneeded workers until the notice period elapsed. Additionally, in the case of permanent plant shutdowns, managers sometimes feared that too much advance warning would lead to the premature exit of employees or to adverse morale and productivity impacts.[4] The pre-1988 advance notice provisions, like others in union–management contracts, represented a compromise between employee and employer desires. The subsequent congressional action illustrates the propensity for federal intervention when employees feel that the balance has not been appropriately struck.[5]

When layoffs are temporary, the issue of recall rights arises. In a recall, the employer brings back into employment workers who were previously laid off.

Most contracts specify that recalls will be in reverse order of layoff, although they may also indicate that an employee will be recalled only if qualified for the new opening. Since layoffs are generally in reverse order of seniority, this contractual feature means that the more senior employee is likely to be recalled ahead of a junior employee.

During the concession bargaining era of the 1980s, it was not surprising that job and income security often was a topic of negotiations. Unemployment was generally high, especially in industries and occupations in which unions are concentrated. Workers were naturally fearful of losing their jobs and being unable to find new employment, given the loose labor market conditions that prevailed. In some cases, unions gave concessions to management in exchange for job or income security assurances. These assurances ranged from promises not to close a specified plant for a given period to more elaborate worker protections.

Perhaps the most far reaching of such programs were those established at General Motors and Ford. These programs provided substantial income protection for workers with at least fifteen years of seniority. Under these systems, the two auto companies have effectively committed themselves to transfer "core" workers to new vacancies and other locations and to provide retraining. The auto programs were negotiated after both union and management officials visited Japan and studied the "lifetime" employment systems used in larger firms in that country.

Grievance Systems and Job Security

Grievance mechanisms (to be discussed in a later chapter) are connected with the job security issue. Workers may be severed from employment for one of two reasons. They may be laid off for economic reasons, for example, when the firm experiences a drop in orders or decides to exit from a line of business, or they may be terminated because of misconduct or incompetence.

Grievance mechanisms can provide protection for workers in both kinds of cases. For example, suppose a contract specifies that senior workers who otherwise would be laid off may bump into other jobs *if* they are qualified. Through the grievance mechanism, a worker may dispute a management finding that he or she was unqualified (and therefore had to be laid off).

Similarly, if a worker is terminated for misconduct, there may be a conflict over whether the alleged misconduct actually occurred, or whether—if it did occur—the misconduct was sufficient to merit a discharge under the terms of the agreement. Again, the grievance mechanism can be used by the adversely affected employee to protest, and possibly reverse, a management action. Virtually all union–management contracts provide for grievance systems, and almost all provide for an outside arbitrator to settle the matter at issue if the union and management cannot arrive at a mutually satisfactory solution.[6]

Workrules and Job Security

Union–management agreements may include "manning requirements" that stipulate the number of individuals or the kinds of workers required to perform certain tasks. From time to time complaints about "featherbedding" have arisen with regard to such workrules. For example, a union insisted on maintaining a railroad fireman whose job had been to shovel coal into the boiler of steam engines, long after steam-powered locomotives had disappeared. This and similar egregious examples have been the subject of well-publicized disputes.

Because workrules involve issues of safety and pace of work as well as employment maintenance, legislative attempts to regulate in this area have been largely unproductive. Courts have been reluctant to try to sort out who is needed on a particular job. Moreover, since unions—as agents of the employees—may emphasize job security demands relative to, say, pay demands, it is unclear that legal restriction on workrule demands is appropriate.[7]

For example, suppose a union insists on a workrule that would raise employment in a workplace by 5% above what the employer would otherwise specify. (Such a demand is typically made when employment is being cut, perhaps because of automation.) From the cost perspective, such a demand is equivalent to a 5% pay increase relative to what the employer would pay given its preferred employment level. Alternatively, the union could have used its bargaining power to try to obtain the pay demand.

Of course, management also has preferences concerning the kinds of proposals it wishes to emphasize. The costs of entrenched workrules may increase over time, as technology and the demands of the product market depart farther and farther from the conditions prevailing when the workrules were first negotiated. A workrule that was originally equivalent to 5% of pay may in time climb in cost to, say, 10%. Management may press the union to reexamine the trade-off in subsequent renegotiations.

During the concession bargaining era of the 1980s, workrule relaxations were often included in negotiations. Management sought increased flexibility in job assignment. Sometimes this goal involved proposals to reduce the number of job classifications. With more workers in a given classification, management could more easily assign workers to diverse tasks.

From the union perspective, management demands for workrule relaxations pose bargaining problems as well as issues of job security. If the union is successful in its pay bargaining, it will raise compensation for employees above the levels management would unilaterally determine. Management might seek to recoup its bargaining losses with various job classifications at a typical worksite by substituting lower wage classifications for higher wage occupations. Relaxing workrules could thus lead to erosion of hard-won bargaining gains rather than increased productivity.

In some situations, particularly cases in which craft unions are involved, workrule relaxations may threaten the union's institutional survival. A major factor in union resistance to eliminating the railroad fireman, for example, was the fact that elimination of the job would also have eliminated the craft union that represented the firemen. When the firemen's union merged with other railroad crafts into a larger union, the institutional hurdle was removed.[8]

Despite the publicity attendant on restrictive union workrules, some research has suggested that productivity is *higher* in the union sector than in the nonunion. Since union wages also tend to be higher, this finding should not be a surprise.

In simple classical theory, if firms are required to pay higher wages, they will follow practices that increase marginal productivity—that is, they will raise the capital-to-labor ratio so that the following condition will hold: wage equals marginal revenue product equals marginal revenue times marginal productivity. A rise in marginal productivity is likely to raise average productivity as well.

Some researchers claim, however, that higher union productivity goes beyond the substitution of capital for labor.[9] They argue that unionized employees become more productive because they have a greater voice in their work environment. Available empirical evidence on this point is mixed; some studies find union-related productivity improvements (that is, improvements that go beyond the classical wage effect) while others find the opposite. Nevertheless, the popular impression that unionization is inevitably associated with lower productivity (compared with nonunion situations) is clearly incorrect. Moreover, according to some economic formulations (discussed later in this chapter), union demands that restrict managerial freedom to set employment levels can be efficient.

Union Security

Although a union represents employee interests, it also has its own institutional interests to protect. Sometimes the line between union institutional interest and employee interest is hazy. Ninety percent of the contracts in the BNA sample included a "check-off" clause, for example. This clause provides for union dues to be automatically deducted from workers' paychecks and remitted to the union.[10] Such a clause saves the union the administrative expense of attempting to collect dues from each individual and helps ensure that the union has an adequate financial base. It could be argued that such a clause benefits the union as an institution by providing lower costs and financial security. It could also be argued that the union will be a better representative of worker interests if it is adequately financed and has lower administrative costs.

Right-to-Work Issue, Free Riders, and Public Goods.   Almost three-fourths of the contracts in the BNA sample had a clause for either a *union shop* or a *modified union shop*. Under a union shop, as a condition of employment all workers are said to be required to join the union within a specified period (usually thirty days). In fact even when such clauses are present, individuals who do not want to join can avoid doing so by offering to pay the equivalent of dues instead.[11] Modified union shops explicitly permit some exemptions, usually for religious objectors to union membership or for nonmembers who were employed when the clause first took effect.

A small number of contracts contained "agency shop" clauses (5%) or "maintenance of membership" clauses (4%). The former does not require formal union membership, but does require payment of a representation fee equivalent to dues and assessments.[12] The latter requires only that union members retain their membership during the life of the contract.

The issue of compulsory union membership (or financial support) has generally gone under the heading of the "right-to-work" (R-T-W) issue. Twenty-one states have R-T-W laws that ban clauses requiring membership or financial support.[13] Typically, when such issues come before a state legislature (or before voters in a state referendum), both sides devote a tremendous amount of money and effort to the issue. Unions generally assume that the presence of R-T-W laws will lower unionization and bargaining strength in the state concerned. There is some evidence, however, that the laws simply reflect local attitudes, which also cause the lower level of unionization.[14]

During campaigns over R-T-W laws, unions use an argument that economists often term the "free rider" problem in connection with a "public good." Economists term certain kinds of government services—such as provision of defense, or traffic regulation, or safe streets—public goods (or "collective goods") because the use of these services cannot be restricted to those who pay for them. Individuals do not have a private incentive to contribute to financing the costs of public goods because they will receive the same amount of service whether or not they contribute. Of course, if no one contributes—that is, if everyone is a free rider—the good will not be provided. Hence there will be a tendency to undersupply public goods unless they are financed through compulsory taxation.[15]

Unions argue, in effect, that they provide a public good to those workers they represent by negotiating better wages, benefits, and conditions than the workers would otherwise receive. Under the law the unions must represent all workers, not just those who belong to the union or pay fees to support it.[16] Therefore, according to the union viewpoint, compulsory membership or fees (analogous to taxes for defense, and so on) are justified.

Not all workers agree with this position. Some may feel that they are not well served by a particular union. Since there are conflicting interest groups within the workplace, for example, skilled workers versus unskilled workers, some groups may feel their preferences are not adequately reflected by the union. Others may have a philosophical or religious objection to unions in general, or just to the union that happens to represent them. For example, workers may not agree with the political positions taken by the union or its leadership.[17] In states where there are no R-T-W laws, workers have the right under the Taft-Hartley Act to petition the NLRB for a "de-authorization poll" by which a majority vote can eliminate a union shop provision.[18]

There is no clear resolution of the conflict between freedom of association (or nonassociation) and the free rider viewpoints. The issue is similar to that faced by the larger society in balancing majority versus minority rights. Sometimes, society permits dissenters to "opt out"; for example, conscientious objectors have been permitted various alternatives to military service during wartime periods of conscription. Sometimes, society does not permit dissension; for example, jail terms are meted out to those who refuse to pay taxes for government policies they do not support.

Apart from the grand philosophical questions, it is interesting to speculate about how many workers may belong to unions that they would decline to join in the absence of a union security clause. No detailed data are published on union representation versus membership in states with and without right-to-work laws. The Current Population Survey, however, does provide some evidence.

Unions in the public sector typically have less legal authority than in the private sector to negotiate union security clauses. Governments have often been reluctant to adopt laws that might require their own employees to join or support private organizations.[19] In 1987 about 15% of public employees who were represented by unions were nonmembers. In contrast, in the private sector, where stronger authority for union security clauses exists, only 9% of union-represented workers were nonmembers.[20] It appears, therefore, that higher proportions of workers become union members where union security clauses are more prevalent.[21]

Management and Union Security.   What is management's interest in union security? There has been no single answer to this question. Different managements have reacted differently, and the response has varied from period to period. Some managements have felt that union security clauses give the union an advantage and have therefore viewed these provisions as simply another bargainable issue. According to this approach, if the union wants a union security clause, it has to pay for the provision by sacrificing something else.

Some managements have decided that a union security clause may serve management interests. With a guaranteed membership base, in their view, the union will behave more responsibly, particularly in regard to grievance handling. In contrast, an insecure union will tend to press all grievances, even those it knows are frivolous and assuredly will be dismissed by an arbitrator. The union will not screen out frivolous grievances, fearing that to do so would anger the grievant and cause him or her to resign.[22] But other views are possible. Management may feel that, with fewer members, a union's bargaining strength may be weakened, ultimately benefiting the employer's side.

Much depends on the climate of industrial relations management is trying to achieve and its perception of union strength over the long haul. In the automobile industry, for example, union security clauses have been in effect for many years at the Big Three companies.[23] The issue over whether such clauses should continue simply does not arise. In fact, since the mid-1970s, there has been an understanding between the union and the companies that management will not oppose unionization in new facilities.[24] General Motors' new Saturn operation, for example, has been arranged so that union representation is a virtual certainty.[25]

In firms in which unions are less entrenched than they are in the automobile industry, management may see benefits in resisting demands for union security. The fact is that major strikes over the union security issue have not occurred for many years. There is a tacit acceptance by both sides of the status quo.

Contract Duration and Related Features

One of the strong demands of management immediately after World War II was that union–management contracts should be legally enforceable. Management wanted to be able to plan on uninterrupted production, that is, no strikes once a settlement was reached, for some agreed-upon time period. With the Taft-Hartley Act of 1947, management got its wish.

Management was also anxious to extend the period of guaranteed labor peace and began to push for multiyear agreements. In that desire, too, management ultimately received what it wanted. For example, in the BNA sample, only

3% of contracts were of only one year's duration; the vast majority were three-year agreements. Ninety-four percent of the contracts contained some form of no-strike pledge, and over 60% of these were unconditional. The others permitted strikes only under limited circumstances.[26]

The grievance and arbitration mechanism noted earlier plays an important role in permitting long-duration contracts to exist. This mechanism provides a method of settling disputes arising from contract interpretation without resorting to strikes and lockouts. Although most grievances arise from cases of individual employee discipline, any contractual matter may be covered by the grievance and arbitration system unless the parties have explicitly excluded it.

Also related to contract duration are clauses specifying future wage and benefit adjustments. These deferred adjustments can keep wages and benefits in line with pay in the external labor market, with general price inflation, or with whatever criteria the parties feel are relevant. In addition to fixed deferred adjustments, the contract may also have contingent adjustments, the most common being the cost-of-living escalator clauses discussed in an earlier chapter.

Finally, some contracts have reopener clauses that permit renegotiation of some feature prior to the contract's expiration date. Fourteen percent of the BNA sample of contracts had such reopeners, most of them dealing with the wage component of the package. Reopeners can be negotiated for any part of the contract and can be made contingent, for example, conditional on a given increase in the Consumer Price Index or some other event.[27]

In effect, reopener clauses represent a compromise on contract duration. It is agreed that most of the contract will remain in effect for its life, but some element of shorter duration is permitted. At the reopener date—unless the entire contract is reopened—there will be fewer issues about which to bargain. For example, wages might be renegotiated, whereas benefits, workrules, and so on continue unchanged. With fewer issues on the table, the chances of an impasse and a strike are reduced.

A commonly cited management objective in pursuing long-term contracts originally was to lower the risk of strikes. Most strikes relate to the renegotiation of a contract, so it may seem evident, at first blush, that with three-year contracts there will be only one-third as many strikes as would occur with one-year contracts. However, the issue is more complicated since the probability of a strike may vary with contract duration. If strikes are more likely after a three-year contract expires than after a one-year agreement, then the amount of striking activity may not be reduced.[28] Rather, strikes may simply be "scheduled" less frequently.

There is some evidence that long-term contracts primarily have bought management less frequent strike scheduling rather than few strikes or days lost to strikes. From the management perspective, this outcome is nevertheless perceived as a good deal. Strikes seem to have a heavy fixed cost attached, so that management would prefer one long strike every three years to three short ones in each of three years.[29] Of course, there is no necessity for a strike to occur whenever a negotiation takes place. In fact new contracts are usually negotiated without a strike. What is at issue is the *risk* of a strike.

Explicit and De Facto Contract Duration

In theory, the entire union–management contract, with all its many features, dies on its expiration date.[30] Yet it is common to find that the successor contract contains much the same language as the expired agreement. Wages and benefits are frequently changed when new contracts are negotiated. Other aspects of the contract may simply roll over from agreement to agreement.

This continuation suggests that the union–management relationship should generally be viewed as ongoing, that is, of no definite duration. Much of the contract has a longer de facto duration than the explicit expiration date found in the contract implies. For example, the job and income guarantees in the automobile industry described above would have little meaning if they were thought by the parties to end every three years. What would it mean to guarantee a worker a long period of job/income security if that guarantee regularly lapsed? Automobile company management and union officials thus have a tacit understanding that while the job/income security program may be revised from time to time, its basic structure will outlive the duration of any one agreement.

In a period when the nature of the union–management agreement comes into question, however, long-neglected contractual features may become issues. During the concession bargaining era of the 1980s, management commonly pressed the union side to alter traditional workrules to make them less restrictive, and to reduce the number of job classifications so that workers could more easily be transferred from task to task. Given the decline in union membership and bargaining strength, management effectively questioned the status quo; it was less sure that there had to be an indefinite, ongoing relationship.

Perhaps, as occurred in some cases, striking workers might be replaced and the firm could revert to nonunion status. Even if achieving nonunion status was not an immediate (or realistic) goal, management pressed issues of flexibility in the use of human resources that—in another era—it might have left untouched. Doubts about union strength, awakened by union concessions at other firms, led to a greater willingness by management to determine by experiment what the relative bargaining power of the parties really was.

10–2 Analysis of Union–Management Bargaining

Economists have long debated how to model union–management wage bargaining.[31] Perhaps the greatest failing in this literature is a concentration on union objectives and a corresponding neglect of management goals and the union–management *interaction* in bargaining. It is not reasonable, when two parties are bargaining and each has the power to inflict costs on the other, to ignore the joint process by which outcomes are determined.

In their analysis economists have also been sidetracked by the temptation to use the simple theory of the firm and apply it to unions. It is true that both a firm and a union face a demand curve. The firm faces a downward sloping demand for its product that represents a trade-off between a high price and a high volume of sales. The union faces a downward sloping demand for labor schedule that represents a trade-off between a high wage and a high volume of employment. There the simple analogy stops.

Elusive Search for Maximizing

In the theory of the firm, it is profit maximization that permits the firm to select the optimum trade-off between price and quantity on the product demand schedule. Given a cost function, the principle that the price/quantity trade-off occurs where marginal revenue equals marginal cost provides an analytic solution. Unfortunately, in the union case, there is not an obvious value index (such as profit) to maximize.

If unions wanted only to maximize wage rates, they would set the wage so high that practically no one would be employed, that is, they would travel—if they could—to the top of the demand curve, as shown in Figure 10–1. Similarly, if unions desired only to maximize employment, they would push wages down to the point at which the employer would have difficulty hiring and retaining workers. Finally, if unions maximized the total payroll, that is, wage times labor input, they would operate at a point at which the absolute value of the elasticity of labor demand equals 1.[32] Such a point happens to occur half way down a linear demand curve of the type shown in Figure 10–1, and thus appears to be a compromise solution, between wage rate maximizing and employment maximizing.

There is no reason to believe, however, that any of these choices, taken alone, is actually a union objective. In the abstract, unions would certainly like to have higher wages, if nothing else had to be sacrificed to obtain them. It is

**FIGURE 10–1
Demand for Labor
Schedule**

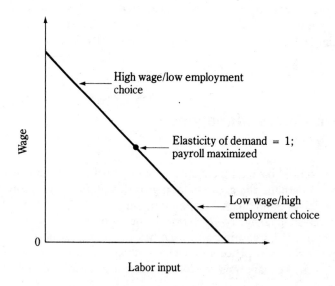

commonly assumed that they would also like more employment (and members), again if no sacrifice were entailed. The real world provides no such simple alternatives, however; nor is there any reason to believe that maximizing the payroll (wage times employment) in the real world is in any sense an optimum choice for the union.

Faced with this dilemma, some economists have proposed models in which the union (or the union's leaders) have a utility function that treats both high wages and high employment as Good Things. The utility function generates an indifference map, just as in consumer theory, and the union picks the point on the demand curve at which the highest indifference curve is attained. Such an approach provides a solution to the trade-off dilemma in theory, but not an especially satisfying one.

Given the assumptions that a union wants both high wages and high employment *and that it readily perceives the trade-off to be made,* the notion of picking the optimum combination on the demand curve raises an analytical problem. Under those assumptions, a point on the demand curve is inherently inefficient (nonoptimum) from the union's perspective. Figure 10–2 shows why.

In Figure 10–2 the firm's demand for labor appears as line D. Suppose that the union obtains the wage-employment combination (w_1, e_1) consistent with point a on demand curve D. It can be shown that there probably is a better point, involving a somewhat lower wage and a somewhat higher employment level, that

**FIGURE 10–2
An Efficient Union
Contract**

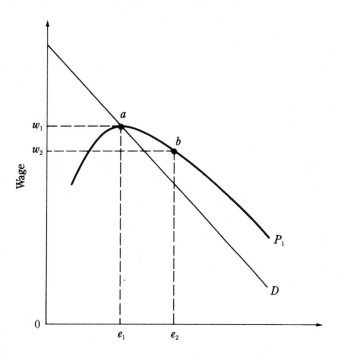

Labor input

is *off* the demand curve and that the firm will not resist. Clearly, if there is a point that is better than *a* from the union's perspective, and if the firm will not resist a move from *a* to that point, the union should make the move.

Traveling through point *a* is the firm's isoprofit line P_1, the line that traces all combinations of wage and employment that would yield the same dollar profit as at *a*.[33] The firm will therefore be indifferent between operating at point *a* and operating at any other point on P_1. To the right of point *a* the line bends downward since a lower wage is required to compensate for decreased employment and output. It bends down to the left of point *a* because the increased employment to the left, while adding some output, is subject to declining marginal productivity and must be compensated by lower wages. Thus *a* is the highest point on P_1.

Effectively, once the union has won point *a*, the relevant menu for it is not along the demand curve *D*, but along P_1. To operate at any point other than *a*, however, the union must negotiate a contract that specifies both wage and employment, not just wage. (If the union fails to specify the employment level along with the wage, the firm will, by definition, stay on its demand curve *D*.) It can be shown that the union generally will prefer to operate to the left of *a* at a point such as *b*, with a somewhat lower wage w_2 and a somewhat higher employment level e_2.

The reader should be able to see why the union will not want to operate to the right of point *a*. Points to the right on P_1 involve lower wage levels and lower employment, clearly not a desirable move from the union's perspective. The choice for the union will thus be either to stay at *a* or move leftwards to a point such as *b*. Generally, when a constraint is relaxed in economics (such as the constraint of staying on *D*), welfare is increased by taking advantage of the loosened constraint and adjusting behavior accordingly. So a point such as *b* is likely to be chosen.[34]

This analysis is useful not because it gives a realistic view of union bargaining, but because it shows the major shortcoming of models that depend on precise union perceptions of economic circumstances and trade-offs. If unions behaved according to such a model, the standard contract they negotiated would of necessity specify the employment level. Except for some reactive workrules, typically triggered by threatened employment cuts, union contracts generally leave the employment specification to the employer. Hence it must be assumed that unions do not perceive the bargaining situation to be as depicted in either Figure 10–1 or the more sophisticated Figure 10–2.

Union Perceptions

Implicit in the notion of a union picking an optimum point on—or off—the demand curve is the assumption that the union *perceives* the downward slope of the demand curve and/or the isoprofit curve, or that it needs to have such a perception in order to bargain successfully. The existence of a downward sloping demand curve for labor, although perhaps obvious to economists, is not necessarily obvious to union officials or to union members. Moreover, a union that did not perceive the trade-off between wages and employment could operate satisfactorily, at least for a time, in a bargaining relationship.

Position Versus Slope of Labor Demand. There are various reasons why union perception of a downward sloping demand for labor or isoprofit curve (the wage-employment trade-off) would be attenuated. First, swings in the number of workers demanded by employers are dominated by aggregate business cycles and orders received by the firm. Put another way, the *position* of the labor demand curve relative to the origin, rather than the curve's slope, is what unions and their members mainly see. Wage changes occur periodically, but do not necessarily correlate negatively with employment changes. Indeed, it is commonly the case that wages and employment rise simultaneously.

Managerial Discretion. Second, although economists tend to view the relationship between wages and employment in mechanistic terms (that is, following from a model), unions will see any connection as related to *discretionary* management decisions. Wage increases create incentives for management actions. When such actions are taken, unions will tend to see the problem as one of adverse (even heartless) management decisions rather than as a direct product of wage increases.

There are two reasons why the demand for labor schedule is downward sloped. One is that wage increases push up costs of production. If these costs are passed on to consumers, they will reduce sales volume. If increased costs cannot be passed to consumers (due to competitive market conditions), they will squeeze profits and tend to induce reduced production and employment. The other reason is the possibility of substitution. If wages rise, there will be a tendency to substitute capital for labor, outside subcontractors for internal production, or lower wage labor (perhaps at a nonunion plant) for union labor.

Raising prices, reducing production, purchasing labor-saving equipment, using alternative facilities, and hiring subcontractors are management decisions. They do not happen mechanically, even if economists and managers view them as inevitable or unavoidable. Unions will tend to see declines in orders as obvious grounds for layoffs. Their response will be to bargain for severance pay, SUB plans, and the other job and income security devices discussed above. When substitutions are threatened, unions may push for controls on the introduction of new technology, workrule restrictions limiting labor-saving possibilities, and limitations on management's right to subcontract or transfer work.

Thus wage objectives of unions will not necessarily be directly checked by employment declines. Management efforts to substitute away from high union wages may simply confirm the impression by union leaders and members that the employer will act deviously if not checked by union pressure. The difference in perceptions between management, employees, and union officials—apart from its importance to an understanding of the bargaining process—is critical to an appreciation of much employer–employee and employer-union tension.

Management will perceive adverse personnel actions taken in response to shifts in demand or relative costs as normal reactions to the market. Employees and their union agents will often see these actions as the results of discretionary management decisions. The worker who experiences the adverse personnel action is likely to blame it on a supervisor or other managerial official who made the decision, or perhaps on a vague "them" in the firm's higher management. Even when union officials believe that forces outside the firm are causing management's response, they may have a very difficult time conveying these beliefs to the employees they represent.

Dominance of Short-Run Perspective.   A third reason why union perceptions of a wage-employment trade-off will be limited is that there is often no substantial trade-off to be had in the short run. As shown in an earlier chapter, labor costs as a percentage of sales are frequently low. In the absence of substitution possibilities, even if a wage increase is entirely passed on to consumers, its impact on prices (and, therefore, on sales volume) may be modest. For example, in a firm in which labor costs are 25% of sales, a 4% wage increase that is fully passed along into prices will translate into only a 1% price increase. Of course, there may be more substantial implications in the long run than in the short. The collective bargaining process, however, tends to focus on the short term.

Historical Evolution.   There is a fourth reason why union perceptions of the economics of the wage-employment trade-off may be limited. This reason is more historical and institutional than intrinsic in the collective bargaining process. It is that American management, from the period immediately after World War II until the 1980s, has not been anxious to deal with unions on matters closely related to management decision making and, more generally, to the economics of the enterprise.

Unions arose in the 1930s, an era characterized by public hostility towards business and calls for restrictions on and regulation of managerial discretion. In addition, some of the major unions in the 1930s and 1940s had communists and other radicals in their leadership. Employers found themselves facing such challenges as sit-ins and worker-occupations of plants. The management community thus feared an overly close involvement of unions in the enterprise. If unions had to be tolerated, management felt, their energies should be channeled away from notions of enterprise control and towards the "terms or conditions of employment" described in the Wagner Act.[35]

Although courts never accepted as narrow a definition of the scope of bargaining as management would have liked in interpreting the Wagner/Taft-Hartley framework, they did accept the basic notion that management had inherent rights to run the enterprise. Generally, the courts have viewed anything dealing directly with wages, fringe benefits, hours of work, employee safety and health, layoffs, promotions, and grievances, to be "mandatory" subjects of bargaining. Employers had to negotiate in good faith on such subjects, although they did not have to agree to any particular demand. Failure to negotiate was an unfair labor practice.[36]

Courts did not, however, interpret employers to be obligated to bargain about the pricing of products, marketing strategy, financial arrangements, or similar matters that were closely related to the overall direction of the enterprise. Of course, decisions in these areas could easily affect employees indirectly. Excessively high prices or poor marketing might reduce sales, for example, thus causing layoffs. But the courts' notion of the appropriate roles for unions and managements meant that such issues were not to be mandatory subjects of bargaining.[37] For better or worse, these policies were to be made unilaterally by management.

Unions seemed to accept these limitations on their functions by the 1950s. Within that prescribed role, they found little need to become familiar with managerial issues or the economic environment in which the firm operated. The union role was simply to make demands on management for improved wages, benefits, and working conditions. Obviously, different unions reacted differently to the narrow view of their function, and some exhibited more economic sophistication than others.[38] But, since unions by and large were not supposed to be concerned with broad managerial decision making, it should not be surprising that concepts such as the long-run elasticity of labor demand were not normally in their tool kits.

Management's Role in Bargained Outcomes

If unions do not perceive the wage-employment trade-off, why do they not bargain their way up the demand curve and into oblivion? Higher wages are better than lower wages. If no employment is perceived to be sacrificed by obtaining higher wages, what would prevent unions from picking such high levels of wages that virtually no union members remained employed? The answer is simple. Management acts to prevent such a result.

Collective bargaining is a two-sided process. Management will resist union demands that cut into profits. Other things being equal, higher wages will cut into profits. Hence management will resist demands for higher wages (or, generally, demands to increase labor costs). This point is both obvious and fundamental.

In collective bargaining each side has the potential to inflict costs on the other. A union-led strike, if successful, will halt immediate production, sales, and profits. If the strike continues for an extended period, it may cause permanent loss of previously cultivated customer relationships. Management must weigh such costs in deciding whether to accept or reject union demands and in making counteroffers.

Even successful strikes, however, are costly to union members. Paychecks stop arriving, health benefits are discontinued, and bills pile up. Generally, workers on strike are ineligible for unemployment insurance or benefits such as food stamps.[39] Also, strikes may not be successful. Employers have a long-standing legal right to attempt to operate in the face of a strike and to hire replacements. When the employer is able to operate with replacements, the strikers may be permanently out of a job.[40] Such situations can destroy the union as an institution. From the union viewpoint even nominally successful strikes can have untoward consequences; the enterprise may be so economically injured that employment prospects are permanently reduced.

Both parties to a collective-bargaining negotiation must take the possibility of a strike very seriously and frame their positions accordingly. The potential costs of error can be great. It pays for management to make some concessions to avoid strike costs. That is why economic studies, as noted in the last chapter, repeatedly find a union-induced wage premium.

On the other hand, unions cannot expect the moon—and they usually do not receive it. Pushing excessive demands will trigger management resistance and possibly lead to heavy costs on union members. Union officials who lead a costly strike and fail to reach their objectives will not experience gratitude from union members. Their political futures may be at risk in such situations, even if the membership was initially enthusiastic and militant about striking. The outcome of collective-bargaining negotiations thus represents a complex balancing of considerations of costs and risks by both sides.

There is a problem, however, inherent in a bargaining process based on the potential infliction of mutual damage. The decisions made will tend to focus much more on short-term strategic bargaining considerations (strike cost minimization) rather than on long-run economics. It is quite possible that the bargaining process, over a long period of time, could produce a sequence of settlements that cumulatively would have unfortunate consequences for both union and management. Markets and employment opportunities might be lost in the long run. Yet, both parties might have been happy with the outcome of each negotiated settlement taken by itself, even if they are unhappy with the eventual consequences.

Strikes

Textbooks on union–management relations commonly point out that most contracts are renegotiated without a strike. This fact might seem to contradict the importance of strategic strike cost considerations in determining bargained outcomes. However, a relatively small number of contracts covers a large fraction of the unionized workforce. In 1987 there were 1,326 contracts covering 1,000 or more workers in the private sector and specifying the terms and conditions of roughly half of the union-represented private workforce. The total number of contracts in existence in 1987 is unknown. The BLS estimated, however, that there were over 177,000 union–management contracts of all sizes in effect in the late 1970s (some of which were in the public sector).[41] Thus whatever happens under the relatively few big agreements containing half of those union-represented private workers is especially relevant to judging the negotiation process.

Strikes in Major Situations.   It is true that, even for the larger contracts, most disputes are settled without strikes. However, strike probabilities are not negligible. During the years 1984 to 1987, the ratio of workers involved in work stoppages to workers included in new union–management settlements averaged about one-tenth for situations covering 1,000 or more employees.[42] This estimate includes public as well as private workers. Some of the workers involved in stoppages may not have been participating in contract-negotiation disputes, but most of them were. Thus, even in the 1980s—when strike activity was much reduced—a worker involved in a major contract negotiation had roughly a one-in-ten chance of participating in a labor dispute.[43] In fact, for the private sector, the odds were significantly higher because of the low propensity of public employees to strike.[44]

The negotiated outcomes in small bargaining units are reached with much lower strike probabilities than those for major contracts.[45] Within industries, however, the outcomes of the major contracts are often imitated, or partly imitated, in small units. In effect, the parties to small contracts have devised a way of holding down their own strike costs; they let someone else (the parties to larger agreements) do their striking for them.[46]

Analysis of Strike Activity.   Strikes have always been a puzzle to economists.[47] In principle, if both parties could foresee the outcome of a strike, it should not occur. The parties could simply accept the terms of settlement they foresee without undergoing the costs of the strike and thus both be better off. According to this view, strikes must be the result of imperfect foresight, that is, mistakes.

The notion of imperfect foresight has been used to model strike duration. For example, in the 1930s John R. Hicks, a British economist, proposed that once union and management had entered into a strike, each side would gradually become more informed about the other's capacity to resist.[48] Figure 10–3 illustrates the Hicksian theory.

Let W_E be the employer's final, pre-strike wage offer and W_U be the union's final, pre-strike wage demand. Since $W_E < W_U$, a strike begins on day 0. As the strike wears on and profit losses mount, the employer gradually becomes more willing to offer more along the schedule E. The employer discovers that union militancy was greater than had been initially estimated. Learning that the employer was more intransigent than it had guessed, the union becomes willing to demand less. It travels along line U of Figure 10–3 as income losses to its members accumulate.[49] The intersection point of the two lines comes at the date (day = T) at which the strike is terminated (settled) and determines the strike's duration ($0T$ days).

If either side can lessen the costs of the strike to it, its curve will become flatter and it will be able to endure a longer dispute with reduced concessions to

FIGURE 10–3
Hicksian Strike
Model

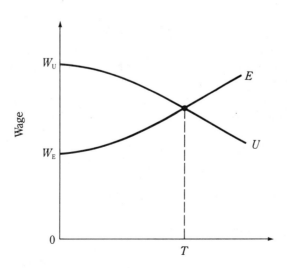

Duration of strike (in days)

the other side. For example, if management is able to maintain production by hiring replacements or if it has successfully arranged a mutual assistance pact (discussed in the previous chapter) with other firms, the costs of the strike to it will be reduced and it will ultimately move not far from its pre-strike wage offer W_E.

Unions, too, may use strategies that reduce the costs of a dispute to them. In some cases they may not engage in a conventional strike at all. They might, for example, stay on the job and engage in "work-to-rule" tactics. Under work-to-rule, employees follow all of the employer's regulations so strictly that production is hindered. Another possibility for the union is to call a series of very short work stoppages, say, for a few hours each, that disrupt production. Workers might also refuse overtime assignments, or call in sick, or just work less efficiently than usual. The idea is to keep workers on the employer's payroll, thus limiting the cost of the dispute to them and to the union.

If successful, such union tactics flatten the U curve on Figure 10–3 and push the eventual settlement towards W_U. During the 1980s, as unions looked for alternative tactics to meet what they perceived was a more aggressive management stance, there was much discussion of these semi-strike approaches.[50] The employer, however, may react with a lockout that nullifies semi-strike strategies.

Information Exchange.   The Hicksian model is useful because it highlights the information exchange that occurs during strikes and during bargaining. In a negotiation, in which each side has the ability to inflict costs on the other, there is an incentive to bluff, to make the opposition believe that willingness to inflict and bear costs is higher than it actually is. This incentive complicates the negotiation process since written and oral demands and offers cannot necessarily be taken at face value.

How can management be sure that the union's declared "final" position is truly final? How can the union be sure that management's "last" offer may not in fact be more flexible than management declares it to be? In principle the union could try to infer management's true position from the firm's financial condition. There is evidence that the more volatile the rate of return on the firm's stock, the greater is the probability of a strike. This finding suggests that as financial information becomes more clouded, the union is more likely to resort to a strike to obtain a sense of management's actual negotiating position.[51]

Since strikes are costly, both sides also have an ultimate incentive to avoid miscommunications. When one party has put its final offer on the table, it needs to have credibility behind that offer so that the other side will not miscalculate. A miscalculation could result in an expensive blunder for both sides, if a needless strike results. The pressure for avoiding miscalculation becomes particularly severe as the contract expiration date approaches. Once that date is reached, an impasse is likely to lead to a strike. That is why labor disputes are often settled just before the strike deadline. Midnight settlements are not unusual, as anyone who has followed newspaper accounts of prominent negotiations knows.[52]

If the deadline passes and the strike does occur, the Hicksian model suggests that communications continue, even if formal bargaining is broken off. Each side can observe the other's strike behavior. Is management able to maintain production, as it initially claimed it could, despite the strike? If not, the union's hand is strengthened. Is the union having trouble keeping its members from crossing the picket line and returning to work?[53] If so, management's hand is strengthened. Strikes, in short, are a form of information exchange, although a costly one.

Limits of the Hicksian-Type Analysis. Although the "mistake theory" of strikes provides some useful insights, it unfortunately also has implications that do not accord with empirical evidence.[54] If strikes are merely mistakes, they should occur at random. In particular, they should not exhibit patterns of correlation with other economic variables. As in the theory of rational expectations in financial markets, the parties involved should quickly learn any correlation patterns and adjust their behavior accordingly, thus eliminating the statistical association.[55]

However, strikes seem to have longstanding statistical relationships with economic variables. For example, they seem to be exacerbated by inflation and boom conditions and to be cooled by recession.[56] In addition, there is some evidence that the stock market can predict the likelihood of a strike.[57] Since stock market transactors presumably have less information than the actual parties to the negotiation, it must be assumed that the parties can make an even better estimate. So why do relations between strikes and economic variables persist, once they are understood?

The empirical evidence will not be so puzzling if it is recalled that the union–management relationship is an ongoing one of indefinite duration. Unlike a potential buyer and seller haggling over the price of a used car, the parties to collective bargaining are tied together permanently. If the potential buyer and seller cannot reach a settlement in a used-car transaction, they simply part company. In sharp contrast, if a union and management reach an impasse over this year's settlement, they must be concerned with what their behavior might imply for future settlements that will eventually have to be negotiated.[58]

For example, if management asserts that it has made a final offer, but then quickly backs down and offers more when threatened with a strike, the union will learn that management is prone to bluff. In backing down and enhancing its offer, management may avert a strike in the current negotiations; but it may actually *raise* the probability of future strikes by having taught the union that management assertions of firmness are not credible. The union may assume in the future that any such assertions are likely to be bluffs and can be safely ignored.

In an ongoing relationship, therefore, both sides must paradoxically exhibit a degree of rigidity in each negotiation in order to reduce the stream of future strike costs. One form of rigidity is to establish a *consistent* pattern of behavior keyed to important and credible variables. Suppose, for example, that the union wishes to establish that it is concerned with protecting the real wage from price inflation. Suppose further that management wishes to establish that it will not grant large wage increases when the outlook for profits is uncertain. If both sides stick to their guns, a procyclical pattern of strike activity is likely to emerge.

At the top of the business cycle, management may start to see indications of the future economic downturn, thus making the profit outlook insecure. On the other hand, inflation pressures on real wages may simultaneously push the union to demand large wage increases. Each party may understand the other's position. Both may even see clearly that a strike is coming and be able to make a rough forecast of the likely post-strike settlement. Both know, however, that to give in without putting up a fight would undermine their future credibility and lead eventually to a higher stream of strike costs.[59]

Public Policies to Reduce Strikes.   In response to a strike wave immediately after World War II, Congress sought to reduce strike activity through various devices incorporated into the Taft-Hartley Act of 1947. First, a procedure—to be initiated by the president—was established for enjoining "national emergency disputes" during an eighty-day "cooling off" period. During that time, a "fact-finding" panel was to explore the issues of the impasse and make a public report. Towards the end of the period, union members would be asked to vote in an election conducted by the National Labor Relations Board (NLRB) to determine whether or not they would accept management's last offer. Various presidents actively used these procedures. By the late 1970s, however, their use had waned, mainly because by that time few (if any) strikes had the potential to create a true national emergency. Presidential interventions blocking strikes have become confined to the railroad industry, a sector falling under a separate piece of legislation, the Railway Labor Act.[60]

Second, Congress required that union–management contracts would continue in force indefinitely unless one party notified the other sixty days in advance that it wished to renegotiate a new contract upon expiration of the old.[61] Since most contracts contain some form of no-strike provision, this requirement would effectively prevent strikes unless advance notice was given. It appears this requirement was imposed because Congress observed that settlements were often reached at the last minute.

Congress naively assumed that the parties somehow were not giving themselves enough time to negotiate and that strikes were occurring because bargaining time had run out. In fact, the analysis of bargaining above makes it clear why last-minute settlements are to be expected.[62] The contract deadline represents a point where bluffs are called and more accurate communication is encouraged.

The third major action taken by Congress in 1947 was the creation of the Federal Mediation and Conciliation Service (FMCS).[63] Pursuant to the Taft-Hartley Act, FMCS mediators offer their services to parties engaged in collective-bargaining negotiations. The mediators have no powers to impose a settlement. Their job is instead to facilitate an agreement, if the parties wish to permit their participation.

Inherent in the bargaining process are the twin requirements that a satisfactory settlement permit the parties to (1) maintain credibility and (2) save face. These goals can be as important as the money value of the agreement, because they will condition the nature of the ongoing union–management relationship. Thus FMCS mediators (or private parties who are also sometimes used as mediators) may be called upon to help craft artful compromises that achieve these two goals.[64]

Suppose, for example, that the union initially swore it would never accept a two-tier wage plan and management swore it would not settle without one. Suppose further that a strike has resulted over this issue and the union now feels that it would be best to accept some version of a two-tier plan. Yet it is stuck with its pre-strike pledge never to accept one. A mediator might be able to suggest an arrangement that gives management a lower wage for new hires, but permits the union to insist that it did not agree to a two-tier wage plan.

Perhaps the mediator can suggest to both sides that a new job classification be created for learners or trainees at a lower wage. New entrants to the firm's workforce would initially be classified as learners or trainees. Thus there would not be two separate tiers of wages, but a single set of wages with learners or trainees at the bottom. The compromise would have much the same effect as a two-tier plan, but both sides could say that the settlement was within their stated objectives.

Mediators must also be mindful of the union's political processes and the pressures those processes place on union leaders. A mediator may be able to interpret the settlement publicly in a way that permits union officials to argue convincingly to their members that the compromise was the best that could be achieved and therefore should be ratified. Although sometimes described as mere go-betweens in a negotiation, successful mediators in fact must exhibit great skill and sensitivity.

Strike Alternatives

The strike threat is the engine that powers contemporary collective bargaining. But, to the parties, strikes can also be a distraction from the economic environment. In a situation in which strike costs and their avoidance are dominant, longer-run concerns such as market share, competitiveness, and resulting employment prospects will not receive the critical attention they deserve.

The neglect of long-run consequences that can affect bargaining is especially paradoxical for unions. Union members are much more likely to have long tenures of employment with their employers than nonunion workers. Because of these long tenures, the stakeholder component of the employment relationship is particularly important for unionized workers. People who have been on the job for a long time are typically more tied to their jobs than newcomers. Hence the long run should be of greater concern for union members than for other workers.

At a unionized firm top managers whose economic prospects look dim may be able to move to other well-paying positions. The managers may thus have less of a stake in the future of the enterprise than its union workers. In a bargaining system powered by the threat of a strike, unions cannot necessarily rely on management to protect the enterprise from excessive bargaining demands in the long run. Long-run economic consequences thus should be high on the union's own agenda.

Given this situation, the question naturally arises whether substitutes can be found for the strike. There really is only one alternative that has been used, and it is quite rare in the private sector.[65] That alternative is interest arbitration.

Interest and Rights Arbitration.   Arbitration comes in two varieties: rights and interest.[66] In both cases the arbitrator (unlike a mediator) is charged with making a *binding* settlement of the dispute. Rights arbitration is used to settle disputes over the interpretation of an *existing* (current) contract—most often in cases of employee grievances—and is by far the most common form of arbitration used in the United States. (This type of arbitration will be discussed in the next chapter.)

Interest arbitration involves the settlement of a dispute aimed at establishing a *new* contract. In principle, interest arbitration can be imposed by government and strikes can be forbidden. Such a policy is known as compulsory arbitration. No current federal statute imposes compulsory arbitration on collective-bargaining parties in the private sector, although there have been instances of ad hoc federal use of the technique in the past.[67] There has never been much sentiment in Congress to establish a labor-relations system (such as exists in Australia) in which compulsory arbitration is the norm.

Privately established interest arbitration can be used to settle private sector disputes without government compulsion. The parties to a negotiation can agree voluntarily to hire their own arbitrators and to be bound by the resulting decision—that is, they can agree that the arbitrator will settle the dispute and that there will be no strikes or lockouts to overturn the arbitration award. Yet the use of voluntary binding interest arbitration by private parties is extremely rare. FMCS data suggest that only about 1% to 2% of the arbitrations known to that agency fall into the interest category.[68]

Rarity of Private Interest Arbitration.   Congress has generally refrained from imposing compulsory arbitration on private parties, partly out of a desire to avoid government intervention generally, and partly because of a fear that such imposition might actually complicate negotiations. For many years standard dogma in labor relations circles suggested that imposition of compulsory arbitration would kill private bargaining. According to this view, arbitrators would simply "split the difference" between the offers of labor and management. Thus both sides would have strong incentives to take extreme positions in order to pull the arbitrator in their respective directions.

Since the parties would take extreme positions, there would be no hope that they would reach a settlement on their own. Arbitration would thus have a "chilling effect" on bargaining. Serious bargaining would not occur because both parties would in effect be talking to the arbitrator, who would later enter the picture, and not to each other. Moreover, once established, compulsory arbitration would also have a "narcotic effect" since the parties would come to depend on it in all disputes.

There are good reasons to believe, however, that this widely accepted negative view of arbitration is unrealistic. First, voluntary binding arbitration is something the parties would chose to use or not use. There is thus no reason why arbitration should become a narcotic or why—if it did—there should be public concern about the private choice of a method of settling a dispute.

Second, researchers have developed evidence that arbitrators in interest cases do not simply split the difference between the labor and management positions.[69]

Rather, arbitrators have their own notions and standards of what a reasonable settlement should be, based on such factors as inflation and the going rate of wage adjustments.[70] In framing their positions, unions and managements can estimate what the arbitrator will think reasonable and position themselves accordingly. Interest arbitration should be viewed as a three-party process with union, management, *and* arbitrator as active participants.[71]

The union will ask for somewhat more than what might be considered reasonable, but not so much more that it would lose credibility with the arbitrator. Management might offer something less than the estimate, but, again, within a credible range. The arbitrator comes somewhere in the middle—not because of a split-the-difference approach—but because the parties have arrayed themselves around the likely decision. There is no guarantee that the result will be positions that are reasonably close to one another. On the other hand, it cannot be presumed that extreme positions are inherent in arbitration.

Obviously, arbitrators do not make decisions in a vacuum, completely unmindful of union and management proposals. They are aware of the parties' offers and take them into account.[72] The fact that arbitrators do have their own norms of settlements acts as a brake on the tendency of the parties to take extreme positions. Thus the feared chilling effect on bargaining need not arise, even when the parties know that they will probably use an arbitrator if the dispute cannot be privately settled.[73] Generally, if there is more uncertainty about the results of interest arbitration than there is about the outcome of negotiations, the parties will be inclined to settle via negotiations.[74]

In any case should the chilling effect remain a concern, private parties can, in principle, develop solutions. For example, final offer arbitration, a variant of conventional interest arbitration, is sometimes used in the public sector (and occasionally in the private) to settle disputes.[75] Under final offer arbitration, the arbitrator must pick the offer of *either* union or management and cannot concoct a compromise. Proponents of this form of arbitration argue that the arbitrator will pick the most reasonable offer of the two. Both parties will therefore have an incentive to take reasonable rather than extreme positions; they may even end up settling the dispute without using the arbitration mechanism.[76]

Future Private Sector Interest Arbitration. The current rarity of interest arbitration in the private sector does not mean that it could not be more frequently used in the future. It is paradoxical that unions and management universally accept rights arbitration as the normal way to settle one class of disputes, but generally ignore or deride interest arbitration as a technique to settle another class of disputes. Historically, the sharp distinction between interests and rights was not always made. Unions and employers in the 1920s sometimes had stand-by umpires upon whom they called to help them resolve problems, regardless of type.

In a period when fundamental assumptions about collective bargaining are being questioned, increased voluntary interest arbitration should be reconsidered as an alternative to strikes. Of course, it would be just as important for arbitrators in such situations to consider the long-term economic consequences of their decisions as it is for unions and managements to do so in conventional bargaining.

Limited evidence suggests that unions are somewhat less willing than managers to use arbitrators with an economics background. They are more likely to prefer arbitrators with legal backgrounds, presumably because lawyers are perceived to be more equity minded.[77] However, the influence of the unfavorable developments of the 1980s began to change union views. In any case more widespread use of interest arbitration represents a potentially more cooperative form of labor–management relations than has been the norm.

10−3 Arrival of the Long Run for Collective Bargaining

Concession bargaining in the 1980s was attributed to various causes. Deregulation in transportation and communications opened up the possibility of new, nonunion competition. Substantial appreciation of the U.S. dollar relative to other currencies in the early 1980s led to increased import competition and to loss of export markets.[78] Under the Reagan administration the political and legal environment for unions became more difficult. A severe recession occurred in the early 1980s, and thereafter the economy remained soft for several years, even in recovery.

Surrounding these factors, however, was a history of a steady increase in union wages relative to nonunion wages during much of the period after the Korean War and in the 1970s. With the introduction of the Employment Cost Index (ECI) in 1976, these trends could not be measured directly and had to be estimated. Table 10−1, based on the ECI, clearly illustrates the relative wage creep of the union-to-nonunion wage ratio until 1982 to 1983, when concession bargaining reversed the trend. The concessions seemed to represent a transfer of previous union wage gains back to firm stockholders.[79]

TABLE 10−1 Private Union and Nonunion Annualized Pay Trends

	Percent Change in Pay								
	1976–1979	*1980*	*1981*	*1982*	*1983*	*1984*	*1985*	*1986*	*1987*
Wages and Salaries									
Union	8.2	10.9	9.6	6.5	4.6	3.4	3.1	2.0	2.6
Nonunion	7.3	8.0	8.5	6.1	5.2	4.5	4.6	3.5	3.6
Total Compensation									
Union	n.a.	11.1	10.7	7.2	5.8	4.3	2.6	2.1	2.8
Nonunion	n.a.	8.9	9.4	6.0	5.7	5.2	4.6	3.6	3.6

Source: Current Wage Developments, vol. 40 (March 1988), pp. 66−67, 74−75, and earlier issues.

In a sense, therefore, the long run arrived for collective bargaining in the 1980s. In another sense it arrived earlier, although it was at first largely unseen. During the 1960s and 1970s, a puzzle emerged regarding union membership. Not only was it declining in the private sector relative to the overall workforce, but it was declining *faster* than could be explained by simple statistical analysis of employment patterns. The obvious explanation, that the slippage reflected a change in industrial mix away from industries in which unions had traditionally been strong, did not account for all of the slippage.[80] A substantial fraction of the erosion was left unexplained.

Moreover, explanations based on changing workforce characteristics are not really satisfactory. Why should unions not have expanded into new industries as these industries arose? Is there something, for example, intrinsically different about workers in, say, high-tech electronics, that makes them immune from unionization? The same question can be asked about blue-collar workers in other new industries where unionization is low. Clearly there must be some other factor accounting for the situation.

Changes in Management Strategy

With the benefit of hindsight, researchers began to unravel the mystery in the late 1970s and early 1980s. In essence, they found evidence of the emergence of a new, nonunion model of human resource management that had developed slowly in the 1960s and flowered in the 1970s.[81] Management had been shellshocked by the growth of unionization in the 1930s and 1940s and had tended to take a passive role in the workplace, responding to union demands if unionized, and to union examples if not. As noted earlier, for example, innovations in fringe benefits were largely the product of union pressure in the 1950s. By the 1960s, however, management began to become more proactive.

Proactive, nonunion management basically followed one of two models. It could innovate in the human resource area and create an environment in which workers saw little benefit in joining unions. That route involved substantial attention to employee communications, potential grievances, the quality of supervision, and in some cases mechanisms for employee involvement in workplace decision making. The approach also involved paying relatively high wages and benefits.[82]

An alternative route was to take an overtly hostile approach to union organizing, even if illegal unfair labor practices might be entailed. For example, firing employees because they are union sympathizers is unlawful in principle. However, the legal penalty—which might not be invoked until after prolonged litigation—is simply reinstatement of the discharged worker with back pay. Although entailing some cost, a few firings might be sufficient to end an organizing campaign. If not, resistance could continue even after the NLRB certified the union as representing a work group. It might be possible, for example, to avoid concluding an initial contract with the union, eventually undermining its status.[83]

Whatever route of resistance management took, it appears that the rising union–nonunion wage premium intensified management's efforts to stay or become nonunion.[84] Although that premium might have caused nonunion workers to become interested in unionizing, the concession bargaining of the 1980s seemed to have the reverse effect. Survey evidence suggests that nonunion workers—perhaps becoming more doubtful about what unions could do for them—turned less favorable toward the idea of unionization during the concession bargaining era.[85] They may have seen unions as harbingers of trouble rather than as protectors of pay and security.

Union Reactions to Adverse Climate of the 1980s

Unions began to react to the perceived management offensive in the 1980s. Concession bargaining to save jobs was one reaction. Although the median voter–union member might have had difficulty appreciating the wage–employment trade-off when the issue was merely a small shift along the labor demand curve, the matter became much clearer when closing an entire plant or a mass layoff was threatened. Detailed perception is not needed in such cases. The question becomes whether the employer's demand curve for labor will exist, not what its slope may be. Threatened by a plant closing or mass layoff, the median union voter could no longer count on rules such as layoffs by reverse order of seniority to protect his or her job and the value of his or her stake in remaining with the employer.

Unions began to be interested in economic and managerial issues previously considered off limits. A far greater degree of self-criticism was evidenced in union officialdom, especially at the national level, than had ever been exhibited previously.[86] The upshot was more willingness to try new ideas.

In the collective-bargaining area, unions experimented with employee ownership, representation on corporate boards, team production approaches, profit sharing, and corporate campaigns. This last approach involved pressuring employers through devices other than strikes, since strikes were often seen as potentially very costly and likely to create job loss. Corporate campaigns have included removal of union funds from banks in a close business relationship to the offending employer, innovative public relations, consumer boycotts, pressure on shareholders, and so on.[87]

Moreover, union officials—at least at the national level—seem to have become more sophisticated about the economic forces that confront the firms with which they bargain. They have become participants in efforts aimed at heading off or channeling hostile takeovers. And they have taken more positive stances toward quality of working life innovations than were typical in the 1970s.

For example, unions have participated in quality circle programs under various names. Under these arrangements, workers and supervisors meet in groups aimed at increasing productivity and maintaining quality standards. Team production methods—sometimes termed the team concept—have also been used in some union situations. Under the team concept the number of detailed job classifications is reduced and workers are given wider responsibility over production. Moves in these directions have not been uniform, nor have the results always been successful. Where such moves have occurred, moreover, union officials have sometimes found themselves charged with selling out to management interests.[88]

These developments and the pressures that sparked them have been the subject of numerous Labor Day feature articles in the popular press. Analogies have been made to turning around a battleship to express the difficulty of changing entrenched patterns of thinking and behavior in the union movement. The challenge is even more difficult than that analogy suggests, since, with the membership losses in the 1980s, the union battleship was plainly taking on water at the same time it was endeavoring to change direction.

As of this writing, therefore, the most that can be said is that the efforts at change have yet to produce evidence of a reversal of past trends. Survey data from the late 1970s suggested that about one-third of nonunion workers in the private sector would vote for union representation in an election if they had the opportunity to do so.[89] Significantly, the proportions are higher than average for young people and women, groups that have not been heavily represented by unions. As of the late 1980s, however, unions had not developed a strategy for recruiting these people in large numbers in the face of a hostile organizing environment.[90]

10–4   Implications for Management

The union sector of the labor force operates differently in many important respects from the nonunion sector. Substantial government regulation is imposed on the union sector, and a climate of legalism pervades union–management relations. Union workers typically earn higher wages and benefits than their nonunion counterparts. A heavy reliance on seniority in determining layoffs, recalls, and other workplace conditions is common in collective-bargaining contracts. Emphasis on the welfare of workers with more seniority is explained partly by the median voter model of the union's political decision-making process.

Outcomes of collective bargaining and trends in union membership can be importantly influenced by the political/legal and economic climates. Unions faced a variety of adverse forces from both sources in the 1980s. The result was a strengthened management hand, a rash of concession bargaining, and declines in union membership. These developments, in turn, triggered an unprecedented soul-searching within the union movement, and the consequences are as yet uncertain.

The shrinkage of the union sector and the evident weakening of union bargaining positions poses an ironic challenge for management. An aging work-force—such as the United States will feature for the balance of this century—is one that will be progressively concerned about job security. In the past the presence of unions has reduced the demand for government regulation—extensive though it is—in the workplace on the grounds that the employer–employee relationship can be determined by collective bargaining. However, with 14% of private wage and salary workers organized (as of 1987), that view is no longer reasonable.

Political moods can vary considerably. The 1980s was a period of government deregulation, at least at the federal level. Even so, Congress moved to protect older workers from mandatory retirement and required advance notification of plant closings and mass layoffs. Some limits on plant closing were also adopted at the state level. Federal legislation in the 1980s gave laid-off workers limited rights to continue their employment-related health benefits.[91] In short, a swing in the political climate could produce a host of new legislative restrictions on management.

There have been signs of discomfort by political leaders and in public discussions over various management practices. American business has been accused of following shortsighted policies that have eroded U.S. international competitiveness. Waves of mergers and acquisitions have been criticized as disruptive. Legislative inquiries have been held into financial scandals.

A climate of union bashing could easily produce a backlash that would adversely affect management's long-term interests. The productivity estimates of the 1980s showed little evidence that efficiency has been markedly improved by union weakness or corporate reorganizations. Thus management has not been able to demonstrate that its human resource policies have, at the aggregate level, laid a basis for a substantial improvement in real incomes.

Unions in the 1960s and 1970s often ignored the long-run implications of their individual decisions and had to live with the consequences in the 1980s. With the benefits of hindsight unions have identified some of their problems, but in a period when it is difficult for them to make substantial changes. Are there no lessons to be learned by management from the experience of its union counterparts?

Consider the following scenario. Suppose by federal and/or state law, employers were required to justify individual firings in court or before some tribunal. As the next chapter will point out, moves in that direction actually developed in the 1970s and 1980s. Suppose also that federal or state law began to mandate the provision of various types of fringe benefits, such as health insurance. Again, the idea is not hypothetical. Massachusetts adopted such a program in the 1980s and proposals for similar legislation in other states and at the federal level were debated. Suppose, finally, that the plant closing notification requirement adopted in the late 1980s was expanded into overt limitations on management's freedom to lay off workers for economic reasons.

Clearly HR managers would not favor such additional restrictions. They would prefer to work out their own company policies regarding what forms of compensation are provided, what standards for discipline should be applied, and if and when layoffs are to occur. Where collective bargaining is used, of course, unions impose certain restraints on management in these areas, but the issues are still worked out locally and privately. If government imposes the restraints and requirements, there may well be less flexibility for management and less attention to local needs than under collective bargaining. That is why organized management needs to think carefully about the long-term implication of a continued decline of organized labor. If employees do not find a way to voice their interests through bargaining, they may turn instead to the political process.[92]

Summary

Union contracts include more than just the specification of wages and benefits. Commonly included is a variety of contractual features designed to protect and maintain both the employer–employee relationship and the union–management relationship. Employment security for individual employees is protected through the grievance mechanism, various workrules, seniority rules, and other devices. The union–management relationship is sustained by union security clauses such as the union shop, by long-term contracts, and by an implicit understanding that the relationship outlasts the written agreement.

Although models of the bargaining process have often looked mainly at union objectives, collective bargaining involves both union and management; a union-only focus is very misleading. Moreover, the political nature of unions is difficult to reduce to the simple maximizing economists generally prefer to contemplate. Unions may be able to operate successfully over an extended period without substantial knowledge of underlying industry or company economics precisely because management's role is to protect the economic interest of the enterprise. In the long run, however, a lack of union ability to analyze the wage–employment trade-off can lead to adverse consequences for unions, as the era of concession bargaining in the 1980s dramatically illustrated.

Union bargaining power has traditionally been grounded in the strike weapon, although other tactics are also applied. Even if a strike is not ultimately called, management will make concessions if it fears a costly enough strike. The occurrence of a strike is more than a random mistake made by the parties about each other's objectives. Strikes sometimes occur, even if both negotiating teams can foresee the likely outcome, because of the need to maintain credible positions over the long run—that is, ongoing strategic concerns can dominate the outcome of any particular dispute.

The primary alternative to strikes is some form of interest arbitration. Interest arbitration, however, has not been popular, especially in the private sector, because of a longstanding fear that the process will chill meaningful bargaining. Recent economic research, however, suggests that the underlying rationale for a chilling effect is flawed. Creative experimentation with interest arbitration should therefore be encouraged.

Declining unionization has been seen by management as an opportunity for increased employer flexibility. The long-term political impact, however, may be just the reverse. Government has shown increasing signs of intervening in the workplace in place of collective bargaining.

EXERCISES

Problem

Find reference to a major strike situation and develop a chronology of what occurred. What were the initial offers and demands of both sides? Why do you think the strike occurred? What role, if any, did mediation play in reaching a settlement? If the employer was a private company with a publicly traded stock, how did the market react as negotiations and then the strike occurred? What was the market reaction to the settlement?

Questions

1. What factors might make union members especially concerned about job security?

2. How does the grievance mechanism in union contracts protect job security?

3. What should be the management position with regard to union security clauses?

4. Are strikes the result of mistakes? Explain.

5. What steps might be taken by public policy to reduce the incidence of strikes?

6. What changes in union and management strategies developed in the 1980s?

7. What issues are raised by the federal requirement that employers provide sixty days' advance notice of plant closings and mass layoffs?

Terms

agency shop	Hicks's strike model	scope of bargaining
bumping rights	interest arbitration	Supplemental
chilling effect	layoffs by reverse order of	Unemployment Benefits
concession bargaining	seniority	(SUB)
eighty-day cooling-off	mediation	Taft-Hartley Act
period	multiyear contracts	union shop
featherbedding	no-strike clause	work-to-rule tactics
final offer arbitration	Railway Labor Act	workrules
free rider problem	right-to-work laws	

ENDNOTES

1. Union workers typically have longer tenures on the job than nonunion workers, thus giving them a special stake in continued employment. See John T. Addison and Alberto C. Castro, "The Importance of Lifetime Jobs: Differences Between Union and Nonunion Workers," *Industrial and Labor Relations Review*, vol. 40 (April 1987), pp. 393–405.

2. Bureau of National Affairs, *Basic Patterns in Union Contracts*, eleventh edition (Washington: BNA, 1986), pp. 41–42.

3. Bureau of National Affairs, *Basic Patterns, op. cit.*, pp. 68–70.

4. Groups representing management, however, tend to urge advance notice to ease the transition for the laid-off employees. See National Association of Manufacturers, *When a Plant Closes: A Guide for Employers* (Washington: NAM, 1983), pp. 12–13. Lack of long advance notice periods as a general practice has been cited by advocates of legislative limits on plant closings at the state and federal levels.

5. The advance notice provisions were originally incorporated into a foreign trade bill vetoed by President Reagan, largely because of their inclusion. The trade bill was then passed without the advance notice provisions and signed into law. A separate bill carrying the advance notice provisions was passed and sent to the president, who permitted it to become law without signing it, thus avoiding a second veto of a popular bill in the 1988 election year.

6. Bureau of National Affairs, *Basic Patterns, op. cit.,* pp. 33–40.

7. The Taft-Hartley Act has an "anti-featherbedding" provision that has proved to be inconsequential in practical application.

8. The Brotherhood of Locomotive Firemen and Engineers became part of the newly formed United Transportation Union in 1969.

9. Richard B. Freeman and James L. Medoff, *What Do Unions Do?* (New York: Basic Books, 1984), Chapter 11; Steven G. Allen, "Human Resource Practices and Union-Management Productivity Differences," working paper for presentation at the Academy of Management meetings of August 1988, Department of Economics, North Carolina State University, July 1988.

10. Bureau of National Affairs, *Basic Patterns, op. cit.,* pp. 100–104. All data cited in this section are taken from this reference.

11. There is thus little practical difference between the union shop and the agency shop discussed later in the text.

12. Some versions of agency shops permit payment of the equivalent of dues and assessments to a private charity rather than to the union. Agency shop clauses are more commonly found in the public than the private sector because they represent a compromise on the freedom of association issue discussed below in the text.

13. The Taft-Hartley Act, Section 14(b), specifically gives states the right to enact such laws. Periodic efforts by unions to persuade Congress to repeal Section 14(b) have been unsuccessful.

14. Henry S. Farber, "Right-to-Work Laws and the Extent of Unionization," *Journal of Labor Economics,* vol. 2 (July 1984), pp. 319–352. There is some evidence that R-T-W laws lower the union wage advantage. See Sandra Christensen and Dennis Maki, "The Wage Effect of Compulsory Union Membership," *Industrial and Labor Relations Review,* vol. 36 (January 1983), pp. 230–238. This is consistent with the general tendency for the wage of union members to be a few dollars higher than the wage of union-represented workers (members and nonmembers combined) in Current Population Survey data.

15. Public (noncommercial) radio and TV broadcasting stations face this dilemma. Anyone can receive their signal. Whether an individual does or does not receive the signal has no effect on the cost of sending it. Nor can such receipt be detected. Hence there is a temptation to watch or listen but not pay. Such broadcasters often engage in public appeals and gimmicks such as auctions and prizes to induce free riders to contribute to the station's upkeep.

16. For example, a union may not legally negotiate a contract providing a pay raise only for its members. Apart from the legal restriction, such a contract might not be wise policy for the union. If the union raised the pay of only union members, the employer would have an incentive to substitute nonunion workers for union members.

17. There are complex legal rules under which a worker forced to pay fees to a union need not pay for political activities. Thus workers have an option other than dropping their membership if they object to the union's political policies.

18. De-authorization polls are sometimes used as indirect decertification elections. The latter completely end the union's status as the exclusive bargaining representative. The NLRB generally will not hold such elections while a union–management contract is in effect. It will hold a de-authorization poll at any time (contract or not), and a union that loses such a poll is on notice that its status with the workers it represents is extremely fragile. In the original Taft-Hartley Act, there was also a requirement that before a union shop could be put into effect, a majority vote in a union shop authorization poll had to be obtained. This requirement swamped the NLRB with work, and in most cases workers voted in favor of the union shop. Congress eliminated the authorization poll requirement in 1951, but retained the de-authorization poll.

19. One study finds that senior workers in the public sector are more likely to become union members than are junior workers. This finding fits well with the notion that unions focus more on the needs of senior workers. See John M. Jermier, Cynthia Fryer Cohen, and Jeannie Gaines, "Paying Dues to the Union: A Study of Blue-Collar Workers in a Right-to-Work Environment," *Journal of Labor Research,* vol. 9 (Spring 1988), pp. 167–181.

20. The data are from *Employment and Earnings,* vol. 35 (January 1988), p. 223. It might be noted that states with right-to-work laws banning union security clauses tend to be those with low unionization rates. That is, most union-represented workers are not located in these states.

21. The issue is more complex than can be discussed here since the attitudes of public and private workers may not be identical.

22. The next chapter discusses the "duty of fair representation" imposed by law on unions. Under this duty unions must fairly represent all in the bargaining unit and can be sued if they do not. Most often, such suits are filed by grievants who are dissatisfied by the union's handling of their case or by a refusal of the union to take the case to arbitration. As a result, unions sometimes feel under legal pressure to pursue grievances they realize have little merit.

23. Of course, where the companies have facilities in states with right-to-work laws, such clauses do not operate.

24. In the mid-1970s General Motors experimented with a southern strategy under which management resisted unionization at new facilities in the south. However, because GM's plants are highly interdependent, the United Auto Workers (UAW) has considerable bargaining clout. After frictions over the southern strategy, the company agreed to remain neutral in future organizing campaigns. The issue arose again at a joint GM-Toyota venture in northern California, which was to operate at a previously closed GM plant. GM management initially indicated that the joint venture was a different company and suggested that former workers might not be rehired. Eventually, an understanding was reached whereby most of the former workers were rehired, thus ensuring UAW representation.

25. GM and the UAW agreed that GM workers from other facilities would be the first hired at Saturn. Since these workers would be UAW members, the arrangement virtually guarantees UAW representation at Saturn. The Saturn arrangement was challenged by the National Right to Work Committee, an employer group that has sponsored right-to-work legislation. The NLRB found, however, that the arrangement passed legal muster.

26. Bureau of National Affairs, *Basic Patterns, op. cit.*, pp. 1–3, 93–99.

27. Reopeners have been based on the outcome of pending litigation or the passage or repeal of some federal legislation.

28. Strikes might be more likely after a long period because potential disagreements have had a longer time to accumulate.

29. See Sanford M. Jacoby and Daniel J.B. Mitchell, "Does Implicit Contracting Explain Explicit Contracting?" in Barbara D. Dennis, ed., *Proceedings of the Thirty-Fifth Annual Meeting,* Industrial Relations Research Association, December 28–30, 1982 (Madison, Wisc.: IRRA, 1983), pp. 319–328; David Card, "Longitudinal Analysis of Strike Activity," working paper no. 2263, National Bureau of Economic Research, May 1987; Sanford M. Jacoby and Daniel J.B. Mitchell, "Employer Preferences for Long-Term

Union Contracts," *Journal of Labor Research,* vol. 5 (Summer 1984), pp. 215–228.

30. Sometimes, as a legal matter, certain contractual obligations live on after the expiration date. This issue sometimes arises in connection with the employer's obligation to arbitrate grievances.

31. The following analysis owes much to Arthur M. Ross, *Trade Union Wage Policy* (Berkeley: University of California Press, 1948). Themes developed below were originally discussed in Daniel J.B. Mitchell, "Union Wage Policies: The Ross-Dunlop Debate Reopened," *Industrial Relations,* vol. 11 (February 1972), 46–61; and Daniel J.B. Mitchell, *Unions, Wages, and Inflation* (Washington: Brookings Institution, 1980), pp. 64–77.

32. In Figure 10–1 let W = the wage per employee and E = the number of employees. Then the payroll $P = WE$. To maximize P, we can differentiate by E and set the result equal to zero. Thus $[(dW/dL)L] + W = 0$ and therefore $-(W/L)(dL/dW) = 1$. The left-hand side of this equation is the elasticity of labor demand. The payroll is maximized when the absolute value of the elasticity of demand equals 1.

33. The isoprofit line shown in Figure 10–2 is one of a family of such lines, with *lower* lines representing more profits. Higher profits are consistent with lower lines, since lower lines represent lower wage costs, given any arbitrary level of employment.

34. The analysis in this section follows that presented in various works including Thomas J. Kniesner and Arthur H. Goldsmith, "A Survey of Alternative Models of the U.S. Labor Market," *Journal of Economic Literature,* vol. 25 (September 1987), p. 1267; and Barry T. Hirsch and John T. Addison, *The Economic Analysis of Unions: New Approaches and Evidence* (Boston: Allen & Unwin, 1986), pp. 14–18. However, use of union indifference curves has been omitted, since collective indifference curves are questionable concepts.

35. In Section 2(9) the Wagner Act defines a labor dispute as a controversy over the terms or conditions of employment.

36. The legal concept of good-faith bargaining is a complex matter that will not be considered further in this volume. The reader can readily see that a judgment of whether bargaining has occurred in good faith can have a strong subjective element. Thus the concept is one of the areas in which legalism has crept into the collective-bargaining system.

37. Management can voluntarily discuss such matters with unions, but unions may not strike to force management to hold such discussions or to accede to demands that might be made over such voluntary subjects. As in the case of good-faith bargaining, the distinction between mandatory and voluntary subjects of bargaining and the determina-

tion of what issues have triggered a strike are legally complex matters.

38. Not surprisingly, unions in industries dominated by small firms and relatively unsophisticated employers were more likely to demonstrate economic expertise in their industries' problems. In effect, unions stepped into a void left by management. Often cited in this regard were unions in the areas of apparel, coal mining, and longshoring.

39. Two states permit unemployment insurance payments to strikers after a waiting period. In addition, in some states, if a labor dispute is determined to be an employer lockout rather than a strike, workers may receive unemployment insurance.

40. "Economic strikers," that is, workers involved in a simple dispute involving contract negotiations, are not legally entitled to their jobs once replaced. They simply have the right to fill any vacancies that may later arise. Of course, if the firm has successfully replaced its striking workforce, there may be no vacancies.

41. U.S. Bureau of Labor Statistics, *Directory of National Unions and Employee Associations, 1979,* bulletin 2079 (Washington: GPO, 1980), pp. 73–75; Joan Borum, James Conley, and Edward Wasilewski, "The Outlook for Collective Bargaining in 1988," *Monthly Labor Review,* vol. 111 (January 1988), p. 11; *Employment and Earnings,* vol. 35 (January 1988), p. 223.

42. Data on strikes and new union settlements were drawn from various issues of *Current Wage Developments.* Included are state and local, private, and postal settlements.

43. Because of limited information on the causes of strikes reported by BLS, it is not possible to segregate strikes due to negotiations from other strikes. However, prior to the 1980s, when BLS collected and published more detailed strike information, most of the workers involved in large strikes were in fact participating in contract-negotiation disputes.

44. A study of private contracts involving 1,000 or more workers in the 1970s found a strike probability of about 13%. See Cynthia L. Gramm, "New Measures of the Propensity to Strike During Contract Negotiations, 1971–1980," *Industrial and Labor Relations Review,* vol. 40 (April 1987), pp. 406–417.

45. In general, small strikes—involving less than 1,000 workers—involve different behavioral responses than large strikes. See Jack W. Skeels, Paul McGrath, and Gangadha Arshanapalli, "The Importance of Strike Size in Strike Research," *Industrial and Labor Relations Review,* vol. 41 (July 1988), pp. 582–591.

46. One study found, for example, that strike propensities were lower when settlements followed traditional patterns. See Martin J. Mauro, "Strikes as a Result of Imperfect Infor-

mation," *Industrial and Labor Relations Review,* vol. 35 (July 1982), pp. 522–538.

47. A review of the economic literature through the late 1970s appears in Michael Shalev, "Trade Unionism and Economic Analysis: The Case of Industrial Conflict," *Journal of Labor Research,* vol. 1 (Spring 1980), pp. 133–173.

48. John R. Hicks, *The Theory of Wages,* 2nd edition (New York: St. Martin's Press, 1966), pp. 136–157. Further discussion of this theory can be found in Robert J. Flanagan, Robert S. Smith, and Ronald G. Ehrenberg, *Labor Economics and Labor Relations* (Glenview, Ill.: Scott, Foresman, 1984), pp. 478–481.

49. An empirical estimate of union concession schedules appears in Henry S. Farber, "Bargaining Theory, Wage Outcomes, and the Occurrence of Strikes: An Econometric Analysis," *American Economic Review,* vol. 68 (June 1978), pp. 262–271.

50. Industrial Union Department, AFL-CIO, *The Inside Game: Winning with Workplace Strategies* (Washington: IUD, AFL-CIO, 1986).

51. Joseph S. Tracy, "An Investigation into the Determinants of U.S. Strike Activity," *American Economic Review,* vol. 76 (June 1986), pp. 423–436.

52. There is no requirement that a union go on strike if negotiations extend past the contract expiration date. Sometimes, if there is a sense that a settlement will be reached shortly, the union may continue to work without a contract. Also, strategic considerations may lead the union to delay a strike until a more propitious time, say, when the firm will have more orders (and would thus lose more business if a strike occurs). The expiration date is a critical point, however; failure to strike in the absence of strong momentum to reach a settlement might communicate union weakness to management.

53. Picketing is a common union strike tactic. It is subject to a variety of legal restrictions and doctrines which, for the sake of brevity, are not reviewed in this text.

54. This statement should not be interpreted as indicating that imperfect information plays no role in explaining strikes. There is evidence that it is a *partial* explanation. See Jean-Michel Cousineau and Robert Lacroix, "Imperfect Information and Strikes: An Analysis of Canadian Experience, 1967–82," *Industrial and Labor Relations Review,* vol. 39 (April 1986), pp. 377–387.

55. Suppose unions initially fail to observe that management's hand in bargaining is strengthened in recessions. They might futilely strike against management proposals during recessions. This hypothetical blindness on the union side would make strikes countercyclical. Over time, however, they would see that such resistance does not produce the desired results and would become more willing to acquiesce. Thus any association between recession and strikes should dis-

appear. Strikes would occur at random in booms and busts. As noted in the text, however, strike activity is associated with the business cycle and is, in fact, procyclical.

56. Albert Rees, "Industrial Conflict and Business Fluctuations," *Journal of Political Economy,* vol. 60 (October 1952), pp. 371–382, was the first to note the procyclical nature of strikes. Later researchers have incorporated inflation into the model and argue that inflationary developments partly explain the cyclical motion of strikes. See Cynthia L. Gramm, Wallace E. Hendricks, and Lawrence M. Kahn, "Inflation Uncertainty and Strike Activity," *Industrial Relations,* vol. 27 (Winter 1988), pp. 114–129; Bruce E. Kaufman, "Bargaining Theory, Inflation, and Cyclical Strike Activity in Manufacturing," *Industrial and Labor Relations Review,* vol. 34 (April 1981), pp. 333–355; Bruce E. Kaufman, "The Determinants of Strikes in the United States," *Industrial and Labor Relations Review,* vol. 35 (July 1982), pp. 473–490. Inflation may systematically erode the real wage of workers in some cases and increase the propensity for labor disputes. See Daniel J.B. Mitchell, "A Note on Strike Propensities and Wage Developments," *Industrial Relations,* vol. 20 (Winter 1981), pp. 123–127.

57. Brian E. Becker and Craig A. Olson, "The Impact of Strikes on Shareholder Equity," *Industrial and Labor Relations Review,* vol. 39 (April 1986), pp. 425–438. References to earlier articles on the subject appear in this paper.

58. The impact of the ongoing union–management relationship on strike activity is emphasized in Melvin W. Reder and George R. Neumann, "Conflict and Contract: The Case of Strikes," *Journal of Political Economy,* vol. 88 (October 1980), pp. 867–886.

59. It has been observed that having a strike in a previous negotiation cuts down the probability of having one subsequently. This observation is consistent with the ongoing learning model described in the text. See John F. Schnell and Cynthia L. Gramm, "Learning by Striking: Estimates of the Teetotaler Effect," *Journal of Labor Economics,* vol. 5 (April 1987), pp. 221–241.

60. The Railway Labor Act also covers the airline industry. As a result neither railroads nor airlines are covered by the Wagner/Taft-Hartley framework.

61. In 1974, amendments to the Wagner/Taft-Hartley framework brought private health care institutions under NLRB jurisdiction. Special features were incorporated, designed to reduce strikes in the health care sector. Among them was a ninety-day advance notice period, rather than the sixty days required in other industries.

62. The result of the Congressional requirement is simply that sixty days before the contract's expiration, a letter will be sent by one side to the other requesting that a new contract be negotiated.

63. A mediation service existed in the U.S. Department of Labor prior to the 1947 Act. Congress feared political involvement of the executive branch in private negotiations and hence created the FMCS as an independent agency outside of a cabinet department.

64. State governments may also have mediation services available to collective-bargaining negotiators.

65. We will not discuss here the so-called nonstoppage strike. In one version of a nonstoppage strike, workers remain on the job, but receive no pay, and management gives away its profits to charity. Thus public inconvenience is avoided while an approximation of strike costs is visited on the parties. There have been a handful of such experiments, but the device seems impractical because the negotiation of the cost formula is so difficult. (If the parties could negotiate the formula, presumably they should be able to negotiate the settlement!)

66. The terminology is said to be of Scandinavian origin. See Frank Elkouri and Edna Asper Elkouri, *How Arbitration Works,* third edition (Washington: BNA, 1973), p. 47.

67. Compulsory arbitration is used in some cases in the public sector. For example, workers at the U.S. Postal Service are covered by such a system. Some state laws require arbitration of interest disputes involving government employees.

68. The FMCS does not supply arbitrators but rather runs a referral service for private arbitrators. Data on the type of arbitration conducted as a result of these referrals appear in the annual reports of the FMCS.

69. Max H. Bazerman and Henry S. Farber, "Arbitrator Decision Making: When Are Final Offers Important?," *Industrial and Labor Relations Review,* vol. 39 (October 1985), pp. 76–89.

70. Elkouri and Elkouri, *How Arbitration Works, op. cit.,* pp. 745–796.

71. David E. Bloom and Christopher L. Cavanagh, "Negotiation Behavior Under Arbitration," working paper no. 2211, National Bureau of Economic Research, April 1987.

72. Max H. Bazerman and Henry S. Farber, "Arbitration Decision Making: When Are Final Offers Important?," *Industrial and Labor Relations Review,* vol. 39 (October 1985), pp. 76–89.

73. The steel industry and the United Steelworkers union established a system of voluntary binding interest arbitration in the 1970s. The parties always managed, however, to reach a private settlement without invoking the arbitration process.

74. On this point, see the discussion in David E. Bloom, "Is Arbitration *Really* Compatible with Bargaining?," *Industrial Relations,* vol. 20 (Fall 1981), pp. 233–244. Risk aversion by both parties is assumed.

75. Final offer arbitration has been used in professional sports to settle disputes between individual players and team owners.

76. There have been suggestions for closed offer arbitration in which, prior to negotiations, the parties would submit sealed contract proposals to an arbitrator, who would not disclose either side's position. The arbitrator would make a decision only on the basis of the sealed positions and only if the parties could not privately arrive at a settlement. Having submitted their sealed offers, the parties would then bargain normally since their offers and counteroffers would not influence the arbitrator. There would be no incentives to take extreme positions in the negotiations since the negotiations and the arbitration process would be kept wholly separate. Whether it would actually be possible to keep the arbitrator ignorant of bargaining developments— as the idea requires—is unclear. One possibility would be for the arbitrator to prepare an award based on the sealed offers prior to negotiations.

77. David E. Bloom and Christopher L. Cavanagh, "An Analysis of the Selection of Arbitrators," *American Economic Review*, vol. 76 (June 1986), pp. 408–422.

78. Issues related to international competition will be discussed in a later chapter.

79. Brian E. Becker, "Concession Bargaining: The Impact on Shareholders' Equity," *Industrial and Labor Relations Review*, vol. 40 (January 1987), pp. 268–279.

80. William T. Dickens and Jonathan S. Leonard, "Accounting for the Decline in Union Membership, 1950–1980," *Industrial and Labor Relations Review*, vol. 38 (April 1985), pp. 323–334.

81. Thomas A. Kochan, Harry C. Katz, and Robert B. McKersie, *The Transformation of American Industrial Relations* (New York: Basic Books, 1986).

82. Fred K. Foulkes, *Personnel Policies in Large Nonunion Companies* (Englewood Cliffs, N.J.: Prentice-Hall, 1980).

83. Paul Weiler, "Promises to Keep: Securing Workers' Rights to Self-Organization under the NLRA," *Harvard Law Review*, vol. 96 (June 1983), pp. 1769–1827; Paul Weiler, "Striking a New Balance: Freedom of Contract and the Prospects for Union Representation," *Harvard Law Review*, vol. 98 (December 1984), pp. 351–420; U.S. General Accounting Office, *Concerns Regarding Impact of Employee Charges Against Employers for Unfair Labor Practices*, GAO/ HRD–82–80 (Washington: GAO, 1982); William N.

Cooke, "The Failure to Negotiate First Contracts: Determinants and Policy Implications," *Industrial and Labor Relations Review*, vol. 38 (January 1985), pp. 163–178.

84. Richard B. Freeman, "The Effect of the Union Wage Differential on Management Opposition and Union Organizing Success," working paper no. 1748, National Bureau of Economic Research, October 1985.

85. Henry S. Farber, "The Decline of Unionization in the United States: What Can Be Learned from Recent Experience," working paper no. 2267, National Bureau of Economic Research, May 1987.

86. Perhaps the most tangible evidence of this change in attitude was a special report published by the AFL-CIO and widely circulated to its constituent unions. See American Federation of Labor–Congress of Industrial Organizations, *The Changing Situation of Workers and Their Unions* (Washington: AFL-CIO, 1985).

87. Charles R. Perry, *Union Corporate Campaigns* (Philadelphia: Industrial Relations Unit, Wharton School, University of Pennsylvania, 1987).

88. For critical comments on quality of working life approaches spawned by changes in union policy, see Mike Parker and Jane Slaughter, *Choosing Sides: Unions and the Team Concept* (Boston: South End Press, 1988); Mike Parker, *Inside the Circle: A Union Guide to QWL* (Boston: South End Press, 1985); Eric Mann, *Taking on General Motors: A Case Study of the UAW Campaign to Keep GM Van Nuys Open* (Los Angeles: UCLA Institute of Industrial Relations, 1987).

89. Richard B. Freeman and James L. Medoff, *What Do Unions Do?, op. cit.,* p. 29.

90. It has been suggested that the comparable worth issue can help unions recruit women members. See Richard B. Freeman and Jonathan S. Leonard, "Union Maids: Unions and the Female Workforce," working paper no. 1652, National Bureau of Economic Research, June 1985. Coming up with an appealing strategy for attracting younger workers is difficult because of the seniority orientation of unions.

91. Former employees are required to pay for the benefits if they want to continue them, but they pay at the employer's group rate.

92. Richard S. Belous, *Union Membership Trends: The Implications for Economic Policy and Labor Legislation*, report no. 86–107 E (Washington: Congressional Research Service, 1986).

Chapter Eleven

CONFLICTS BETWEEN EMPLOYER AND EMPLOYEE GOALS

The two previous chapters have examined collective bargaining, under which the interests of employees *as a group* confront the interests of the employer. There may, however, be discrepancies between the interests of *individual* employees and their employers in both union and nonunion situations. For certain sources of employee discontent, there are often formal or informal mechanisms of resolution within the firm. In addition, employees have increasingly turned to external forums when they feel wronged by an employer's decision.

In this chapter causes of conflicts between employer and employee goals are analyzed, a distinction is made between employee complaints and grievances, mechanisms for resolving conflicts within the enterprise are considered, and finally the trend toward external resolution is probed.

11–1 Economic Modeling and Employee Discontent

The simple economic model of the labor market suggests that there cannot be real conflict between employer and employee goals unless some noncompetitive element is present. Workers in the abstract might want to be paid more for their services than they actually receive. In an atomistic marketplace, however, employees must accept what the auctioneer declares to be the wage that clears the market. The fact that they choose to work at the going wage must mean that, at the margin, workers are being paid what their time is worth to them. Only a noncompetitive element, such as a union or minimum wage law, might lead to rents being paid to workers.

Similarly, atomistic employers would like—other things being equal—to pay less than they actually do for labor. But they cannot pay less than the going rate and expect to hire any workers. Thus in the simple economic model, employers, too, must accept the market wage.

It must also be the case that workers are not overpaid. In the context of the simple auction model the word *overpaid* could only mean being paid more than marginal revenue product. Profit-maximizing employers would not hire workers who, at the margin, did not return a revenue equal to their cost. Only noncompetitive elements, such as employer monopsony or legal ceilings on wages (as during government programs of wage/price controls), could depress wages below marginal revenue product levels.

These same considerations from the simple economic model apply to nonwage conditions of work such as risk of injury or illness, pleasantness or unpleasantness of surroundings, or amicable or uncongenial supervision. The model predicts that wage premiums would compensate workers—in a market clearing sense—for elements in the workplace that lead to disutility. Thus risky jobs would pay more than safe ones and distasteful jobs more than pleasant ones. In this view the market harmonizes employer and employee interests, so long as competition prevails.

Despite this picture of workplace serenity, tensions do arise between employer and employee, even when unions, monopsony, or similar deviations from the auction market are not involved. As in other facets of human resource management, it is necessary to go beyond the simple economic model if we are to understand the underpinnings of employer–employee frictions. It is not necessary, however, to abandon the notion of rationality on the part of employees and employers; rather, it is a matter of introducing fixed costs of decisions, mobility costs, and the inherent vagueness of implicit contracts.

11–2   Complaints and Grievances

Before considering particular examples, it is useful to distinguish between two types of employee expressions of dissatisfaction: *complaints* and *grievances*. Grievances are forms of complaint, but standard HRM parlance defines them as allegations that a right of the employee is being (or has been) violated by the employer. In a union situation, grievances are allegations that a right contained explicitly or indirectly in the union contract is being abrogated by the employer. Union-sector grievances are normally processed through a formal grievance system, with a series of hierarchical appeals to employer representatives. If not resolved through such appeals, grievances can be taken to arbitration for a final and binding resolution by an outside neutral. Such arbitration is termed rights arbitration to distinguish it from the interest arbitration described in the previous chapter.

Grievances in a nonunion setting refer to violations of unilaterally determined management policies—perhaps as spelled out in a company handbook—rather than of provisions of a union–management contract. Generally, nonunion grievance procedures are less formal than those in the union sector; management may simply announce that it has an "open door" approach, meaning that employees can take their grievances to higher management officials, who will be willing to listen. Nonunion grievances usually are subject to final resolution by a top company official such as the CEO. A few nonunion companies, however, deliberately imitate standard union practice and provide for rights arbitration.[1]

Complaints are more general than grievances. Employees may be dissatisfied about almost any condition of work. They may dislike their supervisors, for example, or their benefit packages, or their pay rates. Workers may resent being subject to layoff when business conditions worsen. They may feel that working conditions are too hazardous or be angered by mandatory assignments of overtime work.

Unless company policies or union contracts are being violated regarding supervisory selection, benefits and pay, layoff rules, safety, or work assignments, workers' complaints are not subject to remedy by grievance procedures. Their dissatisfactions, though real, are not complaints over rights, but are akin to the interest disputes described in the previous chapter. The employee wishes that the policy or contract were different from what it actually is and thus is not protesting a violation.

A union-represented worker might want to have the union make demands on the employer to alleviate nongrievance complaints during contract negotiations. Although union officials are sensitive to the desires of members, there is no guarantee that the union will actually place a given complaint on its bargaining agenda. If it does bring the complaint to management's attention, the union may have other items with higher priority about which to bargain; it may drop the complaint from its list of negotiating demands in exchange for something else. Even if the union makes the complaint a top-priority item, it may not be successful in compelling management acceptance of its position.

A nonunion employee can, as an individual, threaten to quit if improvements are not made. Unless the employee possesses a relatively unique talent (as might be the case for a film star, high-level executive, or top scientist), this threat may not produce any results. Nonunion management, however, might be sensitive to employee dissatisfactions—possibly for reasons of union avoidance and possibly as a cost-minimizing strategy—and might take steps to alleviate the problems identified.

Nonunion firms with progressive HRM policies may survey employees to detect complaints and/or train and sensitize supervisors to do so. As in the union case, there is no guarantee that employee complaints will be resolved. Management may be aware of a complaint, and even be concerned about its effect on morale, but may feel that the solution would be too costly to implement.

This chapter discusses one example of a potential source of employee complaints, the quantity and scheduling of working hours. It looks into reasons why hours-related complaints might arise and options that employers might consider as remedies. Then the analysis turns to the processing of grievances under formalized grievance-handling systems. Finally, likely future developments in complaint resolution are considered.

11–3   Example of a Potential Complaint: Working Hours

Hours individuals supply the employer can differ in both quantity and schedule. Individuals can supply more or fewer hours per year, for example, working in some seasons, but not others. Within a week in which hours are supplied, work may be part-time rather than full-time, may or may not include overtime hours, or may or may not involve multiple employers (moonlighting).

Given a level of hours supplied per week, precisely *which* hours of the day are worked is normally important to employees. An individual might work on a day shift or a night shift, for example, or might or might not work on weekends. There are numerous employees who fall into the various categories. In that sense the U.S. labor market is flexible.

Although the labor market can be flexible in the sense that there is a variety of alternative hours and schedules, employees may still have complaints about their assigned working time. One of the characteristics of the labor market, as has been mentioned, is that it often does not clear in the classical sense. Individuals who are willing to work at going wage rates do not all find jobs. This deviation from the simple auction market that always clears has its counterpart in hours and working schedules.

Hours per Week

Just as individuals may have trouble finding any jobs at all, those with jobs may have positions that do not readily match their own preferences with regard to working time. This fact does not mean that individuals will not search for jobs that meet their hours needs, or that empirical surveys will not find evidence that such searching behavior takes place.[2] Nevertheless, some individuals who prefer full-time work to part-time must take part-time employment because they cannot find full-time positions. Others may wish that they could work part-time but, when faced with an alternative of full-time work or no time (no job), opt for the former.

In 1985, for example, questions dealing with preferred worksheet length were added to the Current Population Survey. Employees were asked whether they preferred the same hours that they actually had, with the same pay, to alternatives of either fewer hours with less pay or more hours with more pay. Of those responding, 64.9% preferred the status quo, 7.6% preferred the fewer hours/less pay option, and 27.5% preferred more hours/more pay.[3] In other words, roughly a third preferred an hours/pay option different from the actual situation.

Generally, males were more likely than females to prefer the more hours/more pay option (30.6% versus 25.5%). Higher paid workers, including managers and executives, were more likely than others to prefer fewer hours/less pay. Those working long workweeks were more likely to want fewer hours; those working short workweeks tilted in preference toward more hours.

Faced with this type of evidence, many economists would argue that these stated preferences are not really symptoms of a disequilibrium in the labor market. There is a semantic issue about whether someone who voluntarily takes a job with hours different from those he or she asserts to be preferred is or is not in equilibrium. This is the same semantic issue that has led some economists over the years to argue that unemployment is a voluntary form of leisure, that is, there is no such thing as involuntary unemployment.

In a certain, narrow sense these arguments are correct. Any situation observed in the labor market can be described as voluntary. Inherent in the concept of *employee,* however, is an agreement whereby the employed individual agrees to accept the authority of someone else to impose tasks and conditions.[4] The authority is not absolute; employees may refuse to undertake assignments that involve grave safety or health risks, for example, even if they must quit to do so.[5] Acceptance of authority, however, implies that detailed recontracting (renegotiations of the pay/conditions agreement) will not take place over every issue that arises. In particular, an assignment of working time is typically just that—an assignment that may not be wholly agreeable to the employee.

The real question is whether it is a help or a hindrance to human resource managers to view the labor market as always producing tranquil equilibria with no important implications for the firm. Just because all employment arrangements are ultimately voluntary, should employee dissatisfactions be ignored? The answer is "no." It is useful to view employee dissatisfaction as potentially costly to the employer and to consider appropriate HRM responses.

Indeed, the labor market itself abounds with evidence that employee dissatisfactions with its outcomes are not mere illusions. For example, the Current Population Survey suggests that deviations from preferred hours move cyclically with unemployment. Consider Table 11–1, which compares the movements in the aggregate unemployment rate with movements in the percentage of employees who reported that they worked less than 35 hours because of economic reasons. These reasons consist mainly of employee-reported "slack work" (not enough demand by the employer) and "could only find part-time work."[6] During the course of the 1979–1982 economic slump and the subsequent recovery, overall unemployment and involuntary part-time work moved together.

Since there is no reason to suppose that employee tastes for reduced hours rise with the unemployment rate, it must be concluded that some workers find themselves stuck in job situations that do not match their hours preferences. Specifically, as the unemployment rate rises, workers have progressively more difficulty finding desired working hours. These workers have a complaint about the working arrangements they end up accepting, not a grievance.

The complaint versus grievance distinction, although important in terms of the formal processing of grievances, may not matter very much for human resource management. Workers unhappy with their hours, however that dissatisfaction may be classified, might well quit when economic conditions improve, thus inflicting future turnover costs on the firm. They might also be less productive than other workers, whose hours preferences more closely match those of the employer, a cost that must be borne in the present.

TABLE 11–1 Unemployment and Proportion of Employees Reporting That
They Work Less Than Full Time Due to Economic Reasons,
1979–1987

Year	Total Unemployment Rate*	Employees Working Less Than Full Time for Economic Reasons as Percent of All Employees[†]
1979	5.8%	3.7%
1980	7.1	4.5
1981	7.6	4.9
1982	9.7	6.5
1983	9.6	6.5
1984	7.5	5.7
1985	7.2	5.4
1986	7.0	5.3
1987	6.2	5.0

*Civilian labor force.

[†]Persons at work in the nonagricultural sector.

Note: Full-time work is defined as thirty-five or more hours per week.

Source: Employment and Earnings, vol. 35 (January 1988), pp. 158, 196, and corresponding data from earlier issues.

On the other hand, it is not necessarily the case that workers who find themselves working fewer hours than they would otherwise like will resent the employer or exhibit behavior that reduces firm profitability. Much depends on the circumstances that led to the hours decision and how it is explained to the employees.

Some employers have policies, which they articulate to employees, of reducing hours per week before engaging in layoffs. Such policies often go under the heading of "work sharing." Workers in work-sharing firms may appreciate the job security being offered. They might regard the reduced hours as a temporary measure; the fact that the employer avoids layoffs may be seen as a good-faith continuance of the employer/employee implicit contract during hard times. A few states have actually accommodated their unemployment insurance systems to work-sharing programs, permitting partial benefits to be paid (in specified circumstances) for partial workweeks lost.[7]

Even without formal work-sharing arrangements, it is common practice for employers who normally use overtime work to reduce overtime hours before engaging in layoffs. According to the Current Population Survey, workers are more likely to express a preference for more hours/more pay than for hours/pay reductions. Hence overtime reductions probably create worker dissatisfaction, other things being equal. But when reduced hours are seen as part of a layoff avoidance strategy, workers may on balance appreciate management's effort to maintain employment.

Scheduling of Weekly Hours

Although it is common to think of normal work schedules as "9 to 5," the single most frequent full-time daily schedule is actually "8 to 5."[8] Most work shifts occur during the daytime, although some firms have evening and night shifts. In a formal sense, the heavy general bias toward daytime work is due to the position of the sun in the sky and to the internal biological rhythms of human beings. The precise scheduling of hours within the daytime period, however, is a complex matter.

There is a wider area of determination involved in shift scheduling than just individual employer and employee preferences. For example, when the government announces that there is to be a move from daylight savings time to standard time or vice versa on a specific date, almost every workplace shifts its schedule relative to solar time by one hour. Thus there is a heavy element of *external coordination* involved. Workplaces schedule operating hours at certain times because other workplaces—with which they do business—are also going to be open. In addition, retail businesses such as snack bars adjust their hours to the normal breakfast, lunch, and dinner hours that are produced by the schedules of other workplaces.

The fact that a government announcement greatly facilitates adjustment of schedules to seasonal variations in sunlight (by shifting from daylight time to standard and back) illustrates the value of central authority in such matters.[9] Individual businesses acting alone would have great difficulty making time adjustments unless they knew that all other businesses would make them simultaneously. This need for interfirm coordination helps explain why it is difficult for employers to adjust to the hours-scheduling preferences of workers whose needs do not match normal business schedules.

There are also *internal coordination* problems, that is, problems within the workplace that make it difficult for employers to adapt to the hours needs of individual workers. Many tasks in workplaces depend on teamwork and inherently require most or all of the team members to be present at the same time. Even when formal teamwork is not involved, individuals at the workplace often must interact on a regular basis with other employees. If they were freed from the constraints of external coordination of hours with other firms, employers still might find it extremely costly to permit individual workers to schedule their own hours. Hours scheduling is therefore more likely to reflect the preferences of the *average* employee, rather than those of the individual.

External and internal coordination difficulties explain why "flexitime" or "flextime" schedules, under which individuals (usually within some constraints) determine their hours, are comparatively rare. About 12% of full-time wage and salary workers reported themselves to be on flexible work schedules in 1985. Not surprisingly, the proportions were lowest among blue-collar workers, since production technology such as assembly lines would make individual scheduling very difficult. Managers and professionals tended to have higher incidences of flexible working schedules.[10] A relatively small number of wage and salary workers (as opposed to the self-employed) have arrangements permitting them to provide services at home.[11]

Work Hours and Leisure Hours

The fact that many individuals would prefer longer work *weeks* does not mean that they place little value on leisure. An important issue regarding leisure is how it is taken: in short, regular doses or in periodic large blocks. Having an extra half hour at home per day might not be of great value to many individuals, but having an occasional long weekend or a paid absence of a week or more might be much desired.

In the United States, the accommodation toward leisure preferences since World War II has tended to be in time off, especially in the form of paid vacations and holidays.[12] The existence of paid vacations and holidays (especially the former) is yet another symptom of the ongoing employer–employee relationship; it is hard to imagine what such benefits would mean in the context of a daily labor auction market. (In an auction market, a worker who wanted a day's leisure would simply not auction himself or herself off that day.)

Because holidays involve closing down the business, they raise the external coordination problems cited earlier. Not surprisingly, therefore, government often is involved in declaring national or state holidays. Private employers are not legally required to close on such holidays (or to pay workers for those days if they do close). Yet many do close down their operations, knowing that other firms on which they rely will also be closed.

Vacations, on the other hand, involve the absence of particular individuals, not complete business closings. External coordination issues do not arise. By controlling the number of workers on vacation at any point in time (or attempting to match that number with seasonal production swings), employers can reduce the problems vacation-related absences pose for internal coordination and teamwork.

If 5% of the workforce were typically on vacation on any day, the firm could simply adjust by having a 5% larger workforce than it would if there were no vacationers. Generally, however, employee preferences for vacations will not be spread evenly over the year. For this reason employers often do not permit employees to have complete discretion over when they take their vacations.

Supervisory approval is often required for the scheduling of a vacation. As a result, vacation scheduling can sometimes be a source of employer/employee friction, and HRM guidelines for supervisors may be helpful in reducing conflict. In some situations it may be possible to permit employees to work out their vacation schedules as a group, subject to constraining rules, for example, a given number of workers must always be present on a workday.

Hours and Employer–Employee Frictions

The issues surrounding the scheduling of work and the hours of work have been presented as examples of potential sources of employee complaints. Unless management violates a specified policy in assigning hours, holidays, and vacations, such complaints cannot be formally classified as grievances. Nor will standard grievance mechanisms resolve the resulting frictions. Employees may nonetheless be dissatisfied with management's decisions on hours, and these dissatisfactions may vary with business cycle pressures.

Human resource managers will want to be aware of such dissatisfactions, even if they have difficulty in alleviating them because of external and internal coordination needs. Employees may at least be mollified if explanations of these coordination problems are offered. Indeed, employees may have suggestions for accommodating alternative schedules. Although flexible scheduling is often difficult to accommodate and still comparatively rare, it *is* a growing phenomenon of the workplace, indicating that an employer response to worker preferences is taking place slowly.

11–4   Formal Grievance and Arbitration Procedures

Grievance mechanisms can be found in both union and nonunion settings in the private sector. In the public sector civil service procedures provide similar arrangements, even in the absence of a union. As already noted, private, nonunion grievance processes are less formal than those found in unionized firms, and—except in a few notable cases—nonunion grievances are not subject to final resolution by an outside arbitrator.

The mere fact that an outside arbitrator can be called in to settle an unresolved rights dispute partially accounts for the greater formality of grievance handling in the union sector. More often than not, arbitrators today come from a legal background. Although arbitrators typically do not insist on strict courtroom procedures and rules of evidence, such judicial concepts have had an influence on the way in which contemporary arbitration hearings are conducted. At a hearing, moreover, the representatives of the parties may also be attorneys, reinforcing the legalistic approach. As will be noted, legalism is sometimes viewed as a detriment to the ultimate goal of resolving workplace problems.

It is important to stress, however, that every grievance filed in the union sector does not necessarily require arbitration for its resolution. Arbitration is almost always specified as the final step if all else fails in the union–management contract. Although there is no national census on the subject, it can be assumed that the vast majority of grievances are settled before reaching the arbitration stage. In fact, many potential grievances may effectively be resolved before they are formally filed, or may simply be withdrawn or resolved very early in the process.

Generally, a grievance mechanism involves a series of hierarchical steps, any one of which can be the resolution point.[13] Almost half of all union contracts surveyed in the mid-1980s had a three-step process, and almost all had between two and four steps. In some instances the initial step may entail oral rather than written statements of the grievance and responses from management. Time limits, both for filing and for management's response, are often specified, and they are typically short. Under the Taft-Hartley Act of 1947, even when a union has representation rights, individual workers can present their own grievances to management if they so choose (Sec. 9[a]). As a practical matter most unionized grievants will want a union representative to make the presentation or at least to be present.

If not resolved at the first step, grievances typically proceed to mid-level steps that involve higher level management and union officials. A union–management grievance committee may be designated to meet regularly and consider pending cases. At the final step management might be represented by the director of industrial relations or, in a few instances, by still higher company officials.

Although grievances are often thought to be synonymous with disputes over employee discipline, many other issues can arise as grievances. Again, no national census of grievance issues exists. A partial source of information can be found, however, in reports of the Federal Mediation and Conciliation Service (FMCS). Apart from its duty of supplying parties to interest disputes with federal mediators, the FMCS also provides lists (panels) of private arbitrators to parties in need of such services for rights disputes.[14] FMCS data indicate that discipline *is* the most common source of grievances; in fiscal year 1986, for example, 39% of the issues settled by arbitrators obtained from FMCS panels involved discipline or discharge of employees.[15]

Despite this disciplinary concentration, many grievances relate to the application of seniority (in layoffs, promotions, transfers, and so on), to the use of pay schedules and benefit programs in particular situations, to assignment of work duties, and to management decisions involving the subcontracting of work previously performed in the bargaining unit. Questions of *management rights* (or management's reserved rights) sometimes are raised in the context of grievances and arbitrations. Union–management contracts frequently have language reserving to management unilateral authority in areas not specifically constrained by the contract or itemized for joint resolution. Such clauses may contain general statements about management's right to direct the workforce, manage the business, control production, and make company rules.[16]

In response to a particular grievance by the union over a management decision affecting an individual or group in the workforce, management may reply that it was acting within its area of reserved rights. Also, in some disputes management may take the position that the grievance is not "arbitrable," that is, that it covers a topic or circumstance that is not within the jurisdiction of arbitrator decision making as specified in the contract. In such cases, part of the arbitrator's task is to determine if the dispute is arbitrable under the terms of the agreement.[17]

Thus far grievances and arbitration have been discussed only in formal and abstract terms. In order to illustrate the process more concretely, some examples of issues that might be raised in grievances and possibly end in arbitration are described here.

- *Job classification.* A union–management contract may provide for a variety of wage rates, depending on job classification. An individual employee, whose job duties had in his or her opinion been enlarged over a period of time, might claim that he or she should be placed in a higher paying classification. The employer, however, might contend that the job duties had not changed appreciably or that the changes did not merit a higher classification.

- *Use of supervisors.* Contracts often limit the right of management to use supervisors to perform nonsupervisory tasks except in cases of emergency. These clauses are intended to protect the jobs of nonsupervisory, union-represented workers. The union might grieve what it thought to be use of supervisors in such tasks during nonemergency situations. It might contend that the emergency exception applied only to very unusual situations in which a threat to safety or equipment was involved, for example, a supervisor shutting down a malfunctioning machine that might otherwise be damaged or cause injury. On the other hand, the company might argue that the definition of *emergency* should be understood to include situations in which production deadlines had to be met and insufficient nonsupervisory workers were on hand.

- *Promotions.* Language in the contract may indicate that seniority would be the determining factor in allocating a promotion, if applicants were otherwise qualified. A senior applicant might file a grievance if passed up for promotion, claiming that he or she met the qualifications standard. Management may dispute the grievant's credentials.

- *Night shift differential.* A contract might provide for a lump-sum bonus proportional to wages in lieu of a wage increase for workers with at least one year of seniority. It might also provide that night-shift workers receive a 20% wage premium. The union might grieve if the company failed to reflect the bonus in the premium. Management might respond that other bonuses it had paid—such as perfect attendance awards—had not been factored into the premium during previous contracts, that is, that bonuses had always been based on the straight-time hourly wage on the day shift.

- *Suspension without pay.* A worker might grieve a one-week suspension without pay for smoking in an area containing barrels of inflammable chemicals. The worker might contend that he or she had no way of knowing about the fire danger, since the barrels were not labeled. A supervisor might respond that the worker had been told of the danger and ordered to stop smoking a week earlier when the same barrels were present in another area.

- *Plant closing.* A union might have negotiated language in a contract indicating that before a particular plant could be shut down, management would undertake good faith negotiations with the union to see if the plant could be saved. A grievance might be filed if plant operations ceased without such negotiations and with no announced date for restarting because of what management described as a temporary drop in demand. Management might argue that its obligations involved only permanent shutdowns, not temporary, and that it intended to reopen the plant at some point in the future when demand for its products picked up. The union might argue that it was doubtful that management intended to reopen the plant and that the cessation of production amounted to more than a normal temporary layoff.

Considerations for the Arbitrator

New contracts and contractual provisions are supposed to be negotiated by the parties involved. Arbitrators in rights disputes thus see their task as *interpreting* the existing union–management contract, not creating a new agreement. Just as in the legal setting, where judges see their task as interpreting—not making—the law, the line between interpreting and creating may not always be sharply defined. There is room for subjectivity and even bias in the making of arbitration decisions.[18] If contract provisions were always clear, precise, and unambiguous, it is difficult to imagine what the role of the arbitrator would be, beyond the limited function of fact-finding and determining credibility. The very fact there is a dispute often suggests that some lack of clarity is involved.[19] Resolving that ambiguity inevitably shapes the future meaning of the agreement.

After intense negotiations contracts may be ambiguous because the parties could not reach an agreement on precise language and felt a need to bring their bargaining to a successful conclusion. Some economists who have analyzed contracting in the labor market have emphasized that it is not possible to write a complete agreement, that is, one that covers every possible contingency.[20] Indeed, the necessity of incomplete agreements is a problem that extends to commercial contracting outside of the employment setting and is viewed as an important explanatory factor in corporate organization and practice.[21] In the labor market, when the inherent difficulty of incomplete contracting is compounded by the need to wrap up an agreement and avoid or terminate a strike, it is not surprising that contractual language is not always crystal clear.

In such cases of contract ambiguity, the union and management implicitly expect that an arbitrator will resolve the uncertainties for them at some future date, if they themselves cannot resolve the issue when it actually arises. Again, there are parallels to commercial contracting. It is often the case—to the chagrin of lawyers—that business arrangements leave some matters unresolved, often in the expectation that the parties will handle them later or that good faith on both sides will take care of future disputes.[22]

Perhaps the most critical ambiguity in a typical union–management contract is the provision involving disciplinary actions initiated by the employer. It is common to find provisions that state that discipline and discharge will be undertaken only for "cause" or for "just cause." The language need not always be so vague; in the case of certain employee actions, the cause and effect may be stated exactly, for example, employees not following a specified safety rule on the job will be dismissed.

When such precise contractual language exists, the arbitrator may be largely confined to determining whether the facts occurred as management asserted (whether the employee was, in fact, violating the safety rule). Even in such cases questions may arise as to whether management actually has enforced the rule consistently in the past. In more general cases of discipline for cause (with no further definition), the arbitrator has the task of determining whether cause existed for managerial action.

It would be inappropriate here to attempt to present a treatise on standards applied in arbitration.[23] Some of the kinds of issues facing arbitrators follow.

• *Credibility.* Arbitration hearings usually involve testimony from witnesses. Such testimony may conflict. For example, a supervisor's recollection of what was said to an employee in the course of an oral warning may vary from that of the employee. Two co-workers involved in an altercation may recount the circumstances quite differently. Sometimes conflicting testimony may result from faulty memories, sometimes from the natural tendency for individuals to color their memories in ways that favor their position, and sometimes simply from lying. When reported recollections differ, arbitrators have to make judgments on what the truth is.

• *Past practice.* Management may have made a decision regarding an item not specifically included in the contract. For example, a Christmas bonus that was not referenced in the contract might be terminated by management because of poor business conditions. Whether an arbitrator would deem such a bonus to be an implicit part of the agreement and therefore not subject to change without negotiation might depend on the consistency of awarding the bonus in the past. An occasional bonus might be viewed as less of an obligation than one that had been given without fail, even in bad times, for many years.

• *Rules and reasonableness.* Because not every circumstance can be spelled out in the contract, management has the right to make reasonable rules. Such a right will be deemed to exist even if it is not spelled out in a contractual clause about management's rights. When management's rule-making is challenged in a grievance, "the arbitrator's function is to (determine) whether the employer in administering the rules governing the employee–employer relationship violated the limitations embodied in the collective agreement."[24]

Management-made rules might involve safety standards (requiring the wearing of protective clothing), dress codes (so that customers receive a positive impression of the establishment), record keeping (so that money or inventory is not lost or misplaced), or courtesy (to avoid frictions between employees, between employees and customers, or between employees and supervisors). All of these areas of regulation will be seen in principle as appropriate subjects of rule making by arbitrators.

In some cases, however, a rule involving an appropriate subject—or its application in a particular situation—might be seen as unreasonable.

For example, a rule requiring the wearing of a company uniform is normal and reasonable in many circumstances. But the imposition of a penalty, pursuant to that rule, for being out of uniform might be deemed unreasonable if the employee could show that his or her uniform had been damaged and rendered unsuitable for wearing. Relevant might be the source of the damage; was it caused by negligence of the employee, or was it caused by circumstances beyond the employee's control? Suppose moments before his or her shift was to begin the uniform was damaged by flooding due to a burst water pipe in the employee locker room. In that situation enforcement of an otherwise reasonable rule might well be found to be unreasonable.

Apart from considerations of reasonableness, rules need to be effectively communicated to employees in order to be applied. Furthermore, rules should not be applied in an arbitrary, capricious, or discriminatory manner, for example, to certain employees, but not to others, given similar situations.

• *History of negotiations.* During negotiations the parties may have discussed the interpretation of a contract clause that is now disputed. What they said or did not say while negotiating might help the arbitrator determine what was meant when the language was first inserted into the contract. If the union or management asserted an interpretation during a negotiation but backed off or let the matter drop rather than forcing the issue, the union's or management's reassertion of that interpretation during a subsequent arbitration hearing may not carry much weight. Arbitrators will be loathe to grant one side or the other something it could not win on its own at the bargaining table.

• *Making the punishment fit the crime.* In discipline cases, even where an employee has clearly committed an infraction, management's response can be subject to a test of appropriateness. Commonly used—and viewed as good practice by arbitrators—is the application of "progressive discipline." For example, an employee exhibiting inappropriate behavior on the job might initially be given an oral warning by a supervisor. If behavioral improvements did not ensue, this initial step might be followed with a written warning, then a suspension of several days, and finally—if satisfactory improvement had not occurred—dismissal.

Progressive discipline need not be applied in all cases. Table 11–2 illustrates reported employer policies for six specific examples of employee misconduct or inadequate performance. Generally, the more serious the offense, the more compressed the disciplinary steps involved. Thus most employers used a four-step process for excessive tardiness. At the other end of the spectrum, most discharged immediately in cases of employee theft of company property. Arbitrators expect progressive discipline to be followed except in extreme cases such as theft. A failure to follow progressive discipline might indicate to the arbitrator that a miscarriage of justice had occurred.

The issue is not simply one of following a series of steps. The seriousness of the offense and the circumstances under which it occurred will be important considerations in judging the appropriateness of the penalty inflicted. Discharge of workers is sometimes said by arbitrators to be the workplace equivalent of capital punishment. In taking that view, arbitrators are recognizing the difference

TABLE 11–2   Disciplinary Approaches Reported by Employers

	Percentage of Employers with Policy			
Problem	*1 Step: Discharge*	*2 Steps: Suspension, Discharge*	*3 Steps: Written Warning, Suspension, Discharge*	*4 Steps: Oral Warning, Written Warning, Suspension, Discharge*
Unexcused/excessive tardiness	*	0%	14%	82%
Failure to maintain quality/quantity standards	1%	5%	25%	64%
Refusal to obey order or accept assignment	29%	29%	27%	10%
Possession of illegal drugs	65%	23%	6%	2%
Willful damage to employer's property	76%	17%	3%	*
Theft of employer's property	84%	11%	3%	0%

*Figure is less than 0.5%.

Note: Percentages add up to less than 100% because some employers had no policy or failed to report their policies.

Source: The Bureau of National Affairs, Inc., *Employee Discipline and Discharge,* PPF Survey no. 139 (Washington: BNA, 1985), pp. 17–18.

between the real world labor market and the spot auction market of the simple economic model.

A discharged worker suffers three types of losses. First, there is a direct loss of income while he or she is without work and seeking other employment. Often, state unemployment insurance laws deny or limit payments to workers discharged for cause. Employers pay company-based "experience-rated" premiums for unemployment insurance; their payments will rise if more workers make claims. Hence the employer has an economic incentive to protest unemployment benefit claims of former workers discharged for misconduct.[25] If the employer's position is upheld, the discharged worker may not receive any compensation.

Second, particularly in the union sector, in which many workplace benefits are hinged to seniority, loss of a job means loss of many seniority-related advantages, even if another job is quickly found. A discharged senior worker becomes the most junior employee at the new workplace. He or she may thus be the first laid off in an economic downturn, he or she may be assigned to the least desirable shifts, and he or she may have to work for several years to acquire a vested right to a pension.

An earlier chapter described the efficiency wage approach. As noted, some models in this category involve a pay profile tilted upward with seniority so that new entrants earn below their marginal revenue products in wages and benefits but more senior workers enjoy a pay premium. The rationale for such a pay system is precisely to have a penalty for improper conduct, namely the loss of the seniority premium.

Third, a discharged employee carries a stigma. Potential new employers may be reluctant to hire some other firm's problem worker. The discharge has what economists call a "signaling" effect; it signals to other employers that the job applicant may be of low quality or low productivity, or may disrupt the workplace if hired. Even if these impressions are incorrect—if the employee's discharge was actually not merited—in a world of imperfect information about worker quality, a discharged employee is someone for other employers to avoid. Loss of a job at one employer may thus make it difficult for the worker to find a good job elsewhere in the future.

For minor infractions, therefore, especially for first-time offenses, arbitrators are likely to see discharge as an inappropriate remedy. Employers have other options in discipline such as warning letters, temporary suspensions without pay, and demotions. Indeed, the progressive discipline approach is meant to ensure that discharge is the last resort, not the first, except in cases of the most serious workplace misconduct.

Arbitration Remedies

Arbitrators have discretion in fashioning their decisions. One possibility is that one side or the other is found to be wholly in the right. If management has properly exercised its authority, the arbitrator simply endorses management's decision. If the union's case is completely upheld, the arbitrator so indicates and fashions a remedy that "makes whole" employees who might have been injured by management's improper action.

For example, if a group of employees should have been paid a premium for certain work (say, hazardous duty) but did not receive it, the remedy would be to give them the extra payment retroactively. If an employee was discharged without just cause, he or she can be reinstated with full back pay, seniority and pension rights, and so on. Arbitrators, however, do not award punitive damages; they simply attempt to put matters back to where they should have been, had the improper management action not occurred.

In discipline cases an arbitrator will not impose a stricter penalty than management invoked; a ten-day suspension imposed by management will not be changed by the arbitrator to a thirty-day suspension. Nor will the arbitrator instruct management on how to handle its internal affairs. For example, an arbitrator would typically not advise management to discipline a supervisor who has been shown to have acted improperly relative to the grievant. It is management's job, not the arbitrator's, to see that supervisors appropriately implement their responsibilities.

When arbitrators find that management has acted improperly, they are not bound to grant *complete* relief to the grievant, and often do not. For example, an arbitrator may believe that, while the grievant did commit an infraction worthy of some discipline, management's chosen discipline was excessively harsh. A common remedy in cases of improper discharge, for example, is to reinstate the grievant *without* back pay. Because of the delays in the arbitration process (see below), such a remedy can be expensive to the grieving employee, even if less severe than complete job loss.

Managerial Authority

The grievance and arbitration mechanism takes management's authority over the workplace as a given. Such authority can be limited by the union–management agreement, but ultimately management is deemed to be in control in the hierarchical, superior–subordinate relationship. Except in very unusual circumstances, an employee who is given an order by a supervisor is supposed to follow that order, whether or not he or she believes the order to be proper.[26]

For example, suppose an employee is ordered by a supervisor to continue working during a lunch break. The employee may believe that the union–management contract gives him or her an absolute right to take a break. Simply walking out at lunch time, despite the supervisor's order, would be "insubordination"—even if the employee's interpretation of the contract was later found to be correct. Since insubordination is considered a serious employee offense, the insubordinate act could itself lead to discipline.

In the case of the disputed lunch break, appropriate action for the aggrieved worker would have been to file a grievance but follow the order. Attempts by the employee to remedy the situation through means other than the grievance process (sometimes known as engaging in "self-help") are viewed as improper. In particular, employee actions that undermine supervisorial authority, such as assaulting a supervisor, are likely to be seen as serious infractions by arbitrators. Even in the absence of a specific rule or contract provision dealing with insubordination, these norms of behavior are part of the unofficial law of the shop.

Legal Status of Arbitration

The strike wave after World War II played an important part in passage of the Taft-Hartley Act of 1947 (see Chapter 9). It also focused attention on peaceful means of resolving all forms of labor–management disputes. Most serious strikes then stemmed from interest disputes, not rights disputes. Nevertheless, the fact that arbitration had been adopted as a successful method of handling rights disputes in most contracts was naturally appealing to lawmakers. The Taft-Hartley Act did not require the use of rights arbitration. But it did speak favorably of "voluntary arbitration" (Sec. 201) and supported "final adjustment by a method agreed upon by the parties (as) . . . the desirable method for settlement of grievance disputes . . ." (Sec. 203).

More concretely, the Act created the Federal Mediation and Conciliation Service that helps the parties find private arbitrators.[27] It also gave legal status to union–management contracts, which by that time usually contained no-strike/no-lockout clauses. If those clauses had to be heeded for legal reasons, a need was created for a peaceful dispute-settling mechanism during the life of the agreement. Violation of the no-strike/no-lockout clause could give rise to suits for damages under Taft-Hartley; arbitration was therefore the appropriate remedy for contract interpretation disputes.

Over the years, legal support for arbitration grew. The arbitration language in a union–management contract is seen as a legally binding obligation; management is not free unilaterally to refuse to take cases to arbitration once it has agreed to the standard arbitration clause. Under some circumstances, employers may obtain injunctions against unions that strike, rather than use arbitration, in rights disputes. Following the lead of the U.S. Supreme Court, federal courts generally "defer" to arbitrators' decisions. They are reluctant to second-guess such judgments, in part out of fear that the judiciary might end up becoming a national grievance system.[28]

Under certain circumstances, the National Labor Relations Board will also defer to arbitration in cases raising questions of violations of the laws the NLRB enforces. In some instances, the NLRB will insist on the use of the contract's arbitration procedure before hearing a charge of unfair labor practice arising out of the circumstances. Courts will not necessarily defer to arbitration in cases involving equal employment opportunity (EEO) issues, for example, race and sex discrimination, nor will they require plaintiffs in such cases to use the available arbitration machinery. When EEO-related cases are submitted to that machinery, however, they will be heard by arbitrators, since discrimination in employment decisions typically would also involve violation of the union–management contract.[29] Even if arbitration decisions in EEO cases are appealed to the courts, the arbitrator's opinion might well influence the eventual judicial resolution.

Duty of Fair Representation

The legal system may (inadvertently) actually raise the arbitration caseload. Under the Taft-Hartley Act, unions can be sued by the workers they represent for failure to provide fair representation. In effect, unions acquire the privilege of exclusive representation of workers in the bargaining unit in exchange for an affirmative responsibility towards those workers. For example, suppose a grievance must be appealed from one step of the grievance mechanism to the next within a designated time period. If union officials fail to file a timely appeal, the union can be accused of negligence and be sued for damages by the frustrated grievant.

However, a union decision not to process a grievance or not to appeal it to a higher step or to arbitration need not indicate either negligence or bad faith. The union officials involved may honestly believe that the grievance is frivolous and that pursuing it may be both expensive (with no payoff) and harmful to the climate of labor–management relations. When the labor relations climate is amicable, unions may screen out frivolous grievances, or at least seek to settle them informally. The threat of lawsuits by disgruntled employees tends to make unions leery of performing this important screening role, a result of concern both to unions, who fear expensive suits, and to managements, whose task is complicated by overloaded grievance machinery.

In effect, the duty of fair representation is an issue that is yet another manifestation of the principal/agent problem in the employment area. Unions are—

by law—the agents of the employees (the principals). Through judicial mechanisms, the law seeks to ensure that the agents act for the principals.

Unions have a special problem as agents, however; the principals they represent may have conflicting interests. For example, the union may decide not to push a questionable grievance through to arbitration in the interests of better relations with management or simply to save the union's limited financial resources. In so doing it has basically determined that the interests of the employee group as a whole are in conflict with (and outweigh) those of the grievant. Since the union represents a group of diverse principals, it needs latitude to make such judgments.

Conflicts between principals are prone to arise in matters relating to seniority rights. In a layoff situation suppose a worker claims that management ignored his or her right to bump into another job, thereby displacing a less senior worker. Both workers are represented by the union. Whether it pushes the grievance or not, the union is favoring one principal over the other. Expensive litigation may not be the best way to resolve such questions; as in other aspects of life, perfection may not be attainable.

Criticisms of the Arbitration Process

The widespread use of private arbitration to settle rights disputes in union–management agreements is found in few countries other than the United States. American industrial relations specialists often point with great pride to this innovation. Over the years, however, two criticisms have been leveled at arbitration.

First, as already noted, there have been complaints over increasing legalism and formality in the process. Second, related to this complaint, is the issue of delay and cost. There is some evidence that if one party uses a lawyer as an advocate at an arbitration hearing, it gains an advantage provided that the other side does not use a lawyer. If both sides use a lawyer, the advantage is nullified, although the cost to both sides has increased.[30]

During fiscal years 1980 to 1986, the FMCS reported that cases that went all the way through to arbitration took an annual average of 230 to 377 days from the filing of the grievance to the final decision by the arbitrator. Roughly three months of this time was spent within the parties' own internal grievance machinery. Once the grievance process has been exhausted, it is not unusual for four or five months to elapse before an arbitrator can be picked and a hearing be held. Another month or month and a half may be spent awaiting the arbitrator's decision after the hearing is held.[31]

The direct costs of arbitration, that is, the fee of the arbitrator and his or her travel expenses, averaged $1,476 in fiscal 1986, according to FMCS.[32] These expenses are almost always split 50–50 between the employer and the union. Much larger expenses may accrue indirectly, however, for payment of advocates, pay for time spent off the job by employee witnesses, stenographic services for transcripts (when used), and the intangible—but definite—disruption of the workplace that can result when a grievance festers unresolved for months.

Various solutions have been put forward and tried in response to the criticisms of arbitration. These include a step between the end of the grievance procedure and the invocation of arbitration in which informal mediation of the grievance is tried. Under such an arrangement the parties, with the help of a third party facilitator, attempt to reach a satisfactory solution in a setting without legal trappings. Nothing said or proposed at the mediation session is admissable as evidence at the subsequent arbitration hearing if one is necessary. The parties may thus be freer in exploring avenues of resolution. There is only limited information on the outcome of grievance mediation, but it has received good reviews.[33] Despite its seeming advantages, however, grievance mediation is quite rare.[34]

Forms of expedited arbitration have also been tried. Under these arrangements quick decisions are rendered—perhaps right at the hearing—with agreement that these decisions apply only to the cases at hand and do not set precedents. The chance that a quick-but-erroneous verdict will create future complications is thus reduced.

Difficulties in training arbitrators also contribute to delays in decision processing. The first cohort of arbitrators received their training during the World War II era as a by-product of government intervention and wage controls. Individuals who were employed by the War Labor Board to settle labor–management disputes picked up their trade through that experience, and went on to practice it in the postwar era.

As arbitration became standardized, both labor and management came to recognize that arbitration decisions could have important implications for their relationship. From the management viewpoint a poor arbitration decision might lead to a permanent constraint on managerial flexibility and control or to a substantial outlay of money. From the union viewpoint an erroneous arbitration award could eliminate hard-won bargaining gains and upset the relation between the union and its members.

Thus both parties searched for arbitrators with proven track records and experience.[35] Through past use, word of mouth, and available reporting services, the parties could determine what kinds of issues the arbitrator had decided in the past, and how he or she had ruled.[36] Selection could be made on that basis. Whatever slight financial advantage there might be in hiring an inexperienced arbitrator might easily be swamped by the potential costs of a sloppy decision. It is a system that tends to create backlogs of cases (with resulting delays) for experienced arbitrators, although inexperienced new entrants may have light caseloads. An apprenticeship system of arbitrator training could alleviate this problem.[37]

In spite of complaints about its features, there is a distinct possibility that arbitration of grievances, which has been largely confined to the union sector, may in the future be found increasingly in nonunion settings. Courts have begun to consider complaints about discharge from nonunion employers. It has been argued that use of arbitration by nonunion employers would help shield them from costly court awards in wrongful discharge litigation. In addition, there have been proposals to require by law that discharge disputes be submitted to some form of arbitration. (These issues will be discussed more fully.)

Economic Interpretation

Whenever contracting occurs, some means of resolving disputes over contract interpretation must be created, and a mechanism for contract enforcement be set up. Otherwise, one party or the other to the contract is free to violate its provisions, negating the contracting process itself. The importance of contracting is reflected in reinforcing social norms concerning honesty, fairness, and keeping one's word. In addition, violation of contracts may result in the costs of a poor reputation, that of being a person (or organization) prone to acting in bad faith.

In the nonunion setting, there typically is no written employer–employee contract. Whatever relationship exists is either implicit or expressed in documents that ordinarily are not viewed as contracts, such as, company handbooks outlining HRM rules and procedures. Although nonunion employers—especially those with progressive HRM policies and strong HRM departments—are likely to have grievance mechanisms, these are often the informal open-door programs mentioned earlier.

Not surprisingly, usage of nonunion grievance systems tends to be lower than that of union systems. There are difficulties in creating a formal procedure to enforce implicit obligations. And there are advantages to management in having more discretion in interpreting its obligations to employees than would occur in a formal process capped with judgment from an outside arbitrator.

In union settings, there is more codification of the rights of management and of employees than is found among nonunion employers, even though many areas of ambiguity remain in the most formal situations. However, the potential costs of disagreement over employee rights are much higher in the union sector than in the nonunion sector. If there were no grievance and arbitration mechanism in cases involving unions, contract interpretation disputes might be resolved by strikes. And if strikes could occur in mid-course, that is, during the life of a contract, it is unclear what meaning the contract's agreed-upon duration would have.[38] Effectively, as occurs in some countries, the contract would be operative only until someone became tired of it.

After World War II American management was both threatened by the surge in unionization that had so recently occurred and anxious to regain workplace stability. It wanted contracts of fixed duration that would guarantee labor peace and that would be renegotiated only at specified intervals. The unions of that era, many of which were new institutions looking for recognition and legitimacy, also wanted stable relations with employers. Although the two sides may have agreed on little else after the war, both saw virtue in the grievance and arbitration system that survives to this day.[39]

Unions had still another interest in arbitration, one that remains important today. Although a successful union raises the costs of wages and benefits to the employer, this advantage could be eroded away if employers had full discretion about other aspects of workplace conditions. Faced with higher direct costs of labor, employers would have an incentive to recoup as much as they could of their higher compensation costs by economizing on (degrading) other aspects of the quality of working life.

To prevent such an erosion of conditions, union contracts must be detailed concerning the nonwage component of jobs. For example, jobs and tasks must be carefully described to prevent the employer from using lower paid workers to do the work of higher paid employees. Elaborate contracts require the formal means of interpretation and enforcement that ultimate recourse to binding arbitration provides. In short, the traditional mode of adversarial union–management contracting, when combined with U.S. management's desire for labor peace during the contract's life, requires a grievance and arbitration system or something very much like it.

Exit and Voice

In a buyer–seller context, if one of the parties becomes unhappy with the relationship, there are two basic options. The unhappy party can break off the relationship (exit). Alternatively, he or she can attempt to modify the behavior of the other party by expressing the dissatisfaction and seeking a resolution (voice). For example, a shopper unhappy with the absence of a particular brand in a supermarket can either shop elsewhere, or, alternatively, complain to the store manager.

Which option is chosen—exit or voice—will depend on the relative costs of each. If there are many supermarkets within a short distance, shopping elsewhere rather than complaining may be the easiest solution for the unhappy customer. But in an isolated area with no other nearby markets, the best strategy may be to try to effect a change in the local market's policy on what brands are carried.

The exit/voice model has been applied to the workplace as well as the product market.[40] In the workplace, the exit option for the employee (seller) is quitting.[41] The voice option is trying to alter the policies of management (the buyer) that are causing dissatisfaction. A grievance mechanism is one way for employees to exercise voice. Use of voice rather than exit can be expected in situations where the latter is perceived as costly.

Quitting a job may be costly for an employee. A quit may not carry the stigma of a discharge, but it may have a negative signaling effect nonetheless. For example, because turnover can be costly for firms, someone who changes employers often may be perceived as unstable, as a person who can't hold a job. More important, in the real world labor market, quitting a job may entail a long search for a satisfactory new one, unless the new job is already lined up at the time of the quit. Quitting a job—even if a new one can quickly be found—also entails giving up whatever benefits and privileges past seniority has bestowed.

For union workers the existence of a union pay premium—combined with the strong weight placed on seniority in union jobs—can make quitting a very unattractive option. Alternative nonunion jobs may not pay union wages and benefits. And, because union jobs pay above the market, alternative union jobs may be hard to find; they may already have queues of applicants awaiting any vacancies.

These considerations suggest that the voice option will be important to workers who have nonsalvageable investments in their jobs, especially relatively immobile union workers who enjoy quasi-rents that might otherwise be expropriated by their employers.[42] Union workers tend to express more job dissatisfaction in attitude surveys than nonunion workers, even though they are less likely to leave their employers voluntarily.[43] It may be that unionized employers—seeking to recoup some of the higher costs they carry in wages and benefits—invoke harsher standards of discipline than comparable nonunion firms. In any case, these considerations place added stress on the grievance and arbitration mechanism as an important voice option.

Obviously, having a voice option can be valuable for nonunion employees, too, since the exit option may also be costly for them. There is a value to the employer in providing both options; valued employees may be lost if no channels exist for expressing dissatisfaction. The more formal the grievance process is made, however, the less discretion the employer may have concerning the outcome of dissatisfaction of a particular worker. In some cases the employer may feel it would be better from the firm's perspective if the employee did exercise the exit option.

Were the decision to be placed in the hands of an outside arbitrator, or even decided internally in strict accordance with stated company policy, there is no guarantee that the outcome in these cases would be exit. In effect, nonunion employers may well want the information that the voice option provides, but may not want their managerial discretion limited as a result. For that reason, their internally designed grievance systems are less likely to be so formal that they would restrict managerial flexibility.

11–5   Complaint Resolution in the Future

Employees and employers have both mutual interests and conflicting interests. In the past, coping with these conflicts was primarily a private matter. Bargaining and formal grievance and arbitration mechanisms were the standard approaches in the union sector. In the nonunion sector, less formal grievance mechanisms also were created. Progressive nonunion employers, through surveys and other monitoring mechanisms, attempted to diffuse problems before they became serious sources of friction in the workplace.

Public Intervention

At the outset of this chapter, it was noted that not all employee complaints could be classed as disputes over rights. Many are akin to interest disputes. Employees would like the terms and conditions they are offered to be different (better) than they actually are. One option they have, which involves neither exit from, nor voice within their firms, is to push for legislation mandating resolution of their complaints. Public policy has been less active in both these interest and rights disputes in the United States than in many other countries.

In the interest area policy as established in the 1930s was largely confined to minimum conditions. Federal and state minimum wage laws are the prime examples. Beyond minimums, policy was largely restricted to establishing a framework for collective bargaining—a private system that, it was assumed, would take care of other conflicts.

However, regulation in the United States has never followed the minimum intervention approach completely. Requirements for payment of overtime when hours exceed forty per week, reached beyond the bottom tier of the workforce, as did the mandating of employer participation in unemployment insurance, Social Security, and workers' compensation. Regulatory pressures on the employment relationship began to rise in the 1970s. Perhaps the main example was the federal Occupational Safety and Health Act of 1970 (OSHA) that put into force an elaborate system of mandatory workplace standards for reducing industrial accidents and diseases.

Regulatory pressures in the 1970s also spread into the area of employee benefits. A peculiar mix of mandatory/nonmandatory regulations arose. In the pension area, for example, there was no federal requirement that an employer provide a pension plan for workers (although there were tax incentives to do so). *If* employers did opt to have pension plans, elaborate regulations were enacted setting out how such plans had to be funded, what their vesting and eligibility rules had to be, and mandating federal insurance of certain retirement benefits.

Similarly, in the area of health care, no federal law requires employers to offer health insurance to workers. *If* they do choose to provide such insurance, employers are required to offer employees the option of joining a local health maintenance organization (HMO) in addition to the traditional fee-for-service plans.[44] It was hoped that offering the HMO option would provide greater incentives for containment of the rapidly inflating costs of health care benefits.

In some countries employers are simply required to offer particular benefits.[45] For example, minimum lengths of paid vacations may be specified by law. In the United States there has been a preference for incentives to offer certain benefits but not outright requirements, chiefly through the tax code. There has been a preference for regulating the outcome of a choice, for example, the choice of whether or not to offer a pension, rather than remove the choice and make the benefit mandatory.

However, some conditions *are* mandated in the United States. In the future regulation could tilt toward still more mandatory specifications of exactly what the employment relationship will provide for workers. The decline of collective bargaining has made it more difficult to argue that regulation is not necessary because whatever workplace remedies may be needed can be "negotiated." In the absence of a union representative, negotiations will not take place.

Alternative Forums

A similar evolution with regard to rights disputes may be in the making. Nonunion employees tend to seek to exercise their voice in workplace decisions through external legal channels. In the American context there are a variety of potential channels open for expressing employee voice, even if they were not deliberately created or planned for that purpose.

Wrongful Discharge Litigation.   The rise of wrongful discharge litigation represents a new forum for employee complaints. In states where courts have permitted substantial scope to such litigation, employers have grown cautious about firing workers. The courts have recognized—even if they do not express it in these terms —that workers have a stakeholder interest in their employment relationship.

All states in the United States recognize the employment at-will doctrine. Under this doctrine, employees can quit and employers can discharge for any reason, or no reason, unless some legislative prohibition exists, for example, discharging an employee on the basis of race. State courts are finding a growing list of exceptions to the at-will concept. For example, in a survey in the mid-1980s, courts in thirty-one states were found to construe an exception to at-will employment based on public policy.[46] In other words, employees terminated for, say, refusing to give false testimony at a legislative hearing to cover up employer wrongdoing may have a cause of action against their former employer. In eight states, courts have found that a "covenant of good faith and fair dealing" applies to the employment relationship. Thus an employee fired just before he or she would have become vested in a pension program might successfully sue, if it could be shown that the employer was simply motivated to save pension resources.

Courts in many states will consider statements in employee handbooks as contractual obligations of the employer to the employee. If the handbook promises due process before termination and none was provided, a wrongful discharge may have occurred. Promises made during job interviews or in oral statements to employees at the time of hiring may also bind the employer.

Because of the various opportunities for litigation in the area of wrongful discharge, the management community has pondered a legislative response. Specifically, some employers have toyed with the idea of supporting a limited-liability wrongful discharge arbitration program. Under such a program, complaints over discharges would be channeled to a publicly run complaint system, thereby avoiding jury trials and potentially very expensive verdicts. Management might eventually support this proposal if it feels that the existing system of court adjudication is becoming too costly. A similar development in connection with workers' compensation occurred in the early part of this century.

EEO as a Forum.   Employees are finding forums other than wrongful discharge suits for exercising voice. Equal employment opportunity (EEO) laws provide forums for allegations of discrimination with regard to race, sex, age (forty years and over), religion, national origin, and handicap. Most complaints are filed in the race, sex, and age categories. There is reason to believe that many of the cases filed are really general complaints over workplace decisions. The EEO laws thus provide a limited vehicle for those in the protected groups to exercise some voice, in the absence of other channels.

Age discrimination cases became especially visible in the late 1970s as Congress extended the age of mandatory retirement to seventy years and then eliminated it altogether. Although age and seniority are not the same thing, they tend to be positively correlated. Claims of age discrimination are thus likely to be filed by relatively high-seniority workers who feel wronged by their employer. Not infrequently, the claimants are executives and managers who think they have been passed over for promotions or discharged because the company wants new blood.[47]

Most workers have some place to register a complaint. Those in the public sector have civil service procedures; unionized workers have formalized grievance and arbitration mechanisms; and protected groups have EEO laws. In 1986 only about one-fifth of wage and salary earners were private sector, nonunion white males under forty years old.[48] Even these relatively unprotected workers have the possibility of wrongful discharge litigation in many states.[49] They might also file workers' compensation claims.

Workers' Compensation as a Forum.   Workers' compensation laws provide yet another avenue of employee redress.[50] These laws were created in the early twentieth century at the state level to provide financial compensation for employees injured on the job. Prior to the creation of workers' compensation, employers had various legal defenses if they were sued by injured workers. They could claim, for example, that the worker was injured through his or her own negligence, because of the negligence of some other employee, or simply because the job was inherently risky and the worker assumed the risks entailed by accepting employment. These defenses began to give way to sympathetic juries, and the organized management community opted to support no-fault insurance for employees.

Without having to demonstrate that their employers are at fault, employees can in principle collect specified damages for work-engendered injuries and illnesses (but no pain and suffering awards) under state workers' compensation systems. The circumstances of eligibility for recovery have widened substantially. In recent years, in particular, claims have been filed for cases of "occupational stress" that go well beyond the kinds of injuries and diseases that were originally compensable.[51] Figure 11–1 shows the type of newspaper advertisements that give workers access to forums for complaints about stress.

One form of occupational stress claim alleges that such physical health problems as heart attacks or strokes are brought on by stressful working conditions, usually over an extended period. Undoubtedly, stress at work can contribute to such conditions, but nonwork stresses, genetic predisposition, dietary habits, and so on may also be contributory factors. Claims for this type of stress compensation, and the willingness of workers' compensation authorities to entertain them, can be viewed as the expression of a desire that employers should provide for expenses connected with health problems, even if their connection with the job is uncertain. The claims amount to a public rewriting of the modern employment contract, just as, say, the requirement for overtime pay after forty hours rewrote the contract when it was first enacted.

Stress claims in the psychological area entail compensation for exit from work. In these cases the employee may allege that conditions at the workplace— for example, an overbearing supervisor— created such tension that he or she was unable to work due to anxiety, depression, and so on. Before stress claims became

FIGURE 11–1
Forums for Employees
with Complaints

STRESS on Your JOB?

☆   ☆   ☆

Are you *burned out?*
harassed?
overworked? sick?

Call us now for an
appointment!

555-5000

Job Problems

If you suffer from
NERVOUS ATTACKS,
LACK OF ENERGY, or
DEPRESSION
as a result of

- JOB STRESS
- OVERWORK
- INJURY

Call 555-3410
for a free consultation.

Have you had a **heart attack** or **heart bypass?**

Your medical bills can be paid
if your heart problems were due
in part to job stress.

For free information call

555-1240
Don't wait!

INJURED AT WORK?

UNJUSTLY FIRED?

Free appointment
555-9032

☆   ☆   ☆   ☆

feasible, employees simply left (quit) if workplace conditions became extremely unpleasant. Under such circumstances, the worker might lose the stake he or she had in the job, especially if long seniority was involved. Thus a stress claim may sometimes be an attempt to recoup some of this investment in the job from the employer.

The ability to file claims for stress, for discrimination under EEO laws, or for wrongful discharge creates a degree of voice for employees. Employers are aware that such suits are possible and may therefore be more responsive to employee complaints than they otherwise would be. Litigation can be expensive for the employer, even if its defense is ultimately successful. Legal forums, in short, give nonunion employees the ability to inflict costs on their employers, just as unions can inflict strike costs. This ability provides limited leverage to workers for resolving workplace complaints.

Limitations on Layoffs. Most job loss in the U.S. labor market stems from layoffs, not discharges. If special machinery were created to deal with wrongful discharge, it would not limit such layoffs. (In the next chapter layoffs and job security issues will be discussed more fully.) It is sufficient to note here that pressure for legal restraints on plant closings and mass layoffs mounted in the 1980s. As a result some states adopted relatively weak legislation in this area. In 1988 Congress passed legislation requiring sixty days' advance notice to workers before a plant could be closed or mass layoffs undertaken.

Eventually, the judiciary may also play a role in this area. In at least one case, laid-off workers were successful in achieving an out-of-court settlement against an employer who allegedly concealed plans to close down an operation.[52] An aging electorate during the next ten to twenty years could prove receptive to a regulatory approach toward job security. Such an approach would likely go beyond the limited scope of wrongful discharge and discipline remedies, and would seek to restrict employer freedom to lay off workers during business downturns.

Private HRM Responses

Despite the current and future encroachment of external forces, HRM specialists have options for dealing with employee complaints and grievances. First, when there are union–management contracts specifying a grievance mechanism or when formal complaint systems exist for nonunion employees, these arrangements need to be *monitored*. How many grievances are being filed? Do they vary from worksite to worksite, and if so, why? Are there patterns in the kinds of problems being adjudicated? What kinds of problems seem to be causing the most workplace frictions? Excessive grievances have been linked to poor productivity performance, thus making the tracking of grievances an obvious management concern.[53]

Second, when either union or nonunion systems have been in place for long periods, it is important to *evaluate* their outcomes. Are they, in fact, resolving problems or are they aggravating them? Clearly unproductive are long delays or tensions arising over the use of the systems themselves. Grievance machinery is supposed to reduce the friction that is inevitably found in any workplace. If it is not performing that function, changes are needed.

Alternatives to existing practices are available. The mediation option has already been noted in the union setting, where arbitration is typically the final step in the process. If arbitration has been characterized by high cost and long delays, mediation prior to the arbitration step certainly should be considered. As with any HRM system, mediation needs evaluation. If mediation is installed, it is essential to track the results. Are a substantial fraction of the problems referred to mediation being resolved, thus averting the need for arbitration? If not, mediation simply becomes an additional source of delay. If expedited arbitration is tried, are the decisions simply fast? Or are they also perceived as reasonable when compared with the outcomes of standard rights arbitration?

Third, *alternative remedies* need to be considered. In the case of discharges found to be unjustified, the standard remedy imposed by arbitrators has been reinstatement, perhaps with all or some back pay. Yet the wrongful discharge suits that have been filed by employees often seek monetary damages, not necessarily reinstatement. Reinstatement may not be a viable option, especially for upper level employees. A high level of trust is needed between executives; a forced reinstatement is not likely to be a good remedy for either party. Indeed, even at lower levels of the organization, a forced reinstatement may add to workplace frictions.

Monetary awards and buyouts of problem employees may be an appropriate outcome in disputed discharge cases. In fact, employers contemplating discharge should consider the alternative of a more amicable voluntary departure, lubricated by a monetary settlement. If the employment relationship is viewed as an implicit contract, then an earlier-than-planned termination of that contract can be negotiated in monetary terms, just as occurs in the case of premature termination of other buyer–seller agreements.

Apart from strictly cash payments, employers can ease transitions from their workforces through provision of placement assistance, through flexible policies with regard for absences needed for job search, and through tailored early retirement. As with other HRM approaches, however, there are both costs and benefits. For example, an employer would not want to create the impression among its workforce that buyouts were an entitlement for all departing employees. Also, it would not be desirable for remaining workers to feel that rewards for problem employees exceeded those for workers who were loyal and productive.

The discussion so far has assumed that a grievance mechanism of some type is in place. This assumption is not always valid for nonunion workers. Studies have indicated that nonunion workers in firms that have some unionization are less likely to have complaint systems than those in totally nonunion firms. Indeed, the higher the proportion of union-represented workers, the greater the probability that the nonrepresented workers have no formal grievance handling system available.[54] A survey in the late 1970s found that only 44% of employers had formal grievance procedures for their nonunion employees.[55]

It is probable that the proportion of private nonunion workers with formal grievance arrangements will rise in the future. Contemporary employees are looking for a way to voice their problems; if they do not find such channels within the firm, they will increasingly turn to external remedies. The costs of such external routes can be high for employers. If internal channels are available, however, employees who fail to use them, or who summarily reject their outcomes, will find they have less credibility within the outside channels.

To have a formal grievance system, however, requires guidelines for HRM decisions. Formal grievance systems need formal statements of the mutual obligations of employer and employee. A purely implicit contract, with no documentation, is difficult to adjudicate. The implicit contract must be made more explicit.

Some attorneys are advising employers to state clearly to workers that the firm has no obligations to employees, that employment is at will in the strict classic sense, and that employees can be dismissed at any time and for any reason or no reason. Some firms are heeding that advice and are requiring employees and new hires to sign agreements subjecting them explicitly to discharge without cause.[56] But there are some obvious HRM drawbacks to such a strategy. Would a job applicant be attracted to an employer who openly reserved the right to behave capriciously? For most employers the increasing demand of employees for a voice is likely to be reflected in more carefully crafted and monitored HRM policies and complaint systems.[57]

Summary

The simple, classical economic model of the labor market has difficulty dealing with conflicts between employers and employees. But with a more thorough understanding of the ongoing nature of the employer–employee relationship, it is easy to see why such conflicts occur. Discrepancies between employer and employee goals lead to employee complaints about the job or about employer decisions. Only some of these complaints can be classified as grievances, however. The mechanisms for resolving complaints within firms tend to focus mainly on grievances. Complaints about such matters as the scheduling of work hours—an issue explored in this chapter—are typically not grievances; they are really interests disputes, not rights disputes.

Union-represented employees are almost always covered by formal grievance systems. These systems are multistep procedures that end in arbitration if the problem cannot be solved at earlier stages. Although many nonunion firms have grievance mechanisms, they are commonly less formal than those found in unionized firms and very few use arbitration as a last step. More typically, a high company official makes the final decision in the nonunion setting.

Although there are legitimate criticisms of the arbitration process, such as its legalism and delays, it does provide the employer with some insurance against external resolution of grievances through litigation. Such external resolution has become increasingly common. Thus some nonunion employers may decide to use arbitration as part of their grievance systems in the future. In addition there have been proposals to mandate arbitration of discharges where it is not otherwise provided. For these reasons the process of arbitration must be of concern to all HR executives, even if they do not currently use it.

EXERCISES

Problem

Consider the following circumstances:

An appliance repairman is dispatched to a private home to fix a refrigerator. While there, he is left alone in the kitchen. The woman of the house realizes that she has left her handbag in the kitchen and goes to retrieve it. She opens the purse, declares that a hundred dollar bill is missing, and phones the repairman's employer to complain. The employer immediately sends out an investigator who comes to the house and asks the repairman to empty his wallet. The repairman complies and in his wallet is found a hundred dollar bill, two fifty dollar bills, and some smaller bills and coins. Asked to explain the presence of a hundred dollar bill in his wallet, the repairman claims that he always carried large bills "for emergencies."

Suppose that the employer discharged the repairman and he filed a grievance demanding reinstatement with back pay under a union grievance procedure. Suppose further that the case ultimately came before you as an arbitrator. What criteria might you use in deciding whether to reinstate the grievant as requested or uphold management's action?*

Questions

1. Distinguish between a complaint and a grievance.

2. Why do relatively few employers permit employees to use flextime scheduling?

3. What impact does the business cycle have on part-time work?

4. Why do nonunion grievance procedures rarely end in arbitration? Are there any trends that may change this situation? Explain.

5. Is a unionized employer free to decline to submit an unresolved grievance to arbitration? Why or why not?

Terms

arbitration	insubordination	progressive discipline
at-will doctrine	just cause	rights arbitration
duty of fair representation	make-whole remedy	workers' compensation
EEO	occupational stress	work sharing
exit-voice model	principal-agent model	wrongful discharge

*The situation presented is based very loosely on a case related by arbitrator Gerry L. Fellman.

ENDNOTES

1. David Lewin, "Conflict Resolution in the Nonunion High Technology Firm" in Archie Kleingartner and Carolyn S. Anderson, eds., *Human Resource Management in High Technology Firms* (Lexington, Mass.: Lexington Books, 1987), pp. 137–155.

2. For example, there is evidence that individuals working hours that they characterize as too long or too short receive pay premiums for the mismatch. See Joseph G. Altonji and Christina H. Paxson, "Labor Supply Preference, Hours Constraints, and Hours-Wage Trade-Offs," *Journal of Labor Economics,* vol. 6 (April 1988), pp. 254–276.

3. Susan E. Shank, "Preferred Hours of Work and Corresponding Earnings," *Monthly Labor Review,* vol. 109 (November 1986), pp. 40–44.

4. Herbert Simon, *Administrative Behavior,* third edition (New York: The Free Press, 1976), pp. 130–134.

5. Under the Occupational Health and Safety Act, workers have limited protections against being fired for refusing to perform very hazardous duties.

6. Other reasons, accounting for only a small portion of the total, include "job terminated during week," "new job started

during week," and "material shortages or repairs to plant and equipment."

7. Normally, unemployment compensation systems require that the employee be totally laid off before benefits will be paid. A symposium on the work-sharing topic can be found in Barbara D. Dennis, ed., *Proceedings of the Thirty-Eighth Annual Meeting,* December 28–30, 1985, Industrial Relations Research Association (Madison, Wisc.: IRRA, 1986), pp. 424–456.

8. Earl F. Mellor, "Shift Work and Flextime: How Prevalent Are They?" *Monthly Labor Review,* vol. 109 (November 1986), pp. 14–21.

9. Similar issues arise in connection with adoption of standardized weights and measures, definition of currency units, and so on. The central authority need not always be government; national time zones in the United States were first created by private railroad companies in the nineteenth century because it was difficult to produce train schedules when each town had its own time system. The railroad companies simply announced there would be a clock at the railroad station and the railroad schedule would refer to that clock only. Localities eventually adopted railroad time as their own. When there is no central authority, however, costs may arise, for example, incompatible systems of home video taping (Beta vs. VHS).

10. Mellor, "Shift Work," *op. cit.,* pp. 18–20.

11. Some workers engage in manufacturing at home (industrial homework). There are legal restrictions on such work because it is difficult to enforce minimum-wage and other such laws in a home setting. Under the Reagan administration, some of these restrictions were lifted. See Francis W. Horvath, "Work at Home: New Findings from the Current Population Survey," *Monthly Labor Review,* vol. 109 (November 1986), pp. 31–35.

12. Theresa Diss Greis, *The Decline of Annual Hours Worked in the United States Since 1947* (Philadelphia: Industrial Research Unit, The Wharton School, University of Pennsylvania, 1984); Herbert R. Northrup and Theresa Diss Greis, "The Decline in Average Annual Hours Worked in the United States, 1947–1979," *Journal of Labor Research,* vol. 4 (Spring 1983), pp. 95–113.

13. Information on the structure of grievance machinery in this section is taken from Bureau of National Affairs, Inc., *Basic Patterns in Union Contracts,* eleventh edition (Washington: BNA, 1986), pp. 33–40.

14. The FMCS will supply lists of arbitrators for both types of labor–management disputes: rights and interests. However, almost all the disputes reported are disputes over rights.

15. U.S. Federal Mediation and Conciliation Service, *Thirty-Ninth Annual Report—Fiscal Year 1986* (Washington: FMCS, no date), Table 8. It should be noted that an issue is not the same thing as a case; a case may involve more than one issue. In addition, FMCS reports reflect only the cases that involved arbitrators whose names were supplied on FMCS lists to the parties. Many arbitrations take place without FMCS involvement. Finally, it is possible that there are differences in the mix of issues between grievances filed and that subset of grievances that end up resolved by arbitration.

16. Bureau of National Affairs, Inc., *Basic Patterns, op. cit.,* pp. 80–81.

17. Generally, the arbitrator would hear the dispute over arbitrability and then the facts of the case. In his or her decision, the arbitrator would first rule on the arbitrability issue. If the case was deemed not arbitrable, the decision would end with a statement so indicating. If it was viewed as arbitrable, the arbitrator would then proceed to analyze the facts of the underlying dispute and render a decision. Sometimes management may refuse to participate in the arbitration process if it feels the issue is not arbitrable. Such situations may end up in court, with the union arguing that by refusing to allow an arbitrator to consider the arbitrability issue, management is violating its contractual obligation. Courts are likely to be sympathetic with the union position, in the absence of unusual circumstances.

18. It has been found, for example, that arbitrators are less likely to ratify harsh penalties on female workers than on males. See Brian Bemmels, "The Effect of Grievants' Gender on Arbitration Decisions," *Industrial and Labor Relations Review,* vol. 41 (January 1988), pp. 251–262.

19. There are sometimes cases in which the union will pursue a frivolous grievance, knowing it will lose its case, because it fears that a failure to do so would be unpopular or (as will be discussed below) subject it to litigation. Similarly, management may feel a need to show support for a supervisor, even if it believes the supervisor's action in a given case will not be sustained by an arbitrator.

20. Oliver E. Williamson, *Markets and Hierarchies: Analysis and Antitrust Implications* (New York: The Free Press, 1975), pp. 75–77; Michael L. Wachter and Oliver E. Williamson, "Obligational Markets and the Mechanisms of Inflation," *Bell Journal of Economics,* vol. 9 (Autumn 1978), pp. 549–571.

21. Arbitration of commercial disputes (not related to the employment relationship) is a common practice. On contracting and corporate organization, see Oliver E. Williamson, "The Modern Corporation: Origins, Evolution, Attributes," *Journal of Economic Literature,* vol. 19 (December 1981), pp. 1537–1568, especially 1545.

22. Stewart Macaulay, "Non-Contractual Relations in Business: A Preliminary Study," *American Sociological Review,* vol. 28 (February 1963), pp. 55–67.

23. A widely used and readable text on the subject is Paul Prasow and Edward Peters, *Arbitration and Collective Bar-*

gaining: Conflict Resolution in Labor Relations, second edition (New York: McGraw-Hill, 1983).

24. David E. Feller, "A General Theory of the Collective Bargaining Agreement," *California Law Review,* vol. 61 (May 1973), pp. 663–856. The quote is from p. 748.

25. State laws provide ceilings on unemployment insurance premiums. Those employers who have experienced many layoffs may be at the ceiling rates and may have little incentive to protest claims. Experience rating is discussed in the next chapter.

26. An exception might be an order to undertake a life-threatening action, for example, an order to drive a truck with defective brakes, or an illegal action, for example, an order to commit perjury at a trial or legislative hearing to protect the firm.

27. The FMCS also provides mediators for interest disputes, as discussed in Chapter 10.

28. The courts do not automatically defer to arbitration decisions, but they are reluctant to reverse those decisions, especially if the arbitrator has acted in a professional fashion. The vast majority of arbitration decisions are accepted as binding by the parties and are not taken to court. When they are not, federal courts are bound by three Supreme Court decisions issued in 1960 and popularly known as the "Arbitration Trilogy," that call for a general policy of judicial deferral. For more information, see Walter A. Fogel, "Court Review of Discharge Arbitration Awards," *The Arbitration Journal,* vol. 37 (June 1982), pp. 22–34.

29. For example, a person who was disciplined for reasons of racial animosity rather than for some workplace infraction was clearly not disciplined for just cause. Moreover, many union–management agreements contain nondiscrimination clauses.

30. Richard N. Block and Jack Stieber, "The Impact of Attorneys and Arbitrators on Arbitration Awards," *Industrial and Labor Relations Review,* vol. 40 (July 1987), pp. 543–555. There is a clear implication that both sides could reduce at least one element of arbitration costs by agreeing not to use lawyers. The costs of using a lawyer, however, may differ for the two sides. Management may have in-house counsel at its disposal and may feel it is to its advantage to have a high cost for arbitration so as to cut down on the number of arbitrations.

31. U.S. Federal Mediation and Conciliation Service, *Annual Report, op. cit.,* p. 23, and previous issues.

32. U.S. Federal Mediation and Conciliation Service, *Annual Report, op. cit.,* p. 22.

33. Jeanne M. Brett and Stephen B. Goldberg, "Grievance Mediation in the Coal Industry: A Field Experiment," *Industrial and Labor Relations Review,* vol. 37 (October 1983), pp. 49–69.

34. Only 3% of contracts surveyed in the mid-1980s had grievance mediation. See Bureau of National Affairs, Inc., *Basic Patterns, op. cit.,* p. 37.

35. The preference for experienced arbitrators has been demonstrated in the case of interest arbitration. Presumably, similar preferences should be exhibited for rights arbitration. See David E. Bloom and Christopher L. Cavanagh, "An Analysis of the Selection of Arbitrators," *American Economic Review,* vol. 76 (June 1986), pp. 408–422.

36. In 1987, the AFL-CIO established its own computerized data on arbitrators for its member unions. See "Union Data Bank to Track Arbitrators," *AFL-CIO News,* December 12, 1987, p. 12.

37. Some contracts permit strikes in mid-course, but typically only over certain specified issues. From time to time, unofficial or wildcat strikes occur over matters that should be resolved by the grievance machinery. Union officials are supposed to make an effort to bring about a quick return to work in such cases, and may face legal action by the employer if they do not, especially if it appears that the union played a role in fomenting the strike. As in other facets of life, there are episodes in union–management relations when gaps appear between what is supposed to occur and what actually does.

38. Labor markets in which applicants are told "come back when you have experience" pose problems for long-term recruitment, since experience can be acquired only by hiring. Formal training in school-type settings does not solve the problem. Apprenticeship, whereby the masters in the field provide tutelage to and oversight of new entrants, would give the parties confidence in newcomers.

39. Sanford M. Jacoby and Daniel J.B. Mitchell, "Development of Contractual Features of the Union-Management Relationship," *Labor Law Journal,* vol. 33 (August 1982), pp. 512–518; Sanford M. Jacoby and Daniel J.B. Mitchell, "Employer Preferences for Long-Term Union Contracts," *Journal of Labor Research,* vol. 5 (Summer 1984), pp. 215–228.

40. Richard B. Freeman and James L. Medoff, *What Do Unions Do?* (New York: Basic Books, 1984), chapter 6; Oliver E. Williamson, "The Economics of Internal Organization: Exit and Voice in Relation to Markets and Hierarchies," *American Economic Review,* vol. 66 (May 1976), pp. 369–377; Albert O. Hirschman, *Exit, Voice, and Loyalty: Responses to Decline in Firms, Organizations, and States* (Cambridge, Mass.: Harvard University Press, 1970).

41. For example, it has been found that people who were promoted were less likely to quit than those who were not. The promoted employees were presumably more satisfied with their job and tended not to leave. Individuals who do not receive promotions become dissatisfied and depart. See Loren M. Solnick, "Promotions, Pay, Performance Ratings and Quits," *Eastern Economic Journal,* vol. 14 (January-

March 1988), pp. 51–62. It has also been found that workers who had previously quit jobs to join a firm were less likely to quit the new employer than workers who had been hired while unemployed. The latter group had to take what was available and thus were more likely to be dissatisfied with their lot. When opportunities arose, they would leave. See Andrew Weiss, "Determinants of Quit Behavior," *Journal of Labor Economics,* vol. 2 (July 1984), pp. 371–387.

42. Armen A. Alchian, "Property Rights, Specialization and the Firm," working paper no. 225, UCLA Department of Economics, November 1981.

43. Freeman and Medoff, *op. cit.,* chapter 9.

44. Health maintenance organizations are health care providers who offer comprehensive care for a flat monthly fee through their own facilities. Fee-for-service plans reimburse patients for their medical expenses according to a specified schedule. Employers may offer only an HMO.

45. Foreign practices are discussed in a later chapter.

46. National Association of Manufacturers, *Employment Law in the 50 States* (Washington: CUE/NAM, 1987), p. vi.

47. Michael Schuster and Christopher S. Miller, "An Empirical Assessment of the Age Discrimination in Employment Act," *Industrial and Labor Relations Review,* vol. 38 (October 1984), pp. 64–74.

48. This estimate was made using data from *Employment and Earnings,* vol. 34 (January 1987), p. 219.

49. White males can also file claims that they have been subject to reverse discrimination, that is, illegal preferences for minorities or women.

50. These laws were once known as Workmen's Compensation. The name was made sexually neutral in the 1970s.

51. In most states private carriers provide the insurance to cover these claims even though the adjudication system is government-run. One of the benefits of having a no-fault system was originally thought to be a reduction in the need for lawyer involvement. In fact, there is substantial lawyer involvement in the processing of workers' compensation claims. There is thus a constant search by attorneys who handle such cases to find new avenues of recovery for clients.

52. The case involved the Atari Corporation, a maker of video games, which closed down manufacturing operations in California and moved them to Hong Kong in 1983. See Henry Weinstein, "Atari Settles Landmark Lawsuit," *Los Angeles Times,* June 4, 1986, Part 4, p. 2.

53. Casey Ichniowski, "The Effects of Grievance Activity on Productivity," *Industrial and Labor Relations Review,* vol. 40 (October 1986), pp. 75–89.

54. Ronald Berenbeim, *Nonunion Complaint Systems: A Corporate Appraisal,* report no. 770 (New York: The Conference Board, 1980), pp. 4–5.

55. Bureau of National Affairs, Inc., *Policies for Unorganized Employees,* PPF survey no. 125 (Washington: BNA, 1979).

56. Keith Bradsher, "Firms Ask That Workers Waive Job Security," *Los Angeles Times,* July 31, 1988, Part 1, pp. 1, 18, 20–21.

57. Not surprisingly, in response to growing employer interest in creating complaint systems for nonunion workers, management groups began to advise their members on good practice in this area. See, for example, National Association of Manufacturers, *Settling Complaints in the Union-Free Operation* (Washington: NAM, 1982).

Chapter Twelve

THE EMPLOYMENT MARKET

An earlier chapter analyzed the employment relationship in terms of demand and supply analysis, both from a classical and a more modern economic perspective. It was noted that one of the characteristics of the real world labor market was its tendency not to clear, that is, not to equate demand and supply in the classical meaning of that term. Among the reasons cited for the labor market's departure from the classical model was the cost of employee turnover and efficiency wage setting.

The last chapter reviewed determination and scheduling of labor hours as part of a general discussion of conflicting employee–employer interests. A simple classical view of the labor market again proved to be insufficient. Hours determination involved not only individual employer and employee preferences but also externalities across employers, and problems of imperfect market clearing.

This chapter will provide a further elaboration of demand and supply analysis, relying heavily on empirical information. How do employees and employers find each other? What is meant by "unemployment," and how does it affect the employer–employee attachments of those who are employed? The goal is to provide a realistic picture of the employment market and suggest HRM implications.

12–1 Employment

Previous chapters have drawn repeatedly on data from the monthly Current Population Survey (CPS) for information on the labor market. The CPS provides a wealth of detailed data on individuals in and out of the labor force, based on a sample survey of 59,500 households. Three key statuses are determined for noninstitutional individuals of working age (defined as sixteen years of age and older): (1) employment, (2) unemployment, and (3) not in the labor force.[1] The labor force is defined as the number of individuals in the first two categories. The third classification is the residual population, those who are neither employed nor unemployed.

Each of the three statuses is more arbitrary than its label might at first seem to imply. For example, someone who is actually working for economic gain at the time of the survey should clearly be counted as employed.[2] People who are not working in the external commercial setting are not considered as employed, even though they may be engaged in worthwhile activities. Thus volunteers, homemakers, and students without jobs are not recorded as being employed. However, not all individuals who think of themselves as having a job (and hence as being employed) are actually at work.

Nonworking Workers

Table 12–1 shows that on average about 5% of nonagricultural employees in 1987 were, in fact, not at work during the reference week of the monthly survey. Of these "nonworking workers," over half were on vacation, obviously a seasonal activity that is not spread evenly over the entire year. The remainder were idled due to illness, bad weather, industrial dispute, or what are termed other reasons.

Exactly what these other reasons were is not reported. Employers, especially larger ones, commonly grant leaves for jury duty, bereavement, maternity, and military service. Less common are leaves for paternity and adoption. In addition, employers will sometimes grant leaves (often unpaid) for such personal reasons as alcohol or drug rehabilitation, educational pursuits, work in a political campaign, or social service work. In one survey a few employers even cited serving a jail sentence as a reason for unpaid leave.[3]

TABLE 12–1 Persons with a Job But Not at Work, 1987 (Nonagricultural Workers)

Reason	With a Job But Not at Work as Percent of All Civilian Employees	Percent of Wage and Salary Workers Not at Work Being Paid by Employer*
All Reasons	5.3%	57%
Vacation	3.1	71
Illness	1.2	42
Bad weather	.1	
Strike/lockout	†	27
Other	1.0	

*Excludes private household workers. Ninety percent of those with a job but not at work were nonhousehold wage and salary workers.

†Less than .05%.

Source: Data from *Employment and Earnings*, vol. 35 (January 1988), pp. 158, 195.

A little more than half of those people who had jobs but were not at work were being paid for their absences, mainly as workers on vacation. The converse observation is also significant; about half of the wage and salary workers who are not at work are viewed as employed—and regard themselves as having a job—even though they are receiving no payment from their employers. This view of the employed workforce is symptomatic of the stakeholder attachment of workers to their jobs, an outlook that has been stressed throughout this volume. An individual can have a job yet not be working. American data-collection methods and the ways individuals answer CPS questions about their employment attachments reflect this employee stake.

Also reflecting that stake is the demand for public policies that assure employees the right to hang on to their jobs, even when they are going to be absent from work for long periods. During the 1970s and 1980s, there were repeated calls for mandatory maternity leaves, for example, after which the employee would be reinstated. Some state legislation exists in this field. California law, for example, provides women the right to take up to four months of maternity leave and then be reinstated in a comparable position. Although there is no federal requirement that employers offer maternity leaves, there is a requirement that if an employer does have a leave program for other purposes (such as disability), it cannot exclude pregnancy from the program.[4]

Insufficient Hours

Not all workers who have jobs are necessarily working the hours they wish. In 1987, almost 2% of those who usually worked full time (thirty-five hours or more per week) reported that they were working only part time in the survey week because of "economic reasons." These reasons involved insufficient demand for labor by their employer to maintain full-time work or an inability to find a full-time job. For example, someone who normally worked full time on a five day per week schedule would fall into this category if he or she were suddenly placed on a three day per week schedule due to slack work. Also so-counted would be someone who was permanently laid off part way through the reference week, since he or she would have some work activity to report during that week.

About a fifth of those individuals who normally worked part time in 1987 reported that their part-time status was due to economic reasons, that is, they did not have the full-time work they preferred.[5] As noted in the previous chapter, employee frustration over differences between their actual weekly schedule, and the schedule they would prefer, can pose a human resource problem for employers.[6]

12–2   Unemployment

The word *unemployment* is sometimes used in casual conversation to refer to anyone who does not have a job. Yet there are many people who do not have a job and do not wish to have one, for example, retired persons. Historically, when empirically oriented economists have used the term *unemployment,* they have referred to people who do not have jobs but want to work, that is, people who are involuntarily without employment. Yet because the classical economic model seemed to preclude the existence of involuntary unemployment, arriving at a precise definition posed a significant problem.

Involuntary Unemployment

Economists have pointed out that in a formal sense, unemployment involves an asymmetry between capital and labor.[7] Normally it is expected that capital (the employer) hires labor. Were there no transaction costs, however, workers could just as well hire capital. Thus unemployed auto workers might hypothetically hire a car factory and go into business for themselves if a factory owner refused to hire them. In such an imaginary world, there would be little opportunity for unemployment.[8] But the difficulties involved in an entire factory workforce somehow coalescing itself and hiring the necessary management and capital are self-evident.

The fact that there is always some option for self-employment of unemployed workers, however, is one of the objections purists make to the very concept of involuntary unemployment.[9] Perhaps the unemployed auto worker cannot really join with other idle individuals to hire an auto factory because the costs of forming the necessary coalition are too high. He or she could always offer, however, to cut the neighbors' grass or sell pencils or apples on street corners. Even though such pursuits would pay substantially less than work in a car factory, the unemployed auto worker still chooses not to undertake these tasks and therefore is voluntarily idle.

Still another objection that has been raised to the concept of involuntary unemployment is that unemployed workers ought to bid down the wage for jobs, in effect underselling incumbents. An unemployed worker could, in theory, enter a workplace and offer to work for a few cents an hour below the wage paid to the existing workforce. Economists with a pragmatic orientation have long recognized that such offers would most likely be met with employer responses that there are no vacancies. Yet the notion that the labor market should operate like an auction market (even though it does not) has proved to be an intellectual stumbling block for some theorists. Employee refusal to act as if the labor market were a classical auction is taken as a sign by certain theoreticians that their unemployment is not truly involuntary.

Actual Measurement

During the Great Depression of the 1930s, when unemployment was the most pressing social issue of the day, such debates were quite common in the economic literature. The views expressed then still persist in some circles today, although they would probably be articulated more elegantly than they have been stated above. As the Great Depression continued, empirically oriented economists and statisticians struggled to come up with a definition of unemployment that would permit actual measurement. Ironically, it was not until 1940 (when the Great

Depression was almost over) that the predecessor to the modern Current Population Survey was established to monitor unemployment and other labor force characteristics.

Since 1940 the empirical approach to unemployment has been to sidestep any attempt to classify people on the basis of what the survey taker might have viewed as available alternatives to unemployment. Since cut-the-grass or sell-pencils-and-apples alternatives are always available, no one would ever be counted as unemployed if a strict definition were used. Any less strict version would be inherently subjective and indefensible as a labor market indicator. Instead, those being questioned in the CPS tell their own stories in the form of answers to specific questions.[10] A jobless working-age person is counted as unemployed if he or she meets one of the two following criteria:

1. The individual was available for work during the survey week (except for temporary illness) and had looked for work during the past four weeks.
2. The individual had not looked for work because he or she was on layoff status from a job or was waiting to start a new job within thirty days.

The first criterion under which the vast majority of the unemployed are included—measures unemployment by a self-expressed desire to work *as evidenced by some job-searching activity*.[11] The issue of whether the individual could have found a job if only he or she had searched more diligently is not considered. For example, someone who had received a job offer, but rejected it as unsatisfactory, would still be counted as unemployed.

The CPS survey taker does not dismiss the offer-rejecting individual as being too picky and hence not really unemployed. As will be seen such rejections of offers (including self-offers of grass cutting) may be entirely rational responses of individuals. Much depends on what alternatives the job seeker may expect to uncover by continuing to search for other job offers.

Still another reason for avoiding subjective judgments about the diligence of job search is the notion of queuing. Suppose there are ninety jobs available and a hundred job seekers. Ten of the job seekers will end up as unemployed, because of the labor demand insufficiency. But 90% of the job seekers will be successful in finding work. Had one of the unemployed ten been more aggressive in search, he or she might have been among the successful 90%, and someone else would have been elbowed out of the line and wound up as unemployed. When all is said and done, ten unemployed individuals will remain. The fact that nine out of ten are successful does not mean that the unemployed are volunteering to be jobless. The root cause of their joblessness is, after all, that there are fewer jobs than applicants, not a desire for leisure on the part of job seekers.

The second criterion recognizes the potential linkage between employer and employee during spells of nonemployment, if the employee has an expectation of returning to his or her old job. Formal layoff systems are particularly common in the union sector, but can also be found in nonunion employment. In effect, the second criterion recognizes that it may not pay an employee who believes he has a new or old job lined up to search for some other interim job during a spell of nonemployment. It is really only in the case of workers with formal layoff systems and *predictable* probabilities of layoffs and recalls that the "voluntary" label might arguably be applied. Temporary spells of unemployment might be deemed a feature of the workers' implicit employment contracts with their employers. The CPS, however, counts such laid-off persons as unemployed.

In any case, because of the costs of turnover, workers on layoff who do search for temporary alternative jobs may be rejected by potential employers on the grounds that they will probably quit when their old jobs resume. Why hire someone who will soon be quitting to work for someone else? Empirical evidence suggests that the probability of finding a *new* job is lower for workers with some prospect of recall from layoff than for other workers.[12]

Since, by some definition, all unemployment can be dismissed as voluntary, there is no perfect approach to measuring unemployment. For example, the requirement under the first criterion that those seeking work must cite a search activity within the past four weeks is clearly arbitrary. It could just as well have been set at three weeks or eight weeks.

The looser the criteria (eight weeks rather than three weeks), the higher will the absolute number of unemployed be in any given survey week.[13] Any plausible measure of unemployment, however, will produce the same general *cyclical* responses, that is, more unemployed in recessions and less in booms. Thus, most industrialized countries have adopted some variant of the U.S. approach to unemployment measurement for their own economies.[14]

Job Losers

Perhaps the most common public perception of an unemployed person is someone who has lost a job. Such individuals in fact make up only about 40% to 60% of the unemployed as defined in the CPS, depending on the stage of the business cycle. Times of high unemployment and job scarcity are known as periods of *loose* labor markets. Not surprisingly, job losers become a larger proportion of the unemployed during recessions, when the labor market is loose. Their importance in total unemployment falls during booms when jobs are plentiful and the labor market is termed *tight*. The little poem of Figure 12–1 helps in remembering this confusing terminology.

Table 12–2 illustrates the dominance of job losers in the cyclical fluctuations of unemployment (as opposed to the absolute number of unemployed people). Recall from Chapter 2 that the unemployment rate is defined as the proportion of the labor force that is unemployed, that is, as U/LF where E = the number of employed persons, LF = the labor force, which = $E + U$, and U = the number of unemployed persons. The job loser component accounts for much of the variation in the overall unemployment rate between business cycle peaks (denoted P on the table) and troughs (denoted T). In contrast, unemployment rates for labor force reentrants and new entrants (workers who began to seek work but did not have jobs in the immediate past) show milder fluctuations.[15]

Not all job loss is related to cyclical demand fluctuations. Because of concern over mass layoffs and plant closings in the 1980s, Congress required the Bureau of Labor Statistics to begin a survey of such occurrences. In 1987, about 39% of

FIGURE 12–1
"Dear Abby"

Dear Abby

She's Still Laboring Over Loose Language

By ABIGAIL VAN BUREN

DEAR ABBY: In a recent letter, you incorrectly used the phrase "tight labor market" to refer to a situation where jobs are scarce. Actually, a tight labor market is one in which job openings are *plentiful* and workers who don't like their work can easily quit and find other employment. Economists use the phrase "loose labor market" to describe job scarcity.

Your mistake in terminology is commonly made. So keep the following rhyme in mind:

When the labor market is tight
Tell your boss to fly a kite.
But when the labor market is loose,
Saying that will cook your goose.

DANIEL J.B. MITCHELL
UCLA Professor

DEAR PROFESSOR: You could have fooled me. I erroneously assumed that because the terminology "money is tight" means "money is scarce," the same held true for the labor market. Thanks for wising me up.

Although flying a kite was an electrifying experience for Benjamin Franklin, I wouldn't recommend telling one's boss to fly one under any circumstances.

Source: Taken from the "Dear Abby" column by Abigail Van Buren. Copyright 1986 Universal Press Syndicate. Reprinted with permission. All rights reserved.

layoff events—layoffs resulting in at least fifty unemployment insurance claims in a three-week period—could be classified as demand related in the twenty-nine states surveyed.[16] Eight percent resulted from location or ownership restructurings.[17] Three percent resulted from technical problems such as machinery breakdowns.[18] Twenty-seven percent were linked to seasonal factors.[19] These four reasons accounted for over three-fourths of the layoff events, with the remainder occurring for miscellaneous or unknown causes.

The unemployment rate for job leavers (quitters) shows little cyclical fluc-

TABLE 12–2   Civilian Unemployment Rates by Reason for Unemployment

Category	1973 (P)*	1975 (T)*	1979 (P)	1982 (T)	1987
Total	4.9%	8.5%	5.8%	9.7%	6.2%
Job losers	1.9	4.7	2.5	5.7	3.0
Job leavers	.8	.9	.8	.8	.8
Reentrants	1.5	2.0	1.7	2.2	1.6
New entrants	.7	.9	.8	1.1	.8

*(P) = business cycle peak; (T) = business cycle trough

Note: Details need not sum to totals due to rounding.

Source: Data from U.S. Bureau of Labor Statistics, *Handbook of Labor Statistics,* bulletin 2217 (Washington: GPO, 1985), p. 80; *Employment and Earnings,* vol. 35 (January 1988), p. 172.

tuation in Table 12–2 since it is affected by two opposing influences. People with jobs are less likely to quit them during business cycle troughs, since alternative work is scarce. This factor tends to lower the trough unemployment rate for quitters. On the other hand, those workers who do quit despite the bad times will find it harder to find new jobs and thus will remain unemployed longer than during good times. That factor tends to raise their unemployment rate.

Unemployment Duration

Fear of job loss is an important factor in the lives of many workers. This fear, in turn, affects their relationship with employers and—therefore—the human resource policy of firms. If other factors hold constant, an employer who offers job security, that is, a reduced possibility of layoff, is more attractive to potential job applicants and incumbents than one offering only uncertain prospects of continued employment.

Unemployment is feared in part because of its potential duration. One source of information on unemployment duration is the monthly CPS. Those persons who are identified as currently unemployed by the CPS are asked how long they have been in that condition. The average response has varied from eight to twenty weeks, depending on the business cycle. During periods of high unemployment, the duration recorded rises relative to its level in periods of low unemployment. The long duration during recessions reflects the fact that in loose labor markets finding a job is difficult and the search for work must be extended. In addition, recessions tend to knock individuals who have a high propensity for long unemployment spells off their career ladders.[20]

Two points should be stressed. First, the reported eight week to twenty week responses reflect *interrupted* spells of unemployment—that is, those responding are currently in the midst of being unemployed and many will remain unemployed for additional weeks. If the crude assumption is made that the average respondent is halfway through his or her spell of unemployment, then the unmeasured *completed* spells will be double the length of the measured interrupted spells. Thus average completed spells of unemployment of these workers—after which the worker has found a new job or has dropped out of the labor force—can be taken to be roughly from sixteen to forty weeks in length, again depending on the tightness or looseness of the labor market.

Second, analysts of labor market phenomena have noted that these long durations can hide the fact that many unemployment spells are much shorter than the average spell. When a person enters unemployment, he or she often leaves that status quickly, perhaps within a few weeks. Some people, however, have very long spells that drive up the average. For that reason, the *median* interrupted spell of unemployment reported has been from four to ten weeks in length, compared to from eight to twenty weeks of the *average* interrupted spell.[21]

An alternative approach to unemployment duration is thus to consider how long someone who becomes unemployed can expect to remain in that condition. If the analysis is confined only to new entrants into unemployment, the estimated completed spell should be shorter than if all currently unemployed persons are considered. This feature is due to the fact that long-term unemployed will be disproportionately represented in the CPS sample of currently unemployed individuals.[22]

Estimates of expected unemployment spells for the newly unemployed suggest durations ranging from six weeks during the period of very low unemployment rates in the late 1960s to fifteen weeks during the deep recessions of the mid-1970s and early 1980s.[23] For those with concerns about HRM policy—the readers of this text—the important question is, What is the average duration of unemployment that can be expected by a *job loser* who becomes unemployed? It is that group that is most likely to represent attitudes of current or prospective employees.

Some information on unemployment duration for job losers is available. In 1987, for example, 22% of job losers (other than those on layoff status) reported interrupted spells of unemployment of twenty-seven weeks or more, compared with only 10% for other unemployed persons.[24] A typical worker whose job is permanently terminated can expect to experience several months of unemployment and possibly—particularly in a period of recession—a spell extending beyond a year. Despite the limits of available data, it appears clear that the possibility of unemployment (and attendant income loss and uncertainty) is an important shaper of employee attitudes and motivation.

Debate over the best way to tabulate and present the issue of unemployment duration is best left to specialists and to other books. From the human resource management point of view the key issue is whether unemployment is a significant concern of employees (and, therefore, also of concern to employers). The argument here is that it is, and that workers—who are likely to be averse toward the risk of unemployment-related income loss—will be anxious to avoid layoffs. Thus for many workers, especially those with primary responsibilities for household income, the degree of job security offered by an employer is an important attribute of the total package of working conditions.

Income Losses, Employee Attitudes, and Employer Policy

Sometimes it is argued that unemployment no longer is a serious problem for families because the advent of greater female participation in the labor force has produced the cushion of an extra earner in the household. For example, there is evidence that males feel freer to quit their jobs if they have a working wife.[25] Evidence from the CPS suggests, however, that even with two-earner (husband-wife) families, very substantial drops in family earnings can occur if one family member becomes unemployed, especially if the unemployed member is the husband. A very rough estimate would be that if a two-earner family experiences unemployment of the husband, family wage income will drop by two-thirds. If the wife becomes unemployed, the drop will be roughly one-third.[26]

There is no doubt that two-earner families and the availability of unemployment insurance have made unemployment a less severe problem than it was, say, in the 1930s. As will be discussed below, unemployment insurance will typically make up about 40% to 50% of lost weekly wages after layoff, but its payments usually terminate after twenty-six weeks. Even with the advent of unemployment insurance, the income shocks related to unemployment are still sufficiently large that employees will want to avoid them. Employees will value privately developed internal human resource policies that offer protection from unemployment resulting from fluctuations in economic conditions. They will also be attracted to proposals in the external political setting that require such internal policies to be adopted.

The threat of unemployment, as noted in connection with the efficiency wage model in a previous chapter, also may have a disciplinary effect. A worker dismissed for inadequate or improper performance can anticipate a period of difficulty in finding a new job. Fear of unemployment may thus discourage worker activities likely to be disapproved by management.

For example, in the union sector, strike activity tends to diminish during periods of high unemployment. During the first half of the 1980s, when labor markets were generally loose, absence rates (including those attributed to illness and injury) fell markedly. Apparently workers felt less secure about calling in sick or being absent for other reasons. And employers felt more secure about taking measures to control absences.[27]

Job Security as a Fringe Benefit

Table 12–3 presents evidence on the risk that an employee in a particular occupational group will experience some unemployment during the course of a year. In 1987 the average monthly unemployment rate for all workers was 6.2%. Yet 14.3% of individuals who were in the labor force *at some time* during that year reported experiencing one or more spells of unemployment.

TABLE 12–3 Percent in the Labor Force Experiencing Any Unemployment in 1987

Labor Force Category	Percent Experiencing Unemployment
All who worked or looked for work	13.3%
All who worked	12.9
Executives, administrators, managerial	6.0
Professional specialty occupations	5.7
Technicians and related support	7.6
Sales occupations	11.8
Administrative support, including clerical	10.0
Protective services	8.2
Other services except private household	16.7
Mechanics, repairers	12.3
Construction trades	26.7
Other precision production, craft, repair	11.1
Machine operators, assemblers, inspectors	19.6
Transportation, material moving	19.6
Handlers, equipment cleaners, helpers	25.9

Source: Unpublished data from the U.S. Bureau of Labor Statistics.

Even when confined only to individuals who actually had jobs during 1987 (as opposed to those who looked for work but never had a job), the table shows the probability of experiencing some unemployment was 12.9%. Table 12–3 also suggests that job security has aspects of a fringe benefit. It is known that jobs that pay higher wages also tend to offer higher fringe benefits; for example, an electrical engineer is more likely to have a pension plan than a janitor. As job classification rises in the occupational (and pay) hierarchy of Table 12–3, the risk of having experienced unemployment decreases markedly.

Thus 25.9% of the "handlers, equipment cleaners, and helpers" classification—low-skilled and low-paid workers—experienced some unemployment in 1987 compared with only 6.0% of "executives, administrators, and managers." This discrepancy is *not* merely a blue-collar/white-collar phenomenon. Within the white-collar groupings, sales and clerical workers have higher risks of unemployment than (generally higher paid) managers and professionals. In the blue-collar groups, with the exception of the highly seasonal construction trades, skilled workers show lower unemployment probabilities than unskilled workers.

Some of these discrepancies in proneness to unemployment occur because employers, for reasons discussed earlier, have more reason to hold down turnover costs of the occupations in the higher paid groups. Some of the difference is also due to the general pattern of offering the higher paid workers a variety of desirable job characteristics, including employment security, along with the basic pay rate.

What type of employee would particularly value job security? An important element in determining tastes for security is the probability that it would be difficult to find another job once unemployed. Some research has been done on estimating these probabilities.[28] It appears that the monthly probability of leaving the state of unemployment is lower than average for prime-age persons, that is, persons aged thirty-five to sixty-four, especially for males. It is interesting to note that managers and administrators have particularly low probabilities.

The estimates thus indicate that while the chance of becoming unemployed is fairly low for relatively senior workers and for managers, if unemployment does occur, these workers face an especially long (and perhaps painful) search before their unemployment ends. Individuals who are knocked off a career ladder may find it difficult to locate a job comparable to the job that was lost. It may not be easy for a fifty-year-old displaced executive to pick up and find a new position. Thus the data suggest that employers offer relative security to persons who would be especially hard hit by unemployment and who therefore value protection from such risks.

Note that HRM policies that provide seniority-related security and career ladders paradoxically may worsen the plight of those employees who are dislocated. Policies under which new entrants come in at the bottom of the ladder mean that dislocated senior workers will be forced to start all over again. The possibility of having to face such a loss adds to pressures from employees for HRM policies of seniority-related security. The existence of "internal labor markets"—systems of promotion and career advancement within the firm—thus tends to reinforce itself.

Layoff Systems

As already noted, workers who are on layoff status but are not seeking work are counted as unemployed in the CPS. This practice is followed on the grounds that since such workers have a reasonable prospect of recall, job search for them might not be rational. From the employer's perspective, a layoff system for dealing with the ups and downs of product market demand offers certain attractions. In a world of imperfect information about employee characteristics, rehiring a worker who has previously been employed by the firm may well be cheaper than hiring a new employee off the street. The rehired worker has known productivity characteristics; the new one does not.

Apart from purely information considerations, a rehired worker embodies whatever investment in training and skill upgrading the firm has previously provided.[29] In contrast, a new worker must be brought up to speed by the firm before full productivity is achieved. Thus, the employer saves training costs as well as screening costs by the use of rehires from a layoff pool.

In a period of high unemployment, the chances that a laid-off worker will find a new job before being recalled to the old one are reduced. Nevertheless, an employer with a layoff system will probably want to convey to workers who are being laid off that recall may be expected, or at least what the probability of recall may be. If a laid-off employee is told that he or she has a good chance of recall within a not-too-long period, he or she is likely to remain available to the employer.

It might be expected, therefore, that unemployment spells by laid-off workers will be shorter than those of other job losers. Labor market evidence bears out this expectation. Table 12–4 shows that the length of (interrupted) unemployment spells of workers on layoff status tends to be shorter than length of spells for other job losers. In 1987, for example, over half of all unemployed workers on layoff status reported that their (interrupted) spells of joblessness had thus far been of less than five weeks' duration. The corresponding proportion for other job losers (those not on layoff status) was well under a third.[30]

According to Table 12–4, the significance of layoff unemployment for total unemployment is cyclical. At the trough of the economic slump of the early 1980s, workers on layoff accounted for 20% of all unemployed workers and over a third of all job losers. By 1987, as the economy recovered from the slump, the proportion of all unemployed workers who were on layoff status had dropped to 13%.

Formal layoff systems are more likely to be found in unionized firms than nonunion, indicating that employee preferences as well as employer preferences play a role in the establishment of layoff rules and procedures. The issue of formality may be misleading, however. Formality in the union sector means layoff by reverse order of seniority and recall by seniority order. For reasons discussed earlier, seniority is likely to be a key issue for unions, because of their internal political structure. Thus unions will push employers to obtain seniority-related benefits including job security and recall preference.

Despite such provisions, an employer is likely to prefer to have more discretion in choosing who is laid off and who is recalled. Generally, from the firm's perspective, the optimal rule is to lay off the least productive employees first.

TABLE 12–4   Workers on Layoff Relative to All Unemployed and Job Losers, 1979–1987

		Workers on Layoff as Percent of the Unemployed		Percent of Job Losers with Interrupted Spells of Unemployment Less Than Five Weeks	
Year	Civilian Unemployment Rate	All	All Job Losers	Workers on Layoff	Other Job Losers
1979	5.8%	14%	33%	55%	34%
1982	9.7	20	34	40	25
1987	6.2	13	26	51	30

Source: Data from *Employment and Earnings*, vol. 35 (January 1988), p. 173, and earlier issues.

Similarly, the firm will want to recall the most productive workers in the layoff pool before others are recalled. Nonunion employers, who determine layoff policy unilaterally, are likely to build in more room for managerial discretion.

Even with their more flexible layoff systems, nonunion employers are likely to pay some attention to seniority.[31] Seniority is linked to employee loyalty; the most senior workers have remained with the firm the longest. Under an implicit contracting model, in which loyalty is rewarded, nonunion employers might well give significant (although not determining) weight to seniority in layoff/recall decisions.

An exception to this rule is possible when the value of continuing the implicit contract declines. There is evidence that nonunion employers who are permanently closing facilities and laying off workers are less likely to give weight to seniority than those making temporary layoffs. The former no longer see a value in maintaining the implicit agreement, since the employer–employee relationship is ending. The latter still need to retain employee good will, however.

This factor may account for the findings that many firms gave little advance notice of plant closings before 1988, when Congress imposed a sixty-day requirement on medium-sized and large-sized firms.[32] There is evidence that such notice will benefit affected employees, reducing their periods of unemployment.[33] Yet apparently many employers did not factor this benefit into their HRM policies, perhaps because it entails the severing of the employer–employee relationship.[34]

Unemployment Insurance and Layoffs

In theory insurance carriers could offer workers private insurance policies against the risk of unemployment. However, a large moral hazard problem would occur under such a private system; it would be difficult for a private insurance carrier to verify that a worker who claimed to be unemployed really could not find a new job. People who were planning to drop out of the labor force might try to obtain unemployment insurance benefits in a hypothetical private system. The difficulties in defining unemployment might also encourage a private insurance carrier to challenge excessively the validity of worker claims for payments.

Adverse selection problems would arise, too. Workers who knew that they were likely to be laid off would naturally seek insurance. Of course, moral hazard and adverse selection present difficulties for insurance carriers in other contexts. As these problems mount, however, the ability to offer insurance profitably declines to the point at which no policies are offered. Unemployment insurance seems to be such a case; there are no significant offerings of such insurance from private carriers, nor was there even in the era before it was provided by government.

The only private unemployment insurance arrangements of any consequence that are found in the real world are the Supplemental Unemployment Benefit (SUB) plans specified in some union–management contracts. (These SUB programs were described in an earlier chapter.) SUB plans are monitored by the employer, not an outside carrier, and the employer's operation of the plan is in turn monitored by the union. Opportunities for moral hazard problems to arise on either the employee's or the employer's side are thus limited.

In the absence of unemployment insurance from private carriers, society has chosen to rely on a state-run system. The American unemployment insurance (UI) system was established as a joint federal–state venture during the Great Depression of the 1930s. UI was an important component of the Roosevelt administration's New Deal social insurance arrangements, which also included Social Security.

Generally, the UI system operates today much as it did at its inception. Its intent is still to provide benefits to workers laid off for economic reasons while they search for new employment.[35] The federal government imposes a payroll tax whose revenues can be used *only* to finance a state-run UI program, if the state where the taxes are collected elects to create one.

In principle, a state could refuse to have a UI program. If it did, the state's employers would still be taxed and its unemployed workers would receive nothing. Thus the federal government, through its control of the tax system, effectively makes an offer the states cannot refuse. As of 1988, the tax rate for UI was 6.2% on the first $7,000 of annual wage income.[36]

Almost all wage and salary earners work for employers covered by UI. (Self-employed persons and unpaid family workers are not protected.) Whether an *individual* unemployed worker is actually eligible for benefits depends on his or her work history. To establish eligibility, state UI formulas require minimum time periods of employment and minimum earnings with an employer. New entrants and reentrants to the labor force thus are not eligible, even if they are unemployed according to CPS definitions. Benefit payments are determined by formulas specified in the state programs, which are linked to the worker's recent earnings history. States impose a dollar cap on their benefits that limits the operation of the formulas.

As Table 12–5 shows, UI benefits have averaged between 40–45% of average weekly wages of nonsupervisory and production workers on private, non-agricultural payrolls. Actual earnings replacement ratios are probably somewhat higher, since the unemployed are disproportionately low paid. The ratio of benefits to average weekly earnings shown in the table has tended to rise during business cycle troughs, probably because higher paid workers in the cyclically sensitive manufacturing industries are laid off in such periods.[37] Since higher paid workers are eligible for higher benefits, their presence boosts the average UI benefit.

Typically, state UI systems limit benefits to a maximum of twenty-six weeks. In severe recessions the resulting long durations of unemployment tend to cause unemployed workers to exhaust their benefits before new jobs are found. Until the 1980s, however, Congress often intervened on an ad hoc basis, providing funds for benefit extensions beyond the twenty-sixth week.

In the 1980s a break from the earlier pattern occurred. As Table 12–5 shows, the ratio of UI recipients to CPS-measured job-loser unemployed persons fell from levels above 90% to around two-thirds. This shift resulted from a change in public policy. At the federal level, congressional generosity was restricted by a swing to the more conservative policy of limited social benefits associated with the Reagan administration. Congress was also influenced by the ballooning federal budget deficit of the early 1980s, which had been partly caused by tax cuts and the recession itself. (The UI program is considered part of the federal government budget, even though it is largely administered by the states.) Congress was there-

TABLE 12–5 Unemployment Insurance Coverage and Benefits, 1969–1986

Year	Civilian Unemployment Rate	Claimants Receiving Unemployment Insurance Benefits as a Percent of Unemployed Job Losers	Average Weekly Unemployment Insurance Benefit as Percent of Average Weekly Earnings*
1969	3.5%	92%	40%
1971	5.9	93	42
1973	4.9	96	41
1975	8.5	91	43
1979	5.8	92	41
1982	9.7	65	45
1986	7.2	63	43

*Average weekly earnings refers to nonsupervisory and production workers in the private, nonagricultural sector.

Source: Data from *Economic Report of the President, February 1988* (Washington: GPO, 1988), pp. 294–295, 299; U.S. Bureau of Labor Statistics, *Handbook of Labor Statistics,* bulletin 2217 (Washington: GPO, 1985), p. 80; *Employment and Earnings,* vol. 33 (January 1988), pp. 159, 228.

fore reluctant to undertake funding of potentially costly supplemental UI benefits. The upshot is that by the mid-1980s, the federal–state UI system was undoubtedly less of an influence on the behavior of both worker and employer than it had been previously.

Despite the decline in benefit eligibility, the presence of the UI system still had the potential to affect labor market behavior. Much of the research concerning the impact of UI on the labor market has focused on workers. It has been argued that by providing a subsidy to job seeking, UI may prolong the average duration of unemployment and hence raise the overall unemployment rate.[38] Workers may be encouraged to wait for (infrequent) vacancies at high-wage firms.[39] But the aggregate impact of this influence is ambiguous, since workers who are not eligible for UI will have less competition for the less attractive jobs and may obtain them faster.[40] It has also been argued that the availability of UI benefits may influence some workers who are not really looking for work to declare themselves unemployed for the purpose of obtaining benefits.[41]

From a macroeconomic perspective, the financial cushion provided by UI has often been viewed as a stabilizing influence on national income. It provides income to laid-off workers whose consumption might otherwise fall. To the extent that UI has this effect, it may reduce the unemployment rate below what it would otherwise be during recessions.[42]

While these possible effects of UI are interesting, further analysis of them would take the discussion far afield from HRM policy. Of greater importance for the purposes of this volume is the impact of UI on HRM policy by employers. Three key influences of UI may be cited.

1. During union–management disputes, employers have a disincentive to use lockouts, since in many states locked out workers will be eligible for UI benefits, whereas in most states strikers are not eligible.[43] Thus UI influences employer tactics and bargaining power.

2. Employers have certain incentives to challenge payment of UI benefits to workers discharged for improper behavior, that is workers who were fired for cause rather than laid off for economic reasons. To the extent employers are successful, the penalty of being fired for misconduct is increased, and employer authority over the workplace is thereby enhanced.[44]

3. Under certain circumstances employers have incentives to use layoffs as a means of labor cost adjustment in preference to wage cuts or hours cuts.

Since union–management relations have already been discussed, no further elaboration on the first influence is required. The second and third influences, however, are more general, since they affect nonunion as well as union employers. Both influences are also connected with the practice of "experience rating" in establishing UI tax rates.

The UI system, as already pointed out, is financed by means of a payroll tax. Because the system was originally designed to resemble a private insurance program, the tax rates charged are not necessarily uniform across employers. Those employers deemed to be good risks—those that are not prone to generate substantial claimants of benefits—can be charged lower tax rates than those deemed poor risks. In this regard, the tax rates are analogous to, say, the variations in automobile liability insurance premiums charged to car owners. Car owners with a history of prior accidents are charged more than those with safe records.

States may vary their UI tax rates for individual employers based on the employer's past history (experience) of employee claims for unemployment benefits. An employer whose prior layoff history has generated many such claims will pay a higher tax rate than one with a record of only a few claims. The rules and formulas for determining experience-rated tax assessments are diverse across the states. Nevertheless, a general representation of a "typical" state system of experience rating is depicted in Figure 12–2.

Figure 12–2 shows that experience rating is not perfect in the standard UI system—that is, some employers pay less than would be justified by the risk they impose on the system, whereas others pay more. Usually there is a low minimum tax for employers with very low claimant experience. Thus the tax rate will be only $0a$ for employers whose claims record falls below b in Figure 12–2. Above b, however, the rate rises as the claims record worsens. Even if the claims record rises above c, however, the tax rate will not rise above ceiling rate $0e$. This pattern means that a rise in claims from 0 to b costs the employer nothing in terms of a higher tax rate.[45] A rise from b to c, in contrast, raises employer tax costs. Finally, a rise from c to d again costs the employer nothing.

FIGURE 12–2
Relation of UI Tax
Rate and Claims
Record

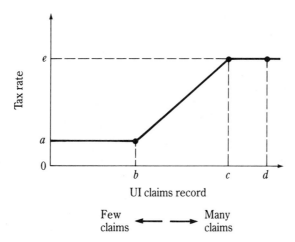

Employers will have a financial incentive to challenge employee claims for benefits if their records fall in the *bc* range. When employers challenge a claim, they usually do so on the grounds that the employee was discharged for cause, for example, misconduct such as theft of company property. State UI regulations generally deny benefits to such claimants, but the employer must be prepared to offer proof of the alleged grounds for discharge.

Thus the second UI influence, outlined in the preceding discussion, is operative only over a certain class of employers (those falling in the *bc* range of claims). Such employers will find it worthwhile to devote resources to examining UI claims against their accounts and to ensure that they have adequate records to document the grounds for discharges.[46] The UI system is yet another influence that causes drift from the historic notion of at-will employment in the American labor market. Even though employers under the at-will doctrine are free to discharge for no reason, under UI they have an economic incentive to follow standards of just cause and to document their actions.[47]

Employers in lines of businesses that are inherently cyclical or seasonal are likely to have histories of many claims against their accounts. A poor claims record will result from cyclical or seasonal adjustments in labor costs via layoffs. The typical employer of this type will probably fall into the *cd* range of Figure 12–2. Because the tax rate on such employers is capped at 0*e*, they pay less than fully experience-rated taxes for UI coverage. There is a net subsidy to the layoffs of these employers that is being financed by tax payments of employers with better records.

This net subsidy reinforces the use of layoffs to reduce labor costs.[48] For example, when a seasonal ski resort hotel lays off its employees at the end of the winter, the laid-off workers will probably be eligible for additional weeks of UI benefits. It is likely that they will actually collect these benefits, since the chance of finding local employment during the off-season period is small.

From the employee's perspective, the benefit of working at the hotel includes both cash wages during the active season and the expected UI benefits during the off-season. Because the hotel does not fully finance the UI benefits, there is a net subsidy to its operations. The hotel can pay lower wages than it would in the absence of UI and still attract sufficient labor. In the long run, the result is more employment in the seasonal, layoff-prone ski-resort industry than would otherwise occur.

Similarly, during an economic downturn a cyclically sensitive industry could consider three options for reducing labor costs: (1) layoffs, (2) reductions in weekly hours per worker without layoffs, or (3) wage reductions without layoffs. The standard UI system, however, will pay benefits only in the case of option 1. Because the employer does not fully finance its UI benefits (since it is likely to be in the *cd* range of Figure 12–2), the UI system effectively subsidizes the choice of option 1 over options 2 and 3.

In recognition of the artificial subsidy to option 1, some states have sought to make 2 more attractive by permitting so-called "work-sharing" options. Under these arrangements, workers may be partially laid off, that is, work only part of their normal weekly hours, and be paid proportionately partial UI benefits. However, the regulations surrounding defining eligibility for work-sharing UI payments have been cumbersome.[49] No attempts have been made to eliminate the artificial disfavoring of option 3 by UI programs. Indeed, severe moral hazard problems would arise were such efforts to be made.[50]

Searching for Jobs and Job Applicants

In a world of perfect and complete information, workers would not spend time searching for jobs, nor would employers have any unfilled vacancies. Workers and firms would instantaneously and costlessly find one another. But with imperfect information, it is likely that both firms and workers will spend time and resources coming together.

Economists have generally modeled the searching process from the worker side. A worker enters the labor market with only an imprecise idea of the actual job offers available. He or she may have an unrealistic notion of what wage his or her labor is likely to fetch in the marketplace. As a result the worker depicted in Figure 12–3a decides not to accept wage offers below W_0 initially (at time t_0).

However, there may not be any jobs the worker can obtain at a wage as high as W_0. (Or, if there is a distribution of wage offers by employers, there may be such a low probability of finding a W_0 offer that none is located.) As time progresses and the worker remains without a job, a more realistic appraisal of the labor market may set in. The worker will reduce his or her "reservation wage" to progressively lower levels as time passes, thus increasing the chance of finding a job.

Thus at time t_1 in Figure 12–3a a wage offer of W_1 would be rejected as too low. (The definition of wages includes all conditions of work—wages plus nonwage benefits.) By time t_2, however, a wage offer of W_1 would be accepted since the worker has learned from experience that higher wage offers are unlikely to be found and that continued search for such offers will probably simply extend the period of unemployment.

FIGURE 12–3
(a) Job Search
Behavior
(b) Vacancy-Filling
Behavior

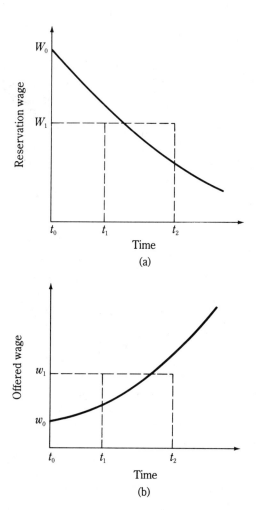

Obviously, the speed with which the adjustment takes place will vary from worker to worker. Some job seekers will start out with realistic expectations about what kinds of offers are likely to be available. Reservation wage schedules for such knowledgeable workers will start lower than those of someone with inflated expectations.

There is evidence that more-experienced workers (presumably with more knowledge about the labor market) search for jobs more efficiently and effectively than those who have less experience.[51] There is also evidence that when the nature of the labor market changes abruptly so that prior knowledge becomes obsolete unrealistic reservation wages are set. During the early to mid-1980s, when high-wage manufacturing industries experienced many layoffs, the resulting unemployed were reluctant to accept the low-wage jobs available in their areas and kept searching for wages to which they were accustomed.[52] From an HRM perspective, this means that recruitment needs of lower paying employers will not

362   *Chapter Twelve*   THE EMPLOYMENT MARKET

necessarily be eased immediately by increased unemployment of formerly high-wage workers. A period of adjustment may be required.

Although economists have neglected the employer search process in filling vacancies, much the same concept could be applied. An employer might initially have an unrealistically low expectation of the price of hiring a worker for a given job. Thus in Figure 12–3b, the initial wage offering might be only w_0.

As time passed and the vacancy went unfilled, the employer might reevaluate and progressively raise the wage offer. At time t_1, a worker who happened along with a reservation wage of w_1 would find the offered wage too low to accept. By time t_2, however, the offered wage would have climbed still higher, so that such a worker would gladly accept the then-prevailing offer.

Search models of the type just described explain what economists call "frictional" unemployment, that is, a minimal level of unemployment that can be attributed to information costs. Similar models might be made for other kinds of markets in which information is imperfect and in which, because of the importance of the transaction, it pays for both buyers and sellers to invest time and money in a searching process. Obvious examples come from the real estate field, for example, markets for houses and markets for apartment rentals. The analogy to frictional unemployment in such markets is the stock of unsold houses at any point in time or the apartment vacancy rate.

Models of searching have some bearing on cyclical fluctuations in unemployment. Some economists have argued that unemployment rises during times of recession because workers are initially unaware that the probability of a job offer at their reservation wage has fallen. In this view a lag in information causes workers to keep their reservation wage schedules too high, thus reducing their chances of finding work and increasing the duration of unemployment.

There are difficulties with such views, however. One problem is that they require too long an information lag. Can it really be the case that workers in 1933 were unaware that the Great Depression, which had begun four years earlier, was upon them? Even in lesser recessions, the same objections hold. In 1982 workers had only to watch the evening news on TV to discover that the U.S. economy had experienced a severe slowdown and that jobs had become scarce.

Simple search models require the presence of unrealistic naiveté on the part of workers to be much help in explaining cyclical unemployment fluctuations. They also do not explain employers' wage rigidity with regard to their current workforces.[53] The implicit contract models and insider–outsider approaches discussed in earlier chapters are much more helpful in this regard.

Another problem with using search models to explain cyclical fluctuations in employment relates to the distribution of wage offers. It is true that a job seeker who has a more realistic view of what offers might be available will obtain work faster. This obvious point might make it seem, therefore, that the problem of unemployment is due mainly to individual behavior regarding reservation wages. As pointed out earlier, however, if a hundred workers are seeking ninety jobs, ten will inevitably lose out. The more realistic worker will have a better shot at the available jobs than the others; he or she will be at the head of the queue. But if all workers were somehow made equally realistic and knowledgeable, there would still be ten unemployed workers left over.

Despite these important limitations, search models do shed certain insights on both sides of the labor market. The model suggests a trade-off process being made on both sides. Workers who embark on job search know in general terms the kinds of jobs they hope to find. In setting the reservation wage, the worker is saying implicitly, "I know that if I lower my sights, I'll find something. But I would rather search longer—even though it costs me the wages from a less attractive job I probably could have obtained—and find a better job. In the long run, the benefits from longer search will outweigh the immediate costs." Similarly, the employer is saying, "I know that if I put a high enough wage on this job offer, I could have a line of applicants that would wrap around the block. I could then pick the best applicant from the pool. But I would rather pay the cost of lost production as long as the vacancy is unfilled and offer a lower wage, since eventually a satisfactory worker will come along. In the long run, the benefits of waiting will outweigh the immediate costs of lost production."

Such statements could be modeled as investment decisions in the face of uncertainty.[54] Decisions on how to set offered or reservation wages involve evaluation of current costs relative to expected future benefits, using an appropriate discount rate. Even without the specification of a precise model, the approach has an implication for HRM policy in filling vacancies. Simply setting some surveyed average wage on a vacancy may not be the best strategy for the employer. There is a time element involved that must be considered.

The employer's question should always be, "How long can I live with this job unfilled?" If the answer is "not very long," a higher wage should be set. If the answer is that it is possible to make do at moderate cost as long as the position remains open, then a more modest offer is appropriate.[55] An employer ought to look periodically at how long job vacancies have typically remained open under current policy with regard to wage offers. The employer should consider changing that policy if the duration seems out of line—either too long or too short—with internal needs.

Unfortunately, information on employer strategies for filling vacancies is much more limited than information on worker methods for finding a job. A series was kept on employer vacancy rates (defined analogously to unemployment rates) by the U.S. Bureau of Labor Statistics for certain industries, until it was discontinued in the 1970s for conceptual and budget reasons.[56] There is evidence, however, that during boom periods, employers make more of an effort to attract workers than during recessions.

The Conference Board, a private business research group, maintains an index of help-wanted advertising based on the number of classified ads appearing in major newspapers in fifty-one cities.[57] Such advertising is one of the most widely used recruitment tools and is regarded by employers as highly effective.[58] It is therefore appropriate to regard help-wanted advertising as a proxy for job vacancies.

As can be seen from Table 12–6, the help-wanted index moves as would be expected, that is, inversely to the unemployment rate. During recessions, employ-

TABLE 12-6   **Help-Wanted Advertising and the Condition of the Labor Market, 1969-1987**

Year	Civilian Unemployment Rate	Help-Wanted Advertising Index (1967 = 100)
1969 (P)*	3.5%	121
1971 (T)*	5.9	83
1973 (P)	4.9	126
1975 (T)	8.5	80
1979 (P)	5.8	158
1982 (T)	9.7	86
1987	6.2	153

*P = business cycle peak; T = business cycle trough.

Source: Data from U.S. Bureau of Economic Analysis, *Business Statistics, 1984* (Washington: GPO, 1985), pp. 44, 60; *Survey of Current Business,* vol. 68 (June 1988), p. S12.

ers advertise for employees less often. This diminution of advertising effort when times are bad reflects both a reduction in available jobs and—as will be shown below—an increase in unsolicited applications from job seekers. The difficulty with the help-wanted index is not in its short-run behavior, but its long-run trend, which is affected by such influences as the decline in the number of urban newspapers.[59] HRM professionals who use the index as a gauge of labor market pressures should concentrate on its short-term fluctuations.

Data from the CPS contain information on job seeker behavior that is of potential relevance to the formulation of employer recruitment strategy. Table 12-7 shows job-seeking methods cited by the unemployed in 1979, 1982, and 1987. (The figures exclude those individuals on layoff status who were awaiting recall to their former employer and were not searching.) Typically, job seekers cited less than two methods of search; the predominant method by far was to approach employers directly.

These figures, in short, bear out the popular image of pounding the pavement looking for work. Of course, employers can also be approached by telephoning the personnel office or sending a résumé. An actual visit to the personnel office by a job applicant is not always necessary for an initial contact.

To the extent that information is available on employer practices, it supports the importance of direct contacts from employees as the key method of recruitment. For nonexempt personnel, over 90% of employers in one survey reported using unsolicited applications at their personnel offices as a recruiting tool. More important for these workers, it was the top-ranked method as measured by the number of new employees recruited.[60]

TABLE 12–7   Searching Methods Cited by the Unemployed*

Search Method	1979	1982	1987 All*	1987 Job Losers*
Public employment agencies	27%	24%	23%	29%
Private employment agencies	6	6	7	8
Employer directly	71	78	75	76
Placed or answered ads	30	35	36	37
Friends or relatives	14	16	17	20
Other	6	5	5	5
Average number of search methods cited	1.5	1.6	1.6	1.8

*Excludes unemployed individuals on layoff status.

Source: Data from U.S. Bureau of Labor Statistics, *Handbook of Labor Statistics,* bulletin 2217 (Washington: GPO, 1985), pp. 86–88; *Employment and Earnings,* vol. 35 (January 1988), p. 177.

There is cyclical variation in the proportion of unemployed workers citing their own approaches to employers as a job-search method. In 1979, a business cycle peak, 71% of job seekers cited such approaches. In trough year 1982, however, the figure had risen to 78%. By 1987, four years into the recovery, the figure had fallen back to 75%. Not surprisingly, therefore, employers can expect more job searchers to come to them when jobs are generally scarce.

Even during boom periods, the fact is that job applicants will be coming to employers. Many employers, therefore, will not find it worthwhile to engage in substantial outreach efforts. Exceptions occur among employers with special needs (such as affirmative action programs) and employers experiencing severe labor shortages. In addition, employers seeking employees with unusual qualities or technical qualifications may need a large applicant pool and thus are unlikely to follow a passive recruitment strategy.

The relatively low use of private employment agencies may be surprising to some readers. Such agencies charge fees for their services, either to the employer or employee, assuming that a successful placement occurs. Apparently both sides prefer to avoid such fees, thus holding down their use of such agencies.

Public employment services that charge no fee to either side have a much higher usage rate. Applicants for UI benefits, however, are required to register with the state public employment service. Not surprisingly, the usage rate for these agencies is higher for job losers (the group within the unemployed that is eligible for UI) than for others.

Still, the reported use of public employment services is far below 100%, even for this group. It appears, therefore, that many job losers do not cite the public employment service as a job-seeking method, even though they have in fact registered with it. Possibly, workers do not perceive the services as likely to produce a placement and thus do not report them to CPS interviewers. Employers indicate that the public employment services are frequently used as recruitment tools but rank them low in actual hires, except of nonsupervisory workers. Even for that group, direct contacts from applicants and help-wanted advertising rank higher in terms of new recruits hired.[61]

12–3   Persons Not in the Labor Force

At first blush, persons identified as not in the labor force, that is, neither employed nor unemployed, might seem to constitute a group irrelevant to the concerns of employers. In fact, within the pool of persons not in the labor force, there are individuals who are potential recruits for jobs. Other people might enter the labor force and seek work (become officially unemployed) if they felt conditions were sufficiently favorable to finding work opportunities.

Persons Who Do Not Want Work

Table 12–8 shows that individuals in the civilian noninstitutional population range across a spectrum marked by their degree of labor market attachment. Of the almost 183 million people who were in this population in 1987, about 63 million were not in the labor force and expressed no current interest in working. Presumably, some of these persons could be enticed into employment if the conditions offered were sufficiently attractive or if their family situations shifted in an adverse direction.[62] By self-declaration, however, their linkage to the labor market was extremely weak. Forty-four percent of these individuals were women who reported being homemakers, and twenty-eight percent were persons who were self-described as retired.[63]

Persons with Some Interest in Work

Another group of persons considered to be not in the labor force indicated that they would like to have had a job but were currently occupied with other nonwork pursuits (such as school or household tasks) or had some work-hindering disadvantage (such as illness or disability). The people in this group (4.7 million in 1987) seemed to be saying that they would have liked a job if one had come their way and had met their particular needs and situations. The desire to work, however, was not sufficiently strong to impel an active search for such jobs. The linkage between this population and the labor market was somewhat stronger than that of those people who said they did not want jobs.

TABLE 12–8   Degree of Labor Market Attachment, 1987 (Civilian Noninstitutional Population)

Degree of Attachment	Number (in millions)
Employed	112.4
Unemployed	7.4
Not in labor force	62.9
Not in labor force but want job now	5.7
Not looking because think cannot get job (discouraged workers)	1.0
Not looking because going to school, in ill health/disabled, keeping house, retired, other reasons	4.7
Not in labor force and do not want job now	57.1
Total civilian noninstitutional population	182.7

Note: Details need not sum to totals because of rounding.

Source: Data from *Employment and Earnings,* vol. 35 (January 1988), pp. 158, 199.

Discouraged Workers

A little over a million individuals indicated that they wanted a job but were not looking for one because they did not think work could be found. These persons, sometimes called "discouraged workers," express a stronger interest in work than the previously cited groups. But they do not meet the test for being counted as officially unemployed since they are not seeking work. Not surprisingly, the size of the discouraged worker pool fluctuates with the number of officially unemployed, since both classifications are related.

Effective Recruitment Pool

Those persons who can cite the requisite work-seeking activity (or who are on layoff status) are counted as unemployed in official statistics. They are still more strongly linked to the labor market than the groups discussed above, even though they did not have jobs at the time of the survey. Of course, the most strongly linked to the employment market in 1987 were the almost 112 million persons who actually had jobs.[64]

These figures carry an important message for employers. Those employers who have policies of actively recruiting new workers are not confined to recruitment from the pool of unemployed individuals. Obviously, employers often recruit employees directly from other employers. (That is, many new recruits transit from job to job without passing through a period of unemployment.) It is also the case that new employees can be obtained from among those persons who are not in the labor force at all. There are people who are neither employed nor officially unemployed, but who nevertheless might accept a job offer.

Table 12–9 illustrates this point. Based on the CPS, the table shows the average previous month status of employed individuals during 1984. About 95% of people employed in a particular month that year were also employed the previous month. (Most of these people, it can be assumed, were in fact employed in the same job from month to month.) In an average month just under 2% of the employed had entered employment after being unemployed the previous month. Over 3%, however, entered employment after not being in the labor force at all in the previous month—that is, more people entered employment from outside the labor force than from the pool of unemployed. Those persons who made the transition from not being in the labor force to being employed were disproportionately female, as the table shows.

Employer Recruitment Strategies

In seeking new recruits, employers can follow a strategy of simply waiting for job applicants. Such people will be unemployed and actively seeking work, or they will be employed people engaged in job search while working, presumably because they are dissatisfied with their current positions. However, an employer who is willing to accommodate the needs of people who are out of the labor force (not searching), but who have some interest in working, will find that a significant labor pool is available.

There are methods of attracting this pool. Use of bonuses to current employees who bring in recruits may succeed in tapping people who otherwise are not seeking work. One study found that 28% of surveyed employers offered such bonuses.[65] Another method is to make employment attractive by accommodating worker needs. For example, the firm can offer flexible hours, create arrangements permitting work at home (say, through computer terminals), or facilitate child care, and so on. The ability to provide such accommodations, and the costs of doing so, will vary across employers. Although the direct labor costs paid to workers may be lower if the employer draws on a pool of individuals who other-

TABLE 12–9   **Average Monthly Shifts into Employment, 1984**

Percent of Employed in Current Month by Source from Previous Month	All Employed	*Employed Males*	*Employed Females*
Employed in previous month	95.2%	96.0%	94.3%
Unemployed in previous month	1.7	1.9	1.4
Not in labor force in previous month	3.1	2.2	4.3

Note: Figures represent averages of monthly data.

Source: Paul O. Flaim and Carma R. Hogue, "Measuring Labor Force Flows: A Special Conference Examines the Problems," *Monthly Labor Review,* vol. 108 (July 1985), p. 11.

wise cannot be in the labor market, there are expenses related to providing this flexibility.

The most obvious costs for individuals whose hours or work site needs must be accommodated are the inherent problems of coordination and control. People whose hours vary substantially from normal work schedules, or who work at home, are difficult to supervise. In addition, if these nonsearchers are to be attracted into regular employment, coverage of worker transportation expenses and other potentially expensive inducements may be needed.

Outreach and the State of the Labor Market

Employers are most likely to engage in outreach to the pool of workers not in the labor force during very tight labor markets, when shortages of workers and unfilled vacancies overcome these costs. Perhaps the most prominent example of such behavior occurred during World War II, when booming production demands for labor (related to the war effort) and reductions in labor supply (due to military conscription of males) forced employers to seek every available worker. The result was a considerable recruitment of women, who at that time had much lower participation rates than they do today, into nontraditional blue-collar jobs.

Even apart from the extreme circumstances of World War II, there are examples of employer outreach. In the late 1980s certain parts of the country began to experience labor shortages. As a result, employers engaged in various outreach strategies. For example, some firms sent buses into depressed urban areas to bring out and hire disadvantaged minority workers who might otherwise not have had job opportunities.[66]

Future Job Desires

In the absence of such efforts, individuals in the not-in-the-labor-force classification may nevertheless become part of the available labor pool. Included in the CPS are questions to such persons about their future work-seeking intentions. Thus in 1987 about 15% of those persons of working age who were not in the labor force indicated that they would be seeking work within the next twelve months.

Eighteen percent of the individuals who indicated they would be seeking work in the future had never worked before. Such persons were mainly young men and women planning to enter the labor market for the first time after leaving school. Almost half, however, had worked during the previous year. These respondents were also typically young, probably students who enter and leave the labor force during their school vacations.[67]

Summary

The employment market has been shown in this chapter to be a fluid system of matching employers and employees. It contains persons of varying degrees of attachment to employment. And it varies in its state of tightness: while both job seekers and unfilled vacancies are always present, the balance between the two changes with the business cycle. The recruitment policies followed by employers will accordingly vary between passivity and active search for new hires, with more active recruitment strategies needed during business-cycle booms.

Fluctuations in labor demand are reflected in the layoff policies followed by employers. The use of layoffs as an adjustment to falling demand is reinforced by the unemployment insurance system. Because of incomplete experience rating, the UI system provides a net subsidy to employers who make heavy use of layoffs. Inability to find work quickly by laid-off job seekers is costly to them and conditions the employer–employee relationship.

Available data suggest that job security is likely to be of concern to many employees. With security of employment, longer employer–employee attachments result. In turn, the potential recoupment periods for "human capital" investments made by both the employee and the employer lengthen, raising the rate of return. Providing job security, however, is potentially costly in the face of demand variability. The next chapter will explore the interconnection between job security and investments in employees.

EXERCISES

Problem

Obtain information from the U.S. Bureau of Labor Statistics or its publications on the unemployment rate for your city or state. Trace the movements of this rate over time. What implications for employers in your area are there in the absolute level of the rate compared with the rate for the United States as a whole? In the *changes* of the area rate over time?

Questions

1. What implications are there for the employment relationship in the concept of workers who are on leave from their positions?

2. What hurdles are there for employees seeking to obtain jobs that provide the number of hours per week they would like to work?

3. What hurdles are there for employees seeking to obtain jobs that provide a schedule of hours that meets their other (nonjob) needs?

4. What role does seniority play in layoff systems?

5. Is the source of recruitment confined largely to individuals who are currently in the labor force? Explain.

6. How does the tax system for unemployment insurance affect the propensity of employers to use layoffs as a method of adjustment to demand fluctuations?

Terms

clearing of the labor market	frictional unemployment	loose labor market
discouraged workers	labor force	Supplemental Unemployment Benefits
employees as stakeholders	internal labor markets	tight labor market
experience rating of unemployment insurance	interrupted spell of unemployment	unemployment
	job search model	unemployment rate

ENDNOTES

1. The institutionalized population that is not included consists of inmates of prisons, mental institutions, sanitariums, and homes for the aged, infirm, and needy. Other detailed information on the Current Population Survey can be found in U.S. Bureau of Labor Statistics, *BLS Handbook of Methods,* bulletin 2285 (Washington: GPO, 1988), pp. 3–12.

2. Self-employed individuals and unpaid workers in family enterprises who worked fifteen or more hours per week are also counted as employed, even though they do not earn wages or salaries.

3. Bureau of National Affairs, Inc., *Policies on Leave from Work,* PPF survey no. 136 (Washington: BNA, 1983), pp. 3, 34.

4. Congress enacted this requirement in 1978 as an amendment to Title 7 of the Civil Rights Act. Issues surrounding equal employment opportunity (EEO) will be discussed in a later chapter.

5. *Employment and Earnings,* vol. 35 (January 1988), pp. 167, 196.

6. Presumably, there are some full-time workers who would prefer part-time work but cannot find such a job. These individuals are not regularly reported in the Current Population Survey.

7. Weitzman, Martin L., "Increasing Returns and the Foundations of Unemployment Theory," *Economic Journal,* vol. 92 (December 1982), pp. 787–804.

8. There could be frictional unemployment in such a situation if there were imperfect and costly information about the labor market. This concept is discussed later in this chapter.

9. For example, consider the view of Robert E. Lucas that "to explain why people *allocate* time . . . to unemployment we need to know why they *prefer* it to all other activities." (italics added) The comment is quoted in Alan S. Blinder, "Keynes, Lucas, and Scientific Progress," *American Economic Review,* vol. 77 (May 1987), p. 131. See also Robert M. Solow, "Unemployment: Getting the Questions Right," *Economica,* vol. 53 (Supplement, 1986), pp. S23–S34, especially S33–S34.

10. Actually, the person responding to the Current Population Survey answers on behalf of all members of the household.

11. In 1987, only 13% of those counted as unemployed were reported to be on layoff, that is, the remaining 87% were covered by the first criterion. Source: *Employment and Earnings,* vol. 35 (January 1988), p. 167. Formal layoff systems are discussed below in the text.

12. Lawrence Katz, "Layoffs, Recall and the Duration of Unemployment," working paper no. 1825, National Bureau of Economic Research, January 1986.

13. The way in which questions are asked and the timing of the questions will influence the results obtained. For example, in the Current Population Survey, there are always eight active "rotation groups." A group enters the sample for four months, drops out for four months, and then returns for four months. It has been found that the unemployment rate reported by the first rotation group (the group that has just entered the survey) tends to be higher than that of the other groups. Reasons for such biases are not known. See National Commission on Employment and Unemployment Statistics, *Counting the Labor Force* (Washington: GPO, 1979), pp. 134–136.

14. Figures on unemployment adjusted to U.S. definitions for various countries appear in the data appendix to the *Monthly Labor Review* and other publications of the U.S. Bureau

of Labor Statistics. In addition, an annual article in the *Monthly Labor Review* describes foreign labor market developments in detail.

15. Officially, there were actually two back-to-back recessions during the 1979–82 economic slump. The table ignores the interim "peak" during this period, which was really a pause on the way down.

16. Demand related is defined here as bankruptcy, contract cancellation or completion, import competition, or slack work. See U.S. Bureau of Labor Statistics, *Permanent Mass Layoffs and Plant Closings, 1987,* bulletin 2310 (Washington: GPO, 1988), p. 5.

17. Included are changes in ownership and domestic or overseas relocation.

18. Included are repairs, automation, energy-related problems, material shortages, and model changes.

19. Included are vacations, weather-related problems, and seasonality.

20. Michael R. Darby, John C. Haltiwanger, and Mark W. Plant, "The Ins and Outs of Unemployment: The Ins Win," working paper no. 1997, National Bureau of Economic Research, August 1986.

21. Analysis of unemployment duration can be found in Hyman B. Kaitz, "Analyzing Spells of Unemployment," *Monthly Labor Review,* vol. 93 (November 1970), pp. 11–20; Kim B. Clark and Lawrence H. Summers, "Labor Market Dynamics and Unemployment: A Reconsideration," *Brookings Papers on Economic Activity* (1:1979), pp. 13–60; George Akerlof and Brian G.M. Main, "Unemployment Spells and Unemployment Experience," *American Economic Review,* vol. 70 (December 1980), pp. 885–893 (comments and replies appear in the December 1983 issue); Michael W. Horrigan, "Time Spent Unemployed: A New Look at Data from the CPS," *Monthly Labor Review,* vol. 110 (July 1987), pp. 3–15.

22. Suppose that there are two classes of individuals. People in group S experience only short spells of unemployment of one week when they become unemployed; people in group L experience long spells of ten weeks. Suppose every week one person from each group becomes unemployed and that this process goes on indefinitely. In the steady state, the unemployed will consist of one person from group S and ten from group L. The average completed spell of those currently unemployed will be 9.2 weeks = $[(10 \times 10) + (1 \times 1)]/11$. The average completed spell of those entering unemployment will be 5.5 weeks = $(10 + 1)/2$. This example is a variant of one appearing in Horrigan, "Time Spent Unemployed," *op. cit.,* p. 4.

23. Hal Sider, "Unemployment Duration and Incidence: 1968–82," *American Economic Review,* vol. 75 (June 1985), pp. 461–472, especially p. 469.

24. *Employment and Earnings,* vol. 35 (January 1988), p. 173. Additional information on unemployment duration for job losers is presented in Table 12–4.

25. Kathryn L. Shaw, "The Quit Propensity of Married Men," *Journal of Labor Economics,* vol. 5 (October 1987), Part 1, pp. 533–560.

26. Median family income of two-earner (husband and wife) families can be compared with median earnings of one-earner families (just husband or just wife) to estimate the contribution of adding a wife (or husband) to the family's earners. Estimates are also available for families in which just the husband is unemployed (and the wife works) or just the husband works (and the wife is unemployed). The two-thirds/one-third estimate in the text is based on such comparisons.

27. Bruce W. Klein, "Missed Work and Lost Hours, May 1985," *Monthly Labor Review,* vol. 109 (November 1986), pp. 26–35.

28. Michael R. Darby, John C. Haltiwanger, and Mark W. Plant, "The Ins and Outs of Unemployment: The Ins Win," *op. cit.*

29. Training is discussed in the next chapter.

30. *Employment and Earnings,* vol. 35 (January 1988), p. 173.

31. Katharine G. Abraham and James L. Medoff, "Length of Service and the Operation of Internal Labor Markets" in Barbara D. Dennis, ed., *Proceedings of the Thirty-Fifth Annual Meeting,* Industrial Relations Research Association, December 28–30, 1982 (Madison, WI: IRRA, 1983), pp. 308–318; Katharine G. Abraham and James L. Medoff, "Length of Service and Layoffs in Union and Nonunion Work Groups," *Industrial and Labor Relations Review,* vol. 38 (October 1984), pp. 87–97.

32. U.S. General Accounting Office, *Plant Closings: Limited Advance Notice and Assistance Provided Dislocated Workers,* GAO–87–105 (Washington: GAO, 1987), pp. 34–39. The 1988 legislation contains a complex set of exclusions for smaller employers and small-scale layoffs.

33. Ronald G. Ehrenberg and George H. Jakubson, "Advance Notice Provisions in Plant Closing Legislation: Do They Matter?," working paper no. 2611, National Bureau of Economic Research, June 1988.

34. It is important to note that there is a distinction to be made between benefiting the employees concerned by advance notice requirements and benefiting society as a whole. Advance notice might provide an advantage to the affected workers by giving them more time to search for a limited number of jobs—to the disadvantage of other job seekers. However, such societal and public policy issues would not be of concern to the individual employer.

35. Workers who quit their jobs may not be eligible for benefits, or may be eligible only for reduced benefits, although

eligibility and benefits (if any) will depend on the circumstances of the quit. Workers who are discharged for misconduct are generally ineligible.

36. The employer can receive a credit of up to 5.4% of the 6.2%, with the remaining 0.8% used to finance federal and state administrative costs of the unemployment insurance system. Some states use wage bases higher than the $7,000 basic amount in order to generate higher revenues for their program. Under experience rating (see below in the text), employers may not in fact pay the full 5.4% and still be given credit for it against their federal tax obligation. State-by-state details on the UI system can be found in annual volumes issued by the National Foundation for Unemployment Insurance and Workers' Compensation and entitled *Highlights of State Unemployment Compensation Laws*.

37. There is evidence that the mix of individuals unemployed changes during cyclical downturns. See Michael L. Darby, John Haltiwanger, and Mark Plant, "Unemployment Rate Dynamics and Persistent Unemployment Under Rational Expectations," *American Economic Review*, vol. 75 (September 1985), pp. 614–637.

38. Finis Welch, "What Have We Learned from Empirical Studies on Unemployment Insurance?," *Industrial and Labor Relations Review*, vol. 30 (July 1977), pp. 451–461.

39. Lawrence M. Kahn and Stuart A. Low, "Systematic and Random Search: A Synthesis," *Journal of Human Resources*, vol. 23 (Winter 1988), pp. 1–19. The fact that there are jumps in job finding that occur among the unemployed at around the time the UI benefits run out suggests that the presence of the benefits does enable workers to prolong their searches. See Bruce D. Meyer, "Unemployment Insurance and Unemployment Spells," working paper no. 2546, National Bureau of Economic Research, March 1988. One experiment found that offering workers a bonus if they found a job early reduced the duration of UI claims. See Stephen A. Woodbury and Robert G. Spiegelman, "Bonuses to Workers and Employers to Reduce Unemployment: Randomized Trials in Illinois," *American Economic Review*, vol. 77 (September 1987), pp. 513–530.

40. Clair Vickery, "Unemployment Insurance: A Positive Reappraisal," *Industrial Relations*, vol. 18 (Winter 1979), pp. 1–17.

41. Technically, the CPS has nothing to do with an individual's eligibility for UI. Thus a respondent who is not really seeking work need not fear that disclosing this information to the CPS survey taker will result in loss of benefits. (Responses to the CPS are confidential.) However, respondents may not know this fact or believe assurances they are given. In any case, since UI payments are contingent on registration with the state employment service, the respondent can always cite such registration as a job-seeking activity.

42. UI effect as a macroeconomic stabilizer is weakened by the system of "experience rating" of UI taxes collected from employers. Average tax rates of employers will rise during recessions under this arrangement. In theory, consumption might not be affected by a temporary fall in income due to layoff. The evidence suggests, however, that consumption and income are linked. See Robert E. Hall, *Consumption*, working paper no. 2265, National Bureau of Economic Research, May 1987.

43. Strikers are eligible for benefits in Rhode Island and New York. State laws vary as to the definition of a striker and the determination of whether a dispute is a strike or lockout. Employers may sometimes be able to create a situation in which the union feels compelled to declare a strike, thus preventing nonworking union members from being eligible for benefits. Unions, in turn, can sometimes try to force a lockout, say, by striking only a key plant and offering to work at other plants.

44. Employers might challenge the eligibility of claimants on grounds other than that they were fired for misconduct.

45. Strictly speaking, as the employer approaches point *b,* it progressively exposes itself to the risk that further layoffs might push it into the rising tax rate range *bc.* There is empirical evidence, however, that employers tend to stay within their tax-rate schedule from period to period. See Denton Marks, "Incomplete Experience Rating in State Unemployment Insurance," *Monthly Labor Review*, vol. 107 (November 1984), pp. 45–49.

46. The state UI systems have appeals tribunals that examine employers' challenges and claimants' protests of denials of benefits.

47. See the previous chapter for more information on the at-will doctrine and wrongful discharge.

48. Robert H. Topel, "On Layoffs and Unemployment Insurance," *American Economic Review,* vol. 73 (September 1983), pp. 541–559.

49. See the symposium on work-sharing UI programs in Barbara D. Dennis, ed., *Proceedings of the Thirty-Eighth Annual Meeting,* Industrial Relations Research Association, December 28–30, 1985 (Madison: Wisc.: IRRA, 1986), pp. 424–464.

50. Imagine a UI system which paid benefits to workers whose wages were cut. An employer paying less than fully experience-rated taxes would have an incentive to hire workers at artificially high wages, and then cut those wages once eligibility of the workers was established, to induce a UI subsidy. If the rules required that UI would be paid only if the wage cuts were in lieu of a layoff, it would be difficult (if not impossible) to provide such proof. Hence, wage-cut benefits would not be paid. If the rules required that the UI authorities would have to disprove assertions that the

wage cuts were in lieu of layoffs, they would never be able to do so and the subsidy would be automatic.

51. Kahn and Low, "Systematic and Random Search: A Synthesis," *op. cit.*

52. Lawrence H. Summers, "Why Is the Unemployment Rate So Very High Near Full Employment?," *Brookings Papers on Economic Activity* (2:1986), pp. 339–383.

53. Suppose currently employed workers are naive about the demand for labor. Their employers would begin to cut pay, as recession loomed. But the naive workers would quit as pay fell, on the (incorrect) assumption that they could find work at the old wage somewhere else. In fact, quit rates fall as the economy goes into recession; they do not rise as the naive-worker hypothesis would suggest.

54. Steven A. Lippman and John J. McCall, *The Economics of Search* (Cambridge, Mass.: Harvard University Press, 1985).

55. It has been noted in a previous chapter that considerations of wage structure and cross-job wage equity may rationally be important to employers. Such considerations could constrain the wage offer decision.

56. Some states elected to continue the program within their jurisdictions. See Katharine G. Abraham, "Structural/Frictional vs. Deficient Demand Unemployment," *American Economic Review*, vol. 73 (September 1983), pp. 708–724.

57. Audrey Freedman and Kenneth Goldstein, "Labor Market Data from The Conference Board" in Barbara D. Dennis, ed., *Proceedings of the Thirty-Eighth Annual Meeting*, Industrial Relations Research Association, December 28–30, 1985 (Madison, Wisc.: IRRA, 1986), pp. 34–41.

58. Bureau of National Affairs, Inc., *Recruiting and Selection Procedures*, PPF survey no. 146 (Washington: BNA, 1988), p. 9.

59. As the number of newspapers in an urban market declines, the index is biased upwards, since the probability that an employer will use the sampled newspaper for help-wanted advertising increases. These and other problems are discussed in Katharine G. Abraham, "Help-Wanted Advertising, Job Vacancies, and Unemployment," *Brookings Papers on Economic Activity* (1:1987), pp. 207–243.

60. Harriet Gorlin, *Personnel Practices I: Recruitment, Placement, Training, Communication*, information bulletin no. 89 (New York: The Conference Board, 1981), pp. 11–12.

61. Bureau of National Affairs, Inc., *Recruiting and Selection Procedures, op. cit.*, pp. 7–9. Among employers, a common view of public employment agencies is that they do not refer the best applicants, that is, better applicants are available through other sources. This poor image may lead to negative signaling of applicants referred by public employment agencies; that is, employers may assume that they are of lower quality.

It might be noted that the CPS estimates of the number of job searching methods used is well below that found in another survey, the National Longitudinal Survey (NLS). It may be that the CPS's reliance on indirect questioning of one member of the household regarding behavior of all household members causes this result. The NLS data suggest that friends and relatives are more commonly used as sources of information about jobs than the CPS reports, especially by young people. See Harry J. Holzer, "Search Method Used by Unemployed Youth," *Journal of Labor Economics*, vol. 6 (January 1988), pp. 1–20.

62. Economists sometimes speak of an added worker effect, the reverse of the discouraged worker effect. (The latter is discussed below in the text.) Added workers are those who have been impelled to enter the labor force because of job loss of someone else in the family. The two effects are likely to work in opposite directions over the business cycle; as the unemployment rate goes up, some workers are discouraged and drop out of the labor force while others are added to it because of the unemployment. However, the discouraged worker effect seems to dominate. Regarding added workers, see Shelly Lundberg, "The Added Worker Effect," *Journal of Labor Economics*, vol. 3 (January 1985), Part 1, pp. 11–37.

63. *Employment and Earnings*, vol. 35 (January 1988), p. 199.

64. The reader is reminded that these figures are monthly averages. Hence there were more than 112 million people who had jobs *at some time* during 1987.

65. Bureau of National Affairs, Inc., *Recruitment and Selection Procedures, op. cit.*, p. 12.

66. Paul Richter, "Northeast U.S. Frustrated by Acute Labor Shortage," *Los Angeles Times*, December 23, 1986, Part 4, pp. 1, 20.

67. *Employment and Earnings*, vol. 35 (January 1988), p. 202.

Chapter Thirteen

TRAINING, HUMAN CAPITAL, AND EMPLOYMENT STABILIZATION

Earlier chapters have reviewed the attachment of individuals to the labor market and to employment. The fact that individuals do become attached to employers for extended periods has important implications for employer investment in employees and employee investments in skill acquisition related to their jobs. Unemployment, which can be a painful experience for workers, is made more so by the potential loss of employee investment in job skills.

This chapter analyzes the process of investment in employees—both by employers and by employees themselves. It then takes up the possibility of employment stabilization. If the probability of employee separation can be lessened, the returns to employer investment in employees would increase, simply because employees would remain longer with the firm, and the recoupment period would be lengthened. One possibility that developed as an important and controversial topic among economists in the 1980s was the use of share-compensation systems to stabilize employment. Such share systems are also discussed in this chapter, since employment stabilization and training are inherently related.

13–1   Job Tenure

How long do people generally work for a single employer? From the viewpoint of an employer considering investing in the training of an employee, or an employee considering investing in his or her own job skills, expected job duration is important. The yield on the investment will be influenced (positively) by the duration of the job. A longer duration means a longer recoupment period during which the returns can be obtained.

Questions about job duration raise problems similar to those relating to the duration of unemployment, discussed in the previous chapter. Although the Current Population Survey (CPS) periodically asks employees how long they have been on their current job, the responses represent *interrupted* spells of employment. The answers do not directly indicate how long an individual who has already been on the job for, say, five years will remain employed there. In other words, the *completed* spell of employment is not tracked.[1]

The median time reported on the current job in 1987 was 4.2 years for all workers; that broke down into 5.0 years for men and 3.6 years for women. Average data are not published, but the mean would be longer than the median; the potential response is bounded by zero on the low side, but has a very long potential duration on the high side.[2] Thus, if it is assumed that the typical respondent is halfway through his or her employment spell, a typical completed spell of employment for males would be 10 + years and for females 7 + years.

Even these figures can be misleading in their HRM implications because of the inclusion of young people in the CPS sample. Young workers who are queried by the CPS cannot have had extended spells with their current employers; they have not been of working age long enough to have been on the job for many years. More important, young workers have a tendency to seek temporary work with very short spells, for example, during school vacations. Even when they have finished their schooling, young workers tend to change jobs more readily than older workers as they seek to find their niche in the labor market. A lack of dependents makes such job changing easier for young people than for their older counterparts in the workforce.

Thus the strength of job attachment is best seen by analyzing older workers, who have had the chance to have had long working lives and who are more likely to have career positions. For males aged 55 to 64 years in 1987, median time on the current job was close to 16 years; over 42% reported having been with their current employer 20 or more years. The corresponding figures for women in that age bracket was a median of over 10 years; over 21% reported employment spells of 20 or more years.

These older individuals are approaching retirement age, so their current employment spells give some indication of their eventual completed job durations. It can be assumed that completed job spells of 20 years for males and 15 years for females are clearly not at all unusual. More precise analysis of CPS data has confirmed the long spells with a single employer that are commonplace in the U.S. labor market.[3]

Employees and employers normally have information as to whether a job situation is long-term or temporary. If it were possible (which it is not) to confine the CPS sample only to workers with career positions in firms with formal HRM procedures, the reported employment spells would be even longer than the available numbers suggest. Thus employers who invest in employees by providing them with training, or employees who invest in themselves by acquiring skills valuable to their employers, often have long potential recoupment periods to recapture such investments.

Once it is established that long durations of employment are not unusual, the precise length of an employment spell may not be critical, thanks to the heavy discounting of returns in years far in the future. For example, the present value of a $1 return paid at the end of each year for a five-year period is $4.33 at a 5% discount rate. For ten years, the present value rises to $7.72. At 15 years, the value is $10.38, and at 20 years, $12.46. As the duration extends, the extra increment of recoupment thus matters progressively less. In making decisions about investing in what economists call *human capital,* that is, in education, training, and skill acquisition, it will not matter very much whether career employees typically stay for 18 or 20 years.

13–2   Education and the Job Market

One fact that is very clear about human capital is that certain kinds of investment in skill acquisition are rewarded in the labor market. Unfortunately, there are no data gathered on the full extent of on-the-job training that occurs (although some limited survey data will be discussed below). What is most readily measured is formal education, that is, years of elementary, secondary, and higher education attained by individuals. Questions about educational attainment, job market experience, and income are part of such surveys as the decennial *Censuses of Population.* From these sources the rewards to education can be documented.

Rewards to Formal Education

In the mid-1980s over seven out of ten 18 year olds were high school graduates. Moreover, roughly half of those who were not graduates by age 18 subsequently completed four years of high school. About three out of ten high school graduates completed four years of college.[4] Thus a substantial investment in formal education is now quite common in the United States.

This heavy investment in human capital is often taken for granted. But it was not always the norm for entrants into the labor market to be highly educated. At the turn of the century, only about 6% of the population completed high school on schedule; practically no one attended college.[5] The vast majority of entrants into the labor market had significantly less than a full high school education.

Indeed, because of the large immigrant inflows entering the United States from Europe and elsewhere during the early part of this century, many industries had workforces in which the ability to use basic English was limited. Not surprisingly, the rewards in the labor market for those who *did* have substantial educations were high at that time, when compared with the rewards for the relatively unschooled.

Despite the advance in general educational attainment, the labor market today still rewards acquisition of education. Rewards come in two ways: job-search success and higher income. The relative advantage of more-educated persons in the labor market may not be as great as was the case in 1900. It is easy to show, however, that people with more educational credentials today have less trouble finding work than those with limited credentials. As in the past, immigrants who acquire English-language ability are rewarded for this learning in the labor market.[6]

In 1987, therefore, among persons aged 16 to 24 years and not enrolled in school, the unemployment rate for high school dropouts was 21.8%. The unemployment rate for high school graduates with no college was "only" 10.7%. And for college graduates the rate was a still lower 5.5%.[7]

Incomes from employment in the modern job market rise with educational attainment. Table 13–1 shows annual earnings of year-round, full-time workers as recorded in the 1980 *Census of Population*. Earnings of 25-year-old to 34-year-old males with four years of college were 22% higher than for males with only four years of high school. Similarly, male high school graduates had a 35% earnings advantage compared with men who had eight or fewer years of education. For females the corresponding ratios were 31% and 29%.

TABLE 13–1 Annual Labor Earnings of Full-Time, Year-Round Workers, by Education and Age, 1979 (Averages)

	Age of Respondent in 1980				Ratio: Peak Income to Age 25–34 Income
	25–34 Years	35–44 Years	45–54 Years	55–64 Years	
Males					
Elementary					
0–8 years	$12,034	$14,449	$15,439	$14,847	1.28
High School					
1–3 years	13,913	16,993	18,264	17,757	1.31
4 years	16,233	19,904	20,869	20,259	1.29
College					
1–3 years	17,399	22,862	24,306	24,514	1.40
4 years	19,859	29,491	33,864	33,218	1.71
5 or more years	22,462	33,919	38,487	37,777	1.71
Females					
Elementary					
0–8 years	$8,032	$8,405	$8,515	$8,611	1.07
High School					
1–3 years	8,748	9,343	9,735	9,747	1.11
4 years	10,340	10,961	11,347	11,432	1.11
College					
1–3 years	11,699	12,746	13,001	13,091	1.12
4 years	13,596	15,454	15,312	15,449	1.14
5 or more years	15,540	18,462	18,868	19,056	1.23

Source: U.S. Bureau of the Census, *Earnings by Occupation and Education*, 1980 Census of Population, PC80–2–8B (Washington: GPO, 1984), p. 1.

Job-Related Skills Versus Signaling

By paying higher salaries to more-educated workers and by offering them greater opportunities, employers seem to be indicating that such workers are more productive. Is it the case, however, that the educational system itself is imparting valuable job-related skills? Or is some other process accounting for the pay/education link? These questions cannot be answered definitively, a fact that by itself is important for HRM policy. The lack of a definitive answer suggests the issue of educational requirements for jobs should be periodically addressed by HRM professionals.

For some occupations, there is an obvious connection between schooling and needed job skills. Doctors learn their trade at medical school, lawyers at law school, and engineers at engineering colleges. High school courses in typing and clerical skills and vocational education classes are also clearly job related.

It is not necessary to confine the examples of productivity-enhancing educational investment to such clearcut occupationally oriented training. The basic elementary level of education also provides skills valued on the job—literacy, ability to do simple arithmetic, and so on. Thus the tie between certain fundamental skills that are useful to employers and certain aspects of the formal education system is not hard to identify.

Many components of education, however, are not so clearly linked to the job market. What about courses in American history, civics, and physical education in high school? What about liberal arts curricula—philosophy, literature, music and art appreciation—at the college level? Are these subjects really providing job-related skills? Just what are employers buying with their pay premiums for education?

Employers' use of educational attainment to ration access to higher paid jobs has long been subject to criticism. Some observers have argued that the U.S. economy is a victim of "creeping credentialism."[8] They argue that educational requirements keep sliding upwards, even though the true underlying qualifications for jobs have not really changed.

It is easy to point to anecdotal evidence of such an upward creep in credentials. For example, at one time doctors and lawyers did not need to acquire a bachelor's degree before going on to professional school. Librarians, social workers, and—dare it be noted?—even managers, seemed able to function satisfactorily with college-level degrees until the MLS, MSW, and MBA became popular. Are employers throwing unwarranted hurdles in the way of young entrants to the job market?

There are reasons to suspect that there is some creep in the educational requirement process. First, for some professional groups, adding requirements for training tends to keep down competition from new entrants by making entry more difficult. Reduced entry, in turn, helps bid up wages for incumbents. Professional groups sometimes seek government aid in adding educational requirements as part of licensing standards, ostensibly to protect the public from poorly trained practitioners. The education industry itself has an interest in having demands for its services maintained and increased by persons seeking to meet professional training standards.

Second, what economists call "signaling" may play a part in establishing educational credentials as sources of labor market rewards.[9] Employers are basically organizations, and they need people who can operate within organizational structures. Student survival in school depends upon possession of certain organizational skills. At a minimum, remaining in high school requires an ability to follow orders, to obey rules, to submit to ratings (grades), to cope with bureaucratic procedures, and to get along with others.

Organizational skills may not be formally taught in school, but students who do not have them are likely to become dropouts. Students who cannot cope with high school—who are chronically tardy or absent, who are disruptive or delinquent, or who simply do poorly academically—find that the barriers to graduation become progressively higher. An employer may feel that screening out dropouts lowers the probability of hiring individuals who could inflict significant costs on the organization. Similarly, labeling job applicants "disadvantaged"— as sometimes occurred under various government-sponsored programs—may have the perverse effect of making employers more reluctant to hire them.[10]

Some of the same organizational skills that serve students well in high school are also needed in higher education. Survival in higher educational settings also requires greater judgment on the student's part than in high school. Major fields and courses must be selected. Trade-offs must be made between time spent on academic pursuits and time spent on social and extracurricular activities. The ability to exercise such judgments in a pressured, but discretionary, environment has parallels with skills needed in many white-collar employment settings. Finally, because employers are organizations, they may well prefer to hire people whose backgrounds do not differ widely from those of people already on the job and from those who will be hired in the future.

It has already been noted that at the turn of the century few people finished high school. In such a world, there was no stigma attached to being a high school dropout. Indeed, the word *dropout*—with its connotation of evading a task that should have been completed—simply did not exist. In the early 1900s an employer would not have viewed someone who had not completed high school as a social deviant who might disrupt the workplace.

Nowadays, however, as noted above, an employer might easily have such concerns about a dropout job applicant. The employer might acknowledge, in the abstract, that there may be dropouts who would make good employees if given the opportunity. In the absence of a severe labor shortage, however, there is little incentive to go through the expense of finding a few diamonds in the rough.

Similarly, in white-collar settings, if most people in the workplace have completed college, they will all share a common experience. Regardless of any technical job skills that may have been learned in college, the common culture that exists among college-educated people may facilitate teamwork and job interactions at the workplace. Furthermore, it is not only employers who may expect employees to fit certain educational norms. Fellow employees might also have such expectations of their co-workers, making interaction with persons whose backgrounds do not match the standard model more difficult. Studies of successful business organizations suggest that they often tend to hire a homogeneous work-force, presumably in an effort to promote trust and cooperation.[11]

If signaling by means of educational credentials is an important element in the labor market, one reason may be that more direct measurements of embodied skills are difficult to make. The employer may have difficulty in gauging the actual organizational skills of job applicants based on résumés, application forms, reference letters, and the other tangible evidence that job seekers commonly provide. In such cases the simplest thing for the employer to do—if it is believed that the needed skills are correlated with educational credentials—is to require the credentials as a proxy for the skills.

The temptation to use credentials may be particularly great during periods of slack labor markets, that is, periods in which unemployment is a problem. When the labor market does not clear and there are many more applicants than vacancies, some method must be developed to ration available vacancies. If educational credentials have any predictive value at all, employers may use them as job-rationing devices for want of other criteria. Some qualified candidates may be eliminated erroneously by credentialism, but if there is no shortage of applicants, the cost of these errors (to the employer, not the applicant) is negligible.

Use of educational credentials (and tests generally) that cannot be shown to be job related or predictive of future job performance are increasingly subject to legal challenge. Judging applicants by credentials and social norms can easily slide into unlawful discrimination based on race or sex. Contemporary HRM professionals are thus well advised to analyze and reconsider whatever educational standards their firms are employing to screen job applicants.

If credentials required for hiring are merely proxies for skills that can be measured directly, use of the more direct measures should be considered instead. If the problem is that productivity is hard to appraise before hiring, it may be possible to develop better monitoring procedures *after* hiring. Better monitoring in the immediate post-hire period can be combined with an initial probationary period during which termination of new hires is relatively simple. This approach could substitute for use of educational credentials as productivity proxies.

Finally, employers can themselves provide training for employees in those areas (including organizational skills) that are clearly job related. Options such as employer-provided training have costs, and employers may feel that the benefits of instituting alternatives to educational credentials do not outweigh these costs.[12] Legal pressures in the area of equal employment opportunity (EEO), however, may override this objection. In any case, as in much of contemporary HRM practice, rigorous evaluations of the costs and benefits of alternatives often have not been undertaken. HRM policies unfortunately are often based on impressions and assumptions rather than on objective analysis.

Other Forms of Learning

Education-related earnings differentials exist in all age brackets. Yet Table 13–1 reveals another important phenomenon. At any given education level, earnings rise with age—up to a point. For males this tendency to rise with age peaks out among 45 to 54 year olds. For women it continues through the 55 to 64 age classification. There seems to be a reward for experience as well as education implicit in the table's numbers.[13]

Three interpretations of the linkage between age and earnings are possible. One is that workers acquire training on the job or during their working lives, outside of the formal educational system. This skill acquisition is then rewarded with higher pay. A second explanation is that workers increase their value to employers simply by becoming more experienced, even if they do not receive actual training. A third explanation is the idea that employers have implicit contracts that link earnings to seniority (which correlates with age) to encourage job performance along the lines discussed in an earlier chapter. Pay is set low at entry level with the implicit promise that good performance will yield higher pay later on.

Before analyzing these explanations, it is useful to look at employee perceptions of where they obtained their training. Table 13–2 is based on a 1983 survey in which workers were asked whether they needed training in order to obtain and perform their jobs. Fifty-five percent answered that they did. These workers were then asked how this training was acquired.

The table shows, not surprisingly, that employees in the professional, technical, managerial, and skilled craft categories were most prone to indicate that they needed training for their jobs. Except for the craft workers, employees in these groups were most likely to cite school as a training source. Informal, on-the-job learning was often cited by technical, managerial, and craft workers as a source of skill acquisition.

Only about a tenth of the workforce (18% of those saying they needed training, that is, 10/55) reported receiving training in a formal company program. Since formal programs are very widespread, especially among larger employers, this finding is startling. It suggests that the learning occurring at work that is most important to employees is what they pick up on the basis of experience on the job.

Training by Employers.   As noted earlier, extensive data on formal training at the workplace are not available. A survey by the Conference Board taken in late 1979, however, provides some information on such training and is summarized in Table 13–3. The survey was based on a sample of firms that was biased towards medium and large employers. It indicated that employer training is common and that it is frequently aimed at new hires, but that it is often used for skill upgrading of incumbent employees as well. Employer training tends to focus on technical job skills for nonexempt workers and on supervisory and interpersonal skills for exempt employees.[14]

Employers provide training in a variety of forums. Much of this training occurs directly on the job, but classroom-type instruction is also used. Formal apprenticeship programs are not unusual for production workers, but are rare for other groups. Training is sometimes conducted by full-time instructional staff, sometimes by persons with other functions in the company (personnel department employees, supervisors, and so on), and sometimes by vendors of equipment to

TABLE 13–2 Sources of Training Reported by Employees

Occupational Group	Percent of Employment by Occupational Group						
	All	*School*	*Formal Company Program*	*Informal On-the-Job Training*	*Armed Forces*	*Correspondence Course*	*Other**
Professional specialty	93%	82%	9%	22%	2%	1%	3%
Technicians and related support	85	58	14	32	5	2	2
Executive, administrative, managerial	71	43	12	39	3	1	3
Precision production, craft, repair	65	16	17	40	5	2	8
Sales	43	15	12	26	1	1	3
Machine operators, assemblers, inspectors	37	6	6	26	1	*	3
Transportation, material moving	36	2	8	26	2	*	3
Service workers†	36	13	9	18	1	*	2
Handlers, equipment cleaners, laborers	16	2	2	13	1	*	1
All‡	55	29	10	28	2	1	3

Note: Some workers may have cited more than one method of training. Hence details may sum to more than 100%.

*Friend or relative or other nonwork-related training.

†Excluding private household workers.

‡Includes private household workers and farming, forestry, and fishing occupations not shown separately.

Source: U.S. Bureau of Labor Statistics, *How Workers Get Their Training,* bulletin 2226 (Washington: GPO, 1985), p. 21.

the employer. Academics and outside consultants are used for certain types of training, mainly involving exempt employees. In addition, many employers have tuition-aid plans for employees who take job-related courses in colleges or vocational schools.

Experience.   It is common to find help-wanted ads specifying that experienced candidates are being sought. Table 13–1 indicates that earnings increase with age, and one possibility is that simply performing a job for a period of time—rather than training per se—adds to employee productivity. The age effect on earnings seems to be more marked among employees who are also more educated and higher paid. Such individuals are unlikely to be receiving substantially more formal training while employed than they had upon leaving school. Thus the notion of an important learning-by-doing effect is quite plausible. People become better at their jobs by performing them over an extended period.

Experience-related learning about the organization, and how best to accom-

TABLE 13–3   On-Site Training by Employers

	Production/Operations Workers	Office/Clerical Workers	Lower Level Exempt
Percent with training	86%	83%	84%
Of those with training	100%	100%	100%
Objectives			
Train new hires	87	83	72
Improve performance of current employees	69	78	82
Prepare employees for new duties	65	66	70
Subjects taught			
Specific job skills	92	84	65
Safety/hygiene	96	53	59
Supervisory skills	19	28	81
Interpersonal skills	17	43	71

Source: Harriet Gorlin, *Personnel Practices I: Recruitment, Placement, Training, Communication,* information bulletin 89 (New York: The Conference Board, 1981), p. 41.

plish tasks within it, may be reflected in another aspect of the earnings numbers of Table 13–1. The fact that male earnings rise with age more than female earnings suggests that employment continuity (particularly employment continuity with a single employer) plays a role in raising earnings. Individuals who remain with organizations for long periods come to know how things are really done and who really has authority, as opposed to the formal statements found in company handbooks and organization charts.

Such organizational knowledge has job-related value, particularly if the person is progressing up a career ladder. At each promotion the individual starts in the new position with more baseline knowledge about the job and where it fits into the organization than an outsider would possess. The widespread phenomenon of promoting from within is partly based on the assumption that insider candidates are more valuable than outsiders.

Implicit Contracts.   A third possible explanation of the age/earnings association is the implicit contract model of the employer–employee relationship, discussed in previous chapters. Under this model, new employees are brought into the firm at comparatively low pay. In effect, they are initially paid less than their marginal revenue products with the understanding that loyalty and good performance will be rewarded later in their careers. The future reward comes in the form of eventual pay levels above marginal revenue productivity.

From the employer's viewpoint, such a system functions as a performance bond, since employees will have a stake in remaining with the firm and will thus want to avoid misconduct and termination. In addition, turnover costs are reduced because recent employees lose their claim to future pay if they quit. Older employees lose their existing pay premiums if they depart before retirement age.

Of the three explanations of the age/earnings correlation, only the implicit contract approach does not directly involve accretion of human capital. But even in the implicit contract case, there is a human capital aspect. The encouragement of long service, as noted earlier, increases the potential recoupment period for investments made by the employer or employee in job skill improvements.

Even in a world in which the implicit contract idea was initially the only employer motivation in structuring pay, skill acquisition would soon enter the picture. Long service, implicit-contract employees are more likely to acquire both formal training and the benefits of experience than those hired with expected short durations of employment. Organizations with career appointment policies can be expected to have an important training element within their HRM function.

How important is the implicit-contract explanation of the pay-experience connection? Unfortunately, a definitive answer cannot be given since the statistical correlation between pay and experience is open to varying interpretations. For example, it has been argued that current employees' time on the job (the interrupted spell) is bound to be positively correlated with time that will eventually be spent on the job (the completed spell). Long completed spells might, in turn, be taken as proxy for having skills that the employer values but that are difficult to measure from available data.[15]

Given available information, including the knowledge that employers do give deference in career advancement to seniority,[16] the most reasonable assumption is that the pay-experience linkage is the product of a mix of forces. It partly represents learning on the job and acquisition of skills. Some of the association is linked to employee characteristics that their employers value and that therefore keep them on the job longer. In other words, there is a good "match" between employer and employee that keeps both sides happy. And some of the pay-experience linkage is due to implicit contracts that reward long and loyal service.

Who Pays for Investments in Human Capital?

Basic education up through high school is largely financed by the taxpayer. Higher education is also heavily subsidized, through state-run universities and colleges, government-operated low-cost financial aid arrangements for students, tax deductions for gifts to colleges and universities, and so on. Significant expenses of education, however, are borne by students beyond high school in the form of tuition, fees, books, and so on, despite the public subsidies.

In addition to out-of-pocket expenditures—and often neglected since they are opportunity costs—are the sacrifices of potential working time. Students who attend college full time, for example, are sacrificing the income they could have earned had they devoted their college hours to the labor market. The same logic applies to any form of training, for example, enrolling in a junior college's vocational track, a secretarial school, or any of the many privately run, for-profit vocational training enterprises. Even if a person works while at school and thus reduces the income loss, the time/effort conflict between work and school may have adverse effects on both.[17]

Individual Investment Decision.   Like any other investment decision, an individual's investment in his or her own human capital can be analyzed in present value terms. There is a sacrifice to be made today in the form of out-of-pocket and opportunity costs. These costs must be weighed against a positive return tomorrow. Consider, for example, a hypothetical individual with a high school degree pondering whether or not to go on to college. He or she could be imagined first making a calculation of the expected present value (at some appropriate discount rate) of four years' worth of tuition and other school-related expenses.

The hypothetical high school graduate would then subtract the present value of these school-attendance costs from the expected present value of the *extra* earnings he or she could expect in the future as a college graduate as opposed to a high school graduate.[18] If the result of the computation is positive, college is a good investment for this individual. To the extent that society subsidizes the costs (through low tuition, cheap loans, and so forth), the more likely it will be that our high school graduate will select the college option.[19]

Not many persons actually make their educational choices with the precise calculations just described. Apart from the uncertainties involved—which are, after all, present in most business investment decisions—there is the matter of personal commitment. Some people enjoy school, some merely tolerate it, and others detest it. Since education is a consumer good as well as an investment good, these individual tastes will play an important part in enrollment decisions.

Despite all of these caveats, economists have found that individual educational decisions do respond to job and income opportunities. Entry level opportunities have been viewed by students as indicators of future lifetime experience, although there is evidence they also look at earnings for a longer term (present value).[20] Enrollments in MBA programs thus grew in the 1970s and 1980s because job opportunities were available to MBAs at attractive salaries and seemed to present good future prospects. Within the field of management education, when opportunities in investment banking and other financial institutions became particularly enticing in the late 1970s and early 1980s, finance became the hot subspecialty for MBAs at most business schools.

Obviously, rate of return to education is not the only factor that determines enrollment trends. Societal trends also condition the choices made. In the late 1960s, over 80% of college freshmen indicated that their very important or essential life goal was to "develop a meaningful philosophy of life," while only a little over 40% said their goal was to "be well off financially." The 1960s also saw such phenomena as college protests against the Vietnam War, hippies, flower children, and other counterculture movements. In contrast, during the conservative 1980s, being well off financially was the goal of over 70% of freshmen students; developing a philosophy of life was the goal of less than half. Given these trends, it is hardly surprising that business became a popular major relative to other subjects.[21]

There are also lags in the process of adjustment of labor supply to labor demand that sometimes create cycles of labor shortages and surpluses. It takes time for information about the labor market to work its way to the student enrollment level. Since training may take several years, there is a lag in emptying the educational pipeline or in filling it. In addition, there may be a reluctance on the part of students to revise their plans in the light of new information. The initial reaction of finance majors to the stock market crash of October 1987 was to shrug it off, even as major Wall Street firms were laying off many employees. Eventually, however, adaptations were made. From whatever source they stem, lags in responding to the market produce a "cobweb model" of adjustment.[22]

Consider, as another example, the government funding cutbacks for R&D and aerospace that soured the labor market for engineers in the early 1970s. Engineering graduates continued to glut the market for several years, as the school pipeline emptied. But the lesson was ultimately learned, and the excess supply of engineers was alleviated. By the late 1970s an engineering shortage started to develop. The pipeline at engineering schools began to fill again in response, but it took several years before those who entered the programs were ready to graduate.

The lags in the adjustment process and the cycles they create have been of the short-term variety, lasting a few years at most. There are also long-run factors that can affect the economic return to education and the choices students must make about careers and education. Most prominent are demographic trends. The baby boom that ran from the late 1940s to the early 1960s crowded higher educational institutions and lowered the return to college education. It also reduced job opportunities of high schoolers, since college grads competed for positions that previously might have been allocated to high school grads. As the effect of the crowding of the educated labor market passes, the return to higher education will probably rise and job prospects for high schoolers will improve.[23]

General Versus Specific Training. Human capital theorists have proposed a distinction between two types of education and training. The kinds of training discussed so far—enrollments in college or engineering school—are examples of *general training*.[24] Such training is distinguished by its applicability to many employers. Simple economic theory (which will be shown below to need important qualification) suggests that employers will not pay for general training because they cannot hope to capture a return on their investment. It suggests, therefore, that the cost of general training will be borne by employees.

Consider an employer looking for a word-processor operator. One option is to go into the labor market and find an experienced operator. The wage to be paid for such a person would reflect the typing and word-processing skills involved. Another option for the employer is to hire someone without any typing and word-processing skills and then provide the needed training. The unskilled person would initially command a lower wage in the labor market than the experienced word-processor operator. This lower wage might seem to be a sufficient cost saving to the employer to pay for the training expenses.

A problem arises, however, with regard to the second option. The unskilled operator becomes skilled as the result of the training and can thus command a skilled wage from other employers. If the original employer that provided the training does not raise the level of pay to meet the market, the now-skilled operator can obtain a word-processing job from some other firm. Thus the investment in training by the employer does not seem to be a good option after all, despite the initially lower wage. As soon as there are any returns to general training to be recouped, the employee—not the employer—can capture them because of the availability of the outside labor market. Again, it must be stressed that qualification will need to be made to this conclusion.

At the other end of the spectrum is *specific training*. Specific training is defined as acquisition of a skill valuable only to a single employer. For example, suppose an employer has developed special in-house computer software to handle its payroll system. Individuals will have to be trained to use this special software since the skills cannot be found on the outside labor market. The simple theory of human capital suggests that the employer will have to pay for this training, since the employee is acquiring a skill with no external use or reward.

In the outside labor market, the newly trained employee will have no more value to employers than before the training occurred. No other firms have the same payroll system. As a result, the employer would at first seem to have no incentive to raise the employee's wage after training. The cost of providing the training is thus captured by the employer in the form of higher productivity, that is, the ability to use the in-house payroll system, without a commensurate wage increase.

Burden of Payment Versus Location of Training.   Before qualifying the general/ specific training distinction, it is important to make clear the notion of paying for training. *The location of training does not indicate who is paying for it.* For example, a firm might pay for training that takes place on the job or in-house. If there are economies of scale in training, the firm might pay for training in some external school setting.[25] Sometimes, employers will even enroll their employees at the training facilities of other employers. External sites may not be in proximity to the job, but the training that occurs at them is still at the expense of the employer. This observation seems self-evident stated from the employer's viewpoint. However, the same statement can be made from the employee's viewpoint, too.

An employee might self-invest in training by paying the tuition of a vocational school or college, but might also bear the expense of training that takes place at a worksite. In theory an employer could charge an explicit tuition to employees who wanted to learn at a worksite location. In practice, however, such tuitions are usually charged indirectly, by having the learner work at a low wage (below the value of his or her productivity) while the training is underway.

The most prominent examples of such arrangements are formal apprenticeship programs, found in such industries as construction. During the apprenticeship period, the apprentice works as a helper to skilled workers, who teach the trade to the newcomer. Other examples can be cited as well. For example, aspiring actors in New York and Los Angeles are willing to work in small theatres for little or no pay to acquire acting experience and in the hope of being noticed. They are investing in themselves while on the job.[26]

Where training takes place is a function of the efficiency with which it can be provided at alternative locations. Some skills are best learned in classroom-type settings provided away from the workplace. Other skills are best learned at worksites. Who pays for skill acquisition is another matter entirely. The two concepts should not be confused.

Optimum Location of Training.   The fact that certain kinds of training are best undertaken at the worksite, while others are suited to classroom-type instruction is often neglected, particularly in regards to management education. Management schools are often criticized for too much book learning, abstraction, and a lack of hands-on experience. As a result, there is a temptation to fill the curriculum with an excess of cases, internships, and so on.

Schools are not worksites, and cannot be transformed into them. Reading and analyzing a case, in which all of the crucial variables and circumstances are laid out with the benefit of hindsight not available to those who actually lived the situation described, is not the same as having to make real-world decisions. School settings are best for honing analytical tools, research techniques, and communications skills. Pressured decision making with absence of full information is best learned by doing, at the worksite—where it normally occurs.

Blending of General and Specific Training.   Although economists make much of the distinction between general and specific training, it is hard to find official acknowledgement of it among employers. Yet some behaviors of employers suggest an appreciation for the difference. During the 1980s there was continuing concern about deteriorating quality of public education at the elementary and secondary level. Employers often complained about having to deal with young workers who lacked essential literacy and arithmetic skills. Nevertheless, compared with other kinds of training, relatively few employers provided workers with remedial basic educational training.[27] Such training would involve archetypal general skills to be provided to a group with inherently high turnover rates.[28]

Perhaps the main behavioral sign of the distinction between general and specific training can be found in the relatively high level of turnover and low pay of clerical employees. Since clerical skills are basically general, employers have little of their own investment embodied in these workers. The salary levels they set for clericals are therefore kept relatively low since the resulting turnover does not cause the employer a substantial loss of investment in training. That is, the costs of turnover are perceived to be small, although it is doubtful that many employers have actually checked out this assumption.

Even with clericals, however—and certainly for other occupational groups—there is *some* employer investment involved in hiring expenses, the costs of basic orientation, and so on. These are specific investments; they do not have a value on the external labor market. Although simple theory at first suggested that employers would not pay wage premiums to workers with specific investments, turnover cost considerations (as discussed earlier) indicate that some wage premium will be provided. Once such a premium exists, employer–employee attachments grow, and employment durations lengthen.

As the length of the expected employment duration extends, employ*ees* will have some incentives to pay for specific training as well as general. The premiums that employers pay to hold down turnover—which are associated with specific investments—create an incentive for employees to make such investments. If they undertake the burden of training, the return will be higher wages. Similarly, the likelihood of a long-term employment duration undermines the notion that employ*ers* will not pay for general training. If the employee is unlikely to leave, the employer's investment in general training might well be recaptured.

In short, wage profiles that rise with seniority and long-term employer–employee attachments blur the distinction between general and specific training in many cases. They also make it difficult to determine exactly who is paying for training. When training occurs in connection with work, the out-of-pocket expenses may well show up on the employer's books. But if employees work at lower pay during the early learning stages of their careers, they may be partially and indirectly financing their own training, general or specific.

Measuring Training Costs.   The analysis suggests that *if* employers were accurately measuring their out-of-pocket training expenses, they might well be obtaining exaggerated estimates of the true costs of training. Hidden subsidies from employees would be missed by such an accounting. This problem is more theoretical than real, however, since employers often do not carefully account for their training costs. Such costs may simply be buried in the budgets of the HRM department or in the expenditures of various line functions.

As noted in an earlier chapter, use of accounting data on training and other costs of turnover with regard to pay setting and other HRM policies is in its infancy for the vast majority of employers. Indeed, for most firms, it has yet to be born. The danger at present is more likely to be that training costs are being neglected, not that they are overstated. Attempts to estimate these costs are thus likely to improve HRM decision making.[29]

13–3   Employment Stabilization

The analysis of human capital formation just presented stressed the importance of job duration—and *expected* job duration—in determining how much investment in employees will take place. Beginning in the 1980s considerable debate about corporate restructuring has occurred. As firms merged or spun off divisions, their HRM systems came under stress. Policies concerning job duration presuppose management continuity. If management cannot be assumed by employees to have continuity, career commitments are uncertain. Employee loyalty and self-investment are likely to be discouraged.

These developments pose a dilemma, not only for HRM professionals, but for America's long-term economic health. On one hand there is a need for flexibility and aggressive management within firms. On the other hand, if flexibility leads to a lack of employee commitment, that overused buzzword—competitiveness—may be harmed rather than furthered.

A key question for HRM policy is whether flexibility and stability can somehow be fostered simultaneously. If firms are under competitive pressure from new entrants, foreign suppliers, changing exchange rates, and technological advances, how can they provide employment stability? This question is posed as a challenge to employers, but it also has a macroeconomic component.

Since the 1930s the public has tended to look to government to solve the problem of unemployment and insufficient labor demand. The Keynesian approach to reducing unemployment has been to stimulate the economy through easy monetary policy (expansion of the money supply and lower interest rates), increased government spending, and tax cuts. All of these devices constitute macro solutions that involve no direct employer input. The theory is simply that employers will be stimulated to hire more workers as the demand for production of goods and services increases.

At the micro level, employers have become somewhat more directly involved in government efforts to reduce unemployment. Programs have included subsidized training for disadvantaged workers to make them more employable.[30] Although such training may be provided directly by government, it sometimes is undertaken by employers with some form of government subsidy. Other subsidized programs reduce the net cost of hiring individuals who might otherwise be chronically unemployed or out of the labor force. These programs, which employees seem reluctant to use, operate through direct subsidy to the employer or tax credits available to the employer for each disadvantaged hire.[31] In principle, workers hired would gain experience and thereby increase their human capital and attractiveness in the labor market.

Problems with Macro and Micro Approaches

Both the traditional macro and the micro approaches have drawbacks. The key problem for the macro approach is the potential stimulation of inflation as a byproduct of increasing the general level of demand in the economy. Inflation is unpopular; when it occurs, government policies of stimulation tend to be reversed and become demand-restricting. The result can be stop-go policies as government alternates between trying to fight inflation and trying to stimulate increased employment. Even small slowdowns in the economy represent billions of dollars in lost output.[32]

Micro approaches, while not directly inflationary, have been criticized on grounds of effectiveness. It has been argued that such programs sometimes fall victim to the general problem of creating optimum incentive systems (discussed in a previous chapter). For example, suppose local government or private operators of micro-level programs are evaluated on the number of job placements of the individuals they are training. The operators may respond by deliberately "creaming" the market, that is, seeking as enrollees individuals with attractive characteristics who would probably have found work anyway. Such strategies will increase the number of recorded placements but do nothing to reduce unemployment.

Similar problems arise with subsidies and tax credits. Employers who receive subsidies to hire certain individuals may simply use these workers in positions they (the employers) would have filled anyway. The subsidized hires effectively displace unsubsidized persons who had (or would have had) the jobs. The queue of job applicants is thus not reduced in length; its constituents are simply reshuffled.

Since neither the micro nor the macro approaches to unemployment reduction have proven as successful in practice as their proponents hoped, it is natural to seek alternatives.[33] There may be linkages between the interest of government in reducing unemployment and avoiding stop-go policies and the interests of employers in combining stability and flexibility. Increasingly, firms have paid attention to compensation systems as devices to improve performance. Economic discussion has thus focused on compensation options that could promote and stabilize employment.

Share Economy Alternative

One suggestion for modifying traditional compensation arrangements has received considerable attention and provoked substantial debate. This suggestion was that a change in the compensation system toward share arrangements such as profit sharing would both stabilize employment and reduce unemployment. Although it had antecedents going back to the 1930s and earlier, this suggestion became identified in the 1980s with the writings of Martin L. Weitzman of Massachusetts Institute of Technology (M.I.T.) and has attracted the interest of a variety of prominent political leaders.[34] Obviously, if the government were to adopt policies aimed at stimulating share systems of compensation, these policies would have a profound impact on employers and HRM specialists.

In the past, profit sharing has been advocated as a device to alter *employee* behavior by providing greater motivation, morale, or identification with the employer. Many HRM analysts, however, have disputed the effectiveness of profit sharing viewed in that way because of the distant connection between individual worker behavior and the overall economic condition of the firm. Weitzman's proposal sidesteps this old dispute. He argues instead that the key impact of profit sharing (and other related compensation systems based on sharing revenues or value added) is on *employer* behavior, not on employee attitudes or productivity.

Potential Employment Stabilization.   The share approach can best be understood in two steps. First, it can be argued that share systems create a *potential* for stabilizing a firm's employment over the business cycle, which might not be available with a conventional wage compensation system. Second, it can be additionally argued—as Weitzman does—that the potential will in fact be realized under sharing because of built-in motivators for the employer. He goes still further and argues that firms with share arrangements would not only *stabilize* employment, but they would also *expand* it, that is, hire more workers than under a conventional compensation system. It is fair to say that there has been wider acceptance of the first proposition than of the second.

To understand the first argument on potential, consider a firm's weekly payroll. This payroll is composed of three multiplicative elements: the average hourly wage W (which can be understood to include fringe benefits), the number of weekly hours worked per worker H, and the number of employees E. Thus:

$$\text{Weekly payroll} = W \times H \times E \qquad (1)$$

Typically, when firms experience a downward adjustment in product demand (and, hence, in labor demand), they react initially by cutting H moderately (perhaps eliminating overtime hours) and then by reducing E (mainly through layoffs). On the other hand, the basic wage schedule underlying W is rarely reduced. Ultimately, therefore, the business cycle is reflected more in variations in E than in wage adjustments.

For example (neglecting fringe benefits for purposes of illustration), suppose a firm pays a straight-time hourly wage of $10/hour, an overtime premium of time and a half, works a 42-hour week (including two hours of overtime), and has 100 employees. Its overtime wage will be $15/hour; thus its average hourly wage W will be $10.238.[35] The firm's weekly payroll will therefore come to:

$$\$10.238/\text{hour} \times 42 \text{ hours} \times 100 \text{ employees} = \$43,000. \qquad (2)$$

Suppose demand for the firm's product declines and management decides it must reduce weekly payroll expenses by $5,000, to $38,000. The firm might first eliminate overtime hours, cutting the workweek to 40 hours. This reduction will cut the labor input by about 4.8% *and* will reduce average hourly pay by $0.238, that is, by about 2.3%, because of the elimination of the overtime premium. Unless the wage schedule underlying W is changed—that is, unless the basic straight-time wage is cut—any further reduction in the payroll must come from a decrease in employment by 5 workers, from 100 to 95. The weekly payroll would then be:

$$\$10/\text{hour} \times 40 \text{ hours} \times 95 \text{ employees} = \$38,000, \qquad (3)$$

that is, equal to the new target amount. Thus of the 11.6% payroll reduction needed, 60% comes from reducing overtime hours and 40% comes from reducing employment.

Of course, an alternative strategy for the firm could be to cut the straight-time hourly wage to $9.50 (a 5% reduction) and to eliminate overtime hours. The original 100 employees could then be retained, but the weekly payroll would still be reduced to the target level:

$$\$9.50/\text{hour} \times 40 \text{ hours} \times 100 \text{ employees} = \$38,000. \qquad (4)$$

As a first approximation, the firm would be indifferent between the two approaches—overtime elimination and layoffs versus overtime elimination and pay cut—since the weekly dollar outcome is the same. In fact, since the firm could probably obtain *some* production value from the 5 workers not laid off in the latter strategy—say, by using them for maintenance operations—it might be satisfied with a lesser pay cut than the full 50¢.[36]

Profits, sales revenues, or value added will tend to fluctuate with the product demand conditions faced by the firm. If the firm's employees had been part of a plan, such as profit sharing, their average hourly wage W would have been partially composed of a share-related bonus rather than just of regular wage payments. The equivalent of a wage reduction to $9.50 might have been accomplished as the share-related bonus fell due to depressed demand.

Suppose, for example, that the straight-time wage had been $9.00/hour and that a profit-sharing bonus equivalent to $1.0238/hour was being paid initially. The weekly payroll (including the bonus) would be $43,000 as before. Now suppose that a fall in demand occurs, reducing profits. If overtime hours were eliminated and the profit-sharing bonus fell to the equivalent of 50¢/hour, the desired payroll reduction to $38,000 would be achieved. Specifically, the calculations are

Before
40 hours @ $9.00/hour × 100 workers   = $36,000
2 overtime hours @ (1.5)($9.00/hour) × 100 workers   = $2,700
42 hours × bonus of $1.0238/hour × 100 workers   = $4,300
     Total   = $43,000

After
40 hours @ $9.00/hour × 100 workers   = $36,000
40 hours × bonus of 50¢/hour x 100 workers   = $2,000
     Total   = $38,000

Thus share systems with bonuses geared to demand-sensitive indexes such as profits, sales revenue, or value added, can provide automatic labor-cost relief to employers. In principle, employers can stabilize employment levels in the face of demand variability by letting the share bonus absorb much of the burden of labor-cost reduction. This outcome, as has been stressed, is a *potentiality*. There is no guarantee in the story as told so far that employers would actually stabilize employment if more labor compensation derived from share arrangements (as opposed to ordinary wages). All that has been shown is that they could do so.

Bargaining over Employment Stability.   One possible linkage between employment stability and a share system could be a formal collective-bargaining agreement in cases in which the firm is unionized. If a union represented the 100 workers employed by the hypothetical employer just described, it could bargain explicitly for an employment guarantee of 100 jobs in exchange for a reduction in the basic straight-time wage and an offsetting share/bonus system. Examples of such developments occurred during the 1980s, as part of the concession bargaining movement.

For example, the 1982 negotiations in the automobile industry between General Motors, Ford, and the United Auto Workers included a profit-sharing/job security element. Mass layoffs and the threat of foreign competition had made job security a key issue. The union negotiated a wage freeze (superseding an earlier contract providing for wage increases), a guaranteed-income stream plan, and profit sharing.[37]

In short, a mandatory connection between a share system and employment stability could be created as part of a written, bargained deal in situations in which unions have negotiating rights. Alternatively, a nonunion employer that followed a unilaterally established full employment policy as part of an implicit contract with its workers might include a share element in its compensation system. The share arrangement would help finance the potential costs of the employment guarantee.

Weitzman and others have argued that the system of bonuses in Japan, where employment security is guaranteed by large firms, functions in this manner.[38] Such behavior is consistent with the widely reported investment in human resources in these firms. In this view, Japanese firms stabilize employment and let bonus fluctuations absorb some of the costs of this HRM policy. Since Japanese firms have been held up as models of a competitiveness that provides both the flexibility to respond to market pressures and employment security, the profit-related bonus proposition is of special interest.[39]

Risk-Averse Preferences and Employee Attitudes. The introduction of a share system as part of the arrangements of employment stabilization can have differential effects on workers.[40] As has been stressed previously, there are both theoretical reasons for, and empirical evidence of, preferential treatment on the job for more senior employees. In a typical layoff situation, junior workers—especially in unionized firms—are more likely to be terminated than senior workers. Hence the costs of employment reductions at a point in time are not evenly borne by the entire workforce. In other words, if employment is to be reduced by 10%, the probability that a junior worker will be laid off is much higher than 10%; the probability of layoff for a very senior worker may be almost zero.

Given these differential probabilities, the value of an HRM policy conducive to employment stabilization will be worth more to junior workers than to senior workers, who already have relative employment security. Of course, there may be great societal value in seeing reduced unemployment by fostering policies that help junior employees avoid layoff risks. But it may be difficult to persuade employers to adopt policies that are of concern mainly to the wider society and to the marginal junior employees.

If there were absolutely no cost to senior workers from a share system of compensation, they would have no reason to oppose its creation. That is, although its benefits to them would be quite limited, there would be little motivation to oppose these minimal benefits if no sacrifice were entailed. The problem is that under share arrangements there will be costs to senior workers in terms of income variability.

Inherent in a share system is fluctuating pay, since the variable to which the bonus is linked (profits, sales revenue, or value added) increases and decreases over time. If profit sharing is used, for example, there will be small or no bonuses during bad years when profits are low or even negative and high bonuses during good times. A share system, in short, brings with it an element of risk for workers.

Usually individuals can be assumed to be risk averse. In the securities market, for example, a bond issued by a highly rated firm can be expected to provide a lower yield than one from a firm on the edge of bankruptcy. The bond market thereby reflects the risk-averse nature of investors.

Similarly, there is every reason to think that employees, like investors in bonds, are risk averse. They may have relatively fixed financial obligations such as mortgage or rent payments. The liquid assets on which they can call if income declines may be limited. Access to capital markets to finance consumption even during periods of temporary income losses may be limited or expensive. For most working households, the chief source of income is from wages; the ability to diversify revenue sources to mitigate risk is limited.

Thus a share system that provides an *expected* annual compensation of, say, $25,000 composed of a sure $20,000 wage and a probable $5,000 bonus will be valued less by workers (given their risk aversion) than a sure $25,000 wage. Worker preferences might require the employer with a share system to pay a higher expected compensation level than would be required under a sure wage system. That is, the firm might have to offer a sure $20,000 wage plus an expected $6,000 bonus to make workers feel indifferent between the share system and a sure $25,000 wage.

Alternatively, if the firm switched from a $25,000 sure wage to an expected but uncertain compensation of $25,000 under a share system, workers might view the switch as equivalent to a pay cut. They might respond as they would to an ordinary pay cut—with higher turnover and lower productivity and morale. In addition, the firm might find it more difficult to recruit new employees because of its risky compensation system.

Share Division and Employee Attitudes.   Under a share system, an earmarked portion of some value measure—profits, sales revenue, value added—is divided among the employees according to a formula. Such an arrangement can lead to worker resistance to expansion of firm employment levels. New hires will add to production and thus to the profits, sales revenue, or value added of the enterprise. But it is unlikely that they will add more than the average contribution of the existing workforce; because of declining marginal productivity they will probably add less. Since bonuses are determined on an average basis, adding workers may well reduce the size of the average bonus for the existing workforce. Current employees may not be receptive to adding claimants (new hires) to the bonus pool, since that dilutes the probable share payment.

Of course, worker dissatisfaction about additional hiring might not have an overt means of expression unless a union is present. However, share systems such as the Scanlon plans discussed earlier are sometimes accompanied by the creation of participative worker voice mechanisms. A parallel is seen between sharing in the financial side of the enterprise and sharing in its direction through quality circles and other means. Thus nonunion workers may have a channel through which resentment can be voiced. If no formal channel is available, employees may manifest resentment through lowered productivity and costly workplace frictions.

Employer Incentive Effects.   The Weitzman argument for a share system depends on two elements: a *potential* for employment stabilization and an *incentive* for the employer to actualize that potential and even increase employment. If such incentives are lacking, speculation about worker attitudes toward such systems might have little practical application. The question of employer incentives to establish share systems is thus obviously crucial.[41]

Weitzman analyzes employer incentives under a share system on the assumption of profit maximization. Profit sharing—a plan based on the profit that variable economic theory suggests the firm will maximize—is the most obvious choice for an illustrative example. As shown earlier, profit sharing is also the most common form of share system actually in existence. In contrast, productivity gain-sharing plans, which are based on sales or value added, are not very common. Apart from theory, then, the greater incidence of profit sharing makes it the most suitable candidate for analysis.

A firm's profits (π) are simply the difference between its revenues (R) and its costs (C):

$$\pi = R - C \tag{5}$$

Profit maximization is determined by differentiating equation (5) by a decision variable and setting the resulting equation equal to zero. In the standard theory of the firm, the firm's decision variable is usually depicted as the quantity of output (Q) to be produced and sold. That is, the firm selects an output target consistent with profit maximization. Differentiating by Q produces

$$d\pi/dQ = (dR/dQ) - (dC/dQ) = 0, \tag{6}$$

which the student will quickly recognize as the familiar marginal revenue = marginal cost condition, since dR/dQ = marginal revenue and dC/dQ = marginal cost.

If a percentage share of profits (s) were taken from firm owners, say, for corporate income taxes, the firm then would maximize $(1-s)\pi$ rather than π because $(1-s)\pi$ is what remains for the owners. But since $(1-s)\pi$ is a constant fraction of π, there will be no behavioral difference for the firm in maximizing π and maximizing $(1-s)\pi$.[42] That is, if the firm maximizes π, it will of necessity also maximize $(1-s)\pi$, and *vice versa*. The firm will make the same output (Q) decision and therefore the same input decisions as it would if s had not been assessed. In particular, if wage rates were reduced, both the π-maximizing firm and the firm maximizing $(1-s)\pi$ would react in the same way. They would both hire more labor.

A profit-sharing plan is like a tax assessment *except that the share s goes to the worker*, instead of to the tax collector. Here is where the difference sets in. Workers will put some value on the share, even if—for reasons of risk aversion—they do not treat the expected bonus as exactly equivalent to a sure wage. *The firm can pay a lower basic wage, because it is also offering the share bonus.* The lower wage, however, means more labor will be hired. Thus, Weitzman argues, having a share system creates an incentive for additional hiring and employment.

Figure 13–1 provides an illustration. The firm's short run demand curve D is depicted as the usual downward sloping line. If the firm had been paying a wage of W_1 before introducing a profit-sharing system, it would have wanted to employ L_1 units of labor. Suppose it now introduces a share system with an expected positive bonus. The base wage it now needs to pay drops to W_2, and it thus wants to employ L_2 units of labor.

Under normal conditions, if just one firm wants to expand its workforce, the labor market could accommodate its needs. But if most firms were induced to adopt a share system, their total increase in labor demand might well exceed available labor supply, thus producing a labor shortage. The firm of Figure 13–1 might thus desire L_2 units of labor after it adopts profit sharing, but it might be able to find only L_S units, where $L_S < L_2$. The creation of a generalized labor shortage is a critical element of the Weitzman proposal, because the shortage provides an incentive for the firm to stabilize employment. Through the shortage the potential for employment stabilization under a share system, as discussed earlier, is realized.[43]

Suppose, for example, that the firm of Figure 13–1 found itself in a labor shortage situation when a moderate reduction in the demand for its product occurred (say, because of a general recession). Its demand for labor might fall to D' under such circumstances. Even with that lower level of demand, the firm would want to employ L_R units of labor, still more than the L_S it actually had. Thus, despite the fall in demand, the firm would not lay off workers, since it did not have enough of them to start. Employment in the firm is thus stabilized in the sense that *a moderate fall in demand creates no labor displacement*.

Having a share system cannot prevent all displacement, however. For example, if there were a large drop in demand to D'', the firm would want only L'' units of labor, less than the L_S it has. It would thus lay off $L''L_S$ units. The share system

FIGURE 13–1
Labor Demand and
Profit Sharing

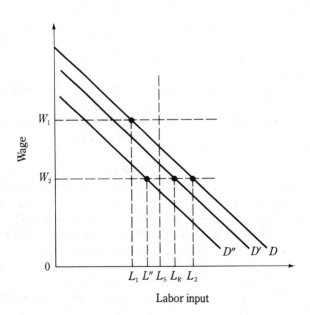

still results in more people employed along demand curve D'' than would be employed under a pure wage system.

Share Systems and Public Policy.   The notion that changing the compensation system could make a contribution toward reducing unemployment and stabilizing employment is very attractive from the societal perspective. Weitzman argues that since there is a public interest in these objectives, society ought to provide incentives for employers to shift to share compensation. The individual firm does not internalize all of the benefits of a share economy; the overall unemployment rate does not depend on the actions of any one firm. Hence firms will not institute a share system on the basis of these social objectives.

In the absence of a subsidy for using a share system, a firm will look only at the traditional arguments for share systems—that they boost employee productivity and morale. If such benefits occur, they are internalized by the firm in the form of greater profits. As noted earlier, however, these arguments have not been sufficiently convincing to induce most employers to shift on a widespread basis to share systems on their own.

Weitzman and others sympathetic to the macroeconomic arguments surrounding share systems thus advocate that tax preferences be given to such arrangements in order to provide the needed societal subvention. A subsidy through the tax system will encourage employers to adopt more share plans than they would based only on the alleged productivity/morale effects. The subsidy, in effect, internalizes the external benefits of having share arrangements.

Skeptics of the Weitzman proposal argue that worker resistance to the employment expansion effects and worker risk aversion would prevent the share economy from having the impact that simple economic theory suggests. In this view, unions would keep firms from expanding employment once the bonus dilution effect was understood. And nonunion firms that followed high-wage policies would limit their hiring in order to prevent the dilution, too. In addition, workers would be so disturbed about the income fluctuations inherent in a share system that employers would not install more such systems, even with a tax-preference subsidy. Taxpayers' money would be wasted in subsidies that would go to firms that had already established share plans for their own internal reasons.

Other critics argue that the simple theory on which Weitzman's argument is based is misleading. If workers are hired for long durations under implicit contracts, and not in spot markets, the employer incentive effects may be quite different from those predicted by Weitzman. If, for example, firms implicitly assured workers that low bonuses in bad years would be made up in good times, the seemingly flexible compensation system would become as rigid as a wage system. The firm's cash saving in labor costs during bad times would be offset by an implicit liability to pay back the saving. A tax-preference subsidy might induce more share plans to be created, but these plans would not have the effects suggested by Weitzman's analysis.

Despite these objections, the Weitzman proposal has a potentially broad political appeal. The effect of a widespread share system of employee compensation cannot be known for sure unless it is actually tried. Hence arguments against the proposal are hypothetical and hard to prove. Moreover, as discussed earlier in this chapter, the prospect of employment stabilization—if not expansion—through share systems became particularly enticing in the 1980s. Job security is an issue for many workers and will become more important in the remaining years of the twentieth century as the U.S. workforce ages. Since neither liberals nor conservatives want to be laid off, the idea of promoting flexible pay is likely to be around for some time, regardless of the political climate, and may well find eventual legislative expression. Indeed, in 1987 the British government modified its tax code to foster profit sharing in response to the Weitzman proposal. American employers and HRM specialists would thus be well advised to expect inducements to shift to share arrangements.

More Share Systems Without Tax Inducements?   Trends sometimes develop in compensation practices without external inducements. Could a trend toward more share bonuses develop, even if no tax preferences were enacted? There are some signs of such developments, signs that HRM professionals would be well advised to watch.

As noted in an earlier chapter, one of the offshoots of concession bargaining by unions in the 1980s was the growth in use of lump sum bonuses. These bonuses are specified in two basic ways: flat dollar amounts (e.g., $1,000/year) or proportions of base pay (3% of each employee's past year's earnings). Bonuses tend to substitute for increases in basic wages and often provide a saving to the employer in fringe benefit costs.

If the use of such bonuses becomes entrenched in the collective-bargaining system over a period of time, a variable element geared to profitability and the general economic outlook for the firm could become part of union bargaining. While the basic wage settlement might show little variation in response to market conditions, the bonus element could vary. In good years contracts might thus begin with relatively large bonuses; in bad times bonuses might be small or nonexistent. Put another way, lump sum bonuses in American contracts could take on features similar to the Japanese bonuses referenced earlier.

Although lump sum bonuses developed mainly in the union sector that encompasses only a relatively small minority of the workforce, past experience suggests that union-sector practices often spread into nonunion employment. Employers seeking means of stabilizing employment might find variable bonuses an attractive option. Fears by employers—based on the experience of the 1980s—that product market conditions are likely to be more erratic in the future than they were in the past make bonuses desirable from the management viewpoint. Bonuses that vary with economic circumstances provide the firm with automatic cost relief during difficult periods; they are not as hard to reduce as wages since the very idea of a bonus is that it is an extra, something that is here today but perhaps not tomorrow.

The use of variable bonuses as an important element in compensation policy could serve to reconcile the need for managerial flexibility and employment stability. It would permit greater investment in human capital, both by employers and employees, because it would permit longer expected employment durations. Such investment, in turn, could contribute to the competitive edge American management has been seeking from its HRM practices.

Other Implications of a Share Economy. Apart from their possible employment and cost effects, share systems could have still other implications for HRM professionals. As noted earlier, there is a linkage between the notion of sharing in an economic sense (financial sharing) and sharing in decisions (managerial sharing). If workers share in profits, for example, they may well come to want a share in the managerial processes that influence those profits. Thus, a move towards a share economy could trigger broad changes in HRM practices. Similarly, firms that have moved toward management-sharing systems, such as quality circles, may eventually find that their workforce would like to share in an economic sense in the fruits of their decisions.

Share systems could have implications for unions and their organizing prospects, too. The bonuses allotted under share systems are ultimately based on accounting data from the firm. There are many potential uncertainties in calculation, particularly with regard to profits. Employees may feel a need for an independent entity to audit the computation. A promised ability to act as an auditor for workers in a share economy could prove to be an appealing organizing tool for unions. Of course, unions would need to develop expertise in areas traditionally left to management in order for them to provide such services.

Alternative Employment Stabilizing Policies

Although the share economy proposal provides one method of employment stabilization, there are other policies, either privately adopted or publicly imposed, that could provide job security. One method that seemed to become more commonly used in the 1980s was the growth of a contingent workforce—without employment guarantees—that could be used to stabilize job prospects for a permanent core group of workers.[44] Through the use of temporary agency workers, direct-hire temporaries, part-timers, and workers hired by subcontractors to whom no ongoing commitment is made, it is possible to protect the jobs of other workers. In effect, the firm staffs for the troughs of demand and lets the peaks be accommodated via changes in the number of contingent workers.

Use of a contingent worker strategy by employers permits investment in the protected core group of workers to be recouped. Of course, little or no specific investment can be made in the contingent workers. Such workers are thus likely to fall into occupational categories of workers with general skills, such as clericals.

While the use of contingent workers is a private decision, another scenario of employment stabilization comes through public policies. A previous chapter discussed the erosion of at-will employment and the rise of wrongful discharge and related legislation. Cases that arise in this area generally involve *individuals* discharged by employers rather than large-scale layoffs. However, just as changing public policy is encroaching on this aspect of managerial discretion, so might it also come to limit layoffs affecting *groups* of workers.

The passage in 1988 by Congress of legislation requiring sixty-days' advance notice of plant closings and mass layoffs could be the first step in the direction of making such terminations of workers more difficult. An aging, and therefore more security-conscious, workforce could make this type of restriction a popular political cause. Changes in the financial sector and related corporate restructurings, mergers, and acquisitions have put pressure on labor markets that could increase the appeal of mandatory layoff limitations.[45]

In an effort to hold back such tendencies, business groups in the 1980s began to stress the need for flexibility in the labor market.[46] Generally, the argument against restrictions on management's laying off workers has been that such limitations will cause firms to restrict hiring to avoid the heavy fixed cost and risk entailed. For incumbent (insider) workers who feel their jobs are threatened, however, this argument may not carry much weight.

13-4   Future Destabilization?

During the 1980s employment fell at Fortune 500 firms even as the overall workforce expanded. Apparently there was a move toward employment in smaller firms. In addition, as Table 13-4 shows, data from *County Business Patterns* indicate that average establishment size began to drop in the United States. What was the cause of this size decline? Was it just short-run pressures—such as recession or foreign competition—that were causing the decrease or were other, longer term forces at work?

Some researchers believe that the production unit of the future will be small and will be characterized by what has been termed "flexible specialization."[47] According to this scenario, customized products, made possible by computer technology, will dominate the marketplace. In a sense the market will return to

TABLE 13-4   Mean Establishment Size, 1973-1985

	Workers per Establishment	
Year	Private Sector*	Manufacturing
1973	15.1	65.2
1979	16.5	67.0
1985	14.2	54.9

*Excludes railroad and self-employed workers.

Source: U.S. Bureau of the Census, *County Business Patterns, 1968–77: 10-Year History,* CBP–77–55 (Washington: GPO, 1981), pp. 1–2; U.S. Bureau of the Census, *County Business Patterns, 1979: United States,* CBP–79–1 (Washington: GPO, 1981), p. 1; U.S. Bureau of the Census, *County Business Patterns, 1985: United States,* CBP–85–1 (Washington: GPO, 1987), p. 1.

the artisan workshop model of the early nineteenth century, although with products using the latest technology.

A small-employer world, with each production unit constantly searching for a competitive niche in the market, is unlikely to be characterized by stable employment patterns. Indeed, many of the human resource policies that have grown up in the twentieth century would be difficult to sustain. If workers move from employer to employer on a regular basis, reliance on a single employer for health insurance, for example, would become difficult if not impossible. Individual employers would not be in a position to invest their own resources in workers.

In a flexible specialization world, employees would have to gain their skills through arrangements such as apprenticeship and/or vocational institutions. Mechanisms such as referral services might be needed to channel workers from employer to employer, as demand shifted. Possibly unions might function in that kind of environment as they did in the nineteenth century (and as they do now in a few industries such as construction), operating apprenticeship programs, hiring halls, and providing health and welfare benefits. Employment stability would be difficult, if not impossible, to achieve.

Is all of this a likely outcome of contemporary trends? That question cannot be answered. History suggests that turning points in industrial development—such as the Industrial Revolution of the late eighteenth and early nineteenth century—take time to unfold. The economy will not move to flexible specialization in a flash, just as the modern corporation did not replace small workshops in a flash in the nineteenth century. Issues of employment stabilization will not vanish in the near future. Indeed, if there is a trend toward flexible specialization, it may exacerbate the stability issue and create demands for public policies to slow down its effects.

Summary

Recognition of employer–employee attachments is critical to understanding the functioning of the labor market and the making of HRM policy. As demonstrated in the previous chapter, employees may be attached to employers even when they are not working. An involuntary breaking of the attachment, particularly in the case of permanent layoff, is costly to employees because of the investment and stake they have in their jobs.

Society attempts to alleviate this problem through such government programs as unemployment insurance. But with an aging workforce it is likely that demands will grow for still more societal protections against layoffs. In addition, proposals for changes in the compensation system to facilitate long and stable employment durations, for example, the Weitzman plan, may well gain in popularity. Longer term trends in the economy that push for a more flexible labor market may, in the short term, create increased demands for employment stabilization, either through private means or through public policies.

Long-duration employer–employee attachments facilitate the training of employees. Both parties have reason to believe that human capital investments can be recouped if they know that the expected duration of employment is long. To the extent that public policies are adopted that push firms to maintain stable employment relationships with their employees, the incentives for skill acquisition will grow.

EXERCISES

Problem

Examine your own choice of educational paths and occupational goals. How much information did you have on the financial rewards available when you made the choice? To what extent did that knowledge influence the choice you made?

Questions

1. What is the significance for human resource management of the long durations of attachment to their employers observed in empirical studies of older workers?

2. Is college education an investment good or a consumer good? Defend your answer.

3. Why do lawyers typically pay for their own educations? Why don't law firms pay to educate their lawyers?

4. What relationship is there between profit sharing in a share economy and firm investment in employees?

5. What demographic factors may be influencing enactment of public policies such as advance notification of plant closings?

6. Why do wages seem to rise with worker experience?

Terms

creeping credentialism
education's effect on
  wages
flexible specialization
human capital

general versus specific
  training
layoff systems
learning by doing
on-the-job versus
  classroom training

signaling in the labor
  market
Weitzman proposal

ENDNOTES

1. The distinction between interrupted and completed spells of employment is the same as that between interrupted and completed spells of unemployment. The latter were discussed in the previous chapter.

2. Source of data is "Most Workers Who Switched Occupations Lost Jobs Through Plant Closings, Layoffs," *Daily Labor Report,* October 10, 1987, p. B4.

3. Robert E. Hall, "The Importance of Lifetime Jobs in the U.S. Economy," *American Economic Review,* vol. 72 (September 1982), pp. 716–724.

4. Source: U.S. Bureau of the Census, *Statistical Abstract of the United States 1988* (Washington: GPO, 1988), pp. 125, 140.

5. U.S. Bureau of the Census, *Historical Statistics of the United States: Colonial Times to 1970,* Part 1 (Washington: GPO, 1975), pp. 379, 383.

6. Walter McManus, William Gould, and Finis Welch, "Earnings of Hispanic Men: The Role of English Language Proficiency," *Journal of Labor Economics,* vol. 1 (April 1983), pp. 101–130.

7. *Employment and Earnings,* vol. 35 (January 1988), p. 166.

8. Ivar Berg, *Education and Jobs: The Great Training Robbery* (New York: Praeger, 1970).

9. Michael Spence, "Job Market Signaling," *Quarterly Journal of Economics,* vol. 87 (August 1973), pp. 355–374.

10. Under one program, disadvantaged job applicants were given certificates that the employer could use to obtain a significant subsidy if the applicant were hired. In fact, the presentation of the certificate seemed to act as a negative signal to employers and reduced the attractiveness of the applicant. See Gary Burtless, "Are Targeted Wage Subsidies Harmful? Evidence from a Voucher Experiment," *Industrial and Labor Relations Review,* vol. 39 (October 1985), pp. 105–114.

11. William G. Ouchi, *Theory Z: How American Business Can Meet the Japanese Challenge* (New York: Avon, 1982), p. 77, points out that the search for homogeneity in the successful firms he analyzed can raise issues of race and sex discrimination.

12. The issue of paying for training is discussed below in this chapter.

13. There are various explanations for the drop-off in income for males in the oldest age bracket shown on Table 13–1. Some of the males may have retired from or lost their primary jobs and may have embarked on second careers. Others may have suffered injury or illness. Cohort effects are also present in the table. The individuals in the oldest bracket are not the same persons as those who are in younger age categories. Each cohort has had a different labor market history.

14. Data from the late 1980s developed by the American Society for Training and Development supports the Conference Board findings. See "The Training Industry," *Los Angeles Times,* January 4, 1988, Part 4, p. 5.

15. Katharine G. Abraham and Henry S. Farber, "Job Duration, Seniority, and Earnings," *American Economic Review,* vol. 77 (June 1987), pp. 278–297.

16. D. Quinn Mills, "Seniority Versus Ability in Promotion Decisions," *Industrial and Labor Relations Review,* vol. 38 (April 1985), pp. 421–425.

17. An area of long-standing concern has been the degree to which holding a job detracts from the school performance of high schoolers. There is evidence that there is such a negative effect, which could mean that the return to education is lowered by work during the educational process. See Philip W. Wirtz, Cynthia A. Rohrbeck, Ivan Charner, and Bryna Shore Fraser, "Intense Employment While in High School: Are Teachers, Guidance Counselors, and Parents Misguiding Academically-Oriented Adolescents?," working paper 1987–4, Graduate Institute for Policy Education and Research, George Washington University, 1987.

18. By considering the post-high school earnings he or she would earn, the individual is in effect taking account of the opportunity costs of college. These earnings would include what would otherwise be earned during the period of college attendance. (Of course, many college students work part time or during the summer while they attend college, so these earnings would also have to be considered.)

19. Note that from the individual's perspective, it matters little whether the returns from education stem from actual skills acquired or from signaling. The cost/benefit calculation will be exactly the same.

20. Mark C. Berger, "Predicted Future Earnings and Choice of College Major," *Industrial and Labor Relations Review,* vol. 41 (April 1988), pp. 418–429.

21. See Alexander W. Astin, Kenneth C. Green, and William S. Korn, *The American Freshman: Twenty Year Trends* (Los Angeles: Higher Education Research Institute, U.C.L.A., 1987), pp. 23–24.

22. Richard B. Freeman, "A Cobweb Model of the Supply and Starting Salary of New Engineers," *Industrial and Labor Relations Review,* vol. 29 (January 1976), pp. 236–248. The cobweb terminology stems from the cobweb-like

appearance of a simple supply/demand diagram incorporating the adjustments.

23. David C. Stapleton and Douglas J. Young, "Educational Attainment and Cohort Size," *Journal of Labor Economics,* vol. 6 (July 1988), pp. 330–361; Wayne J. Howe, "Do Education and Demographics Affect Unemployment Rates?", *Monthly Labor Review,* vol. 111 (January 1988), pp. 3–9.

24. Gary S. Becker, *Human Capital: A Theoretical and Empirical Analysis, with Special Reference to Education,* 2nd edition (Chicago: University of Chicago Press, 1975), pp. 19–37.

25. "The Training Industry," *Los Angeles Times, op. cit.,* p. 5.

26. The pay system (or lack thereof) in such theatres is a constant source of frustration to actors' unions.

27. One survey of firms with fifty or more employees reported that fewer than 19% of employers provided such remedial education compared, for example, to training provided in management development (78.5%). "The Training Industry," *Los Angeles Times, op. cit.,* p. 5.

28. Still another factor may be the technology of effectively providing basic education. Studies of the school system find no strong relation between per-pupil expenditures on education and educational outcomes. On the other hand, external variables such as family background are important to outcomes. It may be, therefore, that employers are uncertain as to how to provide useful basic educational training, even when they are motivated to do so. On educational technology, see Eric A. Hanushek, "The Economics of Schooling," *Journal of Economic Literature,* vol. 24 (September 1986), pp. 1141–1177.

29. Wayne F. Cascio, *Costing Human Resources: The Financial Impact of Behavior in Organizations,* second edition (Boston: PWS-Kent Publishing Co., 1987), pp. 34–37; Eric G. Flamholtz, *Human Resource Accounting,* 2nd edition (San Francisco: Jossey-Bass Publishers, 1985).

30. Sar A. Levitan and Frank Gallo, *A Second Chance: Training for Jobs* (Kalamazoo, Mich.: W. E. Upjohn Institute for Employment Research, 1988).

31. Various reasons have been cited for the low usage of subsidized employment, including simple lack of knowledge of the program. See U.S. Department of Labor and U.S. Department of the Treasury, *The Use of Tax Subsidies for Employment* (Washington: GPO, 1986), pp. 89–102.

32. Some business cycle theorists would argue that the cost of fluctuations is overstated by such calculations. It is difficult in practice to estimate what smoothing out the business cycle would be worth to the average person. However, there is an important distinction between achieving a smoothing around a trend of actual GNP and a smoothing so that the economy stays at some concept of full employment. In the latter case, departures from full employment

cannot by definition be made up. For discussion of modern business cycle theory, see Francis W. Ahking and Stephen M. Miller, "Models of Business Cycles: A Review Essay," *Eastern Economic Journal,* vol. 14 (April-June 1988), pp. 197–202.

33. The implication should not be drawn that there are no government training programs that have succeeded in raising post-training earnings of enrollees. See, for example, Orley Ashenfelter, "Estimating the Effect of Training Programs on Earnings," *Review of Economics and Statistics,* vol. 63 (February 1978), pp. 47–57. It is fair to say, however, that many proponents of such programs had great expectations—that in retrospect were disappointed—about what could be accomplished in lowering the unemployment rate without stimulating inflation.

34. Martin L. Weitzman, *The Share Economy: Conquering Stagflation* (Cambridge, Mass.: Harvard University Press, 1984); Martin L. Weitzman, "Some Macroeconomic Implications of Alternative Compensation Systems," *Economic Journal,* vol. 93 (December 1983), pp. 763–783; Martin L. Weitzman, "The Simple Macroeconomics of Profit Sharing," *American Economic Review,* vol. 75 (December 1985), pp. 937–953; Martin L. Weitzman, "Steady State Unemployment Under Profit Sharing," *Economic Journal,* vol. 97 (March 1987), pp. 86–105. Comments on Weitzman's approach from a human resource perspective can be found in a symposium appearing in the *Industrial and Labor Relations Review,* vol. 39 (January 1986), pp. 285–290. Comments from an economics perspective can be found in a symposium in the *Journal of Comparative Economics,* vol. 10 (December 1986), pp. 414–475. Apart from the literature directly commenting on and criticizing Weitzman, Weitzman's writings have inspired other economists to explore alternative compensation systems and their implications. See, for example, J. E. Meade, *Alternative Systems of Business Organization and of Workers' Remuneration* (Boston: Allen and Unwin, 1986).

35. A typical worker will be employed for 40 hours at $10 per hour and 2 hours at $15 per hour, thus receiving total weekly pay of $430: $430/42 hours = $10.238.

36. As long as the marginal product of labor is positive, the extra workers will in fact produce something of value for the firm.

37. The guaranteed income stream plan in principle guaranteed worker incomes rather than jobs. However, it provided strong incentive for the employers to provide work, since otherwise workers would be paid while idle.

38. Richard B. Freeman and Martin L. Weitzman, "Bonuses and Employment in Japan," *Journal of the Japanese and International Economies,* vol. 1 (1987), pp. 168–194.

39. Not all observers agree with the interpretation of the Japanese bonus system as an *ersatz* profit-sharing arrangement. One criticism is that even if the larger firms enjoy

wage flexibility through their bonuses, wage rigidity in the smaller firm sector has offset this effect in aggregate. See Kazutoshi Koshiro, "Gainsharing, Wage Flexibility, and Macro-Economic Performance in Japan," working paper 87–6, Faculty of Economics, Yokohama National University, June 1987.

40. Objections to the Weitzman plan based on worker preferences as discussed below can be found in Domenico Mario Nuti, "Profit-Sharing and Employment: Claims and Overclaims," *Industrial Relations,* vol. 26 (January 1987), pp. 18–29.

41. The discussion below follows that found in Daniel J.B. Mitchell, "The Share Economy and Industrial Relations," *Industrial Relations,* vol. 26 (January 1987), pp. 1–17.

42. It is not really the case that corporate income taxes have no effect on firm behavior. Real world corporate income taxes, like individual income taxes, are more complex than a simple taking of a constant share *s* of profits or income. Corporate income taxes include preferential treatment for certain kinds of activities and sources of income over others, thus influencing production decisions. Moreover, the analysis in the text is short run. Firms stay in business in the short run as long as they can cover variable costs. In the long run, however, corporate income taxes might influence individual firms' decisions to stay in business by reducing the rate of return to investment in those firms.

43. Normally, it might be expected that firms in a labor shortage situation would eventually raise wages to bid for labor. Such bidding would alleviate the shortage. However, Weitzman's case is somewhat different. Consider the firm depicted in Figure 13–1 operating along demand curve *D* and hiring L_S labor. The cost *C* of hiring an additional unit of labor *L* is $W + s(d\pi/dL)$, that is, the wage plus the share of additional profits that will be paid as a worker bonus. As long as $s > 0$, that is, as long as there is a share system, the firm will be happy to hire any incremental labor *dL* it can find, since it will gain $(1 - s)(d\pi/dL)$ by doing so. In the long run, firms will adjust their wage offers and *s* offers to attract more labor. They will maximize profits where *C* = marginal revenue product of labor. But since $W < C$

when $s > 0$, firms would still be happy—even when they have found their long-run equilibrium positions—to hire more labor and collect the $(1 - s)(d\pi/dL)$ that results. It is just that there is no more labor available. The firm is in equilibrium—it no longer wants to change *W* or *s*—but it still stands by to hire any labor that comes along.

Perhaps the best analogy is with a monopoly in the product market. The monopolistic firm determines its output where marginal revenue (*MR*) = marginal cost (*MC*). But its price *P* is greater than *MR*. The firm would be happy to sell an additional unit of output at price *P* to anyone who wants it, since it collects *P* but pays out only *MC* (where $P > MC$). However, the firm does not find it worthwhile to lower its price to sell another unit. It has a permanent shortage of customers similar to the share firm's permanent shortage of labor.

44. See U.S. Bureau of Labor Statistics, *Business Contracting-Out Practices,* summary 87–8, November 1987; Bureau of National Affairs, Inc., *The Changing Workplace: New Directions in Staffing and Scheduling* (Washington: BNA, 1986); Bureau of National Affairs, Inc., "Special PPF Survey Report: Part-Time and Other Alternative Staffing Practices," *Bulletin to Management,* vol. 39 (June 23, 1988), pp. 1–12; Wayne J. Howe, "Temporary Help Workers: Who They Are, What Jobs They Hold," *Monthly Labor Review,* vol. 109 (November 1986), pp. 45–47; Max L. Carey and Kim L. Hazelbaker, "Employment Growth in the Temporary Help Industry," *Monthly Labor Review,* vol. 109 (April 1986), pp. 37–44.

45. Richard S. Belous, "Flexibility and American Labour Markets: The Evidence and Implications," World Employment Programme Research working paper no. 14, International Labour Office, Geneva, June 1987.

46. Committee for Economic Development, *Work and Change: Labor Market Adjustment Policies in a Competitive World* (Washington: CED, 1987).

47. Michael J. Piore and Charles F. Sabel, *The Second Industrial Divide: Possibilities for Prosperity* (New York: Basic Books, 1984).

Chapter Fourteen

ECONOMIC REGULATION, SOCIAL INSURANCE, AND MINIMUM STANDARDS

By this point in the text, the reader will be well aware of the central role played by public policy, that is, governmental regulation, in the American labor market. Indeed, as a later chapter will point out, this characteristic is not uniquely American; in all developed countries governments have seen fit to intervene heavily in determining the nature of the employment relationship. The laws and regulations that have emerged in the United States, however, are the product of the nation's complex system of legislative-executive-judicial interaction. What makes the American system unique is not the existence of substantial labor market regulation, but rather the way it has developed and is enforced. Because of the importance of public policy to the HRM function, this chapter and the next are devoted to a discussion of selected policies and programs. In this chapter general economic regulation is considered, followed by a review of social insurance programs, labor standards, and occupational safety and health.

14–1 Regulation and the HRM Professional

Whether he or she approves of a particular regulatory program or not, no HRM professional can afford to be uninformed of the many legal requirements and external public policies affecting the labor market. And no general manager, in seeking to evaluate the effectiveness of the HRM function within a firm or organization, should do so unaware of the constraints that legal regulation places on that function. On the other hand, as has been stressed earlier, simply complying with the law's multiple strictures is not a complete HRM strategy. Nor should HRM professionals view their task merely as acting as internal police officers for outside regulatory authorities. There is sufficient latitude within the constraints of public policy to permit the firm to adopt HRM approaches suited to its needs.

Teachers and administrators in public schools often bemoan the fact that they are called upon to deal with social problems that are outside the immediate concerns of educators. Behavioral and other problems that should be dealt with in the home, they say, are being left to the schools. Similar laments are sometimes heard in HRM circles; society, so the complaint goes, is expecting—and requiring—employers to resolve grand social and economic issues that ought to be handled elsewhere. Of course, there is an element of truth to this charge. At the same time, the HRM lament overlooks the centrality of work and employment to the larger social and economic structure.

Perhaps nothing illustrates this point more directly than the expected working life estimates issued by the U.S. Bureau of Labor Statistics (BLS). As Table 14–1 shows, a typical American male at birth could expect to spend 55% of the years of his life active in the labor market, based on 1979–1980 information. For a typical female, the BLS estimate was 38%. Thus working is a major life activity for most people, and many broad social and economic problems will be connected inexorably to employment.

Even those who are not employed—children, homemakers, the disabled, retired persons, and the unemployed—generally receive a major proportion of their income as a byproduct of the labor market. They receive it in the form of support from working members of their families, from Social Security, from pensions, from work-related insurance payments, and from unemployment benefits. Inevitably, the social and economic issues related to income distribution will be connected in the public mind with the labor market, and with the employer–employee relationship.

Indeed, it is difficult to draw a sharp line between those economic policies that are labor market programs, and those that are not. Economic policies that are not generally viewed as examples of labor market regulation nevertheless often have an important impact on employment. Almost any policy that affects the

TABLE 14–1 Worklife Expectancies Based on 1979–1980 Data

Sex and Age	Life Expectancy (Years)	Worklife Expectancy (Years)	Ratio: Worklife to Life Expectancy (Percent)
Males			
At birth	70.0	38.8	55%
At age 25	47.3	33.1	70
Females			
At birth	77.6	29.4	38%
At age 25	54.2	24.0	44

Source: Shirley J. Smith, "Revised Worklife Tables Reflect 1979–80 Experience," *Monthly Labor Review,* vol. 108 (August 1985), p. 27.

product market will also have an impact on the labor market. Thus the politics of public policy in the product market often revolve around whether particular programs that are being advocated will create or destroy jobs.

14–2   Macro Policy

Macroeconomic policy—that is, monetary and fiscal policy—is usually viewed as regulating aggregate demand for the purpose of influencing the rate of unemployment and the rate of inflation. Through tax cuts and increased government spending, fiscal policy can stimulate the economy, expanding production and employment, but also perhaps raising the inflation rate. Expansion of the money supply by Federal Reserve open market operations is also stimulatory to real economic activity and potentially inflationary. A full discussion of macro policy is best left to other texts and to courses in macroeconomics. The field of macroeconomics has been in flux since the 1970s, and new interpretations and analyses have been evolving.[1] However, the interaction between macroeconomic policy and the labor market should be quite clear.

To the extent that macro policy either raises or lowers the general level of economic activity, it changes the level of labor market demand. Pulses of aggregate demand are translated into HRM policies of increased or decreased intensity of utilization of the existing workforce, for example, more or less use of overtime—and into hiring or layoff decisions. Compensation policy is also influenced by induced labor shortages or surpluses, as earlier chapters have noted.

If macroeconomic policy causes an acceleration or deceleration in price inflation, that, too, will have HRM implications. In unionized settings, for example, there may be demands for cost-of-living escalator clauses where none currently exist, or improved escalation formulas where they already do. In both union and nonunion settings, compensation adjustments may be made by employers to protect the real wage or in response to rising wages of other employers.[2]

Apart from wage determination, inflation induced by macro policy has implications for deferred benefit programs such as pensions and life insurance. Issues may arise concerning the status of retired workers whose (unindexed) retirement benefits are deteriorating in real terms, especially in collective-bargaining situations.[3] As discussed earlier inflation may also have a distorting influence on such HRM practices as determining pay increases through evaluation of employee merit.

In short, the conduct of macroeconomic policy has obvious effects on HRM policy at the firm level. The reverse is also true, even if it is less self-evident. The conduct of HRM policy at the firm level affects—and, many economists would say is the motivation for—implementation of active macro policy. If the labor market functioned as a classical economic auction, smoothly and quickly adjusting wages up or down in response to demand, the economy would stay at full employment. Inflation could be painlessly avoided by appropriate monetary policy. Even if inflation did occur, it is not clear that anyone would much care in the context of an auction-type labor market, since no real wage effects would result.[4]

14–3 Product Market Regulation and Deregulation

Labor demand is ultimately derived from product demand. Firms want labor in order to produce goods and services. Government regulation of the product market in ways that influence product demand will inevitably influence labor demand. Even if the initial intent of regulation has nothing to do with any resulting employment effects, those effects will soon enough become evident and will create constituencies for or against particular programs.

Consider, for example, the environmental issue of requiring soft drinks to be sold in returnable deposit containers, rather than in throw-away bottles and cans. Environmentalists tend to favor such requirements on the grounds that deposit laws will discourage discarding of empty bottles and cans on roadsides, in public parks, and so on. Whatever the merits of such regulation, unions representing supermarket employees typically *favor* laws requiring return containers since these create extra work in processing and sorting the returned bottles. In contrast, unions involved in glass bottle production *oppose* deposit/return laws, since recycling reduces the demand for bottles and, therefore, bottle makers.

Some forms of regulation, rather than creating more demand for a service, may instead restrict competition between suppliers. Even though such restrictions can result in higher prices and therefore less production and employment, reduced competition can raise the bargaining power of unions in the protected sector. Similarly, deregulation can reduce that power. In the airline industry, which was deregulated beginning in the late 1970s, postderegulation employment rose more rapidly than in the economy as a whole, but wages fell relative to other sectors.[5] Airline industry unions have been critical of deregulation since it was introduced, generally hoping to enlist public support through arguments related to safety and service to sparsely populated destinations.[6] The employment gains, which sometimes went to nonunion airlines and workers, have mattered less to the unions than the compensation losses and deterioration in working conditions that accompanied declining union bargaining power.

The HRM implications of changes in product market regulation for the employment relationship go beyond unions and bargaining. Employers will adopt different HRM strategies, depending on the nature of product market competition to which they are exposed. Companies with secure, relatively noncompetitive, regulated product markets—such as utilities—are likely to tilt towards HRM policies favoring long-term, career employment and job security. Their managers know that demand for their firms' output will continue without substantial interruption, and so they have every reason to invest both in their employees and in their relationship with their employees. With predictable long-term employment stability will probably go comprehensive fringe-benefit packages. In contrast, firms in volatile, competitive industries may stress temporary, less-assured, flexible, or contingent employment arrangements. Benefit packages are likely to be more spotty, reflecting the more transitory nature of the employer–employee relationship.

Although the connection between the product market and the labor market makes it difficult to draw a precise line around labor market regulation, certain kinds of programs are generally viewed as falling into that category. Earlier chapters have referred to some of these programs, such as the minimum wage. The sections that follow discuss social insurance programs, such as Social Security, and minimum standards programs.

14–4   Social Insurance

Life poses risks and uncertainties, and those perils that threaten a cutoff of income, or a heavy drain on it, are often seen as related to the labor market. Since the labor market is the major source, directly or indirectly, of most people's income, this public perception is not surprising. The result has been adoption of social insurance programs, specifically workers' compensation, Social Security, and unemployment compensation.[7] Much American social insurance dates back to the New Deal era of the 1930s.[8] However, there are elements that predate that period, and others that have been added more recently. The three major social insurance programs are described briefly below.

Workers' Compensation

Workers' compensation is not a federal program. It is composed of state-enacted laws providing benefits to workers who are injured on the job or become ill from occupational diseases.[9] State laws vary in scope. Employment coverage is generally very extensive with exemptions sometimes provided for very small employers, domestic servants, farm labor, and charitable organizations. Generally, employers obtain their mandatory insurance coverage from private carriers. Most jurisdictions permit self-insurance. A few states operate state-run insurance funds to provide the compulsory coverage.[10] As Table 14–2 shows, almost nine out of ten wage and salary earners are covered by workers' compensation.

Program History.   Programs of workers' compensation arose in the early part of the twentieth century, an era in which industrial accidents were of great concern. Injured workers could sue their employers for damages, but they had to show that the employer was at fault. The employer could claim in defense that the worker was at fault, that the worker knowingly assumed the risk entailed in the job, or that some other worker was at fault. These defenses were initially very effective in fending off claims.

As jurors became less receptive to these defenses, however, the management community opted for the present-day "no fault"/limited liability insurance sys-

TABLE 14–2   Coverage of Social Insurance Programs, Mid-1980s*

Program	Population Covered by Program (in Millions)	Ratio: Covered Population to Wage and Salary Workers (Percent)
Workers' Compensation	87.0	88%
Unemployment Insurance	98.2	100[†]
Social Security	93.8	93

*Figures for workers' compensation and unemployment insurance are for 1985. Figures for Social Security are for 1986.

[†]Coverage is almost universal.

Source: U.S. Social Security Administration, U.S. Department of Health and Human Services, *Social Security Bulletin: Annual Supplement 1987* (Washington: GPO, 1987), p. 69.

tem.[11] Under this system, workers need show only that their injury/illness was caused at or by the job to receive benefits. In exchange, suits for damages against employers are not permitted and employees must accept state-designated benefit schedules.

New Types of Claims.   Although the no-fault aspect of workers' compensation was intended to eliminate litigation, litigation in fact occurs—not in court, but before state-operated tribunals. Issues adjudicated can involve whether an injury/illness was or was not work related and the severity of the injury/illness. As noted in an earlier chapter, employers have become concerned about a tendency to widen the definition of work-related injury/illness, particularly in regard to claims of occupational stress. Under stress claims, the employee argues that medical or psychological problems such as heart attacks, strokes, or incapacitating anxiety were induced by job pressures.

In addition, there has been some erosion of the no-fault, specified benefit approach. Enterprising attorneys have filed suits against third parties other than employers. For example, considerable litigation surrounded manufacturers of asbestos products to which employees were exposed while at work.

Both sides—injured worker and employer/insurance carrier—can resort to litigation. In the occupational disease area, for example, where the causal link to the workplace can be questioned, claims by workers are often contested by the employer or carrier. Indeed, one study questions the use of the term *no fault* as applied to such claims, since contesting them is the norm, not the exception.[12]

Safety Incentives.   Workers' compensation premiums for many employers vary depending on claims experience. Some incentives may thus be present to reduce employee exposure to risk of injury or disease.[13] However, if there are compensating wage differentials for risk, that is, if risky jobs pay more than others (other things being equal), provision of workers' compensation benefits would lead to somewhat lower wages, diluting the incentive effect.[14] Still, employers' growing interest in establishing Employee Assistance Plans (EAPs) (discussed in an earlier chapter) seems associated with concerns about workers' compensation costs. In addition, students of occupational stress have suggested approaches to job design that can improve working conditions. These suggestions run from making jobs more predictable to reducing physical stressors such as loud noise and bright light.[15]

The fact that workers' compensation limits claims liability to state-specified benefit schedules may reduce employer incentives to invest in safety, relative to the old common-law system of litigation. In addition, since only the employer is liable under workers' compensation, there may be a misallocation of responsibility between employer and employee in situations when it would have been cheaper for the worker to undertake precautions.[16] Since employees cannot sue for damages resulting from job-related injuries and illnesses through the regular court system, there is no way to know what costs of such a system would be, nor how employers would react to it in terms of expenditures for risk mitigation.[17] Employers have not pressed, however, for a return to the common law system of court litigation, suggesting they view the current workers' compensation approach, whatever its defects, as the cheaper alternative.

Still, premiums for workers' compensation accounted for about 1% of total private-sector compensation in 1987,[18] a proportion that leveled out and declined slightly during the first half of the decade, after rising rapidly. The earlier increased cost trend seems to have been accelerated in the early 1970s, after a federal commission recommended benefit improvements to the states.[19] Benefits for workers and costs to employers, however, vary substantially between state systems, as do administrative procedures.

Information Sources.   Detailed information about the various state systems can be found in *Analysis of Workers' Compensation Laws*, an annual publication of the U.S. Chamber of Commerce. Updates on state programs are also reported annually in the *Monthly Labor Review*. Special publications of the U.S. Department of Labor, issued periodically, also review the highlights of state programs.[20]

Unemployment Insurance

Most paid employees are covered by unemployment insurance (UI), a state-operated, but federally induced program that originated with the Social Security Act of 1935.[21] Under the various state UI programs, workers who are laid off and meet certain standards of eligibility are entitled to weekly benefits for a specified maximum period, generally twenty-six weeks. These benefits are based on prior earnings of the claimant, but are subject to a cap. UI benefits are financed by payroll taxes that are experience rated. Caps and floors on the tax rates facing employers, however, mean that taxes paid by some employers effectively subsidize high rates of layoffs by others.[22] Use of layoffs by employers as a strategy for adjusting to demand fluctuations is encouraged by UI.[23] Because this aspect of UI was discussed in an earlier chapter, only brief highlights regarding other HRM implications of UI are provided here.

Typical HRM concerns with UI involve monitoring claims of laid-off or terminated employees. It may be to the employer's advantage—depending on its experience rating—to challenge such claims. If, for example, the claims involve a worker discharged for misconduct, state law may restrict benefit eligibility, providing the employer asserts that misconduct occurred and is prepared to prove it.

UI may also have an influence on employer strategy in collective bargaining, since two states pay benefits to strikers and some states will pay benefits to workers deemed to be unemployed due to an employer lockout. Where benefits for strikers are paid, strike durations may be increased, strengthening the union's position in negotiations. If benefits are payable for lockouts but not strikes, employers may try to tailor their dispute strategies so that if work stoppages occur, it is the union—not management—that initiates the action.

As in the case of workers' compensation, the precise administrative procedures, employer costs, and employee benefits under UI vary from state to state and can be complex. Annual summaries of the state programs can be found in *Highlights of State Unemployment Compensation Laws*, a publication of the National Foundation for Unemployment Compensation and Workers' Compensation. Other sources of data include the *Social Security Bulletin* and *Unemployment Insurance Statistics*.[24] Updates of state UI programs are reported annually in the *Monthly Labor Review*.

Social Security

Social Security is known primarily as a government-run pension system for workers and their survivors. It is indeed the most important element in the nation's retirement system. But there are also two other key components of Social Security: disability insurance and health insurance. With the exception of certain employees in the public sector, virtually all American workers are covered by these three programs. As can be seen in Table 14–3, in the mid-1980s monthly Social Security benefits stood at roughly one-third the income level of the average private-sector nonsupervisory worker.[25] The increase in relative benefits over the period shown, and the widening coverage of older individuals by Social Security, produced a significant decrease in poverty among the elderly.[26]

Social Security retirement payments are similar in form to those under private defined benefit plans. Benefits are based on past earnings' history and age, and become vested after a specified period. Unlike most private pension arrangements, Social Security is financed on a "pay-as-you-go," rather than an actuarial, basis. As a legal matter the Social Security payroll tax is evenly split between the employer and worker. Thus currently active workers and their employers are taxed to pay for the benefits of current retirees and their dependents. The so-called trust funds for Social Security function more as petty cash accounts—cushions between tax inflows and benefit outflows—than as accumulated assets held in reserve to pay future benefits.

Saving, Deficits, and HRM Policy. It has been argued by some economists that workers tend to substitute Social Security promises of future benefits for private

TABLE 14–3   Social Security Benefits Relative to Monthly Earnings, 1950–1986

Year	Average Benefit for Retiree	Average Benefit for Disabled Worker	Average Benefit as Percent of Average Monthly Earnings*	
			Retiree	Disabled Worker
1950	$30.43	—	13%	—
1960	81.73	$91.16	23	26%
1970	123.82	139.79	24	27
1975	206.49	233.94	29	33
1980	343.67	378.00	34	37
1986	453.42	472.96	34	36

*Average monthly earnings are calculated by multiplying average weekly earnings for production and nonsupervisory workers in the private nonagricultural economy by 4.3452381, that is, (365/12)/7.

Note: In years in which different averages applied for different months, monthly averages were weighted by the proportion of months in the year.

Source: Data from U.S. Social Security Administration, U.S. Department of Health and Human Services, *Social Security Bulletin: Annual Statistical Supplement, 1987* (Washington: GPO, 1987), p. 120; *Economic Report of the President, February 1988* (Washington: GPO, 1988), p. 299.

retirement saving. Because of the pay-as-you-go approach to funding and congressional generosity, workers (and their employers) have historically been required to pay less in taxes (actuarially adjusted) than they have received in benefits. The gap between lifetime taxes and eventual benefits was funded by increased tax rates and by a widening labor force base that paid into the system. Although there have been empirical attempts to pin down the effect of Social Security on national saving, the results have not been at all conclusive.[27]

A major difficulty in trying to estimate the saving effect is establishing what workers would be saving if Social Security had not been created. Would there be an intergenerational understanding, whereby children would support their aging parents? Such arrangements exist in traditional societies and functioned, albeit imperfectly, prior to the creation of Social Security in the United States. If Social Security has simply nationalized a within-family pay-as-you-go understanding, no net saving effect should be expected. If not—if each person would otherwise be putting aside funding for retirement personally or through private pensions—then Social Security could be lowering saving.

Any resolution of this issue is unlikely in the near future. From the viewpoint of firm-level HRM the effect of Social Security on overall saving is only of marginal significance. Its main impact on the firm's HRM function comes only if Congress—in the hope of either fostering saving generally or simply trimming the federal budget deficit—restricts Social Security benefits and/or encourages the creation or expansion of offsetting private work-related savings plans. Although there have been proposals that it should do so, Congress is unlikely to *require* establishment of private pension plans.[28] Hence its main means of encouraging such arrangements is the traditional one of providing favored tax treatment for them. Such tax incentives, however, lead to government revenue losses. Thus the same budgetary constraint that affects Social Security is likely to restrict additional tax-based encouragement of private savings and pensions. Indeed, changes in the tax code in the 1980s restricted use of 401(k) savings plans and Individual Retirement Accounts (IRAs).[29]

Indexation.   Social Security retirement benefits, unlike those of private pension plans, are formally adjusted to reflect changes in the Consumer Price Index.[30] Indeed for a period ending in the mid-1970s, an error in the escalation formula resulted in overindexing, that is, a systematic rise of benefits faster than that warranted by CPI-measured inflation. As Table 14–3 shows, the result was that the economic welfare of retirees rose faster than that of the active working population. This rise enhanced the importance of Social Security as a source of retirement income relative to private pensions and other sources.

The fact that Social Security benefits are indexed to inflation has the effect of *lessening* pressure on employers to place escalators in their own pension plans. Legally mandated funding rules make it extremely difficult to index a private pension plan, and virtually none are directly geared to the CPI.[31] Employers, however, sometimes make ad hoc adjustments for retirees during inflationary periods.[32] Since retirees generally receive a significant fraction of their retirement income from Social Security, employers know that their former workers and dependents have automatically received some inflation-linked benefit increases.

Tax and Benefit Reforms.   Although the overindexing problem was eventually corrected, in the late 1970s and early 1980s stagnant real wages (on which payroll tax revenues are based) led to a sequence of deficits and a funding crisis for the Social Security system.[33] A series of reforms was enacted in 1983, hiking payroll taxes, gradually raising the retirement age (from sixty-five to sixty-seven by 2027), making benefits for higher income persons partially taxable, reducing early retirement benefits, and expanding workforce coverage of the system.[34] The changes produced a diversity of results, but seemed on balance to worsen the retirement income outlook for single individuals relative to married couples and for higher income two-earner families relative to single-earner and lower income families.[35] As a result, even though Congress has not granted further encouragement to private work-related savings arrangements, employers can expect that workers will see greater value in the pensions, 401(k) plans, and similar devices that are available.

Portability.   From the employee viewpoint, belonging to Social Security has an advantage not found in other defined benefit pension plans. The benefits are portable from employer to employer and even carry over into self-employment. Although private defined benefit plans become quasi-portable once the employee has met the vesting requirements, substantial losses in net pension wealth are typically entailed in job changing for long-service workers.[36] Of course, employees who change jobs after short spells of employment may never vest at all in plans under which they are nominally covered.

From the employer's perspective, however, the portability of Social Security may be a disadvantage when compared with alternative private retirement systems. Lack of portability and limited vesting help reduce turnover costs for employers. The presence of Social Security thus reduces the degree to which pensions can be used for turnover control. Its portability also lessens the degree to which pensions can be used for the efficiency wage incentive purposes discussed in an earlier chapter.[37]

Labor Supply. Social Security may reduce the supply of labor in various ways.[38] For older workers, the availability of retirement benefits makes withdrawal from the workforce more feasible than it otherwise would be. In addition, Social Security has a feature that discourages work for benefit recipients. Until the attainment of age seventy, earnings above a specified floor result in partially offsetting benefit reductions. These reductions constitute a de facto heavy marginal "tax" on wages and work that may discourage substantial employment. Finally, the disability provisions of Social Security make it more possible for workers with illnesses or injuries to withdraw more readily from labor force participation.

Normal retirement age under Social Security is sixty-five years. An early retirement option with reduced monthly benefits is available between ages sixty-two and sixty-five. Table 14–4 shows that participation of males aged sixty-five and over has dropped dramatically since the early 1950s. Early retirement for males was introduced in the early 1960s. Thereafter, participation in the age fifty-five to sixty-four group also began to decline.

Of course, retirement and labor force withdrawal of older men was influenced by forces other than the presence of Social Security. Among these forces

TABLE 14–4 Civilian Labor Force Participation Rates of Older Persons, 1950–1987

	Males		*Females*	
Year	*55–64 Years*	*65 Years and Older*	*55–64 Years*	*65 Years and Older*
1950	87%	46%	27%	10%
1960	87	33	37	11
1970	83	27	43	10
1980	72	19	41	8
1987	68	16	43	7

Source: Data from U.S. Bureau of Labor Statistics, *Handbook of Labor Statistics,* bulletin 2217 (Washington: GPO, 1985), pp. 18–19; *Employment and Earnings,* vol. 35 (January 1988), p. 160.

are higher real preretirement incomes and, from the mid-1970s to the mid-1980s, generally higher unemployment rates. Yet retiring workers cluster around ages sixty-two and sixty-five, the Social Security early and normal retirement ages.[39] It is hard to believe, therefore, that the Social Security system did not play an important role in the decisions of these workers to leave the labor market, although there was some evidence in the 1980s of a bottoming out of the effect.[40]

For women the story is more complex, since there has been a rising trend in general female labor force participation. But older women, caught between the increased propensity to participate and the availability of Social Security, which has the opposite effect, have exhibited declining participation since 1960. The availability of early retirement for women produced participation stagnation for the age fifty-five to sixty-four group in the 1970s and 1980s.

Workers can qualify for disability benefits under Social Security, even if the illness or injury is not job related (unlike workers' compensation). The qualifying disability can be mental as well as physical. To be eligible, recipients must have met prior work tests and must be medically precluded by their disability from "substantial gainful work." The degree of generosity or restrictiveness in administering this standard has varied.

In the early to mid-1970s, the number of disability recipients increased rapidly, and appeared to reduce labor force participation for groups below normal or early retirement ages. More restrictive standards, especially during the initial years of the Reagan administration, reduced the number of recipients. Litigation and pressure from Congress, however, led to a subsequent increase in disability recipients.

The Social Security incentives for withdrawal from the labor force at certain ages change the demographic structure within firms. Despite an end to mandatory retirement, Social Security limits the workforce accretion of older workers. As noted earlier, if the employer–employee relationship is viewed as an ongoing implicit contract, with low pay at the beginning and higher pay at the end, some means of ending the relationship is needed. In the absence of mandatory retirement, the incentives from Social Security and private pensions may be that means.

A related issue is the demographic bulge caused by the baby boom generation born in the late 1940s through the early 1960s. By the mid-1990s a larger-than-steady-state fraction of middle-aged workers will be pressing for advancement opportunities. The labor force withdrawal incentives from Social Security—even though reduced by a budget-minded Congress—will dovetail with the needs of this middle-aged group by opening opportunities as still-older workers retire.[41]

Despite pressures from younger cohorts in the firm, employers will not necessarily want to shed all of their older workers, or at least not shed them at the ages that they choose to retire, given the Social Security incentives. To retain older workers, some accommodations to these incentives need to be made in HRM policy. For example, the earnings test for workers under age seventy means that firms that wish to retain their older workers may need to arrange for part-time employment options.

Integration of Private Benefits. The presence of Social Security needs to be considered by employers in benefit administration and design. HRM professionals in firms that offer disability insurance, for example, must consider what their disabled workers will receive from Social Security in formulating their firms' own plans. In general, it can be assumed that if Social Security offers a benefit, employees will place a lower value on increments of that benefit from the employer.[42] Thus Social Security tends to replace benefits employers might otherwise offer.

Congress also takes account of the presence of similar benefits from private employers and Social Security. For example, firms typically provided for reductions in private health insurance for older workers who became eligible for health insurance (Medicare) from Social Security. However, in an effort to reduce budgetary outlays, Congress effectively required employers to provide the first dollar of protection for older workers under Medicare, a reversal of past practice.[43] Even so, firms may continue to provide Medicare supplements to their pensioners. For retirees and dependents, Medicare—not the supplement—pays for the first dollar of coverage. Even in the case of retirees, congressional action can affect employer expenditures.[44]

The most dramatic cases of integration of private benefits with Social Security involve pension plans.[45] There are three chief methods by which private pension designs take account of Social Security. First, there are plans that do not officially include any recognition of Social Security in their formulas, but nevertheless contain benefit levels established in the knowledge that retirees would also draw Social Security benefits. Defined *contribution* plans typically fall into this category. Among workers under defined *benefit* plans in medium-sized and large firms in the mid-1980s, almost four out of ten were under plans with no formal tie to Social Security.[46]

Second, *excess plans* provide benefits based on earnings above a specified level (or provide a higher rate of benefits for earnings above the level). Such plans effectively recognize that Social Security benefits will be paid for those with lower earnings. In some of these plans, the specified level is the Social Security tax ceiling, since workers earning more than the ceiling effectively do not get credit from Social Security for their above-ceiling earnings.

Third, *offset plans* reduce plan benefits by an amount related to Social Security benefits received by the retiree. The reduction is less than dollar per dollar under these plans, and the precise formula may also involve years of service. Once the offset is calculated upon retirement, it is not changed to reflect changes in Social Security benefits.[47]

Nonunion pensions are substantially more likely than union plans to contain formal Social Security integration provisions. Part of the reason may be that nonunion plans will contain higher paid white-collar, professional, and managerial workers, for whom the ceilings on Social Security are important. Also a factor in the lower propensity of the union sector to integrate with Social Security may be the median voter political process within unions.[48] This process may reduce the influence in union decision making of the minority of highly paid union workers.

Income Redistribution and Social Insurance

Although the term *insurance* connotes reduction of risk, social insurance often involves more than simply dealing with economic uncertainty. Also involved is income redistribution. A longstanding theme in American economic policy—reflected, for example, in the Sixteenth Amendment to the Constitution, which permits a progressive income tax—is a notion that government should foster economic equality. Given the political processes that enact economic policy, however, the social programs that result from this theme are often aimed more at benefits for the middle class than for those at the very bottom of the income scale. The same median voter model used to describe the political process in union decision making can also be applied to the larger polity as well. Median voters will be interested in benefits aimed at mid-range incomes.

Despite the interest in the idea of equality, American public opinion has never favored outright confiscation and transfer of wealth. Robin Hood, who took from the rich and gave to the poor, is a more popular figure among children than among voting adults. While a simple economic theory of democracy might suggest that coalitions of 51% of the electorate should form and vote themselves the wealth of the remaining 49%, such bald economic transfers have not been seriously attempted.

When transfers do occur, for example, through the progressive income tax, the rationale is generally couched in terms of fairness and equality of burden sharing.[49] The rich "should" pay more in taxes, it is argued, because the money they pay in taxes is "worth less" to them since they have more of it than the average taxpayer. According to this view, income is subject to diminishing marginal utility. Pure theorists have long had problems with such arguments—it is not really possible to make interpersonal utility comparisons and demonstrate what incremental income is actually worth.[50] The general public, however, has not been bothered by such fine points of reasoning.

Similar to the notion that taxpayers should pay what they can afford is the idea that employers ought to ensure and provide—or be compelled to ensure and provide—certain minimum standards for their employees. Employers can afford to do so, it is argued, in comparison to the average employee, who is likely to be more vulnerable to life's vicissitudes. No one will win a prize in pure economic theory for these propositions, but politicians are not competing for such prizes.

Incidence of Social Insurance Costs

In any case, even though the public—probably including most employers—may feel that job-related social insurance is being paid partially or fully by firms rather than by workers, the standard method of social insurance financing raises questions about this popular perception. Presumably, the idea that the firm pays for something must really be understood to mean that the firm's *owners* ultimately have their profits reduced by the cost of the insurance. But social insurance is generally financed by payroll taxes or premiums related to employment. Profit or income taxes are not the method of choice. Hence there is reason to suspect that the "incidence" or burden of the cost of social insurance falls on employees, not owners.

It is true that when payroll taxes are increased, the official total compensation-per-hour numbers issued by the U.S. Bureau of Labor Statistics tend to blip up. This tendency suggests that in the very short run, the payroll tax is simply added to (not subtracted from) the wage. Such an observation is in keeping with the implicit contract/sticky wage model of pay setting developed in earlier chapters.[51] The basic issue is what occurs to the tax incidence in the long run.

The answer depends heavily on the elasticity of labor supply, which is often assumed to be relatively inelastic with respect to the wage set.[52] In the face of relatively inelastic labor supply curves, economic theory predicts, and empirical evidence suggests, that the incidence of payroll tax and similar payments will fall largely on wages over the long haul.[53] That is, real wages will ultimately be reduced to pay for the costs of social insurance programs.

Consider Figure 14–1. A payroll tax proportional to pay is levied on employers in a labor market characterized by demand curve D and (perfectly) inelastic supply curve S. The tax shifts the effective demand curve down to D', where $D' = D/(1+t)$, and t is the tax rate, for example, .1 or 10%. As a result, the wage falls from W to W'.[54] Labor effectively pays all of the tax in Figure 14–1, even though the tax is officially levied on the employer. Apart from this tax analysis, there are two other reasons to suspect that labor ends up paying indirectly for its own social insurance.

First, the payroll tax payment entitles the employee to benefits that are of some value, even if the employee might prefer the cash to the benefits. Just as payments for voluntary benefits such as pensions can be viewed as part of the total wage—and, hence, deductions from the take-home wage—social insurance

FIGURE 14–1
Effect of a Payroll Tax on Wages

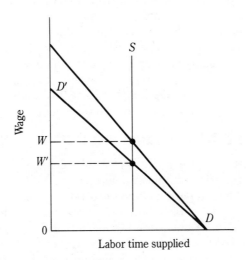

Note: $W = W'(1 + t)$
$D = D'(1 + t)$

benefits can also be so regarded.[55] Second, to the extent that social insurance does raise net costs to the employer, these costs may be passed into product prices, thereby cutting into real wages.

Thus, although there is an income redistribution aspect to social insurance, it is more a matter of transfers between groups of employees rather than transfers from rich to poor per se. Younger workers contribute to the support of retired persons. Employed persons contribute to the support of the unemployed. Able-bodied employees help support the disabled.

There is some tilting of the benefits of social insurance to the lower paid. Retirement benefits under Social Security, workers' compensation benefits, and unemployment insurance benefits replace a larger fraction of the incomes of low-wage workers than those of high-wage workers. Moreover, UI and Social Security benefits are subject to personal income taxation when received by higher income persons, but not when received by those with lower incomes.

Nevertheless, U.S. social insurance programs cannot be characterized as soak-the-rich schemes. Perhaps the best evidence of this proposition is that unemployment insurance and Social Security are financed by *regressive* taxation schedules. Both are funded by payroll taxes up to an annual wage ceiling. Thus higher wage workers (or their employers) pay no tax above the ceiling, making the tax collected a lower proportion of their wage than for lower wage workers.

As in other tax-transfer programs, social insurance will have behavioral effects that go beyond simple income redistribution. There are incentives to undertake steps that minimize taxation and maximize benefits. Since payroll taxes are collected on the basis of wages, not total compensation, there is added incentive for workers to be paid in the form of nonwage benefits rather than in cash.[56] Examples can also be found on the benefit side. As already noted, certain employers have an incentive to rely more heavily on layoffs than on other means to adapt to fluctuations in demand, since their laid-off workers receive an unemployment compensation subsidy.

Because of the behavioral effects induced, social insurance may engender various inefficiencies. Apart from the use of administrative resources, these programs entail a variety of economic costs. The late economist Arthur M. Okun once referred to public policies involving income redistribution as "leaky buckets." A dollar transferred produces less than a dollar's worth of benefits for the recipient.[57] The inefficiency leakage is not necessarily an argument that the programs should not be undertaken. It simply says that society, through the political process, must make a collective decision about whether the social benefits from the programs are worth the costs.

Employer Resistance to Social Insurance Costs

As the various New Deal social insurance programs were being adopted in the 1930s, there was resistance within the management community to the newly imposed arrangements. Today there is little management objection to the basic social insurance arrangements in principle. There is resistance, however, to *increases* in benefits and taxes. If, as economic theory suggests, workers ultimately pay for their own benefits, why should management be concerned with these matters?

Variable Cost Burdens.   Several reasons may be given. First, certain kinds of social insurance impose variable cost burdens across employers. Specifically, workers' compensation and unemployment insurance are experience rated. The more claims there are against the employer, the higher the cost. Even if the average cost of these programs is shifted over time to employees in the form of lower wages, particular employers with above-average (below-average) claims and costs will bear extra costs (or benefit from lower costs) relative to competitors.

Subject to the rules of the programs, it pays for employers to administer the workers' compensation and unemployment insurance aspects of their HRM system. Holding down costs will benefit the firm. Proposed legislative changes in these programs, which make such administration more difficult from the employer's perspective, will be opposed by management organizations. On the other hand, it might be expected that the management community would be less concerned about Social Security taxes—which are not experience rated and are assessed on all employers uniformly—than about other forms of social insurance. Indeed, employers have expressed less ongoing concern about the Social Security program than about unemployment insurance and workers' compensation.

The behavioral responses induced by changes in social insurance programs—especially changes that make them more generous—can also be costly to employers. These costs may not be evenly spread across all employers. For example, workers' compensation benefits are relatively low compared to the wages earned by higher paid workers. Firms employing a highly paid workforce may be little troubled by claims for benefits based on assertions of occupational stress. But firms with lower paid workforces might find that a loosening of standards for occupational stress claims would have a more important impact on their costs of operation.

Short-Run Effects.   A second reason for management opposition to increases in social insurance costs may relate to short-run effects. As noted above, in the short run, when payroll taxes increase, total compensation figures tend to blip up, indicating that the tax is initially added to the wage. Wages are not reduced in the short term to cover the added tax burden. Thus in the short run increased payroll taxes may cut into profits, creating obvious management incentives for opposition.[58]

Tax Illusion?   Finally, there is a third possible reason for management concern about social insurance cost increases, even if the costs are absorbed by employees. A tax-illusion effect may be present; employers are legally obligated to pay the tax, even if its burdens are ultimately shifted completely or partially to employees by the workings of the labor market. The situation depicted in Figure 14–1 involved labor *market* demand and supply curves, not demand curves of individual firms or workers. An *individual* employer would see only a wage of W' prevailing in the labor market plus the tax rate t. The total labor cost to the employer would be $W'(1+t)$.

Such an employer might reason (incorrectly) that if *t* were lower, total compensation would fall accordingly. Although it is true that if the tax rate were reduced *just for that employer*, its profits would be higher, the profit gain will not occur if the tax rate is reduced for all employers in the labor market. As drawn in Figure 14–1, each dollar saved by employers through a tax reduction would be lost to them due to resultant wage increases. With a somewhat more elastic supply curve for labor, reducing taxes would reduce total compensation, but each tax reduction of $1 would produce less than a $1 net cost saving.

The idea of tax illusion will bother theorists who insist that actors in the economic system have perfect insight. As already noted in the case of unions, however, union members—and employees generally—often reason on a personal basis with regard to wages. They reason that if *their* wages were higher, they would be better off; they would thus have trouble appreciating the side effects that might ensue if wages in their firm *all* rose. Employers may well reason in the same manner in thinking about taxes. Informed HR managers, who are aware of the subtle points discussed here, can help focus the firm's energy on legislative objectives that are truly in its interest.

14–5   Other Minimum Standards Regulation

Social insurance can be regarded as part of a national program of minimum workplace labor standards. Employers must offer at least those benefits contained in federal/state social insurance arrangements. For example, employers *must* be part of Social Security's retirement income and disability programs. They can also—*if they choose*—offer private supplements such as pensions or more generous permanent and temporary disability plans. Employers must be part of the unemployment insurance system of the state in which they operate, but they can also choose to offer Supplement Unemployment Benefit plans, as some unionized firms do.

Other forms of minimum standards regulation do not involve a government-run or -sponsored program. At the federal level, some of these regulations involve wages and hours. State-level regulation of wages and hours may involve higher-than-federal standards, or more specialized regulation dealing with such matters as the minimum frequency of pay. For example, California requires that most workers must be paid at least every other week. Apart from social insurance and wages and hours, the other major form of minimum standards regulation involves occupational safety and health.

FLSA Wage and Hour Standards

Earlier chapters have discussed the establishment of a minimum wage and time and a half for weekly overtime above forty hours under the federal Fair Labor Standards Act (FLSA) of 1938 (as amended). Like federal social insurance, the FLSA was a product of the New Deal economic policies of the Great Depression era. The enactment of the FLSA came three years after a much more elaborate New Deal attempt to regulate wages and hours on an industry-by-industry basis was declared unconstitutional by the U.S. Supreme Court.[59]

Minimum Wage.   Because the economic analysis of the minimum wage was discussed in a previous chapter, only a brief review will be presented here. Table 14–5 shows the federal minimum-wage standards in place during 1967 to 1988. As can be seen the minimum wage was moved up from time to time during that period, pursuant to various legislative amendments to the FLSA.

Apart from increases, minimum-wage *coverage* of new groups of workers was expanded. Although the law contains many specialized exemptions, over

TABLE 14–5   **Federal Minimum Wage Rates as Percent of Average Hourly Earnings, 1967–1988**

Effective Date of Minimum Wage Imposition	*Basic Minimum Wage*		*Minimum Wage for Workers Covered Since 1966*	
	Wage Rate	*Percent of Average Hourly Earnings* *	*Wage Rate*	*Percent of Average Hourly Earnings* *
Feb. 1967	$1.40	53%	$1.00	38%
Feb. 1968	1.60	58	1.15	41
Feb. 1969	1.60	54	1.30	44
Feb. 1970	1.60	51	1.45	46
Feb. 1971	1.60	48	1.60	48
May 1974	2.00	48	1.90	45
Jan. 1975	2.10	48	2.00	45
Jan. 1976	2.30	49	2.20	47
Jan. 1977	2.30	45	2.30	45
Jan. 1978	2.65	48	2.65	48
Jan. 1979	2.90	49	2.90	49
Jan. 1980	3.10	48	3.10	48
Jan. 1981	3.35	48	3.35	48
Note: Jan. 1987	3.35	37	3.35	37

*Average hourly earnings data apply to nonsupervisory workers in the private, nonagricultural sector.

Note: Lower minimum wage rates applied to farm workers during 1970–1977.

Source: Data from U.S. Bureau of the Census, *Statistical Abstract of the United States: 1988* (Washington: GPO, 1988), p. 395; U.S. Bureau of Labor Statistics, *Employment, Hours, and Earnings, United States, 1909–84,* bulletin 1312–12, vol. 1 (Washington: GPO, 1985), pp. 5–6; *Monthly Labor Review,* vol. 111 (June 1988), p. 85.

85% of nonsupervisory, private-sector wage and salary earners were covered by the mid-1980s.[60] (Managers and professionals, who would earn more than the minimum anyway, were not covered). Public-sector employees are also subject to FLSA standards.[61] Until 1981 the basic federal minimum generally approximated about half the level of average hourly earnings for nonsupervisory workers in the private, nonfarm sector. No change was made in the minimum wage under the Reagan administration, resulting in a gradual decline in its real and relative value.

The minimum wage has never enjoyed the favor of economists as a group; economic theory suggests that raising a relative wage will diminish the demand for the labor affected, resulting in employment displacement.[62] A queue of job seekers for minimum-wage jobs can be expected to result.[63] Those persons displaced by the minimum wage may not officially appear in the national statistics as unemployed; some may drop out of the labor market and not be counted. Nevertheless, the income losses of the displaced need to be offset against the gains of those who remain employed at the higher wage. In addition, to the extent that they have the latitude to do so, employers may reduce nonwage conditions such as the provision of training for those minimum-wage workers who retain their jobs.[64]

Opponents of the minimum wage tend to seize on such arguments and overstate them. For example, the high unemployment rates of black teens that are often cited in connection with minimum wages seem more closely linked to the shift in the black population to urban areas and away from the agricultural pursuits that once absorbed black teens.[65] Child labor laws, as applied to teenagers, remove certain job opportunities in manufacturing and construction that might otherwise absorb relatively unskilled young workers.[66] These laws also contribute to reduced teen job possibilities.

Even if overstated, issues of potential employment displacement by the minimum wage are compounded by the teenage versus adult division of the low-paid workforce. In the mid-1980s, about 22% of all hourly paid workers who earned the minimum wage of $3.35 or less fell under the government's official poverty line on the basis of their total family income. For teenagers, however, the rate was under 13%, mainly because teenagers are likely to be in families with one or more adult workers.[67] Thus the minimum wage seems to be a blunt antipoverty instrument; most workers at or near the minimum wage are not below the poverty line. And the minimum may hurt some of those who are below the poverty line while benefiting others.

From the HRM viewpoint, however, these arguments over the basic premise of the minimum wage are of little import. The concept of the minimum has been part of American public policy for so long that it can be safely assumed to remain in effect. Indeed, in many respects, the basic argument is really noneconomic. There are other examples of private labor-market contracts that are forbidden, even if voluntarily arranged. The law forbids slavery, even in hypothetical cases in which persons are willing to sell themselves.[68] Prostitution is also generally outlawed. It appears that much the same attitude has formed about working below some minimum wage. Very low wages are a symptom the public would rather not observe.

HRM professionals must assume that minimum-wage legislation will remain on the books, both at the federal and state levels. The magnitude of the wage, and the frequency of its adjustment, however, will be of special concern to employers in low-paying industries such as fast-food restaurants, car washes, and certain retailers. Any firm with some minimum-wage workers will have an interest in minimum-wage developments.

One issue for HRM professionals in situations where there is a mix of minimum-wage workers and higher paid workers is the impact of a minimum-wage increase on the pay of the latter group. Given the norms of equitable treatment that influence pay setting, a hike at the bottom of the pay scale will compress the wage gap between those at the bottom and those higher up, and lead to pressure on employers to restore the previous differential. Firms are unlikely simply to boost the entire pay scale up with the minimum; if they did, the federal minimum wage would effectively set pay for the entire workforce. But employers may grant some pay increases—in order to lessen, not eliminate, compression—to workers whose wages are above the new minimum.[69]

Concern over adverse employment effects of the minimum wage has resulted in special arrangements for subminimum wages for such groups as full-time students, student-learners, and the handicapped.[70] A perennial issue—raised whenever the minimum wage is hiked—is the possibility of adding a provision permitting a general subminimum wage for teenagers.[71] Still another proposal is the suggestion to index the minimum wage to average hourly earnings, thus avoiding periods such as the 1980s of relative minimum-wage erosion. It is over these incremental issues, rather than over the basic principle of having a minimum wage, that HRM professionals in affected industries must be concerned.

Hours Regulation.   As an earlier chapter noted, the FLSA has a much more pervasive effect on American employers through its overtime provisions than through its minimum-wage requirements. Yet these provisions are virtually never debated in Congress or anywhere else, in striking comparison to the continuous debate over the minimum wage. The overtime provision was originally a product of the Great Depression and the problem of the widespread unemployment the depression created. It was thought that by encouraging employers to add shifts, rather than pay their current workers for overtime at a stiff premium, existing work could be spread around to more employees. Since passage of the FLSA in 1938, the U.S. economy has experienced booms and busts. The notion of a forty-hour standard workweek, with overtime thereafter, seems to have become an immovable norm in the labor market.[72]

The overtime provisions have important implications for employment practices. There is an incentive, as the framers of the FLSA planned, to add workers rather than hours, once the forty-hour hurdle is reached. This incentive, however, is not sufficiently strong to end the use of overtime hours. Adding a shift is a lumpy decision with fixed costs, both in terms of obligations to the new employees and the need for rearranging schedules. In addition, there may be premiums to be paid for night work or weekend work not because of federal law, but because of worker time preferences. Estimates of overtime hours per employee in manufacturing suggest that once aggregate average overtime/worker reaches about 3½ hours, further demand for labor is channeled mainly into the hiring of more employees.[73]

Despite the dormancy of the overtime issue, publicized successes in reducing the workweek below forty hours in some European industries may reignite interest in the working-week standard in the United States. Much depends on the course and trend of unemployment. Overtime as a work-spreading device is an issue that is more potent in a slack economy with high, persistent unemployment than in a tight one.

Labor Standards for Federal Contractors

The federal government is a major consumer of goods and services from the private sector. As a consumer, it can require its private suppliers to meet the minimum labor standards of the FLSA. Under the Walsh-Healey Act, for example, suppliers of goods to the federal government can lose their contracts, and even be blacklisted from future contracts, for labor standards violations.[74]

As a consumer, the federal government can also require minimum labor standards for private federal contractors that are *higher* than those of the FLSA. Of course, to the extent that such standards raise the cost of producing for the government, the government will have to pay more for its contracts. Two pieces of legislation, the Davis-Bacon Act of 1931—applicable to federal construction contractors—and the Service Contract Act of 1965 (for services such as equipment repair, building maintenance, food preparation, and so on) require the payment of wages prevailing in the local area to employees hired under federal contracts. The level of prevailing wages is determined by U.S. Department of Labor surveys.[75]

Public debate about such requirements has focused mainly on the cost issue and secondarily on administrative practice. Proponents of prevailing wage standards (chiefly affected unions) argue that federal contracts should not be won by competitive wage cutting. They argue that federal costs are not actually raised by the prevailing wage requirement because more productive workers are employed by higher wage contractors.[76] These two arguments, however, are potentially in conflict; if the productivity effect offset the wage effect, low-wage contractors would not be able to underbid high-wage contractors.

A more sophisticated, theoretically based economic argument is that the federal government might act as a monopsonist in the absence of a legal constraint on such behavior. That is, the government would be tempted to take advantage of its dominance in certain markets for goods and services, push down prices of the goods and services it buys, and thus depress wages. Opponents of prevailing wage standards—most notably the U.S. General Accounting Office—have cited higher costs to the federal government and tendencies by the Labor Department to select upward biased wage samples in determining what wage was prevailing.[77]

Under the Reagan administration, the procedures for determining prevailing wages under Davis-Bacon were changed in ways likely to produce lower wage determinations.[78] Similar changes were made in administration of the Service Contract Act. Although political swings could halt the shift toward reduced minimum labor standards for federal contractors, concern about federal spending and the budget deficit works in the opposite direction.

Occupational Safety and Health

The federal government imposes minimum workplace occupational safety and health standards primarily through mechanisms established by the Occupational Safety and Health Act of 1970 (OSHA).[79] Prior to OSHA, such regulation was mainly in the hands of the states, pursuant to laws dating back to the 1870s. The new law created the Occupational Safety and Health Administration in the U.S. Department of Labor to administer the act and conduct worksite inspections. It also set up the Occupational Safety and Health Review Commission to hear appeals of citations and fines from employers and the National Institute for Occupational Safety and Health (NIOSH) to conduct research and recommend safety and health standards.

Under OSHA, state governments have the option of having their own enforcement programs as long as state standards are at least as strict as the federal rules. States that meet the requirements of OSHA can receive a federal subsidy for their administrative costs. From the employer's perspective, of course, having higher state standards means the potential of inconsistent requirements for worksites in different regions of the country.

Union Role.   Unions played a key role in obtaining congressional enactment of OSHA. It is not surprising that unions would have a special interest in occupational safety and health, since their members are more likely to be in hazardous jobs than nonunion workers.[80] But why would unions have wanted a special statute?

The answer might seem obvious; with a statute in existence, unions could bargain as they traditionally had for wages and benefits and then let OSHA provide the safety umbrella on top of what had been negotiated. This answer is not entirely satisfactory. To the extent that providing safety and health is costly and to the extent that workers value safety and health, OSHA-induced costs may be shifted back to workers by employers, like other fringe benefits. Just as more pension can be expected to mean less wages, other things being equal, so more safety could also mean less wages. Why wouldn't unions prefer to make the trade-off themselves through bargaining, rather than have the federal government impose it?

There could be several answers. First, it may have appeared to unions that OSHA-imposed safety standards would have been added, like gravy, on top of their traditional wage-and-benefit packages.[81] That is, they may not have perceived the possibility of a backward shift in costs, even if economic theory suggests its potential. After all, unions could see that employers opposed a federal statute; if the backward shift had been assured, employers presumably would have been indifferent towards the law's passage. As in other areas of public policy in the labor market, the parties involved often focus on the direct effects and play down (or do not perceive) possible indirect consequences.

A second reason why unions may have pushed for OSHA is that bargaining intelligently for health and safety involves costly technical expertise. Proposing safety standards requires knowledge of industrial engineering and chemistry; proposing health standards requires knowledge of industrial medicine. Moreover, changes in technology introduce new equipment with new hazards into the workplace. New chemicals may threaten workers with potential dangers of exposure. A heavy investment in expertise is involved in simply keeping up with new processes and their consequences, let alone conducting a research program. Under OSHA, these costs are federally borne and centralized.

A third possibility is that OSHA standards, as typically applied, have the effect of increasing employment. The engineering controls needed to reduce noise or chemical exposure may act as a "tax" on capital (not labor), thus raising the demand for employees. A net increase in employment is possible if the substitution effect of higher effective capital costs outweighs the negative effect of higher costs on output. There is limited evidence that OSHA standards have an employment-raising effect.[82]

Finally, the existence of OSHA standards has sometimes proved to be a useful tool for unions in recognition or negotiating disputes with employers. Charges of unsafe working conditions are of obvious concern to workers and can rally their support. Moreover, as part of the general environmental movement that developed in the 1970s, the public is sympathetic to workers who are exposed to health hazards.

Compensating Wage Differentials. Economic theory predicts that wages would adjust to *known* differential risk. If other things are equal, high-risk jobs should pay more than low-risk jobs. As noted earlier, these hypothetical wage premiums are termed *compensating wage differentials* by economists. Demonstrating the existence of such differentials empirically is made difficult by the observed gross *negative* correlation between wage level and occupational risk. Within blue-collar occupations, for example, (low-wage) laborers face greater hazards than (middle-wage) semiskilled operatives, who—on average—face greater risk than (high-wage) skilled trades.[83]

The negative gross correlation does not mean that the theoretical proposition is necessarily wrong. It may simply be that worker preferences for safety, like other fringes, rise with income levels. Or it may indicate that employers tend to shift dangerous work toward low-paid occupations in order to reduce the differentials that must be paid.[84] Some studies have used statistical controls in examining job-related risks and have found evidence of positive compensating differentials for work hazards. However, the evidence has sometimes been ambiguous and, to the extent that positive differentials are found, they seem to be concentrated in the union sector.[85] A complicating factor is that the existence of workers' compensation, by offering injured employees financial compensation, can be expected to weaken the link between riskiness and pay.[86]

As noted at the outset of this section, for job risk to affect wages, there must be worker knowledge of the hazards involved. Evidence exists that—*if* given accurate information on employment hazards—workers will respond appropriately; risk-averse individuals will exit risky jobs.[87] Undoubtedly, firefighters and roofers are aware that they are in risky occupations. Their risks, however, involve injuries that are readily observed and that are easily connected with the job. Occupational diseases, however, often have long incubation periods and their connection with the job may not be at all obvious, even to health professionals. Thus there is evidence to suggest that, to the extent that compensating wage differentials exist, they relate to injury risk, not to disease risk.[88]

The complex nature of the employer–employee relationship also suggests difficulties with placing complete reliance on the labor market to deal with safety and health issues. Employees may come to the job with expectations about reasonable levels of workplace safety. Like other aspects of the relationship, the exact nature of reasonable behavior on the part of the employer is not clearly defined. OSHA is a case in which public policy has been called in to define that behavior more precisely.

Regulations Versus Incentives.   Although a case can be made for public policy in the job safety and health area, the particular regulatory system created by OSHA is not necessarily ideal. OSHA standards tend to be specific, that is, indicating precisely what steps, equipment, and so on, should be undertaken or installed to mitigate a particular hazard. On the other hand, the resources available for OSHA safety inspections are small, as are the fines typically imposed. Economists have criticized this approach to regulation, and two basic issues are raised.[89]

First, there may be more than one way to mitigate a hazard, and it may be more efficient to leave the method chosen to the employer. If the employer is allowed discretion, however, there must be assurance that the method picked is effective. The second issue is thus the need for expected financial penalties, tied to the occurrence of injuries or illness, that are large enough to provide deterrence. A mix of more elaborate inspection resources —aimed at checking on occurrences rather than equipment—and larger fines would be needed.

Unfortunately, the disease aspect of occupational safety and health poses hurdles for such an incentive-based system. Just as workers may have difficulty recognizing the disease risk, so would inspectors assessing fines on the basis of occurrences. The occurrence might take place twenty or more years after exposure to the job hazard. Would the employer be assessed retroactively? What if the employer no longer existed? If the employee had worked for more than one employer at which the disease might have been contracted, how would the fine be allocated between them? What kind of appeals mechanism could be provided to examine events of the distant past while providing due process?

A Bargaining Alternative?   It has been suggested that the federal government should supplant the OSHA model of regulation with private bargaining. Although, as noted above, unions favored the creation of OSHA, the argument has been made that they could be induced to bargain on safety matters and, effectively, replace OSHA by doing so. What would be needed, according to this view, is a sufficient subsidy to be given to unions to develop the necessary health and safety expertise. Additionally, some kind of a limit on union liability to injured workers would be required.[90]

In fact, OSHA *has* distributed some funds for training of union officials in safety matters. Also, unions do engage in safety bargaining, even in the absence of a subsidy. But they do not have the kind of expertise that the enforcement and research arms of OSHA can provide. At any rate, unions represent a minority of workers, even in high-hazard sectors such as manufacturing and construction. How would bargaining be applied in nonunion situations?

Cost/Benefit Analysis?   It has been suggested that economic analysis should play a larger role even within the basic OSHA model of rulemaking. For example, one possibility would be to subject new rules to some kind of cost/benefit analysis. While courts have not demanded complete avoidance of economic considerations in the standard-setting process, they have not accepted a strict cost/benefit approach either, since the statute does not call for it. Costs of regulation enter in court review of proposed OSHA standards indirectly through general judicial insistence that *some* benefits of the rules must be demonstrated and through judicial acknowledgment that achieving zero risk is not a feasible goal.[91]

At any rate, it is easier to call for cost/benefit analyses than to implement a procedure for conducting them. The cost side is more readily handled than the benefit side. Even the cost side has ambiguities, since—as noted earlier—some of the costs to the employer may be shifted back to workers. To value the benefits of a proposed rule, the likely reduction in injuries or illness must be calculated. For occupational diseases, this step is difficult because of long incubation periods and lack of knowledge about the functional relationships involved. As an example, it is often not known whether disease reduction related to chemical exposure is proportionate to exposure reduction, or whether there is a hurdle level of safe exposure, below which no hazard is involved.

Given these difficulties of implementation, suggestions have been made for relying on costs alone. The OSHA authorities might be given an annual "budget" of costs they could impose on employers. Within that budget, presumably, the regulations felt to be most beneficial would be implemented, although precise calculations of benefit would not be needed.[92]

Safety and Health Record.   OSHA established a new data series concerning injuries and illness. As Figure 14–2 illustrates, reported injury and illness fell after the early 1970s. The decline, however, was centered in minor injuries; so-called lost-workday cases, that is, occurrences that led to absence from work showed no trend. On the other hand, death rates do appear to have fallen.[93]

Establishing cause-and-effect relationships from these data is difficult. Some detailed studies have suggested that OSHA regulations do reduce certain types of injuries.[94] Others find, however, that the cost of noncompliance is not sufficiently high to have had a significant effect on injury rates.[95] Apart from the injury-deterrence question is the issue of occupational disease. Data problems related to occupational disease make study of that facet of the OSHA program especially complicated. Employees who contract a disease long after exposure to the workplace hazard may not even be recorded as suffering from a work-related illness. Even if good data were readily available, the full effect of OSHA might not be felt for many years.

OSHA Outlook.   OSHA's effectiveness is difficult to assess, a fact that paradox-

FIGURE 14–2   Injuries and Illness per 100 Full-Time Employees

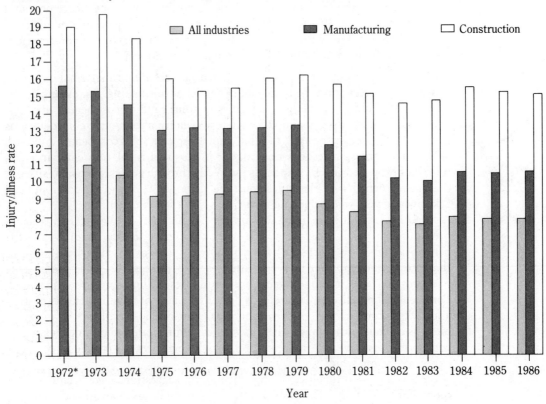

Note: All industries data for 1972 are not available on a basis consistent with later years.

Source: Monthly Labor Review, vol. 111 (August 1988), p. 99; U.S. Bureau of Labor Statistics, *Handbook of Labor Statistics,* bulletin 2217 (Washington: GPO, 1985), p. 412.

ically has insulated the program from criticism. The proposed alternatives to OSHA, moreover, founder on practical difficulties of implementation. Thus HRM specialists would not be well advised to anticipate fundamental changes in the OSHA approach to job safety and health, although there may well be experimentation within the basic model. For example, OSHA has developed approaches that target high risk industries and employers in order to economize on limited inspection resources. The absence of an effective alternative suggests the OSHA model will be retained.

One impact of OSHA has been to thrust HRM policy into an area in which it had previously had little influence: engineering and the application of technology. HR managers of the future will have to acquaint themselves with this unfamiliar territory, since the very design of equipment has assumed importance in the employment relationship.

Safety and health issues also interact with other public policies. Most prominent have been conflicts between equal employment opportunity policy (discussed in the next chapter) and safety standards. In some cases, firms have forbidden women of child-bearing age from assuming jobs where they might be exposed to substances that could adversely affect the female reproductive system or unborn fetuses. Is this sex discrimination or responsible risk management? The guidelines are unclear and may shift with the political winds.

Summary

Public policies that affect the labor market consist of two types: those that are primarily aimed at other objectives but have labor market consequences and those that are deliberately focused on labor market goals. This chapter reviewed macroeconomic policy and product-market regulation and deregulation as examples of the former type of policy. It then turned to a variety of public policies aimed directly at the labor market.

Labor market policies contain both do's and don'ts for employers. Those policies reviewed in this chapter have been primarily of the affirmative nature, that is, thou shalt participate in and provide social insurance. Thou shalt pay at least the minimum wage. Thou shalt follow minimum safety and health standards. Other policies in the labor market, however, focus more heavily on negatives. The next chapter will examine two public policies intended primarily to forbid certain employer behaviors—the hiring of illegal immigrants and discrimination against women and minorities.

EXERCISES

Problem

Although public policies tend to cover employers across the board, certain industries will be more affected by particular policies than others. For example, minimum-wage laws tend to affect industries with substantial fractions of their workforces in low-paid jobs. Using available industry data, see if you can identify industries that you think would be especially concerned with minimum-wage legislation, with workers' compensation and OSHA standards, and with unemployment insurance. (Different industries, of course, may fall into different categories.) See if you can determine how firms falling into the especially concerned industries in your area or state have reacted to proposed changes in these public policies.

Hint: To the extent that policy decisions are decided at the state level (state minimum wage, workers' compensation, unemployment insurance, safety and health if your state operates its own mini-OSHA program), it may be easier to pinpoint the employer reaction in your area.

Questions

1. How does macroeconomic policy impinge on HRM concerns?

2. What impact might you expect product market deregulation to have on an industry's HRM policies and practices? If the industry was heavily unionized prior to deregulation, what special impacts might you anticipate?

3. In what way might workers' compensation induce a safer workplace?

4. How might unemployment insurance procedures affect the course of a union–management dispute?

5. In what ways should designers of a firm's pension policy take account of Social Security?

6. Who pays for programs supported by payroll taxes such as Social Security?

7. Are OSHA standards subject to cost/benefit analysis?

Terms

compensating wage differential

Davis-Bacon Act

disability benefits

employee assistance plans (EAPs)

experience rating and unemployment insurance

experience rating and workers' compensation

Fair Labor Standards Act

integration of Social Security with private pensions

Occupational Safety and Health Review Commission

overtime pay

pay-as-you-go and Social Security

payroll tax incidence

portability of Social Security versus private pensions

ENDNOTES

1. For a review, see Bruce C. Greenwald and Joseph E. Stiglitz, "Examining Alternative Macroeconomic Theories," *Brookings Papers on Economic Activity* (1:1988), pp. 207–260.

2. There is dispute in the empirical macroeconomic literature as to whether wage inflation is best explained through a price-wage or a wage-wage model. Some economists have argued that the empirical evidence suggests that wage and price setting are largely independent. The difficulty with this view is apparent; taken to an extreme, it would suggest massive profit fluctuations as costs and prices moved without relation to one another. For discussion, see Robert J. Gordon, "The Role of Wages in the Inflation Process," *American Economic Review*, vol. 78 (May 1982), pp. 276–283.

3. During periods of inflation, it is not unusual for retirees to receive ad hoc benefit adjustments. Union workers appear to be more likely to receive such adjustments than nonunion. See Steven G. Allen, Robert L. Clark, and Daniel A. Sumner, "A Comparison of Pension Benefit Increases and Inflation, 1973–79," *Monthly Labor Review*, vol. 107 (May 1984), pp. 42–46.

4. Many economists would want to qualify the statements in the text. Some would argue that deviations in the product market from the auction model are just as important as those of the labor market, for example, Olivier Jean Blanchard, "Aggregate and Individual Price Adjustment," *Brookings Papers on Economic Activity* (1:1987), pp. 57–109. Others might question the dynamic implications of freely adjustable wages. Regarding inflation, still others would note that unanticipated inflation (or deflation) could cause income redistribution between debtors and creditors even if real wages were unaffected.

5. According to the national income accounts, full-time equivalent employment in air transportation rose 4.5% per annum between 1977 and 1987, more than double the national rate of 2.0%. But the ratio of compensation per full-time equivalent employee in air transportation to the

overall domestic economy fell from 1.73 to 1.48. Source: *Survey of Current Business,* vol. 68 (July 1988), pp. 80–81; U.S. Bureau of Economic Analysis, Department of Commerce, *The National Income and Product Accounts of the United States, 1929–82: Statistical Tables* (Washington: GPO, 1986), pp. 264, 277.

6. For example, in 1988, unions in dispute with Texas Air Corporation succeeded in prompting a widely publicized federal safety investigation against two carriers owned by the firm: Continental and Eastern. For more on the effects of deregulation on the airline industry, see Herbert R. Northrup, "The New Employee-Relations Climate in Airlines," *Industrial and Labor Relations Review,* vol. 36 (January 1983), pp. 167–181.

7. Some special programs can be classified as social insurance applicable to particular sectors. Worthy of mention are Railroad Retirement (a sort of Social Security system for railroad employees) and black lung compensation, an occupational disease program for coal miners. These programs are not discussed because of their limited applicability.

8. For an historical background, see Irving Bernstein, *A Caring Society: The New Deal, the Worker, and the Great Depression* (Boston: Houghton Mifflin, 1985), chapter 2.

9. Programs exist for the District of Columbia, American territories, and federal employees. There is also a federally operated program for maritime workers.

10. States have various special funds that provide certain kinds of supplementary benefits. The most common is a "second injury" fund for workers who have been previously injured and whose earlier injury is aggravated by a subsequent injury. Such funds are designed to avoid disincentives to the hiring of injured workers on the grounds that their previous injuries will increase employer exposure to the risk of additional claims. Apart from supplements to workers' compensation, a few states have temporary disability funds. Under these programs, workers are able to collect benefits for injuries not covered by workers' compensation (not caused at work) that prevent them from working.

11. Nicholas Askounes Ashford, *Crisis in the Workplace: Occupational Disease and Injury* (Cambridge, Mass.: MIT Press, 1976), pp. 388–389.

12. Peter S. Barth and H. Allan Hunt, *Workers' Compensation and Work-Related Illnesses and Diseases* (Cambridge, Mass.: MIT Press, 1980), p. 187.

13. A self-insured employer obviously bears the risk of claims on a dollar-for-dollar basis. Employers covered through insurance carriers face more complex situations. Very small employers may not be experience rated, since their claims are too few for a carrier to evaluate their riskiness. Instead, they pay state-designated rates based on their industry. Larger firms can arrange for experience-rated coverage. The formulas used, however, seem to provide more than a dollar's premium reduction for each dollar of claims saved by accident avoidance. In a competitive insurance market, the

cross subsidy from high risk to low risk employers would not occur. High-risk firms would be quoted lower rates than under the current system, and therefore the cross subsidy would be eliminated. The cross subsidy prevails, however, because the insurance is sold under detailed state regulation. See Richard B. Victor, *Workers' Compensation and Workplace Safety: The Nature of Employer Financial Incentives,* report R–2979–ICJ (Santa Monica, Calif.: Rand Corporation, 1982).

14. Richard B. Victor, Linda R. Cohen, and Charles E. Phelps, *Workers' Compensation and Workplace Safety,* report R2918–ICJ (Santa Monica, Calif.: Rand Corporation, 1982).

15. Robert L. Kahn, "Work, Stress, and Health" in Barbara D. Dennis, ed., *Proceedings of the Thirty-Third Annual Meeting,* Industrial Relations Research Association, September 5–7, 1980 (Madison, Wisc.: IRRA, 1981), pp. 257–267.

16. Daniel M. Kasper, "An Alternative to Workmen's Compensation," *Industrial and Labor Relations Review,* vol. 28 (July 1975), pp. 535–548. Kasper argues for a system under which both the employer and employee carry insurance and fault is determined by courts.

17. Under workers' compensation, for example, there are no damages for pain and suffering.

18. *Survey of Current Business,* vol. 68 (July 1988), pp. 80, 84.

19. Martin W. Elson and John F. Burton, Jr., "Workers' Compensation Insurance: Recent Trends in Employer Costs," *Monthly Labor Review,* vol. 104 (March 1981), pp. 45–50.

20. U.S. Employment Standards Administration, U.S. Department of Labor, *State Workers' Compensation: Administration Profiles* (Washington: ESA, 1985).

21. The State of Wisconsin had initiated, but had not implemented, an unemployment insurance plan prior to 1935, and some unions had informal unemployment benefit plans for members prior to the 1930s. A few companies also had initiated plans for their employees. The joint federal-state nature of unemployment insurance means that the system's taxes and benefits are part of the federal budget, despite and major role played by states in administering the programs. Proponents of the UI system have called for its removal from the federal budget because its inclusion allegedly causes Congress to restrict the program out of concern with the overall federal deficit. See National Commission on Unemployment Compensation, *Unemployment Compensation: Final Report* (Washington: GPO, 1980), pp. 103–104.

22. Denton Marks, "Incomplete Experience Rating in State Unemployment Insurance," *Monthly Labor Review,* vol. 107 (November 1984), pp. 45–49. The net subsidy goes to industries, such as construction and agriculture, that have strong seasonal unemployment patterns. See Clair

Vickery, "Unemployment Insurance: A Positive Appraisal," *Industrial Relations,* vol. 18 (Winter 1979), pp. 1–17, especially pp. 6–8.

23. A study of UI claims in Pennsylvania and Missouri found that over 30% of the weeks of unemployment of UI recipients ended in recall from layoff. Some workers expected to be recalled when they initially became unemployed, but were subsequently disappointed. Because they expected recall, their search for alternative work was attenuated. See Lawrence F. Katz and Bruce D. Meyer, "Unemployment Insurance, Recall Expectations and Unemployment Outcomes," working paper no. 2594, National Bureau of Economic Research, 1988.

24. The *Social Security Bulletin* is published by the U.S. Social Security Administration. *Unemployment Insurance Statistics* is published by the U.S. Employment and Training Administration of the U.S. Department of Labor.

25. Because Social Security benefits are nontaxable for low-income recipients and only partially taxable for higher income recipients, the after-tax ratios of benefits to active wages would be higher. In addition, married couples receive two payments, typically based on the husband as retiree and the wife as spouse. The average husband-plus-wife benefit was about half of active worker monthly earnings.

26. Sar A. Levitan, Peter E. Carlson, and Isaac Shapiro, *Protecting American Workers* (Washington: Bureau of National Affairs, 1986), pp. 192–193; Laurence J. Kotlikoff, Avia Spivak, and Lawrence H. Summers, "The Adequacy of Savings," *American Economic Review,* vol. 72 (December 1982), pp. 1056–1069.

27. Henry J. Aaron, *Economic Effects of Social Security* (Washington: Brookings Institution, 1982), chapter 4.

28. A Presidential commission appointed by the Carter administration recommended a system of mandatory minimum pensions. Under this proposal, employers would have either set up their own pension plans or contributed to a federally operated supplement to Social Security. See President's Commission on Pension Policy, *Coming of Age: Toward a National Retirement Income Policy,* February 1981, pp. 42–45.

29. Under 401(k) plans, employees voluntarily reduce their take-home pay and the resulting monies go into a savings plan, thus avoiding current taxation. Changes in the tax code lowered the ceiling on amounts that could be diverted into tax-sheltered savings. IRA accounts were individually established, rather than employer-based (although some employers offered IRA arrangements). Payments to IRAs, subject to various limitations, are made in pretax dollars. Tax code changes made higher paid employees who were covered by pensions at their job ineligible for most of the benefits of IRAs.

30. Because of the indexing feature of Social Security, the popular image of a retired person living on a fixed income is misleading. Social Security is likely to be an important part of a retiree's income, and it is *not* fixed in nominal dollars.

31. The requirements of the Employee Retirement Income Security Act (ERISA) for full funding are a barrier to indexing. Actuarially determined funding needs under indexing will be very sensitive to the assumed rate of price inflation, relative to assumed portfolio earnings and future wage growth. Conservative assumptions would require substantial current funding, which trustees are reluctant to commit.

32. Because these payments are treated as one-shot increases in the plan's obligation, the actuarial impact of ad hoc inflation adjustments are relatively small, compared to what formal escalation tend to entail. Firms that make ad hoc adjustments tend to offset inflation only partially. In the inflationary 1970s, one study showed such adjustments offset roughly one-third of the inflation that occurred. See Steven G. Allen, Robert L. Clark, and Daniel A. Sumner, "A Comparison of Pension Benefit Increases and Inflation, 1973–79," *op. cit.,* pp. 42–46.

33. Alicia H. Munnell, "Social Security" in Joseph A. Pechman, ed., *Setting National Priorities: The 1984 Budget* (Washington: Brookings Institution, 1984), pp. 86–87.

34. Newly hired federal employees and employees of private, nonprofit institutions were brought into the system. Those state and local governments that were already in the system were denied the option of leaving.

35. Anthony Pellechio and Gordon Goodfellow, "Individual Gains and Losses from Social Security Before and After the 1983 Amendments," *Cato Journal,* vol. 3 (Fall 1983), pp. 417–442.

36. Alan L. Gustman and Thomas L. Steinmeier, "An Analysis of Pension Benefit Formulas, Pension Wealth and Incentives from Pensions," working paper no. 2535, National Bureau of Economic Research, March 1988.

37. Under the efficiency wage model, the firm pays a lower-than-productivity wage early in a worker's career, compensated by a higher-than-productivity wage at the end. The higher pay later in the career functions as a reward for loyal and satisfactory service, and as a bond that the worker can lose (through dismissal for unsatisfactory performance). Defined benefit pension plans could function as efficiency wages, since their value to the worker increases with service. It is difficult to confirm the presence of efficiency wages directly, since employee marginal productivity must be measured. One study finds a lack of evidence for the efficiency wage model in terms of cash wages, but raises the possibility that benefits (such as pensions) could be the efficiency wage/bond. See Katherine G. Abraham and Henry S. Farber, "Job Duration, Seniority, and Earnings," *American Economic Review,* vol. 77 (June 1987), pp. 278–297, especially p. 295.

38. A review of this issue can be found in Aaron, *Economic Effects of Social Security, op. cit.,* chapter 5.

39. Gary Burtless, "Social Security, Unanticipated Benefit Increases, and the Timing of Retirement," *Review of Economic Studies,* vol. 53 (October 1986), pp. 781–805.

40. Jon R. Moen, "Past and Current Trends in Retirement: American Men from 1860 to 1980," *Economic Review,* Federal Reserve Bank of Atlanta, vol. 73 (August 1988), pp. 16–27.

41. Malcolm H. Morrison, "The Aging of the U.S. Population: Human Resource Implications," *Monthly Labor Review,* vol. 106 (May 1983), pp. 13–19.

42. A qualification to this statement is that workers may not have a clear idea of exactly what their pension benefits are. See Olivia S. Mitchell, "Worker Knowledge of Pension Provisions," working paper no. 2414, National Bureau of Economic Research, October 1987.

43. Under federal regulations, providing less than first-dollar coverage to older, Medicare-covered workers is considered to be illegal age discrimination, if the firm offers health insurance to younger workers.

44. Improvements in Medicare in the late 1980s picked up some expenses for retirees that some firms were paying. Congress, however, required in complex ways that employers either refund the saving they would realize to retirees or use those savings to provide additional benefits for them.

45. Material in this section is drawn from Donald Bell and Diane Hill, "How Social Security Payments Affect Private Pensions," *Monthly Labor Review,* vol. 107 (May 1984), pp. 15–20.

46. U.S. Bureau of Labor Statistics, *Employee Benefits in Medium and Large Firms, 1986,* bulletin 2281 (Washington: GPO, 1987), p. 65.

47. The complex integration formulas partially reflect tax code restrictions. To qualify for tax-favored treatment, pensions are not supposed to be biased towards higher paid workers. Social Security, however, tilts its benefits toward the lower paid. Formulas used for integration effectively reverse some of this tilt, but are designed not to do so in a manner offensive to the tax code.

48. The median voter model was discussed in an earlier chapter.

49. A progressive tax is one under which higher income individuals pay a greater *proportion* of their income in taxes. A regressive tax is the opposite; higher income individuals pay a lower proportion of their income in taxes. As will be noted in the text, the payroll taxes supporting UI and Social Security are regressive.

50. Walter J. Blum and Harry Kalven, Jr., *The Uneasy Case for Progressive Taxation* (Chicago: University of Chicago Press, 1953).

51. Wages are set relatively infrequently—once a year or longer—and hence do not immediately shift in response to a payroll tax increase. In a long-duration model of wage setting,

however, the employer can recoup the tax in some future round of pay setting.

52. There can be various explanations of a low elasticity of labor supply with respect to the wage. It could be that employees see little substitution between wages and leisure, that is, hours not supplied to the labor market. If the income effect of the tax imposed is low, the lack of substitution and income reactions will produce a low supply elasticity. However, it is also possible to have a high level of substitutability between wages and leisure whose effect is offset by a large positive income effect. When the payroll tax is imposed, the leisure effect tends to reduce hours supplied to the labor market, but the income effect (less leisure demanded as income falls) works in the opposite direction. One study concludes that the inelasticity of labor supply is the result of just such an offset. See Jerry A. Hausman, "Labor Supply" in Henry J. Aaron and Joseph A. Pechman, eds., *How Taxes Affect Economic Behavior* (Washington: Brookings Institution, 1981), pp. 27–83.

53. John A. Brittain, *The Payroll Tax for Social Security* (Washington: Brookings Institution, 1972); Richard F. Dye, "Payroll Tax Effects on Wage Growth," *Eastern Economic Journal,* vol. 11 (April-June 1985), pp. 89–100.

54. The tax rate is calculated on the after-tax wage, which lies along the demand curve D'. Hence the old demand curve D can be expressed as $D' + D't$ or $D'(1+t)$, therefore $D' = D/(1+t)$. Thus, if the wage would be $10 per hour in the absence of the tax, a tax rate of 10% would lead to a take-home wage of $10/1.1 = $9.09.

55. One empirical study asserts that workers' compensation premiums reduce nonunion wages on a dollar-for-dollar basis, but found no such tradeoff for union workers. The argument made was that for nonunion workers, the presence of (value of) workers' compensation payments offsets the job hazard premiums that employers would otherwise have had to pay. See Stuart Dorsey and Norman Walzer, "Workers' Compensation, Job Hazards, and Wages," *Industrial and Labor Relations Review,* vol. 36 (July 1983), pp. 642–654.

56. There is an offsetting effect, namely that lower Social Security earnings will eventually produce lower benefits for the employee upon retirement or disability.

57. Arthur M. Okun, *Equality and Efficiency: The Big Tradeoff* (Washington: Brookings Institution, 1975), pp. 91–95.

58. There is an issue of whether employers—in the context of implicit contracting and infrequently adjusted wages—anticipate payroll tax increases in setting pay. If they do, even though compensation may blip up when the tax is first imposed, the tax burden may still fall on wages. Suppose, for example, a firm sets its wage each July 1 for the next twelve months. Suppose further that it knows that on the next January 1 payroll taxes will be increased by 1%. It might set its July-to-June wage 0.5% lower than otherwise, for example, grant a 3.5% increase rather than a 4%

increase, to cover the tax burden. (One percent over six months is equivalent to 0.5% over twelve months.) On January 1 the firm's compensation would still blip up when the added tax was imposed, but the firm would not be absorbing the tax.

59. The National Industrial Recovery Act of 1933 (NIRA) organized firms into industrial groupings that worked out codes of conduct with governmental approval. These NIRA codes contained minimum wage and hour standards, pursuant to an economic theory prevalent at the time that pushing up nominal wages would raise consumption and speed recovery from the depression. The wage-consumption theory was controversial among economists of the time and would not be widely accepted today, although for different reasons. For discussion, see Daniel J.B. Mitchell, "Wages and Keynes: Lessons from the Past," *Eastern Economic Journal*, vol. 12 (July–September 1986), pp. 199–208.

60. U.S. Bureau of the Census, *Statistical Abstract of the United States: 1988* (Washington: GPO, 1988), p. 395.

61. Congress covered certain state and local workers in the 1966 FLSA amendments. The bulk of the others were covered in 1974. However, a U.S. Supreme Court decision prevented coverage of state and local employees until the Court reversed itself in 1985.

62. Reviews of the economic literature can be found in Charles Brown, Curtis Gilroy, and Andrew Cohen, "The Effect of the Minimum Wage on Employment and Unemployment," *Journal of Economic Literature*, vol. 20 (June 1982), pp. 487–528; Finis Welch, *Minimum Wages: Issues and Evidence* (Washington: American Enterprise Institute, 1978); Donald O. Parsons, *Poverty and the Minimum Wage* (Washington: American Enterprise Institute, 1980); U.S. General Accounting Office, *Minimum Wage Policy Questions Persist*, GAO/PAD–83–7 (Washington, GAO, 1983).

63. There is empirical evidence of such a queue. See Harry J. Holzer, Lawrence F. Katz, and Alan B. Krueger, "Job Queues and Wages: New Evidence on the Minimum Wage and Inter-Industry Wage Structure," working paper no. 2561, April 1988.

64. Masanori Hashimoto, "Minimum Wage Effects on Training on the Job," *American Economic Review*, vol. 72 (December 1982), pp. 1070–1087.

65. John F. Cogan, "The Decline in Black Teenage Employment: 1950–1970," *American Economic Review*, vol. 72 (September 1982), pp. 621–638. Cogan emphasizes the decline in agriculture but does indicate that the minimum wage interfered with finding alternative (nonfarm) employment.

66. Teenagers are barred from designated occupations involving potential work hazards. Some states, however, have special school-supervised programs approved by the U.S. Department of Labor permitting such work for 14–15 year olds who are identified as potential dropouts. More information on child-labor laws can be found in Daniel J.B. Mitchell and John Clapp, *Legal Constraints on Teenage Employment: A New Look at Child Labor and School Leaving Laws* (Los Angeles: UCLA Institute of Industrial Relations, 1979).

67. Ralph E. Smith and Bruce Vavrichek, "The Minimum Wage: Its Relation to Incomes and Poverty," *Monthly Labor Review*, vol. 110 (June 1987), pp. 24–30.

68. It may seem that practically no one would sell themselves into slavery, and hence that the prohibition has no HRM implications. In some cases, however, the slavery prohibition prevents enforcement of certain kinds of labor contracts. Individuals who contract to perform a service and then refuse to do so cannot be compelled by law to perform the service, but they can be sued for damages resulting from nonperformance. Although strict slavery is a lifetime arrangement, even short-term contracts involving performance of work will not be enforced.

69. Jean Baldwin Grossman, "The Impact of the Minimum Wage on Other Wages," *Journal of Human Resources*, vol. 18 (Summer 1983), pp. 359–378.

70. Employers must obtain certificates from the U.S. Department of Labor to pay subminimum wages to such groups.

71. The U.S. Chamber of Commerce has supported a youth differential. A difficulty from the public policy viewpoint, however, is that such a differential would encourage substitution of teenagers for low-wage adults, although—as noted in the text—the latter group has a much higher poverty rate. In a book sponsored by a chamber-affiliated foundation, economist Belton M. Fleisher disagreed with the chamber's view on this issue. See Belton M. Fleisher, *Minimum Wage Regulation in the United States* (Washington: National Chamber Foundation, 1983), p. 4.

72. State and local workers can be paid in "comp time," rather than cash, at a rate of time-and-a-half for overtime. Comp time means time off for personal leave. Thus a state and local worker with two hours of overtime in a given week can take off 3 hours at a later date.

73. Of course, the aggregate average overtime/worker figure includes some firms that make extensive use of overtime and others that do not use it at all.

74. Until 1985, federal contractors under Walsh-Healey had to pay overtime after eight hours per day, rather than the looser FLSA standard of forty hours per week. Legislation passed in late 1985 ended the requirement.

75. Some state governments have similar laws for their contractors.

76. Steven G. Allen and David Reich, *Prevailing Wage Laws Are Not Inflationary: A Case Study of Public School Construction Costs* (Washington: Center to Protect Workers' Rights, 1980); *The GAO on Davis-Bacon: A Fatally Flawed Study* (Washington: Center to Protect Workers' Rights, 1979).

77. U.S. General Accounting Office, *The Davis-Bacon Act Should Be Repealed,* HRD–79–18 (Washington: GAO, 1979); U.S. General Accounting Office, *The Congress Should Consider Repeal of the Service Contract Act,* GAO/HRD–83–4 (Washington: GAO, 1983). Relatively few research studies of such laws have been completed. Among them are Armand J. Thieblot, Jr., *The Davis-Bacon Act,* Industrial Research Unit, Wharton School (Philadelphia: University of Pennsylvania Press, 1975); John P. Gould and George Bittlingmayer, *The Economics of the Davis-Bacon Act: An Analysis of Prevailing-Wage Laws* (Washington: American Enterprise Institute, 1980); Armand J. Thieblot, Jr., *Prevailing Wage Legislation: The Davis-Bacon Act, State "Little Davis-Bacon" Acts, and the Service Contract Act* (Philadelphia: Industrial Research Unit, Wharton School, University of Pennsylvania, 1986).

78. For example, past practice by the U.S. Department of Labor had been to designate as prevailing any wage earned by 30% or more of workers in the construction craft in a local area. Generally, such a wage would have been a union rate since it is unlikely to find large blocks of nonunion workers all earning exactly the same wage. The Reagan administration raised the standard to require that a *majority* of workers earn the rate. Otherwise, a weighted average rate is used.

79. For a history of the enactment of OSHA, see Judson MacLaury, "The Job Safety Law of 1970: Its Passage Was Perilous," *Monthly Labor Review,* vol. 104 (March 1981), pp. 18–24.

80. John D. Worrall and Richard J. Butler, "Health Conditions and Job Hazards: Union and Nonunion Jobs," *Journal of Labor Research,* vol. 4 (Fall 1983), pp. 339–347.

81. This notion has been called the ratcheting approach. See James C. Miller III, "Is Organized Labor Rational in Supporting OSHA?," *Southern Economic Journal,* vol. 50 (January 1984), pp. 881–885.

82. Miller, "Is Organized Labor Rational in Supporting OSHA?," *op. cit.,* pp. 881–885. Miller notes that unions share OSHA's preference for engineering controls (modifications to equipment) rather than personal protective devices such as earplugs. The latter would act as a "tax" on labor, rather than on capital, thus reducing the demand for labor through both the substitution and output effects. (Usually, the preference for equipment modification is defended on the grounds that workers may fail to wear the protective devices given to them.)

83. Norman Root and Deborah Sebastian, "BLS Develops Measure of Job Risk by Occupation," *Monthly Labor Review,* vol. 104 (October 1981), pp. 26–30.

84. James C. Robinson, "Hazardous Occupations Within the Job Hierarchy," *Industrial Relations,* vol. 27 (Summer 1988),

pp. 241–250. Robinson finds evidence of such a down-shifting of risk. Note, however, that the argument assumes that low-paid workers will receive absolutely smaller risk premiums than high-paid workers.

85. Various empirical studies are reviewed in William T. Dickens, "Differences Between Risk Premiums in Union and Nonunion Wages and the Case for Occupational Safety Regulation," *American Economic Review,* vol. 74 (May 1984), pp. 320–323.

86. Stuart Dorsey and Norman Walzer, "Workers' Compensation, Job Hazard, and Wages," *Industrial and Labor Relations Review,* vol. 36 (July 1983), pp. 642–654.

87. W. Kip Viscusi and Charles J. O'Connor, "Adaptive Responses to Chemical Labeling: Are Workers Bayesian Decision Makers?," *American Economic Review,* vol. 74 (December 1984), pp. 942–956.

88. J. Paul Leigh, "Compensating Wages for Occupational Injuries and Diseases," *Social Science Quarterly,* vol. 62 (December 1981), pp. 772–778.

89. Charles L. Schultze, *The Public Use of Private Interest* (Washington: Brookings Institution, 1977), pp. 55–57; John Mendeloff, *Regulating Safety: An Economic and Political Analysis of Occupational Safety and Health Policy* (Cambridge, Mass.: MIT Press, 1979).

90. Lawrence S. Bacow, "Private Bargaining and Public Regulation" in Eugene Bardach and Robert A. Kagan, eds., *Social Regulation: Strategies for Reform* (San Francisco: Institute for Contemporary Studies, 1982), pp. 201–220.

91. Lester B. Lave, *The Strategy of Social Regulation: Decision Frameworks for Policy* (Washington: Brookings Institution, 1981), pp. 99–101.

92. Suggestions along these lines can be found in John Mendeloff, "Regulatory Reform and OSHA Policy," *Journal of Policy Analysis and Management,* vol. 5 (Spring 1986), pp. 440–468.

93. Levitan, Carlson, and Shapiro, *Protecting American Workers, op. cit.,* pp. 119–123. Death rates reported by the survey established by OSHA have also declined. See Diane M. Cotter and Janet A. Macon, "Deaths in Industry, 1985: BLS Survey Findings," *Monthly Labor Review,* vol. 110 (April 1987), pp. 45–47. Highway accidents are the most common form of occupational fatality, accounting for 29% of such deaths during 1984–85.

94. William P. Curington, "Safety Regulations and Workplace Injuries," *Southern Economic Journal,* vol. 53 (July 1986), pp. 51–72.

95. Michael L. Marlow, "The Economics of Enforcement: The Case of OSHA," *Journal of Economics and Business,* vol. 34 (2:1982), pp. 165–171.

Chapter Fifteen

RESTRICTING OPPORTUNITY AND ENHANCING OPPORTUNITY: IMMIGRATION CONTROL AND EEO

Some forms of labor market regulation demand that employers *not* do something, rather than establishing minimum standards for what they must do. Two major federal programs fall primarily into this category. These are immigration control policy and equal employment opportunity (EEO) policy. Immigration controls are meant to restrict job opportunities of illegal aliens. EEO is designed to promote job opportunity for protected groups. Immigration controls have a long history in the United States. However, the contemporary HRM function was not much affected by immigration controls until a significant change in the law was adopted in 1986. In contrast, although extensive EEO regulation is a comparatively recent phenomenon, from its inception in the 1960s EEO policy has had widespread effects on the HRM function.[1]

Because the experience with the immigration controls of the 1980s has been limited, this chapter provides only a brief discussion of the issues involved. Its purpose is to alert the reader to a new area of public policy that may further impinge on the HRM function in the future. The discussion of EEO policy is more comprehensive, since there has been more experience with its effects.

15–1 Immigration Control

Many aspects of immigration policy are not directly related to labor market concerns. Foreign policy questions and humanitarian considerations have always been present. The U.S. has historically been a high-wage country relative to most of the world, so that its labor market was and is an enticement to immigration.

During the second half of the nineteenth century and up until World War I, large numbers of immigrants came to the United States. Annual flows of immigrants sometimes exceeded 1% of the domestic population.[2] Thereafter, legal immigration was tightly restricted. Much of the concern about immigration in the 1970s and 1980s has thus been about *illegal* immigration. In addition, immigration—legal and illegal—shifted in the 1970s towards persons with relatively unskilled backgrounds.[3] Limited English language skills also pushed immigrants towards unskilled, low-wage employment.[4] These shifts raised questions about the impact on the domestic labor market for competing labor groups.

Illegal Immigration

Illegal immigrants enter the country either by simply crossing the border illicitly, by entering legally but overstaying visas, or by violating restrictions on working. For obvious reasons, such persons are not readily counted. Recent estimates by the U.S. Bureau of the Census suggest that the stock of illegal immigrants in the United States stood between four and six million as of the mid-1980s. The Bureau estimated that there was a *net* illegal inflow of roughly 200,000 persons annually. A much larger number, however, enter the country and depart in a single year.[5]

Much of the motivation for illegal immigration to the United States is the availability of jobs at better terms and conditions than provided by the immigrant's home country. The immediate proximity of the developed United States and third-world Mexico provides an opportunity for a significant illegal flow. As will be noted in the next chapter, wages in third-world countries are only a fraction of U.S. levels.

Of course, there has also been a significant element of politically motivated immigration, including immigration from Cuba after the establishment of a communist government in that country, and immigration from Southeast Asia after the Vietnam War. Political immigration often means that the new arrival has little or no hope of returning to his or her native country. For such immigrants there may be added impetus to adapt to the American labor market via education and training. In contrast, economically motivated immigrants have the prospect of returning to their native lands and thus may simply sell their (often) unskilled labor without feeling the need for upgrading their human capital.[6]

Mexico has been a major source of economic immigrants in the 1970s and 1980s. In the Mexican case, because of depreciation of the peso and deteriorating internal conditions, the average Mexican wage in manufacturing—translated into U.S. dollars—fell from 30% to 12% of U.S. levels during 1980-1987.[7] Moreover, high Mexican unemployment means that even jobs paying those Spartan wages may not be available domestically to potential young entrants into the Mexican labor force. It is hardly surprising that this large pay and opportunity differential sets flow of labor in motion toward the United States.

Impact on the U.S. Workforce

The impact of immigration, both legal and illegal, has been much debated. In a simple static model of the economy, adding to the supply of labor while holding other factors constant will depress real wages. Dynamic growth models, however, do not necessarily produce such results; the additional labor supply may create sufficient saving to generate the capital needed to hold constant the capital-to-labor ratio. Thus real wages need not fall despite the increase in the labor supply. In that respect a steady increase in the population via immigration is no different from one resulting from native births.

Still more complex models recognize the variegated nature of the U.S. workforce. As with other types of economic change, immigration can create winners and losers within the existing population. Low-skilled workers, who compete directly with the immigrants, may suffer lower real wages and/or job displacement. Immigrants may cluster in segmented job markets so that the primary direct effect of an increase in their supply is a lowering of their own wages.[8] But more skilled workers may be complements in production to the immigrants. Demand for, and real wages of, the higher skilled group may thus increase. There is a general consensus in the economic literature that such mixed effects occur.[9]

Employer Obligations

Until 1987 there were no federal sanctions against employers who knowingly hired illegal immigrants. Employers were under no obligation to ascertain the legal status of any workers. The penalty for working illegally—essentially deportation—fell entirely on the employee, not the employer. Indeed, instances have been reported of employers calling for raids on their own premises by the Immigration and Naturalization Service (INS) during union organizing drives among their employees.

The obligation of employers with regard to illegal workers was changed radically by the Immigration Reform and Control Act (IRCA) of 1986. Under this legislation, which began to be enforced in mid-1987, employers are obligated *not* to employ any illegals who were not on their payrolls when the law was passed. On first impression the new law might seem to have important effects only in certain low-wage industries (such as agriculture, apparel production, and restaurants) and in certain regions of the country (especially the states of California and Texas, which border Mexico). Studies of employment patterns of illegal workers indicate, however, that despite the concentration in certain regions and industries, their usage is surprisingly widespread.

In any case, the 1986 law creates obligations for *all* employers, not just those with prior propensities to hire illegals. Beginning in mid-1987 employers were required to obtain documents from new hires proving their legal employment status. Employers also are required to retain these documents for an extended period and to be able to present them to INS agents.

At the least, therefore, even employers in industries with low usage rates of illegals must cope with significant record-keeping burdens. The law thus presents HRM professionals with new, if routine, responsibilities. Employers discovered to be employing illegals are subject to an escalating set of fines, with criminal penalties for those determined to have a pattern or practice of illegal employment.

Impact of Immigration Controls

The impact of the new immigration-restricting law—if effectively enforced—presumably will be the reverse of those found in the past for less tightly controlled immigration. Competing domestic workers and legal immigrants will benefit through higher wages and/or more job opportunities. Workers for whom demand is complementary to immigrant labor may suffer economic losses.

However, there are important qualifications to be made to this prediction. First, only limited resources will be applied to enforcement; not every violator will be found. Second, the employer penalties are low for initial offenses, suggesting that some employers will take the risk of being caught hiring illegals. Indeed, survey evidence suggests that in the pre-IRCA period many employers thought (mistakenly) that hiring illegals was against the law, but did so anyway. Third, the documentation that employers are required to obtain from new hires can be forged. It is doubtful that employers will be held accountable for accepting forged documents that look genuine. Because there are penalties in the law for discrimination in complying with the law on the basis of national origin, it is doubtful that employers will want to examine closely documents that are not obviously fraudulent.[10]

Years must pass before the impact of the immigration controls can be fully evaluated. However, one estimate—taking account of the limits of enforcement resources—suggests that nonfarm illegal employment might be cut by 15 to 25%.[11] Because of the uncertainty created about the degree of enforcement, the early impact of the program on employment may be greater than the eventual effect.

For HRM professionals, the immigration issue bears watching. If Congress becomes dissatisfied with the results of the new controls, it may impose greater sanctions and put more pressure on employers to act as immigration police. On the other hand, if the law proves ineffective but Congress does not react, then the demographics of the workforce will change as a result of immigration flows. Employers—particularly in areas that have historically received large immigration flows—will increasingly need to cope with issues such as bilingualism in the workplace and managing workers with diverse cultural backgrounds.

If the immigration controls are effective, then certain industries that have relied heavily on low-wage unskilled labor will be adversely affected. They will need to find substitutes for such labor to stay in business. Some may not succeed; others may move abroad to tap on its native ground the labor supply that once came to the United States. In some cases, union organizing may be strengthened, since illegal immigrants were especially hard to unionize.[12] Immigration, in short, is an HRM issue to be watched.

15-2 Equal Employment Opportunity

The equal employment opportunity (EEO) law had its roots in black/white race relations. Although race relations are an ongoing social problem, not just a labor market issue, they grow out of a problem that ultimately had labor market origins. Most American blacks are descended from slaves, involuntary immigrants brought to this country because wages of free labor were high relative to European levels. High American wages, in turn, provided the economic incentive for slavers to kidnap Africans and sell them to employers as an alternative to hiring free labor.

On the eve of the Civil War, slaves accounted for over one-fifth of the U.S. workforce.[13] In the South the proportion was much higher. To maintain a slave labor force, an infrastructure of legal and policing mechanisms was required. Since such measures were not applied to free labor and since such measures violated prevailing norms of treatment that applied to whites, a variety of rationalizations was required to support the institution of slavery. Blacks were viewed as inferior to whites, as preferring menial work, as benefiting from their treatment as slaves, and so on. These ideas from the era of slavery formed the basis of modern racial prejudice.

In the post–Civil War period, competition between freed black labor and white labor played an important part in establishing legal segregation in the South. Notions of appropriate white/black relationships that had arisen under slavery continued as rationales for segregation. Segregation applied to the labor market as well as public facilities such as transportation and schools. Under segregation, formal and informal, blacks were barred from skilled crafts and many other forms of employment.

Much of the black workforce remained in southern agriculture until World War I. The ongoing migration of blacks to the North, where voting was permitted and political influence could be wielded, began to shift public policy. Although the armed forces remained segregated by race during World War II, a presidential executive order promoted antidiscrimination in federally funded defense plants. Although this measure was not considered especially effective, the postwar period saw continued change in the legal and political climate. During the 1950s and 1960s, segregation in public schools and transportation was struck down by a series of Supreme Court decisions. By 1987 blacks constituted about one-tenth of total employment, with only fifteen percent remaining in agriculture.[14]

Racial discrimination against Asians also had labor market roots. In the latter half of the nineteenth century, Asians were viewed by whites, especially in California and the western states, as a competing source of cheap labor. State laws abridged property and other rights of Asian immigrants. At the federal level, the Chinese Exclusion Act of 1882 and subsequent legislation virtually banned new immigration from China. One byproduct of this anti-Asian sentiment was the forced removal of residents of Japanese origin from the West Coast during World War II.

Significant Asian immigration into the United States was not permitted until the 1960s. Since that time the Asian-origin population of the United States has grown rapidly. Although data on workers of Asian origin are not separately published in regular labor market surveys, the 1980 *Census of Population* reported that about 2% of all employees were of Asian background.[15]

Discrimination against Hispanics, like that against Asians, has been linked historically to immigration/labor market concerns. As noted in the previous section, immigration—especially from Mexico—has been more difficult to control because of the physical proximity of the United States and Mexico. The grant of American citizenship to Puerto Ricans in 1917 prevented any limits on their immigration into the mainland United States thereafter. Hispanics constituted about 7% of total employment in 1987, of whom 59% were of Mexican origin, 12% were of Puerto Rican origin, and 6% were of Cuban origin.[16]

Sex discrimination has some labor market origins but is obviously more heavily connected with social, cultural, and religious attitudes. There are obvious cases in which cheap female labor was seen as a threat to male employment in the past, leading to employer, union, or sometimes legislative policies aimed at discouraging or limiting the workforce participation of women. Protective state laws aimed at women and children in the nineteenth and early twentieth century put limits on their hours of employment and job assignments.[17] Generally, the phenomenon of married women working (except on family farms) was seen as a failure of the economic system. Paid work was for single women awaiting marriage.

Initial Federal Regulation in the EEO Area

Discrimination in the workplace was not attacked in federal legislation until the passage of the Civil Rights Act of 1964. Title 7 of the Act forbids discrimination in employment practices on the basis of race, sex, religion, or national origin. Further significant extensions of the law were made in 1972.

As in the case of other labor standards, the federal government can place special requirements on its contractors as a condition of doing business with the government. Under presidential Executive Order 11246 of 1965, federal contractors were required to eliminate the kinds of discrimination forbidden by Title 7. In addition, contractors were required to implement affirmative action plans, a concept discussed in the following section.

Policy Toward Sex, Race, Handicap, and Other Forms of Discrimination

It is often noted that the issue of sex discrimination, which subsequently became a major concern of EEO policy, was dropped into Title 7 as a political ploy. Southern congressional representatives added sex discrimination to the original bill in the hopes of either making the bill more controversial and thus killing it, or diluting the bill's concentration on the race issue. The ultimate inclusion of sex discrimination was not out of line with congressional concerns, however; Congress had shown prior interest in sex-related issues at the workplace. The Equal Pay Act of 1963, for example, outlawed sex-based wage differentials established by an employer for individuals performing essentially the same jobs.

Viewed with hindsight, the inclusion of sex discrimination in the final version of Title 7 can be seen as the product of rising female participation in the workforce. Although female labor force participation rates were not as high in the 1960s as they were in the 1980s, the trend was upwards. The traditional pattern of female withdrawal from employment upon marriage was breaking down.

Women received the right to vote in 1920 through constitutional amendment. They have since shown a higher propensity to participate in elections than men, a fact well known to political representatives. Had sex discrimination not been included in Title 7 as originally enacted, it would have been added at a later date.

Age discrimination is a more complex issue, since—as earlier chapters have noted—age and seniority are often correlated. Complaints about improper treatment of older employees at the workplace often relate to social norms about management obligations to long-service employees. Under the Age Discrimination Act of 1967 (as subsequently amended), discrimination against persons age forty and older is outlawed, and mandatory retirement is forbidden for most employees.

Apart from their obligations under Title 7 and Executive Order 11246, federal contractors are forbidden to discriminate against the handicapped pursuant to the Rehabilitation Act of 1973. Discrimination by contractors is also forbidden against disabled veterans and Vietnam War veterans under the Vietnam Era Veterans Readjustment Act of 1974. As part of their obligations under these various laws and orders, federal contractors are subject to closer scrutiny than other employers. Moreover, because of the large volume of federal purchases and funding, virtually all large firms are federal contractors, as are state and federal governments and many private, nonprofit organizations.

State and local governments often adopt EEO policies of their own, both for firms that do business with them and for other employers. In some cases these policies may go further than federal requirements, for example, antidiscrimination restrictions regarding individuals with AIDS that were adopted by some jurisdictions in the 1980s. HRM professionals thus must be aware of public policies from a variety of sources.

Administration and Enforcement

The Equal Employment Opportunity Commission (EEOC), established by Title 7, handles complaints pursuant to that title (race, sex, religion, and national origin) plus age discrimination and Equal Pay Act complaints. Compared to other federal agencies such as the NLRB, the EEOC is not a powerful agency—a characteristic resulting from the political compromises reached to obtain passage of the original Civil Rights Act. It primarily investigates and mediates; most EEO complaints, if pursued, are either settled privately or litigated in the courts. On the other hand, the reach of Title 7 is very broad; it covers all but the smallest employers (public and private) plus unions, union hiring halls, employment agencies, and apprenticeship programs.

Employers, unions, and others who are found to have violated EEO requirements can be required to pay damages to victims, to hire or rehire them, to promote them, or to make changes in HRM policies. Where large numbers of individuals are involved in class-action suits, awards or settlements may run into the millions of dollars, apart from litigation expenses. The potential costs involved, the bad publicity that can result from EEO litigation, and the possible extensive court involvement in internal firm policy, are sufficient to attract the attention of HRM specialists. Indeed, as will be argued in the following discussion, EEO has had a profound effect on the practice of HRM, similar to that of the rise of unions as a challenge to management during the 1930s.

Pursuant to amendments to Title 7 enacted in 1972, the EEOC can support suits filed by individuals or, in certain cases, litigate on its own. The courts, however, not the EEOC, have final authority in determining remedies. In contrast, in the labor relations field the NLRB can issue its own cease-and-desist orders and fashion its own remedies. The EEOC is also obligated to defer to state and local agencies that have EEO jurisdiction, if such agencies exist and meet designated standards.

The other major federal agency is the Labor Department's Office of Federal Contract Compliance Programs (OFCCP), which monitors federal contractors pursuant to the various applicable orders and laws. As noted, federal contractors are subject to more detailed scrutiny and requirements than other employers, and it is the OFCCP that carries out this monitoring function. As a practical matter, the OFCCP seems to focus its attention on larger firms within the universe of those doing business with the federal government.[18] Failure to meet federal EEO requirements can mean loss of government contracts and debarment from future bidding on contracts.

Impact of Antidiscrimination Rules on HRM Policy

It is important to stress that *discrimination* in the EEO context is a very broad term. *Any* action that might be taken with regard to employees could potentially be taken in a discriminatory manner. Charges could thus be made that the firm has a discriminatory recruitment policy, a discriminatory screening and testing policy, a discriminatory pay policy, a discriminatory benefit plan, a discriminatory employee evaluation program, a discriminatory promotion system, and that it discriminates in the manner it provides training or in the way it conducts layoffs. Thus *the entire array of HRM policies is subject to EEO review.*

Any employee can file EEO charges, as can rejected job applicants or discharged former workers. Although most EEO policy is centered on blacks, Hispanics, and women, white males can file suits alleging "reverse discrimination." It is not necessary to prove that a discriminatory intent was involved for a plaintiff to win an EEO case.

Of course, a showing of "disparate treatment" of women or minorities in hiring, promotion, or other employment decisions will demonstrate intentional discrimination. But showing of discriminatory *results*—intended or not—may be sufficient. A seemingly neutral HRM policy that has a "disparate impact" on minorities or women, even if not purposefully designed to do so, is regarded as discriminatory. Methods of establishing discriminatory impact often involve statistical analysis of firm and local labor market data. Remedies for affected individuals are generally of the make whole variety: hiring or reinstatement, back pay, promotion, and credit for lost seniority.

EEO cases can involve multiple interests. The workforce may be divided by EEO charges, with resultant workplace tensions, particularly if the remedy sought by the plaintiff(s) would disadvantage some other employee or employees. Because of the extensiveness of EEO regulation, some examples of its impact on selected HRM functions are provided here.

Help-Wanted Advertising.   Prior to the enactment of EEO legislation, help-wanted ads sometimes specified the race of the applicants being sought, for example, "whites only." Newspapers typically divided their ads into separate sections of jobs for men and for women. Such blatant practices are extremely rare today. However, consider the implications of an ad seeking "recent college grads" or one requesting the services of a "gal Friday." Might not age or sex discrimination be inferred from these phrases? There are not many recent college grads over age forty. Thus "recent college grads" may be a code phrase indicating older workers need not apply. And many men might be reluctant to apply for a position as a "gal Friday."

Sound policy with regard to advertising suggests that an HRM specialist sensitive to EEO requirements should screen proposed advertising by the firm for hidden messages.

Screening.   Applicants for jobs may be required to take a test of some type. A higher than average failure rate of minorities or women may lead to the test being considered discriminatory *unless* the test can be "validated." A test can be validated if it can be shown that higher scores predict better job performance.

Proving the connection between scores and performance, particularly in the case of general verbal/math aptitude tests, may be difficult. Statistical methodology may be required to validate general tests. However, tests that ask for demonstration of a job-specific skill, such as typing for a typist, are generally valid.

Apart from tests, employers may require presentation of credentials, such as a high school diploma. Again, it is not always evident that such credentials are predictive of job performance. Is a high school diploma, for example, needed to function as a janitor? However, credentials that are closely related to skills—a medical degree for a doctor, a driver's license for a trucker—are unlikely to be challenged.

The interviewing process necessarily involves subjective judgments on the part of the person conducting the interview. A firm in which the interview process results in a disproportionate rejection rate of minorities or women may find its practices challenged by persons not hired. There is an obvious bias in EEO regulation for the application of objective, relevant measures. Subjective judgments and techniques are certainly not forbidden, but their outcomes need to be monitored.

Title 7 includes a very limited possibility of legitimately excluding persons from particular jobs on the basis of sex. It provides for such exclusion only when sex is a "bona fide occupational qualification" (BFOQ) for the job. Occupations such as restroom attendant fall under this exception. However, defenses such as customer preference are not accepted. Thus airlines—which once barred males from jobs as flight attendants on the grounds that passengers preferred stewardesses to stewards—were not permitted to continue the practice.

Training. Opportunities for training provided by an employer can be a valuable benefit for employees, leading to opportunities to advance within the firm. Employers may be more reluctant to provide training for women than for men, on the assumption that women are less likely to have a long career with the firm during which the training investment can be recouped. On average, women do have a higher propensity than men to quit.[19] Generalizing on the basis of group averages, however, can be seen as discriminatory when applied to individuals. Careful examination must thus be made of the mechanisms by which decisions to train are taken. Monitoring of the outcomes of those mechanisms is also needed.

Pay Policy. The Equal Pay Act of 1963 requires that separate male and female wage rates not apply to substantially equivalent work.[20] Prior to this legislation, different male and female wage rates for the same job were sometimes found in company practices and union contracts. (The female rate was inevitably lower.) As in the case of overtly discriminatory help-wanted advertising, such blatant practices rarely occur today. However, issues can arise over whether two job titles—one containing mostly men and the other mostly women—involve basically the same tasks. If they do, the pay schedule must be the same, regardless of job title. It is function—not title—that matters.

An earlier chapter described the comparable worth issue (sometimes also known as pay equity).[21] In its usual formulation, comparable worth goes beyond equal pay for the same work. It asks that disparate jobs be compared by some uniform standard. The resulting evaluation of worth should then be applied to the various jobs. Typically, job evaluation plans, which are designed to make such interoccupational comparisons, are advocated as the tool for determining comparable worth.

As a legal matter, comparable worth has *not* emerged as an EEO requirement in litigation thus far. Courts have accepted the outside labor market as a legitimate guide for setting pay. Some private settlements of pay equity cases, mainly in the public sector, have been made, however. Paradoxically, comparable worth claims and pressures are most likely to be raised in the context of government and large private employers who probably pay above-average wages.[22] Employers may be vulnerable to comparable worth litigation if it can be demonstrated that they deliberately set wages for predominantly female jobs lower than for male jobs merely because women were in those jobs (as opposed to market reasons).[23]

The Canadian province of Ontario passed a law in 1987 requiring employers to apply comparable worth in pay setting through job evaluation. Australia implemented a version of comparable worth through its compulsory arbitration system in the early 1970s. A comparable worth law, however, is not in the immediate offing in the United States. Nonetheless, foreign developments may eventually influence American lawmakers and judges. HRM specialists need to be sensitive to the issue, even though its current legal status is dubious.

Benefits.   The design of benefit plans has been influenced by EEO policy, especially with regard to pregnancy. Until the late 1970s it was not uncommon for employers to remove benefits for pregnancy from programs such as disability insurance and sick leave. Reversing a Supreme Court decision, Congress made such pregnancy exclusions illegal under Title 7. Employers are not required to have disability or sick leave plans. If they do, however, pregnancy must be treated the same as other medical conditions.

Retirement and life insurance plans have also been affected by EEO regulation. Female life expectancy is notably longer than male. Based on 1985 data, a white female at birth could expect to live about 79 years, compared with 72 for a white male; the figures for nonwhites were 75 and 67. At age 65, a women could expect to live about four years longer than a male.[24] The result is that a given amount of life insurance is actuarially cheaper to provide for females than for males. A defined benefit pension for females is, however, more expensive to fund.[25]

At one time some employers adjusted benefits to reflect these sex-based differences or—if they had contributory plans—adjusted the contributions employees were required to make. Such practices are now viewed by the U.S. Supreme Court as illegal generalizations about the sexes. Employers may not charge different contribution rates based on sex, or provide unequal monthly pensions or life insurance policies.[26]

Federal contractor obligations with regard to the handicapped have influenced the trend toward establishment of Employee Assistance Programs (EAPs) for alcohol and drug abusers. Although substance abuse and addiction is a handicap, current alcohol or drug abusers whose problem hinders job performance or safety are not protected by the handicapped requirements. Employers may find it wise, however, to provide an EAP vehicle to permit the affected employee a chance to resolve his or her problem.

Job Design.   Title 7's ban on religious discrimination and the Rehabilitation Act's requirements for federal contractors regarding the handicapped may influence the way jobs are designed. Employers must make "reasonable accommodation" with regard to job requirements that may conflict with religious beliefs. Issues may involve scheduling of work on the Sabbath, allowing time off for religious holidays, and dress and appearance standards. Employers may, however, cite "undue hardship" as a defense against demands for such accommodations.

Federal contractors must also make reasonable accommodation to the physical needs and abilities of the handicapped. Included here may be access arrangements for work stations and restrooms, special equipment, and task reallocation between members of a work group. Substantial costs of making such accommodation may be a defense for not doing so. Generally, however, a wider view of accommodation has been taken regarding handicapped needs as opposed to religious needs.

Working Conditions and Evaluation.   The issue of sexual harassment has arisen both in connection with the general tone of work group relations and the process of employee evaluation. Most typically in such cases, male supervisors are accused of harassing female subordinates. The supervisor may hold out the promise of favorable merit reviews or promotions in exchange for sexual favors. Alternatively, threats of making negative evaluations may be used to obtain sexual favors. Since such conduct is aimed only at one sex, it violates EEO regulations, even if the employer has explicit rules against sexual harassment.

Employers may also be held liable for harassment (sexual or racial) of non-supervisory employees against other nonsupervisors. In effect, the employer is responsible for the climate of working relationships. Indeed, even harassment by outsiders—by customers or by employees of subcontractors who are working on the premises—may lead to employer liability.

Because ignorance of incidents by the employer may not be an excuse when harassment occurs, HRM professionals need to establish both systems of monitoring (of supervisors and nonsupervisors), systems of complaint (for use by individuals who are harassed), and mechanisms of workplace training and sensitization about the harassment issue. Although explicit antiharassment policies that are not enforced do not offer legal protection to the employer, it is important nevertheless that antiharassment policies be formulated. Enforcement systems—with penalties where warranted—work best where explicit rules are in place and where information on the rules has been promulgated.

Affirmative Action and HRM Policy

Although this section began by including EEO under the heading of policies that ban certain HRM practices, some EEO elements require that the employer do something rather than not do something. The reasonable accommodation requirements for religious minorities and the handicapped are examples. The major example, however, and the one that has provoked the greatest controversy, is *affirmative action* (AA).

Affirmative action can mean simply reaching out to attract applicant pools of women or minorities where these groups are underrepresented in the employer's workforce. For example, a firm might place help-wanted advertisements in a minority newspaper or open up an employment office in a minority neighborhood. AA is a requirement for federal contractors. In addition, courts sometimes order it as a remedy for past discrimination, and it may be included in "voluntary" labor–management agreements, company policies, or out-of-court settlements.

The controversy over affirmative action comes from its requirement that employer goals and timetables be established. Such schedules specify numerical objectives of greater minority and female representation within the workforce or within particular sectors of the workforce (such as skilled crafts or professional occupations). They also include a time frame in which the objectives should be met. The employer may fall short of these goals (such discrepancies are not infrequent), but in such cases reasons for the shortfall may be requested.

Under the Reagan administration, prior affirmative action policy was criticized as producing reverse discrimination through job quotas and as giving preference on a basis other than merit. Yet that administration never moved to end the affirmative action requirements that previous presidents had established.[27] Although divided by the issue, the Supreme Court has continued to endorse the AA concept within limits.

Essentially, it appears that affirmative action programs will be permitted in situations in which access to *new opportunities* is involved. Thus, affirmative action is accepted as appropriate in hiring, promotions, or training. In situations in which application of affirmative action results in *job loss* for existing employees, however, it may not be permitted.

Thus a bona fide union seniority system might include a provision requiring layoffs by reverse order of seniority. An employer that had raised the proportion of minorities or women in the recent past pursuant to an affirmative action program might see its efforts undone if the most junior people were laid off. But it would not be free simply to override its contractual seniority system obligations in the name of affirmative action. Such action would result in tangible job losses for some to benefit others.

Because of the sensitive political nature of affirmative action, it is possible that future Supreme Courts will see the issue quite differently. Employers who have such plans have generally not been anxious to see substantial changes in the rules, let alone more uncertainty about them. The establishment of numerical standards, and the achievement of those standards, is something that can be managed by the firm. An employer that achieves its OFCCP-approved goals under the current system is certain of compliance with federal standards. A looser, less defined standard would create a management problem. As a result, political conservatives who deplore affirmative action find themselves at odds with the management community on this issue.

Social Discrimination and Employer Policy

It is important to distinguish between social discrimination, which affects the characteristics of potential employees, and discrimination *within* the firm. Social discrimination may manifest itself by making individuals less productive to employers than they otherwise would be. For example, provision of inferior schooling to minority children, leading to less education or lower quality education, might reduce employee value.[28] So might a less stable family background. Nondiscriminatory employers would pay less to the affected individuals (or not hire them) because these persons are worth less to the firm.

Social discrimination may also take more subtle forms, such as creating expectations in individuals about sex roles in careers and marriages. These expectations cause the individuals who hold them to invest in different levels of education, to search for particular kinds of jobs, and to follow different patterns of workforce attachment. The key characteristic of social discrimination is that it changes the endowments or job-related characteristics of individuals before they arrive at the employer's door. As a result of their endowment—but not necessarily because of employer prejudice—the individuals experience different treatment in the labor market in terms of success in finding work, attaining occupational status, and achieving wage level.

Employer Discrimination

The roots of EEO policy developed out of concern about discrimination by employers. Employers' discrimination consists of unequal treatment of individuals by virtue of race, sex, and so on, despite their equal endowments of job-related attributes. In empirical tests of discrimination, now often found as part of EEO litigation as well as in academic research, a statistical relationship might be developed of the general form:

$$\text{Job Outcome} = f(\text{Job-Related Endowments})$$

where job outcomes might be the probability of hire or the pay level, and job-related endowments might include education, years of experience, or other relevant characteristics. If the function $f()$ differs by race or sex, discrimination might be inferred.

As can readily be seen from the equation, the concept of discrimination is more easily conceived than measured. The use of statistical evidence in EEO cases has created a growth industry for economic and statistical consultants. Issues arise over the appropriate variables to include, measurement techniques, and biases in particular estimation methods.[29] Judges find themselves in the uncomfortable position of weighing probabilities in cases in which the precise mechanism of discrimination is not identified.[30]

One example of the problems raised by statistical interpretation arises in the case of numerical performance appraisals received by employees in the course of their employment. In principle, these ratings are measures of on-the-job output, rather than just background endowments. A case can thus be made for including them in any analysis of how individuals are treated on the job. If claims are made that promotional opportunities are being denied to women or minorities, an employer might want to use the appraisal ratings as evidence of nondiscrimination. If there is prejudice in the rating process, however, equivalently productive individuals will not receive the same ratings. On the other hand, excluding the ratings will cause omission of actual performance information. Such methodological disputes may end up being decided by judges, who are not always masters of econometric technique.

Economic Models of Discrimination

An important reason why statistical approaches to discrimination by employers produce uncertain results is that discrimination is difficult to fit into a simple economic model. Without a clear model, it is hard to justify a particular tool of measurement. The difficulty arises from the basic question of *why* employers should discriminate in the first place.

Note first that if *only one* employer discriminated in a large, classical labor market, there would be no practical effect. An individual employer who did not hire blacks or females for certain jobs would hire whites or males instead. But other (unprejudiced) employers would hire the rejected blacks or females not employed by the prejudiced employer. The biases of a single employer would thus result simply in a reshuffling between firms of the race or sex composition of the labor force. No noticeable impact on wages or anything else would follow from this isolated discrimination.

If *all or most* firms discriminate, however, then the group against which the discrimination is directed will suffer economic loss. Wages will be lower for the affected workers. In effect, employers require a (negative) compensating pay differential to hire members of the target group. Adding search costs to the model may lead to higher unemployment rates and other real-world symptoms of employer discrimination. Another paradox then enters the picture. With lower wages for otherwise comparable workers, profit maximizing employers should rush to hire the affected group in place of other workers. A model of discrimination would thus seem to imply that firms are not profit maximizing, in violation of the usual classical assumption.

Two basic routes can be proposed out of this dilemma. One is to suggest that employers maximize their utility, not their profits. Profits are an input into the employer's utility function, but so is the satisfying of prejudice, according to this approach. Hence widespread employer tastes for discrimination are said to explain the phenomenon.[31] A second possibility is to find reasons why discriminatory behavior might foster profit maximization, and, hence be a rationale within the classical economic model.

Employer Tastes

A major problem with the tastes explanation is the separation of ownership and control in the modern firm. Shareholders do not come in contact with the firm's workforce, so it is difficult to understand why they should be concerned with anything but profitability. Of course, salaried managers might have discriminatory tastes. If these tastes are exercised, however, a principal/agent problem is created. Management—the agent for the shareholders—is not maximizing profits for its principals. Rather, by not hiring the cheaper adversely affected group, it is diverting potential profits to satisfy management's own preferences.

A second conceptual problem is that even if employer preferences in existing firms are dominated by prejudiced tastes, thus pushing the firms away from profit maximization, new (unprejudiced) firms could enter the market and outearn their older competitors. In particular, it is not clear within the context of the classical model why the victims of discrimination do not form their own firms and compete against prejudiced firms. Ultimately, models of discrimination due to employer prejudice must be sustained by background social discrimination that inhibits entrepreneurship and access to capital markets.[32]

Alternative Explanations

Under certain assumptions discrimination could be compatible with profit maximization. One possibility is that employers are "made" to discriminate by unions. *Union discrimination* can certainly be documented historically, particularly among skilled crafts.[33] Prior to EEO regulation, blacks and Asians were sometimes excluded from certain trades; separate male and female job classifications and pay grades were found in some union contracts. Although the most overt forms of discrimination have ended, some elements of earlier practices linger on. However, the union explanation of general discrimination in the labor market founders on three facts.

First, important unions—particularly industrial unions—historically opposed discriminatory practices by employers. This opposition stemmed from radical ideology in some unions, which viewed themselves as uniting the working class. It also stemmed from the practical need to organize all workers in a firm in order to gain recognition and bargaining power. Second, statistical studies suggest that— at least with regard to blacks—unions in modern times have tended to promote greater equality of wage distribution by pushing up wages in industries in which blacks are concentrated.[34] Third, most of the workforce is nonunion.[35]

The presence of unions may have had effects on employer behavior with regard to hiring, apart from the direct preferences of unions or of their members. Employers in the past found it in their interests to use racial divisions to weaken unions, which might otherwise have had greater bargaining power. In the early part of this century, black workers from the South were sometimes recruited to northern factories as strike breakers. Some of the subsequent tension between white and black labor stemmed from such incidents.

Despite the past history, a union or union-relations story is not a satisfactory explanation of contemporary employers' discrimination. Meshing discrimination with profit maximization requires other explanations. One possibility is *customer preference*. Firms that are in retail trade might find it profitable to discriminate in hiring if their customers are prejudiced. For example, if white customers are uncomfortable with black salesclerks or black bank tellers, employers might accommodate to customer preference, as they do in other aspects of marketing. Indeed, blacks do tend to be underrepresented in sales occupations and retail employment.[36] Even nonretail firms might find it in their economic interests to adjust to prevailing social prejudices in the communities and neighborhoods in which they operate.

Employee preference might also play a role in determining an employer's policy. A firm with a significant investment in its existing workforce members is likely to cater to their views. If these views are prejudiced, the firm may want to avoid adverse productivity effects that might be engendered by, say, racial tensions.[37]

There are many examples of resistance by workers in traditionally white or male occupations to the introduction of blacks, other minorities, or women. The problem is compounded by the team production mode often found in the work setting; all members of the team must cooperate and trust each other. Introduction into the team of persons who are not trusted by the incumbents could lower productivity.[38]

Finally, the notion of *statistical discrimination* may explain employer discrimination. As noted in an earlier chapter, employers might be unable to measure the productivity of prospective employees. Detecting and removing low-productivity workers after hiring can be costly. Thus firms look for clues about future performance before hiring workers or before promoting workers into new jobs.

Accordingly, if belonging to a particular race/sex group is correlated in the experience of the firm with lower productivity, the firm may generalize this idea to all members of that group. Insurance companies find that it pays to generalize about risk in establishing insurance premiums. For example, teenage males as a group have above-average rates of traffic accidents, so all teenage males are charged above-average rates for automobile coverage. It is too costly for the carriers to make individual assessments of each boy's likely risk and thus rational to generalize. If generalizing about potential employees is cheaper than making detailed individual investigations, employers might also make actuarial-type decisions in hiring and promotions.

With statistical discrimination, the accuracy of the generalization may not be the key element in determining its rationality. Suppose there are two groups with identical distributions of productivity, but that there are costs of determining or predicting the productivity of any individual within the group. Suppose further that employers are more familiar with predictors of productivity in one group compared to the other. They might rationally tilt their hiring and promotion decisions toward the known group in which assessments are less costly.[39]

EEO Costs

The cost impact on the firm of imposing EEO regulations will vary, depending on the nature of the discrimination process. It might appear that if discrimination is profit-maximizing, as most of the models described suggested, then removing discrimination would be profit-reducing. That, however, is not necessarily the case.

For example, if employer discrimination is due to customer preference and if EEO antidiscrimination provisions are uniformly enforced, no one firm is likely to lose any business by following EEO rules. When all firms are forced simultaneously to end discriminatory practices, prejudiced customers cannot take their trade elsewhere. Short of not consuming at all, they must accept the new situation. In effect, coordinated EEO enforcement acts as a monopsony element in the product market that favors nondiscrimination in the labor market.

Suppose, alternatively, that discrimination is of the statistical type and is due to the fact that employers are less able to determine the future productivity of potential recruits from certain groups. Suppose further that the productivity distributions are the same for all groups. Forced use of the unknown group will, in fact, raise the marginal products of those previously excluded. A net gain in social efficiency could result.[40]

Much depends on the sequence of events. If employee preferences for discrimination were driving employer policy, there may be initial frictions and loss of output during the period of integration. But if a learning process takes place, after which prejudices recede, the employer will have a wider labor market from which to select future employees. EEO policy, enforced over a period of time, could change attitudes, expectations, and labor market institutions. Although discrimination might be rational for unconstrained employers initially, it might be irrational (not profit-maximizing) at a later date after EEO policy has been enforced.

Despite the uncertainties involved in modeling discrimination in the workplace, there is a lesson to be drawn for EEO policy. All models ultimately require an interaction of social and employer discrimination. The two types of discrimination may reinforce each other so that, over time, discriminatory policies and attitudes become entrenched. It is likely, therefore, that discrimination cannot be overcome except by widespread pressure from public policy. Reliance on The Market alone will not by itself change deeply embedded HRM practices. Discriminatory practices can exist comfortably within a market system, and an external push may be required to change these practices. Once changed, however, market forces need not push for the resurrection of past practices.

Labor Market Trends

Labor market data from the 1970s and 1980s suggest that aggregate indicators were improving for females relative to males, but not for blacks versus whites. Figure 15–1 shows the employment-to-population ratios by race and sex. For all groups, the business cycle impact is clearly evident; employment falls relative to the noninstitutional civilian population during the recessions of the mid-1970s and early 1980s. It rebounds during recoveries. But apart from these cyclical

FIGURE 15–1 Employment-to-Population Ratios (Civilian Labor Force, Age 16 and Older)

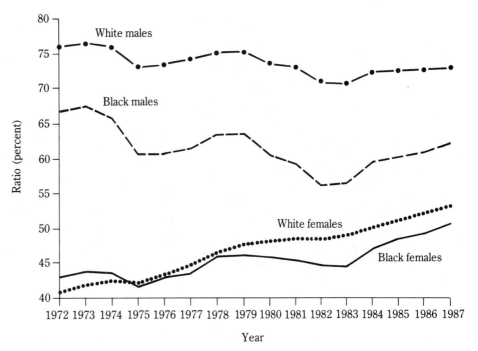

Source: Data from U.S. Bureau of Labor Statistics, *Employment and Earnings*, various issues, and *Handbook of Labor Statistics*, bulletin 2217 (Washington: GPO, 1985), Table 2.

effects, male employment has been falling relative to female. Employment dips during recessions are most severe for black males and least severe for white females who, as a group, have made the most dramatic employment gains.

Unemployment data show a similar pattern. There are regular cyclical patterns of relative unemployment by race and sex. Figure 15–2 depicts the ratio of black-to-white unemployment rates. Black female rates have risen relative to white female rates over the period shown while black male rates show little trend. Yet as Figure 15–3 illustrates, female unemployment rates have fallen relative to male rates. This tendency resulted in part because the labor market for males worsened during the 1980s, due to structural shifts in industry employment patterns.

Although employment and unemployment data measure gross success in job finding, earnings data provide information on the *quality* of work once it is found. Earnings data reflect a mix of influences such as occupation, industry, firm size, and unionization. In general, an improvement in the pay ratio of blacks to whites

FIGURE 15–2   Black-to-White Unemployment Rate Ratio (Civilian Labor Force)

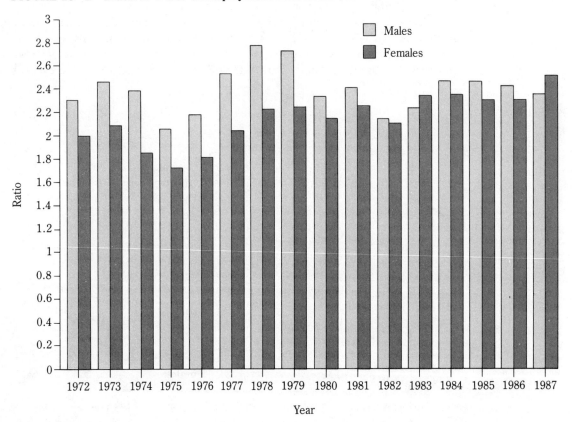

Source: Data from U.S. Bureau of Labor Statistics, *Employment and Earnings,* various issues, and *Handbook of Labor Statistics,* bulletin 2217 (Washington: GPO, 1985), Table 3.

**FIGURE 15–3
Female-to-Male
Unemployment
Rate Ratio
(Civilian Labor
Force)**

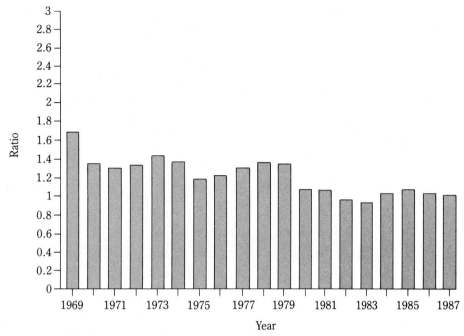

Source: Data from U.S. Bureau of Labor Statistics, *Employment and Earnings,* various issues, and *Handbook of Labor Statistics,* bulletin 2217 (Washington: GPO, 1985), Table 2.

or females to males represents an improvement in the employment situation for blacks or females.

Figures 15–4 and 15–5 show the black-to-white earnings ratios for full-time male and female employees, respectively, during the 1970s and 1980s.[41] Some improvement occurred for both groups in the earlier years, but there is little trend thereafter for black females and a slight deterioration for black males. In contrast, the female-to-male earnings ratio (Figure 15–6) began to rise in the late 1970s, roughly the period when agitation over the comparable worth issue began to swell.[42]

Concerns have been expressed that women will disproportionately enter the contingent labor force and thus be subject to lower pay and few benefits.[43] There is no precise definition or measurement of the contingent labor force; part-time workers are the closest approximation available. Since the data in Figure 15–6 are confined to full-time workers, it might be the case that the trend shown hides developments among part-timers (who are disproportionately female). During the 1979–1988 period, however, when the female-to-male earnings ratio was rising for full-timers, it also rose for part-timers. Moreover, full-time female employment rose faster than part time.[44]

Obviously, many forces—especially the tightness or slackness of the labor market and changes in industrial structure—influenced the aggregate data just reviewed. For example, it has been argued that the rising female/male earnings

**FIGURE 15–4
Nonwhite or Black
Male Earnings as
Percent of White
Male Earnings**

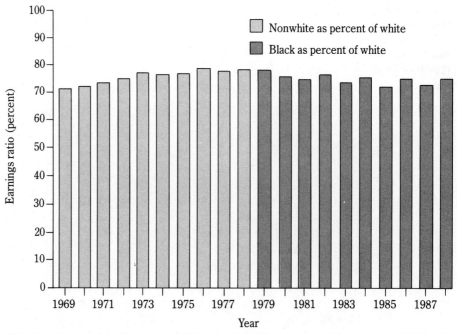

Note: Data refer to usual weekly earnings of full-time workers. Estimates are as of May for the period 1969–1978 and as of second quarter thereafter.

Source: Data from U.S. Bureau of Labor Statistics, various press releases, and *Labor Force Statistics Derived from the Current Population Survey: A Databook,* vol. I, bulletin 2096 (Washington: GPO, 1982), p. 726.

ratio in the 1980s was more the result of a deteriorating job market for males than of an improved one for females.[45] Moreover, a substantial fraction of the female/male and black/white discrepancies in labor market treatment results from different job-related endowments rather than from employment discrimination.[46] Nevertheless, there is room for optimism concerning future female employment developments.

One factor stressed by many economists is job-market experience. Generally, this factor augurs well for female/male wage comparisons in the future, since women have been gaining in labor market experience. With rising participation rates, women will be using that experience more fully in the labor market.[47] During the 1970s young women showed a dramatic increase in expectations that they would be working later in life.[48] On the other hand, falling workforce participation among black males is an omen of future difficulties.

Effects of EEO Policy

Although there were broad social and economic trends that seemed more favorable to females than to black males in the 1970s and 1980s, it is still important to ask whether EEO policy had a noticeable impact in making the labor market different from what it otherwise would have been. *In fact, research studies suggest that EEO and affirmative action have had an effect and that it has been in the*

**FIGURE 15–5
Nonwhite or Black
Female Earnings
as Percent of
White Female
Earnings**

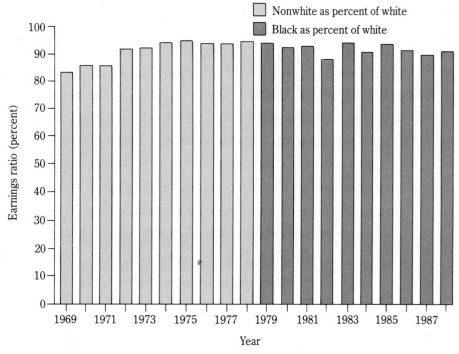

Note: Data refer to usual weekly earnings of full-time workers. Estimates are as of May for the period 1969–1978 and as of second quarter thereafter.

Source: Data from U.S. Bureau of Labor Statistics, various press releases, and *Labor Force Statistics Derived from the Current Population Survey: A Databook,* vol. I, bulletin 2096 (Washington: GPO, 1982), p. 726.

expected direction. Yet the timing of the impact of EEO policy does not necessarily correlate with the intensity of enforcement nor with the administrative efficiency of the enforcement agencies.

Significant improvements for black workers, for example, seemed to come in the late 1960s, shortly after EEO policy went into effect. The lesson appears to be that EEO policy has worked as much or more by focusing the attention of management on race and sex problems as it has by implementation of any particular policy or procedure.[49] This pattern may be reflected in the upward drift of the female/male pay ratio after the comparable worth issue surfaced. Although the comparable worth doctrine has not received court endorsement, the focus on the issue may have convinced HRM specialists to address the question before it became a problem for their employers.[50]

EEO and the Status of Human Resource Management

EEO policy, like other federal regulatory programs adopted in the 1960s and 1970s, put added stress on the HRM function within firms. When regulatory policies are created, firms must adjust by hiring experts to keep up with the new

FIGURE 15–6
Female-to-Male
Earnings Ratio for
Full-Time Workers

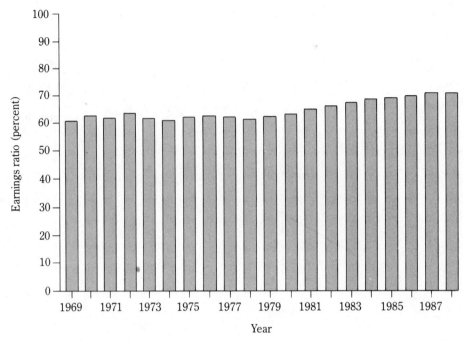

Note: Data refer to usual weekly earnings of full-time workers. Estimates are as of May for the period 1969–1978 and as of second quarter thereafter.

Source: Data from U.S. Bureau of Labor Statistics, various press releases, and *Labor Force Statistics Derived from the Current Population Survey: A Databook,* vol. I, bulletin 2096 (Washington: GPO, 1982), p. 726.

requirements. In that respect all of the regulatory programs discussed in this chapter and the preceding one have raised the status of the HRM function, the HRM department, and HRM professional within the firm.

But EEO is something special. It is not just a creator of a demand for experts. Its impact can be compared with the effect of the rise of unionization in the 1930s and later, since EEO touched all elements of HRM practice within firms. Moreover, it pushed internal firm policy toward formalization and central control or monitoring.

When a firm is challenged in court, or by a regulatory agency, with regard to an EEO matter, the firm will generally be better off showing that it follows centralized, controlled, and objective HRM policies. In the case of hiring, for example, a firm that leaves such decisions entirely in the hands of line managers runs a risk. Line managers are under pressure to meet production targets; they may well hire through informal networks of friends or through referrals by current employees. Such hiring procedures will generally not be neutral with regard to race and sex; they will bias the applicant pool towards people similar to those already in the firm's employ.

Similarly, firms who leave it to line managers to discharge unsatisfactory employees may create problems for themselves. Detailed documentation on the reasons for discharges may not be kept by line managers, whose main goal is to rid themselves of a troublemaker. Without such documentation, however, it will be hard to refute charges that disciplinary actions were really taken for discriminatory reasons.

The fact that EEO policy pushes the firm toward centralized and formalized HRM policies does not mean that all firms adopt such management styles. There are obvious advantages in decentralization and in leaving decisions with line managers, who are close to the production scene and who have an incentive to meet firm production goals. As with everything else in economic life, EEO pressures create a trade-off for the firm. Different firms select different points along the trade-off spectrum.

Even decentralized styles of management, however, can be influenced by EEO objectives. Line managers can be trained to recognize the potential costs that incorrect decisions on their part can inflict on the firm. The reward and penalty system can be designed to reflect the firm's EEO, as well as production, objectives. In such situations HRM specialists operate as trainers, monitors, and evaluators of line decisions; they do not make such decisions themselves.

15-3 Public Policy Environment

Some readers at this point must wonder whether the list of regulatory programs that affect the HRM function has been exhausted in the last chapter and this one. Complex as the programs discussed so far seem, they are but a sampling of the public policies that affect the employment relationship. For example, there are specialized programs that affect fringe benefits. An earlier chapter mentioned the influence of the tax code on the kinds of benefits offered. These incentives reflect a congressional desire to foster a private system of health and welfare programs run by employers. And there are also other programs aimed at regulating employee benefits.

Because of federal concerns about retiree security, firms that offer pension plans and similar arrangements are subject to the Employee Retirement Income Security Act of 1974 (ERISA). Those with defined benefit pensions must insure their plans against bankruptcy with the federal Pension Benefit Guarantee Corporation (PBGC), and they must meet various standards of funding and vesting.

The federal government has an interest in controlling health care costs, because of its involvement in Medicare and other medical programs. Under federal legislation, companies that offer health insurance must generally provide employees with the option of belonging to a Health Maintenance Organization (HMO), if an HMO is available in their area.[51] Partly as a result of federal involvement, and partly because their own health insurance costs have been rising, many firms have active health care cost containment programs of their own.

Federal policy is also concerned about unemployment, particularly high youth unemployment and unemployment among welfare recipients. As a result it has fostered various programs aimed at subsidizing, through tax credits and other means, employers who hire targeted groups. State and local governments have related programs.

As these examples illustrate, the list of public policies that affect the workplace is long. When a government interest is felt, a labor market solution is often sought. Some resulting programs impose mandatory burdens on firms; others provide financial inducements to modify HRM practices.

If future predictions about public policies that will affect HRM are to be made, it is thus necessary to consider likely future public concerns. The aging of the population, which will occur over the next few decades, will place added stress on income security. Income security and job security are closely related. As a result, proposals are surfacing for restricting employer freedom to lay off and discharge employees. The requirements, enacted in 1988, that employers provide 60 days' notice of plant closings and mass layoffs are symptomatic of this movement.

The growing proportion of women in the workforce will continue to raise issues concerning comparable worth, pregnancy leaves, sexual harassment, and similar matters. Changes in industrial structure, and the resulting job displacement, have renewed public interest in job training and vocational education. The degree to which the regular educational system prepares students for the transition to the workforce will also be a key concern.

Forward-looking HRM specialists attempt to monitor those social trends that can lead eventually to pressures on internal firm policy. But futurology is risky. The overused term *flexibility* best describes the posture HRM specialists should take with regard to future developments. An ability to quantify the effects of potential programs and alert top management to their internal consequences is important. Also very important is an ability to see the potential conflicts between proposed management strategies and the requirements of public policy.

If the firm has severe problems with regulatory proposals or actual programs, it may find outlets for expression of its needs through trade associations and business groups. Forecasting future public policies with confidence may not be possible. But firm survival may rest on coping with those policies and even influencing them.

Summary

Some public policies serve to restrict job availability. Included under this heading are, for example, restrictions on the employment of child labor. But the most prominent new public policy restricting employment of a target group is the Immigration Reform and Control Act of 1986. This statute prohibits employers from hiring illegal aliens on the assumption that such a prohibition will enhance wages and opportunities of citizens and others entitled to work.

In fact, the impact of immigration on the job market is complex. It can enhance the welfare of workers whose jobs are complements to the kinds of jobs taken by immigrants; and it can reduce the welfare of those who compete in the labor market with immigrants. Thus the economic effects of IRCA, if tightly enforced, will be mixed. There is, in addition, a significant issue of how strict enforcement will be and can be, given the limited resources available to police IRCA's requirements and weaknesses in the standards regarding proof of entitlement to work.

While IRCA seeks to curb job opportunities of a target group, the various EEO laws and executive orders are aimed at improving them for minorities and women. Initially, EEO policy was stimulated by the American racial problem, an aftermath of black slavery. Modern EEO regulation, however, is also devoted in a major way toward sex discrimination. Discrimination on the basis of religion, national origin, age, handicap, and other factors is also covered.

Economic modeling of discrimination in the workplace raises many questions. It does distinguish, however, between social discrimination—which affects employee skills, interests, and abilities—prior to entry into the labor market and employer-initiated discrimination, which treats equals unequally. Statistical studies have found evidence of improved workplace treatment of women and minorities since the 1960s, when EEO became a major federal program. Women have exhibited increased labor force participation and the female-to-male pay ratio rose during the 1980s. Black women in full-time positions earn about ninety percent of what their white counterparts make. On the other hand, black unemployment rates remain high relative to whites.

EEO laws and executive orders have had a major impact on the conduct and status of the HRM function within the firm. The effect is comparable to the impact of unions in an earlier era. Both unions in the 1930s and 1940s and EEO in the 1960s and 1970s elevated the status of HRM professionals relative to line managers and tilted notions of good human resource policy toward formalized and centralized approaches. Virtually any human resource policy or program is now subject to EEO review.

EXERCISES

Problem

In 1987, women constituted about 45% of total civilian employment. Yet only 13% of employed engineers were women. Although there is underrepresentation of women in other scientific and mathematical fields, it is nowhere near the level of engineering. For example, about a third of mathematical and computer analysts and about a fourth of natural scientists are women.[52] Suppose you were an HR executive in an industry such as aerospace, which is a heavy user of engineering personnel and is a major supplier to the federal government. Your record regarding the hiring of women into engineering pursuant to your affirmative action plan is being questioned by officials of the OFCCP. What steps might you take to increase female representation in your engineering ranks? Consider such aspects of your HR procedures as recruitment, screening, training, and retention. What costs might you encounter in implementing policies in these areas? What other HR problems might arise?

Questions

1. In what way do immigration controls affect employers who have not had a history of employing immigrants, legal or illegal?

2. Will native labor necessarily benefit from a tightening of immigration restrictions? Defend your answer.

3. What distinction would you make between affirmative action and antidiscrimination policy?

4. How have EEO requirements affected HRM functions related to the hiring of new employees?

5. How might the preferences of nonsupervisory employees lead to discriminatory practices by management, in the absence of EEO constraints?

6. How do restrictions on age discrimination interact with concerns about job security?

Terms

Age Discrimination in Employment Act
bona fide occupational qualification
comparable worth
disparate impact
disparate treatment
EEOC
Equal Pay Act

health care cost containment
Immigration Reform and Control Act
OFCCP
reasonable accommodation to religious practice
reasonable accommodation to the handicapped

seniority versus affirmative action
sexual harassment
statistical discrimination
Title 7, Civil Rights Act
validation

ENDNOTES

1. As the text will note, EEO policy can in principle be traced back to World War II. Its impact was extremely limited until a legislative breakthrough in the 1960s occurred as part of the civil rights movement of the period.

2. U.S. Bureau of the Census, *Historical Statistics of the United States: Colonial Times to 1970* (Washington: GPO, 1975), Part 1, pp. 8, 105–106.

3. Barry R. Chiswick, "Is the New Immigration Less Skilled Than the Old?," *Journal of Labor Economics,* vol. 4 (April 1986), pp. 168–192.

4. Sherrie A. Kossoudji, "English Language Ability and the Labor Market Opportunities of Hispanic and East Asian Immigrant Men," *Journal of Labor Economics,* vol. 6 (April 1988), pp. 205–228.

5. Jeffrey S. Passel, "Estimating the Number of Undocumented Aliens," *Monthly Labor Review,* vol. 109 (September 1986), p. 33; U.S. President, *Economic Report of the President, February 1986* (Washington: GPO, 1986), pp. 218–219.

6. George J. Borjas, "The Earnings of Male Hispanic Immigrants in the United States," *Industrial and Labor Relations Review,* vol. 35 (April 1982), pp. 343–353.

7. These data, and other related international wage statistics, are discussed more fully in the next chapter.

8. George J. Borjas, "Immigrants, Minorities, and Labor Market Competition," *Industrial and Labor Relations Review,* vol. 40 (April 1987), pp. 382–392.

9. For reviews of these issues, see Michael J. Greenwood and John M. McDowell, "The Factor Market Consequences of U.S. Immigration," *Journal of Economic Literature,* vol. 24 (December 1986), pp. 1738–1772; U.S. President, *Economic Report of the President, February 1986, op. cit.,* chapter 7; Clark W. Reynolds and Robert K. McCleery, "The Political Economy of Immigration Law: Impact of Simpson-Rodino on the United States and Mexico," *Journal of Economic Perspectives,* vol. 2 (Summer 1988), pp. 117–131, especially p. 125.

10. Barry R. Chiswick, "Illegal Immigration and Immigration Control," *Journal of Economic Perspectives,* vol. 2 (Summer 1988), pp. 101–115, especially pp. 111–113.

11. John K. Hill and James E. Pearce, "Enforcing Sanctions Against Employers of Illegal Aliens," *Economic Review,* Federal Reserve Bank of Dallas (May 1987), pp. 1–15. The law provides for importation of foreign workers in agriculture under certain conditions. A special "adverse effect wage rate" is established by the U.S. Department of Labor—in effect a minimum wage for farmers—for employers of immigrant labor under this program to avert a depression of domestic wages by the immigrants.

12. Prior to IRCA, union officials complained that employers threatened with unionization would call for INS raids of their own premises to remove union activists. Given IRCA's employer penalties, employers would be unlikely to use such a tactic.

13. U.S. Bureau of the Census, *Historical Statistics of the United States: Colonial Times to 1970,* Part 1 (Washington: GPO, 1975), p. 139.

14. *Employment and Earnings,* vol. 35 (January 1988), p. 191.

15. U.S. Bureau of the Census, *General Social and Economic Characteristics: United States Summary,* 1980 Census of Population, PC80–1–C1 (Washington: GPO, 1983), Part 1, Table 125.

16. *Employment and Earnings,* vol. 35 (January 1988), pp. 191, 204.

17. Women and children were often grouped together in the mind of legislators of the period. State protective laws that vary by sex were struck down as being in conflict with the federal EEO legislation to be discussed below.

18. Jonathan S. Leonard, "Affirmative Action as Earnings Redistribution: The Targeting of Compliance Reviews," *Journal of Labor Economics,* vol. 3 (July 1985), pp. 363–384.

19. A study comparing newly hired men and women found that while time on the job reduced the likelihood of quitting for men, the quit probability rose with time for women.

See Mark E. Meitzen, "Differences in Male and Female Job-Quitting Behavior," *Journal of Labor Economics,* vol. 4 (April 1986), pp. 151–167.

20. Differences between males and females doing the same job that result from merit awards, progression plans, and piece rates are not forbidden.

21. See also Henry J. Aaron and Cameran M. Lougy, *The Comparable Worth Controversy* (Washington: Brookings Institution, 1986).

22. Robert S. Smith, "Comparable Worth: Limited Coverage and the Exacerbation of Inequality," *Industrial and Labor Relations Review,* vol. 41 (January 1988), pp. 227–250.

23. In the cases of firms that have been in business for long periods of time, there may be a history of pay differentials which—if unearthed—could be taken as evidence of pay discrimination. For example, there may be memos written years ago which justify low female pay rates for certain jobs on the grounds that women don't need as much money as men.

24. U.S. Bureau of the Census, *Statistical Abstract of the United States: 1988* (Washington: GPO, 1988), pp. 70–71.

25. The pension cost differential is cushioned by the inclusion of survivor's benefits. A short-lived male employee is likely to be married to a younger, long-lived female. The extra costs for her tend to offset the lower costs for him. Similarly, a long-lived female employee is likely to have an older, short-lived husband.

26. Estimates of the differential costs the unisex benefit decisions have made for the pay of men and women have not been made. There are many complicating factors, including the dependent issue cited in the previous note. With regard to pensions, although women are more expensive if they reach retirement age, they tend to have shorter average job tenures than men. Thus they are less likely to vest their pension benefits and are likely to have shorter service periods, if they do vest. It is interesting to note that blacks have shorter life expectancies than whites, but employers did not make racial adjustments in their benefit plans to reflect this difference.

27. In principle, President Reagan could have revoked earlier executive orders and ended the affirmative action requirement for federal contractors.

28. In the early 1950s, at around the time of the Supreme Court's school desegregation decision, instructional expenditures per pupil in southern white schools was about two-thirds higher than that in black schools. See Finis Welch, "Black-White Differences in Returns to Schooling," *American Economic Review,* vol. 63 (December 1973), pp. 893–907, especially p. 900.

29. See, for example, the symposium on the subject of statistical tests for employment discrimination (part of a volume devoted to "Statistical Inference in Litigation"), appearing

in *Law and Contemporary Problems,* vol. 46 (Autumn 1983), pp. 171–267; Masanori Hashimoto and Levis Kochin, "A Bias in the Statistical Estimation of the Effects of Discrimination," *Economic Inquiry,* vol. 18 (July 1980), pp. 478–486; Walter Fogel, "Class Pay Discrimination and Multiple Regression Proofs," *Nebraska Law Review,* vol. 65 (2:1986), pp. 289–329; Joseph L. Gastwirth, "Statistical Methods for Analyzing Claims of Employment Discrimination," *Industrial and Labor Relations Review,* vol. 38 (October 1984), pp. 75–86.

30. The statistical techniques usually involve identifying a difference in job-related outcomes for one group relative to another. The source of the difference in outcomes may not be known, however. All that may be said is that the chance that the difference in outcomes is caused by random processes is very small. Orley Ashenfelter and Ronald Oaxaca, "The Economics of Discrimination: Economists Enter the Courtroom," *American Economic Review,* vol. 77 (May 1987), pp. 321–325.

31. An early statement of this approach can be found in Gary S. Becker, *The Economics of Discrimination,* 2nd edition (Chicago: University of Chicago Press, 1971 [1957]), pp. 16–17.

32. It might be noted that international trade theory—some of which is described in the next chapter—suggests that even barriers to factor acquisition (such as limits in obtaining capital) would not necessarily prevent real wages from being equal in an economy composed of, say, all-male and all-female firms. If female firms in the aggregate had lower capital-to-labor ratios than the aggregate of male firms, they would specialize in labor-intensive goods, exporting them to the male economy in exchange for capital-intensive goods. Under certain assumptions, the capital-to-labor ratios at the firm level would equalize within the two sectors, thus equalizing productivity and real wages.

33. A criticism of unions with regard to treatment of blacks, with historical references, can be found in Herbert Hill, "The AFL-CIO and the Black Worker: Twenty-Five Years After the Merger," *Journal of Intergroup Relations,* vol. 10 (Spring 1982), pp. 5–78.

34. Orley C. Ashenfelter, "Racial Discrimination and Trade Unionism," *Journal of Political Economy,* vol. 80, part 1 (May-June 1972), pp. 435–64; Orley C. Ashenfelter and Lamond I. Goodwin, "Some Evidence on the Effect of Unionism on the Average Wage of Black Workers Relative to White Workers, 1900–67" in Gerald G. Somers, ed., *Proceedings of the Twenty-Fourth Annual Winter Meeting,* Industrial Relations Research Association, December 27–28, 1971 (Madison, Wisc.: IRRA, 1972), pp. 217–224.

35. A comparison of union and nonunion plants in California suggested that unions did not hinder employment opportunities of women and minorities. See Jonathan S. Leon-ard, "The Effects of Unions on the Employment of Blacks, Hispanics, and Women," *Industrial and Labor Relations Review,* vol. 39 (October 1985), pp. 115–132.

36. One study finds that black professional basketball players earn less than equivalently talented whites, and connects this discrepancy to white fan (customer) preferences. Attendance at games (and therefore team profitability) rises if white players are substituted for blacks. See Lawrence M. Kahn and Peter D. Sherer, "Racial Differences in Professional Basketball Players' Compensation," *Journal of Labor Economics,* vol. 6 (January 1988), pp. 40–61.

37. It has been argued, for example, that once it becomes obvious that female-dominated jobs are lower paid, males will have an incentive to act as gatekeepers, resisting the entrance of women into "their" occupations. In addition, socialization might keep women from applying for better paying male jobs, even if wage premiums could be obtained. See Myra H. Strober and Carolyn L. Arnold, "The Dynamics of Occupational Segregation among Bank Tellers" in Clair Brown and Joseph A. Pechman, eds., *Gender in the Workplace* (Washington: Brookings Institution, 1987), pp. 107–148, especially pp. 110–119. The authors note parallels between how real estate markets are able to maintain separate neighborhoods for whites and blacks, even without legal support for doing so. If everyone knows where they "belong," and if there is a sense that hostility might ensue if unwritten borders are crossed, the separate neighborhoods can maintain themselves, even if land prices and rents differ between them.

38. Ouchi notes that the highly successful American "theory Z" firms he identified had top management teams composed of "unremittingly white, male, middle class" membership and the firms tend to be racist and sexist. He found even greater racism and sexism among successful Japanese firms. These characteristics are attributed to the high degree of trust among managers on which the firms rely. See William G. Ouchi, *Theory Z: How American Business Can Meet the Japanese Challenge* (New York: Avon Books, 1982), pp. 77–79.

39. Shelly J. Lundberg and Richard Startz, "Private Discrimination and Social Intervention in Competitive Labor Markets," *American Economic Review,* vol. 73 (June 1983), pp. 340–347.

40. *ibid.*

41. Available data provide nonwhite (rather than black) earnings information until the late 1970s, and black data thereafter. Nonwhites are roughly 90% black.

42. One of the first statements of comparable worth as a legal issue appeared in early 1979. See Ruth G. Blumrosen, "Wage Discrimination, Job Segregation, and Title VII of the Civil Rights Act of 1964," *University of Michigan Journal of Law Reform,* vol. 12 (Spring 1979), pp. 399–502.

43. Susan Christopherson, "Labor Flexibility: Implications for Women Workers" in Rosalind M. Schwartz, ed., *Women at Work* (Los Angeles: UCLA Institute of Industrial Relations, 1988), pp. 3–24.

44. Female and male part timers are very different in age profile. However, the gross ratio of part-time female-to-male usual weekly earnings stood at about 1.08 in 1979–II and 1.11 in 1988–II. *Source:* U.S. Bureau of Labor Statistics, press release USDL 88–369, August 2, 1988, and earlier releases.

45. Lester C. Thurow, "The New American Family," *Technology Review,* vol. 90 (August/September 1987), pp. 26–27.

46. Randall K. Filer, "Male-Female Wage Differences: The Importance of Compensating Differentials," *Industrial and Labor Relations Review,* vol. 38 (April 1985), pp. 426–437.

47. One study argues that female job experience has been rising over a long period, but paradoxically not for working women. That is, the gains have been among women who are not currently working, *but have worked in the past.* As participation rates rise, however, the probability increases that nonworking women will convert to working status. See James P. Smith and Michael P. Ward, *Women's Wages and Work in the Twentieth Century* (Santa Monica, Calif.: Rand Corp., 1984). See also June O'Neill, "The Trend in the Male-Female Wage Gap in the United States," *Journal of Labor Economics,* vol. 3, Part 2 (January 1985), pp. S91–S116.

48. U.S. President, *Economic Report of the President, January 1987* (Washington: GPO, 1987), pp. 215–216.

49. Jonathan S. Leonard, "Employment and Occupational Advance under Affirmative Action," *Review of Economics and Statistics,* vol. 66 (August 1984), pp. 377–385; Jonathan S. Leonard, "What Promises are Worth: The Impact of Affirmative Action Goals," *Journal of Human Resources,* vol. 20 (Winter 1985), pp. 3–20; Jonathan S. Leonard, "The Impact of Affirmative Action on Employment," *Journal of Labor Economics,* vol. 4 (October 1984), pp. 439–463; Jonathan S. Leonard, "The Effectiveness of Equal Employment Law and Affirmative Action Regulation" in Ronald G. Ehrenberg, ed., *Research in Labor Economics,* vol. 8, Part B (Greenwich, Conn.: JAI Press, 1986), pp. 319–350; Paul Osterman, "Affirmative Action and Opportunity: A Study of Female Quit Rates," *Review of Economics and Statistics,* vol. 64 (November 1982), pp. 604–12; Orley Ashenfelter and James Heckman, "Measuring the Effect of an Antidiscrimination Program" in Orley Ashenfelter and James Blum, eds., *Evaluating the Labor-Market Effects of Social Programs* (Princeton, N.J.: Industrial Relations Section, Dept. of Economics, Princeton University, 1976), pp. 46–84; Richard B. Freeman, "Changes in the Labor Market for Black Americans: 1948–72," *Brookings Papers on Economic Activity* (1:1973), pp. 67–120.

50. Aaron Bernstein, "Comparable Worth: It's Already Happening," *Business Week,* April 28, 1986, pp. 52, 56.

51. These requirements are spelled out in the Health Maintenance Organization Act of 1973. HMOs are health care providers who charge a flat monthly fee, regardless of usage. Thus they have a strong incentive to hold down costs.

52. *Employment and Earnings,* vol. 35 (January 1988), p. 181.

Chapter Sixteen

INTERNATIONAL SIDE OF HUMAN RESOURCE MANAGEMENT

Although the United States has been a major player in world trade and investment since the end of World War II, public awareness of that role was dim until the 1980s. Then a substantial increase in the volume of imports, combined with lagging performance of U.S. exports, substantially raised the level of consciousness. Much of the discussion of the need to be competitive that occurred revolved around competition *with other countries*.

As is often the case when topics become hot, short-term trends become the focus, and apocalyptic visions prevail. It became fashionable to place the blame for America's international problems on deficiencies in management and on the HRM function in particular. This chapter will stress the point that the foreign sector difficulties that developed in the 1980s were largely the result of forces beyond the control of management. It will also note that, over the long term, HRM cannot be seen as insulated from international pressures.

16–1 Alternative to the Comparative Approach

There are two ways of looking at the HRM aspects of the international economy. One is to compare American HRM practices with those abroad. The insights thus gained have two values. First, they point to the fact that there are alternatives to standard American HRM practices. In other countries things are done differently. Thus those HRM professionals who are seeking new ideas to apply in the United States might well find them abroad. Second, international insights are useful to American HRM professionals employed by multinational enterprises since they need to know just how HRM matters are normally handled in particular host

472

countries. Failure to understand local customs and expectations could produce unfortunate results.

One approach, therefore, in reviewing the international aspects of HRM is to take the so-called comparative approach. Some general HRM texts include a chapter that attempts to take their readers on a world tour, going country by country and describing the key features of HRM practice in each. Others go on a topical tour instead; they take up particular issues such as job security and then compare in detail how various countries deal with that topic.

While the traditional comparative approach has great value, it cannot be adequately undertaken in a single chapter. The American system alone has taken up the bulk of this text; how much justice in coverage could be done to HRM practices around the whole world in a few pages? Thus it is best to leave the comparative approach to separate texts and courses devoted exclusively to that topic.[1]

A detailed country-by-country approach is also not attempted. Instead, this chapter will first take up those aspects of foreign HRM practice that often differ markedly from those in the United States. Following that discussion, the chapter will turn to the impact of the international sector on U.S. HRM practices.

16–2 Variations from American Practices

Economic forces have been stressed throughout this volume as explanations of HRM policy. Although these forces exist universally, the social, legal, and political systems of different countries have produced variegated responses to them. A nation's stage of economic development is also an important HRM determinant. Clearly, HRM practice in a third-world economy that has a semiliterate, impoverished population is going to be quite different from that found in a developed economy with a high standard of living.

For American-oriented HRM professionals, three areas of difference in foreign practice are likely to stand out when compared with the United States. These are (1) the role of unions and collective bargaining, (2) the degree and style of economic regulation of the labor market, and (3) social expectations about the nature of the employer–employee relationship. A brief discussion of each is provided below as a checklist for American managers who may be embarking on international careers.[2] Listed are HRM areas that need attention because the foreign responses to them cannot be assumed to follow American practices. They are thus potential pitfalls for managers and HRM professionals who have had experience and training only in the U.S. context.

Unions and Collective Bargaining

As has been discussed, unions have represented a declining fraction of the U.S. workforce since the mid-1950s. Although dramatic strikes still can provoke newspaper headlines, the degree of public attention to unions and collective-bargaining issues has generally waned. Yet at earlier points in American history, especially during the 1930s, union–management relations were an explosive area, eventually triggering substantial government intervention in the form of the Wagner Act of 1935 and its subsequent modifications.

Unions and Politics.   In some countries, union–management relations are still a central arena of social tension and government involvement. Although American unions involve themselves in politics, it is often the case abroad that the local union movement or movements are heavily involved with political parties that may sometimes control the government. Labor parties in Britain, Australia, Israel, and the Scandinavian countries are examples. The result may be a governmental climate that actively fosters unions when the labor-affiliated party is in control. In such countries sharp oscillations in public policy towards unions can occur when elections bring in new governments. Thus the election of the Conservative Thatcher government in Britain led to an adverse climate for unions there in the 1980s, after a period of union growth in the 1970s.

Unions abroad often have a more left-wing orientation than American unions. They may be affiliated with the local Communist Party or other radical groups. Foreign unions may also be linked to religious communities such as the Catholic Church. Their agenda may encompass wide-reaching economic, political, and social change, not just current relations with particular employers. Although there have certainly been radical elements in the American labor movement, on balance there has been a greater focus on workplace issues and lesser attention to social transformation in the United States than in many other countries.[3] These differences in orientation can influence the quality of the labor–management climate that HRM professionals must face.

Union Suppression.   In countries where authoritarian regimes prevail, independent unions are often suppressed or discouraged. On the other hand, membership in—and employer recognition of—government-controlled unions may be encouraged or required. A mix of motivations is involved, or at least cited, in such circumstances. The government may hope to prevent independent unions from arising as sources of political opposition. It may also point to alleged needs of economic development, especially in the case of third-world countries, as a rationale for keeping tight control on union activity. For example, strikes or too high wages might be said by the authorities to have a potentially adverse effect on exports or on general economic welfare.

Lack of Exclusive Representation and Contracting.   The American/Canadian system of representation by exclusive bargaining agents and of long-term contracts is not generally found elsewhere in the world. In many nations more than one union may represent a group of workers, sometimes leading to rivalry and competition between the organizations. Craft-based unionization may be more common in some countries than in the United States, so that an industrial unit is represented by several occupationally oriented unions. There may be informal local bargaining through a shop steward representing the different groups, while the national unions engage in company- or industry-wide bargaining.

In the U.S./Canadian system, the outcome of successful bargaining is a legally enforceable written agreement, typically of two or three years' duration, between the employer and the exclusive representative. Obtaining such an agreement can be more difficult in countries in which multiple unions are involved. In any case, American-style long-term agreements are much less common abroad. Moreover, contracts will not necessarily have the same legally enforceable status that they do in the United States. Agreements effectively come to an end when new union demands are made.

Systems of Extension.   Unions abroad may directly influence the wages paid by employers with whom they have no formal relations. In some countries, once settlements are reached between major employers and unions, the agreements are "extended" by law to other employers. The extension system tends to insulate union workers from the competition of nonunion employees, since the latter's wage is geared to the union sector through the extension process. Perhaps the most extreme variant of extension is to be found in Australia, where a system of compulsory arbitration through special labor courts sets wages and wage adjustments for almost nine out of ten workers, whether or not their firms are organized by unions.[4]

Systems of Worker Representation.   Outside the United States representation of employees in company decision making is sometimes required by law through elected plant-level works councils or through worker representatives on company boards (known as codetermination). In principle any worker might be elected. Often, however, unions will run slates of candidates for positions of representation. Through works councils or codetermination systems unions may thus have an alternative means of interaction with management.

The closest the United States has ever come to such an approach was the stimulus given by the federal government to establishment of employee representation plans during World War I. Such arrangements were never mandated, however, just encouraged. During the 1930s, employer-sponsored employee representation systems (so-called company unions) were outlawed by the Wagner Act.

The United States thus moved away from any form of employee representation other than through collective bargaining, while other countries adopted a more mixed approach.[5] Only in the 1980s, with the growth of interest in quality circles and similar arrangements, has alternative representation been discussed in the United States. Of course, such arrangements are neither mandated nor fostered by American law.[6]

Centralization and Incomes Policy.   Certain countries have evolved systems of highly centralized bargaining in which national pacts are negotiated by top union and employer associations—sometimes with government involvement—and then implemented in a widening pattern at the industry, firm, and local plant level. Centralized bargaining has often been linked with attempts by government to hold down wage increases for anti-inflation motivations. These attempts have often been termed incomes policies (generally a euphemism for wages policy). On occasion they are also known as social accords, a phrase that generally implies a government–union–employer deal covering areas such as taxation and social insurance as well as anti-inflation wage guidelines.[7]

Centralization means more than just having a central organization of unions such as the AFL-CIO in the United States. It also implies that the central body has significant authority over its constituent unions. Such authority—for example, the right to represent member unions in negotiations—has never been given to the AFL-CIO by its member unions. It has been argued that foreign centralized union federations, which are needed for incomes policies and accords, are encouraged by economic climates of export dependency. In such climates the general need to maintain competitiveness focuses attention on overall economic welfare and away from employer-by-employer bargaining.[8]

Internationally Coordinated Bargaining?   At the international level unions in different countries have attempted to coordinate their negotiations with multinational corporations, a transnational variation on centralization of bargaining.[9] A number of international trade secretariats—confederations of national unions in particular industrial sectors—in some cases have acted as forums for such coordination. An example is the International Metalworkers' Federation, an organization that covers such industries as automobile production.

In theory, from the union perspective, bargaining strength could be enhanced vis-à-vis a multinational employer if all unions around the world who dealt with it coordinated their demands. The firm would be unable to shift production to nonstriking facilities or to low-wage plants. But there are very strong practical barriers to such international coordination. After all, unions are not always able to coordinate their bargaining effectively *within* countries. At the international level there are hurdles to overcome of divergent interests, ideology, legal systems, and language.

Claims of success in achieving true coordinated international bargaining must thus be treated with skepticism.[10] Union interests and ideologies may diverge across international boundaries, making coordination very difficult. However, when countries are in close economic union, for example, the European Common Market, unions may be able to bring pressure on multinational firms operating in more than one of the member states.[11] Indeed, there has been growing concern among unions in the Common Market over the need for stepped-up cooperation as national markets are integrated.

Employer Attitudes.   It is often said that in most countries where independent unions are permitted, aggressive American-style antiunion campaigns by employers are discouraged by the prevailing social milieu.[12] In countries with a more radical history of unions and politics than the United States, such antiunion tactics are not adopted, according to this view, because employers prefer accommodation to confrontation.[13] These employer attitudes may be changing, but there is still truth to the notion that harsh conflict over union representation rights is generally less visible in other western countries than in the United States.

Foreign employer attitudes and strategies are not fixed in concrete. Just as the United States sometimes looks to foreign HRM practices for ideas, so foreigners sometimes follow U.S. examples. Antiunion resistance by American employers has been noted with interest abroad and may spill over into other countries. U.S.-based multinational firms may in fact be exporting this aspect of American practice to other countries.[14] As noted earlier, British unions—traditionally powerful influences in the workplace—were placed on the defensive during the 1980s, a period of both Conservative Party government rule and high unemployment.

Economic Regulation of the Labor Market

There are many types of government regulation of the labor market in the United States, including minimum wage and overtime requirements, mandatory provision of workers' compensation, occupational safety and health rules, and so on. Counterparts of such rules exist in most developed countries and (on paper at least) in many third-world countries.[15] Indeed, the United States has pushed less developed countries that enjoy special tariff preferences in the American market to meet certain labor standards.[16] Whether in developed or in third-world countries, however, the forms labor market regulations take and their extensiveness can vary widely.

Social Insurance and Other Benefits. Social insurance systems in some countries are more elaborate than in the United States. Health insurance, for example, may be provided through a national medical system. Special monetary allowances may be paid for large families. These arrangements may be linked to the workplace through payroll taxes, and their existence may influence the kinds of voluntary fringe benefits employers offer (just as the U.S. Social Security system influences the design of private American pension plans).

Apart from social insurance, certain kinds of benefits, notably vacations, that are left to employer (or employer–union) discretion in the United States, are legally mandated in some countries.[17] Survey evidence suggests there may be a greater preference for leisure in Western European countries than in the United States.[18] Thus it is not surprising that the political process responds by requiring leisure-related benefits.

Public Enterprises. Government-owned enterprises are more common in many countries than in the United States. Transportation and utilities are often government run. The government may also own mines, petroleum resources, automobile and metal manufacturing plants, broadcasting systems, and financial institutions. Where there is a significant sector of government ownership of commercial enterprises, HRM policies of the government-as-owner/employer may be imitated by private firms.

State influence on HRM practice can thus extend beyond formal legal regulation. The government may see itself in its employer's role as setting an example for the private sector. Political swings between governments of the right and left may influence both the size of the state-run sector and the degree to which it is used as a pattern setter for private HRM practices.

Styles of Regulation. Even when formal legal regulation applies to the labor market, the method of government–business interaction surrounding enforcement and interpretation is often different abroad as compared with the United States. At the federal level the American regulatory model is usually based on passage of a statute to be enforced by a board, commission, or agency with a system of appeals tribunals. Decisions of the enforcement body are also appealable into the general court system on a variety of grounds, ranging from proper statutory interpretation to constitutionality. The relationship between the regulated and the regulator is supposed to be at arms' length. Cozier relationships are often seen as signs of undue influence by government or even as symptoms of outright corruption. At the very least special deals by government for particular industries, even declining ones, are viewed as anticompetitive and inappropriate.[19]

The foreign model of labor market regulation (and economic regulation more generally) is less likely to be arms' length. Indeed, it may be seen as a virtue to have close interaction between the regulator and the regulated, and there may be a long history of such relationships.[20] Deals and understandings may be reached between unions, employers, and government before new programs are enacted. Litigation and appeals are less common than in the United States. Foreigners often look with wonder and incomprehension at the American regulatory system with its adversarial, arms' length approach, and its complex interplay of the executive, legislative, and judicial branches of government.

Labor Standards and the ILO.   An influence on government regulation in many countries is the International Labour Organisation (ILO). The ILO was created immediately after World War I as part of a general effort to foster international cooperation. After World War II, the ILO became affiliated with the United Nations. ILO member states are represented in tripartite fashion by union, management, and government delegations. The ILO makes recommendations for labor regulation and passes conventions concerning labor standards that member states may ratify.[21] It has no enforcement powers but can conduct embarrassing investigations of abuses.

Views of the Employer–Employee Relationship

Throughout this text, the complex nature of the employer–employee relationship has been stressed. It has been noted that employee expectations of what the relation entails will condition the formation of HRM policies. These expectations, however, vary from society to society. Lifetime employment contracts at larger firms with company-provided housing and social benefits in Japan are an expression of a particular set of expectations in that country. In the American context, Japanese practices are often viewed as excessively paternalistic. Americans thus seem to vacillate between praising all things Japanese and publicizing exposés of deficiencies in Japanese HRM practices.[22] The composite advertisement in Figure 16–1 reflects the interest of American HRMs in one Japanese practice.

Job Security.   One of the most sensitive issues surrounding the employer–employee relationship is the question of when that relation may be terminated by the employer. An earlier chapter reviewed the gradual erosion in the United States of the at-will doctrine, the legal doctrine that employees may be terminated for good, bad, or

FIGURE 16–1
Composite of
Advertisements Widely
Received by Human
Resource Managers in
Early 1980s

QUALITY CIRCLE
TRAINING, INC.

One-Day Seminars
One-Week Training for QC Leaders

Now Your Company
Can Take Advantage of Proven
Japanese Productivity-Boosting
QUALITY CIRCLES!

* * *

It doesn't matter what line of business you're in!
Quality Circles will
• motivate your employees!
• increase quality!
• raise productivity!
For the Seminar Schedule in Your Area, Call
1-800-555-1400

---

no reason at all. Many countries, however, place legal restrictions on both individual terminations and layoffs, and these restrictions go far beyond recent American court interpretations.

Foreign employers may be held to a standard for discharge similar to the just cause notion applied by American arbitrators in interpreting union–management agreements. Specialized labor courts abroad may hear appeals from terminated employees who allege that the local version of just cause was not present in their cases.[23] Monetary damages for, or possibly reinstatement of, discharged workers may be ordered by these courts in cases of improper firings.

Restrictions on economic layoffs also may apply. Firms may be required to provide long notices and to award substantial severance pay before layoffs are permitted. Government policy to discourage layoffs may operate both through legal restrictions and a "frown"—that is, employers may be aware that the government would be unhappy about massive layoffs, even if the layoffs are technically legal. Foreign-owned multinational firms must be especially sensitive to the views of host governments and local public opinion and thus are vulnerable to regulation by frown.

Pressures for Flexibility.   In the face of declining labor demand, an anti-layoff policy can initially reduce unemployment. But it also tends to protect the jobs of insiders (those who already have jobs) at the expense of outsiders (new entrants to the labor market) who are seeking work.[24] In addition, employers may be more reluctant to hire permanent workers if such hiring entails a potentially costly indefinite obligation. The job guarantee may effectively act as a tax on new hires.

The result of tough anti-layoff rules may thus be increased use of contingent workers—part-timers, temporaries—who do not receive job security guarantees, or more intensive use of core workers through longer hours. Alternatively, there may be more subcontracting of work to small employers or foreign suppliers who are outside the bounds of legal regulation. Increases in off-the-books employment, a hidden economy that escapes rules and taxation, may occur as well.

As unemployment rates rose in many countries during the 1980s, concern was heightened about the ability of local employers to adjust to changing patterns of market demand. Often, the debate fell under the general heading of flexibility or adaptability in HRM.[25] Interestingly enough, a political consensus over the desirability of such flexibility developed often regardless of the political coloration of the government in power. As a result, some restrictions on employer ability to lay off or redeploy resources were relaxed.[26] Governments with a more liberal political orientation (using the American definition of *liberal*) were more likely to insist that the needed flexibility should be obtained through retraining of redundant workers (possibly with state subsidy of the training) than were conservative governments.

Information Sources

It should be evident to the reader that American HRM policies and practices cannot uniformly be transplanted to foreign soil. Successful implementation of HRM policy requires knowledge of the local legal, political, and social system, as well as economic conditions. HRM professionals in large, multinational enterprises keep themselves abreast of national institutions, developments, and economic trends in the countries in which their firms have operations. A variety of data and information sources are readily available.

Official institutions such as the Organisation for Economic Cooperation and Development (OECD) and the International Labour Organisation put out publications providing country-level and comparative reviews of trends relevant to HRM.[27] The U.S. Department of Labor can be a source of useful information. American embassies abroad have commercial and labor attachés who keep up with current events in the HRM area. Foreign embassies and consulates in the United States may be helpful.

Selected Sources of International HRM Data

International Labour Office of the International Labour Organisation
- *Yearbook of Labour Statistics*
  Data on wages, employment, unemployment, work stoppages, occupational composition of the workforce, occupational

injuries, inflation. Supplemented by the quarterly *Bulletin of Labour Statistics.*

U.S. Bureau of Labor Statistics

- *Monthly Labor Review*
  Data for selected countries on manufacturing pay, output per hour, and unit labor costs. Labor force data on employment, unemployment, and participation based on American definitions. Historical data appear in the periodic *Handbook of Labor Statistics* and the *Economic Report of the President.*
- *U.S. Department of State Indexes of Living Costs Abroad*
  Estimates of the cost of living in major cities of the world relative to Washington, D.C. Data are used to adjust salaries of U.S. government employees stationed abroad and could be used to adjust pay of employees stationed abroad by multinational firms.

International Metalworkers' Federation

- *The Purchasing Power of Working Time*
  Wage comparisons in selected metalworking industries in terms of purchasing power.

Other Sources of Publications

International Monetary Fund
Organisation for Economic Cooperation and Development
United Nations
Other international organizations

Private reporting services also provide useful information. Noteworthy examples are the quarterly country reports published by the Economist Intelligence Unit, which contain general information on economic and political trends, including those affecting the employment relationship. In addition, foreign universities may have centers of industrial relations that put out reports on local HRM practices and developments.

16-3 International Impact on Domestic HRM

At an abstract level it might be argued that the existence of a foreign trade sector has no particular implication for U.S. HRM practice. After all, the presence of a foreign sector just means that there are more markets to sell in and to buy from. What difference does it make to a firm if the competition is from foreign or domestic sources?

Although competition in the market is similar in its effects regardless of source, the international sector does have a special impact. First, factor market conditions abroad—especially those related to the labor market—may be substantially different from those faced by domestic competitors. In particular, in many parts of the world wages are only a fraction of American pay levels. Second, the degree of foreign competition that is faced can be importantly influenced by domestic policies such as tariffs and quotas. Pure free trade is an abstraction; all countries follow so-called commercial policies that influence what they buy and how much they sell abroad.

Economic Analysis of International Trade

There are numerous textbooks available on international trade, and it would be inappropriate here to attempt to duplicate their analyses.[28] However, the basic highlights of international economic analysis can be usefully summarized.

- The economic analysis of international trade usually begins with the assumptions that countries can trade goods (exports and imports), but cannot trade factors of production, that is, labor and capital. Obviously, these assumptions are oversimplifications. Labor does flow across international borders in the form of both legal and illegal immigration. Capital flows internationally, both in the financial sense (the purchase and sale of financial assets such as stocks, bonds, and bank accounts) and in the real sense (export and import of capital goods such as industrial machinery). Nevertheless, factor mobility—especially labor mobility—is much more restricted across national borders than it is within them.

- Given the factor-immobility assumptions, the pattern or structure of trade is determined by "comparative advantage." In the absence of factor flows, there is no absolute standard of value. What matters, in determining who exports what goods, is the *relative* cost of production. In a two-good, two-country model, if wheat is relatively cheap in the United States as compared with cloth, and if cloth is relatively cheap in the United Kingdom as compared with wheat, the United States will export wheat in exchange for cloth from the United Kingdom. The United Kingdom—as the other party to the transaction—will export cloth to and import wheat from the United States.

- Trade produces potential benefits for countries by relaxing a production/consumption constraint. In the absence of trade, anything a country wants to consume must be produced domestically. Trade opens up the possibility of consuming more of some goods than are produced at home (importing). To pay for the deficit of production, the country produces more of other goods than are consumed and exports the balance. Countries can specialize in production according to their international comparative advantage, while consuming in accordance with their internal tastes.

- The lifting of the consume-only-what-you-produce constraint changes the pattern of production within countries. Industries that enjoy a comparative advantage find the demand for their products increased. Those with a comparative disadvantage face a decline in demand and, possibly, a complete cessation of production.

- The existence of international investment flows further relaxes the constraints in a dynamic sense. Countries can purchase more than they produce domestically and borrow abroad to finance their trade deficits—that is, for a time they can import a greater value of goods than they export. In exchange, however, they must eventually repay their debts (plus interest) by running an export surplus in a later period.

- Since the possibility of international investment flows means that countries can run net export surpluses or deficits in any given period, the size of their foreign trade sector can vary relative to their domestic sector. In other words, in periods of net export deficits (value of imports exceeding value of exports), those industries that produce exports or import-competing goods will shrink in size relative to those producing goods and services that cannot be traded internationally, for example, haircuts. During periods of net export surpluses, the opposite will occur; the foreign trade sector will expand relative to other sectors.

- By changing the pattern of production, trade has complex effects on internal income distribution. In the short term, wages, employment, and profits in particular industries may be increased or reduced by trade. In the long run, the general prices of factors of production, including real wages, may be altered.

  In short, although a country as a whole may in some sense benefit from trade, trade will produce both winners and losers in the economy. Contrary to the popular impression, economic theory does *not* predict that large subgroups in society—such as the labor force relative to the owners of capital—will necessarily benefit from freer trade. Particular interests may or may not benefit, depending on assumptions.[29]

- By modifying trade flows through tariffs, quotas, subsidies, and other devices, government policies can influence the domestic structure of production and therefore the distribution of income and the pattern of employment. Employers and employees are thus likely to have an economic interest in how the government conducts its trade policies.

Trends in International Commerce and Labor Costs

To understand the forces surrounding the international marketplace, the principles of economic analysis must be combined with knowledge of empirical trends and institutions. In that sense the international setting is no different from the domestic. In order to provide the necessary background for analyzing the international impact on American HRM practice, some key trends are discussed below.

Importance of Exports and Imports. Compared with many countries, the United States has a relatively small international sector. Exports of goods and services accounted for less than 10% of American GNP in 1987. The U.S. import-to-GNP ratio was just over 12%.[30] Some countries, especially smaller nations located within large trading areas, have much higher ratios.

The ratio of exports or imports to GNP, however, does not fully measure the importance of trade to an economy. International prices, for example, can spill over into the prices of domestically produced goods. General Motors cannot ignore prices charged by Toyota in setting its own prices. Pricing ability, in turn, is reflected in General Motors's HRM decisions on wages, new hires, and layoffs. Much of manufacturing, mining, and agriculture in the United States is affected, directly or indirectly, by international trade because of actual or potential foreign competition. These sectors accounted for 23% of GNP in 1987 and about a fifth of all employees.[31] Moreover, other sectors were involved in trade as suppliers to the trading sector or in the transportation and sale of exports and imports. Finally, international competition in parts of the service sector has been steadily increasing.

Multinational Enterprises.   Generally, the post-World War II period has seen a substantial expansion of trade and investment by virtually any measure. Of particular interest has been the growth of direct investment, that is, the establishment of subsidiaries of multinational firms around the world, as well as in the United States. U.S.-based nonbank multinational firms employed 17.9 million persons in the United States in 1987. Foreign-based multinationals employed 3.0 million.[32]

The extension of multinational firms across national boundaries creates a channel of communication of HRM practices and strategies. While national differences in the HRM area are very important, the fact that single corporate entities operate in the face of different national systems creates potential for consideration of alternatives. It is always possible for a country to resist international pressures for conformity and uniformity—as the United States has resisted adoption of the metric system—but the pressure is present nonetheless.

Although studies of multinational firms generally do not indicate that they automatically import the HRM practices of their mother country, over the long run they may act as a transmitter of HRM techniques. Research on multinationals indicates that they often staff jobs that have a heavy cultural content—such as HRM professional positions—with persons from the host country.[33] Even so, at the most general level, employers around the world face common problems of recruitment, screening, evaluation, training, pay setting, grievance handling, and productivity management. If an HRM approach appears to be effective in one country, there is reason to try that approach elsewhere. Perhaps the most prominent experiment along these lines in the United States has been the joint General Motors–Toyota automobile assembly plant that blended Japanese and American HRM practices in its operation in northern California.[34]

The existence of multinational firms can sometimes be used by third parties to influence labor practices in foreign countries. Most notable were pressures on U.S.-based multinationals to adopt the Sullivan Principles with regard to treatment of black employees in South Africa. These principles were designed to assure as much opportunity for blacks as possible under the South African apartheid system. By the mid-1980s, however, pressures on American multinational firms had generally shifted toward divestment of South African holdings rather than adherence to the Sullivan Principles.

Host countries may sometimes pressure multinational firms to adopt certain HRM policies as a condition for doing business. All countries expect multinationals to comply with local labor laws and regulations pertaining to the labor market and the employment relationship. However, especially in third-world countries, host governments may encourage the promotion of nationals into key management roles. They may also seek training and skill acquisition for the nonsupervisory workforce.

Exchange Rate Fluctuations. One of the sharp differences between the domestic and the international setting is the presence of nationally based monetary systems. American firms operating within the United States utilize a common dollar standard. They have no need to worry about fluctuations of, say, the "California dollar" versus the "Ohio dollar." Only one currency is used in all parts of the United States. Firms operating across international boundaries, however, face very different monetary conditions.

At the international level, separate currencies are employed in almost every country. From the end of World War II until the early 1970s, most countries maintained fixed exchange rates relative to one another, under the so-called Bretton Woods system.[35] The exchange rate between, say, the U.S. dollar and the British pound was not allowed to deviate from an agreed-upon par value, except in a very narrow range. Changes in the official par values of currencies occurred only at infrequent intervals.

During that era exchange rates were maintained at their official values by government intervention in the currency market. When a country's currency was in excess supply and therefore tending to depreciate (fall in value) relative to its par value with the dollar, its monetary authorities would buy up the excess supply, using its own dollar reserves or by borrowing dollars externally.[36] Similarly, when a country's currency was in excess demand, and therefore tending to appreciate (rise in value), its monetary authorities would buy up the excess by selling dollars.

Although firms had to consider the possibility of occasional currency value changes, the fixed exchange rate system made trading in the international arena more like domestic trade. If currency values were fixed, then trade could occur almost as if there were one world currency. However, the fixed exchange rate system broke down in 1971[37] and an attempt to resuscitate the system ended unsuccessfully in early 1973. No single international exchange rate system has since developed. Exchange rates between currencies have generally been much more flexible since the early 1970s than before.

Since the breakdown of fixed exchange rates, some countries have attempted to peg their currencies' values to the dollar or another currency unilaterally. Some have followed a policy of pegging their currencies' values relative to a basket or average of other currencies, rather than to any one currency. Some have intervened in currency markets in an attempt to smooth out currency fluctuations. Others have left it largely to demand and supply in the currency market to determine their exchange rates. The United States has generally followed such a *laissez-faire* strategy, with occasional episodes of intervention. In all likelihood, these diverse exchange rate policies will continue to characterize the international monetary system indefinitely.[38]

The result of greater exchange rate fluctuations has complicated decision making on where to produce, where to invest, and how to evaluate relative national labor costs. Many economists would argue that over long periods of time the particular exchange rate system in use is irrelevant. According to this view, international trade and investment will be governed eventually by the fundamentals of comparative cost.

The long run may be a long time in coming, however. In the meantime, exchange rates are likely to be of concern to firms operating in the international marketplace. Indeed, a significant part of future pressure for labor market flexibility in the United States and elsewhere is likely to be the result of exchange rate changes. Available evidence suggests that the foreign exchange market is vulnerable to speculative swings and other instabilities.[39]

Labor Costs and Exchange Rates.   Perhaps the most dramatic illustration of the importance of exchange rate changes was the experience of the United States in the 1980s. The dollar began appreciating relative to other currencies after 1980. Economists have attributed much of this appreciation to federal tax cuts and resulting budget deficits.[40] The federal budget deficit was a form of national dissaving that resulted in a sucking into the United States of net foreign saving. That is, Americans invested less abroad and foreigners invested more in the United States. Net demand for the dollar (to acquire claims on the United States) rose, causing dollar appreciation, thereby putting American exporters and import-competing firms at a substantial disadvantage.

When the dollar appreciated, American export prices rose as seen by foreigners in terms of their currencies. U.S. exports became less competitive on world markets and export performance deteriorated. From the American viewpoint, the prices of foreign imports measured in dollars fell, stimulating a switch from American products to foreign supplies. These trends can be seen in Figure 16–2, which illustrates the movements of real exports, real imports, and the real dollar exchange rate.[41]

Although the dollar reversed its upward course in early 1985, it had already sparked an ongoing debate concerning declining U.S. competitiveness and its HRM implications. Imports rose rapidly, and continued doing so even after the dollar's appreciation reversed. Exports stagnated during the dollar's rise, then began to increase again as the dollar's real exchange value fell.

Table 16–1 illustrates the impact of the appreciation of the U.S. dollar on foreign manufacturing wages in seven countries relative to American wages. During 1980 to 1985, American wages on a total compensation basis rose at 6% per annum, slower than the rate of wage inflation in six of the seven countries as measured in their own currencies. In six out of seven countries, local wages rose faster than U.S. wages in terms of real purchasing power. But the appreciation of the U.S. dollar caused foreign wages, *when translated into dollars*, to rise more

**FIGURE 16–2
Real Exchange
Rate, Exports,
Imports**

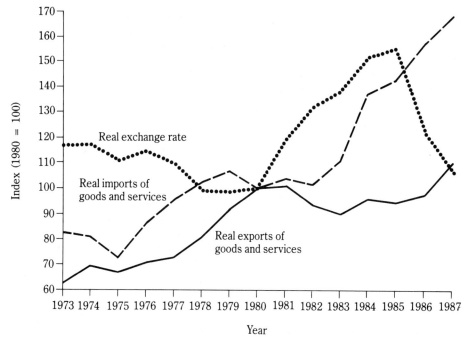

Year

Note: The real exchange rate is a weighted average of exchange rates of ten currencies relative to the U.S. dollar, each adjusted by national trends in consumer prices.

Source: Economic Report of the President, February 1988 (Washington: GPO, 1988), pp. 251, 371.

slowly than U.S. wages.[42] In fact, in five out of the six cases, foreign wages actually *declined* in dollar terms.

This situation dramatically reversed when the dollar declined in value during 1985 to 1987. The depreciating dollar pushed foreign wages, measured in dollars, up substantially. Wage inflation in the United States was quite moderate during this period, but the exchange rate dominated the relationship between U.S. and foreign wages.

Wage movements by themselves do not give a complete picture of shifts in competitiveness. Costs other than wages also are relevant, although, of course, such costs also will be influenced by exchange rates. Even when the focus is on labor costs, wages must be adjusted for productivity—as described earlier—to calculate unit labor costs. However, as Table 16–2 shows, during 1980 to 1985 unit labor costs (the ratio of the wage rate to productivity) fell in all but one of the countries listed when measured in U.S. dollars. The dollar appreciation is again the principal explanation of this development. Similarly, during 1985 to 1987, foreign unit labor costs rose rapidly relative to those in the United States because of dollar depreciation.

It is clear from Tables 16–1 and 16–2 that the loss of American competitiveness during 1980 to 1985 cannot be attributed to some failure of U.S. HRM practices. Despite all of the breast-beating about loss of the American work ethic, lack of labor–management cooperation, top-heavy supervision, and excessive

TABLE 16−1 **Exchange Rate Movements and Rates of Pay Change, Manufacturing, 1980−1987, Eight Developed Countries**

Country	Annualized Rate of Change, 1980–1985				Annualized Rate of Change, 1985–1987			
	Wages in Local Currency	U.S. Dollar per Local Currency Unit	Wages in U.S. Dollars	Real Wages*	Wages in Local Currency	U.S. Dollar per Local Currency Unit	Wages in U.S. Dollars	Real Wages*
United States	6.0%	—	6.0%	.4%	2.3%	—	2.3%	− .5%
Canada	8.2	− 3.1%	4.9	.7	4.2	1.5%	5.7	0.0
Japan	4.6	− 1.1	3.5	1.8	3.2	28.4	32.4	2.8
France	12.5	− 14.0	− 3.3	2.6	4.1	22.3	27.1	1.2
Germany, West	5.6	− 9.2	− 4.2	1.6	4.3	27.9	33.4	4.3
Italy	16.8	− 14.8	− .5	2.7	4.8	21.4	27.2	− .5
Sweden	9.7	− 13.2	− 4.8	.3	7.1	16.5	24.7	2.6
United Kingdom	8.9	− 11.0	− 3.1	1.5	7.9	12.4	21.3	4.0

Note: Wages refer to hourly compensation of production workers including wages, benefits, and payroll taxes.

*The real wage is the local wage divided by the local consumer price index.

Source: U.S. Bureau of Labor Statistics, press release USDL: 88–326, July 6, 1988.

American pay levels, the loss of U.S. competitiveness was due primarily to macroeconomic forces: dollar appreciation and federal budget deficits. To burden American HRM practitioners and practices with the blame for rising import competition is unfair and misleading. Similarly, it would be wrong to credit the increased competitiveness that appeared after 1985 to some startling HRM innovations. Overemphasis of short-term phenomena related to exchange rates diverts attention from longer range competitive issues that *do* have HRM implications.[43]

Relative Wages in the Long Run.   One of the long-term issues that arises in the international area is the ability of American firms to compete when wages are substantially below U.S. levels in much of the world. Will American wages be forced down to foreign levels by international competition? This question can be viewed from both an analytical and empirical perspective.

Economic analysis of international commerce sees trade in goods and trade in factors of production as potentially equivalent. If labor and capital did flow costlessly across international borders, there would be a tendency for factor prices to equalize around the world. In particular, as labor moved from low-wage to high-wage countries, the average level of wages would be bid down in the latter and up in the former. Indeed, high-wage countries often restrict in-migration to protect the wages of their resident labor forces from such direct competition.

Less obvious is the possibility that even without factor mobility, trade in

**TABLE 16-2   Trends in Manufacturing Unit Labor Costs, 1980-1987,
Eight Developed Countries**

	Annualized Percent Change in Unit Labor Costs	
Country	*1980-1985*	*1985-1987*
United States	1.7%	-1.0%
Canada	.8	5.0
Japan	-2.0	28.7
France	-6.8	23.6
Germany, West	-7.3	31.4
Italy	-5.6	24.4
Sweden	-8.3	23.0
United Kingdom	-8.4	15.8

Note: Figures refer to production workers.

Source: U.S. Bureau of Labor Statistics, press release USDL: 88-326, July 6, 1988.

goods could have much the same equalizing effect. If high-wage countries import goods from low-wage countries, labor from the low-wage countries is embodied in the imports. The imports displace labor that might have been used in the high-wage country to produce those goods in the absence of the imports. Thus, receiving goods from low-wage countries is similar to receiving labor from them, in terms of the impact on the labor market.[44]

Consider, for example, the inflow of cheap Mexican labor into the United States. Attempts by the United States to impede this flow provide a stimulus for U.S. firms to set up assembly plants just inside the Mexican border, and then import the assembled products into the United States.[45] In effect, if the people cannot come to the plant, the plant comes to the people. And if the people cannot be imported, the products that incorporate their labor can be. Of corse, the reverse is also true; exports of U.S. goods can be viewed as an embodied export of U.S. labor.

Some data do point to a tendency for foreign and U.S. wages to equalize. Table 16-3 shows manufacturing wages in the seven countries featured in previous tables as a percentage of U.S. wages. Foreign wages rose relative to American wages during the 1960s and 1970s. Although year-to-year figures jumped around with the end of fixed exchange rates in the early 1970s, it is nonetheless clear that a long-term wage convergence with the United States has occurred among developed countries.

During most of the period shown, this phenomenon did not come about because real wages in the United States were falling towards world levels. American real wages moved generally in line with American productivity during 1960

TABLE 16–3   Foreign Wages as Percent of American, Manufacturing Sector, 1980–1987, Eight Developed Countries

	Total Hourly Compensation as Percent of U.S. Level			
Country	*1960*	*1970*	*1980*	*1987*
United States	100%	100%	100%	100%
Canada	80	83	90	89
Japan	10	24	57	84
France	31	41	92	92
Germany, West	32	56	125	125
Italy	24	42	82	92
Sweden	45	70	126	112
United Kingdom	32	36	74	67

Note: Total compensation includes wages, benefits, and payroll taxes. Figures refer to production workers.

Source: Calculated from data appearing in U.S. Bureau of Labor Statistics, *Handbook of Labor Statistics,* bulletin 2217 (Washington: GPO, 1987), Table 133, and unpublished data provided by the U.S. Bureau of Labor Statistics for 1987.

to 1980. During those years, the tendency toward wage equalization in the developed world seemed to stem mainly from the faster rate of productivity growth abroad relative to that in the United States. The faster foreign productivity growth, in turn, was associated with rising foreign capital/labor ratios.[46]

In the 1980s as the dollar substantially appreciated, U.S. real wage growth did lag behind productivity. As discussed in a previous chapter, this period was an era of concessionary wage bargaining and a downward shift in American wage norms. Studies of earlier periods suggest that relative wage slippage in trade-impacted industries can result from foreign competition.[47]

The wage lag during the period of dollar appreciation, however, was not concentrated in manufacturing, the center of import competition, suggesting that product market pressure from the international sector was not the sole explanation. Also, concession bargaining was not disproportionately found in the trade sector. In fact, trade-sensitive industries were less prone to concessionary wage bargaining than others.[48]

Good wage data are less readily available for third-world countries than for developed countries. However, the picture of world wage convergence with the United States among the developed countries does not necessarily apply elsewhere. It is possible for less developed countries to show marked wage growth relative to the United States even if they start from low bases. (Note that in Table 16–3, Japan's relative manufacturing wage went from only 10% of the U.S. level in 1960 to 84% of the U.S. level by 1987.) Starting from a low base does mean, however, that wage catch-up will take a long time to occur—if it occurs at all.

Some very low-wage countries have featured wage growth faster than the United States; others have not.

The gaps between U.S. and third-world wages are large in absolute terms, as Table 16–4 illustrates.[49] Obviously, if a firm can obtain its capital abroad at the same cost as in the United States, and if all nonlabor production costs (adjusted for the cost of transportation) are the same as in the United States, the markedly lower wage in the third world will give production there a clear cost advantage. For certain kinds of assembly-intensive products, such as home electronic equipment, lower wages abroad have given the edge to foreign suppliers.

Yet it is often the case that nonlabor costs are not the same abroad as in the United States. In 1987, 63% of U.S. imports came from *developed* countries— not from low-wage third-world countries.[50] Although the fraction varies from year to year, it has shown no long-term downward trend, despite the well-publicized rise of export-oriented manufacturing in such Pacific rim countries as Taiwan, Korea, Singapore, and Hong Kong. Thus the proposition that the United States cannot compete unless its wage levels fall to third-world levels is not supported by the U.S. trade pattern. Certain U.S. industries cannot compete, however, and have drastically contracted in employment and production. These are industries in which labor costs are the major factor in production cost differentials.

Protection and Real Wages.　　While the notion of U.S. wages dropping to third-world levels is not plausible, it is possible that trade could have a retarding effect on real-wage growth. Economic theory has long featured models in which trade could lower real wages (and trade restrictions—such as tariffs and quotas—could raise them).[51] There is evidence that the United States has tended to provide tariff protection to industries intensive in the use of unskilled labor.[52] This tendency suggests an effort to protect the wages and employment of those most vulnerable

TABLE 16–4　Hourly Compensation Relative to the United States in Six Third-World Countries, Manufacturing, 1975–1987

	Hourly Compensation as Percent of U.S.		
Country	*1975*	*1980*	*1987*
Brazil	14%	14%	11%
Mexico	31	30	12
Hong Kong	12	15	16
South Korea	5	10	13
Singapore	13	15	18
Taiwan	6	10	17

Note: Figures refer to production workers.

Source: U.S. Bureau of Labor Statistics, unpublished data provided to the author.

to foreign competition, since through the 1970s, at least, it was the low-wage industry in the United States that was most prone to import competition.[53] However, the long term effect of protection on wages generally is difficult to pin down empirically. The proposition that protection could raise *some* people's wages is more definite.

Limits on foreign competition make possible higher domestic prices for protected items than would otherwise prevail. The greater profitability that protection permits is not necessarily going to be passed along to workers as higher wages. Protection directly affects the product market, not the labor market, and protected employers will not necessarily see any need for raising pay. If workers in a protected industry are represented by a collective bargaining agent, however, they may be able to obtain some of the "rents" afforded by protection in terms of higher wages. Indeed, the union involved may be a vocal proponent of the import restricting policy.

Tariffs, Quotas, and Wage Bargaining.   There are two basic kinds of explicit protective devices in use.[54] Tariffs are taxes on imports and are collected at the time of entry. The tariff/tax raises the landed price of foreign goods, making them less price competitive with domestic substitutes. Quotas, in contrast, place an absolute limit on the number of imported items that will be permitted to enter the domestic market. Once the quota is sold out, domestic suppliers no longer face foreign competition and are therefore free to increase their own prices. Tariffs are administered by the importing country, whose government collects the resulting revenue. Quotas may be administered by the importing country, but are sometimes handled by foreign exporting countries under the terms of "orderly marketing agreements."[55]

Even though tariffs restrict foreign competition, they do not eliminate it. Domestic producers are limited in how much they can raise prices by the potential attraction of more imports. As the domestic price is raised, the alternative foreign price—even with the added tariff—looks more and more attractive to consumers. The absolute quantitative restriction under a quota, in contrast, eliminates such competition. Once the quota is exhausted, domestic consumers cannot buy the foreign alternative at any price.

To the extent that unions can bargain for a share of the gains from protection in terms of higher pay, they will probably prefer quotas to tariffs. The passing along of wage increases into prices will be easier if the volume of foreign sales is absolutely limited. Indeed, American unions have generally pushed for quotalike quantitative limits on imports rather than for tariffs.[56]

Usually, the union motivation in seeking protection is a mix of both pay and employment objectives. The union seeks to prevent job loss of its members from import competition as well as to protect its bargaining position. In principle, job protecting could be done as well by tariffs as by quotas. Job protection via tariffs, however, is more complex, since foreign sales will be determined by (unknown) demand elasticities, exchange rates, and the (uncertain) reaction of domestic pricing to the tariff. Quotas, in contrast, fix the number of foreign units sold, making their effects more definite. Thus unions are likely to prefer quotas to tariffs, regardless of the mix of their pay versus employment motivations.

Often unions and management—even if they have trouble agreeing on other issues—see eye to eye on the need for protection from imports. But this agreement is not always total; sometimes their views diverge—for example, the firms involved may be multinationals and may be in a position to import themselves; or, because they have operations abroad, they may be fearful of triggering a trade war between the U.S. and other countries, which could hurt their affiliates.[57] Firms are tied to a domestic industry by capital investments; unions and workers have stakes in the industry that have been stressed in previous chapters. Sometimes the tie embodied in the latter stake is stronger than that engendered by past capital investments. Thus unions may sometimes be stronger advocates of protection for particular products than the firms that make them. Indeed, in some cases they may be the only advocate.

16–4   HRM and International Competitiveness

HRM policies cannot be held accountable for the sharp loss of American competitiveness in the early 1980s, as has been stressed. The blame for that loss falls on macroeconomic policies—mainly the federal budget deficit—and on exchange rates. Over the long run, however, American HRM practices—both at the firm level and in terms of public policy—can influence competitiveness. Competitiveness, in turn, will ultimately influence the American standard of living.

As economists would be quick to note, under a flexible exchange rate system, exchange rate adjustments will occur to equate supply and demand for the U.S. dollar. If at the prevailing exchange rate, American exports fall short of imports and if foreigners are unwilling to hold the resulting increments of claims on the United States, the exchange value of the dollar will fall until demand and supply for it are again equated.

Equilibrium of a sort is thus guaranteed, even if U.S. competitiveness declines. Falling real exchange rates, however, tend to reduce American living standards in two ways. First, such depreciations are usually accompanied by declines in the "terms of trade," the ratio of export prices to import prices.[58] Such terms of trade deteriorations mean that—with a unit of exports worth less in relative terms—it takes more American resources to buy a unit of imports. Seen from the viewpoint of the typical employee, this means declining real wages measured in terms of imports and import-competing goods, at least in the short run.

Second, long term declines in U.S. competitiveness are likely to show up as problems for the manufacturing sector. If the manufacturing sector weakens both as a source of exports and of import-competing goods, the U.S. overall pattern of production will shift toward agriculture and primary products (to pay for imports and interest on America's net debt to foreigners). Employment opportunities in manufacturing will be reduced, and employment will thus tilt toward the lower wage sectors of the economy.

Deterioration of the U.S. trade balance during the first half of the 1980s contributed to such developments, although it was not the only cause. Were such a process to continue indefinitely, it would act as a long-term retardant on real-wage growth and therefore on overall living standards. Rising anger over foreign competition and import displacement could trigger a protectionist movement in Congress. Sliding American competitiveness on world markets could thus have unfortunate consequences in the area of international relations and foreign policy, as well as on the domestic economy.

Trade Adjustment Assistance: Background

Even in the best of circumstances, some industries will be losers in the international marketplace. As already noted, there are certain industries in which labor costs are the main element of cost competition. Third-world countries, with labor costs ranging from a tenth to a third of American levels, are going to have an advantage that will be very hard to overcome in such cases. Some U.S. workers will be displaced as a result.

The United States has had a program of trade adjustment assistance (TAA) for workers and firms injured by foreign competition since the early 1960s. Adopted when U.S. manufacturing was heavily export-oriented, originally this program was enacted to obtain labor support for wide-ranging trade legislation. The Trade Expansion Act of 1962, a bill strongly supported by the Kennedy administration, provided for presidential negotiation of tariff reductions with the recently formed European Common Market and with other countries. At the time, the AFL-CIO generally supported the bill but needed a provision to assist those affiliates experiencing import problems.[59]

Under the Trade Expansion Act, the worker component of trade adjustment assistance was supposed to provide supplements to unemployment compensation and funds for retraining to displaced workers who could show that their displacement was due to imports. The imports, in turn, had to be attributable to a concession, for example, a tariff reduction, made by the United States. Proving the cause-and-effect relationships, however, proved exceedingly difficult, and no TAA petitions were approved until the early 1970s.[60]

Congress again considered the adjustment assistance issue in 1974. At that time the president again sought legislative authority to negotiate with foreign countries for further reductions in international trade barriers. By then, imports were perceived as a threat to important elements of manufacturing, and—in particular—by organized labor, which had heavy concentrations of members in that sector. A liberalized TAA program was included in the authorization bill, mainly in the hope of blunting labor's opposition, rather than of gaining its support.[61]

The new TAA provision eased the requirements for proving cause-and-effect links between imports and displacement, and dropped the requirement that the imports had to be due to a trade concession by the United States. As a result a substantial increase in approvals of petitions for TAA occurred, and by the early 1980s TAA had become a major factor in government policy toward displaced workers.

In fiscal year 1980 almost 685,000 workers were certified by the U.S. Department of Labor as eligible for benefits, at a cost of over $1.6 billion.[62] Thereafter, substantial restrictions were placed on the program by the Reagan administration, which initially hoped to do away with TAA entirely. Congress balked at a complete elimination, and the program was kept alive until the mid-1980s, when it was again expanded. Legislation enacted in early 1986 extended the program through 1991.[63]

Issues Surrounding Trade Adjustment Assistance

TAA raises an issue of equity. Under its provisions, a worker displaced by foreign competition is eligible for special government assistance.[64] An identical worker displaced by domestic competition is not eligible.[65] This peculiarity results from the political motivation of TAA; it has been viewed as a device to foster adoption of trade liberalizing bills by Congress—or to fend off protectionist legislation. In effect it has been a tool to buy off opposition to trade liberalization from adversely affected groups.

Usually the political motivation behind TAA has not been stated so baldly. Arguments have been made that since "society" has determined that a liberal trade policy is generally beneficial, a kind of social contract is established whereby those who are hurt (so that others may gain) should be compensated. It has also been noted that trade-dislocated workers tend to be older than average, with low levels of education and skill. They have been characterized as having greater difficulties than other workers in finding new employment after displacement.[66] Thus trade-displaced workers have been portrayed as more deserving of assistance than others.

If—despite these rationales—TAA is viewed primarily as a political device, concerns about its actual effectiveness in aiding the displaced are not likely to receive substantial attention. Indeed, TAA as actually implemented has been criticized as featuring slow processing of applications and delays in providing training to those who receive eligibility certifications. Even when the program was at its height, it was found lacking in actually helping displaced workers to readjust and in targeting those workers who most needed assistance.[67]

TAA has also been criticized for weakening, rather than strengthening, the motivation for trade-displaced workers to adjust to available opportunities. By extending unemployment insurance benefit payments, it is said, TAA creates an incentive to delay the inevitable, that is, to prolong the period of unemployment.[68] Since individuals whose employments are displaced by imports have empirically been prone to long durations of joblessness,[69] further delays in adjustment can compound the problem. One suggestion has been to condition TAA on receipt of a new job, and then make the payment according to a formula that compensates for any reduction of wages that has occurred.[70] Such a system would not preclude provision of a training or mobility allowance to assist in finding employment.

However, particularly during periods of high unemployment, Congress may be reluctant to eliminate ongoing income support payments from TAA.

Employment Security

One criticism of American business practices in the face of international competition is that U.S. firms are too quick to retreat. Consider the comments of economist Lester C. Thurow, dean of the Sloan School of Management at M.I.T.:

> Every country has a comparative advantage—the thing it does best. . . . What American firms do best is go out of business. . . . No one goes out of business faster or with less regret than American firms.[71]

Thurow argues that in other countries, employers are less free to lay off workers, either by law or custom. Going out of a line of business because of foreign competition involves costly payments to employees or costly placement of them in other jobs. As a result they continue seeking competitive strategies aimed at world markets rather than retreat from the field. Thurow views Japanese firms as taking an offensive strategy; they seek to regain leadership in markets in which they are slipping or threatening to slip. He sees European firms as adopting defensive postures, seeking to hold on to their market shares, but not necessarily striving for leadership.

American firms, Thurow suggests, face relatively low costs of layoff. Even if employees have economic stakes in their jobs, the implicit contracts involved are not legally enforceable. Moreover, Thurow argues, American firms know that their European and Japanese competitors are unlikely to drop out of a market because of their employment commitments. This knowledge makes it all the more likely that the American firm will withdraw. Finally, Thurow proposes, if for some reason the current management of an American firm is reluctant to abandon a market, takeover artists will assume control of the firm and do the job for them, probably ridding themselves of the incumbent managers along the way.

How valid is the Thurow critique? Experts would undoubtedly want to make many qualifications and would consider Thurow's position overstated or incomplete. Foreign firms do not literally protect every job. Moreover, the economic slump of the early 1980s and subsequent employment stagnation in Europe triggered a greater willingness to restructure industry abroad than had previously existed.[72]

The asymmetric reaction of the U.S. balance of trade to the appreciation and then depreciation of the dollar, however, is supportive of Thurow's view. When the dollar appreciated after 1980, the U.S. trade balance quickly and markedly deteriorated (as would be expected); imports increased substantially relative to exports. When the dollar depreciated after early 1985, however, the reverse did not occur; the U.S. trade balance did not quickly and markedly improve. Although exports did pick up, it nevertheless appeared that U.S. firms were not standing by, ready to recoup lost markets quickly when the opportunity reappeared.[73]

The interrelationship between a company's policies regarding the HRM area and its basic business strategy is highlighted by the Thurow proposition. Internal policies with regard to employment security constrain and condition the degree to which the firm is tied to particular lines of production. The more employment security is offered, the more labor becomes like a fixed cost. The more labor is like a fixed cost, the cheaper it is to continue production, even in the face of adverse market conditions. Using labor that would otherwise remain idle on the payroll involves a very low marginal cost.

Compensation Systems

In an earlier chapter it was noted that the form of compensation can be an important element in defining the employer–employee relationship. A flexible compensation arrangement, such as profit sharing, can make it easier for firms to provide employment security in the face of fluctuating product market conditions. If the expansion of the international marketplace poses more uncertainty for firms, then consideration of the compensation system is clearly warranted.

Share arrangements shift some of the risks of the product market into the labor market, that is, onto the employees. A willingness to remain in the product market—even in the event of adverse competitive conditions—becomes less costly for the firm. That willingness is linked to job security. Share systems recognize that although the employees have an investment stake in the firm, the value of their stake, like that of ordinary investors, depends on the economic conditions facing the firm. There is evidence that where capital market deregulation occurs, and a greater focus is placed on short-term profitability, wage flexibility is forced to increase.[74]

Considerable Western interest has been expressed in the Japanese semiannual bonus payment system for employees. As illustrated in Table 16–5, Japan has exhibited very low unemployment rates, even in recession, and relatively little fluctuation in unemployment.[75] It has been argued that the bonus system—which has elements of profit sharing—is one factor that permits Japanese firms (and therefore the Japanese economy) to absorb external demand shocks more easily than firms elsewhere.[76]

Japan is not the only country to show a low unemployment rate in Table 16–5, however. Sweden, a country that does not have a Japanese-style bonus system, also stands out. Both Sweden and Japan have relatively homogeneous labor forces, a factor that helps keep the absolute level of unemployment down. Sweden has had a long history of welfare state programs aimed at holding down unemployment through retraining, subsidies to encourage mobility, and so on.

The countries that showed the worst record in the 1980s are certain Western European countries that seemed unable to pull themselves out of the slump that began in the early years of the decade. In some cases these are the countries with official and semiofficial restrictions on layoffs, but without flexible compensation systems and without Swedish-style adjustment programs. As has already been noted, *external* restrictions on the right to lay off can translate into reluctance to hire, especially in an uncertain economy.[77]

A system of self-imposed reluctance to lay off, combined with a flexible,

TABLE 16–5   Civilian Unemployment Rates in Eight Developed Countries, 1979–1987

	Rate of Unemployment		
Country	1979	1982	1987
United States	5.8%	9.7%	6.2%
Canada	7.4	11.0	8.9
Japan	2.1	2.4	2.9
France	6.0	8.3	11.1
Germany, West	3.0	5.8	6.9
Italy	4.4	5.4	7.9
Sweden	2.1	3.1	1.9
United Kingdom	5.4	11.3	10.3

Note: Unemployment data have been adjusted to American definitions.

Source: Monthly Labor Review, vol. 111 (June 1988), p. 107.

share-type pay system seems less likely to restrict hiring than the Western European model. Workers have a stake in the firm, which is recognized, but the value of that stake is not rigidly set and reflects prevailing economic circumstances. The entrepreneurial element of compensation is in keeping with an aggressive stance in the product market rather than a defensive posture or a willingness to drop out in hard times.

Productivity: The International Setting

Productivity is a key variable in determining competitiveness. In absolute terms a productivity advantage can offset the cost disadvantage of a higher wage by bringing down unit labor costs. In terms of trends higher rates of productivity improvement can make possible rising real wages without eroding a country's competitive position.

Absolute Productivity Differentials.   It is extremely difficult to obtain data on absolute productivity differentials by industrial sector across countries. A very crude all-sector measure is simply GNP per employee.[78] In the mid-1980s GNP per employee in northern Europe and Japan generally fell into a range of 75% to 95% of the American level. British and Italian GNPs per employee were about 60% of the U.S. level. South Korea's GNP per employee was about one-sixth the American level.

In absolute terms the United States has thus been able to offset its higher wages—compared with those of other countries—with higher productivity. Its ability to enjoy such an offset has fallen over the long term, however, as other nations catch up in productivity levels. As Table 16–6 shows, the long-run rate of productivity *growth* in U.S. manufacturing has been slower than those of its developed competitors. Thus absolute differentials have narrowed.

Productivity Catch-Up. That there should be a catch-up in productivity is not surprising. Before World War II American productivity was substantially higher than that of other developed countries, due to heavier capitalization and the application of the most modern technology. For example, a study of American versus British productivity as of the late 1930s revealed that U.S. output per worker was more than twice the British level in such products as radio equipment, automobiles, glass containers, and paper. It was 1.4 to 2 times higher in cotton goods, cigarettes, hosiery, footwear, and beer production.[79] Damage to European and Japanese industrial plants during World War II added to the American productivity advantage.

But the effects of wartime damage were not permanent. The damage was eventually repaired, and newer vintage capital equipment (embodying the latest technological advances) replaced what was lost in the war. Rates of investment abroad moved foreign capital-to-labor ratios up towards American levels. Even though the United States emerged in the postwar period as a principal source of technological innovation, the technology could be—and was—transmitted to other countries.

Of the eight countries shown in Table 16–6, the United States exhibited the slowest manufacturing productivity growth rate during 1960 to 1987. In the 1980s the rising dollar and resulting international competition put special pressure on the United States to improve its productivity performance. U.S. produc-

TABLE 16–6 **Trends in Manufacturing Output per Hour in Eight Developed Countries, 1960–1987**

Country	*Annualized Percent Change in Output per Hour*			
	1960–1973	*1973–1979*	*1979–1987*	*1960–1987*
United States	3.2%	1.4%	3.4%	2.8%
Canada	4.5	2.1	2.2	3.3
Japan	10.3	5.5	5.1	7.7
France	6.5	4.8	3.2	5.1
Germany, West	5.8	4.3	2.6	4.5
Italy	7.5	3.3	4.6	5.7
Sweden	6.4	2.6	2.9	4.5
United Kingdom	4.2	1.2	4.7	3.7

Source: U.S. Bureau of Labor Statistics, press release USDL: 88–326, July 6, 1988.

tivity in manufacturing rose relative to the American service sector, which was not as directly affected by foreign competition.[80]

Unexplained Slippage.   All countries, not just the United States, experienced a productivity slowdown after 1973. It appears that the slowdown abroad, as in the United States, cannot be fully explained by measuring changes in capital and labor inputs. The available evidence suggests, however, that in the United States, the unexplained element in the slowdown was larger than those of Western Europe and Japan.[81]

It would be unfair, especially since the cause of the slowdown is not fully known, to blame HRM practices in the United States for the American slippage since 1973. On the other hand, the possibility of *improvements* in HRM as a way of accelerating the American productivity trend relative to other countries ought not to be neglected. The most positive approach is to look at the record of past productivity performance as both a challenge to HRM professionals and an opportunity.

Alternative HRM Strategies.   Competition from the foreign sector is going to be a continuing factor in transforming the American industrial scene. In theory the United States could insulate itself from the external economy through tariffs, quotas, and similar arrangements. Although there may be swings in the degree of protection afforded to U.S. firms, there is little likelihood that the United States will simply opt out of international competition. Just as firms are forced by foreign competition to reexamine their strategies in marketing, production, and product development, so must they reconsider their HRM policies.

The possibility of fostering a longer term, although more flexible, linkage with employees has been stressed in previous sections. In such a relationship there must be greater pay flexibility and greater flexibility in the use of employees. One model of flexibility in employee deployment is simply to hire and fire employees as different needs arise. For reasons stressed earlier, such a system is likely to produce disincentives for job-related investments in training. An alternative model features job security, flexible pay, and generalized training on the job, aimed at producing multiskilled workers who can be redeployed as market demands change.[82]

HRM and Changes in World Production Patterns.   There is no single answer for all industries. In some cases the hire/fire model, combined with use of temporaries, part-timers, and other loosely linked employees, may prove to be the best approach from the employer's viewpoint. These will be industries in which a heavy training commitment is not required for production. Note, however, that such industries are likely to be characterized by low-wage and low-skill workers.

Industries of that variety, if exposed to international trade, are extremely vulnerable to low-wage competition from developing countries. In the United States, such industries will at best be import-competing, not export leaders. At worst, even with the flexibility inherent in a hire/fire approach, they may nevertheless be uneconomic. Thus the search for HRM innovations that foster international competitiveness is unlikely to produce fruitful results in these sectors.

Studies of American trade patterns suggest that among the sources of U.S.

comparative advantage is the relative abundance of skilled workers in the United States. When compared with its imports, American exports have historically been more intensive in the use of skilled labor and less intensive in the use of unskilled labor.[83] The biggest contrast in labor utilization, however, is not between U.S. exports and imports, but between the trade sector (both exports and imports) and the rest of the economy. Because of the manufacturing orientation of trade, it uses more production workers and production-related professionals (for example, engineers) and fewer service-sector oriented occupations such as clerical work.

Industries with trade-linked occupations, particularly those that are not inherently dependent on low-wage, unskilled workers, have the most to gain from considering alternatives to the hire/fire model. One projection of likely future world industrial development (discussed in a previous chapter) is identified with Michael J. Piore and Charles F. Sabel.[84] They argue that mass production industries will give way to those employing flexible specialization. There will be more custom-designed products, according to this view, facilitated by computer technology and (re)programmable machines. The driving force behind this shift, Piore and Sabel argue, is that in the developed world, rising prosperity in the post–World War II era has saturated the market for mass-produced consumer goods. The successful competitor, therefore, is the one who finds market niches and who continues to innovate in product development and design.

What are the implications of such a shift in the mode of production for HRM? One is a need for flexible pay arrangements, as discussed above, since a firm constantly turning out new and revised products cannot count on continuous prosperity. A second is a need for broadly skilled workers, capable of shifting job tasks and collaborating with technicians.[85] An open question is the optimum scale of production under flexible specialization. If custom production means smaller firms, the ability of any one firm to pay for the overhead entailed in an active HRM function is reduced. In effect, therefore, the HRM function must itself become more productive, performing its role with less bureaucracy and cost.

Summary

It is appropriate to close this volume with a chapter on the international aspects of HRM. Until the 1980s many of the topics discussed in this chapter—exchange rates, international comparative labor costs, and productivity—would not have been thought appropriate for an HRM text. To the extent that an international component entered the discussion, it would simply be a comparison of how similar HRM functions were carried out in various countries. But with the greater integration of the world economy, HRM cannot stand apart from international market trends.

Although HRM interest can no longer be confined solely to variations in practice from country to country, there is still much to be said for the international comparative approach. The fact that practices do vary—that the same function can be carried out in many different ways—is important. It is a reminder not to take national characteristics as given. Perhaps that is the most crucial lesson to be learned: there is a menu of HRM practices available, and no one country has a permanent lock on the best approach to HRM problems. While national traditions and culture may limit the choice on the menu, there are always options and alternatives available.

EXERCISES

Problem

Select a country in which you have an interest. Draw up an HRM profile, statistical and descriptive, from the international sources described in this chapter. Compare the long-run trends in productivity growth and labor costs in your selected country with those of the United States. What factors explain the differences between the United States and your chosen country? If you have an interest in a particular industry, repeat this process (obtaining as much information as you can) for the industry in your selected country and in the United States.

Questions

1. What key differences can be cited between foreign and U.S. practices with regard to union–management relations?

2. Employers abroad have called for greater flexibility in the labor market. What types of flexibility are being sought?

3. What important differences can be cited between U.S. and foreign practices with regard to determination of employee benefits and working conditions?

4. Why are exchange rates of concern to HRM managers? How might movements in exchange rates be relevant to the choice of compensation system?

5. What are the areas of common and divergent interests of employees and employers with regard to protective measures such as tariffs and quotas?

6. Why have unions been more likely to prefer quotas over tariffs as a form of protection?

Terms

codetermination
extension of labor
   agreements
flexible specialization
incomes policy

International Labour
   Organisation
international trade
   secretariats

quality circles
trade adjustment assistance
unit labor costs
works councils

ENDNOTES

1. See, for example, Hervey Juris, Mark Thompson, and Wilbur Daniels, eds., *Industrial Relations in a Decade of Economic Change* (Madison, Wisc.: Industrial Relations Research Association, 1985); Greg J. Bamber and Russell D. Lansbury, eds., *International and Comparative Industrial Relations: A Study of Developed Market Economies* (Boston: Allen & Unwin, 1987).

2. Since historically foreign firms have not been permitted to operate in communist countries, except under very limited circumstances, discussion of HRM practices in those countries is not included. However, changes toward more market-oriented policies in China and the Soviet Union may lead to greater economic interaction with western countries. For references, see Lucie Cheng and Siwei Cheng, "Human Resource Management in the People's Republic of China" in Eric G. Flamholtz and T.K. Das, eds., *Human Resource Management and Productivity,* volume II, International Perspectives (Los Angeles: UCLA Institute of Industrial Relations, 1985), pp. 97–116; I.B. Helburn and John C. Shearer, "Human Resources and Industrial Relations in China: A Time of Ferment," *Industrial and Labor Relations Review,* vol. 38 (October 1984), pp. 3–15; Emily Clark Brown, *Soviet Trade Unions and Labor Relations* (Cambridge, Mass.: Harvard University Press, 1966); Arcadius Kahan and Blair A. Ruble, eds., *Industrial Labor in the U.S.S.R.* (New York: Pergamon Press, 1979); Ichak Adizes, *Industrial Democracy: Yugoslav Style; The Effect of Decentralization on Organizational Behavior* (New York: Free Press, 1971).

3. The differences between the American labor movement and those abroad with regard to political orientation are sufficiently marked that scholars refer to American exceptionalism, in effect labeling the U.S. case as an aberration.

4. Daniel J.B. Mitchell, "The Australian Labor Market" in Richard E. Caves and Lawrence B. Krause, eds., *The Australian Economy: A View from the North* (Washington: Brookings Institution, 1984), pp. 127–193.

5. Henry P. Guzda, "Industrial Democracy: Made in the U.S.A.," *Monthly Labor Review,* vol. 107 (May 1984), pp. 26–33.

6. U.S. Department of Labor, Bureau of Labor-Management Relations and Cooperative Programs, *U.S. Labor Law and the Future of Labor-Management Cooperation: Second Interim Report—A Working Document* (Washington: U.S. Department of Labor, 1987).

7. Robert J. Flanagan, David Soskice, Lloyd Ulman, *Unionism, Economic Stabilization, and Incomes Policies: European Experience* (Washington: Brookings Institution, 1983).

8. Michael Wallerstein, "Union Centralization and Trade Dependence: The Origins of Democratic Corporatism," working paper no. 126, Institute of Industrial Relations, UCLA, July 1987.

9. Daniel J.B. Mitchell, *Essays on Labor and International Trade* (Los Angeles: UCLA Institute of Industrial Relations, 1970), chapter 4.

10. Herbert R. Northrup and Richard L. Rowan, "Multinational Collective Bargaining Activity: The Factual Record in Chemicals, Glass, and Rubber Tires, Part I and II" *Columbia Journal of World Business,* vol. 9 (Spring 1974 and Summer 1974), pp. 112–124 and 49–63, respectively; Herbert R. Northrup, "Why Multinational Bargaining Neither Exists Nor is Desirable," *Labor Law Journal,* vol. 29 (June 1978), pp. 330–342.

11. Jacques Rojot, *International Collective Bargaining: An Analysis and Case Study for Europe* (Deventer, Holland: Kluwer, 1978).

12. Jack Barbash, Discussion of "U.S. Industrial Relations in Transition: A Summary Report" in Barbara D. Dennis, ed., *Proceedings of the Thirty-Seventh Annual Meeting,* Industrial Relations Research Association, December 28–30, 1984 (Madison, Wisc.: IRRA, 1985), pp. 292–293.

13. Lloyd Ulman, "Who Wanted Collective Bargaining in the First Place?" in Barbara D. Dennis, ed., *Proceedings of the Thirty-Ninth Annual Meeting,* Industrial Relations Research Association, December 28–30, 1986 (Madison, Wisc.: IRRA, 1987), pp. 1–13.

14. John J. Lawler, "Union Growth and Decline: The Impact of Employer and Union Tactics," *Journal of Occupational Psychology,* vol. 59 (1986), pp. 217–230.

15. Third-world countries often are unable or unwilling to enforce the labor standards legislation they enact. Smaller employers may operate outside the standards, while larger, visible (often foreign-owned) enterprises comply. See Rafael Alburquerque, "Minimum Wage Administration in Latin America," *Comparative Labor Law,* vol. 6 (Winter 1984), pp. 57–66.

16. The motivation behind this pressure was to blunt criticism of labor exploitation as a source of trade advantage. See Steve Charnovitz, "Fair Labor Standards and International Trade," *Journal of World Trade Law,* vol. 20 (January-February 1986), pp. 61–78.

17. Richard S. Belous, *An International Comparison of Fringe Benefits: Theory, Evidence, and Policy Implications,* report 84–815 E (Washington: Congressional Research Service, 1984).

18. Oliver Clarke, "The Work Ethic: An International Perspective" in Jack Barbash, Robert J. Lampman, Sar A. Levitan, and Gus Tyler, eds., *The Work Ethic—A Critical Analysis* (Madison, Wisc.: Industrial Relations Research Association, 1983), pp. 121–150, especially pp. 139–141.

19. Mark W. Frankena and Paul A. Pautler, *Antitrust Policy for Declining Industries* (Washington: Bureau of Economics, Federal Trade Commission, 1985).

20. For some examples, see Charles F. Sabel, Gary Herrigel, Richard Kavis, and Richard Deeg, "How to Keep Mature Industries Innovative," *Technology Review,* vol. 90 (April 1987), pp. 27–35.

21. Although the United States first joined the ILO in 1934, it rarely ratified any ILO conventions. Most of those few that were ratified dealt with maritime labor standards, a clearly international issue. Reluctance to ratify other standards was based on a feeling in Congress that a loss of sovereignty over internal policy might result. The United States withdrew from the ILO in the late 1970s in protest over anti-Israeli actions taken by the organization and alleged pro-communist bias on other matters. It rejoined in 1980. In 1988, the United States ratified two ILO conventions, one dealing with a non-maritime issue. This action was seen as a change in policy regarding the sovereignty issue by the United States. For further information, see Tadd Linsenmayer, "U.S. Ends ILO Moratorium by Ratifying Two Conventions," *Monthly Labor Review,* vol. 111 (June 1988), pp. 52–53; and Joseph P. Goldberg, "The Landmark Provisions of the Ratified ILO Conventions," *Monthly Labor Review,* vol. 111 (June 1988), pp. 53–55.

22. James N. Ellenberger, "Japanese Management: Myth or Magic," *American Federationist,* vol. 89 (April-June 1982), pp. 3–12; Satoshi Kamata, *Japan in the Passing Lane: An Insider's Account of Life in a Japanese Auto Factory* (New York: Pantheon Books, 1982). The latter was reviewed in *Time* as a "powerful indictment" of Japanese HRM practices ("Bleak House," *Time,* February 14, 1983, p. 62).

23. Benjamin Aaron, ed., *Labor Courts and Grievance Settlement in Western Europe* (Berkeley, Calif.: University of California Press, 1971); Jack Stieber, "Protection Against Unfair Dismissal: A Comparative View," *Comparative Labor Law,* vol. 3 (Spring 1980), pp. 229–240.

24. The insider/outsider approach has been discussed in earlier chapters. See Assar Lindbeck and Dennis Snower, "Cooperation, Harassment, and Involuntary Unemployment: An Insider-Outsider Approach," *American Economic Review,* vol. 78 (March 1988), pp. 167–188.

25. Organisation for Economic Cooperation and Development, *Flexibility in the Labor Market: The Current Debate* (Paris: OECD, 1986); Guy Standing, "Labor Surplus and Labor Flexibility: A European Perspective" in Howard Rosen, ed., *Job Generation: U.S. and European Perspectives* (Salt Lake City: National Council on Employment

Policy, 1986), pp. 23–55. European union leaders prefer the word *adaptability* to *flexibility* because the latter term in Europe has taken on a management-orientation. "European Labor and Management Welcome Switch from 'Flexibility' to 'Adaptability' Bargaining," *Daily Labor Report,* October 26, 1987, pp. C1–C2.

26. Martin Vranken, "Deregulating the Employment Relationship: Current Trends in Europe," *Comparative Labor Law,* vol. 7 (Winter 1986), pp. 143–165.

27. The OECD has its headquarters in Paris, and the ILO in Geneva. However, both organizations have sales representatives in Washington, D.C. University libraries are likely to carry both OECD and ILO publications.

28. See, for example, Peter H. Lindert, *International Economics,* eighth edition (Homewood, Ill.: Irwin, 1986).

29. James C. Hartigan and Edward Tower, "Trade Policy and the American Income Distribution," *Review of Economics and Statistics,* vol. 64 (May 1982), pp. 261–270.

30. *Survey of Current Business,* vol. 68 (July 1988), p. 40.

31. *Survey of Current Business,* vol. 68 (July 1988), pp. 78, 81.

32. Ned G. Howenstine, "U.S. Affiliates of Foreign Companies: Operations in 1986," *Survey of Current Business,* vol. 68 (May 1988), p. 60; Obie G. Wichard, "U.S. Multinational Companies: Operations in 1986," *Survey of Current Business,* vol. 68 (June 1988), p. 85.

33. R. Hal Mason, Robert R. Miller, and Dale R. Weigel, *International Business,* second edition (New York: Wiley, 1981), pp. 416–417.

34. U.S. Bureau of Labor-Management Relations and Cooperative Programs of the U.S. Department of Labor, *New United Motor Manufacturing, Inc., and the United Automobile Worker: Partners in Training,* labor–management cooperation brief no. 10, March 1987.

35. Bretton Woods is a town in New Hampshire at which a major international monetary conference was held in 1944, during World War II. By that time, the allied powers were beginning to plan for the nature of the postwar economy.

36. The International Monetary Fund (IMF) was created after World War II as a financial intermediary whereby countries with balance of payments surpluses could—through complicated mechanisms—lend to deficit countries. The IMF has been modified since its original creation, and it now plays a somewhat different role in international monetary affairs. In addition, other means of borrowing reserves were developed in the post–World War II period.

37. The reasons for the breakdown are complex and need not be developed here. In essence, fixed exchange rate systems require a great deal of international cooperation and coordination of domestic economic policies. Otherwise, currency values are threatened by chronic excess demand or

supply. The U.S. dollar was in chronic excess supply during the late 1960s and early 1970s, and the Nixon administration was unwilling to apply the painful domestic austerity policies that would have been necessary to maintain the fixed exchange rate system.

38. The journal *International Financial Statistics* carries a monthly listing of national currency policies.

39. Jeffrey R. Shafer and Bonnie E. Loopesko, "Floating Exchange Rates After Ten Years," *Brookings Papers on Economic Activity* (1:1983), pp. 1–70.

40. *Economic Report of the President, January 1987* (Washington: GPO, 1987), p. 111.

41. Real exports and imports are the values of exports and imports of goods and services as reported in the national income accounts, divided by the relevant price deflators. The real exchange rate refers to a Federal Reserve Board index of exchange rates of ten major currencies with the U.S. dollar. It is adjusted to take account of relative inflation in the United States and the other countries. To understand this adjustment, if the dollar appreciates 10% relative to another country's currency, the impact on U.S. competitiveness can only be measured if the rate of inflation there relative to the United States is known. Suppose that prices in the United States rise by 4% and prices in the foreign country rise by 6%. Then, as an approximation, the real appreciation of the dollar was actually only 8% [10% − (6% − 4%)]. That is, American prices seen by the foreign buyer rose by the 10% appreciation plus the 4% inflation for a total of 14%. However, the foreigner must compare the 14% dollar price increase with the 6% home price rise. The difference is a net relative price shift of 8% in favor of foreign suppliers.

42. Note that the appreciation of the dollar during 1980 to 1985 appears in the table as a negative number, since the number of dollars per unit of foreign currency decreased. Similarly, the depreciation of the dollar during 1985–1987 appears with a positive sign in the table.

43. For more analysis of these issues, see Robert Z. Lawrence and Robert E. Litan, "The Protectionist Prescription: Errors in Diagnosis and Cure," and Paul R. Krugman and Richard E. Baldwin, "The Persistence of the U.S. Trade Deficit," *Brookings Papers on Economic Activity* (1:1987), pp. 289–310, and 1–43, respectively.

44. Readers who have studied international trade will recognize that the text is alluding to the Samuelson factor-price equalization theorem. This theorem, which originally evolved out of the so-called Heckscher-Ohlin model of international trade, is discussed in Lindert, *International Economics, op. cit.,* chapter 4.

45. It also provides a stimulus for the Mexican government to provide economic incentives for firms to build border plants, so as to offer employment to the native population.

46. Daniel J.B. Mitchell, "International Convergence with U.S. Wage Levels" in Barbara D. Dennis, ed., *Proceedings of the Thirty-Sixth Annual Meeting,* Industrial Relations Research Association, December 28–30, 1983, pp. 247–255. Of course, there were other influences on foreign productivity than just capital/labor ratios.

47. Ann C. Orr and James A. Orr, "Employment Adjustments in Import-Sensitive Manufacturing Industries, 1960–1980" in Barbara D. Dennis, ed., *Proceedings of the Thirty-Sixth Annual Meeting,* Industrial Relations Research Association, December 28–30, 1983 (Madison, Wisc.: IRRA, 1984), pp. 230–238.

48. Daniel J.B. Mitchell, "Alternative Explanations of Union Wage Concessions," *California Management Review,* vol. 29 (Fall 1986), pp. 95–108; Wayne Vroman and John M. Abowd, "Disaggregated Wage Developments," *Brookings Papers on Economic Activity* (1:1988), pp. 313–338; Wayne Vroman and Susan Vroman, "Wage Adjustments to Increased Foreign Competition" in Barbara D. Dennis, ed., *Proceedings of the Fortieth Annual Meeting,* Industrial Relations Research Association, December 28–30, 1987 (Madison, Wisc.: IRRA, 1988), pp. 35–43.

49. The figures refer to production workers. Wage gaps between the United States and the countries shown might well be reduced if white-collar workers were included. See Richard S. Belous, *Labor Costs in Different Cities Around the World,* report 85–1097 E (Washington: Congressional Research Service, 1985).

50. *Survey of Current Business,* vol. 68 (June 1988), p. 48.

51. Wolfgang F. Stolper and Paul A. Samuelson, "Protection and Real Wages," *Review of Economic Studies,* vol. 9 (November 1941), pp. 333–357.

52. Don P. Clark, "The Protection of Unskilled Labor in the United States Manufacturing Industries: Further Evidence," *Journal of Political Economy,* vol. 88 (December 1980), pp. 1249–1254.

53. Stephen A. Rhoades, "Wages, Concentration, and Import Penetration: An Analysis of the Interrelationships," *Atlantic Economic Journal,* vol. 12 (July 1984), pp. 23–31.

54. There are also a variety of hidden barriers to trade, such as safety standards, which vary from country to country, and other regulations. These hidden restrictions are often termed "nontariff barriers." Because they are hidden and hard to quantify, efforts at reducing nontariff barriers have proven difficult.

55. Foreign countries may agree to limit their own exports under threat of harsher measures by the importing country. They may also be in a position to collect some rents domestically by agreeing to the arrangement. The restriction of export sales can have a monopolistic effect, raising the price of those units they are permitted to sell. Thus, although the number of units sold is reduced by the orderly

marketing agreement, and mark-up per unit can be increased. A prominent example of an orderly marketing agreement was a restriction by Japan of automobile exports to the United States, agreed to under American pressure in the early 1980s.

56. American unions have not always favored trade restrictions. Up through the early 1960s, they often looked kindly on trade. This attitude in that period should not be surprising because heavily unionized industries then were often export oriented. See Peter Donohue, "A Monopoly on Brains: Trade Liberalization's Endorsement and Political Action by the Congress of Industrial Organizations and the American Federation of Labor, 1943–1951," working paper, Department of Economics, San Francisco State University, 1987.

57. A trade war is a situation in which countries retaliate against one another by imposing trade barriers such as tariffs.

58. There is no theoretical requirement that depreciation lead to a decline in the terms of trade. However, this association is an empirical regularity. If U.S. import prices are viewed as determined largely by foreign costs, and U.S. export prices as determined largely by domestic costs, it is easy to see why depreciation of the dollar (the raising of foreign costs in terms of dollars) would cause American terms of trade to deteriorate.

59. Daniel J.B. Mitchell, "Labor and the Tariff Question," *Industrial Relations,* vol. 9 (May 1970), pp. 268–276.

60. A special temporary TAA program was adopted for the automobile industry in the mid-1960s after a U.S.-Canadian agreement established free trade in new cars between the two countries. This program, unlike the more general TAA version, did pay benefits in the late 1960s.

61. The history of TAA is discussed in Daniel J.B. Mitchell, *Labor Issues of American Trade and Investment* (Baltimore: Johns Hopkins University Press, 1976), chapter 3.

62. U.S. Congress, Office of Technology Assessment, *Trade Adjustment Assistance: New Ideas for an Old Program, Special Report* (Washington: GPO, 1987), p. 25.

63. Legislation in 1988 extended TAA to oil and gas workers, who were previously ineligible because they produced a "service" rather than a "product."

64. The TAA program, which was extended in 1986, provides for seventy-eight weeks of payments at the same rate as state unemployment insurance. Typically, unemployment insurance is provided for only twenty-six weeks, so that TAA gives workers up to an extra year of benefits. They also become eligible for retraining programs.

65. Charles R. Frank, Jr., *Foreign Trade and Domestic Aid* (Washington: Brookings Institution, 1977), chapter 10.

66. American Enterprise Institute for Public Policy Research, *Reauthorization of Trade Adjustment Assistance* (Washington: AEI, 1983), chapter 4; Malcolm D. Bale, "Adjustment Assistance: Dealing with Import-Displaced Workers" in Walter Adams et al., *Tariffs, Quotas & Trade: The Politics of Protection* (San Francisco: Institute for Contemporary Studies, 1978), pp. 149–161.

67. U.S. General Accounting Office, *Restricting Trade Act Benefits to Import-Affected Workers Who Cannot Find a Job Can Save Millions,* HRD–80–11 (Washington: GAO, 1980).

68. Walter Corson and Walter Nicholson, "Trade Adjustment Assistance for Workers: Results of a Survey of Recipients Under the Trade Act of 1974," *Research in Labor Economics,* vol. 4 (1981), pp. 417–469.

69. Douglas L. Kruse, "International Trade and the Labor Market Experience of Displaced Workers," *Industrial and Labor Relations Review,* vol. 41 (April 1988), pp. 402–417.

70. Robert Z. Lawrence, *Can America Compete?* (Washington: Brookings Institution, 1984), pp. 131–133.

71. Lester C. Thurow, "Take the Money and Run: U.S. Firms Are Best at Going Out of Business," *Los Angeles Times,* Part 4, August 16, 1987, p. 3.

72. William Schweke and David R. Jones, "European Job Creation in the Wake of Plant Closings and Layoffs," *Monthly Labor Review,* vol. 109 (October 1986), pp. 18–22.

73. Attempts have been made to determine if there was a permanent loss of market share of U.S. firms at home and abroad after the dollar appreciation of 1980–1985. Krugman and Baldwin find no solid evidence that such a permanent loss occurred. However, it is extremely difficult to make such a determination—based on a single episode—using the techniques they apply. Their evidence does suggest that the lag in improvement in the U.S. trade balance due to dollar devaluation was longer than might have been expected, based on previous relationships. See Paul R. Krugman and Richard E. Baldwin, "The Persistence of the U.S. Trade Deficit," *Brookings Papers on Economic Activity* (1:1987), pp. 1–43, and discussants' comments on pp. 44–55.

74. Richard S. Belous, "Flexibility and American Labour Markets: The Evidence and Implications," working paper no. 14, World Employment Programme Research, International Labour Office, June 1987.

75. There have been arguments made that even when nominally converted to American methodology, the Japanese unemployment rate (as reported in Table 5) is understated by the U.S. Bureau of Labor Statistics. It has been said, for example, that displaced Japanese workers are more prone than Americans to drop out of the labor force, and, hence, are not counted as unemployed. Or they become underemployed, working fewer hours than desired. If discouraged workers are included in an expanded definition of the unemployment rate, the Japanese and American rates on that basis are roughly comparable. See Constance Sorren-

tino, "Japan's Low Unemployment: An In-Depth Analysis," *Monthly Labor Review*, vol. 107 (March 1984), pp. 18–27; Constance Sorrentino, "Japanese Unemployment: BLS Updates Its Analysis," *Monthly Labor Review*, vol. 110 (June 1987), pp. 47–53.

76. Richard B. Freeman, and Martin L. Weitzman, "Bonuses and Employment in Japan," *Journal of the Japanese and International Economies*, vol. 1 (1987), pp. 168–194; Takatoshi Ito and Martin L. Weitzman, "Lessons to be Learnt from Japan," *Financial Times*, January 21, 1987, p. 17.

77. As might be expected, there are skeptics concerning this explanation of high European unemployment in the 1980s. One argument that is made is that American HRM practices involve some commitment to employees, even if not legally required. However, a self-imposed commitment can be altered (or renegotiated, if pursuant to a union contract). A legally required practice cannot be changed short of legislative modification. For a skeptical view, see Michael J. Piore, "Perspectives on Labor Market Flexibility," *Industrial Relations*, vol. 25 (Spring 1986), pp. 146–166.

78. Many difficulties arise with this measure. Value added in government is defined as the labor cost. Thus, government productivity cannot be measured. International comparisons will be distorted by differences in the size of the government sector across countries. The usual difficulties of exchange rate fluctuations also arise. The estimates that follow in the text are based on GNP estimates (divided by civilian employment) in 1986 (1984 for South Korea) converted at prevailing exchange rates. Source for GNP data is U.S. Bureau of the Census, *Statistical Abstract of the United States: 1988* (Washington: GPO, 1988), p. 804–805. Employment data except for South Korea are from *Monthly Labor Review*, vol. 111 (August 1988), p. 97. For South Korea, employment data are from International Labour Office, *Yearbook of Labour Statistics: 1986* (Geneva: ILO, 1986), p. 344.

79. G.D.A. MacDougall, "British and American Exports: A Study Suggested by the Theory of Comparative Costs," *Economic Journal*, vol. 61 (December 1951), pp. 697–724.

80. Edward F. Denison of the Brookings Institution has argued in an unpublished work that manufacturing productivity improvement, and its differential relative to other sectors, has been overstated by methodology used to estimate quality improvements in computer output. Even after adjustment for the computer effect, however, some differential remains between manufacturing and nonmanufacturing.

81. Angus Maddison, "Growth and Slowdown in Advanced Capitalist Economies: Techniques of Quantitative Assessment," *Journal of Economic Literature*, vol. 25 (June 1987), pp. 649–698, especially p. 676.

82. There is some evidence that U.S. nonsupervisory workers receive less job training than those in Japan. See Richard M. Cyert and David C. Mowery, eds., *Technology and Employment: Innovation and Growth in the U.S. Economy* (Washington: National Academy Press, 1987), p. 141.

83. Data on the 1950s through 1970s can be found in Daniel J.B. Mitchell, "The Occupational Structure of U.S. Exports and Imports," *Quarterly Review of Economics and Business*, vol. 10 (Winter 1970), pp. 17–30; Daniel J.B. Mitchell, "Recent Changes in the Labor Content of U.S. International Trade," *Industrial and Labor Relations Review*, vol. 28 (April 1975), pp. 355–375; and Lindert, *International Economics, op. cit.*, p. 78.

84. Michael J. Piore and Charles F. Sabel, *The Second Industrial Divide: Possibilities for Prosperity* (New York: Basic Books, 1984).

85. Piore and Sabel, *The Second Industrial Divide, op. cit.*, pp. 271, 273.

INDEX